Community and Evolutionary Ecology of North American Stream Fishes

Community and Evolutionary Ecology of North American Stream Fishes

Edited by

William J. Matthews and David C. Heins

University of Oklahoma Press : Norman and London

Library of Congress Cataloging-in-Publication Data

Community and evolutionary ecology of North American stream fishes.

Bibliography: p. 269
Includes indexes.
1. Fishes, Fresh-water—North America—Ecology.
2. Fishes, Fresh-water—North America—Evolution.
3. Stream ecology—North America. 4. Fishes—
North America—Ecology. 5. Fishes—North America—
Evolution. I. Matthews, William J. (William John),
1946– . II. Heins, David C. (David Carl),
1948– .
QL625.C66 1987 597′.05′097 87-40213
ISBN 0–8061–2073–8

Publication of this work has been made possible in part by a grant from the National Science Foundation and grants from Tulane University and the University of Oklahoma.

The paper in this book meets the guidelines for permanence and durability of the Committee on Production Guidelines for Book Longevity of the Council on Library Resources, Inc.

Contents

Editors' Preface

We first discussed the possibility of organizing a symposium to address recent progress in ecology of North American stream fishes in April 1983 at the annual meeting of the Southwestern Association of Naturalists in Little Rock, Arkansas. After considerable discussion about scope, taxonomic limits, and magnitude of ongoing research, we agreed that the time was right to attempt to bring together the many researchers engaged in empirical studies of stream fish ecology and those approaching the subject from more theoretical points of view. The decision to hold the symposium in conjunction with an annual meeting of the American Society of Ichthyologists and Herpetologists (ASIH) came easily, for no other organization includes so many individuals so knowledgeable about stream fishes. At the 1983 ASIH meeting in Tallahassee, we spent much of our time between papers speaking with potential participants, getting ideas and feedback on symposium content, learning of new persons whose work was not known to us, and the like. We were impressed with the virtually unanimous feeling of the active researchers in the area that there was need for a face-to-face meeting of the principals in the ongoing research in stream fish ecology in North America. With this active support, we were granted approval by ASIH to organize the symposium for the 1985 annual meeting held in Knoxville 10–12 June 1985.

To our gratitude, the Ecology section of the National Science Foundation (NSF) concurred with our request for support for the symposium, specifically agreeing to fund travel for the keynote speakers and for invited participants without access to other funds, and to provide a publication subsidy for the proceedings of the symposium. Our home institutions, Tulane University and the University of Oklahoma, also agreed to help underwrite costs of publication. After consideration of numerous publication outlets, we were pleased to have the opportunity to work with the University of Oklahoma Press in the preparation of this volume. Our goal with respect to publication was simple: to produce a high-quality volume useful to the research community at an affordable price. Toward this end, we are grateful to Doris Radford Morris, John Drayton, and the staff of the Press.

Why a symposium at this particular time, and why on "Community and Evolutionary Ecology of North American Stream Fishes"? There exists a huge body of information on stream fishes that has accrued through ichthyological field studies spanning more than a century; but particularly in the last decade studies of stream fishes have advanced from the descriptive to the quantitative and, in some cases, from observational to experimental. Research on North American stream fishes is characterized by a long history of empirical studies, with a major recent increase in studies addressing or attempting to advance ecological theory (Heins and Matthews, this volume). Particularly since 1975, much progress had been made in stream fish ecology in North America but by diverse researchers, many of whom had never met in person. The year 1985 seemed an appropriate time to take stock of progress, exchange ideas, and ensure that future studies are placed in a profitable ecological perspective. It was also our perception that a gap remained to be bridged between empiricists and theoreticians within the discipline and that the symposium might encourage a marriage of these viewpoints.

The symposium was designed to provide a forum for presentation of new syntheses or of original research in six areas of stream fish ecology: (1) community dynamics, (2) distributional patterns or faunal alterations, (3) life history strategies and tactics, (4) population biology or genetics, (5) physiological ecology, and (6) functional morphology or ecomorphology. We solicited participation in the symposium by making contact with individuals known to us to have made major contributions in those subdisciplines, plus a few graduate students whose work commanded attention. We made every attempt to include all who were active in the field, but in such subjective judgments errors are made. To any whom we have slighted we offer apologies. From the outset it was our purpose to have the symposium represent the current status of stream fish ecology in North America. Thus we made no attempt to influence the distribution of papers across subdisciplines. We believe that the particular combination of papers, clearly not balanced evenly among the six subdisciplines, does represent approximately the recent levels of research activity in these areas.

Fishes of streams provide an exciting, tractable, and accessible theater for ecological studies. Natural streams abound throughout North America, from deserts to the Arctic, with a tremendous variety of fishes, habitat types, and, likely, regulatory mechanisms. Most North American streams are simple enough logistically for research by small groups (compared, for example to "big lake" studies). Many are clear so that study can be by direct observation (snorkel and mask and SCUBA), and the wide array of stream sizes and physical configurations makes at least some ideal for manipulative field experiments. In North America, many streams have a more complex fish fauna than do natural lakes; thus a given site in a small stream may have many more coexisting species than do neighboring sites in lentic waters. Streams are physically open systems, with more potential for colonization of drainages, migrations within drainages, or faunal filtering than exists among lakes. However, although they are physically interconnected systems with potential long-range movements of fishes, the tens of thousands of stream kilometers on this continent with physical barriers and the proclivity of many small fishes for headwaters make streams or springs ideal places to examine isolated populations and adaptation to local environments.

As open, flowing systems with directional geomorphological processes and movements of materials, streams are highly dynamic and subject to abrupt longitudinal variation. Within short reaches (e.g., 10 to 20 km) a stream can present vastly different habitats that vary in size, structural complexity, stability, substrates, physicochemical properties, and food availability and thus differ trenchantly in characteristics of fish assemblages. Many streams are subject to unpredictable perturbations like floods and droughts and seasonal abiotic stresses to which fish must be adapted. Primary productivity and input of allochthonous materials can be highly pulsed, imposing on the entire aquatic biota a shifting resource base. Stream fishes are thus offered a temporally variable, diverse variety of foods; they can adopt active foraging or sit-and-wait feeding. Stream fishes are also offered a tremendous variety of situations in which to mate, deposit eggs, and place young. Complex adaptations in reproductive repertoires and mating systems have thus evolved. Finally, by offering a wide variety of current speed regimes and sizes and complexities of habitats, streams invite ecological radiation and adaptation in fishes not found in lentic waters of this continent.

Streams and their fishes therefore offer ecologists highly diverse physical and biotic systems for studies that focus either on the fishes as organisms or on the testing and development of general ecological principles. For some studies, complexity may inhibit rather than promote progress. However, it is clear that in recent decades many ecologists have accepted the challenge of research with North American stream fishes, taking advantage of the many positive conceptual and logistical attributes of these systems. Yet many of the basic processes regulating stream fish ecology, such as movements, breeding systems, life history strategies and tactics, predator-prey relationships, competitive interactions, or local adaptations, remain poorly understood. Perhaps most important, we are only recently beginning really to study fish as components of and forcing factors in whole stream ecosystems.

A symposium is only as good as its individual participants. We thank all of the many persons who participated in or helped make a success of the symposium sessions in Knoxville. In particular we thank Dave Etnier for his role as local chairman of the ASIH annual meeting (and for his courage in the face of a certain amount of chaos); Stephen T. Ross and Tony Echelle, who served with us as chairpersons of sessions; Ross Kiester, Tom Schoener, and Clark Hubbs, for stimulating keynote addresses and a summary; Garth Redfield, of the NSF, who provided a profitable workshop for all symposium participants; and Frances Gelwick, for helping collate the Literature Cited. We appreciate the detailed critical reviews (a minimum of two per paper) by the persons listed hereafter and the prompt and cooperative responses of all the contributors in the preparation of manuscripts for the volume. We are especially grateful for the time and effort spent by the independent reviewer for the Press. We are indebted to Robert C. Cashner and Frances Cashner, who were the index editors.

From the first, in organizing the symposium and editing this volume, we have shared equally in all the work that had to be done. Sequence of editorship for the volume and of authorship of the introductory chapter was thus decided by a coin toss.

We thank those persons who kindly served as reviewers of manuscripts submitted for the volume (asterisks indicate review of more than one manuscript): James W. Atz, John C. Avise, Reeve M. Bailey, Royce Ballinger,* Thomas L. Beitinger, Daniel R. Brooks, Donald C. Buth, Robert C. Cashner,* Glenn H. Clemmer,* Thomas Coon, Frank B. Cross, Larry B. Crowder, Edward M. Donaldson, Michael Douglas, Jerry F. Downhower, Anthony Echelle,* John A. Endler, Kurt Fausch, C. Robert Feldmeth, James D. Felley,* Terry Finger, Douglas Fraser, Shelby D. Gerking, Carter R. Gilbert, Owen T. Gorman, Mart R. Gross, Charles R. Hocutt, Richard J. Horwitz, Robert Hoyt, Raymond B. Huey, James Karr, Allen Keast, Hiram W. Li, John J. Magnuson, Richard L. Mayden, S. J. McNaughton, Edie Marsh, Rudolph J. Miller, Gary Mittlebach, W. Linn Montgomery,* Peter B. Moyle,* Larry Page, Barbara Peckarsky, William L. Pflieger, Eric R. Pianka, Mary V. Price, David Reznick, Henry W. Robison,* Stephen T. Ross,* William M. Schaffer, Isaac J. Schlosser,* Gary D. Schnell, R. J. Schultz, C. Lavett Smith, Michael H. Smith, Franklin F. Snelson, Jr., Roy Stein, Arthur J. Stewart, Richard E. Strauss,* Stephen T. Threlkeld, Bruce Vondracek, Paul W. Webb, Earl E. Werner, Henry M. Wilbur, James D. Williams, Earl G. Zimmerman.

Kingston, Oklahoma — William J. Matthews
New Orleans, Louisiana — David C. Heins

Community and Evolutionary Ecology of North American Stream Fishes

1. Historical Perspectives on the Study of Community and Evolutionary Ecology of North American Stream Fishes

David C. Heins and William J. Matthews

The study of stream-fish ecology in North America has origins in the initial faunal surveys of the late 1700s and early 1800s by naturalists such as Lesueur, Mitchill, and Rafinesque (Myers, 1964). Annotated reports from these early surveys included limited information on the natural histories of the fishes, many of which were described for the first time.

During the early to mid-1800s a number of naturalists in the East completed comprehensive treatises on the fishes of different states or regions and included considerable information on natural history. Among these were Kirtland, who treated the fishes of Ohio; DeKay, who wrote on the fishes of New York; and Storer, who compiled volumes on the fishes of Massachusetts and of North America (Myers, 1964). These and other similar efforts were the precursors of modern state and regional treatments of fishes that also contain a great deal of general information on the ecologies of the fishes discussed therein (e.g., Trautman, 1957, 1981; Cross, 1967; Pflieger, 1975; Scott and Crossman, 1973; Moyle, 1976; Becker, 1983.)

The western "railroad" and "boundary" surveys of the mid-1800s (Hubbs, 1964) further added to knowledge of the ecology of North American stream fishes. The result was that by the late 1800s much general ecological information had been amassed on the common stream fishes of North America, particularly on the distributions and habitats of those in the eastern part of the continent. This knowledge was reflected in the ecological anecdotes found in some of the important taxonomic treatises that appeared at the turn of the century, such as *The Fishes of North and Middle America* (Jordan and Evermann, 1896–1900) and *The Fishes of Illinois* (Forbes and Richardson, 1908).

Shortly before these major works appeared, other scientists, most notably Forbes (1880a, b, 1883), began publishing quantitative ecological data. Interest in the development of general principles in stream-fish ecology also began about this time when one of the foremost early ecologists, Victor E. Shelford, published his classic study (Shelford, 1911) on distributional limits in stream fishes.

For ichthyologists, the years from about 1875 to 1925 were characterized by intensive study that was strongly influenced by David Starr Jordan (directly or through his students), resulted in group revisions and faunal studies (particularly in the late 1800s), and might be called the Jordan era in North American ichthyology. As shown above, they were also auspicious years for the study of stream-fish ecology. However, they were followed by a period characterized by emphasis on taxonomic, systematic, and distributional studies of stream fishes.

As the Jordan era came to a close in the early 1900s, the "Michigan school" arose under the influence of Carl L. Hubbs, Jordan's last graduate student. Ichthyological activity from the 1930s through the 1950s was dominated by the still uncompleted task of describing new species, revising interpretations of systematic relationships, and exploring many of the fish faunas of western North America. Despite this emphasis of North American ichthyologists, Hubbs, one of the foremost researchers of the time, also made important contributions to principles of ecology and evolution in stream fishes (e.g. Hubbs, 1922, 1926, 1934, 1941). Nevertheless, during the years when ecology was emerging as a quantitative, analytical science, the interest of most ichthyologists was primarily taxonomy, systematics, and distributional zoogeography, and ecologists made few ventures into the study of fish ecology.

There were important exceptions to this trend. Forbes's pioneering studies were followed by a number of important ecological studies on stream fishes at the Illinois Natural History Survey, including work by Thompson and Hunt (1930) on intermittent streams and by Larimore et al. (1959) on the effects of drought. William Starrett (1950a, b, 1951) also produced notable studies on the ecology of minnows, darters, and other small fishes, the significance of which is only now becoming fully appreciated. Numerous papers by Raney, Lachner, and co-workers (e.g., Raney and Lachner,

1946, 1947) developed a strong data base on the ecological life histories of some eastern stream fishes. Clark Hubbs and K. Strawn (1957) performed manipulative experiments to study the effects of environmental factors on the fecundity of the greenthroat darter. Funk (1955) and Gerking (1959) provided major conceptual advances about the distributions and movements of stream fishes. Huet (1959), in Europe, promoted concepts of longitudinal zonation in streams that were thought-provoking for North American ecologists. Added to these important advancements by ichthyologists were contributions from systems and behavioral ecologists such as those by Burton and Odum (1945) and Winn (1958). While this sampling of papers is not exhaustive, it does show that the study of stream-fish ecology was slow to develop in comparison to other aspects of ichthyology or to ecology in general. As a result, the list of major ecological studies on North American stream fishes before the 1960s is not long.

This pattern continued until the mid-1970s, as important contributions continued to appear intermittently. But there were signs of emerging changes. Following Northcote's (1954) paper, Gee and Northcote (1963), and Keast (1966) began work relating to resource partitioning in North American stream fishes. Chapman (1966) provided a general review of the factors regulating salmonid populations in North American and European streams. Kuehne (1962) and Sheldon (1968) published important papers on longitudinal zonation and species diversity in stream fishes. Gunning and Berra (1969) and Berra and Gunning (1970) added information on stream-fish movements, repopulation, and home ranges. Smith and Powell (1971) published the first multivariate analysis of the composition of stream-fish assemblages. Studies on resource partitioning, competition, and population dynamics of European stream fishes such as those by Maitland (1965), Mann (1971), and Jones (1975), some of which preceded similar North American investigations, were also completed during these years. However, it was not until the mid- to late 1970s that the study of stream-fish ecology in North America showed marked changes in tenor.

The last decade has witnessed a significant number of studies in which North American stream fishes were used to test general ecological ideas or ecological theories were applied rigorously in stream-fish ecology. The increase in empirical and theoretical studies occurred amid an explosive proliferation of quantitative studies in stream-fish ecology in North America. In all of the recent work there clearly is a growing tendency to place the study of stream-fish ecology in a theoretical context, to compare stream-fish ecology with that of other aquatic systems or other vertebrate groups, or to develop general principles. One measure of progress in stream-fish ecology is that the research now keeps pace with the major theoretical studies and controversies in ecology as a whole. The important papers in North American stream-fish ecology of the last decade are numerous; therefore, we will emphasize the ideas that have developed.

Community Ecology

Since about 1975 there has been a widespread interest in community dynamics of North American stream fishes. Theoretical works by Hutchinson (1959), MacArthur (1972), and others; the studies of Hartley (1948) in Europe, Keast (1966), Zaret and Rand (1971), and Mendelson (1975); and a review by Schoener (1974) provided germinal ideas or impetus for numerous studies on resource partitioning, competition, predator-prey interactions, and stability in stream-fish communities. The energetic research on stream-fish ecology in these areas has naturally led to divergent views of the generality of patterns, causal mechanisms, and appropriate theories. Information and ideas resulting from the recent community-level stream-fish studies need synthesis and integration into a cohesive theoretical framework.

One major issue that has arisen from recent research is the question of the role of competition in resource partitioning within stream-fish systems, and many stream-fish ecologists are at the fore in evaluating the importance of competition (versus abiotic factors) in structuring communities. Early papers on streams of the tropics (Zaret and Rand, 1971) and North America (Mendelson, 1975) supported a competition-based view of resource partitioning in fish communities. Numerous papers followed that suggested resource partitioning to be common in a wide variety of stream-fish communities (Baker and Ross, 1981; Finger, 1982a; Wynes and Wissing, 1982; Paine et al., 1982; Matheson and Brooks, 1983), facilitating coexistence of similar species. Tallman and Gee (1982) found intraspecific resource partitioning to be adaptive for fishes in small streams. However, Harrell (1978) and Matthews and Hill (1980) found habitat use or partitioning much less structured in a fluctuating stream environment than has often been reported in more stable environments.

Sale (1979), working on coral-reef fishes, cautioned against uncritical acceptance of competition as the cause of observed differences in resource use among species. Werner, whose work on resource partitioning in lentic fishes (Werner et al., 1977; Hall and Werner, 1977; Laughlin and Werner, 1980; related papers) also stimulated much of the research in streams, cautioned (pers. comm.) that the basic assumptions made for fish in lakes may not be valid for those in streams, if they are actually nonequilibrium systems. Two coexisting darters studied by Schlosser and Toth (1984) varied independently in distribution and abundance because of morphological differences as related to microhabitat use and responses to variations in streamflow, not interspecific competition. Matthews (1985) found that varying abilities of darters to hold position in flowing water, owing to morphological differences, facilitated their spatial segregation in an upland stream. Physiochemical stress or gradients may strongly influence microhabitat selection of fishes in prairie rivers or in upland headwaters (Matthews and Hill, 1979; Matthews and Styron, 1981). Miller (1983) and Baltz and Moyle (1984) reported segregation of coexisting stream species on resource axes but that competition was not required to explain the patterns. Angermeier (1982) found evidence of competition in a stream-fish community in Illinois but that competition was not the primary regulator of community structure. Ross (1986) reviewed 233 papers (75% published since 1974) on resource partitioning in fish communities in a wide variety of habitats. He found numerous factors other than competition that could explain the observed patterns of resource partitioning. Also, Ross found a strong suggestion that artifacts of sampling techniques complicate many studies on resource partitioning.

Despite the recent controversy, competition seems to be real in some stream situations. Recent field manipulations by Greenberg (1983) are consistent with the hypothesis that competition regulates distribution of darters in streams. The conclusions of Echelle et al. (1976) and Page and Schemske (1978) that competition regulates distribution of several darter species seem unshaken by recent arguments over the role of competition or of biotic versus abiotic factors in community organization. Further, Baltz et al. (1982) showed that temperature can mediate the outcome of competitive interactions between stream fishes. The final conclusion regarding the importance of competition is likely to be more complex than originally envisioned, and its importance is likely to vary over space and time and among taxa.

The tendency in stream-fish ecology to question the causes of observed resource segregation paralleled the trend away from uncritical acceptance of competition-based explanations that pervaded community ecology in general. As confidence in the role of competition eroded, researchers began to examine the basic organizational patterns of stream-fish communities or assemblages and the factors that regulate their structure. This work led, in a seemingly inevitable fashion, to a debate over the importance of abiotic and biotic factors as controlling elements in community structure. Habitat complexity, physiochemical characteristics, competition, and predation are among the factors that have been considered. Gorman and Karr (1978) reemphasized the important influence of habitat complexity on the structure of stream-fish assemblages. Smith and Powell (1971) and Moyle and Li (1979) suggested that competition and predation play a secondary role in community organization, with physical phenomena most important. Schlosser (1982a) hypothesized that the relative importance of recolonization dynamics, physical variability, competition, and predation in regulating community structure in small streams is likely to vary considerably among habitat gradients.

Models of the regulation of stream-fish communities have been reevaluated as an outcome of the debate involving apparently contradictory evidence on the factors regulating the structure of stream communities. This led to debate over the extent to which stream-fish assemblages are regulated by stochastic events. Grossman et al. (1982) concluded that many North American stream-fish communities are stochastic and that equilibrium-based models of community structure could not be applied to such streams.

The paper stimulated numerous rebuttals, particularly Yant et al. (1985), who argue that there is little variation in stream-fish communities and strongly disagree that they are "stochastic." Karr and Freemark (1983) (although referring to birds) argued that the entire "stochastic versus deterministic" line of investigation may be misleading, in that communities can be nonequilibrium yet predictable on the basis of knowledge of environmental conditions. The extrapolation of this reasoning to streams, in which physical conditions have long been considered important, is likely. However, different kinds of streams might have fish assemblages regulated by different mechanisms. For example, trout streams in California may be deterministic (Moyle and Vondracek, 1985), whereas some streams in glaciated areas may tend toward stochastic control (cf. Grossman et al., 1982; but see Matthews [1986a] for a contrasting view).

While the details of veracious community regulation models for stream fishes await elucidation, one critical question that must be addressed involves the stability of stream-fish communities over time. One of the strongest arguments for stream-fish communities as stochastic systems is that streams are commonly subject to unpredictable perturbations, such as floods and drought (Grossman et al., 1982). Harrell (1978), Coon (1982), Ross and Baker (1983), and Schlosser (1985) suggest that floods can alter community structure or the age structure of populations of stream fishes. In contrast, Matthews (1986a) found that an upland stream-fish community was highly stable and persistent across a decade, despite the occurrence of the "flood of the century." Ross et al. (1985) found also that one of the worst drought and heat waves on record in Oklahoma caused no lasting change in composition of a small stream-fish community. Finger (1982b) showed consistency in local stream-fish assemblages over microscale distances. Schlosser (1982b) argued that stability of small fish communities is likely to be a function of interactions between channel morphology and flow regime. Moyle and Vondracek (1985) showed that simple fish assemblages in western streams were quite stable, in contrast to those in some midwestern streams.

Structure of fish communities also has been shown in this decade to relate directly to tolerance of physical stress, as suggested long ago by Thompson and Hunt (1930) and numerous others. Tolerance of some species to oxygen or temperature stress corresponds closely to their distribution within watersheds (Ultsch et al., 1978; Matthews and Styron, 1981; Ingersoll and Claussen, 1984), and other recent authors suggest that both zoogeographic range limits and local distributions of species of fishes may correspond to differences in their physicochemical tolerances.

Predator-prey interactions in streams also have been considered as a factor that may control community structure. For example, a number of studies have shown that predation can influence the presence and abundance of prey organisms. Predator-prey interactions in streams can influence fish-community dynamics, although this has received less direct assessment in North American streams than have other community-level interactions. Fraser and Cerri (1982), Cerri and Fraser (1983), and Fraser and Emmons (1984) report from field and laboratory experiments that predators can directly influence distributions in streams of the fish species they prey upon, forcing small fishes into inferior habitats. Power and Matthews (1983) and Power et al. (1985) have shown that predation by largemouth bass influences habitat use by grazing minnows (*Campostoma*), which in turn alters distribution of algae in small streams.

Ecomorphological aspects of resource partitioning and community structure have been given only limited attention despite divergent views on the importance of ecomorphology. Gatz (1979a, b, 1981) has argued that stream-fish communities, like those of birds (Ricklefs and Cox, 1977), bats (Findley, 1973, 1976), and other mammals (Smartt, 1978), can be analyzed in detail on the basis of multivariate ecomorphology. Mahon (1984) found that an ecomorphological approach provided relatively good ecological interpretations in North American and European stream-fish communities. However, Miller (1983) and Paine et al. (1982) found that ecomorphology did not reflect observed differences in food use by darters, and Felley (1984) showed that morphological characters selected a priori did not adequately predict ecological relationships in complex cyprinid assemblages.

Coincident with the increased activity in fish-community ecology in the last ten years have been studies of long-term changes in North American fish faunas (see this volume) or of the distributional ecology of fishes as related to environmental correlates. Improved computing capabilities have made possible multivariate studies (e.g., Echelle and Schnell, 1976; Rose and Echelle, 1981) investigating species associations and distributional patterns of fishes within drainages.

Evolutionary Ecology

Evolutionary ecology of North American stream fishes in the last decade has largely focused on life-history traits, mating systems, and population genetics. Stimulated by the work of Fisher (1930), Lack (1947, 1954) and especially Cole (1954), early attempts to formulate general theories on the evolution of life-history parameters centered on reptiles and birds. The vigorous activity in this general area of interest in evolutionary ecology peaked in the 1970s, at about the time a number of studies on fishes began to appear.

Studies on fishes (Svardson, 1949; Williams, 1959; Murphy, 1968; Schaffer and Elson, 1975; Schaffer, 1979; Hirschfield, 1980; Stearns, 1980, 1983, 1984; Reznick, 1981, 1982a,b, 1983; Reznick and Endler, 1982; Trendall, 1982) have made important contributions to an understanding of life-history traits, but most of these papers do not deal with North American stream species. Critical work on life histories of North American stream fishes is limited. Ironically, as Stearns (1977) points out, the literature on fishes is substantial and includes large sample sizes, but few studies of North American stream fishes have gone beyond the data to consider ecological relationships and general concepts. Further, fishes have greater phenotypic plasticity than other major vertebrate taxa (as Stearns [1977] also notes), and this, coupled with possibly large sample sizes, makes fishes desirable systems for life-history study. Two such systems, comprising important North American stream-fish groups, the minnows and the darters, are currently under study. Clark Hubbs and colleagues (e.g., Hubbs and Strawn, 1957; Hubbs et al., 1968; Marsh, 1984, 1986) have been investigating the nature and significance of reproductive patterns in darters of the Southwest. Heins (e.g., Heins, 1979, 1985) has begun similar studies for minnows and darters in southeastern streams. These and other recent studies by Garrett (1982), Farringer et al. (1979), and Baltz and Moyle (1982), which have contributed to knowledge of life-history tactics of pupfish, minnows, and tule perch, respectively, have demonstrated significant geographic variation (or variation that corresponds to differences among environments) in the life histories of these fishes. However, much work remains to determine the patterns of variation in life-history traits, to establish the causal factors, and to develop syntheses related to general life-history theory.

Nevertheless, study of the life-history traits of North American stream fishes, which seeks to test or to develop general concepts, still lingers, while conceptual issues continue to be addressed with other taxa or, in a few instances, fishes from other geographical areas (e.g., Kaplan, 1980; Crump, 1981, 1984; Trendall, 1982; Kaplan and Cooper, 1984; Zammuto and Millar, 1985). Perhaps one factor that has been involved in the slow pace of work on North American stream fishes is our poor understanding of some aspects of their life histories. For example, Hubbs and Strawn (1957), Hubbs (1983, 1985a), Page, (1983), and Gale and Deutsch (1985) have debated the occurrence of multiple clutches in darters; and only recently Heins and Rabito (1986) have demonstrated the occurrence of multiple clutches in the genus *Notropis*.

In contrast, much of the recent work on life histories of North American stream fishes has focused on mating systems or the behavioral aspects of breeding tactics. Kodric-Brown (1977, 1981), Loiselle and Barlow (1978), Constantz (1979), Dominey (1980), Downhower (1980), Gross and Charnov (1981), Downhower et al. (1983), Grant and Colgan (1983), Ross (1983), and Gross (1979, 1982, 1984, 1985) have made significant contributions to assessment of mating systems or breeding behaviors, with several examples of variation related to local environments. Loiselle and Barlow (1978) compared the mating systems of fish with those of birds. Gross (1984) provides a summary of the information he and others have gathered on alternative mating strategies and tactics in salmonids and sunfishes; he also reviews theories used in analyzing such behavioral strategies and tactics.

One of the more exciting areas of stream-fish ecology in North America in the last decade has involved the investigation of genetic patterns in population ecology—local adaptations and evolution, and genetic systems. Electrophoretic analyses and other biochemical techniques have permitted research that was not possible a few years ago, and the importance of understanding the genetics of local stream-fish populations readily became apparent with the publication of the results of studies in this area. Echelle et al. (1975, 1976) found gene flow highly restricted in two darter species of small streams, with much local variation in genic composition. Smith et al. (1983) found stream-fish populations much more genetically dynamic than previously expected, with strong genetic-environmental correlates. Vrijenhoek (1978, 1979), Vrijenhoek et al. (1977, 1978), and Schultz (1977, 1982) have made major contributions in evolutionary ecology of clonal fish populations. Zimmerman and his students (Richmond and Zimmerman, 1978; Zimmerman and Richmond, 1981; Calhoun et al., 1982) found a surprising rate of local genetic adaptation in a thermally altered stream reach, with direct correspondence between the genetic change and temperature selection. In Zimmerman's studies we find examples of ecologically adaptive local evolution in a fish species in less than 40 years.

Conclusion

The studies cited herein and similar studies we have not cited are largely concerned with descriptions of patterns observed in one or more settings. In this respect we are reminded of the introductory comments by Robert H. MacArthur in *Geographical Ecology* (1972), who said, "To do science is to search for repeated patterns, not simply to accumulate facts." For the study of stream-fish ecology to progress in the coming years as rapidly as it has in the last decade, studies might begin to concentrate on the analysis of repeated patterns through hypothesis testing (sensu MacArthur [1972]; see the introduction to part 2, "The Patterns"). In such analysis the processes that contribute to the repeated patterns may also be brought to light through experimentation. In all of this, researchers should attempt to integrate interactions between biotic and abiotic factors. Another approach that seems to provide the potential for important contributions to our understanding of stream-fish ecology is the integration of studies on life histories, population dynamics, and community patterns. Finally, any viewpoint in research that perpetuates the past conceptual isolation of fishes from ecosystems is likely unprofitable. Integrated research that begins with basic geomorphology and hydraulics and considers interactions of fish within stream ecosystems as a whole is most likely to increase understanding of the role of fishes in lotic environments. Such approaches may allow resolution of conceptual issues that have arisen in the recent past and will continue to arise in the years to come as naturalists doing science seek to develop general principles in stream-fish ecology.[1]

[1] This chapter benefited from comments of Bob Cashner, Tony Echelle, Carter Gilbert, Gerald Gunning, Clark Hubbs, Peter Moyle, David Reznick, and Ike Schlosser, who critically read a draft of the manuscript. Elizabeth Day Heins helped with the word processing of the manuscript.

2. Axes of Controversy in Community Ecology

Thomas W. Schoener

Abstract

This paper recognizes seven axes of controversy in community ecology: unpatterned versus patterned, random versus nonrandom, physical versus biological, interactive versus noninteractive, density-independent versus density-dependent, nonequilibrial versus equilibrial, and stochastic versus deterministic. The terminology defining these axes has a variety of origins—natural phenomenology or causality, statistical inference, and mathematical theory. As such, the axes can often show strong correlations. These correlations have sometimes led to a blurring of the distinction between certain axes; however, no axis is identical to any other—each describes a substantive and separate controversy. Existence of these controversies can be viewed as supporting the existence of real differences between ecological communities. Two recently popularized research strategies—the mechanistic and pluralistic approaches—are suggested as facilitating the eventual explanation of such differences.

It is no news that community ecologists have recently been embroiled in a great deal of controversy. What have we been arguing about? The major issues can be induced from the contents of several recent volumes (Price et al., 1984; Strong et al., 1984; Diamond and Case, 1986), although no chapter in those volumes focuses explicitly on the kinds of controversies.

At the risk of being moderately repetitious, I would like to reorganize and supplement the recent overviews of community-ecological issues in a way that adopts such a focus. In particular I will identify, discuss, and interrelate seven axes of controversy.

Table 2.1 identifies each controversy by using labels for the two extremes of the appropriate axis, e.g., "stochastic" versus "deterministic." This procedure risks straying into semantics, but I believe that all the axes have some reality in more substantive ways. The axes are neither exclusive nor exhaustive but rather represent phraseology common in the recent literature, and their diverse origins preclude any elaborately structured organizing logic. Some are mainly phenomenologically based (e.g., unpatterned versus patterned) or mainly based on natural causes (e.g., physical versus biological). Others are based on some theoretical model structure (e.g., nonequilibrial versus equilibrial) and/or are mainly statistically based (e.g., random versus nonrandom). Others are not as easy to classify as to origin (e.g., density-independent versus density-dependent), and, indeed, attempts to evaluate a controversy on the basis of one kind of origin with respect to another kind of origin has led to second-order controversy about methodology and validation, to say nothing of confusion. For example, how does one statistically confirm density dependence, easily defined in mathematical models? Or what is the theoretical justification for arguing that competition (Hairston et al., 1960) or predation (Menge and Sutherland, 1976) is predominant at the base of a food web? (more about these approaches to community ecology appears in Schoener, 1986a).

I now proceed through the axes of controversy in the order given in table 2.1, leaping ahead and backtracking where necessary to identify the empirical and logical relations between them. As will be obvious to aficionados, some of the

Table 2.1. Axes of Controversy

1. Unpatterned versus patterned
2. Random versus nonrandom
3. Physical versus biological
4. Interactive versus noninteractive
5. Density-independent versus density-dependent
6. Nonequilibriai versus equilibrial
7. Stochastic versus deterministic

axes are especially prominent in the literature on stream-fish community ecology, and I highlight these cases. At the end I attempt to show how two recently arising approaches to community ecology, the mechanistical and pluralistic approaches, while not resolving the controversies, greatly enhance their scientific interest.

The Controversies

Axis 1—Unpatterned Versus Patterned

This axis is a phenomenological axis that describes to what extent there exist particular patterns in ecological communities. Examples of purported patterns abound: for variation in space, the species-area relationship (reviews in Connor and McCoy, 1979; Schoener, 1976; Schoener and Schoener, 1981) is exemplary; for variation in time, the temporal constancy of species lists (lack of turnover, sensu MacArthur and Wilson, 1963) or species abundances (degree-of-abundance concordance, e.g., Grossman et al., 1982) is exemplary. To the extent that certain kinds of variation are low, e.g., variation about the species-area curve, we claim to have found a pattern—a claim that can sometimes be substantiated by a simple statistical test; e.g., is a regression coefficient significantly different from zero? Such patterns, as Roughgarden (1983) has suggested, are better regarded as phenomena demanding explanation than as explanations themselves, although they can certainly be used as links in an explanatory chain.

When determination of the existence of a pattern mainly involves selection of an appropriate "traditional" statistical test, this axis by itself is probably the least controversial, since such issues generate relatively minor disagreement (e.g., Hendrickson, 1981; Rahel et al., 1984; Schoener, 1984). When the appropriate test is a more complicated, Monte Carlo procedure, controversy is greater, and issues overlap those of axis 2 (below), which deals with null models. Moreover, to account for an observed pattern, we typically hypothesize that some causal process—competition, noninteractive habitat preference, and so on—might be responsible. Such processes may themselves form parts of other, more controversial axes, i.e., those dealing with natural causes (axes 3 and 4). It is sometimes overlooked that lack of pattern also demands some kind of explanation, and we shall return to this below.

As has been emphasized especially recently in community ecology, presence of a pattern need not imply certain very "active" kinds of ecological processes—randomness in some sense can be all that is necessary. Resolution of such issues leads into the next axis of controversy.

Axis 2—Random Versus Nonrandom

Although an ecological pattern might be statistically significant in the above sense, its features may not differ significantly from the output of some neutral or null model (e.g., Caswell, 1976; Strong et al., 1979; review in Harvey et al., 1983). (A null model, by definition, attempts to exclude the effects of at least one process or phenomenon; "null" implies that something is missing.) Somewhat loosely, the pattern is then said to be consistent with random expectation, although, of course, factors other than the ones excluded may be involved. An example of a highly successful null model is the Hardy-Weinberg Equilibrium Model of population genetics.

Most null models used in community ecology have become controversial. An example of one that is not controversial is Simberloff's (1970) treatment of the species-per-genus ratio. Various investigators observed that smaller areas (e.g., small islands) had fewer species per genus than larger areas; more intense competition on the former was given as a possible explanation. This pattern can be confirmed by comparing means between small and large areas using a simple t-test, as in the discussion of axis 1. However, Simberloff pointed out that the pattern is expected purely on the basis of those areas having fewer species; random selection of species with respect to genus showed that, if anything, residual effects have a pattern opposite to the one claimed.

More controversial null models are those of Simberloff and Boecklen (1981) and Strong et al. (1979). The former paper claims correctly that investigators have often failed to justify statistically their conclusions that size ratios among species are larger or more constant than expected by chance. Their test, however, has been argued to fail in various ways, e.g., in the shape of the null distribution of sizes used (Colwell and Winkler, 1984; Schoener, 1984; Case et al., 1983; but see Boecklen and NeSmith, 1985). Most serious is the criticism that, by allowing the data to determine the end points of the assumed null distribution of sizes, the definition of a large ratio changes in such a way that the outcome of the test for larger-than-expected ratios depends almost entirely, for small numbers of species, on the degree of ratio constancy (Schoener, 1984a). For example, the ratios 1.75 and 2.50 are not significantly larger than expected, but the ratios 1.01 and 1.01 are. The Strong et al. (1979) procedure is in my opinion substantially better. It combines species (or other taxa) from a number of communities and then draws randomly from the resulting pool to form artificial communities. Some statistical test is then used to assess whether the artificial communities differ from the actual ones. This procedure has also been criticized, however, on the basis that species similar in size to others may have been exterminated by competition everywhere, so that the remaining pool already incorporates the effect of competition and is therefore not "null" (Colwell and Winkler, 1984). The importance of this argument, of course, depends on the likelihood of total extermination of a species, typically smaller the more extensive the area considered (e.g., Schoener, 1984a).

Many other null procedures exist, and the general technique is now making its way into stream-fish community ecology (e.g., Matthews, 1982). In my opinion, the infusion of null models is an improvement over the previous "numerological" situation; not only are such procedures better defined, but they are all we are ever going to have to test certain types of evolutionary hypotheses that are impractical to test by experimentation. Because null models typically make certain strong phenomenological assumptions, it is best to use a variety of more or less independent (and sensible) null models in any investigation (Schoener, 1982).

Axis 3—Physical Versus Biological

This axis and the next are axes of natural causes, in the sense that they are derived from direct observation of natural phenomena rather than from some intermediate mathematical or statistical construct. The tension between physical and biological factors in structuring communities has been a classical theme for some time in ecology, for example, in attempts to account for latitudinal diversity gradients (e.g., Slobodkin and Sanders, 1969). The theme is taken up in various ways in this volume (e.g., Fisher and Pearson, chap. 9; Matthews, chap 14; Ross, et al., chap 6; Schlosser, chap. 3; Coon, chap. 10).

In a somewhat narrow sense, physical factors involve those of macro- and microclimate. Their meaning can be extended to include structural properties of the environment, e.g., substrate properties. In both cases, but especially the latter, they are not entirely separable from biological factors, i.e., those owing to the existence of other organisms. For lotic systems particularly important physical factors are temperature, oxygen, and discharge rate; particularly important biological factors are food resources, competitors, predators, and parasites. Many of the chapters in this book illustrate that stream-fish communities, sometimes separately, but especially in toto, are intermediate to an unusual degree in the extent to which one or the other type of factor predominates (see also below). The interaction between the two kinds of factors may therefore be expected to be especially interesting. For example, Schlosser (chap. 3) points out that larger pools allow more large fishes to exist, which, because of "escape in size" from predation, predilects a system toward one controlled largely by competition.

Some rather substantial data linking this axis 1 (unpatterned versus patterned) exist for stream-fish communities. In studies by Ross et al. (1985, chap. 6) streams or portions of streams having harsher physical conditions, particularly high temperatures and drought, had communities more discordant in temporal abundance changes than those of less harsh areas. An explanation was offered in terms of the likelihood of more physically dominated environments being more stochastic (axis 7 below).

Axis 4—Noninteractive Versus Interactive

This axis orders communities according to the degree to which other species in the community matter in determining the ecological properties of a given species. Toward the noninteractive portion of the axis are communities in which one or more physical factors, noninteractive habitat preferences, intraspecific competition, and cannibalism are predominant. Toward the interactive portion of the axis lie communities strongly influenced by one or more of predation, parasitism, competition, and mutualism. Note that only one of the noninteractive factors is nonbiological, so that this axis and the last are only partly correlated. Simberloff (1983) has been especially prominent in advocating that the first and second noninteractive factors are sufficient to explain most community patterns. This view, as discussed in detail elsewhere (Schoener, 1986b), represents a very strong form of reductionism.

Field manipulations have been especially prominent in recent years in attempts to resolve controversies orderable along axes 3 and 4. Natural experiments (sensu Diamond, 1986) are also of substantial help, with the proviso that in such experiments nature, rather than the experimenter, selects the experimental and control arenas in a way that is assumed (but often not shown) to be random with respect to factors of interest. A fairly large number of field experiments have been done on both interspecific competition (Connell, 1983; Schoener, 1983a) and predation (Sih et al., 1985); fewer seem to exist on physical factors, although these have not been reviewed. In addition, a number of experiments on the interaction between competition and predation have been performed (Sih et al., 1985). Very few field experiments covered in recent reviews were done on stream fishes. Of 164 interspecific competition studies done through 1982, only 1 (Fausch and White, 1981) was on stream fishes (Schoener, 1983a); of 139 papers describing predation experiments published during 20 years in 7 journals, only 2 (Fraser and Cerri, 1982; Allan, 1982) were on stream fishes (Sih et al., 1985). Somewhat more field experiments were done on stream invertebrates, and a substantial number more were done in lentic systems. The field-experimental approach is now beginning to take hold in stream-fish ecology, as evidenced by Matthews et al. (chap. 16).

Field experiments can reveal many effects, and those performed have typically found at least something. Simple addition or removal experiments in the short term have two drawbacks, however: (1) the mechanism of the interaction may not always be obvious, and (2) they reveal present, or instantaneous, effects only, not necessarily those important over evolutionary time.

Among other things, the first drawback may be especially important where indirect effects—those operating through intermediate variables—are expected. Indirect effects between biological components have received the most attention so far, both theoretically and empirically. For example, Holt (1977) showed how two prey species of a particular predator can act as apparent competitors, and Brown et al. (1986) have reviewed the numerous important indirect effects now shown to exist in the desert-granivore system.

Indirect effects that include physical variables must also be important in a very basic sense. Suppose, for example, that temperature is varied in an experiment and population growth of a particular species is enhanced—does this support the action of a physical or biological factor? The answer, of course, is that it depends on whether temperature affects the target species directly (e.g., via metabolic rate, growth rate, reproductive output, and so on, as in Hlohowskyj and Wissing, chap. 13), or indirectly (via a food resource); in the latter case both physical and biological factors can be said to be important. The analogous situation in competition experiments occurs when the existence of consumptive (resource) versus other kinds of competition is at issue—in the sense just given, all resource competition can be said to involve indirect effects. The single field experiment on interspecific competition in stream fishes implicated territorial competition as the mechanism, though, of course, all mechanisms listed in Schoener (1983a) can be expected as more experiments are performed.

The second drawback sometimes is not recognized because of the still occasional confusion between the past and present existence of some process, particularly competition. Suppose, for example, that we get no effect in a short-term experiment on interspecific competition. This allows us to conclude that no instantaneous or present competition (of a certain magnitude [Toft and Shea, 1983; Schoener, 1985]) is detectable. This in turn can arise from the following factors inter alia: (1) predators or parasites hold populations at sizes too low for them to compete, (2) physical factors do likewise, and (3) the species do not overlap much in their use of resources, i.e., do not show strong resource partitioning. The first two factors can be tested for with more experiments. The third, if it exists, could be due to intense past competition. In such a situation experimentation is not useful for a test unless evolutionary time is available; the null-model approach discussed above would seem the most sensible alternative (related hypotheses about past competition can sometimes be tested by experimentation, however—see Hairston's [1980] work on salamanders).

One might counter the argument concerning the impracticality of an experimental test of whether competition induced resource partitioning as follows: a substantial amount of present competition is needed to maintain the partitioning, and this should be detectable in the short term. Given the low statistical power of many experiments, this counter seems often unlikely even if the competition is chronic. If it is intermittent, however, even an experiment with high power will fail if done at the wrong time. The degree of intermittency of interspecific competition, and the implications thereof, has also been a matter of controversy (Wiens, 1977; Schoener, 1982). In the one relevant set of direct observations available, that on the Galápagos finch *Geospiza fortis* (Boag and Grant, 1981), intermittent but severe selection had a strong directional effect on size. Indirect observations on resource overlap as it varies with resource abundance also appear to support the intermittent but nonetheless strong effect of competition: in 28 of 30 studies greater resource overlap was found between species during "fat" seasons or years than during "lean" ones. Ironically, stream fishes (e.g., Power, 1981) constitute one of the two exceptions, for somewhat idiosyncratic reasons having to do with substantially more restricted habitats available during the lean (in this case, dry) season. In contrast, the study of Felley and Felley (chap. 8) on the Calcasieu drainage fits the general pattern: each species contracts to its preferred (and more or less unique) habitat during the dry season, when resources are low.

Axis 5—Density-Independent Versus Density-Dependent

This axis of controversy constituted the prominent ecological issue in the late 1950s and much of the 1960s; it dominated the famous 1957 Cold Spring Harbor Symposium volume, and it was extensively discussed by, among others, Andrewartha and Birch (1954) in their milestone volume. Although now giving way to other issues, the controversy is still very much alive among lotic ecologists, as evidenced by the paper of Shiozawa (1983).

Roughly speaking, density dependence occurs when individual net reproductive rate is a function of the number of individuals in the same population; the definition is extended in obvious ways to include interspecific cases. The definition can be given precise mathematical notation, as follows. For differential-equation representations of population growth, if f in

$$(1/N)(dN/dt) = f \tag{2.1}$$

is a function of N, density dependence occurs. For difference-equation representations, if f in, for example,

$$(N_{t+1} - N_t)/N_t = f \tag{2.2}$$

is a function of N_t, density dependence occurs. Typically, controversies revolve around negative density dependence, that is, whether f is negatively related to N or N_t.

While thus easily represented in mathematical models, statistical confirmation of density dependence is replete with pitfalls. The main problem lies in the fact that estimates of the left-hand portions of eqs. 2.1 and 2.2 involve the variable N, which is also involved in the right-hand portion by hypothesis, provided density dependence occurs. An inverse relation between the left-hand portion and N can therefore mean either or both (1) that the population shows negative density dependence or (2) that there exists a statistical artifact, since the left-hand side will decrease with N even where all variables are random. A much better procedure, although still not entirely satisfactory, is to plot log (N_{t+1}) versus log (N_t) and statistically compare the slope to 1, the value expected when density independence occurs (Morris, 1959). This method, however, becomes increasingly unreliable as random variation in N increases (reviewed in Slade, 1977). A number of more sophisticated techniques have been proposed (Bulmer, 1975; Jolicoeur, 1975; Ricker, 1973, 1975; Slade, 1976); these have been compared in an extensive analysis by Slade (1977).

Logically, one expects a strong association between this axis and axis 3, provided competition is involved—competition implies negative density dependence. For predation the situation is more ambiguous, depending in particular on whether predator saturation exists. Axis 4 can also be related in obvious ways to a definition of density dependence extended to populations of other species.

Axis 6—Nonequilibrial Versus Equilibrial

This axis and axis 7 order perhaps the most heated controversies at least as regards terminology, not only in stream-fish ecology but perhaps especially in stream-fish ecology (Grossman et al., 1982; Yant et al., 1984; Rahel et al., 1984; Herbold, 1984; Grossman et al., 1985). The principal problem is that, even more than axis 5, these two axes constitute mathematical metaphors when applied to the real world; their meaning is obvious in mathematical models but not as obvious in biological data or as related to natural causes.

Equilibrium occurs in mathematical models of the sorts represented by eqs. 2.1 and 2.2 when $dN/dt = 0$ or $N_{t+1} = N_t$, respectively. These models have as dependent variable number of individuals of some population, and, depending on independent variables, equilibrium occurs via negative feedback from intraspecific competition, from interspecific competition, and/or from predation. Other models have different dependent variables, i.e., number of species (the MacArthur-Wilson [1963] Equilibrium Model) and number of places occupied by a species (the spatial heterogeneity models of Levins and Culver [1971], Slatkin [1974], and Levin [1974]). Moreover, one can have a point equilibrium (in which abundance stays constant) or an equilibrium set such as a cycle (in which abundance rotates over a constant set of values). Despite these multifarious mathematical meanings, the issue as recently applied to ecological communities (e.g., Wiens, 1977, 1984) is typically restricted to the two kinds of competition and to point-equilibrial cases: Is the number of individuals in a population limited by the amount of resources and by (perhaps) the number of individuals of other species using that resource and/or by some kind of interference competition?

Wiens's (1977) counter-Malthusian answer was that it often is not. In a later paper Wiens (1984) emphasized the frequency of disturbance as determining where on the equilibrium continuum particular communities lie. This frequency is now being estimated for some stream-fish communities, as the chapter by Li et al. (chap. 25) exemplifies.

The question of equilibrium as restricted above can be related to the various other axes. If the answer is yes, then we necessarily have negative density dependence (axis 5). If the answer is yes, we are probably more likely to have pattern than no pattern (axis 1; see Schoener, 1986d, for a justification). If the answer is yes, we have biological rather than physical influences, at least as direct effects (axis 3). If other species are important, we have an interactive situation (axis 4). These simple relations are subject to some reservations, however.

First, species populations may be not at equilibrium but at similar proportional distances from it. Then one can have a "moving equilibrium," which if precise enough can give patterns that can be related to local conditions. This is particularly likely when species are using a common resource set, i.e., when a guild exists in Root's (1967) sense, because the resources of the various species will then covary over time. Thus the relation to axis 1 need not be the one just claimed.

Second, whether or not a population is at equilibrium depends not only on resource variability and other manifestations of disturbance but also on the population's ability to track it. Where that ability is slight, pattern (axis 1), density-dependence (axis 5), and biological factors (axis 3) will be of little importance. But where that ability is great, all of the above can operate strongly even in the face of great variation in physical factors (axis 3). We know little about such abilities, although intuitively we would expect arthropods and other invertebrates to be better able to track a resource than long-generationed organisms such as most fishes and birds. Yet, perhaps surprisingly, in the only precise study on vertebrates available, that of Grant (1985) on Galápagos finches, very rapid resource tracking was shown. In this system precipitation affects the seed crop, which affects finch populations. Despite great variation in rainfall, itself apparently stochastic (see axis 7), species populations were near equilibrium with their resources and with one another.

Third, while the number of individuals of a set of species may usually be at equilibrium, the number of species may not, or vice versa. In the first case a community is invasible by one or more species (e.g., Roughgarden, 1974); in the other case populations may rise and fall but the number of species stays constant ("species turnover" in the MacArthur-Wilson [1963] model, as found in many studies [review in Schoener, 1983b]). Thus, if a different definition of equilibrium from the restricted one given above is used, a different conclusion could easily be drawn.

Axis 7—Stochastic Versus Deterministic

It is this axis that perhaps embodies the most controversy in stream-fish community ecology, a controversy that is certainly in part semantic. What does "stochastic" mean? I am indebted to Robert Silverberg (1975), the science-fiction writer, for the following etymology:

> According to the Oxford English Dictionary this word was coined in 1662 and is now *rare* or *obs*. Don't believe it. It's the OED that's *obs*., not *stochastic*, which gets less *obs*. every day. The word is from the Greek, originally meaning "target" or "point of aim," from which the Greeks derived a word meaning "to aim at a mark," and, by metaphorical extension, "to reflect, to think." It came into English first as a fancy way of saying "pertaining to guesswork," as in Whitefoot's remark about Sir Thomas Browne in 1712: "Tho' he were no prophet . . . yet in that faculty which comes nearest it, he excelled, i.e., the stochastick, wherein he was seldom mistaken , as to future events."

The word now enjoys common usage in describing a set of mathematical techniques or models.

Stochastic mathematical models incorporate probabilities, where an event or state has a certain chance, but not certainty, of occurring during some time interval. May (1973) distinguishes two general classes of such models:

1. Models of *environmental stochasticity* incorporate variation into one or more "environmental" parameters, such as carrying capacity. The idea is to simulate variation owing to, say, weather factors. The commonest such model uses "white noise"; a disadvantage is that such variation is uncorrelated from one instant to the next. Other sorts of environmental models also exist, e.g., those incorporating autocorrelated variation. In environmental-stochastic models, variation in output is not affected by population size.
2. In contrast, models of *demographic stochasticity* have populations whose fluctuations (coefficients of variation over time) scale roughly as $N^{-1/2}$ (see below). The models deal with whole individuals (not fractions, as in deterministic analogs), and they specify probabilities of events such as birth and death occurring in some small unit of time. Such models simulate sample-size effects, in which the smaller the number of individuals, the greater the departure from the deterministic situation and the more likely, say, population extinction (Sheldon [chap. 25] exploits this concept).

In all stochastic models a probability distribution of outcomes, rather than a single outcome, is expected at any point in time; sometimes, but not always, this distribution approaches a "stationary" state; i.e., its properties stabilize over time.

Note that "deterministic" can be viewed simply as an end point of the stochastic continuum in the sense that, for example, environmental variation is zero or population size is infinite (in probabilist parlance, the deterministic case has measure zero). The reason that deterministic models are often used rather than stochastic ones is that the latter are much more intractable mathematically; it is often difficult to determine how the model behaves, which would seem a necessary prerequisite for simulating nature. When stochastic models must be used is a sometimes difficult matter of judgment (Gurney and Nisbet, 1984).

Given these mathematical concepts, it is possible to make some headway into determining what a natural manifestation of a stochastic factor might be. For demographic stochasticity the situation is easy—variation occurs because of small sample-size effects. For environmental stochasticity the situation becomes murkier, almost metaphysical (see, for example, the discussion of probability in Feller, 1968, chap. 1). Is something about a factor intrinsically stochastic? Or is a probability used because there are too many variables having small effects to tease apart and incorporate into a deterministic model? Moreover, some of the variables may not fall under the explanatory bailiwick of the science in question; ecology, for example, typically considers major weather factors as inputting from some black box, the latter being the explanatory province of meteorologists, to the extent that it can be explained at all. Moreover, some of the variation may be historically determined to the degree that its origins are unobservable. In short, the prevailing rationalization seems to be not to deny deterministic causal chains when using stochastic models but to argue that they are too numerous and intricate to represent except by probabilities. Again, when to separate variables deterministically and when to throw them into probability statements are a matter of judgment that depends inter alia on how much is known and the statistical power of the system; the less we know and the sparser our data, the more desirable a stochastic approach becomes.

Having tried to sharpen the meaning of "stochastic," we may now relate this axis of controversy to the others. In one of the many senses of "random" (axis 2), the present axis would seem almost identical—the dependent variable and some or all independent ones in stochastic models are "random variables" in a statistical sense. However, in the sense we have used "random," i.e., indistinguishable from the output of an appropriate null model, the relation is more consequential than identical, in the following way. All other things being equal, the more the actual data are variable because of the influence of stochastic factors, the less statistically distinguishable, typically, they are likely to be from null expectation. The situation is tricky, however, because of the somewhat circular nature of many null models; that is, because many null models use the data to form null expectations, variability in the former affects variability in the latter, so that one may be scaled to the other. Any particular relation of axis 2 to axis 7 must be carefully reasoned on an ad hoc basis.

It seems to be generally accepted, although usually without comparable data from the same system, that physical factors are more likely to be stochasitc than are biological ones, so that a fairly strong relation exists between axis 3 and the present axis. Perhaps also physical factors are more likely to be unknown to biologists in their etiology or more likely to be outside their domain of expertise, so that in the sense above they are more likely to be modeled as stochastic. Again, evaluation of this relationship depends on how indirect effects of physical factors are classified (see discussion under axis 4). These remarks apply to environmental stochasticity (for a discussion of environmental variation with respect to genetics, see Falconer, 1981, p. 124). The degree to which demographic stochasticity relates to axis 3 depends on whether populations controlled mainly by physical factors are likely to be smaller than those controlled mainly by biological factors. Perhaps they are, but I know of no compelling logic or data. On the other hand, it is possible to argue that, within the biological part of the continuum, populations controlled mainly by predation are more likely to be influenced by demographic stochasticity than are those controlled mainly by competition (Schoener, 1986d). This is because, on average, for the same kind of organism, the former populations should be smaller in size.

There would seem to be little relation of the present axis to axis 4, noninteractive versus interactive. Stochastic concepts apply as well to populations considered in isolation as to communities of populations. It is possible to have highly deterministic occurrences of species having largely nonoverlapping habitat preferences, for example, provided those species are close to carrying capacity. Examples for lizards on islands are given in Schoener and Schoener (1983). On the other hand, were species to act independently and were carrying capacities seldom achieved, demographic stochasticity could prevail even in the face of strong habitat preferences.

Likewise, little necessary relation of the present axis to axis 5, density-independent versus density-dependent, exists. Stochastic versus deterministic representations can apply in principle to models or situations at any point along the density-dependence continuum. Correlations between axes 5 and 7 are likely to result mainly via intermediary axes, especially axis 3, physical versus biological.

The relation of the present axis to axis 6, nonequilibrial versus equilibrial, can best be approached by examining properties of the respective mathematical representations. A stochastic model generates a distribution of values of N about the equilibrium point of the appropriate deterministic analog. In demographic models the coefficient of variation of this distribution scales as $N^{-1/2}$ (May, 1973; Turelli, 1986; J. E. Cohen, pers. comm.). In environmental models, no general relation between the population-size variance or coefficient of variation and the magnitude of environmental fluctuations, σ^2, is known to exist (Turelli, 1981, 1986; pers. comm.; Roughgarden, 1979). For example, a logistic model for a fluctuating r and K (eq. 20.42 in Roughgarden, 1979) has the variance sometimes decreasing with increasing σ^2, while the coefficient of variation always increases (Turelli, pers. comm.). In many models the coefficient of variation and/or the variance of population size over time does increase with increasing σ^2 (Turelli, 1986; Goel and Richter-Dyn,

1974, chap. 4, eqs. 14a, b).

Typically, population-size variation in the field is measured as the coefficient of variation of N or as the standard deviation of log (N) (Connell and Sousa, 1983; Schoener, 1986d). The biological implication of the above models is that such variation is directly related to the degree of demographic stochasticity and, in certain environmental models, is known to be directly related to the degree of environmental stochasticity, this sometimes depending on how fluctuations are measured. Hence there may be a very strong relation between the present axis and axis 6, with the additional proviso that in the mathematical models population sizes below *and* above deterministic equilibria (or means of population-size distributions) are considered, whereas biological discussions typically emphasize the "below-equilibrium" state.

Finally, and somewhat technically, the above-mentioned distribution, if stationary, provides a stochastic analog to the point equilibrium of deterministic models (May, 1973).

The above discussion illustrates how axes 6 and 7 can be closely related when applied to data, but the two are far from identical conceptually (contra Grossman et al., 1982, p. 438).

The relation of the present axis to the phenomenological axis, unpatterned versus patterned (axis 1), would typically seem relatively straightforward. If perception of pattern is less likely, the greater the variance in some measure of the pattern, then stochastic factors, considered as factors other than the one being measured or described, are by definition the hidden determinants of such variance. However, stochastic factors can produce pattern in certain senses; for example, a large number of independent factors acting multiplicatively on population size gives a lognormal distribution of abundances (May, 1975). Hence we need to specify carefully the type of pattern being evaluated. Moreover, a particular stochastic input, e.g., a stochastic physical factor, may or

Table 2.2. Ordination of Real Communities Along Organismic Axes

Axis	Ranked Communities*											
01. Body size (small → large)	HMit	THer ISpi		IVas EAlg		SFis ILiz MVas	PFis	PAlg IBir CFis	Chet CBir			CTre
02. Source of new individuals (closed → open)*‡		ILiz PFis		CHet		IVas MVas	CTre	IBir†		THer ISpi HMit CBir	SFis PAlg	CFis EAlg
03. Generation time (small → large)	HMit	THer ISpi EAlg	IVas		SFis CFis PFis ILiz CHet	CBir IBir	PAlg MVas					CTre
04. Mobility (sessile → mobile)	PAlg EAlg CTre IVas MVas		HMit THer	ISpi		ILiz	PFis CFis	CHet	SFis IBir†		CBir	
05. Homeostatic ability (low → high)	HMit ISpi THer		EAlg IVas	SFis ILiz	MVas PFis PAlg	CFis CTre					CBir IBir CHet	
06. Number of life stages (small → large)	CBir IBir CHet				ISpi ILiz		SFis PAlg EAlg CFis CTre PFis IVas MVas		HMit	CHer		

*Temperate stream fishes are boxed. CBir = shrub steppe, continental birds; CFis = coral-reef fishes; CHet = continental desert heteromyids; CTre = continental forest trees; EAlg = ephemeral intertidal algae; HMit = hummingbird mites; IBir = tropical island birds; ILiz = island lizards; ISpi = subtropical-island orb spiders; IVas = interstitial vascular plants; MVas = matrix vascular plants; PAlg = perennial intertidal algae; PFis = pond and lake fishes; SFis = temperate stream fishes; THer = temperate herbivorous insects (details of these communities in Schoener, 1985b, table 28.1).

†Galápagos study.

‡Islands considered separately.

may not give a pattern, depending on the modulation the biological community provides. Coefficients of concordance in abundance, for example, may be high over time if members of a community respond to physical factors similarly. On the other hand, if they do no not, concordances can be low. Three studies of stream-fish communities—Herbold (1984), Schlosser (chap. 3), and Finger and Stewart (chap. 11)—suggest that differences between species in life-history features such as breeding times produce discordant abundance changes.

Two Emollients for the Controversies

Faced with this multiplicity of interrelated controversies, how have community ecologists responded? Some have become pessimistic; a few verge on nihilism. However, ecology has weathered spates of pessimism before; typically, pessimism self-destructs and is eventually replaced by a new wave of optimism. Accordingly I would like to end optimistically. I think there are at least two new waves in community ecology, where the newness is largely with respect to emphasis or enthusiasm, rather than invention. These are the pluralistic approach and the mechanistic approach.

The Pluralistic Approach

Pluralism explicitly recognizes and emphasizes differences between ecological communities (Schoener, 1986c). "Primitive" characteristics are those intrinsic to the species and location in question; they can be divided into organismic and environmental. A pluralistic theory attempts to relate differences in these characteristics to differences in "de-

Table 2.3. Ordination of Real Communities Along Environmental Axes

Axis	Ranked Communities[a]										
E1. Severity of physical factors (high → low)		ISpi EAlg			SFis CFis IVas	PAlg MVas CTre	THer	CBir	PFis	CHet IBir ILiz	
E2. Trophic position (low → high)		IVas MVas PAlg EAlg CTre		CHer HMit	ISpi	SFis THet IBir CBir CFis		PFis ILiz			
E3. Resource input (open → closed)[b]		ISpi	ILiz			CBir CFis	SFis IBir[c]			CHet PFis	THer CTre EAlg PAlg IVas MVas HMit
E4. Spatial fragmentation (broken → continuous)[b]		HMit THer	IVas		MVas	EAlg	PAlg		SFis CFis	IBir ISpi PFis ILiz	CHet CTre CBir
E5. Long-term climatic variation[d] (high → low)	CBir CRre (D)[e] THer MVas IVas	CHet	SFis PFis PAlg EAlg				IBir[c]	ISpi ILiz		HMit CTre (H)[f]	CFis
E6. Partitionability of resource (low → high)	PAlg EAlg		IVas	MVas CTre		THer	SFis HMit CFis		ISpi	CHet IBir CBir ILiz PFis	

[a]Temperate stream fishes are boxed. Abbreviations as in table 2.2.
[b]Islands considered separately; adults or life stages similar to adults—e.g., later instars of spiders or hemimetabolous insects—considered only.
[c]Galápagos study.
[d]Seasonal, or over a period of about 10 years.
[e]D = Davis.
[f]H = Hubbell.

rived'' axes, such as species diversity and temporal constancy of a population size. By its nature pluralism is positive with regard to between-community variation in major controlling factors and the many-faceted theory necessary to account for such variation. An explanation for the lack of pattern in some characteristic is as essential as an explanation for its presence. No place in pluralism exists for true nihilism, unless the theory becomes too complex.

The particular kind of a community most amenable to this approach is the ''similia community,'' which consists of a set of species in some place similar in their organismic characteristics. A recent conference attempted, among other things, a first classification of some similia communities with respect to organismic and environmental characteristics. Tables 2.2 and 2.3 present the results. Stream fishes were not represented at the conference; however, I have inserted into the tables average positions for temperate stream-fish communities as discussed in this volume. Note that stream fishes are mostly intermediate with respect to the various characteristics.

My treatment of stream-fish communities as a single entity masks the considerable differences that might exist between them. It would be possible to construct a set of tables analogous to tables 2.2 and 2.3 restricted entirely to stream-fish communities. Some of the discriminating characteristics would likely be different; for example, discharge rate, stream temperature, and breeding times might be added. Moreover, units considered communities in the present volume might have to be divided to meet the criteria of a simila community. For example, fishes vary in size, and this variation can affect major controlling factors. In Schlosser's (chap 3) and Gorman's (chap. 5) studies smaller fishes are considered more likely to be affected by predation and physical factors, larger ones by competition. In Gorman (chap. 5) juveniles and adults are treated separately with respect to habitat preference. So far, the nearest to a pluralistic approach for stream fishes is Schlosser's (1982a and chap. 3) scheme, in which upstream and downstream habitats define a continuum. The key environmental axis is the degree to which deeper areas (large pools and the like) are available in sufficient quantities to support specialists in such areas. These specialists tend to be large; thus an environmental (depth-heterogeneity) and and organismic (body-size) axis are correlated. In turn, these primitive axes can be related to derived ones: the downstream communities are less controlled by predation and more by competition, are more diverse, and show less fluctuation in abundance.

The Mechanistic Approach

This approach attempts to construct a theory for higher ecological levels—population and community ecology—by utilizing concepts from lower levels—particularly behavioral and physiological ecology. As such, it is avowedly reductionistic (Schoener, 1986b). It stands in contrast to the descriptive approach to population and community ecology. For example, rather than the logistic equation, a similar equation, but one derived from lower-level assumptions about feeding, might be used.

Mechanistic ecology provides a vehicle for pluralism by being explicit about how the various organismic and environmental characteristics affect higher-level phenomena. Higher-level objects, such as carrying capacities, for example, can be decomposed into lower-level objects, such as feeding rates and metabolic costs. Such decompositions provide a variety of explanatory interpretations of carrying capacity and lead us away from the ''sufficient parameter'' approach of Levins (1966). Underlying this withdrawal is a distrust that most models will be ''robust,'' also in the sense of Levins (1966).

A recent symposium in ''American Zoologist'' (1986) highlighted some of the mechanistic research now being done. Again, stream-fish ecology was not represented, but the extensive research program of Werner, Hall, and colleagues on pond fishes was included. By obvious analogy, stream-fish ecology is ready for an infusion of mechanistic ecology, and, indeed, certain research in the present volume is tending in this direction. For example, Angermeier argues that habitat preferences may result from a trade-off between feeding and avoidance of predators. This notion is very similar to Price's (1986) ideas for desert heteromyid rodents, and tests of it may take similar forms.

In conclusion, the axes of controversy in community ecology can be viewed through pluralistic and mechanistic glasses as objects of scientific interest, not objects of distress. Rather than using axes to polarize and isolate, they can be used to order data in a way that ultimately facilitates understanding.[1]

[1] I thank B. Herbold, W. Matthews and M. Turelli for comments on a previous draft. The work was supported by NSF grants and the University of California at Davis.

3. A Conceptual Framework for Fish Communities in Small Warmwater Streams

Isaac J. Schlosser

Abstract

Spatial and temporal variation in the structure of the fish community along a gradient of increasing habitat heterogeneity and pool development is described. Based on the pattern, a conceptual framework is presented that attempts to integrate the relative roles of physical versus biological processes in regulating fish community structure in small warmwater streams. The framework suggests that future theoretical advances in lotic fish ecology will require syntheses that incorporate differences in regulating processes (1) *between* communities, because of the influence of channel morphology on environmental stability, age-size structure of fish populations, and predator abundance, and (2) *within* communities, because of the influence of fish size on susceptibility to predation, high flow regimes, and harsh winter conditions.

The goals of community ecology are to record the patterns that occur in nature, elucidate the casual processes underlying these patterns, and generalize the explanations for the patterns as far as possible (Wiens, 1984). In an emerging discipline such as ecology, divergent views frequently develop regarding the patterns that exist and the processes producing them (Roughgarden, 1983; Strong, 1983). Advances in such a discipline will occur primarily as a result of syntheses that reconcile apparently opposing perspectives (Salt, 1983).

Recently very divergent views have been presented regarding the importance of physical versus biological processes in regulating the structure of stream-fish communities. Some researchers emphasize the importance of temporal variability in community structure and the critical role of physical variability (Grossman et al., 1982). Other research has documented both the relative stability of species composition in stream-fish communities (Moyle and Vondracek, 1985) and the importance of biological interactions (Fraser and Cerri, 1982; Power and Matthews, 1983).

These differences in perspective reflect the complexity of natural communities. Fortunately most ecologists increasingly realize that processes related to both physical disturbance and biological interactions are involved in determining community organization (Sousa, 1984b). The relative importance of these processes is strongly influenced by spatial habitat heterogeneity, frequency and intensity of physical disturbance, and life-history attributes of the organisms being considered (Connell, 1975, 1978; Karr and Freemark, 1983, 1985; Sousa, 1979, 1984a, b; Strong, 1983; Wiens, 1984).

This chapter represents an attempt to reconcile the diverse perspectives in the literature regarding the importance of physical variability versus biological interactions in regulating stream-fish communities by (1) briefly illustrating how the composition and temporal dynamics of the fish community change among stream reaches with distinctly different attributes of spatial habitat heterogeneity and temporal variability in the physical environment and (2) presenting a hypothetical conceptual framework that attempts to integrate the relative roles of abiotic and biotic processes in regulating fish community structure along physical gradients.

Study Area

Jordan Creek is a second-order warmwater stream in Vermilion County, Illinois, which drains a glaciated area of 25–30 km^2. Topography is level in the upper portion of the watershed but rolling in the lower regions. Predominant (80%) land use in the drainage basin is row-crop agriculture. Subsurface springs maintain some flow even in relatively dry years, and complete ice cover over the stream is common during winter periods. The stream has an abundant and diverse fish fauna represented by a variety of taxa and trophic groups (table 3.1; see also Larimore et al., 1952).

Distinct stream reaches can be distinguished in the water-

Table 3.1. Predominant fish species in Jordan Creek and Their Trophic Classifications*

Common Name (Abbreviation)†	Scientific Name (Trophic Group)
Darters	
1. Orangethroat darter (Ot)	*Etheostoma spectabile* (Bi)
2. Johnny darter (Jd)	*Etheostoma nigrum* (Bi)
3. Greenside darter (Gd)	*Etheostoma blennioides* (Bi)
4. Fantail darter (Fd)	*Etheostoma flabellare* (Bi)
5. Rainbow darter (Rd)	*Etheostoma caeruleum* (Bi)
Minnows	
6. Creek chub (Cc)	*Semotilus atromaculatus* (Gi)
7. Stoneroller (Sr)	*Campostoma anomalum* (Hd)
8. Bluntnose minnow (Bm)	*Pimephales notatus* (Omn)
9. Hornyhead chub (Hh)	*Nocomis bigutattus* (Gi)
10. Striped shiner (Ss)	*Notropis chrysocephalus* (Gi)
Sunfish	
11. Bluegill (Bg)	*Lepomis macrochirus* (Ip)
12. Rock bass (Rb)	*Ambloplites rupestris* (Ip)
13. Smallmouth bass (Sm)	*Micropterus dolomieui* (Ip)
14. Longear sunfish (Le)	*Lepomis megalotis* (Ip)
Suckers	
15. Creek chubsucker (Cs)	*Erimyzon oblongus* (Bi)
16. Northern hogsucker (Hs)	*Hypentelium nigricans* (Bi)
17. White sucker (Ws)	*Catostomus commersoni* (Bi)

*Trophic groups include herbivore-detritivores (Hd), omnivores (Omn), generalized insectivores (Gi), benthic insectivores (Bi), and insectivore-piscivores (Ip). See Schlosser, 1982a, for a definition of trophic groups.

†See fig. 3.1

shed on the basis of channel morphology (table 3.2). The modified upstream area is a low-gradient (0.65 m/km) stream consisting of uniform raceways created by channelization and only poorly developed pools. Unstable silt-sand substrates occur throughout this reach. The natural upstream area has a relatively undisturbed, moderate gradient (0.95 m/km) channel with reasonably well developed small pools and riffles and sand-gravel substrates. The downstream area is a natural high-gradient channel (4 m/km) that has large rocky riffles and well-developed sandy bottom pools with undercut banks.

Methods

Sampling occurred from March 1978 to November 1979: early spring (March–April), late spring or early summer (May–June), late summer (August–September), and autumn (October–November). Normally three stations, each 100 m long, were sampled in the modified and natural upstream areas. The number and lengths of stations were chosen to include the range of habitats occurring in the stream. Because of the greater habitat heterogeneity in downstream areas, five stations, each 100 m long, were normally sampled. The primary exception to this sampling regime occurred in spring 1979, when only one station could be sampled in the downstream area because of frequent high-flow conditions.

Habitat heterogeneity and habitat volume were measured for each sampling date and station. Habitat heterogeneity (H′) was measured in three dimensions: depth, current, and substrate. Sampling protocol and calculation of habitat heterogeneity followed Gorman and Karr (1978). Habitat area was calculated as the product of the length and mean width of the station (m^2). Habitat area times mean depth was used as an indication of habitat volume (m^3).

Since upstream stations had little instream cover and a uniform narrow channel, fish were sampled in these areas with a minnow drag seine (1.2×6 m) with a 4.8-mm mesh. Block seines were placed at the upper and lower ends of the station before sampling. Each station was seined until capture rates declined to near zero. Normally this involved five seine hauls. New species were not added after four seine hauls and 90% of the individuals eventually collected were captured after five seine hauls (Schlosser, 1982a). Large rocks and undercut banks prevented the use of drag seines in downstream areas. A 7-m electric seine powered by a 60-cycle AC generator with a maximum capacity of 1,500 and 8.7 amp was used. Block seines (4.8-mm mesh) were placed at the upper and lower ends of the station. Each station was electroseined twice, and fish were picked up with 4.8-mm-mesh dip nets. Approximately 90% of the species and 80–90% of the individuals eventually captured were collected in the first two seine passes (Schlosser, 1982a).

To ensure that differences in the characteristics of the fish community in upstream versus downstream areas were not related to differences in sampling methods, I electroseined the natural upstream habitat with the most complex habitat after drag seining. Electroseining increased the number of fish caught by only 1%, indicating that drag seining missed few fish. Furthermore, both drag seining and electroseining had a similar lower limit of capture efficiency for small fish of approximately 20 mm total length.

A detailed discussion of the sampling procedures, their relative efficiencies, and potential influences of sampling biases on the results can be found in Larimore, 1961; Schlosser, 1982a, b; and Schlosser, 1985. It should be emphasized, however, that, while both drag seining and electroseining resulted in quantitative underestimates of community parameters, the basic qualitative conclusions regarding differences in community pattern and temporal dynamics of pattern in various reaches of the watershed do not appear to be due to sampling biases.

The Patterns

The patterns will be illustrated here only briefly, since they have been discussed in part in previous publications. Those readers desiring greater detail should refer to Schlosser (1982a, b, 1985).

Spatial and Temporal Variation in Habitat Heterogeneity and Habitat Volume

Habitat heterogeneity increased in downstream reaches (table 3.2) because of less human disturbance and the de-

Table 3.2. General Characteristics of the Channel Morphology in Three Reaches of Jordan Creek, Vermilion County, Illinois

Stream Reach	Mean Channel Width (m)	Channel Morphology	Mean Habitat Heterogeneity*	Mean Habitat Volume†
Modified upstream	3.6	Predominantly raceways, no pool or riffle development	2.07 (17.2)	106.3 (38.4)
Natural upstream	4.0	Moderately well-developed pools and riffles	2.84 (5.0)	130.3 (44.4)
Downstream	8.0	Well-developed large pools and riffles	3.15 (7.1)	182.0 (22.0)

Source: Adapted from Schlosser, 1982a.

*Habitat heterogeneity (H') measured in three dimensions: depth, current, and substrate. See Gorman and Karr, 1978, and Schlosser, 1982a, for details. Number in parentheses represents the coefficient of variation in H' over the two-year sampling period.

†Volume (m^3) of water in 100 m of stream. Number in parentheses represents coefficient of variation in habitat volume over the two-year sampling period.

velopment of a structurally complex channel with large, stable pool habitats. Temporal variability in habitat heterogeneity was greater ($P < 0.05$; see Lewontin, 1966, regarding procedure for comparing CV values) in modified upstream areas than either natural upstream or downstream areas. Habitat volume was more variable (but not significantly $0.05 < P < 0.10$) in both of the upstream reaches than in the downstream reach (table 3.2). Additionally, the relative magnitude of temporal variation in habitat heterogeneity and habitat volume was evaluated. Habitat volume was more variable ($P < 0.05$) than habitat heterogeneity in all reaches of the stream (table 3.2).

These results indicate that a distinct physical gradient occurred in Jordan Creek. A gradient that ranged from modified upstream areas with low habitat heterogeneity, poorly developed pools, low habitat volume, and accentuated temporal variation in the physical environment to downstream areas with high habitat heterogeneity; large, well-developed pools; large habitat volume; and low temporal variation in the physical environment (table 3.2).

Species Composition

As expected, species composition of the fish community changed considerably along the physical gradient (fig. 3.1). Minnows were predominant, both numerically and by biomass, in upstream areas. A significant decrease in minnow abundance occurred in the downstream area (fig. 3.1). Decreased minnow abundance was associated with a large increase in biomass of sunfish and suckers. The shift in biomass composition resulted in a basic shift in trophic structure of the community from generalized insectivores to insectivore-piscivores and benthic insectivores (fig. 3.1, table 3.1). High biomass but low numbers of fishes in the downstream area (fig. 3.1) reflected a shift in community composition toward fewer, larger individuals (see also fig.3.2).

Comparisons of community similarity based on numerical abundances were used to assess the degree of temporal variation in species composition in each reach during the two-year period. Considerable controversy exists regarding the best

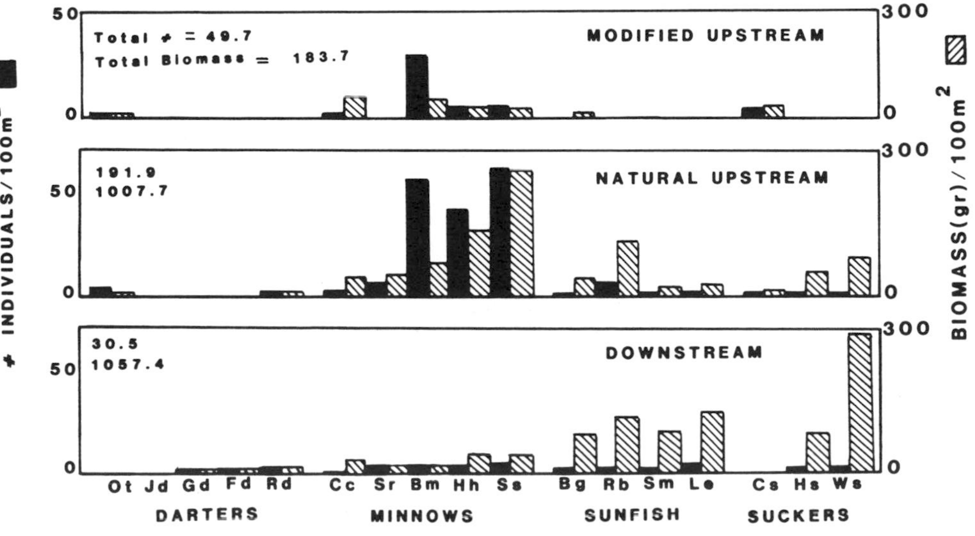

Fig. 3.1. Numbers of individuals and biomass for the predominant species in Jordan Creek. Data from June 1978. Species abbreviations and trophic classifications of species are provided in table 3.1.

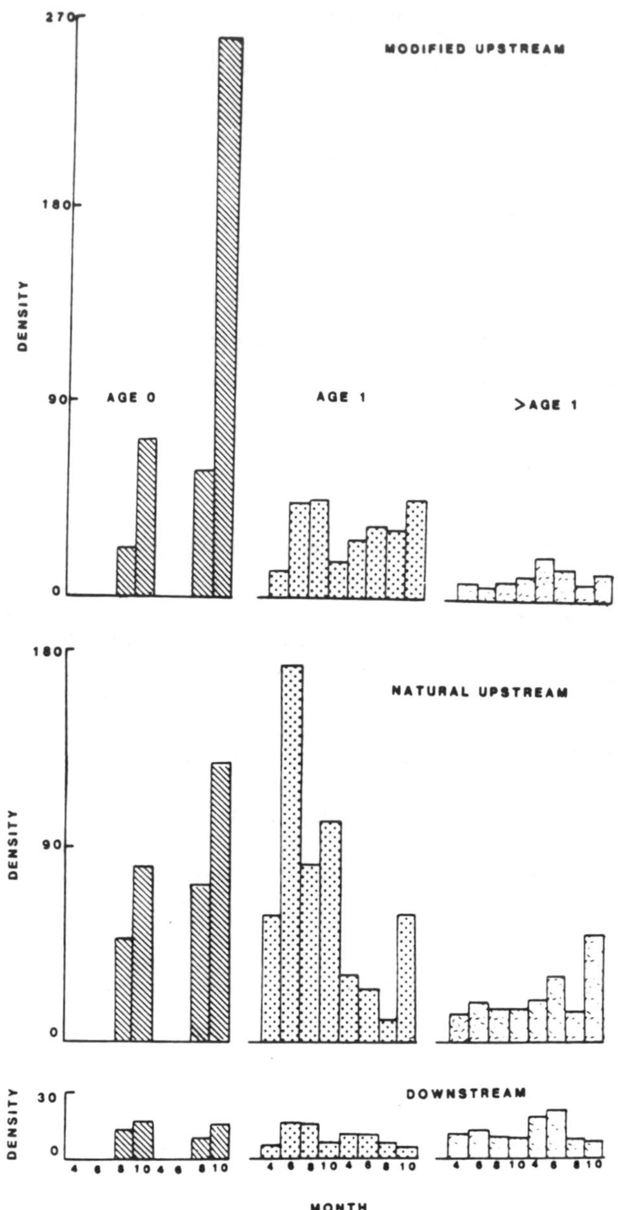

Fig. 3.2. Density (no./100 m^2) of age 0, age 1, and >age 1 fish in three reaches of Jordan Creek.

statistical approach for assessing community similarity (Grossman et al., 1982; Rahel et al., 1984; Jumars, 1980; Ghent, 1983), but most researchers have used either rank correlation indices or contingency table analyses. Both approaches have their limitations. Rank correlation has an increased probability of a Type I error, rejection of a null hypothesis when it is true (Grossman et al., 1982). Contingency table analysis has an increased probability of a Type II error, acceptance of the null hypothesis when it is false (Ghent, 1983). In an attempt to overcome this problem, I used a rank correlation approach with a conservative critical value ($P = 0.01$) for rejection of the null hypothesis. Comparisons of species ranks across all sample periods in each reach (Kendall's coefficient of concordance [*W*]; Sokal and Rohlf, 1981) indicated a significant association in species ranks in the modified upstream ($r = 0.78$, $P < 0.001$), natural upstream ($r = 0.78$, $P < 0.001$), and downstream ($r = 0.67$, $P < 0.001$) areas.

Fish Density (no./100 m^2)

Considerable spatial variation in fish density occurred along the physical gradient (table 3.3). Fish density tended to increase from the modified to natural upstream area and decrease in the downstream area. However, there was substantial temporal variation in the pattern (table 3.3). A comparison of coefficients of variation in fish density over the two-year period (table 3.3) indicated that modified upstream and natural upstream areas did not differ ($P > 0.05$) in temporal variability of fish density but that fish density in both upstream areas was more variable ($P < 0.05$) than in the downstream area. Fish density in the modified upstream area was nearly 5 times more variable than the downstream area (table 3.3). Greater temporal variability of fish density in upstream areas was attributable to two components: greater seasonal variation and greater annual variation (table 3.3). Seasonally, fish density in upstream areas was lowest in late winter or early spring and highest in autumn. Annually, the upstream areas differed in the season of greatest variability in fish density. Modified upstream areas exhibited the largest annual variation in autumn. Natural upstream areas exhibited the largest annual variation in early summer.

Age Structure

Variability in fish density was primarily attributable to spatial and temporal variation in density of age 0 (juvenile) and age 1 fishes (fig. 3.2). Increased fish density in natural relative to modified upstream areas was primarily caused by the addition of age 1 fish. Decreased fish density in the downstream area resulted from a major decrease in density of both age 0 and age 1 fishes.

Greater seasonal variation of fish density in upstream areas was primarily related to greater seasonal variation in abundance of juvenile recruits. Fish density was lowest in spring because of decreased abundance of fishes during the age 0 to age 1 transition in winter (table 3.3, fig. 3.2). Fish density was highest in autumn because of increased abundance of juveniles throughout the summer (table 3.3, fig. 3.2). Greater annual variation of fish density in upstream areas was associated with annual variation in the density of age 0 fish, especially in modified upstream areas, and age 1 fish, especially in natural upstream areas (fig. 3.2).

The downstream area did not exhibit accentuated periods of juvenile recruitment (fig. 3.2). This resulted in greater seasonal and annual stability of fish density and age structure in this region of the stream (table 3.3, fig. 3.2).

Table 3.3. Mean Fish Density (No./100 m^2) in Jordan Creek

Stream Reach	Date								CV*
	4/78	6/78	8/78	10/78	4/79	6/79	8/79	10/79	
Modified upstream	21.9	59.3	84.7	123.3	49.2	55.6	105.8	373.9	108
Natural upstream	79.4	254.0	154.0	223.0	63.6	67.7	104.3	192.7	52
Downstream	25.5	38.3	45.2	43.4	38.9	30.7	30.2	37.9	19

*CV represents the coefficient of variation in fish density over the two-year sampling period.

Species Richness and Species Density

Because of increased stream width in downstream areas (table 3.1) and the hypothesized relationship between species richness and area (MacArthur and Wilson, 1967; Schlosser, 1985), both species richness (number of species/station) and species density (number of species/100m^2) were evaluated (fig. 3.3). Species richness tended to increase from modified to natural upstream areas but was similar in natural upstream and downstream areas. In contrast, species density tended to be highest in natural upstream habitats (fig. 3.3).

However, substantial temporal variation occurred in both species richness and species density (fig. 3.3). A comparison of coefficients of variation in species richness and species density over the two-year period indicated that modified and natural upstream areas did not differ ($P > 0.05$) in temporal variability, but both reaches were more variable ($P < 0.05$) than the downstream area. Greater temporal variability in upstream areas was associated with lower species richness and species density in late winter or early spring and increased species richness and species density in summer and autumn (fig. 3.3).

The Conceptual Framework

Fish Communities Along Physical Gradients in Small Warmwater Streams

A major attribute of spatial heterogeneity in small-stream ecosystems is the degree of pool development (Leopold et al., 1964; Sheldon, 1968; Schlosser, 1982a). Pool development is also critical with respect to temporal heterogeneity because it has major effects on habitat volume and temporal stability of the physical environment (Schlosser, 1982a). Based on the results in this chapter and other previously published data (Schlosser, 1982a, b; Schlosser and Toth, 1984; Schlosser, 1985), a simple conceptual framework for viewing fish communities along a gradient of increasing habitat heterogeneity, pool development, and habitat volume in small warmwater streams can be proposed (figs. 3.4, 3.5).

The model is proposed to provide a preliminary conceptual framework for viewing stream-fish communities that will stimulate others to test, adapt, and refine its components for their particular fauna and geographic region. It should also be explicitly pointed out that the association between physical

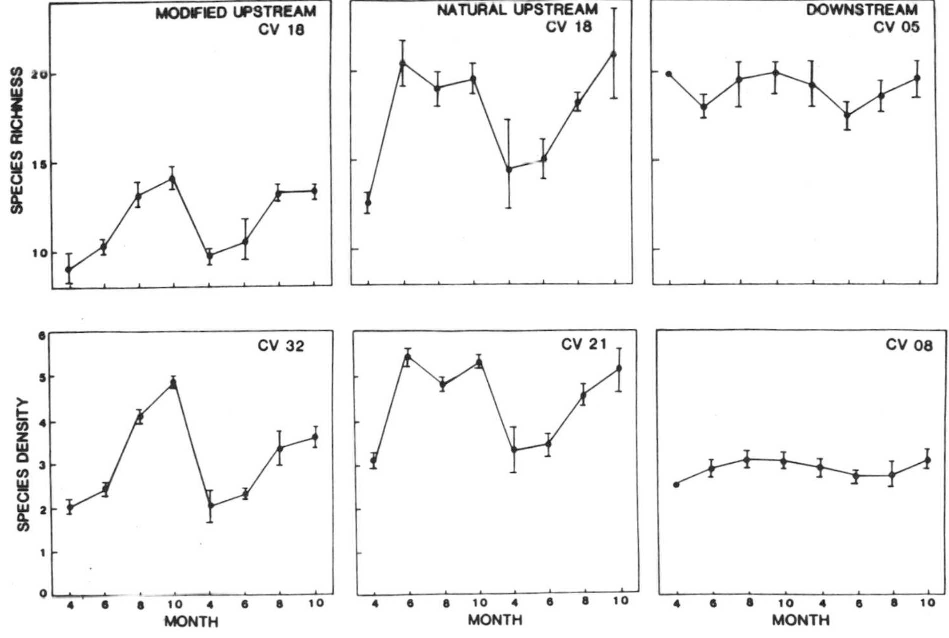

Fig. 3.3. Species richness (no. species/100 m of stream length; $\bar{x}$ + 1 SE) and species density (no. species/100 m^2; $\bar{x}$ + 1 SE) in three reaches of Jordan Creek. CV represents the coefficient of variation in species richness or species density during the two-year sampling period.

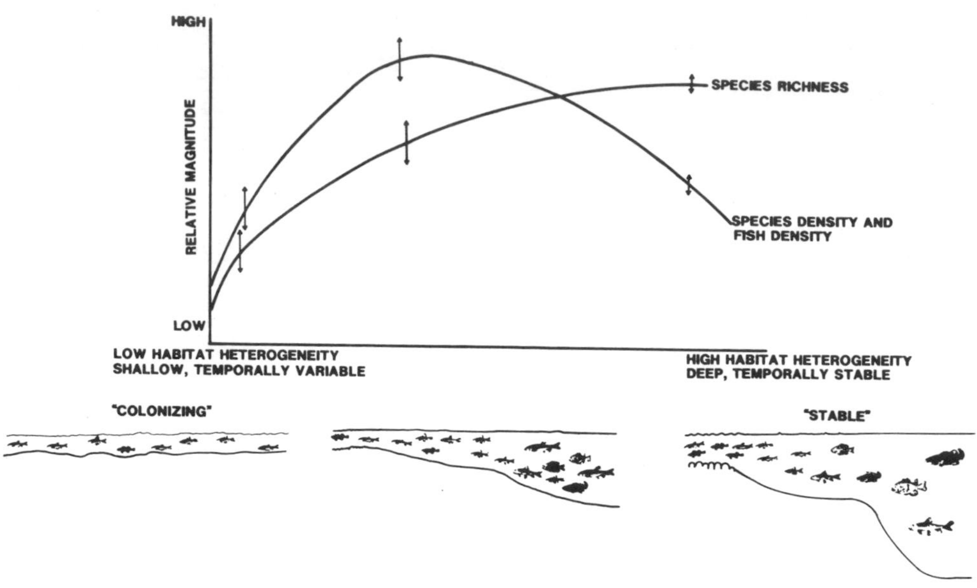

Fig. 3.4. Hypothetical pattern of select fish community attributes along a gradient of increasing habitat heterogeneity and pool development in a small warmwater stream. The patterns of species composition and size structure of fishes in the community are shown at the bottom of the figure. Arrows indicate relative temporal variability in the parameters.

factors and fish community structure illustrated in the model is reasonably well supported by the data in this and related studies, barring major methodological artifacts. On the other hand, the hypothesized nature and importance of biological interactions in the model are largely "guided" speculation based on the limited amount of experimental data in the literature. This alone should illustrate to the reader where future research is critically needed.

In areas with poorly developed pools, predominantly shallow depths, and low habitat volume, species richness, species density, and fish density are low because of the absence of deeper habitats needed by older age classes and pool species (fig. 3.4). The uniform shallow habitat results in a simple community with most fish being juvenile minnows (fig. 3.5). Large fish appear to avoid these shallow reaches because of either space limitations or increased susceptibility to terrestrial predators (Power, 1984a). As habitat heterogeneity, pool development, and habitat volume increase moderately, species richness, species density, and fish density increase because of the addition of older age groups of cyprinids and younger age groups of centrarchids and catastomids (fig. 3.4; Sheldon, 1968; Schlosser, 1982a).

Lack of large pool refugia in these upstream areas results in considerable emigration/mortality of fish during winter, resulting in lowest fish densities in early spring (Toth et al., 1982). Fish abundances increase throughout the spring and summer because of recolonization, especially by age 1 individuals, and juvenile recruitment (fig. 3.5). However, high flow regimes in spring and summer potentially cause considerable annual variation in recolonization by age 1 fishes and reproductive success. The unstable physical environment resulting from the combination of harsh winter conditions and fluctuations in streamflow results in considerable seasonal and annual variation in species richness, species density, fish density, and age structure (see also John, 1963, 1964; Hanson and Waters, 1974; Harrell, 1978; Toth et al., 1982; Schlosser, 1985). Fluctuations in species composition may or may not occur (Grossman et al., 1982), depending on (1) the nature and timing of the physical disturbance, (2) the range of life-history patterns within the community, and (3) whether the life-history patterns have stages or strategies to cope with the particular environmental disturbance (Sousa, 1984b; Moyle and Vondracek, 1985; Schlosser, 1985). Species such as the bluntnose minnow (*Pimephales notatus*) and striped shiner (*Notropis chrysocephalus*), with rapid maturity, prolonged breeding seasons, high reproductive rates, and strong dispersal capability of young, seem to predominate in these "colonizing" communities (figs. 3.1, 3.5).

Competition rather than predation is hypothesized to be the critical biological interaction influencing community dynamics in these shallow areas because of the simple trophic complexity and predominance of younger age classes (fig. 3.5). Competition appears to limit summer growth, prewinter size, and potentially winter survival in juvenile fishes (fig. 3.5, Schlosser, 1982a, b). However, the intensity of competition is likely to be both seasonally variable, as resource levels, metabolic rates, and demand/supply ratios change; and annually variable, as juvenile recruitment, fish density, and age structure fluctuate (table 3.3, fig. 3.2; Wiens, 1977; McIntire and Colby, 1978; Schlosser, 1982a, b).

Development of large, deep pools results in major changes in both community structure and the biological interactions hypothesized to be most critical in regulating community processes (figs. 3.4, 3.5). Species richness continues to increase with increasing habitat heterogeneity but at a slower rate because younger age classes of most pool species have already been added to the community (fig. 3.4). More important, the age/size structure, species composition, and trophic structure of the community undergo pronounced shifts toward fewer, larger centrarchids (insectivore-piscivores) and catostomids (benthic insectivores). Overall, small fishes exhibit reduced density in the stream, being restricted to

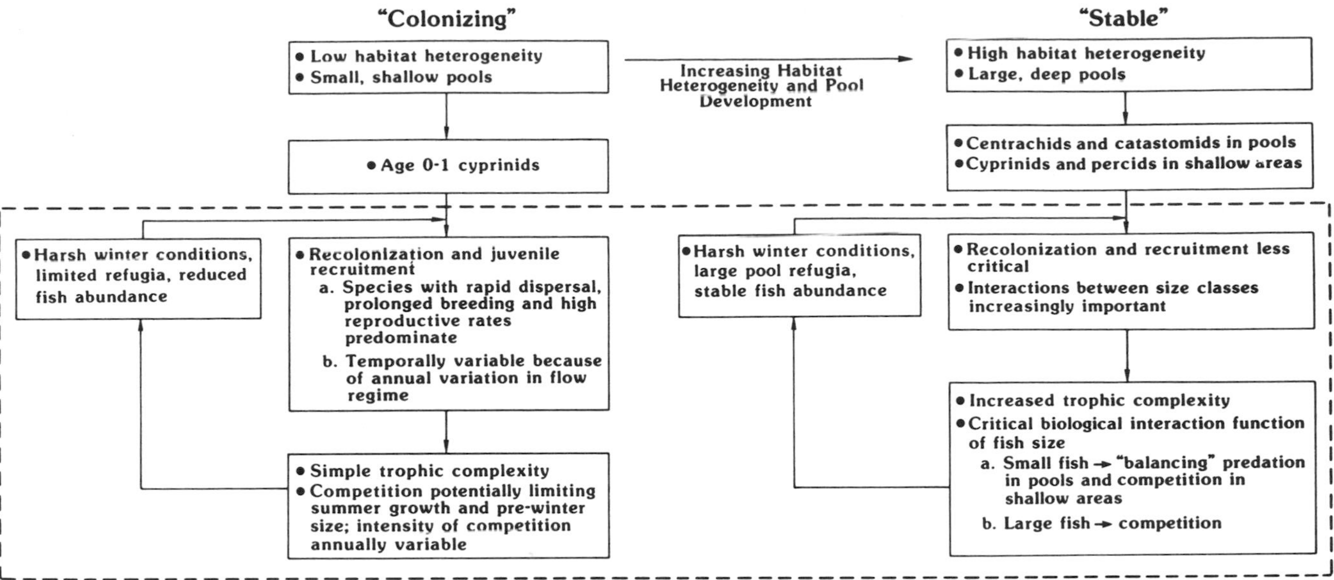

Fig. 3.5. Hypothetical conceptual framework of processes determining fish community structure along a gradient of habitat heterogeneity and pool development in a small warmwater stream. Critical ecological processes are outlined in the dashed box.

spatially isolated, shallow refugia (Schlosser, 1982a; fig. 3.4). The simplest explanation for smaller fishes being limited to shallow areas is that predaceous centrarchids cause short-term changes in abundance and spatial distribution of their prey (figs. 3.4, 3.5). Power and Matthews (1983) and Schlosser (unpub. data) provide experimental evidence for such an interaction. Increased predator pressure results in major decreases in cyprinid abundance, fish density, and species density (fig. 3.4). However, the predator pressure is also hypothesized to increase the intensity of competitive interactions among smaller fishes by forcing them into spatially restricted, shallow refugia (figs. 3.4, 3.5; see also Sih, 1980; Werner et al., 1983). Among older/larger size classes, fish predation is likely to be of limited importance in determining distribution and abundance because of the effectiveness of size as a refuge from predation (Werner et al., 1983; Werner and Gilliam, 1984). Rather, competition and habitat-related differences in foraging efficiency are hypothesized to be the critical biological processes potentially influencing large individuals in pool habitats (Werner and Hall, 1976a, 1977, 1979; Mittelbach, 1981; Werner and Gilliam, 1984).

The fish community in areas with large, well-developed pools is relatively "stable" over time (fig. 3.4) because (1) juveniles are a comparatively small component of the community, reducing the influence of the seasonal pulse in recruitment on age structure and fish density, and (2) large pools provide a stable refuge from harsh winter conditions or low flow conditions in summer, reducing the importance of emigration/mortality and recolonization (fig. 3.4).

It should be emphasized, however, that the apparent "stability" of downstream areas is strictly relative to the stability of upstream areas and the magnitude of physical disturbances occurring during the two-year study period reported here. For example, a severe drought would likely cause a major shift of community pattern along the upstream-downstream gradient (Larimore et al., 1959; Ross et al., 1985). Upstream communities of predominantly younger age groups would be shifted downstream into areas that were previously considered "stable," causing major temporal changes in age structure, fish density, species density, and species composition (Schlosser, 1985). Detecting such shifts in community structure requires multiyear sampling efforts because their frequency of occurrence will depend on geological attributes of the watershed, stochastic climatic factors, and position of the stream reach along the gradient (Horwitz, 1978).

Variation Between and Within Fish Communities in Regulating Processes

Recently physical disturbance and biological interactions have individually been implied as primary factors regulating the structure of stream-fish communities (Moyle and Li, 1979; Matthews, 1982; Fraser and Cerri, 1982; Grossman et al., 1982; Power and Matthews, 1983; Yant et al., 1984; Moyle and Vondracek, 1985). The conceptual framework proposed in this chap. (figs. 3.4, 3.5) indicates that integrating these equally important processes into an effective synthesis will require distinguishing regulating processes at two different scales: between and within communities (Menge and Sutherland, 1976; Peckarsky, 1983).

The relative importance of physical versus biological processes in regulating community structure appears to change dramatically between communities along environmental gradients (see also Connell, 1975, 1978; Karr and Freemark, 1983, 1985; Wiens, 1984). At one extreme ("colonizing" community, characteristic of upstream areas; fig. 3.5) we see frequent stochastic effects of climatic variation, a temporally variable community pattern, considerable opportunism, and abiotic limitation. Biotic interactions are hypothesized either to be of limited importance (predation) or to exhibit considerable seasonal and annual variation in intensity (competition). At the other extreme (''stable'' community, characteristic of downstream areas; fig. 3.5) we see infrequent stochastic effects of climatic variation and a relatively stable community pattern, with biotic interactions hypothesized as playing a major role in regulating community attributes.

Similarly, within fish communities the nature and relative importance of physical versus biological processes in regulating community organization appear to change along gradients of increasing fish size. Among smaller fish predation and physical disturbance owing to harsh winter conditions and high-flow regimes are hypothesized to be more critical, while among larger fish competition is hypothesized to be more important (fig. 3.5; Menge and Sutherland, 1976).

Conclusions

Our understanding of stream-fish communities will profit most from studies that use multiple working hypotheses aimed at distinguishing how the relative importance of physical versus biological regulating processes changes between and within communities. The critical problem faced by lotic fish ecologists is not development of new hypotheses but development of innovative techniques to assess effectively the validity of currently available hypotheses. In particular, studies combining (1) detailed long-term analyses of the influence of hydrologic regime and channel morphology on differences between communities in recruitment, immigration/emigration, mortality, and age structure (Moyle and Vondracek, 1985) with (2) well-designed experiments that assess the influence of size class interactions within communities, especially competition and predation, on the spatial distribution, growth, and survival of younger age classes (Cerri and Fraser, 1983; Power and Matthews, 1983; Werner et al., 1983; Werner and Gilliam, 1984) will likely lead to major theoretical advances in lotic fish ecology.[1]

[1]Paul Angermeier, Jim Karr, and an anonymous reviewer made useful suggestions for improving the manuscript. I am especially indebted to Barbara L. Peckarsky for her thorough review of the paper. All remaining errors are my own. Special thanks go to a number of individuals, too numerous to list separately, who helped with the fieldwork. Papers by Joseph Connell on community dynamics of coral reefs and tropical forests considerably influenced development of the conceptual aspects of the chapter. Completion of this research would not have been possible without the encouragement of Barbara Porter Schlosser. The United States Environmental Protection Agency (Grant #R806391) and the National Science Foundation (BSR-8320371) supported this work.

4. Life-History Patterns and Community Structure in Stream Fishes of Western North America: Comparisons with Eastern North America and Europe

Peter B. Moyle and Bruce Herbold

Abstract

The fish faunas of the streams of eastern North America, western North America, and Europe are compared to find similarities and differences in the way the communities are structured. The communities of cold headwater streams are similar in all three regions and usually contain a salmonid species, a sculpin (*Cottus*), and one to three species of cyprinids or catostomids. At lower elevations the fish communities of Europe and western North America bear a greater resemblance structurally to each other than either does to those of eastern North America. Streams in the latter area are dominated by large numbers of small, short-lived species in which parental care is common, extensive migrations are not common, and extreme trophic specialization is the exception. In western North America and Europe species richness is low, most species have large body sizes and are long-lived, parental care is not common, spawning migrations are common (but presence is variable), and most species appear to exhibit trophic or other specializations. This similarity is apparently the result of Pleistocene and post-Pleistocene events that created harsh environments for fishes having only limited refugia.

The freshwater fish fauna of North America west of the Rocky Mountains is strikingly different from that of eastern North America. The eastern fauna is extremely rich in species, and many of them are widely distributed in the Mississippi-Missouri River basin, which dominates the area. In streams, most of these species are small as adults (less than 10 cm standard length) (Mahon, 1984). By contrast, western fish faunas are depauperate, with a high degree of endemism in isolated drainages (Miller, 1958; Moyle, 1976; Smith, 1981b). A high proportion of the fishes have large body sizes (> 30 cm SL) as adults (Smith, 1981a, Moyle et al., 1982). In many respects the western fish faunas resemble those of Europe more than those of eastern North America. European fish faunas are likewise depauperate and contain many fishes with large adult body sizes. Endemism is low in central Europe but increases in southern peripheral areas, such as the Iberian Peninsula, the Balkans, and Italy (Muus, 1967; A. Wheeler, pers. comm.), where maximum body sizes also tend to be less. Mahon (1984, 1985) has demonstrated that the fish assemblages (= taxocenes) of central Europe are fundamentally different in structure from those of eastern North America. In this chapter we examine the nature of the stream-fish assemblages of western North America and compare then with those of eastern North America and, where possible, with those of Europe. We address the following questions:

1. Are the fish communities of coldwater streams in different zoogeographic regions more similar to each other than those of warmwater streams?
2. Are differences in species richness among regions simply a function of area?
3. What are the differences in body size, and related life-history parameters, among the fish faunas of the different regions?
4. Do different methods of reproduction dominate in the different areas?
5. Are the fishes of western North America and Europe more migratory than those of eastern North America?
6. Is there a greater proportion of trophic specialists in the depauperate fish faunas?

Coldwater Communities

In streams with high-mountain headwaters it is common to describe the fish communities in terms of three or four fish zones, each zone containing a more or less distinct assemblage of fish associated with a set of gradient-related environmental characteristics (Moyle and Li, 1979). Under close scrutiny the zones are often hard to define or locate precisely, but the least ambiguous in most schemes is the Trout Zone, which occupies the headwaters. In North America it is occupied by trout (Salmonidae: *Salmo* or *Salvelinus*), sculpin (Cottidae: *Cottus*), suckers (Catostomidae: *Catostomus*), dace (Cyprinidae: *Rhinichthys*), and often a drift-feeding cyprinid (table 4.1). The exact composition of this community varies from place to place. However, a four- or five-species system does seem to develop if lack of barriers permits the invasion of cold tolerant taxa other than salmonids and the water is cold (rarely exceeding 20° C) and swift enough to prevent further invasion by other fishes. In Europe and northern Asia, trout, sculpin, and minnow (*Phoxinus*) are part of this community, loach (Cobitidae, mainly *Noemacheilus*) more or less occupying the role of *Rhinichthys*. Both *Noemacheilus* and *Rhinichthys* are active benthic predators (e.g., Welton et al., 1983, Baltz et al., 1982). Moyle and Vondracek (1985) showed that a California version of this community was highly deterministic; it was persistent through time, was resilient when perturbed, and showed a high degree of trophic and microhabitat segregation among the species. Presumably the coldwater assemblages in other regions are similarly deterministic, for microhabitat and trophic segregation among the fishes are usually observed (e.g., Jones, 1975; Johnson and Johnson, 1982; Welton et al., 1983). This is in marked contrast to the warm- and cool-water faunas, which, as we will show, differ markedly among regions.

In western North America the same families that make up the Trout Zone fauna (Salmonidae, Cottidae, Catostomidae, Cyprinidae) are also dominant at lower elevations. Salmonids and cottids are most important in the more northern coastal drainages, while cyprinids are most important in the southern and interior drainages (Yaqui, Colorado, Sacramento-San Joaquin, Truckee). From the Klamath River northward the species characteristic of headwaters are also likely to be part of the more complex fish communities of the larger streams (because of cold water temperatures), while in the more southern drainages they tend to drop out at lower elevations (see maps in references given in table 4.1). In eastern North America the salmonids and cottids only rarely join the the lower-elevation communities, which are made up mainly of members of the families Cyprinidae, Catostomidae, Percidae, and Centrarchidae. In Europe the situation is more like that of western North America, with species characteristics of the Trout Zone confined to headwaters in central and southern areas (e.g., Huet, 1959) but joining the more complex fish assemblages at lower elevations in northern areas.

Table 4.1. Fish Species Characteristic of Coldwater Streams in Various Drainages of North America and Europe[a]

Location	Trout (Salmonidae)	Sculpin (Cottidae)	Dace (Cyprinidae)	Sucker (Catostomidae)	Other Cyprinidae	Other Fishes	Source
Colorado	*S. clarki*	*C. bairdi*	*R. osculus*	*Ca. platyrhynchus*	*Gila* spp.?	P. *williamsoni*[b]	Miller et al., 1982
Sacramento	*S. gairdneri*	*C. gulosus* or *C. pitensis*	*R. osculus*	*Ca. occidentalis*			Moyle, 1987
Truckee	*S. clarkii*	*S. beldingi*	*R. osculus*	*Ca. tahoensis*	*Rh. egregius*	*C. platyrhynchus*	Moyle and Vondracek, 1985
Klamath	*S. gairdneri* a/o *S. clarki*	*C. klamathensis*	*R. osculus*	*Ca. rimiculus* or *Ca. snyderi*			Moyle, 1976
Columbia	*S. gairdneri* a/o *S. clarki*	C. spp.[c]	*R. osculus* a/o *R. cataractae*	*Ca. macrocheilus* plus others	*Rh. balteatus*	*P. williamsoni*[b]	Bisson and Bond, 1971 Hawkins et al., 1983
Fraser	*S. gairdneri* a/o *S. clarki*	*C. cognatus*	*R. falcatus*	*Ca. columbianus*	*Rh. balteatus*	?	Scott and Crossman, 1973
Yukon	*Sv. malma*? *Sv. alpinus*?	*C. cognatus*		*Ca. catostomus*		?	
Michigan	*Sv. fontinalis*	*C. bairdi, cognatus*	*R. atratulus*	(*Ca. commersoni*)		*Etheostoma nigrum*	Fausch and White, 1981
New York	*Sv. fontinalis*	*C. bairdi*	*R. atratulus*	*Ca. commersoni*	*Se. atromaculatus*	*Se. margarita*[d] and others	Greeley, 1972 Johnson and Johnson, 1982
Kentucky	*S. gairdneri*	*C. carolinae*	*R. atratulus*	*Ca. commersoni*	*Se. atromaculatus*		Minckley, 1963
Ohio	*S. gairdneri*	*C. bairdi*	*R. atratulus*	*Ca. commersoni*	*Se. atromaculatus*	*Notropis chrysocephalus*[d] and others	Swaidner and Berra, 1979
Central Europe	*S. trutta*	*C. gobio*	*Noemacheilus barbatulus*[f]		*Phoxinus phoxinus*		Huet, 1959
England	*S. trutta*	*C. gobio*	*N. barbatulus* a/o *Gobio gobio*			*S. salar* and others	LeCren, 1969; Mann, 1971 Jones, 1975

[a]Generic abbreviations are: S = *Salmo*; Sv = *Salvelinus*; C = *Cottus*; R = *Rhinichthys*; Ca = *Catostomus*; Rh = *Richardsonius*; P = *Prosopium*; Se = *Semotilus*.
[b]Salmonidae.
[c]Twelve species recorded from drainage.
[d]Cyprinidae.
[e]Introduced.
[f]Cobitidae.

Table 4.2. Percent Species in Three Standard-Length Groups in Western Drainages as Compared to Eastern and European Drainages*

Drainage	*N*	Size Class (cm, SL) <10	10–30	30+	Source
Western North America					
Yaqui	16	44	31	25	Hendrickson et al., 1980
Colorado	19	37	5	58	Miller et al., 1982; Minckley, 1973
Sacramento	16	25	13	62	Moyle, 1976
Truckee	9	22	22	56	Moyle, 1976
Klamath	14	29	7	64	Moyle, 1976
Columbia	34	24	35	41	Scott and Crossman, 1973
Fraser	24	17	21	62	Scott and Crossman, 1973
Skeena	21	10	10	80	Scott and Crossman, 1973
Yukon	18	11	11	78	Scott and Crossman, 1973
Mackenzie	22	32	18	50	Scott and Crossman, 1973
Eastern North America					
Upper Grand (Ontario)	33	45	36	18	Mahon, 1984
Mississippi (Missouri)	182	41	32	27	Pfleiger, 1975
Europe:					
Nida (Poland)	25	16	52	32	Mahon, 1984

*(Only species that occupy more than 10% of the drainage were included in the analyses.

Species Richness

Mahon (1984) demonstrated that the number of species in a given drainage area or stream length was consistently higher in Ontario than in Poland, a result that can be generalized when streams of eastern North America are compared with those of Europe. In the arid interior drainage basins of western North America the number of species is considerably less than that in Europe (Smith, 1978), although it is slightly higher in the Columbia River (table 4.2). Roughly 50 species can be expected in a 10,000-km^2 drainage in Ontario, 30 in central Europe, 17–20 in a western coastal drainage, and 5–10 in a western interior drainage. The Ontario figure is considerably lower than would be expected for drainages farther south, below the glaciated areas. These figures imply a definite species-area relationship for these regions, which Mahon (1984) obtained for Polish streams. For Ontario streams he found a direct relationship until larger streams were reached, where the number of species leveled off. In the West we could find no relationship between number of species and drainage area ($r^2 = 0.34, P < 0.14$; fig. 4.1). Most drainages (except the Columbia) had about the same number of species.

Body Size

Adult body size is an obvious yet important factor to look at when we are comparing the structure of temperate stream-fish communities because it is correlated with a number of life-history characteristics (Moyle and Li, 1979; Smith, 1981a; Mahon, 1984). We use maximum adult body size attained as the measure of body size in this chapter even though few individuals of a species ever approach that size, especially in suboptimal environments. Our assumption is that maximum body size reflects typical body size of most

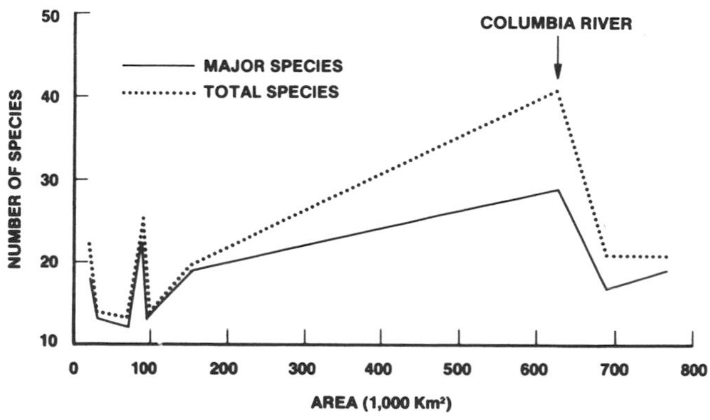

Figure 4.1. Number of species plotted against area for nine river systems of western North America. Major species are those that occupy more than 10% of the drainage.

species. Species with large adults (> 30 cm SL) usually live longer, reproduce at older ages, have longer reproductive spans, have higher absolute fecundities, and are more likely to have the adults and juveniles sharply segregated ecologically than are species with small adults (< 10 cm SL). Small species usually live less than 2 or 3 yr, spawn in their first or second year, and are unlikely to make extensive migrations. From the perspective of life-history tactics (Stearns, 1977), large species of stream fishes have an advantage if adult survivorship is high (with life spans of 5–10 yr) and the probability of successful reproduction in any given year is low. Small species have an advantage if adult survivorship is variable, but conditions necessary for successful spawning occur at least once every two years. Obviously other factors join with life-history tactics to determine adult body size; Miller (1979), for example, has discussed the many advantages of small body size in fishes. Mann et al. (1984) showed that fishes can vary their life-history tactics in response to environmental conditions. Small fishes in productive environments may have short life spans, early maturity, and multiple spawnings, while the same species in less productive environments may delay maturity, spawn just once a year, and live longer. In fact, most stream-fish communities contain a mixture of species with different adult body sizes. Nevertheless, it is obvious that in different regions the relative abundances of fishes with large and small body size differ (table 4.2).

In eastern North America the stream-fish fauna is dominated by small and medium-sized (< 30 cm SL) fishes (e.g., Becker, 1983, and other regional works). If Missouri is selected as representative of this region because of its central location and diversity of habitats, including large rivers, we find that only 27% of the fishes exceed 30 cm SL as adults (Pflieger, 1975). In the Grand River drainage of Ontario the percentage drops to 18% (Mahon, 1984), presumably because the large river habitat is absent; this percentage seems to be typical of smaller river systems throughout the East. The small species are predominantly cyprinids (especially *Notropis* spp.) and darters (Etheostominae), while the intermediate-sized species are predominantly cyprinids, suckers (Catostomidae), catfishes (Ictaluridae), and sunfishes (Centrarchidae). The large species are a varied collection; the most conspicuous seem to be the centrarchid basses (*Micropterus*), pikes (Esocidae), large catfishes, and suckers. Oddly, many of the largest (> 60 cm SL) fishes belong to relict families or genera (e.g., Acipenseridae, Polyodontidae, Lepisosteidae, Amiidae, *Cycleptus* of Catostomidae).

Mahon (1984) found that the fish community of the Nida River in Poland was dominated by intermediate-size and large cyprinids (84%) while small species were relatively scarce (Mahon, 1984). A similar pattern seems to exist for European streams in general. Overall, only about 28% of the European fish fauna consists of species that do not exceed 10 cm as adults (even when the large lake-dwelling and subarctic species are omitted and a number of small species with very restricted ranges are included), while about 40% of the fauna is comprised of species that exceed 30 cm SL as adults (Muus, 1967). Most of the larger species are cyprinids. However, in small streams many of these species will not exceed 20 cm SL, although they may live 5 to 7 years (e.g., Lobon-Cervia and Penczak, 1984). In isolated areas these smaller fishes may in part be distinct species (A. Wheeler, pers. comm.).

In western North America over half the species in most drainages are large, and less than 30% are small (table 4.2). Two apparent exceptions to this rule are the Mackenzie River, the northernmost drainage considered, and the Río Yaqui, the southernmost. The fish fauna of the Mackenzie shows that river's recent connections to the Mississippi basin; it contains such fishes as *Hiodon alosoides*, *Esox lucius*, *Notropis atherinoides*, *Notropis hudsonius*, *Phoxinus neogaeus*, *Percopsis omiscomaycus*, and *Cottus cognatus*, all widely distributed in the Mississippi basin (Scott and Crossman, 1973). The high percentage of large fishes is due to the nine widely distributed salmonid species. The Río Yaqui also has a fauna derived in part from the Mississippian fauna, through geologically recent connections with the Rio Grande (e.g., *Notropis*, *Campostoma*, *Ictalurus*), although it also shares some species with the Colorado River (*Gila*, *Catostomus*) and with drainages to the south (*Poeciliopsis*, *Cichlasoma*) (Hendrickson et al., 1980). The comparatively high percentage (37%) of small fishes in the Colorado River is the result of counting four small species (three cyprinids, one poeciliid) that are confined to the Gila River in Arizona, the largest southern tributary to the Colorado. Two of these species (*Agosia chrysogaster* and *Poeciliopsis occidentalis*) are also shared with the Río Yaqui. The comparatively low percentage (41%) of large species in the Columbia drainage is largely the result of proliferation of *Cottus* species in this enormous drainage, combined with the presence of three species of *Rhinichthys*, one of which is most likely an invader from the Mississippi drainage (*R. cataractae*).

Although the proportion of large fishes in western rivers is high in all drainages, the types of large fishes change from south to north. In the north the number of salmonid species, especially anadromous species, increases, while the number of large cyprinid species decreases. This seems to be a simple function of greater proportion of cold, clear waters in the downstream reaches of the more northern rivers, which provide optimal habitat for salmonids but less than optimal habitat for most cyprinids. Large cyprinids that complete their entire life cycle in the stream also may have less of an evolutionary advantage in the more northern areas because precipitation is less strongly seasonal and river flows are less variable, hence reproductive success is more constant. To examine this idea, we examined south-to-north trends in maxium body size within the piscivorous genus *Ptychocheilus* (four species) and within the large chublike cyprinids *Gila*, *Orthodon*, *Pogonichthys*, *Acrocheilus*, *Mylocheilus*, and *Lavinia*. In both groups there is a decline in maximum body size toward the north (fig. 4.2). This trend runs contrary to the general trend of decreasing size with lower latitude in cyprinids noted by Miller (1979).

To see whether the differences in body sizes in the three regions were due mainly to the differences in the abundances of different fish families, we examined the trends in size classes of the largest family in all regions, the Cyprinidae. In Europe 66% of the cyprinids are large species; in eastern North America, 2%; and in western North America, 36% (41% if Río Yaqui and Mackenzie River are excluded).

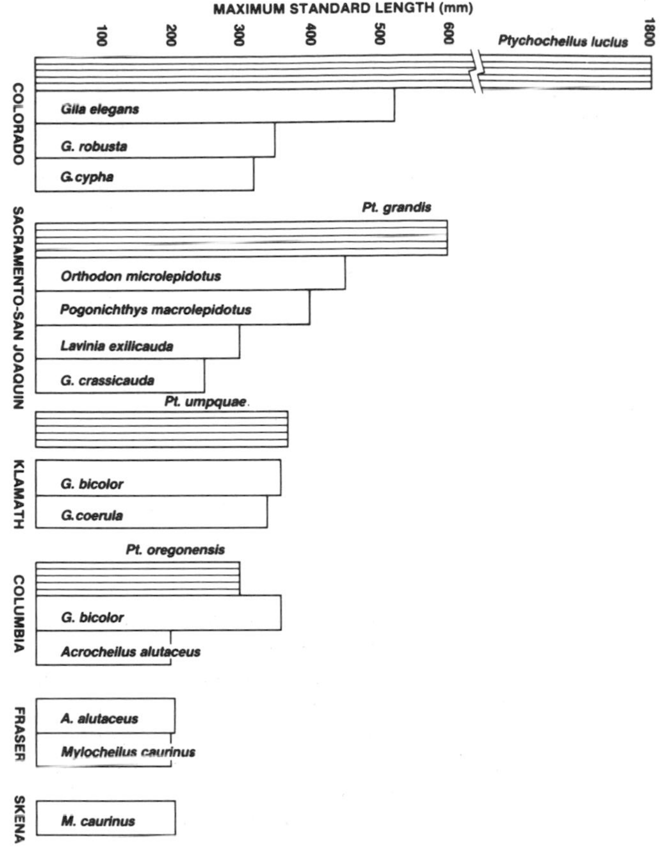

Figure 4.2. Maximum standard lengths of large cyprinid fishes in major drainages of western North America, arranged south to north. *Ptychocheilus umpquae* does not occur in the Klamath River but occurs in the Umpqua River to the north.

Methods of Reproduction

Mahon (1984) compared the reproductive behavior of fishes in Ontario and Polish streams using the reproductive guild classification system of Balon (1975). He found that a much higher percentage (39%) of the Ontario fishes guarded their eggs than did the Polish fishes (8%). When we determined the reproductive guilds of Missouri fishes (from Pflciger, 1975), the percentage was somewhat lower (32%) than in Ontario but still higher than in any western drainages (table 4.3). In Europe and western North America fishes scatter their eggs on the substrate and exhibit no postspawning care of the embryos or young (Lelek, 1981; Moyle, 1976). However, there does seem to be a slightly higher percentage of fishes that either bury their eggs (brood hiders) or are live-bearers in western North America than in Europe or eastern North America. In the three western drainages with the highest percentages of guarders (Sacramento–San Joaquin, Klamath, Columbia), the guarders are mostly sculpins. If just the Cyprinidae are examined, no species in Europe and western North America exhibit brood care, while 33% of eastern species are brood hiders or guarders.

Migratory Patterns

The degree to which stream fishes make spawning migrations is probably related to their size and reproductive habits, although the migratory patterns of most stream fishes are poorly known. Energetically, large fishes that have little or no parental care are much more likely to be able to accumulate the fat stores necessary to make extensive migrations for spawning than are small species with parental care. Thus Mahon (1984) presents circumstantial evidence that extensive migrations are common among Polish stream fishes, especially cyprinids, but whether or not this pattern is characteristic of European fishes in general is questionable (R. H Mann, pers. comm.). In eastern North America most sucker

Table 4.3. Percent Species in Western Drainages and the Central Mississippi Drainage with Different Degrees of Parental Care*

Drainage	*N*	No parental care (%)	Brood hiders (%)	Guarders (%)	Live-bearers (%)
Yaqui	14	64	7	14	14
Colorado	19	84	5	5	5
Sacramento	16	56	13	25	6
Truckee	9	78	11	11	0
Klamath	14	50	21	29	0
Columbia	28	54	21	25	0
Fraser	22	59	27	14	0
Skeena	20	45	45	10	0
Yukon	18	67	28	5	0
Mackenzie	22	77	5	18	0
Mississippi*	141	59	9	32	0
Grand (Ontario)	33	45	15	39	0
Nida (Poland)	25	88	4	8	0

*Species used in the analyses are those that occupy at least 30% of each drainage. See table 5.2 for sources of information.
†Fishes of Missouri only; 41 species for which reproductive habits uncertain were omitted from analysis.

species make extensive migrations for spawning, as do some intermediate-sized cyprinids (e.g., Montgomery et al., 1983). Otherwise most large species seem to have restricted home ranges (Gerking, 1959), and most small species probably spend their lives in relatively small sections of stream (Mahon, 1984, Grossman et al., 1985). However, Funk (1955) showed that many large species were highly variable in their movements; some individuals were sedentary, while others were highly mobile. Even small species contain mobile individuals, for they seem to be able to colonize rapidly stream sections depleted by natural or human-related causes.

In western North America extensive migrations by the large cyprinids and catostomids are documented mainly in the Colorado and Sacramento–San Joaquin drainages, but they probably occur in other drainages as well, especially among the catostomids. In the Colorado River movements of over 100km have been documented for Colorado squawfish (*Ptychocheilus lucius*) (Miller et al., 1982). Similar movements have been observed for Sacramento squawfish (*Ptychocheilus grandis*; B. Vondracek, pers. comm.), Sacramento sucker (*Catostomus occidentalis*; N. Villa, pers. comm.), and for other species in the drainage (Moyle, 1976). Smith (1982) recorded rapid recolonization of long sections of a California river by both juveniles and adults of four native cyprinids and a sucker when flows were restored following a drought. In western streams almost all major spawning migrations by nonsalmonids take place in the spring, when meltwater from the winter snowpack on the mountains greatly increases streamflows. This enables the adult fish to move up into streams that would otherwise be too small for them; after spawning they move back downstream. This behavior often segregates adults and young, the small streams serving as nursery areas. This is also the general pattern of the salmonids that dominate the more northern rivers. Overall, it appears that small species are less likely to be migratory than are large ones but that many, perhaps most, stream fishes are variable in their migratory habits.

Trophic Specialization

Moyle et al. (1982) noted that most adult fishes of the Sacramento–San Joaquin basin are fairly specialized in relation to diet or habitat or both, a pattern that also seems to be true of fishes of the Colorado basin (Schreiber and Minckley, 1981; Miller et al., 1982) of the Truckee (Lahontan) drainage (Moyle and Vondracek, 1985), and probably of western drainages in general. However, juveniles of large species feed mainly on aquatic invertebrates and show a great deal of overlap with each other and with the diets of small species (Moyle, unpub. data).

Dietary studies of temperate stream fishes in general show the fishes to be highly opportunistic and able to take advantage of abundant sources of food, especially aquatic invertebrates. In Deer Creek, California, larvae of a large mayfly (*Isonychia*) are important, when abundant, in the diets of fishes ranging from large Sacramento squawfish (*P. grandis*) to small riffle sculpin (*Cottus gulosus*) (Moyle, unpub. data). Thus studies of fish diets made on warm summer days in normal-flow years (when most studies are made) may reveal little about the ability of fishes to feed in specialized ways. In another California stream the limited study of Li and Moyle (1976) indicated that overlap in diet was considerably less in early winter than in summer. It is possible that a high degree of specialization in diet is advantageous mainly during periods of extreme environmental conditions, such as severe drought, when competition for limited resources is likely to be most severe.

One way to obtain an idea of the amount of trophic specialization that occurs in each region is to compare the structure of the pharyngeal teeth of members of the family Cyprinidae in each region. The Cyprinidae is the most species-rich family in each region, and the structure of the pharynegal teeth is generally regarded as reflective of diet (Moyle and Cech, 1982). Most unspecialized pharyngeal teeth are adapted for processing insects and other invertebrates without excessively hard shells; such teeth are moderately stout to slender, hooked at the tip, and in one or two rows. Examples of specialized teeth include the bladelike teeth of squawfish (*Ptychocheilus* spp.), the molariform teeth of peamouth (*Mylocheilus caurinus*), and the flattened teeth of the brassy minnow (*Hybognathus hankinsoni*). To compare regions, we classified the pharyngeal teeth as specialized or unspecialized. The classification was based on the descriptions of teeth of 38 eastern North American cyprinids in Becker (1983), drawings and descriptions of teeth of 19 European cyprinids in Wheeler (1969, 1978), and descriptions of teeth of 13 western North American cyprinids in Moyle (1976). Of the European cyprinids 63% had specialized teeth, as did 46% of the western cyprinids and 21% of the eastern cyprinids. This indicates that trophic specialization may indeed be more common among western North American and European stream fishes than among those of eastern North America. However, such specialization is at least partly a function of size; all the specialized species in the west are large, while all the eastern cyprinids are small or medium-sized. Also, in a number of the western cyprinids (e.g., *Mylopharodon conocephalus*, *Acrocheilus alutaceus*, *Mylocheilus caurinus*) the juveniles possess more or less unspecialized teeth, while the adults possess specialized teeth.

Discussion

Overall, it is evident that the structure of fish communities in cold headwater streams is very similar in western North America, eastern North America, and Europe. The more complex communities at lower elevations in Europe and western North America are surprisingly similar in their characteristics (table 4.4), despite their independent origins. Both differ markedly from the stream communities of eastern North America. Curiously, the successful introduction of numerous other species of fish into the three regions suggests that differences and similarities among the regions were the result of past, rather than present, environmental conditions. Thus at least six species of warmwater fishes from eastern North America are now found in Europe (Muus, 1967), while four species of European cyprinids have become es-

Table 4.4. Comparisons of Some General Characteristics of Fish Faunas of Eastern North America, Western Europe, and Western North America*

Characteristic	Mississippi Drainage	Western Europe	Western North America
Species richness			
Sample richness	High (10–30+ species usual)	Low (usually < 10)	Low (usually < 10)
Cumulative richness	High; increases rapidly in small streams, then levels out	Low; increases as stream size increases	Low; increases as stream size increases
Morphology	Small species predominate, esp. benthic forms and fusiform nektonic forms	Large species predominate; many deep-bodied	Large species predominate; many specialized body shapes present in south, fusiform salmonids in north
Life history			
Bionomics	Short lives, maturation, low fecundity, short reproductive spans predominate	Long lives (2+ years), late maturation, high fecundity, long reproductive spans predominate	Same as Europe
Parental care	Brood hiders and guarders common	Mostly no parental care	Mostly no parental care but brood hiding, live-bearing common in some drainages
Migration	Most species have limited movements; some large species make spawning migrations	Spawning migrations common, but occurrence variable	Spawning migrations common, but occurrence variable
Trophic specialization	Most species relatively unspecialized invertebrate feeders	Adult morphology indicates specialization; dietary studies do not	Specialists common

*Based in part on table 8 in Mahon, 1984.

tablished in eastern North America, although the range of most of these species is limited (Moyle, 1985). In much of western North America introduced eastern species dominate the fauna, and two species of European cyprinids are well established; fishes from other parts of the world are established as well (Moyle, 1985; Moyle et al., 1985). Although a number of native fishes have become extinct as the result of introductions, the net impact has been an increase in species number. Even the fish communities of "trout" streams have been enriched through reciprocal transplants of salmonids from the three regions.

Much of the reason for the observed structures of the fish communities in the three regions may lie in Pleistocene events (Smith, 1981a; Mahon, 1984). Much of the northern portion of eastern North America was repeatedly covered with glaciers, but the Mississippi-Missouri River drainage, with its numerous tributary systems, remained intact and served as a refuge and center of fish evolution. The tributaries provide numerous opportunities for isolation and subsequent speciation of fish populations to take place (as is taking place now in the Ozark [Pfleiger, 1975] and Appalachian mountains [Jenkins et al., 1972]). Such speciation events, followed by breakdown of isolation, are presumably a major reason for the high species richness of the Mississippi drainage, when combined with its great age. This may also account for the proliferation of small species, since there are probably more opportunities for small species to become isolated and persist (in small streams) than for large species. Small species, with their shorter generation times, may also be able to speciate more rapidly (Mahon, 1984).

Northern Europe was also covered with continental glaciers during this period, as were the southern mountain ranges. The lowlands of central Europe were then presumably inhabited mainly by coldwater fishes, which dispersed northward (through cold dilute seas) and upward in elevation as the glaciers melted. Unless there were thermal refugia in central Europe, the present warmwater fish fauna presumably invaded from the large and more southerly Danube drainage, through headwaters of Elbe and Rhine rivers (Wheeler, 1977, pers. comm.). The warmwater fishes probably persisted in more southern areas, such as the Iberian Peninsula, the Balkans, and the Caspian and Black sea regions, as indicated by the endemism in these areas. In any case, the Pleistocene was undoubtedly a climatically stressful time for the European fish fauna, even in the refuge areas. This would place a premium on two general types of fishes: those that can thrive in cold, swift water (the Trout Zone fishes) and those that can seek out thermal and quiet-water refugia and be able to persist without successful reproduction through several years of adverse conditions. The latter group are exemplified by the long-lived large cyprinids.

In western North America the drainages north of the Columbia were probably largely covered by the continental glaciers and were recolonized by large migratory salmonids moving through salt or brackish water and by fishes from the Mississippi and/or Columbia drainages by way of meltwater connections (e.g., glacial Lake Agassiz for the Mackenzie River, [Scott and Crossman, 1973]) or by headwater captures and connections that are common in a geologically active area. From the Columbia River south, however, the effects of Pleistocene glaciation were less direct, and were reflected in increased precipitation, which increased streamflows, making them more constant, and created numerous large lakes in interior basins (Smith, 1981a, b). This increase in aquatic habitat occurred despite the rapid rise of the Sierra Nevada and coastal mountains, which blocked the interior flow of airborne moisture from the Pacific Ocean. Before and during the Pleistocene the fish faunas of most western drainages were much richer than they are today (Smith, 1981b). Thus, as the glaciers melted and rainfall in the West decreased, the southwestern drainages dried up rapidly, and widespread extinction of fishes occurred. The water became increasingly seasonal in its availability, with streams relying on meltwater from the mountains for persistence; thus high flows could be expected in late winter and spring and low flow in the summer. High year-to-year variability in flows also became the rule, with long-term droughts common. The fishes that persisted under these conditions were, as in Europe, those that could thrive in cold, swift water, those that were highly migratory (e.g., anadromous salmonids), and those that could survive adverse conditions in big river or lake refuges (large, long-lived cyprinids and catostomids). Trophic specialization may have permitted survival of some fish species during periods of limited resources, when competition might be most severe. Some species may also have persisted because of their ability to tolerate high temperatures and alkalinities in drought-stricken streams and lakes (e.g., *Archoplites interruptus*, *Lavinia symmetricus*, *Gila bicolor*, *Cyprinodon* spp.) or because of their unusual reproductive strategies (*Hysterocarpus traski*), (Baltz and Moyle, 1982).

Thus the similarities between characteristics of the fish communities of western North America and Europe can be explained as adaptations of life-history strategies to adverse environmental conditions. Presumably in both areas, the fauna was reduced during the Pleistocene, with conditions favoring the larger, longer-lived species. In eastern North America the Mississippi-Missouri drainage provided an enormous refuge for fishes of all sizes in which speciation, especially in small streams, could continue unabated.

Conclusion

The main conclusion that can be reached from this study is that the dramatic events of the Pleistocene played a large role in shaping the structure of the fish communities of north temperate regions. The effects of Pleistocene events were most severe in Europe and western North America because of the comparative isolation of drainage basins. This resulted in considerable convergence in community structure. This latter conclusion is obviously based on a thin foundation of evidence. We suggest, however, that, if it is correct, then the following predictions should be true:

1. The structure of salmonid-dominated fish assemblages in coldwater streams in general should be deterministic, as discussed by Moyle and Vondracek (1985). A true comparison among regions should involve long-term studies, using comparable methods.
2. In streams whose flows have been regulated by human activities to make them more predictable, large fishes should reproduce at smaller sizes and younger ages than fishes in nearby unregulated streams, at least in western North America. This assumes that enough time has passed for some selection to have taken place to alter the population structure.
3. In streams of comparable size and latitude, the year-to-year variability in growth rates of large cyprinids should be greatest in western North America and least in eastern North America, with Europe in between. To be valid, comparisons of growth would have to be made over the same 10–20–year period. Carp might be a good subject for this comparison, since they have been introduced into all three regions.
4. Oophagy should be more common among the fishes in streams of eastern North America than among those in the other regions. In response to this, species of fish without parental care should spawn earlier in the year than those with parental care. The largest species should be the earliest spawners.
5. Juvenile fish (> 25 mm SL) should show a higher degree of habitat segregation from adults in western North America and central Europe than from those in eastern North America.
6. During times of food shortages (e.g., drought) fishes of western North America and Europe should show a divergence in diets, while those of eastern North America should show a convergence in diets.

Finally, it would be instructive to compare the characteristics of freshwater fish communities in the temperate regions of eastern Asia and of the temperate regions of the southern hemisphere with those discussed in this chapter.[1]

[1] The insightful, if acerbic, comments of D. M. Baltz, L. Brown, B. S. Goldowitz, and B. Vondracek are appreciated, as are reviews of the manuscript by A. Wheeler, R. H. K. Mann, R. Mahon, G. D. Grossman, R. A. Daniels, and R. Cashner.

5. Habitat Segregation in an Assemblage of Minnows in an Ozark Stream

Owen T. Gorman

Abstract

Habitat partitioning in an assemblage of minnows in an Ozark stream was described in an observational field study. Six habitat variables were used: depth, current speed, substrate, lateral position, longitudinal position, and vertical position. Analysis focused on the five numerically dominant minnow species, with separate treatment of adults and juveniles. Current speed and longitudinal position delimited a suite of still water (pool) microhabitats used collectively by the dominant adult species. Depth and lateral position separated near-edge from open-water species. As a group the dominant adult species used a similar array of open-water pool microhabitats, but juveniles, with one exception, used near-edge microhabitats in pools and raceways. The two groups formed complementary habitat guilds. Within guilds segregation was almost entirely by vertical position. Substrate provided little information on species segregation. Maintenance of segregation within guilds is explained by differential habitat selection and competitive interference among species. The pattern of segregation between guilds can be explained by varying levels of predation risk associated with body size in near-edge versus open-water habitats.

Habitat, food, and time are often major axes of niche partitioning in natural communities (Schoener, 1974, 1982). Evidence from numerous past studies indicates that habitat is a major dimension in determining niche relationships in stream-fish communities. Unfortunately, most studies of stream-fish communities have been based almost entirely on seining surveys. This method is inappropriate for detailed analysis of microhabitat use patterns in fish communities because the sampling obliterates information on small-scale distributional relationships among species. Some studies using seining techniques have provided inferential assessments of habitat relationships in whole communities (e.g., Sheldon, 1968; Gorman and Karr, 1978; Baker and Ross, 1981; Schlosser, 1982a; Felley and Hill, 1983). Other studies using more detailed sampling techniques have provided more thorough assessments of habitat use among only a few species (e.g., Mendelson, 1975; Matthews and Hill, 1980; Finger, 1982a; Fraser and Cerri, 1982; Matthews et al., 1982a; Paine et al., 1982; Surat et al., 1982; Wynes and Wissing, 1982). More recently, studies using direct observational techniques have provided detailed analyses of habitat segregation in whole assemblages (e.g., Gorman, 1983; Moyle and Vondracek, 1985).

Emphasis on a predictable relationship between community composition and habitat structure reflects the view that stream-fish communities are organized by deterministic processes such as competition and predation (Grossman et al., 1982; Moyle and Vondracek, 1985) and thus adhere to the general tenets of competition theory (MacArthur and Levins, 1967; MacArthur, 1972; Schoener, 1974, 1982; Diamond, 1978). However, this deterministic view of stream-fish communities has been challenged by some investigators who contend that fish communities appear to be nonequilibrium systems regulated by stochastic processes (Grossman et al., 1982, 1985) or are assembled randomly (Matthews, 1982). These recent studies provide the alternate viewpoint that fish communities conform to the stochastic model of community organization (Connor and Simberloff, 1979; Strong et al., 1979; Strong, 1980, 1983; Simberloff, 1983). However, some ecologists have argued that most attempts to demonstrate the importance of stochastic processes in community organization and structure have been equivocal because the null models proposed were unrealistic or the data were inappropriate or inadequate (Schoener, 1982; Roughgarden, 1983). For example, the study by Grossman et al. (1982) of an Indiana stream-fish community has been criticized by Herbold (1984) for using an unrealistic model, by Rahel et al. (1984) for an arbitrary definition of the community, and by

Yant et al. (1984) for faulty design and inaccurate data.

In this chapter I present results of a detailed field study of habitat partitioning in an assemblage of minnows in a warmwater stream. To adhere as closely as possible to the assumption of equilibrium conditions for deterministic models of communities, a relatively undisturbed, stable, spring-fed stream was chosen for investigation. Also, the stream is isolated from downstream reaches so that the community is unaffected by migrants. I focused my research on the five numerically dominant minnow species, which formed a natural habitat guild that used a similar array of still-water microhabitats. The field approach consisted of direct observation of habitat use by fishes over a number of habitat variables. In the analysis of field data I evaluated the level of segregation for each habitat variable and examined patterns of habitat use by the entire assemblage of small, actively swimming species, by subsets, and by individual species. The purpose of the analysis was to identify the most important (or informative) variables of habitat segregation and to evaluate patterns of community organization, with particular consideration of the roles of predation and competition.

Methods

Study area

Roubidoux Creek, a fourth-order tributary of the Gasconade River (sensu Horton, 1945), is situated in the central Missouri Ozark region in Texas and Pulaski counties. The relatively long (60 km), narrow (9–17 km) watershed (area = 740.7 km^2) receives an average annual precipitation of 1,070 mm. The topography is rugged and consists of low hills (76–122–m relief) with steep, rocky slopes and narrow valleys rarely more than 300 m wide. Approximately 90% of the watershed is forested; about 80% is contained within the Mark Twain National Forest. Thus most of the watershed is in a relatively undisturbed state.

The stream depth ranges from < 0.1 m in riffles to > 1.5 m in downstream pools. Channel width ranges from < 0.5 m in headwater riffles to > 10 m in downstream pools. Substrates consist largely of chert fragments and occasional expanses of resistant sandstone or limestone bedrock.

Owing to numerous springs along the channel, sustained flow is relatively stable (approx. 1 m^3/sec at mid-drainage), usually not varying by more than a factor of 2 annually, except during brief periods of high rainfall (< 24 h), when discharge can exceed 100 m^3/sec in downstream reaches. The stability of the stream-bed structure is indicated by only minor changes in the configuration of pools and riffles at three mid-drainage stations over a five-year period, 1979–83 (Gorman, unpub. data). Thus the spring-stabilized baseflows indicate a moderately stable physical environment for the resident fishes and contribute to the unusual clarity of the water. About 25 km from the mouth Roubidoux Creek disappears underground through gravel bars, leaving the lower 40% of the drainage with a dry stream bed. This feature isolates Roubidoux Creek from the Gasconade River and eliminates seasonal influxes of migrant fishes into the community.

The research was conducted at three mid-drainage study stations, each of which consisted of approximately 200–400 m of stream channel. These stations were chosen on the basis of their overall similarity of habitat structure and community composition. Observational fieldwork at each station was conducted twice in 1981 and once in 1982 during middle to late summer (July to September) for a total of 22 days.

Habitat Measures

During each visit 100–200 point-sample measurements of five habitat variables were taken on a grid in those sections of the stream where fish were to be observed. The sampling procedures were adapted from Gorman (1976) and Gorman and Karr (1978). Study sections included at least one riffle and pool that encompassed approximately 100 m of stream channel. Point-sample measurements were taken systematically with a standard measuring pole (2 m long, 18 mm diameter, divided into cm increments) as follows: starting 10–20 cm from the left bank, points were sampled at 1-m intervals along a cross-stream transect. Cross-stream transects were taken at 3- or 5-m intervals moving upstream. Transects were permanently marked with flags in streamside vegetation to allow resampling at a later date. To avoid bias in the location of a point sample, the pole was dropped from 0.5 m above the stream bottom, and then values for the habitat variables were recorded, and a 1-m wire survey flag was temporarily installed to mark locations for fish observations.

Four variables provided measures of available microhabitat distributed horizontally over the sample points: depth, current, substrate, and lateral position (Gorman, 1983). Depth was measured in centimeters, and current and substrate (substr) were classified into categories. There were five current categories: zero (< 0.02 m/sec), very slow (0.02–0.10 m/sec), slow (0.10–0.25 m/sec), moderate (0.25–75 m/sec), fast (0.75–1.25 m/sec), and torrential (> 1.25 m/sec). These current categories were empirically derived by correlating ranges of observed current speeds with different stream habitats, i.e., edges, pools, raceways, and riffles (Gorman, 1976). Current categories were determined by observing the pattern of water movement about the habitat measuring pole. Water-movement patterns were calibrated with a current meter. Substrates were classified structurally (adapted from Cummins, 1962). Categories 0 to 8 correspond to alluvial-bed material of increasing size from silt to bedrock: 0, silt (< 0.06 mm); 1, silty sand (0.06–0.10 mm); 2, sand (0.10–0.20 mm); 3, gravel (0.20–16 mm); 4, pebble (16–32 mm); 5, rock (32–100 mm); 6, cobble (100–256 mm); 7, boulder (> 256 mm); 8, bedrock. Lateral position (latpos) was measured as distance in tenths of meters from the nearest stream edge. A fifth variable, longitudinal position (longpos or lgpos), provided a measure of macrohabitat and was categorized as one of three major stream habitats: 0, pool; 1, raceway; 2, riffle. Measures of available habitat were taken solely by the author.

Underwater observation of fishes provided data on the sixth and final microhabitat variable, vertical position. This fish-dependent variable provided a measure of an individual's relative vertical position in the water column. The vertical-position categories were empirically derived from preliminary observations in Roubidoux Creek and also from previous familiarization with stream fishes. Preliminary observations indicated that small pelagic fishes recognized vertical positions that remain relatively constant with changing depth. For example, *Notropis zonatus* tends to use the middle zone of the water column of pools regardless of depth (pers. obs.). The vertical position categories reflect two orientations and adaptive morphologies in stream fishes: benthic and pelagic. Some fishes are morphologically adapted to and feed on the substrate (e.g., *Campostoma anomalum*), while others are more pelagic (e.g., *N. zonatus* (pers. obs.; Pflieger, 1975). Five vertical zones were recognized: 0, in contact with the bottom (benthic); 1, close to but not in contact with the bottom (near benthic); 2, lower one-third of water column above position 1 (lower pelagic); 3, middle one-third of water column (mid-pelagic); 4, upper one-third of water column but not at or near surface (upper pelagic); 5, at or near the surface.

Fish Observations

The Roubidoux fish fauna contains 36 species, a typical number for a fourth-order Ozark stream, but only 26 species were commonly encountered in the study stations (Gorman, 1983). On the basis of the results of several years of seining surveys (Gorman, 1983), I chose the 5 numerically dominant minnow species for detailed study (table 5.1); *Notropis zonatus* (bleeding shiner), *Notropis boops* (bigeye shiner), *Notropis nubilus* (Ozark minnow), *Nocomis biguttatus* (hornyhead chub), and *Campostoma* spp. (stonerollers). *Campostoma* included two species that were difficult to separate in underwater observations: *C. anomalum* (central stoneroller) and *C. oligolepis* (largescale stoneroller). Seining samples indicated that approximately 70% of the *Campostoma* in the three mid-drainage study stations were *C. oligolepis* (Gorman, 1983). Preliminary observations suggested that these minnows formed a natural habitat "guild" (sensu Root, 1967) because they were most often found together in the same areas of horizontally distributed microhabitats.

While most of my attention focused on adults, I also observed and analyzed young-of-the-year (YOY) of the five common species. YOY were treated separately because they are morphologically and ecologically different from adults. Therefore, I will refer to them as "ecological species" (sensu Polis, 1984) to facilitate analysis and discussion. Four miscellaneous species were included in an analysis of the entire assemblage of small, actively swimming species (table 5.1): *Notropis greenei* (wedgespot shiner), *Pimephales notatus* (bluntnose minnow), *Fundulus catenatus* (northern studfish), and juvenile *Lepomis megalotis* (longear sunfish). These miscellaneous species either were much less abundant than the common minnows (the two minnows and cyprinodont) or were behaviorally and ecologically distinct (the sunfish) (Gorman, 1983). With the inclusion of YOY and miscellaneous species the total number of ecological species studied was 14. Sizes of the species are provided in table 5.1, and more detailed descriptions are given by Pflieger (1975).

Habitat use by fishes was determined by direct observation. Equipped with snorkel and wetsuit, I observed fish underwater along flagged transects in a systematic fashion between 1100 and 1600 h on bright, sunny days. Several hours or a day after habitat sampling, I entered the stream in downstream areas from which minnows were absent (in deep pools at least 50 m downstream from observation areas) and moved slowly upstream to the flagged transects. This period allowed fish to accommodate to my presence, and if fish appeared to be affected, observations were halted until they appeared to ignore me. Because of the coarse and relatively clean substrates in Roubidoux Creek, my gentle movements stirred up very little particulate matter that would attract fish. Also, the use of a wetsuit allowed me to float in water as shallow as 10 cm without making contact with the bottom. At no time did the fish appear to be affected by the thin wire flags. Approximately 50 h of training in underwater observation were required to develop skills in rapid and accurate identification of fishes and their use of vertical positions. Over 100 h were logged in conducting underwater observations on habitat use by fishes. All observations were made by the author.

At a distance of approximately 2 m from a transect, I systematically observed fish at each flagged habitat sample

Table 5.1. Fishes Studied in Roubidoux Creek

Species	Size* (mm)	Basic Habitats
Most common species		
1. *Notropis zonatus*	75–120	Pelagic zone of pools and raceways
YOY†	30–60	
2. *Notropis boops*	40–70	Pelagic zone of pools
YOY	20–30	
3. *Notropis nubilus*	60–75	Near benthic zone of pools and raceways
YOY	30–50	
4. *Nocomis biguttatus*	75–150	Pelagic zone of pools and raceways
YOY	30–50	
5. *Campostoma* spp.	75–140	Benthic zone of pools and raceways
YOY	30–60	
Miscellaneous species		
6. *Pimephales notatus* (includes YOY and adults)	40–75	Near benthic zone of pools
7. *Notropis greenei* (includes YOY and adults)	45–75	Pelagic zone of raceways and riffles
8. *Fundulus catenatus* (includes YOY and adults)	30–75	Pelagic zone of pools
9. *Lepomis megalotis* (includes YOY and yearlings)	40–90	Near benthic zone of pools

*Size ranges are representative of fish in the stream from July to September. Sizes given are total lengths.
†YOY = young-of-the-year.

point. Moving from left to right across a transect, I stopped and censused fishes in an area approximately 1 m^2 about each flagged point. A point census consisted of relaying of information on the vertical position and species of each individual observed in "snorkelese" to an onshore assistant. These point censuses were taken as rapidly as possible to obtain near-instantaneous records of habitat use by fishes around each point. Also, this observational procedure allowed continuous observation of fishes with minimal movement and disturbance of fish. After finishing a transect, I drifted downstream 3–4 m and waited several minutes before starting the next transect. This pause was taken as a precautionary measure to ensure that the fish were unaffected by my presence.

To check the subjectivity of my visual censusing, sets of photographs (color slides) of the flagged points were taken with an underwater camera. The procedure was the same as for direct observations except that a photograph was taken to record habitat use by fish. All photographs were taken from a mid-pelagic position approximately 2 m from a flagged point. Adjacent flagged points were included in the borders of the photograph as reference points. These photographs were analyzed for information on species, number of individuals, and vertical position. Since data derived from photographs were not statistically different from those from direct observations, ($P > 0.10$, Chi-square test of independence) both sets of data were pooled for analysis.

Analysis of Field Data

Because few significant differences were found among the data sets from the three stations (Chi-square test of independence, $P > 0.10$), they were combined. The combined data sets were then analyzed by use of frequency histograms. This analysis provided information on the general patterns of habitat utilization by groups or individual species. The groups analyzed were (1) the entire assemblage of ecological species (referred to as the 14-species set), (2) the 5 numerically dominant adult minnows, (3) the 5 numerically dominant adult minnows plus the YOY of *N. zonatus* (referred to as the six-species set), and (4) the YOY of the five numerically dominant minnows. I have included the YOY of *N. zonatus* in the set of six species because these YOY were very common and used the same suite of microhabitats as adult species.

More detailed evaluation of habitat use was provided by chi-square tests and a niche analysis using the percent similarity (PS) measure (Schoener, 1970; Abrams, 1980; Feinsinger et al., 1981). Chi-square goodness-of-fit tests were used to determine whether habitat utilizations of species sets or individual species were significantly different from the distribution of available habitat. In these analyses each of the expected (available) and observed distributions used in goodness-of-fit tests was standardized to a sum value of 100. This standardization resulted in more conservative statistical tests because the sample sizes used in most comparisons were $>> 100$. Because the classification of vertical positions is fish-dependent, its availability could not be quantified. Therefore, the vertical distributions of species or species sets were compared to an even distribution. In the niche analysis the PS measure provided a measure of selectivity or niche breadth for each species over each habitat variable. Also, the PS measure provided a measure of overall utilization of a habitat variable by comparing the collective utilization of a species set to the availability of that variable.

In a second phase of the niche analysis the degree of segregation among the species over each habitat variable was evaluated. Chi-square tests of independence were used to detect significant heterogeneity in the utilization of habitat variables by the different sets of species. Then, with the use of the PS measure, each species' utilization distribution for each habitat variable was compared to every other species' utilization distribution, and a matrix of overlap values was constructed. From this, mean overlap values were obtained for each habitat variable. This second analysis was done separately for each species set.

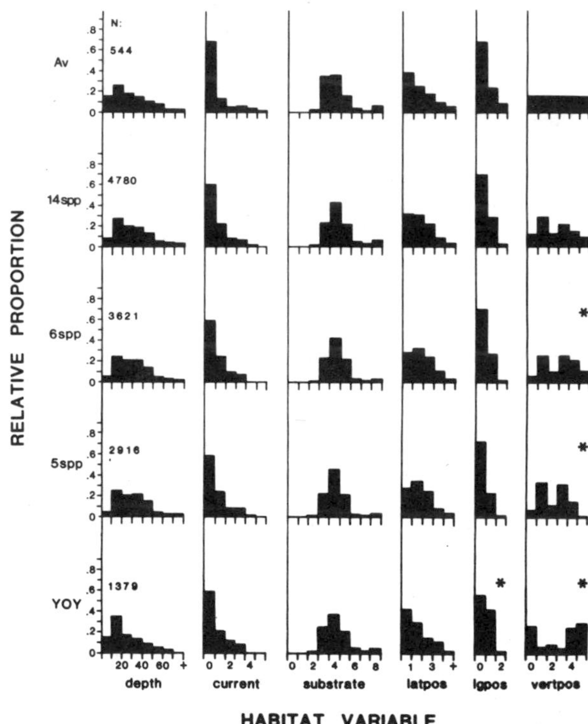

Figure 5.1. Available habitat and composite habitat utilization by species groups. Asterisks denote distributions significantly different from expected (available habitat) using a chi-square goodness-of-fit test, $P < 0.05$ (see "Methods"). AV—measured available habitat; 14 spp.—entire assemblage of small, actively swimming species; 5 spp.—the five numerically dominant adult minnow species; 6 spp.—the same as 5 spp., but with the addition of the YOY *Notropis zonatus*; YOY—young-of-the-year of the five numerically dominant adult species. For explanation of habitat variables see "Methods." Sample sizes are noted in the first column.

Results

General Patterns of Habitat Utilization

Available habitat was described from 544 sample points (figure 5.1). The typical available microhabitat can be described as shallow ($\bar{x}$ depth = 30.6 cm), still water ($\bar{x}$ current = 0.71 units, or < 0.10 m/sec), with a pebble bottom ($\bar{x}$ substrate = 4.1 units, or 16–32–cm size), and relatively close to the stream edge ($\bar{x}$ lateral position = 1.84 m). The typical macrohabitat (pool, race, riffle) was pool habitat ($\bar{x}$ longitudinal position = 0.40 units).

The overall utilization distributions of the six habitat variables by the 14 species set ($N = 4780$) were not significantly different from the distribution of available habitats (χ^2, $P > 0.10$), and the PS measure of similarity ranged from 84 to 94% (fig. 5.1, table 5.2). However, some of these distributions contain noteworthy (often significant) category deviations. First, depths < 10 cm were underused, indicating that fish tend to avoid very shallow areas (χ^2, $P < 0.05$). Second, underuse of very deep water (> 70 cm) and lateral positions > 4 m indicate that most fish avoid deep areas far from stream edges. Third, the community as a whole slightly avoided the strongest currents (4–5) and riffle habitats, used intermediate currents (2–3) in a nonselective manner, and favored the use of still-water areas (currents 0–1; χ^2, $P < 0.05$). If fish moved randomly and passively, virtually all individuals would be found in still-water areas (which was not observed), but if some fish actively select currents with an energetic cost and are found distributed randomly over a range of currents (as was observed), that distribution does not reflect a lack of habitat selection by individual fish. Fourth, among vertical positions, greater use of the benthic zone 1 (significant χ^2, $P < 0.05$) and the mid-pelagic zone 3 contrasts with an underuse of the lower and upper pelagic zones 2 and 5, respectively. This pattern reflects the benthic and pelagic orientations and feeding modes observed in my preliminary studies. Examples of benthic associates include *Campostoma* and *N. nubilus*, while *N. boops* and *N. zonatus* are examples of pelagic fishes (fig. 5.2). Adaption to both zones appears unlikely owing to design constraints on morphology and may explain the apparent underuse of the intermediate vertical position 2. Near-surface positions may be avoided by larger pelagic fish because of increased vulnerability to avian predators, e.g., kingfishers or herons.

As a next step in the analysis the microhabitat utilizations of the species subsets were examined for deviations from the general pattern (table 5.2, fig. 5.1). Because of numerical dominance, the subsets of 5 and 6 species did not have significantly different patterns of habitat use compared to the 14-species set (chi-square test of independence, $P > 0.10$). However, the 5-species subset had some notable exceptions. In the vertical position variable, categories 0, 2, and 5 were underused, resulting in a strongly bimodal distribution with greater use of near-benthic and mid-pelagic positions. Also, there was slightly greater use of areas > 2 m from the edge.

A more useful comparison is between sets of the five adult minnow species and their YOY (table 5.2, fig. 5.1). Except for the current and substrate distributions, the microhabitat use by YOY was generally significantly different from the five adult species' utilizations (χ^2, $P < 0.05$). Juveniles used shallower water, near-edge areas, and raceway habitats to a greater extent than their adult counterparts. Also, the juvenile vertical position distribution differed by showing

Table 5.2. Summary of Niche Analysis from Field Observations[a]

Habitat Variable	Overall Utilization[b]			Selectivity[c]			Overlap[d]		
	14 spp.	YOY	6 spp.	14 spp.	YOY	6 spp.	14 spp.	YOY	6 spp.
Depth	0.898 NS	0.916 NS	0.899 NS	0.647 12/14	0.560 4/5	0.734 4/6	0.527 *	0.369 *	0.727 *
Current	0.879 NS	0.758 NS	0.863 NS	0.766 9/14	0.798 4/5	0.818 2/6	0.669 *	0.730 *	0.784 *
Substrate	0.869 NS	0.906 NS	0.848 NS	0.750 7/14	0.703 3/5	0.839 1/6	0.681 *	0.549 *	0.849 *
Lateral position	0.903 NS	0.926 NS	0.894 NS	0.774 10/14	0.709 4/5	0.825 4/6	0.695 *	0.632 *	0.806 *
Longitudinal position	0.940 NS	0.822 *	0.939 NS	0.770 13/14	0.769 5/5	0.851 5/6	0.689 *	0.690 *	0.794 *
Vertical position	0.836 NS	0.710 †	0.842 ‡	0.368 14/14	0.387 5/5	0.375 6/6	0.243 *	0.184 *	0.165 *

[a]These tables are summarizations of the niche analysis in Gorman (1983). Species groups are: 14 spp. = entire assemblage of ecological species, YOY = young-of-the-year of the five numerically dominant species, 6 spp. = five numerically dominant species plus YOY of *N. zonatus*.

[b]Summary of overall habitat utilizations by species groups. Significant deviations from expected (available habitat, fig. 5.1) using the chi-square goodness-of-fit test are noted: NS, not significant; * significant for $p < 0{:}001$; † significant for $p < 0.01$; ‡ significant for $p < 0.05$.

[c]Summary of mean habitat selectivities (a measure of mean niche breadth) by species groups. The number of significant species' selectivities in each group using the chi-square goodness-of-fit test are noted (figs. 5.1–5.3).

[d]Summary of mean overlap in habitat utilization by species pairs within groups. Significant deviations in species' habitat utilizations within groups are noted as in "Overall Utilization."

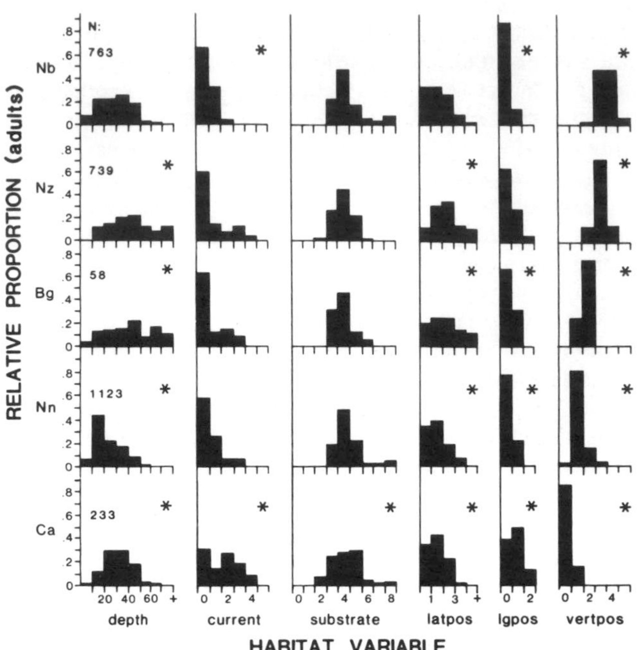

Figure 5.2. Habitat use by the numerically dominant adult species. Asterisks denote distributions significantly different from expected (available habitat, fig. 5.1), using a chi-square goodness-of-fit test, $P < 0.05$ (see "Methods"). Species shown (top to bottom): Nb = *N. boops*, Nz = *N. zonatus*, Bg = *N. biguttatus*, Nn = *N. nubilus*, Ca = *Campostoma* spp. For explanation of habitat variables see "Methods." Sample sizes are noted in the first column.

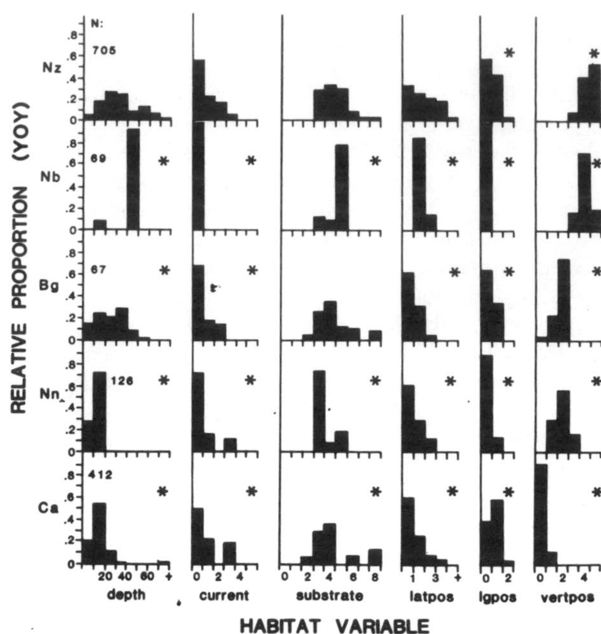

Figure 5.3. Habitat use by YOY (young-of-the-year) of the numerically dominant minnow species. Asterisks denote distributions significantly different from expected (available habitat, fig. 5.1) by use of a chi-square goodness-of-fit test, $P < 0.05$ (see "Methods"). Species shown (top to bottom): Nz = *Notropis zonatus*, Nb = *N. boops*, Bg = *N. biguttatus*, Nn = *N. nubilus*, Ca = *Campostoma* spp. For explanation of habitat variables see "Methods." Sample sizes are noted in the first column.

greater use of benthic and surface positions, whereas the mid-pelagic zones were greatly underused. The differences in the microhabitat utilizations of adults and juveniles resulted in their segregation into different suites of microhabitats: juveniles were most common in shallow-edge microhabitats with quiet water in both pools and raceways, while adults mostly used deeper areas of pools farther from edges. The patterns of microhabitat use by adults and juveniles are complementary; their combined utilizations (approximately equal to all species combined) more closely match the overall availability of microhabitats (table 5.2, fig. 5.1).

Microhabitat Use Among Species

While the overall use of microhabitats by the entire assemblage reflected habitat availability, individual species showed considerable habitat specialization (table 5.2, figs. 5.2, 5.3). The greatest specialization was manifested in the vertical-position variable, as indicated by the smallest mean niche breadths among the species sets (0.368–0.387) and by the largest number of significantly different selectivities within each group. The next level of specialization was provided by the depth variable (niche breadth = 0.560–0.734). The remaining variables (current, substrate, lateral position, longitudinal position) were similar in having relatively greater niche breadths (0.703–0.851), reflecting less specialization.

The degree of segregation between species is reflected by the mean overlap (PS measure) in utilization of habitat variables (table 5.2). Vertical position provided the lowest mean overlaps among the species sets (0.165–0.243). The depth variable yielded the next-lowest mean overlap (0.369-0.727), and the remaining variables generally showed greater overlaps (0.549–0.849). Chi-square tests revealed that all species sets had significantly heterogeneous patterns of utilization for all variables, but these tests do not have the power to make pairwise comparisons among species.

The niche analysis shows that, of the six habitat variables considered, vertical position provided the most information on habitat segregation in the community, especially within species subsets. A clear pattern of vertical segregation is indicated by the distinct layering of the six-species set and the five YOY species (figs. 5.2, 5.3, far-right column). When the data set was restricted to the six species, the mean overlap in vertical position decreased from 0.243 to 0.165, while overlap on other variables increased from 0.527–0.695 to 0.727–0.849 (table 5.2). These results indicate that the six species were fairly similar in their use of horizontally distributed microhabitats but were highly segregated in their use of vertical positions. Thus the six-species set appears to constitute a natural-habitat guild.

For the community as a whole, no single habitat dimension provided complete segregation of all species. However, inspection of a combination of habitat variables provided greater separation of some species (figs. 5.2, 5.3). For example, *N. bigutattus* and their YOY had similar vertical positions, but they complemented each other in that the adults used deeper-water areas farther from the stream edge, while YOY used shallow water close to the edge. A similar pattern of lateral complementarity occurred between *N. nubilus* and *Campostoma* and their YOY. The vertical position of *N. nubilus* was tightly sandwiched between *N. biguttatus* and *Campostoma*, but *N. nubilus* was more abundant in shallower water closer to stream edges. Also, in contrast to *N. nubilus*, *Campostoma* was more abundant in raceways. The YOY *N. boops* also had a vertical distribution that overlapped considerably with two other species—YOY *N. zonatus* above and its adult counterpart below. In contrast to *N. boops* and YOY *N. zonatus*, YOY *N. boops* was uniquely restricted to deep-water areas within 2 m of the stream edge. *Notropis boops* had a vertical position just above *N. zonatus* and overlapped considerably, but *N. zonatus* was more abundant in deeper water farther from stream edges. In all cases the effect of vertical overlap was reduced by horizontal microhabitat segregation. Species with little vertical overlap such as *N. biguttatus* and *N. zonatus* tended to utilize the same horizontal microhabitats. Species pairs occurring in the same areas but with greater vertical overlap (e.g., *N. boops*—*N. zonatus* and *N. nubilus*—*Campostoma* and *N. biguttatus*) were also very different in body size (approximate ratio 1:2), which may indicate some trophic segregation. Finally, horizontal microhabitat complementarity between adults and juveniles of the same species reduced overlap in vertical position (figs. 5.2–5.4). However, *N. zonatus* and their YOY had considerable overlap in use of horizontally distributed microhabitats but had highly complementary vertical distributions. In summary, all species appeared to be well segregated when a combination of vertical position, depth, and lateral position variables was considered.

Discussion

General Patterns of Segregation

The results of this study provide a basis for a more thorough evaluation of habitat partitioning in stream fishes than has been generally presented from seining and trapping studies. The Roubidoux Creek assemblage of small, actively swimming fishes used virtually all of the available habitat space, a result that supports the theoretical suggestion by Sale (1974) and Lawlor (1980) that the composite resource (habitat) utilization by a community should approximate the distribution of available resources. Subsets of the community, however, used habitat in significantly different ways.

Because most species (and individuals) in the assemblage used still-water areas and most still-water areas were found in pools, consideration of the longitudinal position variable aided in defining a guild of species collectively using pool microhabitats. The most conspicuous members of this guild include the numerically dominant minnow species (*N. boops, N. zonatus, N. biguttatus, N. nubilus, Campostoma*) and to a lesser extent the YOY species (note that *Campostoma* and YOY also used raceway habitat extensively).

Within the pool macrohabitat two microhabitat variables, depth and lateral position, were useful in describing horizontal segregation of species (fig. 5.4). Together these variables describe distinct "patches" of microhabitat arranged horizontally in two dimensions as viewed from above. Generally, smaller fishes (most YOY species and small-sized species) tended to use near-edge, shallow microhabitats, while larger adult species primarily used deeper pelagic zones. This size-based segregation further divides the pool guild into two subgroups: (1) the near-edge habitat guild of small YOY species and (2) the pelagic habitat guild of the dominant minnow species (the six-species set).

The vertical position variable provided the most information on segregation, especially within guilds. Without the vertical dimension added by this variable, most guild members would be poorly segregated because they shared similar arrays of horizontally arranged microhabitats (fig. 5.4). The relative importance of vertical segregation may reflect constraints on a species' adaptation to more than one vertical position, i.e., benthic, pelagic, and surface zones. Also, the level of predation risk associated with different vertical positions may place additional constraints on suitable body size and morphology (see below).

Substrate provided little information on habitat segregation, possibly because of low substrate diversity or because

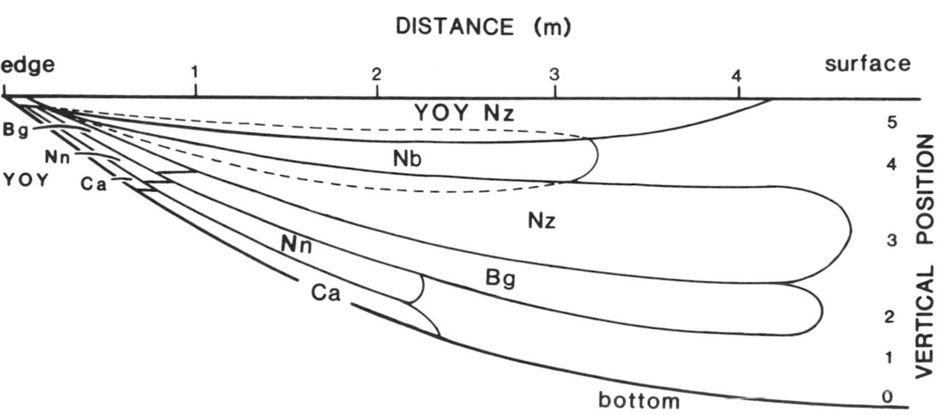

Figure 5.4. Diagrammatic representation of horizontal and vertical microhabitat distribution of Roubidoux minnows. Habitat variables represented include lateral position, relative depth, and vertical position. Species represented include the five numerically dominant minnow species and their YOY, except for YOY *Notropis boops*, which was omitted because of small sample size and unusual microhabitat use. Species shown: Nb = *N. boops*, Nz = *N. zonatus*, Bg = *N. bigutattus*, Nn = *N. nubilus*, Ca = *Campostoma* spp. Overlap in vertical distribution by *N. boops* is indicated by dashed lines. Data for this figure are taken from figs. 5.2 and 5.3.

modal substrates were preferred by the species studied. *Campostoma*, a substrate grazer, was the only member of the six-species set to select substrate size (figs. 5.2, 5.3). Substrate might be a more important variable of segregation for other components of the entire community (e.g., weakly swimming benthic species such as darters, sculpins, and madtoms).

In summary, a combination of variables describing a horizontal array of microhabitats and vertical position provided nearly complete segregation of the six species comprising the guild (mean overlap ≤ 0.165). These results emphasize the importance of detailed description of habitat segregation with the use of a number of variables. Those variables that provide little information can always be discarded later. Also, a description of segregation based on a few variables assumes that the environment is relatively homogeneous or that all species use habitat in a fine-grained manner.

Niche Complementarity in Adults and YOY

YOY of three species (*N. biguttatus, N. Nubilus,* and *Campostoma*) were segregated horizontally from adults by the use of shallow, stream-edge microhabitats in pools and raceways. This segregation of YOY should serve to minimize competition and predation from adults, and the small scale and high surface-to-volume ratio of these edge microhabitats should maximize feeding efficiencies and growth rates. Also the small size of YOY fish makes them less vulnerable to predators that frequent edge habitats (e.g., snakes and wading birds). Within these edge microhabitats YOY of each species manifested vertical distributions parallel to those of adults. Thus YOY represented a distinct habitat guild, separate but horizontally complementary to adults. Complementarity in YOY *N. zonatus* differed in that they used a similar array of horizontal microhabitats as the adults but were segregated by a higher vertical position (figs. 5.2, 5.3). In this case YOY *N. zonatus* behaved as a distinct member of the adult minnow guild. Overall, the juveniles of each species were segregated from their adults and functioned as distinct ecological species in the community.

Body Size, Habitat Scale, and Predation Risk

Fishes in Roubidoux Creek appear to adjust their habitat use on the basis of a proportional relationship between relative body size and the scale of the habitat; in other words, smaller fish use smaller habitats. Thus large minnows (e.g., *N. zonatus, N. biguttatus*) used areas of deeper water farther from the stream edges, small minnows (e.g., *N. boops, N. nubilus*) used areas closer to edges, and YOY used shallow-edge microhabitats. Additionally, pelagic species (*N. boops, N. zonatus,* and YOY *N. zonatus*) ordered their vertical positions on the basis of size, the smallest (YOY *N. zonatus*) at the surface and the largest (*N. zonatus*) at midwater (fig. 5.4).

Similar patterns observed in streams and lakes have been attributed in part to predation (Keast, 1966, 1978; Fryer and Iles, 1972; Werner et al., 1977; Helfman, 1978; Schlosser, 1982a; Power, 1984). In Roubidoux Creek larger minnows (e.g., *N. zonatus, N. biguttatus, Campostoma*) would be more vulnerable to terrestrial predators (herons, kingfishers, and water snakes, which were always present at each study area; pers. obs.) if they used microhabitats or vertical positions that placed them close to the aquatic-terrestrial interface. Smaller pelagic minnows and YOY are probably less vulnerable to such predation risk because they are difficult to see from above the water surface (pers. obs.). The small size and nearly transparent or silvery bodies of such upper-water column species as *N. boops* and YOY *N. zonatus* probably aid in their camouflage from both terrestrial and aquatic predators. While the deeper, mid-pelagic or benthic zones farther from the stream edges represent "safe habitat" for larger minnows, these fish probably represent a predation threat to smaller fish, so that shallow, near-edge areas represent "safe habitat" for small or juvenile fish (e.g., YOY of *N. biguttatus, N. nubilus, Campostoma*).

Overlying this assortment of microhabitat use by body size among minnows is a higher level of segregation. In the summer 60–80% of large areas in Roubidoux Creek were essentially devoid of minnows (Gorman, 1983). These minnow-free areas were occupied by large predacious centrarchids and consisted of open areas > 4 m from edges in large, pondlike pools, and smaller, deep pools strewn with boulders and tree limbs. Instead, minnows and other small fish used smaller-scale habitats such as riffles, raceways, small pools, shallow areas near stream edges, or stream channels < 3 m wide. These habitats appeared to be relatively safe from predation by large fish. Alternatively, smaller-scale habitats may be avoided by large piscivorous fishes because of increased vulnerability to terrestrial predators. Power and Matthews (1983) and Matthews et al. (chap. 16) have observed similar distributional patterns for *Campostoma* in Oklahoma streams. In summary, the influence of predation risk may partly explain three levels of spatial segregation among fishes in Roubidoux Creek: (1) small fishes in surface-edge microhabitats, (2) intermediate-sized fishes in smaller macrohabitats (small pools, riffles, raceways), and (3) large fish in larger macrohabitats (pondlike pools and deep pools with cover).

Segregation Within Guilds

While predation appears to govern segregation among subsets of the community, other factors such as innate habitat selection and competitive interference may govern segregation within guilds. Sufficient habitat segregation by the smaller fishes may be critical for coexistence, especially since predation risk appears to sharply reduce the amount of "safe" habitat. Thus predation may ultimately enhance competitive interactions among guild members. This contrasts with studies of intertidal communities where predation acts to alleviate interspecific competition (Paine, 1966; Menge and Sutherland, 1976; Lubchencho, 1978).

Evidence that both habitat selection and interspecific interactions contribute to segregation among Roubidoux fishes is presented elsewhere (Gorman, 1983). To summarize that work, I found many significant interactions between species pairs of the six-species guild in the field. Generally, interactions between species pairs were asymmetrical; about half the interactions were interferences, and half were associations. Laboratory experiments corroborated field results and further demonstrated that segregation was due to innate habitat selection modified by interspecific interactions. The interactions were found to be species-specific and highly predictable. These results indicate that the segregation of species in the field is dynamic—the observed pattern is a product of the innate habitat selection by species modified by an average of interspecific interactions over time and space.

The results of the field and laboratory studies suggest that the members of the six-species guild are coadapted—their fine-tuned interactions ensure adequate segregation and efficient use of resources that should also allow prolonged coexistence of the assemblage. Not surprisingly, the relative composition of the five most common minnow species of Roubidoux Creek varied only 17–32% ($\bar{x}$ = 23%) over the four-year period 1980–83 (reciprocal of PS measure; Gorman, 1983). These results are not surprising if stream-fish communities are governed by deterministic processes such as competition and predation. The widespread distribution, endemism, and long-term persistence of the members of the Roubidoux minnow assemblage in the Ozark region (Pflieger, 1971) suggest that the Roubidoux assemblage is not randomly assembled (sensu Matthews, 1982) and that coevolutionary adjustments have maintained the assemblage over time (Gorman, 1983).[1]

[1] The research described here was taken from a dissertation presented to the Department of Systematics and Ecology, University of Kansas, in partial fulfillment of the requirements for the degree of doctor of philosophy. Frank B. Cross, Michael S. Gaines, Robert D. Holt, and James R. Karr provided useful comments on earlier drafts of this manuscript. Special thanks goes to my wife, Wendy L. Gorman, for her unwaivering support and assistance at home and in the field. For providing an occasional helping hand in the field thanks go to Scott Cambell, Joseph T. Collins, Frank B. Cross, Michael L. Johnson, Harold A. Kerns, Stuart C. Leon, Richard L. Mayden, William L. Pflieger, and E. David Wiseman. This research was supported in part by a University of Kansas General Research Grant, 3515-X0-0038, and by a National Science Foundation Doctoral Dissertation Improvement Grant, DEB 8017734.

6. Microhabitat Partitioning of Southeastern Stream Fishes: Temporal and Spatial Predictability

Stephen T. Ross, John A. Baker, and Kathleen E. Clark

Abstract

Microhabitat segregation is commonly documented in stream-fish assemblages, but few studies have addressed temporal-spatial changes in resource use. Also, the potential importance of such partitioning to the assemblage may vary depending on its position along a gradient of equilibrial to nonequilibrial control mechanisms. We attempt to determine whether a stream-fish assemblage changed temporally (over a nine-year period) or spatially (over a 14-km stream section) in microhabitat use. The study area is in Black Creek, in southeastern Mississippi.

Stream discharge varied both seasonally and annually over the study; however, at no time were physical conditions harmful to fishes. Ranks of species' abundances were concordant over both space and time; likewise, actual abundances of the 15 numerically dominant species did not show significant temporal changes. On the basis of the nature of the habitat and the faunal constancy, we position the Black Creek fish assemblage nearer the equilibrium end of a nonequilibrial-equilibrial gradient of community control.

While the fauna did not show significant spatiotemporal variation, patterns of microhabitat use did change. We evaluated microhabitat changes in two ways. First, we used the classification phase of discriminant function analysis (DFA) to classify cases to species, on the basis of microhabitat use. The functions were built from spatial and temporal "control" data and were then applied to the remaining "test data." Second, we tested for univariate changes in spatial or temporal habitat use of individual species. Both the multivariate and the univariate approaches indicated greater spatial than temporal change. To a large degree spatial changes reflected species' responses to varying environmental conditions at the different stream sections. The greatest amount of temporal change occurred on variables that were less important to the segregation of species in microhabitat use.

Microhabitat segregation is an important means of resource partitioning in North American stream-fish assemblages. For instance, Ross (1986) found that, of nine studies that examined habitat partitioning of three or more species, all showed at least some degree of habitat segregation. Habitat partitioning is, however, only one way in which fishes may subdivide resources. Overall, trophic separation seems equal in importance to habitat separation for stream-fish assemblages (Ross, 1986).

A problem with demonstrations of "ecological pattern" is that studies may be of limited temporal and spatial duration (Likens, 1983; Wiens, 1984). Because of this, apparent differences in species' resource use may actually be of minor importance to the long-term functioning of an assemblage. Overall, resource partitioning studies of stream-fish assemblages have been of short duration, averaging 15 months (range = 1–60; N = 17) between initiation and end of fieldwork (Ross, 1986). To our knowledge there are no long-term studies of temporal persistence of stream-fish resource use.

Resource partitioning studies have generally not addressed the relative position that an assemblage occupies along a gradient of equilibrial to nonequilibrial control mechanisms (Grossman et al., 1982). Because biotic interactions may have little significance to assemblage function in an unstable situation, such information is critical to the interpretation of resource partitioning. An important determinant of the degree of biotic control in stream communities may be the level of physical harshness (Peckarsky, 1983), with communities in benign streams controlled primarily by biotic interactions (Ross et al., 1985).

In this study we attempt to determine whether realized niches (Hutchinson, 1978; MacMahon et al., 1981) of fish species changed temporally, over a nine-year period, or spatially, over five stream sections. It is not our purpose to present a detailed study of niche partitioning among the species. First, we document seasonal and annual changes in the stream environment, as indicated by stream discharge. From these data we place the stream within a gradient of harsh-benign habitats and then test for temporal and spatial changes in the rank order of the numerically dominant species and in the abundance of individual species, and position the taxocene within a nonequilibrial-equilibrial gradient of possible community control (sensu Wiens, 1984). Finally, we describe microhabitat use of stream fishes and then ask whether species are predictable in microhabitat use over space and time.

Study Area

The study region of Black Creek is in Lamar County, in southeastern Mississippi. Black Creek lies within the Pine Hills physiographic region of the Gulf Coast Plain (Cross et al., 1974), and is tributary to the Pascagoula River. We studied five stream sections included within a 14.2-km portion. Section 1 was at Mississippi highway 589 and was the most upstream location. Approximate intersectional distances were: 1–2 = 7.6 km; 2–3 = 3.2 km; 3–4 = 1.7 km; 4–5 = 1.7 km. Sections ranged from 60 to 100 m in stream length and were all order 4 (Hynes, 1970), with gradients of 1.1 to 1.2 m/km^{-1} and annual mean discharges (determined from channel morphology; Leopold et al., 1964) ranging from 6.8 m^3/s at section 1 to 13.9 m^3/s at section 5. Stream widths for sections 1–5 averaged 10, 11, 13, 16 and 14 m, respectively.

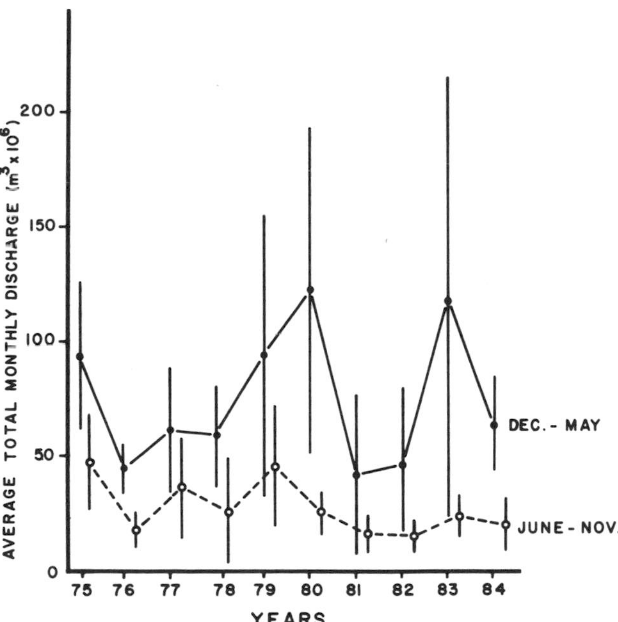

Fig. 6.1 Annual and seasonal variation in flow rates for Black Creek, near Brooklyn, Mississippi. Data are six-month averages of total monthly discharge for the dry season (June–November) and the wet season (December–May). Vertical lines are 95% confidence intervals.

To our knowledge, this region of Black Creek has never been dewatered; however, the stream is characterized by elevated flow rates and flooding of the fringing floodplain from December to May (especially February, March, April, and December), and low flow from June through November (especially June to October; Ross and Baker, 1983). During the study the total monthly discharge for both high- and low-flow periods varied between years. (fig. 6.1). Peak discharge was relatively low in 1976 and again in 1981 and 1982, and high in 1979, 1980, and 1983, although monthly variability was great in these years.

Methods

The five sections were sampled semiannually to quarterly from January 1976 to January 1981; sections 1–2 were sampled again in September 1984. Overall we took 71 section-date samples. Our field procedure was to collect fishes from all seinable, discrete microhabitats present at each section (see Baker and Ross, 1981). We sampled microhabitats as they were encountered, working from downstream to upstream areas, when possible, to minimize disturbance of adjacent sites. In each section we sampled from 5 to 10 microhabitats, for a total of 466 microhabitats over the entire study. We used a bag seine 6.1 m × 1.2 m, 3.1-mm mesh, for most collections; occasionally during 1976–8 we used a smaller seine (3.6 m × 1.2 m, 3.1-mm mesh), or dipnets. Where possible, we took two seine hauls in each microhabitat, one upstream and one downstream. Because of the variable shape of the microhabitats, block netting before sampling was not feasible. All fishes were fixed in 10% Formalin and preserved in 45% isopropanol.

For each microhabitat-date combination we measured surface current speed, mean depth, maximum depth, substratum size, litter, cover and vegetation amounts, bank shape, and shading. These measurements were averages taken from the central region of each microhabitat and were determined following Baker and Ross (1981), with the following clarifications. The amounts of litter and vegetation and the amount of cover other than vegetation were visually scored on a scale of 1 (absence) to 2 (very high amounts). The substratum was scored on a scale corresponding to the progression of the phi scale (Cummins, 1962), ranging from clay (1) through sand (4), gravel (8) to rubble (10). Bank shape was scored on a scale of 1 to 5: 1 = low beach, 2 = 30° slope, 3 = 60° slope, 4 = 90° slope, and 5 = undercut bank. Shading was scored on a scale of 1 to 4: 1 = full sun, 2 = partial shade, 3 = temporary full shade, and 4 = permanent full shade. Such visual estimates had the advantage of being readily recorded in the field and were consistent across all samples.

Our experimental design was to test for differences across the five stream sections using combined data from all years, and to test for differences across time using combined data from all sections. We tested for significant changes in ranks of species' abundances between sections and years using Kendall's coefficient of concordance (W), following Siegel (1956). Because the same microhabitats were sampled in each section over the entire study, with essentially constant sampling effort in a given section, we present abundance data simply as the total number of fishes taken in each section-date collection. We compared annual changes in abundance of individual species and annual and spatial changes in microhabitat variables using the Kruskal-Wallis statistic (Siegel, 1956).

We analyzed patterns of species occurrence on a geographic level by principal components analysis (PCA) of a correlation matrix of species presence for each stream section-year combination. PCA with Varimax rotation was accomplished with the Statistical Package for the Social Sciences (SPSS7.05; Nie et al., 1975).

To determine the relative position of species in multidimensional niche space (Hutchinson, 1957), we used discriminant function analysis (DFA; SPSS9.1; Hull and Nie, 1981), followed by a Varimax rotation of meaningful functions. DFA is a multivariate statistical technique useful in identifying the sets of variables (e.g., microhabitat measurements) that best delimit predetermined groups (e.g., species; Green, 1971, 1974, 1979). For purposes of the multivariate analyses, each species occurrence in a microhabitat, along with the associated environmental variables, constituted a data entry (= case). To lessen the bias caused by poor representation of any species in our samples, we chose, a priori, to include only those species occurring in three or more section-date combinations and nine or more microhabitat-date combinations for each stream section, following Green (1971). The variables mean water depth, litter amount, and shade had homogeneous variances over the 25 fish species used in the analysis (Bartlett box F, SPSS9.1, $P > 0.05$). A transformation ($Y = \ln [X + 1]$) eliminated heteroscedascity for bank slope and substantially reduced it for the remaining five variables.

Once the discriminant equations have been derived, each data case can be assigned to an "ecological" species (by use of the classification function of DFA), on the basis of its microhabitat variable scores. Because the actual identity of each case is known, this provides a measure of the resolving power of the analysis (Klecka, 1975). To assess predictability of microhabitat use of species over space or time, we used the "select" function of the SPSS9.1 DFA program to build discriminant functions from only one stream section or year of the study ("control" cases) and then used these functions to classify all remaining ("test") cases to species based on their microhabitat variable scores. To increase the resolving power of the DFA, we ran separate analyses on each of the two major taxonomic groups: Cyprinidae and Percidae.

We chose 1976 data to serve as the temporal basis for the discriminant functions because sections were sampled more often in 1976, and our goal of examining temporal change made it logical to start at the beginning of the study period. For analysis of spatial change we used section 1 as the basis, since this section afforded the highest species number and was sampled more times than the other sections. For the sake of comparison we further reduced the species used in the classification analyses to the 15 more abundant species used in the univariate analyses of spatial and temporal microhabitat changes and temporal changes in abundance.

A decrease in classification success could be due to a change of the species in multivariate niche space, or it could be an artifact of (1) a change in the frequency of ecologically similar species, (2) a change in the number of species being classified, (3) a change in the number of cases being classified, and (4) sampling error. To control for item 1, we weighted species in both the control and the test analyses to the most frequently occurring species. Thus species proportions did not change during the analysis. To control for item 2, we held the number of species constant in the spatiotemporal comparisons. There was no relationship between the number of randomly chosen test cases and the classification success when the number of species and the control cases used to build the discriminant functions were held constant (for spatial data with section 1 as a control; $r = 0.57$; $N = 10$; $P > 0.05$). Finally, sampling error could affect the outcome if control cases did not adequately describe microhabitat use of each species. This was partly controlled by our criteria for the entry of species in the analysis.

Results

Species Abundance and Faunal Composition

The Black Creek ichthyofauna within the study area is diverse, with 49 species captured during this study (table 6.1). We have also taken an additional 7 species with other sampling gear (Ross and Baker, 1983; Ross, unpub.). Minnows (Cyprinidae) were the numerical dominants, comprising 64.7% of the total number of fishes collected. Other numerically important families were darters (Percidae, 13.7%), topminnows (Cyprinodontidae, 8.8%), basses and sunfishes (Centrarchidae, 7%), catfishes (Ictaluridae, 2.1%), and mosquitofish (Poeciliidae, 1.2%). Together these six families made up 97.5% of the number of fishes collected from the five sections on Black Creek. Twenty-five species met our initial criteria for inclusion in the subsequent analyses.

Spatial Variation in Species Composition. Section 1, the most upstream area, supported the most species (40), while sections 2–5 were similar, with a range of 27–32 species (table 6.1). Cyprinids were numerically dominant in all sections, but other families varied in importance.

PCA of yearly collections showed that section 5 was the most distinct and that section 1 was moderately so, while sections 2–4 broadly overlapped (fig. 6.2). Factor loadings indicated that PC 1 was a time-space interaction, with higher positive loadings for the years 1976 to 1977 for sections 2–4. PC 2 showed primarily a longitudinal effect, with higher loadings characteristic of section 5 and lower values characteristic of section 1. Thus on the basis of the presence of the studied fish species, the five sections demonstrate a weak longitudinal continuum, but with broad overlap in faunal composition.

Rank abundances of species were highly correlated between sections ($W = 0.73$; $\chi^2 = 86.8$; $P < 0.001$) for the 25 species (table 6.1). Consequently, both qualitative (PCA) and quantitative measures indicate that the 14-km section of Black Creek varied little in species composition.

Table 6.1. Fishes collected from the Upper Region of Black Creek, Mississippi, Sections 1–5, 1976–1984

Species	Number	Percent	Sections* 1		2		3		4		5	
			N	*r*	*N*	*r*	*N*	*r*	*N*	*r*	*N*	*r*
Ichthyomyzon gagei	10	0.08	+		+		+		–		–	
Anguilla rostrata	4	0.03	+		+		–		+		–	
Esox niger	26	0.21	+		–		–		+		+	
E. americanus	14	0.11	13	21.0	0	23.0	0	22.5	1	22.5	0	23.5
Ericymba buccata	153	1.23	3	25.0	56	8.5	2	17.5	9	16.0	83	7.0
Hybopsis winchelli	3	0.02	–		+		–		–		+	
H. storeriana	2	0.02	–		–		–		–		+	
Notemigonus crysoleucas	3	0.02	–		–		–		–		+	
Notropis emiliae	13	0.10	+		–		–		+		–	
N. volucellus	261	2.09	38	16.0	77	6.0	4	16.0	31	10.0	111	4.0
N. venustus	1,783	14.31	179	6.0	205	3.0	186	1.0	312	2.0	901	1.0
N. welaka	43	0.35	+		–		–		–		–	
N. longirostris	100	0.80	4	23.5	0	23.0	6	15.0	1	22.5	89	6.0
N. texanus	1,340	10.75	749	2.0	330	2.0	39	7.0	122	5.0	100	5.0
N. roseipinnis	4,319	34.66	1,827	1.0	918	1.0	173	2.0	945	1.0	456	2.0
N. chrysocephalus	6	0.05	–		–		–		–		+	
N. atherinoides	1	0.01	–		–		–		–		+	
Erimyzon tenuis	24	0.19	+		–		–		–		–	
Hypentelium nigricans	26	0.21	+		+		+		+		+	
Minytrema melanops	5	0.04	+		+		–		–		–	
Noturus leptacanthus	237	1.90	56	13.0	56	8.5	7	12.5	67	6.0	51	9.0
N. gyrinus	15	0.12	+		+		+		–		+	
N. funebris	3	0.02	–		+		–		–		–	
N. nocturnus	6	0.05	+		–		+		+		–	
Labidesthes sicculus	163	1.31	145	7.0	4	17.5	0	22.5	7	17.0	7	18.0
Fundulus olivaceus	1,075	8.63	585	3.0	123	5.0	130	4.0	190	3.0	47	10.0
F. notti	23	0.18	+		–		–		–		–	
Gambusia affinis	160	1.28	78	10.0	0	23.0	7	12.5	10	15.0	65	8.0
Aphredoderus sayanus	59	0.47	57	12.0	1	19.5	1	19.0	0	24.5	0	23.5
Elassoma zonatum	54	0.43	43	14.0	5	16.0	0	22.5	4	19.5	2	21.0
Micropterus punctulatus	18	0.14	+		+		+		+		+	
M. salmoides	38	0.30	20	20.0	4	17.5	0	22.5	3	21.0	11	7.0
Ambloplites ariommus	21	0.17	+		+		–		+		–	
Lepomis gulosus	3	0.02	+		–		+		–		–	
L. macrochirus	385	3.09	281	4.0	34	13.0	20	10.0	19	12.0	31	12.0
L. punctatus	26	0.21	26	17.0	0	23.0	0	22.5	0	24.5	0	23.5
L. megalotis	237	1.90	104	9.0	33	14.0	25	8.0	36	9.0	39	11.0
L. microlophus	36	0.29	23	18.5	0	23.0	2	17.5	4	19.5	7	19.0
L. cyanellus	36	0.29	23	18.5	1	19.5	7	12.5	5	18.0	0	23.5
L. marginatus	15	0.12	+		–		+		–		–	
L. humilis	4	0.03	–		–		+		+		–	
Pomoxis annularis	1	0.01	–		–		–		+		–	
Ammocrypta beani	280	2.25	60	11.0	72	7.0	105	5.0	30	11.0	13	16.0
Percina sciera	62	0.50	7	22.0	11	15.0	7	12.5	15	13.0	22	14.0
P. nigrofasciata	821	6.59	184	5.0	184	4.0	153	3.0	131	4.0	169	3.0
P. vigil	4	0.03	–		–		–		–		+	
Etheostoma swaini	234	1.88	140	8.0	54	10.0	24	9.0	12	14.0	4	20.0
E. zonale	107	0.86	4	23.5	38	12.0	0	22.5	51	7.0	14	15.0
E. stigmaeum	201	1.61	39	15.0	52	11.0	40	6.0	46	8.0	24	13.0
Total	12,460											
Number of Species	49		40		29		27		32		31	

*Total abundances (*N*) and ranks (*r*) of species included in the subsequent analyses are given for each section. Rarer species not included in the analyses are indicated by a (+) if they were collected at a section and a (–) if they were not. See text for inclusion criteria.

Table 6.2. Geometric Means ($\log_e [n + 1]$) and Percent Occurrence (in Parentheses) of Numerically Dominant Fishes from Sections 1–5, Black Creek, Mississippi.

Species	1976		1977		1978		1979		1980		1981		1984	
	$\bar{x}$	(%)	$\bar{x}$	(%)	$\bar{x}$	(%)	$\bar{x}$	(%)	$\bar{x}$	(%)	$\bar{x}$	(%)	$\bar{x}$	(%)
Ericymba buccata	0.29	(23.5)	0.99	(57.1)	0.75	(26.7)	0.17	(25.0)	0.36	(30.0)	0.14	(20.0)	—	—
Notropis volucellus	0.51	(41.2)	1.11	(42.9)	1.10	(46.7)	1.14	(58.3)	0.67	(50.0)	0.32	(20.0)	1.15	(50.0)
N. venustus	1.81	(76.5)	2.60	(100)	2.61	(93.3)	2.80	(83.3)	3.17	(100)	1.74	(80.0)	2.28	(100)
*N. texanus**	2.83	(94.1)	2.34	(100)	1.14	(53.3)	1.48	(66.7)	1.54	(70.0)	1.53	(60.0)	2.20	(100)
N. roseipinnis	3.60	(100)	3.49	(100)	2.94	(100)	3.00	(83.3)	3.57	(90.0)	1.89	(60.0)	5.12	(100)
Noturus leptacanthus	0.84	(58.8)	0.08	(42.9)	1.26	(73.3)	0.88	(66.7)	1.05	(50.0)	1.24	(80.0)	1.96	(100)
Labidesthes sicculus	0.93	(47.1)	0.62	(28.6)	0.25	(20.0)	0.32	(16.7)	0.46	(20.0)	—	—	1.24	(50.0)
Fundulus olivaceus	2.28	(94.1)	2.36	(85.7)	1.84	(86.7)	1.74	(83.3)	2.78	(80.0)	1.71	(100.0)	1.42	(50.0)
Gambusia affinis	0.21	(17.1)	0.38	(28.6)	0.91	(46.7)	0.49	(33.3)	0.55	(40.0)	0.14	(20.0)	1.93	(50.0)
Lepomis macrochirus	0.82	(52.9)	0.53	(42.9)	0.84	(60.0)	0.93	(58.3)	2.02	(80.0)	1.21	(80.0)	1.20	(50.0)
*L. megalotis**	1.00	(64.7)	1.84	(100)	1.44	(80.0)	0.84	(58.3)	0.52	(30.0)	0.14	(20.0)	0.55	(50.0)
*Ammocrypta beani**	0.84	(58.8)	1.54	(71.4)	0.93	(73.3)	1.56	(91.7)	1.72	(100)	0.64	(60.0)	1.67	(100)
Percina nigrofasciata	2.33	(100)	2.60	(100)	2.12	(86.7)	2.04	(100)	2.15	(100)	2.88	(100)	2.42	(100)
Etheostoma swaini	1.11	(58.8)	0.92	(57.1)	0.84	(66.7)	0.51	(50.0)	0.78	(50.0)	1.84	(80.0)	0.90	(50.0)
E. stigmaeum	0.83	(64.7)	1.57	(85.7)	0.85	(60.0)	1.00	(66.7)	0.77	(70.0)	1.79	(100)	1.24	(100)

Note: Yearly data combine all section-date combinations.
*Significant change in abundance ($P < 0.05$) for 1976–81, as determined by the Kruskal-Wallis one-way analysis of variance.

Temporal Variation in Species Abundance and Composition. Temporal effects contributed to the structure of PC I (fig. 6.2), indicating that the presence of species in a section varied between years. We further examined temporal changes in percent occurrence and total abundance of individual species, and temporal change of the assemblage, through rank-order analysis. Data from all sections were combined for these analyses; however, we limited the analyses of total abundance to the 15 species that comprised 1% or more of the total fish collection (following Ross et al., 1985). Data for 1984 were not used in the statistical analyses because only sections 1 and 2 were sampled in that year.

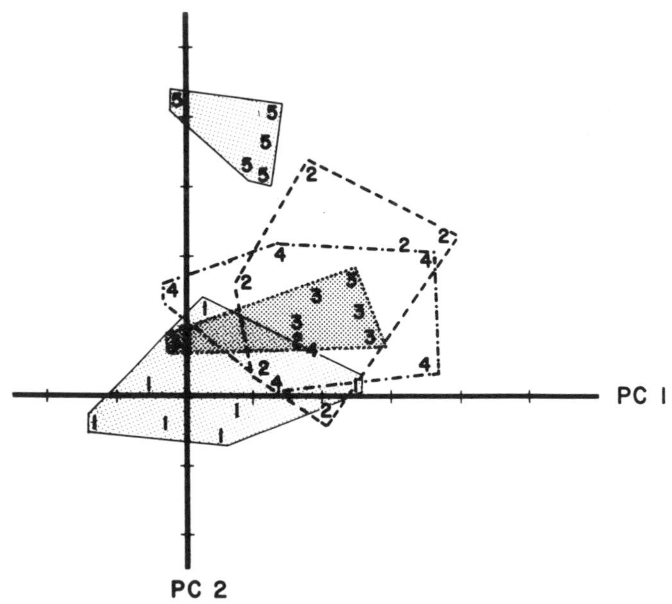

Fig. 6.2. Principal component analysis of the five stream sections based on the occurrence of fish species. Hash marks on the axes equal 0.2 standard deviation.

Twelve of the 15 species did not vary significantly in annual abundance, the exceptions being *Notropis texanus, Lepomis megalotis* and *Ammocrypta beani* (table 6.2). Changes in percent occurrence in section-date collections generally followed changes in abundances. The assemblage likewise did not show significant annual variation, even when data for 1984 (in which we sampled only sections 1 and 2) were included (table 6.3). Rank orders of species were significantly correlated between years ($W = 0.77$; $\chi^2 = 129.5$; $P < 0.001$; 1976–81). Thus over the 14-km length of Black Creek encompassed by our study, both the actual abundance of numerically dominant fishes and the relative numerical ranks of species in the assemblage were stable between years. The minor change in the presence of fish species at individual sections, as suggested by PCA, was due primarily to fluctuations in rarer species, all of which tended to have low ranks and which were not among the 15 species included in the analysis of total abundances.

Microhabitat Analysis

Species showed significant interspecific differences across all nine microhabitat variables (table 6.4). Means were determined from $\log_e$-transformed data for variables with heteroscedastic variances, although species differences over each variable were compared by the Kruskal-Wallis test. The order of variable entry in the stepwise DFA showed that species were separated primarily on the basis of association with aquatic vegetation, current speed, and substratum size.

Overall, the first three discriminant functions explained 86% of the total variance. Following rotation, we interpret the first function as a gradient of the amounts of aquatic vegetation and to a lesser extent cover, and the second function as a gradient from shallow habitats with coarse substrata and limited amounts of litter to deeper habitats with fine substrata and abundant litter. The third function arrayed habitats on the basis of current speed, bank slope and amount of shading (table 6.5).

Table 6.3. Annual Changes in Rank Order of Total Abundance of Fishes from Sections 1–5, Black Creek, Mississippi

Species	1976		1977		1978		1979		1980		1981		1984	
	N	*r*	*N*	*r*	*N*	*r*	*N*	*r*	*N*	*r*	*N*	*r*	*N*	*r*
Esox americanus	2	24.5	0	24.0	6	22.5	1	22.0	5	24.0	0	23.0	0	22.0
Ericymba buccata	12	18.0	33	10.0	97	6.0	3	20.0	7	23.0	1	18.0	0	22.0
Notropis volucellus	18	14.5	56	6.0	82	7.0	75	6.0	17	14.5	4	14.5	9	11.5
N. venustus	195	5.0	137	2.0	461	2.0	535	2.0	358	2.0	79	3.0	18	5.0
N. longirostris	5	21.0	0	24.0	53	11.0	9	17.0	25	11.5	8	11.0	0	22.0
N. texanus	673	2.0	102	5.0	108	5.0	242	3.0	121	5.0	66	4.0	28	3.0
N. roseipinnis	979	1.0	291	1.0	566	1.0	1,011	1.0	875	1.0	100	1.0	497	1.0
Noturus leptacanthus	43	10.0	18	12.5	67	9.0	27	11.0	52	8.0	17	9.0	13	7.0
Labidesthes sicculus	81	7.0	18	12.5	12	19.5	22	12.0	19	13.0	0	23.0	11	9.0
Fundulus olivaceus	293	3.0	117	3.0	171	4.0	115	4.0	330	3.0	33	6.0	16	6.0
Gambusia affinis	8	19.0	7	16.5	65	10.0	20	13.0	13	19.0	1	18.0	46	2.0
Aphredoderus sayanus	3	23.0	0	24.0	6	22.5	10	16.0	39	9.0	0	23.0	1	18.0
Elassoma zonatum	20	13.0	1	21.5	15	17.5	1	22.0	10	21.0	6	12.5	1	18.0
Micropterus salmoides	5	21.0	5	19.5	5	24.5	8	18.0	14	17.5	1	18.0	0	22.0
Lepomis macrochirus	47	9.0	9	14.0	39	13.0	42	8.0	211	4.0	27	8.0	10	10.0
L. punctatus	5	21.0	6	18.0	11	21.0	1	22.0	2	25.0	1	18.0	0	22.0
L. megalotis	64	8.0	45	9.0	79	8.0	32	10.0	14	17.5	1	18.0	2	15.5
L. microlophus	18	14.5	5	19.5	5	24.5	0	24.5	8	22.0	0	23.0	0	22.0
L. cyanellus	2	24.5	1	21.5	15	17.5	0	24.5	17	14.5	0	23.0	1	18.0
Ammocrypta beani	38	11.0	58	7.0	39	13.0	60	7.0	70	7.0	6	12.5	9	11.5
Percina sciera	13	16.5	7	16.5	19	16.0	6	19.0	11	20.0	4	14.5	2	15.5
P. nigrofasciata	200	4.0	108	4.0	210	3.0	94	5.0	92	6.0	92	2.0	25	4.0
Etheostoma swaini	82	6.0	21	11.0	39	13.0	14	14.5	25	11.5	48	5.0	5	13.5
E. zonale	13	16.5	8	15.0	12	19.5	14	14.5	32	10.0	16	10.0	12	8.0
E. stigmaeum	33	12.0	47	8.0	38	15.0	33	9.0	15	16.0	30	7.0	5	13.5

Table 6.4. Means of the 25 Fish Species on the Nine Microhabitat Variables, 1976–1984, Sections 1–5, Black Creek, Mississippi

Species	Minimum Samples	Surface Current* (cm/s)	Mean Depth (cm)	Depth Diff.* (cm)	Sub-stratum* (Coded)	Litter (Coded)	Cover* (Coded)	Vege-tation* (Coded)	Shade (Coded)	Bank Slope* (Coded)
Esox americanus	10	2.4	52.0	13.1	2.9	3.4	3.0	2.8	1.2	1.8
Ericymba buccata	21	10.8	65.5	19.8	3.8	2.2	1.2	1.0	1.5	1.6
Notropis volucellus	40	5.3	53.3	17.5	4.0	3.1	1.6	1.3	1.6	1.7
N. venustus	181	13.8	59.2	19.5	4.3	2.4	1.5	1.1	1.8	2.2
N. longirostris	24	12.9	55.9	17.4	3.8	2.4	1.2	1.2	1.3	1.6
N. texanus	117	9.1	57.8	17.8	3.6	2.8	1.7	1.4	1.7	4.5
N. roseipinnis	184	10.1	62.6	20.1	3.8	2.6	1.7	1.3	1.8	2.5
Noturus leptacanthus	55	33.6	43.4	13.5	4.7	2.2	2.3	1.9	2.0	2.9
Labidesthes sicculus	41	6.6	59.6	20.0	3.3	3.2	2.1	1.7	1.5	2.3
Fundulus olivaceus	163	7.3	53.5	19.4	3.7	3.1	1.8	1.4	1.8	2.1
Gambusia affinis	34	6.1	51.1	20.5	3.7	3.3	1.9	1.6	1.5	1.7
Aphredoderus sayanus	17	3.3	43.2	17.1	3.3	3.8	2.8	2.8	1.7	1.9
Elassoma zonatum	22	2.3	49.0	14.8	3.2	3.7	2.4	2.2	1.5	1.7
Micropterus salmoides	26	2.9	52.9	21.0	3.6	3.5	2.4	1.7	1.6	2.2
Lepomis macrochirus	67	3.8	51.8	19.6	3.5	3.3	2.2	1.8	1.7	1.9
L. punctatus	10	0.4	33.5	15.0	2.9	4.1	3.3	3.4	1.6	1.2
L. megalotis	61	5.2	60.8	19.6	3.7	3.2	1.7	1.3	1.6	2.0
L. microlophus	15	1.4	49.3	16.8	3.4	3.6	2.5	2.0	1.5	1.6
L. cyanellus	18	5.7	55.8	17.4	3.1	3.2	2.0	2.0	1.8	1.9
Ammocrypta beani	87	12.6	59.9	21.8	3.8	2.5	1.3	1.0	1.9	2.3
Percina sciera	34	19.2	54.7	18.9	5.2	2.2	1.8	1.3	1.8	2.5
P. nigrofasciata	216	15.1	53.2	16.9	4.1	2.5	1.7	1.4	1.8	2.4
Etheostoma swaini	77	14.5	52.7	16.3	3.7	3.0	2.0	1.8	1.9	2.6
E. zonale	29	41.2	45.6	10.0	5.8	1.6	1.8	1.4	1.8	3.8
E. stigmaeum	90	10.2	57.5	21.1	4.3	2.8	1.5	1.2	1.8	2.3

Note: See text for explanation of coded characters. Variables were tested for significant differences across species by the nonparametric Kruskal-Wallis test. All species showed significant differences across each variable ($P < 0.001$ [$P < 0.05$ for "Shade" only]).

*Geometric means of log-transformed variables.

Table 6.5. Variable Loadings on the First Three Discriminant Functions, Following Rotation*

Variable	Discriminant Functions I (40.1%)	II (21.1%)	III (19.3%)
Vegetation amount	0.65	0.09	0.37
Current speed	−0.08	0.23	0.62
Substratum size	0.04	0.59	−0.21
Bank slope	0.02	−0.03	0.61
Litter amount	0.17	−0.53	0.29
Shade	0.02	−0.12	0.54
Cover amount	0.32	0.24	−0.26
Mean depth	−0.22	−0.23	0.05

*The percent of total variance explained by each function is shown in parentheses. Variables are listed in the order in which they were included in the stepwise analysis. Data are from sections 1–5 of Black Creek, Mississippi, 1976–84.

Species centroids (mean discriminant scores) along the first three discriminant functions (fig. 6.3) showed a progression from *Lepomis punctatus, Aphredoderus sayanus* and *Esox americanus*, which occupied highly vegetated areas possessing fine substrata and slow current speeds, to *Ericymba buccata, Ammocrypta beani*, and *Notropis longirostris*, which occurred in open, nonvegetated habitats with coarser substrata and moderate current speeds. Three species, *Etheostoma zonale, Noturus leptacanthus*, and *Percina sciera*, had high positive scores on DF II, indicating their occurrence in habitats with coarser substrata and low amounts of litter; two of these, *Etheostoma zonale* and *Noturus leptacanthus*, had high positive scores on DF III, indicating their association with high current speeds. *Etheostoma swaini* also had a high positive score on DF III, but this was more reflective of its occurrence in habitats with moderate current speeds and relatively high bank slopes and

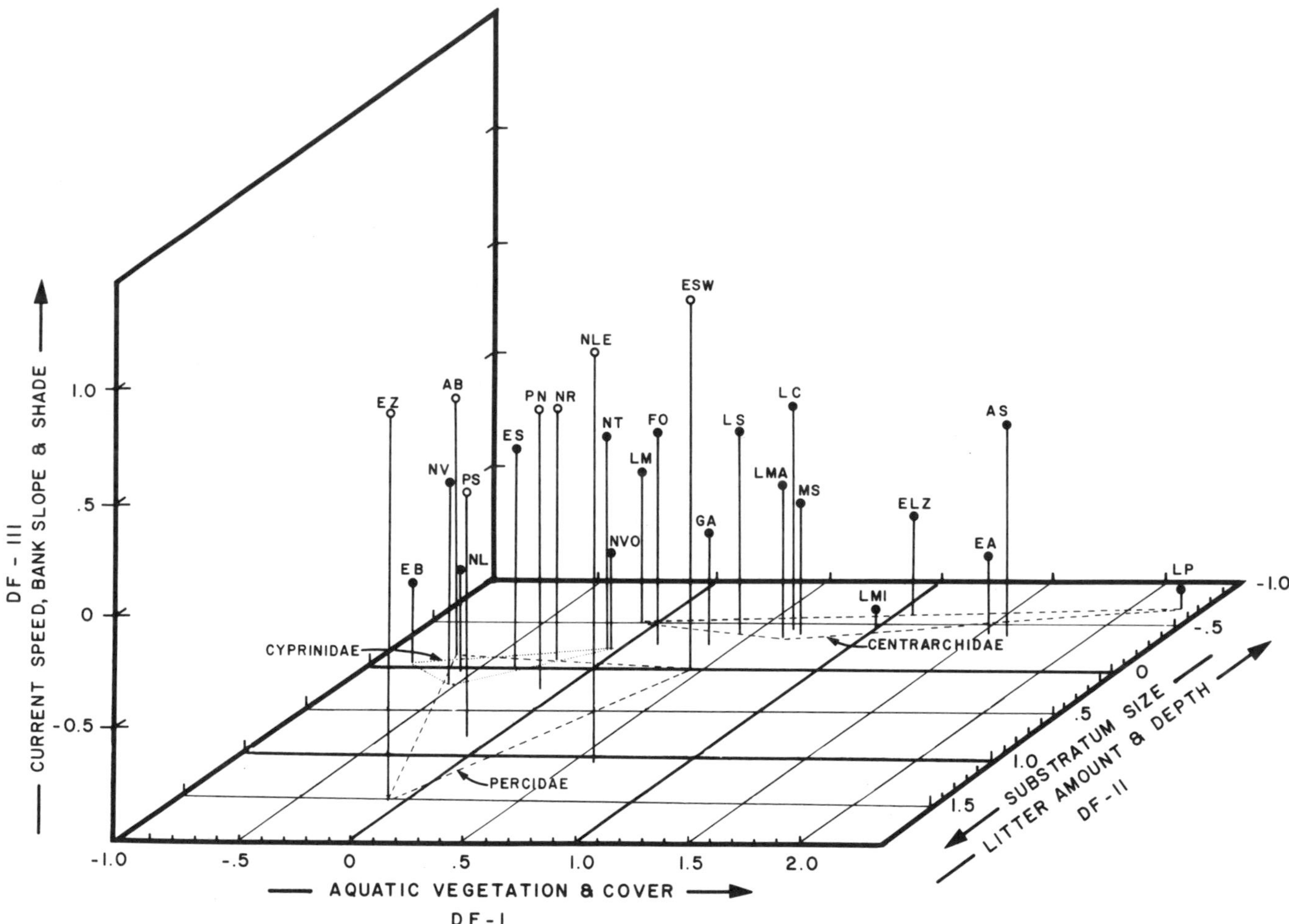

Fig. 6.3. Species' centroids along the three rotated discriminant functions. The labels on each axis describe the major structure of the functions; arrows indicate direction of increasing magnitude or amounts of the variable. Open circles = species with positive scores on DF-III; solid circles = negative scores on DF-III. Species codes are: AB = *Ammocrypta beani*; AS = *Aphredoderus sayanus*; EA = *Esox americanus*; EB = *Ericymba buccata*; ELZ = *Elassoma zonatum*; ES = *Etheostoma stigmaeum*; ESW = *E. swaini*; EZ = *E. zonale*; FO = *Fundulus olivaceus*; GA = *Gambusia affinis*; LC = *Lepomis cyanellus*; LM = *L. megalotis*; LMA = *L. macrochirus*; LMI = *L. microlophus*; LP = *L. punctatus*; LS = *Labidesthes sicculus*; MS = *Micropterus salmoides*; NL = *Notropis longirostris*; NLE = *Noturus leptacanthus*; NR = *Notropis roseipinnis*; NT = *N. texanus*; NV = *N. venustus*; NVO = *N. volucellus*; PN = *Percina nigrofasciata*; PS = *P. sciera*.

Table 6.6. Species' predictability in microhabitat use over space and time, based on the classification function of multiple discriminant analysis*

Faunal Group	Spatial Predictability			Temporal Predictability		
	Control (Sec. 1) (%)	Test (Sec. 2–5) (%)	% Change	Control (1976) (%)	Test (1977–84) (%)	% Change
Assemblage (15)	22.8	8.8	−61.4	21.7	12.7	−41.5
Cyprinidae (5)	48.6	15.4	−68.3	48.9	21.5	−56.0
Percidae (4)	53.9	24.3	−54.9	47.4	33.7	−28.9

*The numbers of species used in each analysis are shown in parentheses and are the same species as those listed in table 6.7.

shade amounts than of association with high current speeds.

The three numerically dominant families were ecologically distinct, with centrarchids arrayed primarily in the region of slow to moderate current speeds and higher amounts of vegetation, and cyprinids in the areas of moderate current speeds, with lower amounts of vegetation and litter. Percids overlapped with cyprinids on DF I but generally had higher scores than cyprinids on DF II and III, indicating their occurrence in habitats with swifter currents and coarser substrata.

The ability of the discriminant functions to identify correctly species on the basis of their ecological characteristics was, however, limited, since only 18% of the 1,639 species-microhabitat associations were successfully classified. This indicates that species overlapped considerably in habitat use and also supports field observations that in any discrete microhabitat more than one species was usually collected. The resolving power was not altered by partitioning the analysis by season. Classification success for summer and fall collections remained at 18%, while classification success of winter and spring collections decreased to 16%.

Spatial Changes in Microhabitat Use. Classification analysis (DFA based on section (1)) indicated a change in microhabitat use between stream sections for the 15 species (table 6.6). On the basis of ecological data from section 1, 22.8% of the cases were correctly classified to species. These cases form a benchmark of the ability of the analysis to discriminate between species. When data from the other sections were classified, only 8.8% were correctly assigned to species, indicating a decline of 61% in classification success. The order of variables entered in the stepwise analysis for the control cases was vegetation amount, bank slope, current speed, cover amount, shade, litter amount, mean depth, and substratum size, indicating their relative importance in separating species in niche space.

Analysis by family showed that cyprinids and percids had approximately equal decreases in microhabitat predictability over the five sections. Only two centrarchids were included among the 15 most abundant species; therefore, this group is not analyzed separately. The cyprinid DFA for spatial predictability was based on 5 species, *Ericymba buccata, Notro-*

Table 6.7. Spatial (*S*) and Temporal (*T*) Changes in Microhabitat Parameters by the 15 Numerically Dominant Fishes in Black Creek, Mississippi[a]

Species	Surface Current (cm/s)		Mean Depth (cm)		Sub-stratum (Coded)		Litter (Coded)		Cover (Coded)		Vege-tation (Coded)		Shade (Coded)		Bank Slope (Coded)	
	S	*T*	*S*	*T*	*S*	*T*	*S*	*T*	*S*	*T*	*S*	*T*	*S*	*T*	*S*	*T*
Ericymba buccata	ns[b]	ns	ns	ns	ns	ns	ns	ns	ns	ns	ns	ns	ns	ns	ns	ns
Notropis volucellus	ns	ns	ns	ns	[c]	ns	ns	ns	[d]	[c]	[e]	ns	[d]	ns	ns	ns
N. venustus	ns	ns	ns	[c]	[e]	ns	[c]	ns	ns	[c]	[d]	ns	[e]	ns	ns	ns
N. texanus	ns	ns	ns	[c]	ns	ns	ns	ns	[c]	[c]	[e]	ns	[e]	[c]	ns	ns
N. roseipinnis	ns	ns	[d]	[e]	[e]	ns	ns	ns	[d]	[e]	[e]	ns	[e]	ns	ns	ns
Noturus leptacanthus	[e]	ns	ns	[c]	[e]	ns	[e]	ns	[c]	ns	[d]	ns	[d]	ns	ns	ns
Labidesthes sicculus	ns	ns	[c]	[c]	ns	ns	ns	ns	ns	ns	ns	ns	[c]	ns	ns	ns
Fundulus olivaceus	ns	ns	ns	ns	[e]	ns	ns	ns	[c]	ns	[e]	ns	[e]	[d]	ns	ns
Gambusia affinis	[c]	ns	ns	ns	[e]	ns	ns	ns	[d]	[c]	[e]	[c]	[d]	ns	ns	ns
Lepomis macrochirus	[d]	ns	ns	ns	[d]	ns	ns	[c]	[c]	ns	[e]	ns	[c]	[d]	[c]	ns
L. megalotis	[c]	ns	ns	ns	[c]	ns	ns	ns	[d]	ns	[e]	ns	[e]	[c]	ns	ns
Ammocrypta beani	[c]	[c]	[c]	[c]	[d]	[d]	ns	ns	[c]	ns	ns	ns	[e]	ns	[c]	ns
Percina nigrofasciata	[e]	ns	[e]	[c]	[e]	[e]	[e]	ns	[e]	ns	[e]	ns	[e]	[d]	ns	[c]
Etheostoma swaini	[d]	ns	[c]	ns	[c]	[c]	[e]	ns	[c]	ns	[e]	ns	[d]	[e]	[d]	ns
E. stigmaeum	ns	ns	ns	ns	[e]	ns	[c]	ns	ns	ns	[e]	ns	[e]	[d]	ns	ns

[a]Data analyzed by the Kruskal-Wallis Test.
[b]*ns* = $P > 0.05$.
[c]$P \leq 0.05$.
[d]$P \leq 0.01$.
[e]$P \leq 0.001$.

pis volucellus, Notropis venustus, N. texanus, and *N. roseipinnis*. Percids used in the spatial family-level analysis were *A. beani, P. nigrofasciata, E. swaini*, and *E. stigmaeum*.

Because the discriminant functions for the spatial analysis were formed with data from section 1 only, the order of entry of variables in the stepwise analyses may provide a more limited measure of microhabitat resources on which species differed than the initial overall analysis, which included data from all species, sections, and dates. However, it is appropriate to use the control data from the spatial analysis only for comparison with univariate measures because variables that changed least over the five stream sections would tend to be those most useful in discriminating between the species in the overall analysis.

Univariate analysis of the 15 species showed that 58% of the species-microhabitat combinations varied significantly between sections, on the basis of the Kruskal-Wallis Test (table 6.7). Spatial changes in species' microhabitat scores were not related to the importance of the variables in species niche separation, with 48% of significant changes occurring along the four variables (vegetation, bank slope, current speed, and cover) entered first in the stepwise DFA of the control cases. Most species differed spatially in their association with vegetation, and these changes reflect variation in the amount of vegetation between section 1 (higher amounts) and the other sections. Cyprinids showed less spatial change in microhabitat use (43% of the species-microhabitat combinations varied) than did percids (78% of the combinations varied significantly).

Temporal Changes in Microhabitat. Realized niche space of the assemblage varied over the nine years, for the overall classification success decreased by 41% between the control and the test data (table 6.6). The 15 species were the same species as those used in the spatial analysis. The order of variables entered in the stepwise analysis for the control cases were current speed, vegetation amount, bank slope, water depth, shade, litter amount, substratum size, and cover amount. Microhabitat predictability for minnows was approximately half that shown for darters.

Univariate analysis of microhabitat variables for the 15 species showed that only 22% of the species-microhabitat combinations changed over time (table 6.7). Minnows also followed this pattern, only 20% of the species-microhabitat combinations showing significant temporal change. However, univariate analysis for darters demonstrated somewhat greater change, 31% of the species-variable combinations having significant temporal change. Proportionally less change (38%) occurred along the four variables most important in ecological differentiation of the 15 species (current speed, vegetation amount, bank slope, and water depth).

Microhabitat Variability and Stream Discharge. Mean annual microhabitat values for the assemblage (all species combined) varied independently of annual changes in stream discharge, with one exception. Vegetation amount was negatively correlated (r_s = -0.77; $P < 0.05$) with total stream discharge during low-flow months. Thus as discharge decreased, fishes became more associated with submerged vegetation.

Within the temporal and spatial scales of our study, both multivariate and univariate analyses suggested greater spatial than temporal change in microhabitat use of the assemblage. The greatest amount of temporal change occurred on variables that were less important in the DFA, indicating that species were less variable in use of microhabitat parameters on which they differed most interspecifically.

Discussion

The physical environment of Black Creek, while seasonably variable in discharge and water quality (Ross and Howell, 1982), has not, in our experience, presented conditions limiting to aquatic life. Considered on Peckarsky's (1983) model of stream-community structure, the upper region of Black Creek would fall nearer to the benign end of the benign–harsh gradient.

The fish assemblage of Black Creek did not show significant changes in the rank order of species in either spatial or temporal dimensions. Similarly, only three species showed significant changes in numerical abundance between years. One of these, *N. texanus,* is known to exploit the fringing floodplain, and its abundance is correlated with the amount of spring river discharge (Ross and Baker, 1983). Thus, while there are individual exceptions, the Black Creek fish assemblage (defined as the 15–25 more abundant species) showed both temporal and spatial stability (sensu Connell and Sousa, 1983). Following the reasoning of Grossman (1982) and Grossman et al. (1982), the assemblage may exist nearer to the equilibrial end of a nonequilibrial–equilibrial continuum of community control. While Strong (1983, p. 641) cautioned that high concordance of species, "could be expected for independently coexisting species that were all greatly affected by the same overwhelming autecological factors," we are not aware of such factors in Black Creek. Thus the fish assemblage of Black Creek may be primarily controlled by biotic factors, such as competition and/or predation.

Ross et al. (1985) found that stream-fish assemblages from physically less harsh environments showed greater assemblage stability than those from harsher environments. In contrast, Schlosser (1985) determined that there were no between-year associations for 15 warmwater fish species comprising the fauna of a second-order Ohio stream, although the latter differed in having extremely low flows during the fall months.

The Black Creek fishes showed pronounced interspecific differences in microhabitat use as evidenced by their positions in multivariate niche space and by their responses to individual variables. However, the low classification success of DFA, even when restricted to specific families, indicates that the species overlap in microhabitat use. To an unknown degree the lack of high microhabitat separation of the species could also be due to our choice of variables. For instance, in the same region Baker and Ross (1981) demonstrated that eight species of cyprinids showed high microhabitat separation, primarily by differences in vertical water-column position (a variable that we were unable to include in the present analysis). The two species that were similar in microhabitat use (*E. buccata* and *N. longirostris*) differed in times of major feeding activity. Using DFA, Baker and Ross successfully classified 62% of the cyprinids for 1975–77, in contrast to the comparable value of 49% reported in the present study. Moyle and Senanayake (1984) also found that an assemblage of tropical stream fish separated primarily by vertical water-column position.

Our comparison of temporal and spatial variation is meaningful only within the limits of this study because we see no way to equate units of area with time. Multivariate and univariate analyses of temporal and spatial predictability in microhabitat use gave concordant results. There was less temporal than spatial change in successful classification of species based on ecological data (thus we infer less ecological change), and fewer individual species showed significant temporal, compared to spatial, differences on univariate microhabitat parameters. The two approaches, however, have very different emphases. DFA does not emphasize all biologically relevant factors, but only those serving to separate species (Carnes and Slade, 1982). Univariate measures undoubtedly included both those of little importance in resource separation of species (as judged by the entry of variables in stepwise DFA), and those of overall little biological significance to a particular species. For instance, *N. roseipinnis* showed significant spatial variation in substratum size, yet Baker and Ross (1981) demonstrated that this species typically occurs in the water column, with little apparent affinity with the stream bottom. Consequently, a significant spatial or temporal change along a particular variable may mean not that a species is actually altering its position in niche space but that the variable in question carries no ecological meaning. The habitat offered at each of the five sections differed (Ross and Howell, 1977; 1982), and many species that occurred over all five sections did so by using statistically different microhabitats. Because the microhabitats at any given section have generally shown little change over time (Ross, unpub. data), univariate measures of temporal change may have consequently shown fewer significant differences. The results do underscore the importance of controlling for spatial variation in long-term studies of fish assemblages.

Species showed both temporal and spatial changes in microhabitat use. However, temporal changes along univariate measures were generally less for variables most important in ecological separation, although this relationship did not hold for spatial changes. We cannot determine whether this represents an effect of ongoing biotic interaction working to reduce variation or is simply due to historical effects and morphological restriction of ecological traits. Our evaluation that the assemblage lies nearer to the equilibrium end of the equilibrial–nonequilibrial gradient would suggest that biotic mechanisms might be important.

Many studies of fish resource partitioning attempt to interpret interspecific differences in resource use as due solely to local spatiotemporal interactions and ignore the evolutionary history of species. That biotic interactions do occur and are at times important has been well documented (e.g., Werner and Hall, 1976a, 1977; Hixon, 1980; Larson, 1980; Edlund and Magnhagen, 1981; Baltz et al., 1982; Werner, 1984). However, each species in an assemblage represents a long, spatially integrated, and potentially independent evolutionary history, and at any given point in space or time a species may not even be well adapted to its environment (Jaksic, 1981). Thus species of local assemblages may show varying levels of independence in resource use and be predictable in resource use across space and time to the extent allowed by environmental variation. Also, studies of resource partitioning in fish assemblages show a strong historical effect, with more distantly related species pairs having greater resource separation than do more closely related pairs (Ross, 1986). Such results suggest that current biotic interactions, as affecting resource use, may be minimal or sporadic (e.g., Wiens, 1977; Strong, 1983; Wiens, 1984) in many systems and may play a secondary role to historical and environmental effects.

A similar, but somewhat more extreme, view has recently been taken by James et al. (1984), who also emphasize that ecological processes are taking place on a broad geographical scale. They suggest (p. 17) that community ecology needs a new model, "one that does not interpret resource data according to the Hutchinsonian constraint that observed differences between species in a local community are attributable a priori to present or past interspecific interactions." An answer to whether the reduction in temporal variation along variables most important in species separation is real, and, if so, by what mechanism it occurs, will ultimately require manipulative field experiments.[1]

[1]This study would not have been possible without the cooperation of many people. We thank P. Attaway, T.C. Modde, C. F. Rakocinski, S. M. Byers, A. Cofrancesco, W. M. Brenneman, and M. S. Peterson for help with fieldwork; R. Leonard and J. Hubbard for help with data analysis; and E. J. Tharpe for providing prepublication streamflow records for Black Creek. Fieldwork on Black Creek was supported from 1975 to 1977 and 1978 to 1981 by grants to STR from the South Mississippi Electric Power Association (SMEPA). We are particularly grateful to C. A. Webb, Jr., of SMEPA, for his interest and support of the Black Creek studies.

7. Spatiotemporal Variation in Habitat Selection by Fishes in Small Illinois Streams

Paul L. Angermeier

Abstract

Associations between stream fishes and habitat features were identified through analyses of principal components. Although most species usually exhibited distinct associations with certain habitat features, associations often broke down in comparisons between years in the same reach, between reaches of the same stream, and between streams of different drainages. Habitat selectivity was greatest in structurally simple reaches, where much of the available habitat was avoided. Centrarchid species consistently preferred pool habitats, and the degree of habitat selectivity exhibited by centrarchids was inversely related to reach depth. In contrast, cyprinid species were inconsistent in their habitat associations and their degree of selectivity. Differences in habitat use exhibited by these widespread taxa may be related to constraints on growth and survival owing to body shape and success in finding food and avoiding predators. Spatiotemporal differences in fish-habitat associations make it necessary to exercise caution when assessing assemblage persistence and inferring processes of community organization. An accurate assessment of persistence requires that the assemblage be viewed over appropriate spatiotemporal scales. Inferences regarding the relative importance of stochastic and deterministic processes in community organization must be drawn in the context of resource availability and species-specific patterns of resource use.

Habitat features have long been recognized as major determinants of distribution and abundance of vertebrate species (e.g., Grinnell, 1917). Indeed, species-specific patterns of habitat association are basic to the concept of an ecological niche and often provide inferences regarding the relative importance of the various selective pressures an animal faces (see James et al., 1984, for a discussion of habitat and niche concepts). The adaptive basis for selecting particular habitat configurations from those available is likely to be complex, with the relative importance of different selective pressures varying through space and time. However, the most important pressures probably include physicochemical stress, competition associated with food acquisition, and avoidance of predation (Connell, 1975). Habitat features considered most important to the distribution and abundance of stream fishes include depth, current, substrate, and cover.

Associations between these features and fish abundance were reported even in the earliest ichthyological accounts from Illinois (Forbes and Richardson, 1908; Shelford, 1911) and have been corroborated in more recent studies of individual species as well as entire assemblages. Behavioral observations on darters (Winn, 1958; Smart and Gee, 1979; Paine et al., 1982), minnows (Mendelson, 1975; Baker and Ross, 1981), and sunfishes (Probst et al., 1984) in streams indicate that subtle differences in habitat use among species and size classes are common, although considerable overlap also occurs. On a broader scale, fish species diversity is often positively correlated with habitat complexity (Gorman and Karr, 1978; Schlosser, 1982), with depth often being the most important habitat variable in this relationship (Sheldon, 1968; Evans and Noble, 1979).

Few authors have addressed the topic of spatiotemporal variation in fish-habitat associations (but see Matthews and Hill, 1980). Yet the strength of such associations may directly affect interpretations of spatiotemporal variation in fish populations, as well as the types of inferences drawn regarding processes of community organization. Stream ecologists currently face the problem of sorting out the relative importance of stochastic and deterministic processes in regulating assemblage structure. One of the first questions asked when addressing this problem is, Is the assemblage persistent? Some authors (Grossman et al., 1982; Moyle and Vondracek, 1985) have approached this question through long-term studies of a few, relatively small sample sites. Consequently, their conclusions regarding stability of entire fish populations rest on the assumption that fish-habitat associations are relatively static.

In this chapter I examine the validity of that assumption for fish species in small Illinois streams. My objectives are threefold:

1. To identify associations between fish and particular habitat features.
2. To compare habitat associations of the same species from different years and study reaches.
3. To relate (through inference) patterns of variation in habitat associations to probable processes of community organization.

Midwestern streams are well suited for addressing these topics because their diverse fish faunas virtually ensure that a broad array of ecological strategies are represented in the fish assemblage. Thus patterns resulting from both stochastic and deterministic processes may be expected.

Study Streams

Two streams in east-central Illinois were studied, Jordan Creek and Range Creek. Jordan Creek is a second-order tributary of the Salt Fork of the Vermilion River; Range Creek is a third-order tributary of the Embarras River. Two study reaches, differing in channel morphometry and riparian characteristics, were selected in Jordan Creek. In the upstream reach gradient is slight (0.7 m/km), and pool-riffle development is poor. The stream is narrow (3 to 5 m wide) and bordered on both sides by 5 to 10 m of shrubs and trees. In the downstream reach gradient is higher (4 m/km), and pools and riffles are well developed. The stream is wider (4 to 8 m) and bordered by 10 to 50 m of woodland and pasture. Subsurface springs supplement flow in both reaches of Jordan Creek. Both reaches support diverse fish faunas of 25 to 30 species, including cyprinids, centrarchids, catostomids, and percids. Further details of Jordan Creek and its fauna are given in Larimore et al. (1952) and Schlosser (1982).

Channel morphometry and riparian characteristics of Range Creek are similar in the four study reaches in its watershed. The low-gradient (< 1 m/km) channel is 3 to 7 m wide with poorly developed pools and riffles. The channel is bordered on both sides by 5 to 20 m of woodland. Range Creek supports a diverse fish fauna of 25 to 30 species, many of which also occur in Jordan Creek.

Methods

Sample Reaches

Range Creek data were collected in May, June, August, and November 1979, and in July and October 1980. Habitat evaluations and fish collections were performed on the same day for all sample sites. Sample sites coincided with naturally occurring riffles, runs, and pools and ranged from 8 to 40 m in length. Sample sites were contiguous within each of the four study reaches, and the total length of channel sampled in a study reach ranged from 90 to 140 m. Not all study reaches were sampled on each sampling date; a total of 93 sites were sampled.

Data were collected from upper Jordan Creek in June, August, and October 1981. Habitat evaluations of all sample sites were performed on the same day, which was usually the day before initiation of fish collection. Because well-defined pools and riffles occurred rarely in upper Jordan Creek, all Jordan Creek sample sites were set at 35 m long. Sample sites were contiguous in upper Jordan Creek but widely dispersed in lower Jordan Creek. Riffles were avoided during selection of sample sites in lower Jordan Creek because these habitats did not occur in upper Jordan Creek. A total of 93 and 39 sites were sampled in upper and lower Jordan Creek, respectively.

To provide a broader array of habitat choices than occurred naturally for Jordan Creek fishes, I manipulated the abundance of woody debris in most sample reaches. Woody debris (logs, branches, etc.) was a primary source of fish cover, especially in upper Jordan Creek. Three types of manipulation were performed with similar frequency; all three began with the removal of all naturally occurring debris from the sample site in May of the sample year. Then the sample site received (1) no additional debris, (2) additional branch structures, or (3) additional board structures. Artificial structures used in (2) and (3) were standardized units designed to provide cover for fish and colonization surfaces for invertebrates (see Angermeier and Karr, 1984, fig. 1). Although not all sample sites received the same number of additional structures, the number of structures (and absence of other debris) in each site was maintained throughout the sample year. Removal of naturally occurring woody debris had negligible impact on other habitat characteristics in lower Jordan Creek (Angermeier, 1983) but significantly affected depth and current features and occurrence of benthic detritus in upper Jordan Creek, especially in 1980 (Angermeier and Karr, 1984).

Habitat Evaluation

Depth, current, substrate, and cover were evaluated along a series of transects across each sample site before fish were collected. Transects were 3.5 and 2.5 m apart in Range Creek and Jordan Creek, respectively. All habitat variables were measured at 1-m intervals along each transect, starting at 10 cm from one edge of the stream. Water depth was measured to the nearest 1 cm. Surface current was estimated from the distance (mm) that water climbed the leading edge of a vertical meter stick; this distance is exponentially related to actual velocity (Schlosser, 1982). Benthic substrates were classified as clay-silt, sand, gravel, cobble, or rock. The presence of benthic organic material (e.g., leaves, twigs, roots) was noted, as was the presence of potential fish cover (e.g., undercut banks, woody debris, submersed vegetation). The number of habitat measurement locations ranged from 12 to 77 and from 42 to 117 for sample sites in Range Creek and Jordan Creek, respectively.

Habitat features of each site were summarized by eight habitat variables: mean and standard deviation of depth, current, and substrate; proportion of bottom covered by organics; and proportion of channel associated with cover. Depth and current measures were taken directly from field data. Substrate categories were assigned numerical values of 1 (clay-silt) through 5 (rock) before statistical analyses. Proportions of habitat measurement locations with benthic organics and cover were arc-sine–transformed before statistical analyses. All eight variables were used to distinguish sample sites in principal components analyses.

Fish Collection

Sample sites were blocked at both ends with 0.5-cm mesh nets before fish were sampled. A fish sample in Range Creek comprised three hauls with a 1.4 × 6.7-m bag seine (0.5-cm mesh). Using a similar capture method, Schlosser (1982) obtained 75 to 85% of the individuals and species in three seine hauls that were eventually caught after eight hauls. Jordan Creek fish were sampled with two passes of a 7-m electric seine, powered by a gasoline generator (25 ampere, 110 volts, alternating current). Stunned fish were collected with dip nets or from the block nets. Two passes of the electric seine were sufficient to collect 85 to 95% of the individuals and species eventually caught in five passes (Angermeier, 1983). Three to six Jordan Creek sites were sampled within a day; sampling proceeded in an upstream direction. Fish from all collections were identified to species, and most were released 10 to 15 m downstream from the sample site in which they were captured.

Multivariate Analysis

Principal components techniques were used to evaluate associations between fish abundance and habitat features. For comparative purposes all fish collections were grouped into one of four data sets: Ranger Creek, upper Jordan Creek—1980, upper Jordan Creek—1981, and lower Jordan Creek. These data sets provided a comparison of fish-habitat associations at three spatiotemporal scales: (1) in the same stream reach during hydrologically different years, (2) in structurally different reaches of the same stream in one year, and (3) in structurally similar reaches of streams from different river systems. Numerous species were omitted from the analysis because I judged their occurrence in sample sites to be too low for meaningful interpretation. Only those species occurring in at least half the collections in a data set were considered in further analyses (table 7.1). All fish abundances were converted to densities (number of fish per 100 m^2 of surface water) before analysis. Densities ranking in the upper 25th percentile of their respective data sets were used to map species positions in habitat space defined by principal components.

Results

Each of the four sets of habitat data describes a stream structurally distinctive with regard to depth, current, substrate, and cover features. Range Creek was characterized by slow current, sand substrate, and relatively abundant organic material (table 7.2). In 1980 upper Jordan Creek was very shallow, with slow current and little cover, but in 1981 it was deeper, with faster current and more cover (table 7.2). Lower Jordan Creek was generally deeper than other study reaches and featured the fastest current, the coarsest substrates (gravel and cobble), and the least benthic organic material (table 7.2). In overall habitat complexity Range Creek ranked lowest, lower Jordan Creek ranked highest, and upper Jordan Creek was intermediate.

Although sample sites differed with respect to many habitat features, depth and current were the most important contributors to variation in habitat structure. Principal components analyses indicated that sample sites were best dis-

Table 7.1. Densities of Fish Species Captured in at Least 50% of the Samples Collected for Any of the Four Data Sets Analyzed

Species	Density (fish/100m^2)*			
	Range Creek	Upper Jordan Creek 1980	Upper Jordan Creek 1981	Lower Jordan Creek
Esox americanus, grass pickerel			10- 2	
Fundulus notatus, blackstripe topminnow	23- 7	23- 5	8- 3	
Hypentelium nigricans, northern hogsucker				5- 3
Campostoma anomalum, central stoneroller	37- 6			
Ericymba buccata, silverjaw minnow	578-54			
Nocomis biguttatus, hornyhead chub		342-73	117-13	28- 4
Notropis chrysocephalus, striped shiner		119-27	181-15	102-11
N. umbratilis, redfin shiner	81-11			
Pimephales notatus, bluntnose minnow	135-28	450-40	117-10	111- 8
Semotilus atromaculatus, creek chub	233-79	26- 3		
Ambloplites rupestris, rock bass		9- 3	7- 3	3- 2
Lepomis cyanellus, green sunfish	90-15			
L. macrochirus, bluegill	65- 8	48-3	11- 2	
L. megalotis, longear sunfish			15- 4	10- 4
Micropterus dolomieui, smallmouth bass				4- 2
Etheostoma caeruleum, rainbow darter				6- 2
E. nigrum, johnny darter	31- 6	12- 3		

*Upper and lower boundaries for the upper 25th percentile of densities are given for each species.

Table 7.2 Mean Values for Habitat Variables Used to Describe Sample Sites in Four Data Sets

Habitat Variables	Range Creek	Upper Jordan Creek 1980	Upper Jordan Creek 1981	Lower Jordan Creek
	N = 93*	*N* = 37	*N* = 56	*N* = 39
$\bar{x}$ depth (cm)	24.0	15.0	22.0	27.0
SD depth (cm)	15.0	9.0	12.0	14.0
$\bar{x}$ current (mm)	0	0	1.0	3.0
SD current (mm)	1.0	1.0	2.0	4.0
$\bar{x}$ substrate	2	1.9	1.6	3.3
SD substrate	0.5	0.7	0.7	1.3
Percent benthic organics	36.0	26.0	28.0	14.0
Percent cover	14.0	7.0	14.0	11.0

**N* indicates the number of sample sites over which means were calculated.

tinguished along synthetic axes that were usually heavily loaded by depth and current measurements (table 7.3). Mean substrate size also occasionally achieved strong loadings on principal component axes. This pattern was observed for each of the four original data sets, as well as for combinations of data sets (combined data sets are used below for direct comparison of fish-habitat associations within the original four data sets). Only in the data for upper Jordan Creek—1981 did habitat variables other than depth and current heavily load either of the first two principal components. The consistent structure of habitat data matrices facilitated comparisons of fish-habitat associations among data sets.

Plots of sample sites supporting the top 25th percentile of fish densities onto two-dimensional principal component space illustrate patterns of habitat selection (figs. 7.1–7.4). The juxtaposition of species-specific polygons relative to available habitats indicates the configuration of habitat selected, while the relative size of species-specific polygons is inversely related to the degree of habitat selectivity.

Fish species in Range Creek were consistently concentrated into pools (i.e., sample reaches with relatively slow current). Although some Range Creek fish (e.g., bluegill, green sunfish, redfin shiner) selected relatively deep habitats, others (e.g., creek chub, central stoneroller, johnny darter) exhibited little preference along the depth gradient (fig. 7.1). No Range Creek species was most abundant in sample reaches with relatively shallow water or fast current. In upper Jordan Creek—1980, where pools were much shallower than those in Range Creek (table 7.2), fish selected habitats on the basis of both depth and current. As in Range Creek, slow current was preferred over fast current, but in contrast to Range Creek, some species (e.g., hornyhead chub, johnny darter) were most abundant in relatively shallow sample sites (fig. 7.2). Habitat selection along depth and current gradients was less apparent in upper Jordan Creek in 1981 than in 1980. Longear sunfish and rock bass were most abundant in relatively deep, slow sample sites, but other species were abundant in a wide range of depth and current conditions (fig. 7.3). Grass pickerel was equally abundant in all available habitats (fig. 7.3). Habitat selection was least apparent in lower Jordan Creek, where smallmouth bass and rock bass were most abundant in relatively slow reaches, but other species were abundant under a variety of depth and current conditions (fig. 7.4). Species-specific polygons assumed the smallest proportions of available habitats (i.e., fish were most selective) in upper Jordan Creek—1980 and Range Creek ($\bar{x}$ = 0.18 and 0.29, respectively), where current was slow and habitat complexity was relatively low. Species-specific polygons assumed relatively large proportions of available habitat in lower Jordan Creek and upper Jordan Creek—1981 ($\bar{x}$ = 0.45 for both), where current was faster and habitat complexity was greater. Linear distances (in principal component space) between species'

Table 7.3. Loadings of Eight Habitat Variables on the First Two Principal Components Used to Distinguish Sample Sites for Original and Combined Data Sets and Percent of Total Variance Accounted for by Each Component

Data Set	PC	$\bar{x}$ Dep	SD Dep	$\bar{x}$ Cur	SD Cur	$\bar{x}$ Sub	SD Sub	% BO	% Cov	% Variance
Range	1	0.46*	0.48*	−0.33	−0.33	−0.44	−0.18	0.23	0.25	38
	2	−0.34	−0.30	−0.56*	−0.56*	0.01	−0.26	0.20	−0.24	24
Upper Jordan—1980	1	0.55*	0.56*	−0.07	−0.12	−0.30	−0.04	0.41	0.33	36
	2	−0.11	−0.04	−0.64*	−0.64*	−0.27	−0.08	−0.30	−0.01	27
Upper Jordan—1981	1	0.45*	0.45*	−0.45*	−0.42*	−0.37	−0.02	0.27	0.09	45
	2	−0.25	−0.26	−0.24	−0.28	−0.32	−0.55*	−0.28	−0.50*	24
Lower Jordan	1	0.11	0.09	−0.54*	−0.56*	−0.25	−0.33	−0.40	0.20	34
	2	−0.54*	−0.59*	−0.03	−0.04	0.27	0.26	−0.30	−0.36	30
Upper Jordan, 1980 and 1981	1	0.53*	0.53*	−0.21	−0.21	−0.39	−0.02	0.34	0.28	38
	2	−0.17	−0.13	−0.60*	−0.60*	−0.17	−0.20	−0.19	0.36	26
Upper and lower Jordan	1	0.08	<0.01	0.46*	0.46*	0.53*	0.45*	<0.27	−0.08	37
	2	−0.62*	−0.62*	0.16	0.15	−0.08	−0.23	−0.11	−0.33	28

*Variables used to label axes in figs. 7.1–7.6.

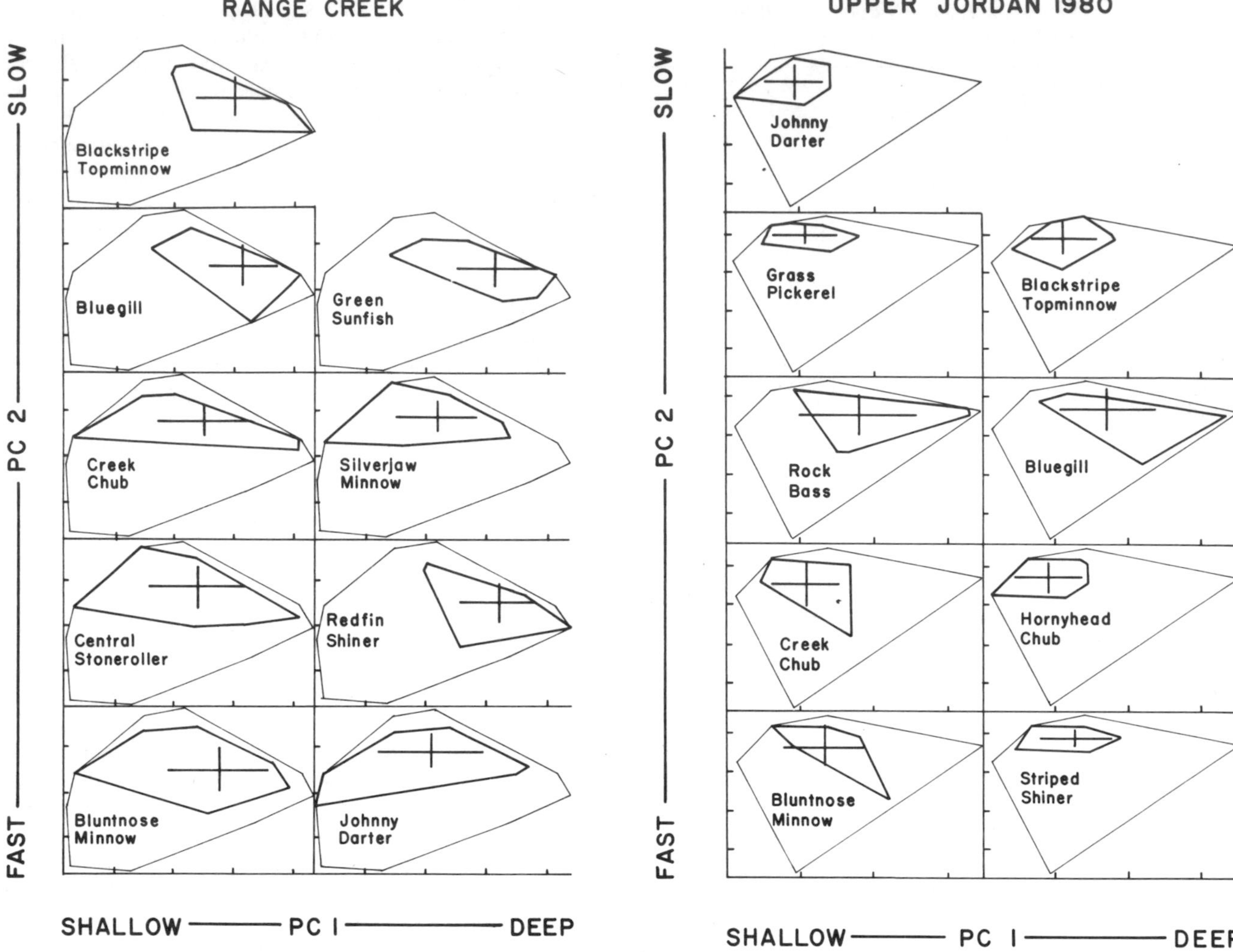

Fig. 7.1. Graphic presentations of centers of abundance for nine fish species of Range Creek. Graph axes are the first two principal components of an analysis based on habitat variables given in table 7.3. The large polygon, identical for each graph, circumscribes all sample sites. The small polygon in each graph circumscribes the 25% of sample sites where densities of the respective species were highest. Crossbars on each graph illustrate the mean and standard deviation of the coordinates of circumscribed sites.

Fig. 7.2. Graphic presentations of centers of abundance for nine fish species of upper Jordan Creek in 1980. Format is the same as that in fig. 7.1.

centers of abundance exhibited similar patterns and ranged from $\bar{x} = 0.88$ in upper Jordan Creek—1980 to $\bar{x} = 1.52$ in upper Jordan Creek—1981 (table 7.4). Thus not only were fish more concentrated in real space in Range Creek and upper Jordan Creek—1980 than in upper Jordan Creek—1981 and lower Jordan Creek (table 7.1), but they were also more tightly packed along important habitat gradients because much of the available habitat was avoided.

A more direct means of illustrating spatiotemporal shifts in habitat selection by fish is to map sample sites from different data sets onto the same principal components axes (figs 7.5, 7.6). This method not only illustrates the changes in relative position and size of species-specific polygons already described but also indicates that a variety of species may exhibit distinct patterns of habitat use under different stream conditions. Indeed, habitat-use patterns of the same species in different years or different streams may be more distinct than habitat use by different species at the same time or place.

Inspection of the principal components plots in figs. 7.1–7.6 suggests that fish species vary substantially in their tendency to associate with particular habitat features. For example, contrarchids were consistently most abundant in relatively deep sites with slow current (i.e., pools), but cyprinids were more variable in positions they selected along depth and current gradients. This visual impression is supported by comparisons of the proportions of available habitat

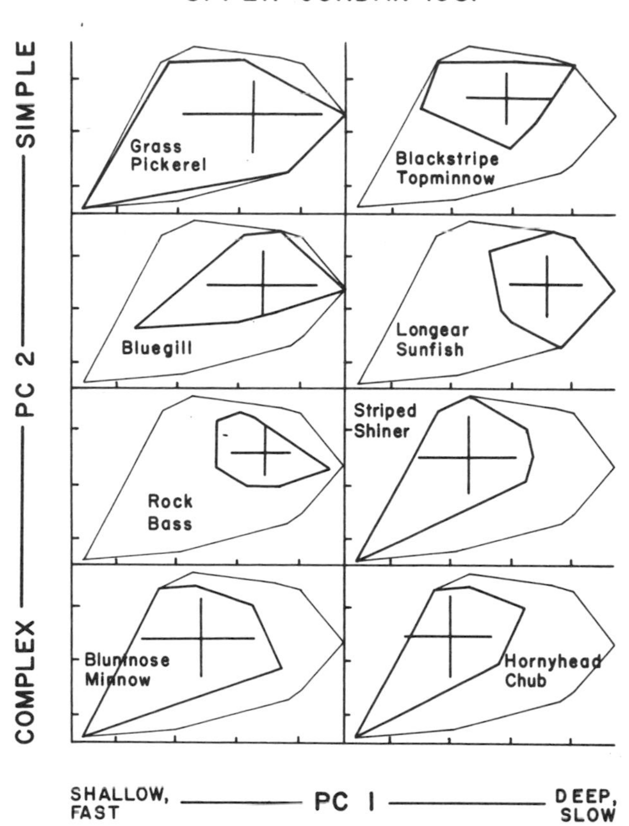

Fig. 7.3. Graphic presentations of centers of abundance for eight fish species of upper Jordan Creek in 1981. Format is the same as that in fig. 7.1.

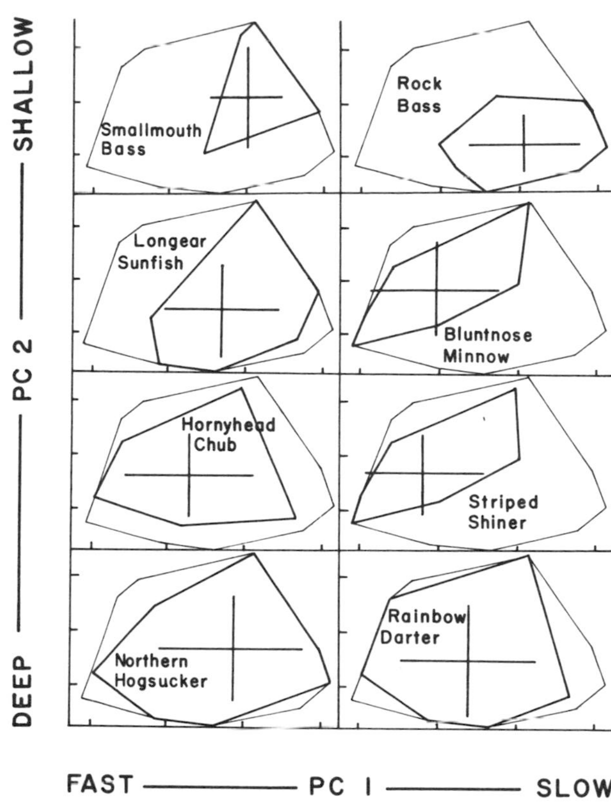

Fig. 7.4. Graphic presentations of centers of abundance for eight species of lower Jordan Creek in 1981. Format is the same at that in fig. 7.1.

Table 7.4. Summary Statistics for Linear Distances (in Two-Dimensional Principal Component Space) Between Species' Centers of Abundance in Range Creek and Jordan Creek

	Range Creek	Upper Jordan Creek		Lower Jordan Creek
		1980	1981	
Number of species pairs	36	36	28	28
Mean distance	1.07	0.88	1.52	1.42
Standard error	0.11	0.08	0.17	0.12

*The mean for upper Jordan Creek—1980 was significantly different from the means for upper Jordan Creek—1981 and lower Jordan Creek (*t* test; $P < 0.05$), but no other pairwise comparisons of means revealed significant differences.

(in principal component space) circumscribed by species-specific polygons in figs. 7.5 and 7.6. These figures illustrate species-specific differences in the degree of habitat selectivity for fish in upper Jordan Creek in different years (fig. 7.5), and for fish in upper and lower Jordan Creek in the same year (fig. 7.6)(remember that a relatively small species-specific polygon indicates strong habitat selectivity). Differences between the proportion of available habitat circumscribed by species-specific polygons in the paired data sets were less pronounced for centrarchids than for cyprinids (i.e., habitat selectivity varied less for centrarchids between years and study reaches than for cyprinids). The average between-year difference in the relative size of species-specific polygons (in fig. 7.5) for centrarchids was 0.12, whereas the relative size of cyprinid polygons differed by 0.31 on the average. Similarly, differences in the proportion of available habitat circumscribed by centrarchid polygons in the two study reaches (in fig. 7.6) average 0.11, but the proportion of available habitat circumscribed by cyprinid polygons differed by an average of 0.18 between reaches. Furthermore, all centrarchids in figs. 7.5 and 7.6 exhibited less habitat selectivity in

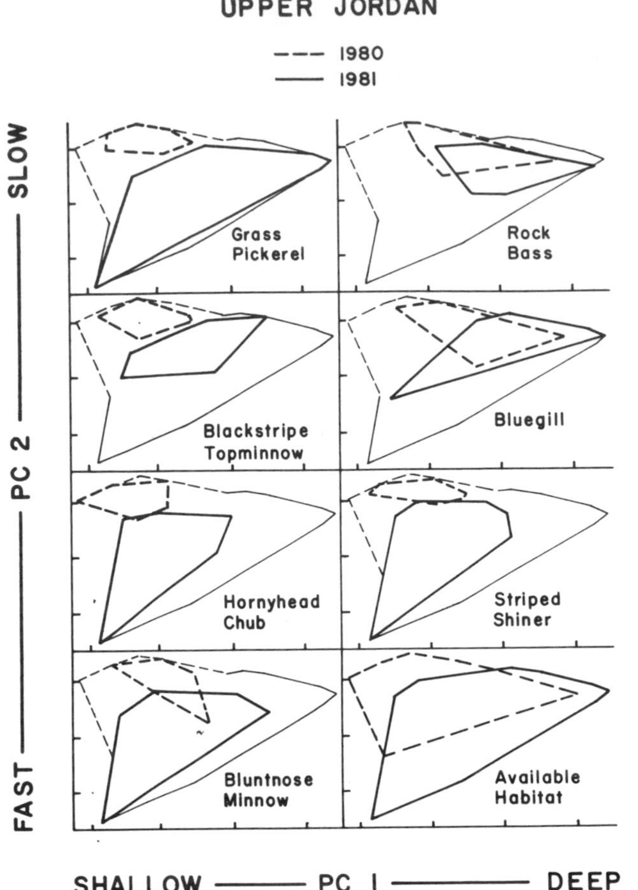

Fig. 7.5. Graphic comparisons between 1980 and 1981 for centers of abundance of seven Jordan Creek fishes. Polygons circumscribing all sample sites (lower right) as well as those where respective species were abundant are displayed on the same principal component axes.

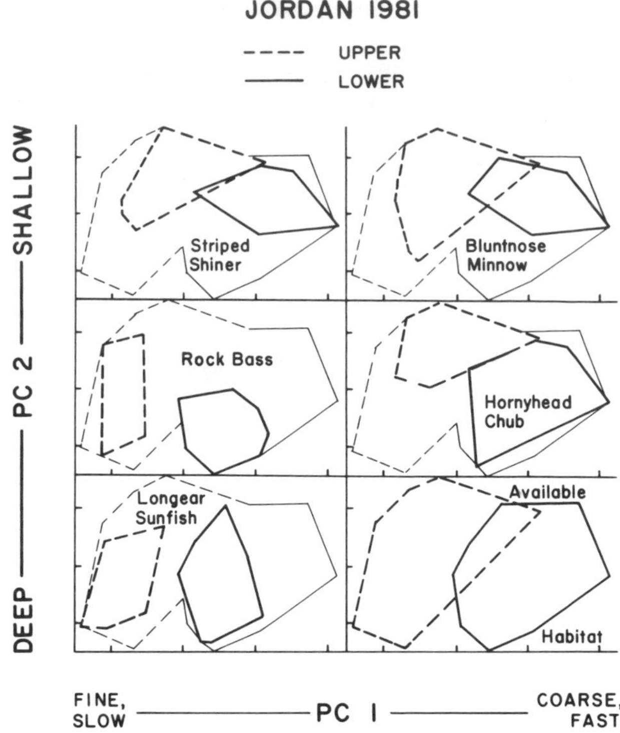

Fig. 7.6. Graphic comparisons between upper and lower Jordan Creek for centers of abundance of five fish species. Format is the same as that in fig. 7.5.

the data set for which sample sites were deeper (i.e., 1981 in fig. 7.5 and lower Jordan Creek in fig. 7.6). In contrast, cyprinids generally exhibited the least habitat selectivity in data from upper Jordan Creek—1981, a pattern inconsistent with gradients of depth or current. Thus centrarchids consistently maintained preference for pool habitats, but habitat selectivity by cyprinids was more variable through time and space.

Discussion

Seasonal and annual variation in discharge is substantial in most streams and is often extreme in headwater reaches (Horwitz, 1978). Moreover, habitat availability for fish (as indicated by characteristics of depth, current, substrate, and cover) is a direct function of discharge. Thus most stream fishes encounter a wide variety of habitat conditions during their lifetimes, even if they remain in the same location. The extent to which fluctuations in habitat characteristics (often unpredictable) affect growth, survival, and reproduction is of major importance to the success of a fish species in lotic environments. Consequently, life histories of species that are widespread and regionally abundant are likely to be relatively insensitive to habitat differences between years and streams. The fish species studied here, all with extensive geographic ranges, usually exhibited preferences for particular habitat configurations, but the kind of habitat selected and the degree of selectivity often varied between years and study reaches. Evidence from the literature suggests that this pattern is typical of many North American fishes. In their survey of Champaign County, Illinois, Larimore and Smith (1963) observed that associations between fish species and habitat features varied among streams. Matthews and Hill (1980) reported that habitat segregation and species associations among numerically dominant fishes of an Oklahoma river were transitory, habitat selectivity being directly related to the severity of physicochemical conditions. In addition, relationships between fish-species diversity and habitat complexity have been shown to vary among different reaches of the same stream, and seasonally in the same reach (Schlosser, 1982). Thus observed fish-habitat associations, even if well defined at any particular time, may not be sustained over larger spatiotemporal scales. It remains unclear, however, whether relatively rare species are as flexible in their habitat use as abundant species seem to be, and whether abundance is strongly correlated with plasticity in habitat use among fish species.

Although adaptive bases for habitat selection by animals are usually related to physiological stress, competition for food, or predation (Connell, 1975), explanations for the basis of fish-habitat associations in this study are speculative. Because no major differences in physicochemical features of the water were apparent between years and study reaches, it seems unlikely that factors related to physiological stress can account for observed patterns of habitat use. Some Illinois fishes spawn in habitats distinct from those they otherwise occupy (Smith, 1979), but this factor should be unimportant in this study because sampling periods overlapped little with spawning periods of most species. Thus observed patterns of habitat use probably resulted from the trade-offs between finding food and avoiding predators. Most of the fish in this study rely largely on aquatic invertebrates for food, but a few (e.g., grass pickerel, smallmouth bass) also regularly consume fish (Angermeier, 1982, 1985). Although aquatic invertebrates are typically most abundant in relatively fast, shallow reaches (Minshall and Minshall, 1977; Slobodchikoff and Parrott, 1977), fish in upper Jordan Creek—1980 and Range Creek were most abundant in slow, deep sites. Avoidance of shallow habitats in these reaches may have been related to susceptibility of fish to bird and mammal predators when they are in shallow water (Kramer et al., 1983; Power, 1984). The basis for habitat selection was probably most complex in lower Jordan Creek, where densities of large piscivorous fish were greatest. The occurrence of large (> 35 g) grass pickerel or centrarchids ranged from 20% of the sample sites in Range Creek to 90% in lower Jordan Creek. Thus the relatively low level of habitat selectivity observed for fish in lower Jordan Creek may have reflected a complex balance of maintaining foraging opportunities yet avoiding predators from inside and outside the stream.

Results of this study suggest that centrarchids and cyprinids, both abundant in many North American streams, have achieved success through different ecological strategies. Centrarchids consistently preferred deep habitats with little current (i.e., pools) and appeared least selective in lower Jordan Creek, the deepest study reach. The laterally compressed body form of most centrarchids makes them better adapted for lenticlike pool habitats than for fast-flowing habitats, where energetic expenses of maintaining longitudinal position may be prohibitive. Although all stream fishes must choose habitats where energy consumption exceeds expenditure, few taxa are likely to be more constrained in their range of energetically profitable habitats strictly owing to a structural feature of the environment (i.e., current). Thus concepts of habitat profitability for fish, such as those developed for lentic systems (Werner et al., 1983), may also apply in lotic habitats (also see Fausch, 1984). The hypothesis that growth and survival of centrarchids in Jordan Creek are habitat-limited is also supported by stomach-contents analyses, which indicate that centrarchids typically enjoy greater foraging success than cyprinids (Angermeier 1982; 1985). Discrepancies in foraging success between these taxa are most pronounced during low-flow periods of late summer. The fusiform body shape of the cyprinids in Jordan Creek adapts these species for maneuvering in a wide variety of habitat conditions. The highly flexible associations between cyprinids and habitat features in this study suggest that growth and survival of cyprinids are limited not directly by habitat characteristics but perhaps by food availability, risk of predation, or both. Experimental studies by other researchers (Cerri and Fraser, 1983) demonstrate that some cyprinids are adept at balancing these potentially conflicting demands on fish behavior. Spatiotemporal differences in cyprinid-habitat associations may reflect spatiotemporal shifts in the habitats, providing cyprinids with favorable balances between finding food and avoiding predators. Although not addressed in this study, size-specific differences in patterns of habitat association should also exist for centrarchids and cyprinids. In particular, juvenile centrarchids, which are more fusiform than adults, should be less confined to pools than are adults. Conversely, as cyprinids grow large, risks of being eaten by other fish diminish, and they should exhibit less avoidance of pools. Results of other analyses of fish distribution in Jordan Creek (Schlosser, 1982; Angermeier and Karr, 1984) are consistent with these hypothetical patterns.

A challenging theoretical problem currently facing stream ecologists is to sort out the relative importance of stochastic and deterministic processes in community organization. Central to this problem is the concept of assemblage persistence, which must be judged in the context of appropriate spatiotemporal scales (Connell and Sousa, 1983). In practice, emphasis on different scales of community patterns may produce qualitatively different interpretations of how a community is organized (Grossman et al., 1982; Yant et al., 1984; Rahel et al., 1984). The minimum time scale that allows meaningful interpretation of assemblage persistence is the length of time it takes for complete replacement of individuals in the assemblage (Connell and Sousa, 1983). The minimum spatial scale over which assemblage persistence should be considered is less well defined but probably approximates the area that includes a breeding population of each community member. Results from Jordan Creek indicate that fish from the same population may exhibit different levels of habitat selectivity in different years or reaches, and some species (e.g., cyprinids) exhibit little fidelity for particular configurations of habitat features. Consequently, long-term studies conducted over a limited range of the habitats available to populations in an assemblage may not accurately depict fluctuations in population density. For example, up- or downstream shifts in a population's center of distribution in response to annual differences in discharge might be misconstrued as population instability. This sort of inadequacy in sampling design increases the likelihood of judging the assemblage to be in a nonequilibrial state. However, deterministic processess (e.g., competition, predation) may still be important in nonequilibrial communities (Karr and Freemark, 1983; Yant et al., 1984). Coexistence of ecologically similar stream fishes may be maintained through a mechanism analogous to that proposed by Hutchinson (1961) to account for coexistence of planktonic algae. In particular, annual stochasticity in the hydrologic regime may prevent highly interactive species from eliminating each other. Although environmental conditions may strongly favor certain fish species at any one time, it is unlikely that conditions in most streams remain stable long enough (i.e., several years) for biotic exclusion to occur. In summary, processes of community organization can be accurately inferred from patterns of distribution and abundance only when such patterns are viewed over appropriate spatiotemporal scales and in the context of resource availability and species-specific patterns of resource use. Continued advancement in our understanding of organizational processes in stream communities probably depends on development of innovative experimental approaches to studying the mechanisms associated with those processes.

[1] I am grateful to all the laboratory and field assistants, especially K. Bisbee, whose toil made this study possible. J. R. Karr, G. G. Mittelbach, D. J. Orth, and an anonymous reviewer made numerous helpful comments on an earlier draft. Fieldwork was conducted through support of two University of Illinois Graduate Fellowships to P. L. Angermeier and United States Environmental Protection Agency Grant R806391 to J. R. Karr. The manuscript was prepared through support of United States Enivronmental Protection Agency Grant CR-810745 to J. R. Karr and a Virginia Commission of Game and Inland Fisheries grant to R. J. Neves.

8. Relationships Between Habitat Selection by Individuals of a Species and Patterns of Habitat Segregation Among Species: Fishes of the Calcasieu Drainage

James D. Felley and Susan M. Felley

Abstract

Multivariate studies of habitat partitioning attempt to identify axes that summarize patterns of habitat use by species. An assumption of these studies is that environmental gradients represented by such axes are of importance in habitat selection by individuals of a species. We tested this assumption for fishes of the Calcasieu drainage of southwestern Louisiana in the wet season (winter and spring) and the dry season (summer and fall). Using factor analysis, we identified three axes (representing stream size, current speed, and amount of debris and cover) that described habitat partitioning among species. We compared the distribution of conditions relative to these axes to distributions of 11 common species in the drainage. Almost all species occupied subsets of available current speeds and amount of debris and cover, showing that these variables are important to habitat choice by individuals of these species. Only the cyprinid species consistently selected subsets of available stream sizes; most other common species were distributed randomly with respect to this variable. In the dry season most of the common species were found closer to their preferred environments than they were in the wet season. This constriction of habitat use was paralleled in most species by a switch from invertebrate prey to detritus (perhaps owing to a decrease in invertebrate populations in the dry season).

Recent studies of habitat segregation in fish assemblages (Baker and Ross, 1981; Felley and Hill, 1983; Moyle and Senanayake, 1984) have used multivariate methods to detect variables important in habitat selection by species. The methods employed (generally some type of discriminant or factor analysis) describe habitat use by analyses of species means (preferences) for a suite of environmental variables. Differential habitat use within an assemblage is summarized by multivariate axes that identify those forms with contrasting habitat preferences (a species' preferred environment being that where it is most likely to occur). Baker and Ross (1981) investigated species overlap on such axes, Felley and Hill (1983) demonstrated recurring trends of habitat partitioning in different seasons, and Moyle and Senanayake (1984) included an analysis of habitat preferences in an ecological study of a tropical stream fauna. An assumption of these types of studies is that the identified multivariate axes reflect real and important environmental variables that affect habitat choices by each species in the assemblage. However, the relevance of such axes to habitat selection by particular species in the assemblage has not been demonstrated.

In this study we identified trends of habitat partitioning among species of a large drainage in southwestern Louisiana in the wet and dry seasons. We then determined whether axes that summarize habitat partitioning within the assemblage reflect environmental variables of importance to habitat selection by particular species of the assemblage. For each of 11 common species we (1) identified the variables important to habitat selection, (2) characterized seasonal changes in habitat use according to these variables, and (3) described seasonal changes in use of different food types.

Materials and Methods

The Calcasieu drainage includes most of southwestern Louisiana (Douglas, 1974). There have been few ecological studies of the area (Carver, 1975; Lafleur, 1956; Mills, 1976). The headwaters drain sandy hills forested by pine and agricultural land devoted to pasture, soybeans, and rice. Gradients are relatively low throughout the drainage (ranging from 0 to 2 m/km at our sampling locations), and stream bottoms generally consist of silt, clay, or sand. The water at locations where we collected fishes was usually turbid (mean = 40, range 7–60 cm, Secchi disk depth) with low pH (mean

= 6.5, range 5.1–7.4) and low conductivity (mean = 126, range 15–250). Estuarine conditions begin where the Calcasieu River flows into Lake Charles; above this point a manmade barrier prevents saltwater intrusion. There are two identifiable seasons in the region, a cooler, wet season, November through May, and a hot, dry season, June through October.

Fishes were collected from sites throughout the Calcasieu drainage upstream of the saltwater barrier, from 78 locations in the wet season (January to May) and 61 during the dry season (July through September) of 1984. Each location was sampled only once in a season. We used a seine (3.7 × 1.5-m, 3-mm mesh) to collect fishes from one identifiable microhabitat at each location, following Felley (1984) and Felley and Hill (1983). We identified a microhabitat as an area homogeneous for substrate type, current speed, presence or absence of macrophyte vegetation (emergent or submerged), presence or absence of cover in the water (cover was defined as structure or vegetation in which fishes might hide), presence or absence of cover at the shoreline, and presence or absence of debris (leaves and sticks on the bottom). Substrate type was coded 0–5 (silt, clay, sand, gravel, rubble, boulders). Current speed was measured in cm/sec with a mechanical (General Oceanics) flowmeter. Vegetation, shoreline cover, cover, and debris were each coded 1/0 for presence/absence. Additional variables measured at each location were clarity (Secchi disk depth, cm), pH, conductivity (μmho/cm), and dissolved oxygen (measured by Winkler titration, ml/l). Stream order (ranging from 1 to 6) and stream gradient were measured for each location from 1:250,000 topographic maps. Before analysis we corrected for wide seasonal variation in temperature, as follows: we calculated temperature means for all locations sampled in five defined periods (January–February, March–April, May, July–August, September). From each location's temperature we subtracted the mean for the period in which the location was sampled. Thus locations were characterized as being warmer or cooler than the average for that period.

The species included in this study were those that were seine-vulnerable (i.e., small) and regularly encountered in the drainage (collected from at least five locations in a particular season). Fishes were preserved in 10% Formalin and identified and counted in the laboratory. Gut contents were examined for 9 species (*Notropis emiliae, Notropis fumeus, Notropis texanus, Notropis umbratilis, Notropis venustus, Pimephales vigilax, Gambusia affinis, Lepomis macrochirus* and *Lepomis megalotis*. Up to 10 individuals of each of these species were examined from each location. Gut contents were divided into five categories—detritus, benthic invertebrates, midwater invertebrates, surface prey, and large-prey items (crayfish, shrimp, and fishes). This last category was quite rare in these species, and was not included in further analyses. Percentage of volume of these categories was estimated for each individual (from the area of a gridded petri dish covered by the food type), as was percentage of the gut filled with food. We then compared food use of a species in the two seasons.

The methods used to identify patterns of habitat use by fishes in the Calcasieu drainage follow Felley (1984) and Felley and Hill (1983). A species' "preference" for an environmental variable was defined as the state of the variable where individuals of the species were most likely to be found. So defined, this is the species' environmental preference in its realized niche (Hutchinson, 1957; the subset of the fudamental niche utilized in the presence of competitors and predators). As Werner and Hall (1976a) demonstrated, a species' environmental preference may differ in its fundamental niche as compared to its realized niche. In the absence of competitors, *L. macrochirus* was most likely to be found in vegetation along the edges of the pond; in the presence of *L. cyanellus, L. macrochirus* was displaced from vegetated areas and was most abundant in open water.

A species' preference is estimated by the mean of the variable over all individuals collected. In a particular season preferences for all environmental variables were calculated and used in further analyses for those species collected at five or more locations. Individuals included in analyses were adults and juveniles. We did not consider differential habitat use of different age groups, though this has been demonstrated (Matthews and Hill, 1979; Moyle and Vondracek, 1985).

A correlation matrix was generated from all species' preferences for measured environmental variables. Factor analysis (principal components analysis with Varimax rotation; Mulaik, 1972) was then used to identify sets of interrelated variables (only those factors with eigenvalues greater than 1 were rotated). Patterns of covariation among species preferences may arise because of physical correlations among the variables themselves, or because the variables affect some aspect of the fishes' physiology (Felley and Hill, 1983). Factors are artificial variables to which the measured variables (species preferences) are variously correlated. We used the jackknife method (Mosteller and Tukey, 1968) to determine significance of correlations of measured variables with factors, following the recommendations of Clarkson (1979). We interpreted each factor as a representation of a range of contrasting types of habitat use among species.

Factors are variables and can be represented as axes. Factor-scoring functions were used to plot the species included in the analysis on these axes. A species' score on an axis is the same thing as the species' mean on that axis and represents the species' preferred habitat on that axis. Species with high positive scores and species with high negative scores use contrasting habitats. The scoring functions were also used to compute the scores of locations on these axes. Plotting of location scores allowed us to determine the distance of any location from a species' preferred location on those axes. Assigning a location's score to individuals of the species collected there allowed us to calculate species variances on these axes.

Factor analysis of a correlation matrix generated from species preferences implies that all variables (preferences) were standardized (Sokal and Rohlf, 1981) using the mean and standard deviation of the species preferences. Values of environmental variables measured at a location had to be similarly standardized to calculate the location's score on a particular axis. Thus a location's value for each environmental variable had to be standardized with the use of the species mean and standard deviation for that variable. All computations and analyses were performed on an IBM 4341

Table 8.1. Fish Species Collected in the Calcasieu Drainage During the Wet (January–May) and the Dry (July–October) Seasons of 1984*

Species	Season			
	Wet		Dry	
	No. Collected	(No. Locations)	No. Collected	(No. Locations)
Dorosoma cepedianum	14	(5)	8	(2)
D. petenense	—		61	(5)
Anchoa mitchilli	—		634	(5)
Notemigonus crysoleucas	24	(9)	25	(3)
Notropis atherinoides	—		80	(6)
N. emiliae	99	(18)	35	(13)
N. fumeus	74	(16)	144	(14)
N. lutrensis	42	(5)	33	(6)
N. sabinae	50	(7)	100	(4)
N. texanus	155	(16)	442	(23)
N. umbratilis	255	(23)	280	(11)
N. venustus	536	(19)	262	(19)
N. volucellus	18	(11)	25	(7)
Pimephales vigilax	83	(15)	104	(12)
Aphredoderus sayanus	18	(15)	1	(1)
Fundulus blairae	29	(5)	36	(5)
F. chrysotus	13	(5)	1	(1)
F. notatus	17	(5)	42	(10)
F. olivaceus	31	(18)	21	(14)
Gambusia affinis	506	(48)	844	(42)
Labidesthes sicculus	23	(7)	238	(16)
Elassoma zonatum	22	(5)	8	(3)
Lepomis cyanellus	9	(5)	8	(3)
L. gulosus	24	(9)	2	(1)
L. macrochirus	178	(33)	149	(17)
L. marginatus	14	(6)	10	(5)
L. megalotis	68	(20)	53	(20)
L. microlophus	34	(8)	18	(8)
L. symmetricus	17	(7)	5	(2)
Ammocrypta vivax	21	(5)	26	(9)
Etheostoma chlorosomum	47	(16)	31	(9)
Percina sciera	10	(8)	9	(6)

*Only the species used in analyses are shown.

computer, using the Statistical Package for the Social Sciences (SPSS; Nie et al., 1975).

Results

Of the 32 regularly encountered species in the drainage (table 8.1), the 11 most frequently encountered were *N. emiliae, N. fumeus, N. texanus, N. umbratilis, N. venustus, P. vigilax, Fundulus olivaceus, G. affinis, L. macrochirus, L. megalotis,* and *Etheostoma chlorosomum*. These "common" species were collected from 10 or more locations in both seasons (*E. chlorosomum* was collected from 9 locations in the dry season). Preferences for all species collected at 5 or more locations in a season were used as raw data in factor analysis of that season. Raw data are available from the authors.

In both seasons the three identified factors related habitat partitioning to stream size, current speed, and amount of debris and cover (table 8.2). Only those variables with statistically significant correlations were used to interpret the factor.

Factor I of both seasons contrasted species that preferred larger, high-order streams with low gradient to species found more often in smaller, upstream areas with higher gradient. Thus this factor represented habitat partitioning by species according to environmental differences associated with stream size and order. Species preferring upstream areas were *N. umbratilis, G. affinis,* and *E. chlorosomum*; characteristic of downstream areas were the clupeids, *Notropis atherinoides, P. vigilax, Fundulus notatus,* and *Labidesthes sicculus*.

Factor II in the wet season and factor III in the dry season demonstrated habitat partitioning according to current speed. Variables that correlated with this factor in both seasons were current speed and substrate type. Species preferring calm water with fine substrates were *Fundulus blairae, G. affinis,* and *Lepomis marginatus*. *Ammocrypta vivax* and *Percina sciera* were forms that preferred fast water and coarser substrates.

Finally, factor III in the wet season and factor II in the dry season demonstrated habitat partitioning on the basis of amount of debris and cover. Variables that correlated with

Table 8.2. Component Loadings of Environmental Means for Fish Species of the Calcasieu Drainage During the Wet (January–May) and Dry (July–September) Seasons*

Season	Component					
	I		II		III	
Wet	Stream depth	0.93	Vegetation	−0.78	Shore cover	0.59
	Stream width	0.96	Substrate type	0.91	Cover	0.75
	Stream order	0.80	Current speed	0.76	Debris	0.87
	Stream gradient	−0.81				
Dry	Stream depth	0.93	Vegetation	0.76	Clarity	0.77
	Stream width	0.97	Shore cover	0.92	Substrate type	0.78
	Temperature	0.80	Cover	0.83	Current speed	0.83
	Conductivity	0.63	Debris	0.67		
	Stream order	0.88	Dissolved O_2	0.80		
	Stream gradient	−0.92				

*The representations in the table are the principal components rotated to simple structure. Only the statistically significant loadings (significance determined by the jackknife procedure) are shown.

this factor included cover, shoreline cover, and debris. Species preferring areas with much cover and debris were *N. texanus, F. blairae,* and *P. sciera;* those preferring areas clear of debris and cover were *N. umbratilis, P. vigilax,* and *A. vivax.*

We plotted location scores on these three types of axes in both seasons. Figure 8.1, as an example, illustrates the distribution of location scores (grouped by 0.25 standard deviation units) for the stream-size factor. The average collection site tended to be in a small stream. However, a wide range of conditions was available to fishes relative to this

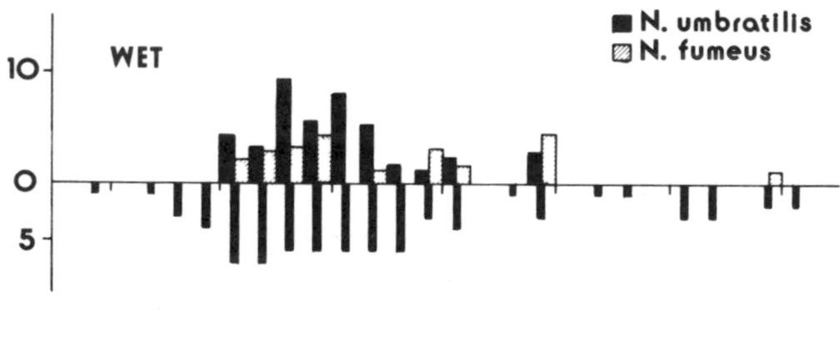

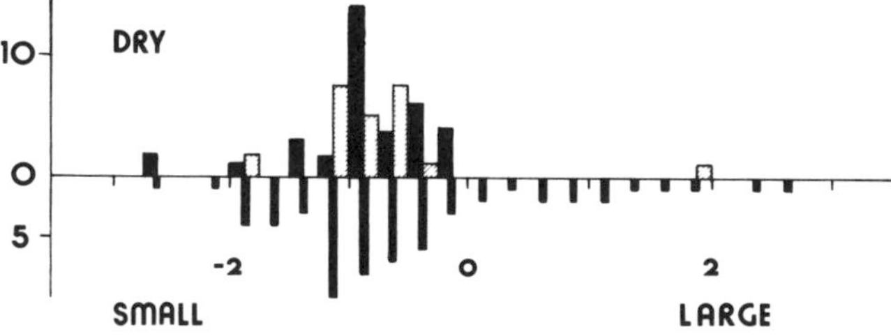

Fig. 8.1. Distributions of *Notropis fumeus* and *N. umbratilis* and locations according to their scores on the stream-size factor in the wet and dry seasons. On the *y* axis for each season, numbers of locations are plotted below 0, while square roots of species abundances are plotted above. The *x* axes represent the stream-size factor and are given in standard deviation units. Location scores and species abundances were grouped by 0.25 standard deviation units.

axis. The standard deviations of the distribution of location scores on the stream-size axis in each season are given in table 8.3, as are standard deviations of location scores on the other two types of axes. As with the stream-size factor, a wide range of conditions was available to fishes relative to current speeds and amount of debris and cover. We also plotted the number of individuals of *N. fumeus* and *N. umbratilis* at different locations (fig. 8.1). We used the square root of species numbers so as to compress the *y* axis, but the standard deviations of the untransformed species' distributions on the different axes are given in table 8.3. Standard deviations ranged widely (0.32–2.11) among the common species.

If an environmental variable represented by a factor were of no importance to a particular species' selection of its preferred habitat, then the species should occur across the full range of conditions relative to that variable. In that case the species' distribution would be dictated by the distribution of locations relative to this variable, and the variance of the species' distribution should equal that of the locations. Conversely, a species choosing a subset of the available habitat represented on an axis will have a variance less than that of the locations. We chose to examine these two alternatives for the 11 common species of the drainage.

We used Levene's test (Levene, 1960) to test null hypotheses of equality of location and species variances. Van Valen (1978) addressed the question of tests of variance equality, suggesting a number of tests (Levene's test was one) appropriate for situations where the variances to be tested do not come from normal distributions. We followed Van Valen's suggestion, since we had no reason to assume that either locations or species abundances were distributed normally. Levene's test is essentially a *t*-test, and multiple tests create a situation of compounding type I error. To counter this, we considered the null hypothesis of equal variances to be rejected only if the calculated *t* value exceeded the tabulated value at $P = 0.001$ (methods for determining this alpha value are found in Sokal and Rohlf, 1981). Since we were interested in those comparisons only where a species' variance was less than the location variance, we conducted one-tailed tests of variance equality.

Table 8.3. Means (Scores) and Standard Deviations of the 11 Most Common Species of the Calcasieu Drainage on Factors Describing Habitat Partitioning Among the Regularly Occurring Species of the Drainage and Standard Deviations of Location Scores on These Factors*

Species	Season	Type of Factor: Waterway Size	Current	Debris and Cover
		Mean (SD)	Mean (SD)	Mean (SD)
Notropis	Wet	1.34 (1.52)	0.19 (0.78)	−0.97 (2.11)
emiliae	Dry	−0.76 (0.96)	−0.75 (2.03)	−0.34 (1.34)
Notropis	Wet	−0.56 (1.08)	−0.37 (0.78)	−0.21 (1.73)
fumeus	Dry	−0.69 (0.40)	1.49 (0.57)	−1.34 (0.83)
Notropis	Wet	0.03 (1.24)	−0.17 (0.87)	0.64 (1.67)
texanus	Dry	0.44 (1.00)	−0.56 (1.29)	0.28 (1.48)
Notropis	Wet	−1.16 (0.54)	0.27 (0.91)	−1.24 (1.89)
umbratilis	Dry	−0.78 (0.32)	0.90 (0.93)	−1.65 (0.65)
Notropis	Wet	0.81 (1.21)	−0.30 (0.79)	−0.14 (1.63)
venustus	Dry	−0.48 (0.61)	−1.17 (1.20)	−1.18 (0.79)
Pimephales	Wet	1.08 (1.68)	−0.21 (0.93)	−2.06 (1.97)
vigilax	Dry	1.12 (1.42)	−0.21 (1.03)	−1.30 (0.89)
Fundulus	Wet	−0.60 (1.20)	−0.04 (0.76)	1.51 (1.35)
olivaceus	Dry	−0.94 (0.81)	0.94 (0.86)	−0.92 (1.27)
Gambusia	Wet	−0.93 (1.04)	0.38 (1.05)	0.58 (1.83)
affinis	Dry	−0.66 (1.11)	0.87 (0.86)	0.17 (1.63)
Lepomis	Wet	0.58 (1.69)	1.10 (1.04)	0.28 (1.59)
macrochirus	Dry	0.57 (1.04)	0.61 (0.88)	1.01 (1.49)
Lepomis	Wet	0.46 (1.75)	0.11 (0.61)	−1.12 (2.13)
megalotis	Dry	0.77 (1.34)	0.70 (0.99)	−0.30 (1.36)
Etheostoma	Wet	−0.80 (1.53)	−0.37 (0.90)	−0.12 (1.83)
chlorosomum	Dry	−1.21 (0.74)	−0.22 (1.48)	−0.58 (0.85)
Locations	Wet	(1.46)	(1.28)	(1.99)
	Dry	(1.09)	(1.45)	(1.51)

*On the three types of factors, negative scores indicate preferences for small streams, fast current, and areas with little cover and debris, respectively. Positive scores indicate the converse.

Table 8.4. Significance Tests of Distributions of Individuals for the 11 Most Common Species on Factors Describing Habitat Use by the Fish Species of the Calcasieu Drainage

Seasons	Waterway Size: Locations Wet	Locations Dry	Seas.	R_s Wet	R_s Dry	Current: Locations Wet	Locations Dry	Seas.	R_s Wet	R_s Dry	Debris and Cover: Locations Wet	Locations Dry	Seas.	R_s Wet	R_s Dry
Notropis emiliae		*X*	*X*			*X*		*X*				*X*			
N. fumeus	*X*	*X*	*X*			*X*	*X*	*X*		−0.77**	*X*	*X*	*X*	−0.67**	
N. texanus	*X*		*X*		−0.53*		*X*				*X*	*X*	*X*		
N. umbratilis	*X*	*X*	*X*	−0.72**	−0.66**	*X*	*X*	*X*			*X*	*X*	*X*		−0.53**
N. venustus	*X*	*X*	*X*	−0.39**		*X*	*X*	*X*			*X*	*X*	*X*		
Pimephales vigilax					−0.53*	*X*	*X*		−0.42**			*X*	*X*		
Fundulus olivaceus						*X*	*X*				*X*				
Gambusia affinis	*X*		*X*			*X*	*X*	*X*			*X*		*X*		
Lepomis macrochirus					−0.65**	*X*	*X*	*X*			*X*		*X*		
L. megalotis					−0.57**	*X*	*X*	*X*							
Etheostoma chlorosomum						*X*					*X*	*X*	*X*	−0.47**	−0.60**

Note: Levene's test of variance equality was used to compare species variances with location variances in both seasons. Significance of tests is given under "Locations." Difference in a species' variance in the wet and dry seasons was similarly tested (significance given under "Seas"). The between-seasons tests were performed on species variances transformed as (species variance/location variance) to correct for differing location variances in the two seasons. For Levene's test results, *X* represents $P < 0.001$. Under R_s is given the rank correlation of numbers of individuals with distance of a location's score from the species' mean score (representing its preferred environment on that factor). Only signifícant correlations are reported (* = $P < 0.05$, ** = $P < 0.01$).

Every species had a significantly smaller variance in both seasons, on at least one of the three axes (table 8.4). Overall, most species tended to select a smaller range of current speeds than was available. Fewer species seemed to select habitat according to amount of debris and cover, and of the 11 species only the cyprinids were consistently limited to particular stream sizes. In general the cyprinids seemed to be more selective of or limited to certain habitats, on the basis of numbers of significant tests. *Fundulus olivaceus, G. affinis,* the sunfishes, and *E. chlorosomum* were less selective.

Some of the common species showed seasonal shifts. In the dry season *N. emiliae* and *N. venustus* were found in smaller streams with high gradients more often than in the wet season. In the dry season the two forms were also found in faster water, while *N. fumeus* moved to slow water. *Fundulus olivaceus* tended to be found in less debris-choked areas during the dry season. These shifts were reflected in the species' score on an axis (table 8.3) in the two seasons.

We also investigated changes in species variances in the two seasons, using Levene's test. Before these tests, we transformed species variances as (species variance/location variance) to correct for differing location variances in the two seasons. A species' variance might be smaller in one season merely because there was less variation in available habitat in that season. We tested null hypotheses of variance equality in the two seasons using two-tailed tests (a species' variance might either increase or decrease from one season to another). Of the significant changes in variance, most (14 of 21) involved decreases in species variances in the dry season (table 8.4). Thus most forms were more likely to be found closer to their preferred environment in the dry season than in the wet season. A few species showed increases in variance in the dry season, on one axis or another. On the stream-size axis *N. texanus* and *G. affinis* increased the range of habitats in which they were found. On the current speed axis *N. emiliae* and *N. venustus* (two species that showed a shift on this axis) had an increase in variance in the dry season, as did *L. megalotis*. *Notropis texanus, G. affinis,* and *L. macrochirus* had increased variances on the debris and cover axis. Only *F. olivaceus* showed no change in variances between seasons on any axis.

If a particular habitat axis is important to a species, the species should be less common in habitats that are different from its preferred habitat. For those sites where a species was collected, we computed Spearman rank correlations (r_s; Sokal and Rohlf, 1981) between number of individuals and the difference between a location's score and the species' score on that axis. A significant negative correlation indicates that the species is progressively less common in habitats more different from its preferred habitat. Table 8.4 presents these correlation coefficients. Most of the species for which significant correlations were found were cyprinids. Also, most significant correlations (8 of 13) were found for species distributions in the dry season (again suggesting that these species are more tied to their preferred habitats in the dry season).

We examined gut contents for 9 of the 11 species (all except *F. olivaceus* and *E. chlorosomum*), and these species consumed a wide range of foods (table 8.5). Species that seemed to specialize on surface foods included *N. fumeus* and *N. umbratilis*. *Gambusia affinis* and *L. macrochirus* fed substantially on midwater invertebrates (mostly copepods and cladocerans), while *L. megalotis* tended to eat benthic invertebrates. *Notropis emiliae* and *P. vigilax* concentrated primarily on detritus. These food preferences were especially obvious in the wet season. In the dry season all species consumed more detritus and fewer invertebrates. This increase in detritus consumption was especially marked for *N.*

Table 8.5. Food Types of Nine Common Fish Species of the Calcasieu Drainage in the Wet and Dry Seasons

Species	Seas.	N(%)	Animal Prey: Surface % (%)	Animal Prey: Midwater % (%)	Animal Prey: Benthic % (%)	Detritus % (%)
Notropis emiliae	Wet	52(10)	8.3 (7.1)	13.6 (31.0)	31.8 (38.1)	46.3 (57.1)
	Dry	26 (4)	0.0 (0.0)	14.2 (22.7)	23.2 (36.4)	62.7 (86.4)
Notropis fumeus	Wet	50(10)	64.1 (65.0)	0.6 (5.0)	33.7 (62.5)	1.6 (5.0)
	Dry	53 (8)	37.4 (42.2)	8.7 (13.3)	21.0 (31.1)	32.8 (62.2)
Notropis texanus	Wet	63(18)	20.5 (31.1)	5.0 (6.7)	39.1 (53.3)	34.8 (55.6)
	Dry	114(17)	5.2 (9.3)	3.4 (11.3)	9.9 (23.7)	81.5 (86.6)
Notropis umbratilis	Wet	100(27)	56.9 (56.2)	3.3 (8.2)	39.8 (60.3)	0.0 (0.0)
	Dry	61(11)	59.1 (58.0)	13.8 (26.0)	14.2 (20.0)	12.9 (30.0)
Notropis venustus	Wet	82(29)	30.5 (41.5)	0.0 (0.0)	54.0 (62.3)	15.6 (30.2)
	Dry	70 (5)	12.1 (23.1)	1.7 (1.5)	15.4 (32.3)	70.8 (80.0)
Pimephales vigilax	Wet	33 (7)	21.0 (26.9)	1.0 (7.7)	35.6 (50.0)	42.4 (76.9)
	Dry	41 (2)	2.5 (5.1)	0.0 (0.0)	17.5 (25.6)	80.0 (92.3)
Gambusia affinis	Wet	222(42)	20.3 (23.3)	57.3 (68.3)	17.6 (25.6)	4.9 (10.0)
	Dry	187(31)	15.8 (18.6)	10.9 (19.2)	5.8 (9.6)	67.4 (71.2)
Lepomis macrochirus	Wet	68(12)	10.9 (14.3)	48.9 (69.6)	27.8 (57.1)	12.4 (37.5)
	Dry	74 (7)	4.7 (9.0)	34.9 (58.2)	30.0 (53.7)	30.4 (47.8)
Lepomis megalotis	Wet	48(15)	7.9 (18.2)	13.4 (18.2)	72.3 (81.8)	6.4 (2.4)
	Dry	41 (1)	9.1 (12.5)	3.4 (7.5)	69.9 (90.0)	17.6 (55.0)

Under *N* is listed the number of individuals whose gut contents were examined (the number of individuals with empty guts is given in parentheses). For each species in each season are listed the percentages of aggregate volume and (in parentheses) the percentage of occurrence of each of the four food types.

fumeus, *N. texanus*, *P. vigilax*, and *G. affinis*. It may be that all species were experiencing a food shortage owing to a decline in the invertebrate fauna. Daiber (1982) included an overview of work demonstrating the poor food value of detritus to various aquatic organisms. Possible explanations for detritus feeding by the fishes of the Calcasieu drainage are that detritus either was an alternative food or was ingested incidentally during food searches. Considering the predominance of detritus in the guts of most species (except for *N. umbratilis* and *L. megalotis*), the second alternative is unlikely.

Discussion

Fishes of the Calcasieu drainage partition habitat according to three different environmental factors. The same variables were significantly associated with these factors in both seasons, suggesting that patterns of habitat segregation in the drainage are consistent between seasons, despite the inclusion of different species in each analysis. In the wet season eight species were included that were not regularly collected in the dry season; in the dry season three species were included that were not found regularly in the wet season.

The three environmental axes demonstrated in our study reflect environmental variables shown to be major contributors to habitat partitioning of fishes in other studies. Shelford (1911), Sheldon (1968), and Whiteside and McNatt (1972) showed the importance of longitudinal zonation (reflected in the stream-size factor); Curry and Spacie (1984), Moyle and Vondracek (1985), and Page (1983) have documented the importance of current speed in habitat segregation of various stream fishes; Angermeier and Karr (1984) have experimentally demonstrated the importance of debris and woody structure to occurrence of stream fishes. Multivariate studies of habitat segregation by Baker and Ross (1981), Felley and Hill (1983), and Moyle and Senanayake (1984) demonstrated factors involving stream size, current speed, and amount of debris and cover.

What has not been demonstrated by multivariate descriptions of habitat partitioning (such as those listed above) is the importance of the various axes to an individual species. Does each species react as though all axes were equally important in habitat selection? We identified the axes of importance for each of the common species by comparing the distribution of individuals of a species to the distribution of conditions relative to each axis. We found that each of the common species selected a particular subset of available conditions on the current speed axis. Similarly, most species selected limited subsets of available conditions relative to the debris and cover axis. The distribution of individuals of *L. megalotis* on this axis was not significantly different from the distribution of habitats; amount of debris and cover may not be of great importance to habitat selection by *L. megalotis*. Waterway size seemed to be the least important axis in affecting the distributions of these species. Only the cyprinids consistently selected a subset of available stream sizes. The cyprinids (actively swimming and widely ranging forms) were generally the more active habitat selectors, as demonstrated by variance comparisons and rank correlations of abundance with distance from a preferred habitat. For the more sedentary sunfishes and darters (Gerking, 1959), as well as *F. olivaceus* and *G. affinis*, evidence of active habitat selection was not as obvious.

Variance comparisons between seasons indicated that the dry season is generally a stressful period for fishes in the drainage. Most of the common species had smaller distributional variances in the dry season, as individuals clustered about their preferred habitats on a particular axis. Ross and Baker (1983) showed that the wet season is a time of plenty for many stream fishes of the southeastern United States. Flooded lowlands offer new food resources and unexploited habitats, and many species respond by moving into these unutilized areas. Conversely, Matthews and Hill (1980) found that during periods of physicochemical stress fishes of an Oklahoma river constricted their habitat use. Schoener (1982) considered such patterns of niche expansion and constriction in the light of competition; in the "lean" season species retreat to resources or environments in which they are competitively superior. Of course, in the fishes investigated here, such a retreat to "best available" environments might be movement to habitats within the species' tolerance limits, or to areas free of predators.

Diets of nine of the common species confirm that the dry season is truly the "lean" season for fishes of the Calcasieu drainage. Most species fed heavily on invertebrates in the wet season but were more reliant on detritus in the dry season. Angermeier (1982), Starrett (1950), and Whitaker (1977) found similar trends of species switching to detritus in summer and fall in streams of the midwestern United States.

In the Calcasieu drainage the switch from invertebrate prey to detritus is apparently due to a seasonal decrease in numbers of invertebrates. The benthic invertebrate groups of greatest importance to the fishes studied here were the Oligochaeta, Ephemeroptera, Trichoptera, Odonata, and Diptera. Carver (1975) and Lafleur (1956) sampled stream benthos in portions of the Calcasieu drainage with Peterson dredges (0.93 m^2). In the months we classify as the wet season, Carver found 34 individuals of these taxa per sample, 22 in the dry season. Lafleur found 18 per sample in the wet season, 8 in the dry season. If surface and midwater invertebrates follow such a trend (as stomach contents would suggest), then the dry season is a season of food shortage for the fishes of the Calcasieu drainage.

Though fishes might retreat to "best available" environments to escape predators or intolerable physicochemical conditions, it may be that constriction of habitat use in the dry season is a response to food shortages. Zaret and Rand (1971) showed that in the dry (lean) season species of a tropical stream specialized on "exclusive" foods, resulting in segregation according to food types. By contrast, species in the Calcasieu drainage may retreat to "exclusive" habitats, since the decrease in invertebrate prey in the dry season might preclude specialization on any one type. Fishes seem to compensate for the lack of invertebrate food by eating detritus. The question why species of the Calcasieu drainage undergo habitat constriction in the lean season suggests hypotheses that await experimental testing.

In conclusion, we showed that three axes of importance to habitat segregation among species are of varying importance to habitat selection by individuals within a species. Of the common species in the drainage most selected habitats on the basis of current speed and amount of debris and cover. Only the cyprinids consistently selected habitat on the basis of stream size. Most of these species showed evidence of habitat constriction in the more stressful dry season.

Habitat choice by fishes in the Calcasieu drainage appears to be a dynamic process. Different species select habitats according to different environmental parameters and seasonally change their habitat use (in terms of habitat shifts and distribution along environmental gradients). Karr and Freemark (1983) showed such a dynamic pattern of habitat use in tropical birds as these species sought habitat optima. Yant et al. (1984) suggested that fish assemblages may respond similarly to their environments. The patterns of habitat use we find in fishes of the Calcasieu drainage support their view.[1]

[1]We thank Michael Vecchione for comments on the manuscript. A McNeese State University grant provided funds for supplies, equipment, travel, and computer time.

9. Patterns of Resource Utilization Among Four Species of Darters in Three Central Kentucky Streams

William L. Fisher and William D. Pearson

Abstract

Patterns of resource use among four *Etheostoma* species from three central Kentucky streams were examined for evidence of resource partitioning, niche shifts, and competition. The order of decreasing abundance of species for each stream, was North Rolling Fork, *E. flabellare*, *E. caeruleum*; South Fork Green River, *E. flabellare*, *E. bellum*, *E. caeruleum*; Fishing Creek, *E. rufilineatum*, *E. caeruleum*, *E. flabellare*. In all three streams juveniles and adults of *E. caeruleum* and *E. flabellare* exhibited spatial segregation on the basis of mean depth and current velocity, but not substrate type. Although *E. bellum* occupied a wider range of habitats than its congeners in South Fork Green River, the three species in this stream were generally segregated by depth and current velocity within the riffle. *Etheostoma flabellare* and *E. rufilineatum* showed considerable overlap in Fishing Creek, but these two species showed little overlap with *E. caeruleum*. The four species differed in the mean number and relative proportions of benthic invertebrates they consumed. *Etheostoma flabellare* consumed larger prey than did *E. caeruleum* in all three streams, while *E. bellum* and *E. rufilineatum* utilized prey of intermediate size compared with the former two species. Juveniles of all species tended to eat smaller-sized prey than did the adults. Adults, and to a lesser extent juveniles, of all species partitioned the available food and/or habitat resources. In Fishing Creek *E. flabellare* may have shifted toward larger-sized prey and experienced depressive competition as a result of the presence of *E. rufilineatum*.

Competition for resources between coexisting species traditionally has been considered important in shaping the structure of biological communities (Hutchinson, 1959; MacArthur, 1972; May, 1974; Cody and Diamond, 1975; Roughgarden, 1983). This assumption, however, has recently been the subject of intense debate (Connor and Simberloff, 1979; Connell, 1980; Weins and Rotenberry, 1980b; Simberloff, 1983; Strong, 1983), and abiotic factors (i.e., physical disturbance and gradual environmental change) are also considered to be major determinants of community structure. Presumably both biotic and abiotic factors have exerted selective pressures resulting in ecological differentiation and thus have provided coexisting species a sufficient number of ways to partition their resources.

Although studies of resource partitioning are numerous, relatively few have dealt with freshwater fish communities (cf. Schoener, 1974; Werner et al., 1977; Keast, 1978a; Laughlin and Werner, 1980; Baker and Ross, 1981). Recent studies of resource partitioning among coexisting darter species (Percidae: Etheostomatini) have focused mainly on feeding interrelationships (Smart and Gee, 1979; Wynes and Wissing, 1982; Hlohowskyj and White, 1983; Miller, 1983; Martin, 1984), although some (Paine et al., 1982; Matthews et al., 1982; Schlosser and Toth, 1984) have included elements of habitat partitioning and population dynamics.

In the present study we examine (1) whether patterns of spatial and trophic resource utilization between two species of darters, *Etheostoma caeruleum* and *Etheostoma flabellare*, are consistent between communities across three separate drainage systems and (2) whether the presence of an additional abundant species, *Etheostoma bellum* in one drainage and *Etheostoma rufilineatum* in another, affects their use of resources. These patterns are examined for evidence of resource partitioning, niche shifts, and competition among the four species.

Materials and Methods

Study Sites

Sampling was conducted from June 1982 to July 1983 at field sites in three central Kentucky streams. North Rolling Fork, a tributary in the Salt River drainage, is in the Knobs subsection of the Bluegrass Region. The stream flows through rolling agricultural lands and is underlain primarily by shale and limestone rocks. Above the study site (Marion County) the North Rolling Fork is 173.8 km long, has a gradient of 1.09 m/km, and drains 248 km^2. Both South Fork Green River (Green River drainage) and Fishing Creek (Cumberland River drainage) drain limestone, siltstone, and shale rocks of the Mississippi Plateau. Agriculture and silvaculture are the predominant land-use forms in both drainages. Above our study site (Casey County) the South Fork Green River is 18.2 km long, has a gradient of 6.01 m/km, and drains 184 km^2. Fishing Creek, above our study site (Pulaski County), is 29.8 km long and has a gradient of 4.09 m/km and a drainage area of 131.4 km^2.

Spatial Analysis

To determine spatial and habitat associations of each darter species, we sampled one riffle in each stream (North Rolling Fork, 37°30′22″N, 85°08′34″W; South Fork Green River, 37°12′52″N, 84°58′00″W; Fishing Creek 37°11′45″N, 84°42′30″W) twice each season from July 1982 to July 1983, except in April 1983, when flooding prevented sampling. Using a Coffelt BP-3 backpack DC-pulsed electroshocker and a dip net, fish were collected from the riffle and its immediate borders which the adjoining upstream and downstream pools. Sampling began at the downsteam end of the riffle and continued upstream. Fish were shocked and collected from an approximate meter-square-area plot every 2 m across transects established at 6 m intervals upstream. The number of fish captured per 30 sec of shocking in the meter-square areas was the catch-per-unit effort (CPUE) used to estimate relative abundances. Fish from each sample were placed in a separate holding net and identified and measured at the completion of each transect. The fish were returned to the stream after the riffle had been completely sampled.

After collecting the fish, we scored each sample plot of the transects for three features of the habitat structure. Surface substratum was identified with the use of an underwater viewing scope and categorized into the two predominant substrate types according to a modified Wentworth scale (Cummins, 1962): (1) vegetation, (2) silt, (3) sand, (4) gravel, (5) pebble, (6) cobble, (7) boulder, and (8) bedrock. Current velocity was measured with a Pygmy-type flowmeter near the substratum at one representative location within each plot. Water-column depth was also measured at the flow-reading locality.

Spatial overlap of coexisting species in each stream was computed from Schoener's (1970) formula:

$$S = 1 - \tfrac{1}{2} \Sigma \mid P_{xi} - P_{yi} \mid ,$$

where S is niche overlap, P_{xi} is the proportion of species x occurring in the ith plot and P_{yi} is the proportion of species y occurring in the ith plot. Values range from 0 (no overlap) to 1 (complete overlap).

Habitat variables were weighted on the number of individuals sampled in each plot (i.e., all individuals collected from a plot were assigned the same set of habitat measurements made for that plot). Water-column depth and current velocity data were $\log_{x+1}$–transformed, and pairwise comparisons were made between each species using a Students t-test. A Mann-Whitney U-test was used to test for species differences in substrate types.

Dietary Analysis

For analysis of stomach contents, 5 to 15 individuals of each darter species were collected from a riffle near the one used for habitat analysis. Collections were made twice each season from June 1982 to March 1983, except in April 1983. Fish collected for stomach analysis generally represented the entire size range of darters in each monthly sample. To prevent regurgitation, fish were killed in MS-222 (an ectothermic vertebrate anesthetic) and later fixed in 10% Formalin. In the laboratory the stomach contents were removed, and prey were identified to the lowest taxonomic level possible (usually genus). Body lengths and head-capsule widths of intact prey items were measured to the nearest 0.1 mm with an ocular micrometer.

Niche breadth for species populations was computed using Levin's (1968) index:

$$B_i = 1/\Sigma \, P_j^2,$$

where B_i is niche breadth for species i and P_j is the proportion of food j consumed by species i. All P_j^2's are summed over j food types. For an index of prey size we multiplied head-capsule width by body length, and a square-root transformation (Sokal and Rohlf, 1981) was performed on these data. Prey size was statistically compared between coexisting species using a Students t-test.

Length-frequency histograms were constructed from monthly population data to separate juveniles (young-of-the-year) from adults. Juveniles were determined to be those individuals less than 32–mm standard length (SL) for *E. caeruleum*, 28–mm SL for *E. flabellare*, 30–mm SL for *E. bellum*, and 32–mm SL for *E. rufilineatum*.

Results

Seasonal Abundance

In North Rolling Fork, *E. flabellare* (total number collected [N] = 997) was more abundant than *E. caeruleum* (N = 332) during all seasons. Juveniles of both species entered the population in midsummer and peaked in abundance during autumn and winter. Total population densities were greatest during the summer and autumn months, when riffle area (mean area [$\bar{x}$] = 384 ± 142 m^2) and current velocities were lowest and water temperatures were highest, and least in winter and spring, the period of maximum current velocity and riffle size ($\bar{x}$ = 629 ± 62 m^2) and minimum water temperatures. Other, less common darters collected from the riffle included: *Etheostoma blennioides*, *Etheostoma nigrum*, *Etheostoma spectabile*, *Etheostoma zonale*, and *Percina caprodes*.

Etheostoma flabellare (N = 314) was the numerically dominant species in South Fork Green River; *E. bellum* (N = 188) and *E. caeruleum* (N = 182) were almost equally abundant. Juveniles of *E. caeruleum* and *E. flabellare* first appeared in the population in midsummer and were most abundant during autumn and winter months. Juveniles of *E.*

bellum were sparse in the riffle throughout the year but were most frequently taken in the spring and summer. Seasonal abundance patterns were similar among all three species. Lowest abundances occurred during the winter, when maximum riffle area ($\bar{x}$ = 901 ± 78 m^2) and current velocity were coupled with minimum water temperatures. Peak abundances occurred during the summer and autumn months, when riffle area ($\bar{x}$ = 647 ± 166 m^2) and current velocity declined, while water temperatures were higher. Other, less abundant riffle fishes in this stream were *E. barbouri*, *E. blennioides*, *E. rafinesquei*, *E. zonale*, *P. caprodes*, and *Cottus carolinae*.

The most abundant species in Fishing Creek was *E. rufilineatum* (*N* = 541), followed in order by *E. caeruleum* (*N* = 129) and *E. flabellare* (*N* = 47). The recruitment and seasonal abundance patterns of *E. caeruleum* and *E. flabellare* juveniles in Fishing Creek were similar to those seen for these species in the other two streams. Juveniles of *E. rufilineatum* first appeared in late summer, and recruitment continued through the autumn months. Both *E. caeruleum* and *E. rufilineatum* exhibited a winter and spring depression in abundance that corresponded with an increase in riffle area ($\bar{x}$ = 531 ± 93 m^2) and current velocity and low water temperatures. Both species increased in abundance during the summer and autumn months, when water temperature was higher, and current velocity and riffle area ($\bar{x}$ = 426 ± 43 m^2) declined. Juveniles and adults of *E. flabellare* were uncommon and reached their peak abundance in September. Additional darter species occasionally collected from this stream included: *E. simoterum* (formerly *E. atripinne*), *E. blennioides*, *E. obeyense* and *P. caprodes*.

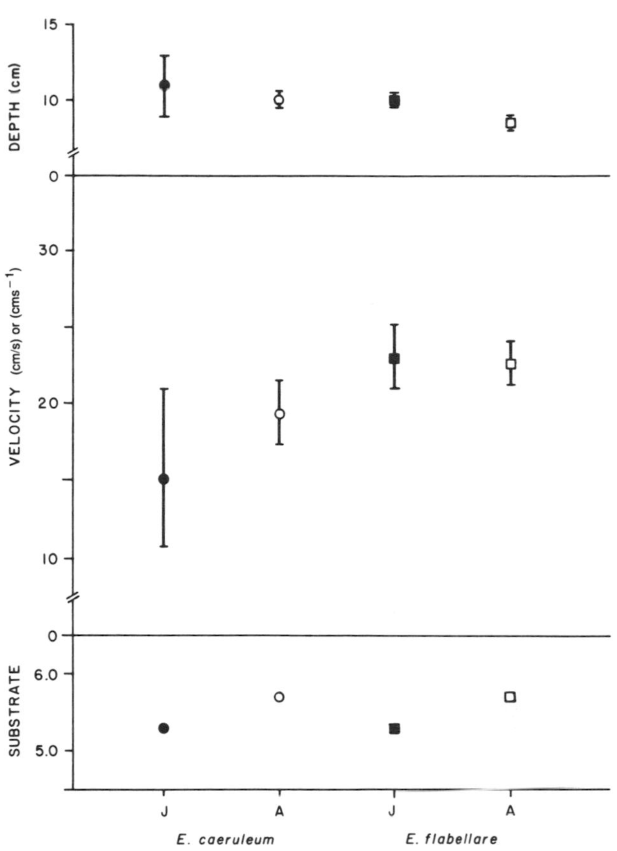

Fig.9.1. Water-column depth, current velocity, and median substrate types for juveniles (J) (solid symbols) and adults (A) (open symbols) of two *Etheostoma* species in North Rolling Fork, Kentucky, July 1982–July 1983. Symbols and vertical lines represent back-transformed means and 95% confidence intervals, respectively. Substrate types: 5 = pebble; 6 = cobble.

Spatial Overlap

In general, the coexisting darter species were relatively segregated in all three streams, as indicated by the low spatial overlap values (table 9.1). The greatest overlap occurred in North Rolling Fork between *E. caeruleum* and *E. flabellare*, and the least in Fishing Creek between *E. flabellare* and *E. rufilineatum*. Seasonal overlap mirrored seasonal abundance trends: maximum values during summer and fall months and minimum values during winter and spring.

Table 9.1. Median Spatial Overlap Values for Five *Etheostoma* Species Pairs from North Rolling Fork, South Fork Green River, and Fishing Creek, Kentucky

Stream	Species Pairs*				
	E. bellum × *E. caeruleum*	*E. bellum* × *E. flabellare*	*E. caeruleum* × *E. flabellare*	*E. caeruleum* × *E. rufilineatum*	*E. flabellare* × *E. rufilineatum*
North Rolling Fork			0.411 (0.113–0.666)		
South Fork Green River	0.204 (0–0.308)	0.280 (0.094–0.461)	0.100 (0.025–0.413)		
Fishing Creek			0.105 (0.0–0.414)	0.248 (0.050–0.403)	0.065 (0.0–0.287)

*Ranges of values in parentheses.

Habitat Associations

A comparison of habitat types selected by *E. caeruleum* and *E. flabellare* adults from North Rolling Fork (table 9.2, fig. 9.1) indicated a significant difference between mean water-column depth ($P < 0.001$) and current velocity ($P < 0.010$), but no difference between median substrate types ($P > 0.464$). Juveniles of these species (table 9.2, fig. 9.1) were taken from similar depths ($P > 0.265$) and substrate types ($P > 0.111$), but significantly different current velocities ($P < 0.012$).

In South Fork Green River, the occurrences of *E. bellum* and *E. caeruleum* adults (table 9.2, fig. 9.2) did not differ in mean depth ($P > 0.181$) but were significantly different in the mean current velocities ($P < 0.001$) and median substrate types ($P < 0.019$) they occupied. The juveniles of these species (table 9.2, fig. 9.2) were found at different depths ($P < 0.031$) and current velocities ($P < 0.034$) but similar substrate types ($P > 0.676$). Significant differences in all three habitat types occurred between the adults of *E. bellum* and *E. flabellare* (table 9.2, fig. 9.2), mean depth ($P < 0.001$), current velocity ($P < 0.001$), and median substrate type ($P < 0.001$). However, *E. bellum* and *E. flabellare* juveniles (Table 9.2, fig. 9.2) occupied similar mean depths ($P > 0.398$), current velocities ($P > 0.508$), and median substrate types ($P > 0.957$). As observed in North Rolling Fork, the juvenile and adult populations of *E. caeruleum* and *E. flabellare* in South Fork Green River (table 9.2, fig. 9.2) differed significantly in mean depth (juveniles, $P < 0.036$; adults, $P < 0.001$) and current velocity (juveniles, $P < 0.002$; adults, $P < 0.050$), but did not differ significantly in median substrate type (juveniles, $P > 0.544$; adults, $P > 0.191$).

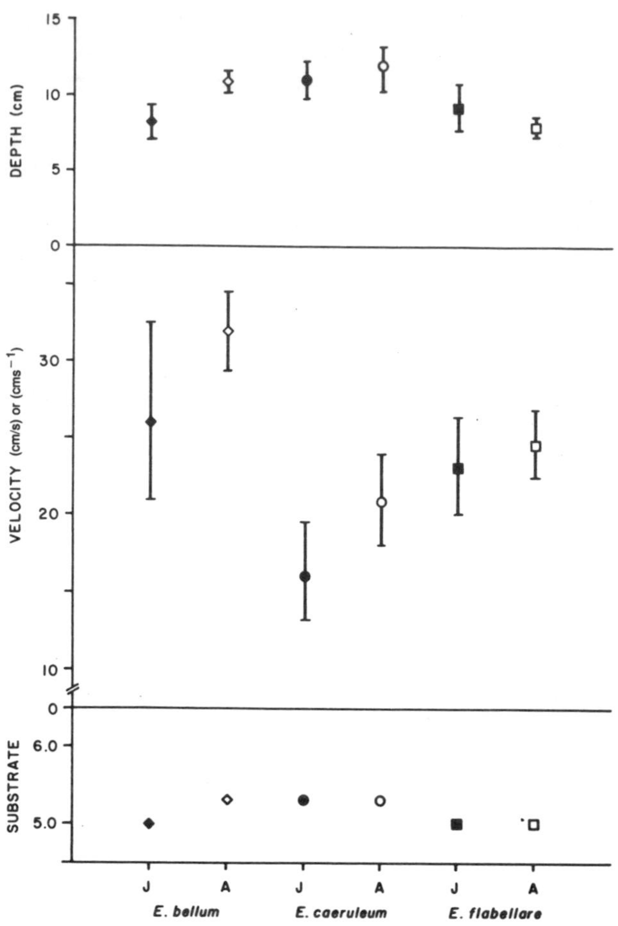

Fig. 9.2. Water-column depth, current velocity, and median substrate types for juveniles (J) (solid symbols) and adults (A) (open symbols) of three *Etheostoma* species in South Fork Green River, Kentucky, July 1982–July 1983. Symbols and vertical lines represent back-transformed means and 95% confidence intervals, respectively. Substrate types: 5 = pebble; 6 = cobble.

Table 9.2. Untransformed Means (± 1 SD) of Habitat Parameters for Juveniles and Adults of Four *Etheostoma* Species in North Rolling Fork, South Fork Green River, and Fishing Creek, Kentucky

	North Rolling Fork				South Fork Green River						Fishing Creek					
Habitat	*E. caeruleum*		*E. flabellare*		*E. bellum*		*E. caeruleum*		*E. flabellare*		*E. caeruleum*		*E. flabellare*		*E. rufilineatum*	
	J	A*	J	A	J	A	J	A	J	A	J	A	J	A	J	A
N†	39	293	423	554	19	169	96	86	141	173	27	102	8	39	105	436
Depth (cm)	11.8 ±8.2	9.6 ±4.4	10.1 ±5.4	8.5 ±4.3	7.4 ±2.6	11.2 ±6.2	11.6 ±6.4	12.2 ±6.3	10.1 ±6.9	8.4 ±6.0	16.0 ±4.6	11.6 ±5.3	9.1 ±4.9	7.4 ±3.7	11.3 ±5.4	8.4 ±4.9
Current velocity (cms)	20.5 ±14.1	25.3 ±18.0	29.5 ±17.3	27.4 ±17.1	28.1 ±13.2	35.2 ±17.4	20.7 ±13.8	23.5 ±12.5	28.9 ±20.0	27.8 ±17.4	13.8 ±9.3	18.5 ±10.0	42.2 ±17.9	34.5 ±22.7	28.7 ±20.5	35.3 ±19.9
Dominant substrates‡	5, 6	6, 5	6, 5	6, 5	5, 6	5, 6	5, 6	5, 6	5, 6	5, 6	5, 6	6, 5	6, 5	5, 6	6, 5	6, 5

*J = juveniles; A = adults.
†N = weighted sample size.
‡Substrate types: 5 = pebble, 6 = gravel. Listed in order of importance.

The populations of *E. caeruleum* and *E. flabellare* juveniles and adults in Fishing Creek (table 9.2, fig. 9.3) differed significantly in mean depth (juveniles, $P < 0.001$; adults, $P < 0.001$), current velocity (juveniles, $P < 0.001$; adults, $P < 0.001$), and median substrate type for adults ($P < 0.004$) but not for juveniles ($P > 0.651$). The mean depths and current velocities at which juveniles and adults of *E. caeruleum* and *E. rufilineatum* were found (table 9.2, fig. 9.3) differed significantly (juveniles, $P < 0.001$; adults, $P < 0.001$), but median substrate types did not (juveniles, $P > 0.252$; adults, $P > 0.921$). Juveniles and adults of *E. flabellare* and *E. rufilineatum* (table 9.2, fig. 9.3) occurred at similar mean depths (juveniles, $P > 0.208$; adults, $P > 0.283$) and current velocities (juveniles, $P > 0.074$; adults, $P > 0.536$). Substrate type associations were similar for juveniles of these species ($P > 0.792$) but different for adults ($P < 0.001$).

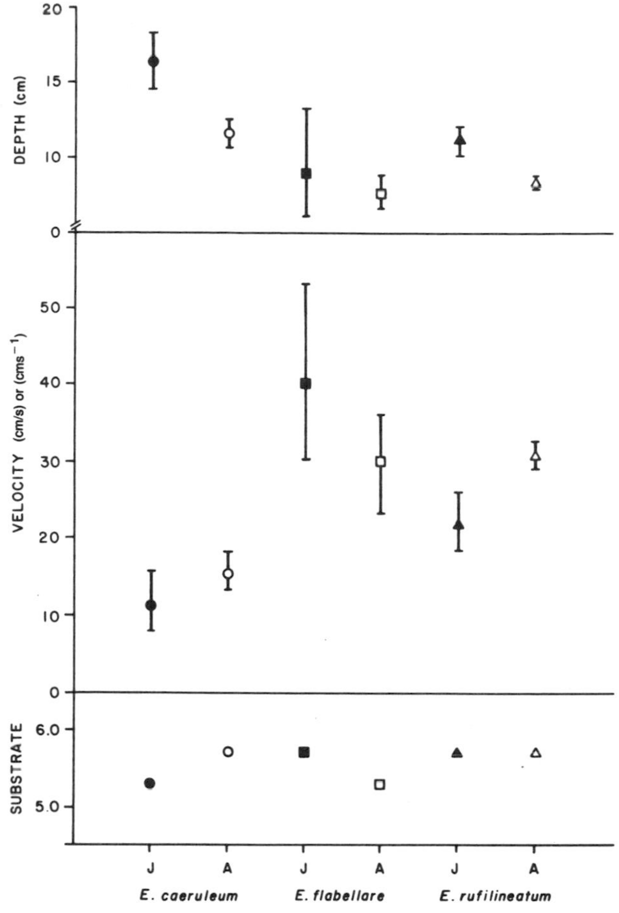

Fig. 9.3. Water-column depth, current velocity, and median substrate types for juveniles (J) (solid symbols) and adults (A) (open symbols) of three *Etheostoma* species in Fishing Creek, Kentucky, July 1982–July 1983. Symbols and vertical lines represent back-transformed means and 95% confidence intervals, respectively. Substrate types: 5 = pebble; 6 = cobble.

Diet Composition

The diets of juveniles and adults of all four species were similar and consisted mainly of benthic invertebrates. However, there were differences in the relative proportion, as well as the total and mean number, of invertebrates consumed by each species in the three streams (Table 9.3).

In North Rolling Fork, *E. caeruleum* adults fed mainly on chironomid larvae and pupae, hydracarinads, and some ephemeropteran nymphs, averaging more than four times as many items per stomach than *E. flabellare* (table 9.3), which fed on chironomid larvae, several genera of ephemeropterans, and winter stoneflies (e.g., *Nemoura*, *Taeniopteryx*, and *Allocapnia*). Juvenile diets were similar but less varied than adult diets.

Both *E. bellum* and *E. caeruleum* adults consumed, on the average, three to four times as many prey items as *E. flabellare* in South Fork Green River (table 9.3). Juveniles and adults of *E. bellum* fed primarily on chironomids, Hydracarina, and ephemeropteran nymphs. Adults also consumed simuliid and trichopteran larvae (e.g., *Hydroptila* and *Symphitopsyche*). *Etheostoma caeruleum* juveniles and adults had very similar diets and ate mostly chironomid larvae and pupae and hydracarinads. Although chironomid larvae were the most abundant food items eaten by *E. flabellare*, larger

Table 9.3. Mean Number of Food Items and Diet Breadths for Juveniles and Adults of Four *Etheostoma* Species in North Rolling Fork, South Fork Green River, and Fishing Creek, Kentucky

	North Rolling Fork				South Fork Green River						Fishing Creek					
	E. caeruleum		*E. flabellare*		*E. bellum*		*E. caeruleum*		*E. flabellare*		*E. caeruleum*		*E. flabellare*		*E. rufilineatum*	
	J	*A**	*J*	*A*	*J*	*A*	*J*	*A*	*J*	*A*	*J*	*A*	*J*	*A*	*J*	*A*
$N^{\dagger}$	8	58	11	62	6	74	18	39	36	36	23	47	27	29	18	58
$\bar{x}^{\ddagger}$	14.6	23.6	11.7	5.2	13.0	19.4	24.8	28.5	11.9	6.7	9.7	6.7	8.6	6.6	11.3	11.4
$B_i^{\S}$	1.19	1.25	1.54	1.91	1.48	1.57	1.27	1.27	1.20	1.55	1.35	1.73	1.46	2.39	1.39	3.30

*J = juveniles; A = adults.
†N = number of stomachs examined.
‡$\bar{x}$ = mean number of food items.
§B_i = diet breadths.

prey organisms (i.e., ephemeropterans, plecopterans, and trichopterans) consituted a comparatively large portion of juvenile and, to a greater extent, adult diets.

The mean number of food items consumed by all three darter species in Fishing Creek was nearly equal (table 9.3). As in North Rolling Fork and South Fork Green River, *E. caeruleum* adults fed mainly on chironomid larvae and pupae, hydracarinads, and some ephemeropterans (e.g., *Isonychia* and *Baetis*), while chironomids were the predominant food item of the juveniles. *Etheostoma flabellare* juveniles and adults ate nearly equal numbers of plecopteran (e.g., *Amphinemoura* and *Allocapnia*) and ephemeropteran nymphs (e.g., *Isonychia*, *Pseudocloeon*, and *Baetis*), with juveniles consuming more chironomids. The diet of *E. rufilineatum* adults differed from the other two species in that it contained more ephemeropterans (e.g., *Pseudocloeon* and *Isonychia*), trichopterans (e.g., *Cheumatopsyche* and *Symphitopsyche*), and simuliid larvae and fewer chironomid larvae. The diet of juvenile *E. rufilineatum* was similar to those of the other two species.

Diet Breadth

The diets of juveniles of all four species were generally less varied than those of the adults, as indicated by the diet breadth values (table 9.3). *Etheostoma flabellare* consumed a greater variety of food items than *E. caeruleum* in all three streams; however, the diets of *E. bellum* and *E. rufilineatum* were generally more varied than those of their congeners.

Prey Size

In North Rolling Fork, the mean prey sizes of *E. flabellare* juveniles and adults were significantly different ($P < 0.001$) from those of *E. caeruleum* juveniles and adults (table 9.4, fig. 9.4). This pattern also occurred for these two species in South Fork Green River and Fishing Creek (table 9.4, fig. 9.4), all comparisons being significantly different ($P < 0.001$). In South Fork Green River, *E. bellum* adults used

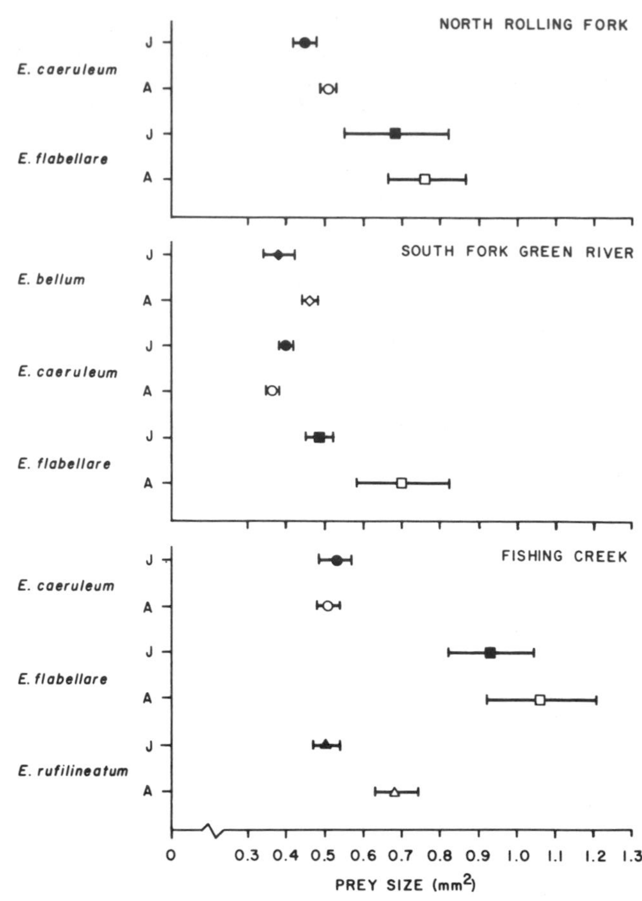

Fig. 9.4. Mean prey size (mm^2) for juveniles (J) (solid symbols) and adults (A) (open symbols) of four *Etheostoma* species from North Rolling Fork, South Fork Green River, and Fishing Creek, Kentucky, June 1982–March 1983. Symbols and horizontal lines represent back-transformed means and 95% confidence intervals, respectively.

Table 9.4. Untransformed Means of Prey Size for Juveniles and Adults of Four *Etheostoma* Species in North Rolling Fork, South Fork Green River, and Fishing Creek, Kentucky

Stream	Species							
	E. bellum		*E. caeruleum*		*E. flabellare*		*E. rufilineatum*	
	J	A*	J	A	J	A	J	A
North Rolling Fork			0.47 ± 0.22† (145)	0.59 ± 0.94 (1,294)	0.89 ± 1.34 (123)	1.02 ± 1.70 (299)		
South Fork Green River	0.40 ± 0.15 (60)	0.53 ± 0.90 (1,411)	0.43 ± 0.45 (813)	0.41 ± 0.45 (695)	0.56 ± 0.71 (422)	1.01 ± 2.33 (233)		
Fishing Creek			0.58 ± 0.51 (215)	0.64 ± 1.37 (294)	1.14 ± 1.64 (219)	1.28 ± 1.61 (174)	0.54 ± 0.45 (191)	0.85 ± 1 (594)

*J = juveniles; A = adults.
†Means (±1 SD); prey size in mm^2; number of prey items in parentheses.

prey intermediate in size with respect to *E. caeruleum* ($P <$ 0.001) and *E. flabellare* ($P <$ 0.001) adults, while the juveniles of *E. bellum* overlapped significantly with *E. caeruleum* ($P <$ 0.020) but not with *E. flabellare* ($P <$ 0.593) (table 9.4, fig. 9.4). *Etheostoma rufilineatum* adults exhibited a similar pattern in Fishing Creek, differing significantly from adults of *E. caeruleum* ($P <$ 0.001) and *E. flabellare* ($P <$ 0.001) (table 9.4, fig. 9.4). The juveniles of *E. rufilineatum* fed on prey similar in size to *E. caeruleum* ($P >$ 0.310) but smaller than E. flabellare ($P <$ 0.001).

Discussion

The seasonal abundance patterns of juvenile and adult darters from all three streams were similar. Greatest densities occurred during the summer and autumn periods of low flow, restricted riffle habitat, and high water temperatures, whereas, darter densities were lowest in winter and early spring, when stream discharge and subsequent available riffle habitat increased and water temperature decreased. These fluctuations in abundance reflect not only physical changes in the environment but also recruitment and seasonal migratory movements (Schlosser, 1982; Schlosser and Toth, 1984) and to some extent may be an artifact of the sampling technique (i.e., decreased electrofishing efficiency at lower stream temperatures and higher discharges [Reynolds, 1983]).

In general, *E. caeruleum* and *E. flabellare* juveniles and adults appeared to be segregated within the riffle by depth, current velocity, and, to a lesser extent, substrate type, the former species occupying the deeper, slower-flowing regions, the latter occurring in the shallow, swifter-flowing areas. These patterns varied somewhat seasonally, both species occupying similar habitats during low-flow periods in late summer and autumn, when spatial overlap was greatest. Juveniles and adults of *E. bellum* occupied a wide range of habitats, including the deeper, fast-flowing runs in South Fork Green River. This was reflected in the greater spatial overlap that occurred between *E. bellum* and both *E. caeruleum* and *E. flabellare* than between the latter two species together and in the overlapping habitat between juveniles of *E. bellum* and *E. flabellare*. While *E. caeruleum* and *E. rufilineatum* juveniles and adults were segregated by depth and current velocity, there was considerable overlap in the habitats occupied by *E. flabellare* and *E. rufilineatum* in Fishing Creek. The low spatial overlap between the latter two species may have resulted from the disparity in their abundance.

Juveniles and adults of *E. caeruleum* generally consumed more items and smaller-sized prey (i.e., chironomid larvae and Hydracarina) than *E. flabellare*, which fed on fewer, larger-sized prey items (i.e., Ephemeroptera, Plecoptera, and Chironimidae larvae). The diet composition and prey size of *E. bellum* and *E. rufilineatum* populations were generally intermediate to those of their congeners, the former being more similar to that of *E. caeruleum* and the latter resembling that of *E. flabellare*, especially in its use of larger-sized prey items (i.e., Ephemeroptera and Trichoptera). With the exception of *E. caeruleum* in South Fork Green River and Fishing Creek, juveniles of all species consumed smaller-sized prey items and overlapped more often than did the adults of the same species.

These data indicate that *E. caeruleum* and *E. flabellare* partition habitat and food resources by within-riffle segregation in water-column depth and current velocity, and by selecting prey that differ proportionally in taxonomic composition and size. These patterns were consistent for both species in all three streams, even though the apparent range of available resources varied (pers. obs.) in each stream. Habitat partitioning between *E. caeruleum* and *E. flabellare* has been observed on a macrohabitat scale (Hlohowskyj and White, 1983), as in this study, as well as on a microhabitat scale (Schlosser and Toth, 1984; Paine et al., 1982). Partitioning of food resources has also been reported between *E. caeruleum* and *E. flabellare* (Adamson and Wissing, 1977; Paine et al., 1982; Hlohowskyj and White, 1983) on the basis of prey types, and among other coexisting species of darters (Thomas, 1970; Lotrich, 1973; Small, 1975; Smart and Gee, 1979; Matthews et al., 1982; Miller, 1983; Martin, 1984). However, Schlosser and Toth (1984) found no evidence of food resource partitioning between *E. caeruleum* and *E. flabellare* in an Illinois stream. Although other studies have suggested that habitat partitioning may be more important than food partitioning in stream fishes (Gibbons and Gee, 1972; Mendelson, 1975; Gorman and Karr, 1978; Gatz, 1979), our results and those of Paine et al. (1982) indicate that both are important.

Under equilibrium conditions the addition of species to a community without a concomitant increase in the breadth of available resources can occur only through increasing the degree of overlap between species, increasing specialization among species, or increased environmental heterogeniety (Ricklefs, 1979). If none of these conditions is met, the productivity of one or more of the species will be reduced. In this study there was typically one numerically dominant species in each stream. *Etheostoma flabellare* appeared best able to exploit the resources of North Rolling Fork and South Fork Green River, as did *E. rufilineatum* in Fishing Creek. Overall, space did not appear to be limiting in South Fork Green River, since the study riffle had the largest total area but only the second-greatest abundance of individuals. Furthermore, each species appeared to be specializing in a particular habitat type and prey size, thereby reducing overlap. In Fishing Creek, *E. rufilineatum* and *E. flabellare* overlapped significantly on the variables depth and current velocity, and *E. flabellare* appeared to have shifted toward larger-sized prey items compared with those used by this species in the other study streams. Considering the apparent success of *E. flabellare* in exploiting the resources in North Rolling Fork and South Fork Green River, the low productivity of this species in Fishing Creek may be the result of depressive competition (MacNally, 1983) imposed upon it by *E. rufilineatum*. This hypothesis is not definitive because of a lack of data on population characteristics (e.g., comparative survival, fecundity, relative fitness, and production) for *E. flabellare* in each stream and warrants further study.

Differences in resource use have often been considered to be evidence for competitive interactions (MacLean and Magnuson, 1977); however, Thomson (1980) cautions against making such inferences because intrapopulation variability could cause a niche shift to occur on a nonlimiting resource. We did not examine intrapopulation interactions in this study; however, others (Gibbons and Gee, 1972; Moshenko and Gee, 1973; Tallman and Gee, 1982) have documented the importance of intraspecific partitioning in the structuring of stream-fish populations. Furthermore, in temporally variable environments (i.e., warmwater streams) interspecific competition may be relatively unimportant (Connell, 1980; Weins and Rotenberry, 1980; Schlosser, 1982; Schlosser and Toth, 1984). The institution of long-term ecological studies will be necessary to assess the relative importance of abiotic and biotic factors in the structuring of warmwater stream-fish communities.

[1] We are grateful to K. Fisher, B. Fisher, J. Mayfield, R. Doyle, and B. Palmer-Ball for their assistance in the field. The manuscirpt benefited greatly from helpful comments and criticisms by J. Mayfield, C. Peterson, and two anonymous reviewers. This study was supported by a Sigma Xi Grant-in-Aid of Research, awards from the University of Louisville Academic Excellence Commission, and the Water Resources Laboratory, University of Louisville.

10. Responses of Benthic Riffle Fishes to Variation in Stream Discharge and Temperature

Thomas G. Coon

Abstract

Populations of benthic fishes were studied at two sites on a Minnesota stream over a five-year period. Variations in discharge and temperature were more extreme at one site than at the other. Between-year variation of population densities of three darter species and a sculpin species was high and relatively equal at both sides. Age structure and recruitment success of the most abundant species, *Etheostoma flabellare* varied at both sites; however, they varied more at the site with greater environmental variability. Between-year variation in recruitment success depended on the timing and severity of summer flooding and differed between sites in most years. Adult mortality rates appeared to be greater at the more variable site in years with extremely cold winters. Young-of-the-year *E. flabellare* grew to a larger size in their first year, primarily because of an earlier spawning season and a longer growing season, but growth of age I fish at the less variable site erased the difference formed in the first year of growth. The interspecific differences in responses of benthic riffle fishes to environmental fluctuations are consistent with the hypothesis that the dynamics of these communities are dominated by disturbances.

The idea that environmental extremes play a key role in regulating stream-fish populations has a long and colorful history (e.g., Forbes, 1887; Paloumpis, 1958; Moyle and Li, 1979; Grossman et al., 1982; Rahel et al., 1984). The particular influences of floods, droughts, extreme temperatures, and extremes in water quality depend on the timing and severity of these events, the differential tolerances of species to these disturbances, and the proximity of neighboring populations from which colonists can disperse.

Recent interest has focused on the structure and dynamics of fish assemblages in streams that experience frequent disturbances, particularly extremes in discharge. High variation in discharge may result in reduced species richness (Horwitz, 1978; Schlosser, 1982a); a shift to smaller, younger fishes with more generalized, insectivorous diets (Schlosser, 1982a); and frequent change in the ranking of species abundances (Grossman et al., 1982; Ross et al., 1985). However, Moyle and Vondracek (1985) found that floods in a Sierra Nevada stream did not affect species-abundance ranks, even though total fish abundance was reduced by floods.

Population studies are needed to understand further the mechanisms underlying these assemblage-level responses. In particular, it is important to determine whether different species respond to particular disturbances in different ways. If all species are affected in the same way by a flood or drought (as reported in Moyle and Vondracek, 1985), disturbances may have little influence on assemblage structure. However, if species are affected to different extents by particular disturbances, depending on their timing and magnitude, and if disturbances occur on a frequent but unpredictable schedule, the disturbances may play a primary role in determining assemblage structure. For example, in floodplain communities early season floods favor the reproduction of early spawners, and late floods favor late spawners (Starrett, 1951; Ross and Baker, 1983).

Whether or not populations covary in response to disturbances, more information is needed on the demographic effects of disturbances. Variation in density may result from variation in reproduction, juvenile survivorship (recruitment), adult survivorship, and individual growth and maturation rates. For example, floods and droughts can affect populations of small fishes by interrupting spawning (Winn, 1958) and by reducing both juvenile (Schlosser, 1985) and adult survivorship (Toth et al., 1982; Schlosser and Toth, 1984). In addition, patterns of resource utilization can be altered by these disturbances (Lotrich, 1973; Goulding, 1980; Matthews and Hill, 1980), which may affect individual growth rates (e.g., Werner and Hall, 1977). In combination these effects should result in populations with abbreviated age structures in streams exposed to frequent disturbances compared to populations in more benign systems. Walsh and Burr (1985) found this pattern in comparing populations of stonecat (*Noturus flavus*) in streams with stonecat populations in Lake Erie. In contrast, stream populations of large fish, such as centrarchids, catostomids and salmonids, are relatively unaffected by floods (Gerking, 1950) unless the floods destroy important habitats (Fajen, 1962; Waters, 1983).

The purpose of this chapter is to compare the responses of benthic fish populations to fluctuating environmental conditions in two locations that differ in the amplitude of variation in discharge and temperature. In particular I address the following questions:

1. Do population densities vary more at the location with greater environmental extremes?
2. Is the between-year variation in population densities due to variation in recruitment, adult mortality, individual growth, or some combination of these?
3. Do population densities covary at each location in response to envirnmental extremes?

Study Sites

The two study sites were on the South Branch Root River, in Fillmore County, Minnesota. This river flows through a forested canyon in the karst region of southeastern Minnesota, where the karst features affect stream discharge and temperature by withdrawal of water to subterranean flow and by additions from coldwater springs.

The downstream site, in Forestville State Park, was 18 river km below the upstream site at Mystery Cave. Owing to its more upstream position and its greater dependence on surface runoff (see Coon, 1982, for details), extremes in temperature and discharge were greater at the Mystery Cave site (table 10.1). Much of the discharge at Forestville is contributed by coldwater springs, which moderate water temperature and discharge. Thus seasonal and daily temperature extremes were greater at Mystery Cave (table 10.1). In midwinter the water at Mystery Cave was supercooled, and the stream was covered with ice. Surface ice never formed at Forestville during the course of this study, and the temperature never dropped below 2° C.

Discharge was greatest in spring and early summer and lowest in autumn and winter at both sites. I measured discharge at each site on nine dates over a two-year period. The date-paired discharge measurements were significantly different between sites (t = 3.667, DF = 8, $P < 0.01$), with discharge greater at Forestville (table 10.1).

Table 10.1. Summary of Temperature and Discharge Data at Two Sites on the South Branch Root River, Minnesota, 1980–1981

Site	Temperature Extremes (° C)		Discharge (m^3 /sec)				
	Min.	Max.	$\bar{x}$	N	CV_q %	Min.	Max.
Mystery Cave	−0.3	27	1.50	9	87.4	0.20	4.65
Forestville	2.0	24	2.11	9	69.7	0.63	5.52

The temporal variation in discharge at the sites was compared in two ways. The discharge coefficient of variation (CV_q) was used to compare the total variation in discharge relative to the mean discharge between sites. Extreme discharge values also were compared to evaluate the difference between sites in flood and drought conditions.

The CV_q estimates were corrected for bias and compared by the method of Sokal and Braumann (1980). The CV_q values were high at both sites, and although CV_q at Mystery Cave (87.4%) was greater than at Forestville (69.7%), the difference was not statistically significant (t = 0.419, DF = 8, $P > 0.50$).

The minimum discharge measurement was obtained at both sites on 10 July 1981 following a relatively dry winter and spring. The minimum discharge at Mystery Cave (0.20 m^3/sec) was less than at Forestville (0.63 m^3/sec). On this date the mean riffle depth at Mystery Cave (0.13 m) was significantly less than that at Forestville (0.20 m; t = 7.468, DF = 198, $P < 0.001$). Under more extreme drought conditions in 1985 the difference between sites was even greater. At Mystery Cave, riffles became extremely shallow with undetectable flow, yet water continued to flow at measurable velocities and at greater depths over riffles at Forestville (C. Alexander, unpub. data). The stream channel was dry immediately below the Mystery Cave site during the 1985 drought period.

The maximum discharge was measured at both sites on 20 July 1981, following a two-week period of intense rainfall. The flood was receding by 20 July, but the strong currents prevented efforts to measure discharge at higher river stages. Again, discharge was greater at Forestville.

Another important aspect of flooding is the time required for discharge to rise from preflood levels to the maximum flood discharge during flashfloods. At least two flashfloods occurred during the course of this study. Although discharge was not measured during these floods, other information indicates that flashfloods develop more rapidly at Mystery Cave than at Forestville. Dye studies have shown that the water-travel time from Mystery Cave to Forestville during high flows is 10 to 12 h (C. Alexander, unpub. data). Because of the more upstream position of Mystery Cave in the watershed, the surface runoff of flashfloods is likely to increase flows at Mystery Cave sooner than at Forestville. Furthermore, the greater influence of springs at Forestville is likely to slow the rate of increase in current velocities compared to the rate of increase at Mystery Cave. In summary, the Mystery Cave site responds sooner to intense rainstorms and reaches maximum velocity more rapidly.

The major effect of springs at Forestville was to moderate water temperature and discharge. Thus, although the same floods and weather patterns influenced both sites, seasonal and daily extremes were greater at Mystery Cave than at Forestville.

In other ways, the two sample sites were similar. I measured microhabitat characteristics (stream width, depth, current velocity at 0.6 X depth, and substrate composition) at 50 randomly selected locations in each of two riffles at each site on three dates in July (Coon, 1982). Because the two riffles at

Table 10.2. Summary of Riffle Habitat Characteristics at Two Sites on the South Branch Root River, Minnesota, July 1981

Site	N	Depth (m)		Width (m)		Current Velocity* (m/sec)	
		$\bar{x}$	s	$\bar{X}$	s	$\bar{x}$	s
Mystery Cave	298	0.20	0.070	11.9	2.117	0.33	0.2142
Forestville	298	0.29	0.086	11.8	1.737	0.44	0.2081

*Current velocity measured at 0.6 × total depth.

Table 10.3. Percent of Substrate Samples Containing Particles of Each Substrate-Size Class at Two Sites on the South Branch Root River, Minnesota, July 1981

Site	N	Substrate-Size Class (mm)*				
		<0.3	0.3–3	3–30	30–300	>300
Mystery Cave	298	10.1	37.9	35.9	88.9	33.6
Forestville	298	13.1	24.1	50.0	89.3	41.6

*Samples could contain more than one substrate type.

each site were similar in all characteristics measured, the data from the two riffles at each site were combined for comparison of the two sites (tables 10.2, 10.3). Stream width did not differ between sites, but owing to the greater discharge at Forestville riffles were slightly deeper and faster than at Mystery Cave (table 10.2). Also, the substrate at Forestville contained slightly more gravel and boulders and less sand than that at Mystery Cave (table 10.3).

Methods

Benthic fishes were collected from the two sites over five years (June 1979 to July 1984). The sampling frequency varied between years, but samples were taken at least once in the period June–August for every year except 1982 at Mystery Cave and 1982 and 1983 at Forestville. Data from two intensive sampling periods (November 1979–November 1980, monthly samples; and June–August 1981, biweekly samples) indicated that the summer samples were adequate to allow assessment of relative abundance, age-class size, and annual growth increments.

At each site I sampled fish populations in two successive riffles, each 50–70 m long. Two riffles were used to ensure sufficient sample sizes for comparing populations between sites. Fish were collected from the entire riffle habitat with a large, fine-mesh (3.2-mm) kick net. The amount of time spent sampling at each site was used as a measure of sampling effort. Sampling effort ranged from 0.7 to 3.5 h per sample, owing to differences in the time needed to obtain an adequate sample size for determination of age structure. Mean sampling times at Mystery Cave (1.7 h) and Forestville (1.4 h) were not significantly different (t = 1.296, DF = 27, $P > 0.20$). Captured fish were preserved in a 10% Formalin solution or were identified, measured (total length), and returned to the stream. Preserved fish were measured (total length) later.

Fish captured in miniature minnow traps for a microhabitat study in 1981 and 1984 (Coon, 1982) were included in the age-class and growth-increment comparisons to increase sample sizes, but they were excluded from the density comparisons. Paired trap and kick-net samples yielded similar estimates of relative age-class abundance for the species included here.

I estimated relative abundance as catch per hour of sampling effort (CPUE). Spearman rank correlation coefficients (r_s) were calculated to determine whether the abundance of individual species covaried through time between the two sites and whether the abundance of coexisting species covaried within each site. In addition, the magnitudes of variation in abundance for each species were compared between sites by a comparison of coefficients of variation (CV_a). I used the CV_a bias correction for sample size, and I applied a $\log_e$ transformation to normalize the abundance data before applying the t-test described by Sokal and Braumann (1980).

Etheostoma flabellare was the most abundant species in kick samples at both sites and was the only species for which sufficiently large samples were obtained regularly to use in age structure, recruitment, and growth comparisons. Fish ages were determined by length-frequency analysis; these estimates were corroborated by an examination of scales from 30 to 50 fish at each site. Variation in age structure of *E. flabellare* populations was evaluated by chi-square analysis of age × year contingency tables for each site. Age 0 fish were excluded from this analysis owing to variation in the timing of their appearance in summer samples. Comparisons of adult mortality between sites were based on changes in these age structures.

I measured recruitment as the relative abundance (CPUE) of age 0 fish in post spawn samples collected in the months August–July. Age 0 fish did not appear consistently in samples until August. Their abundance remained relatively stable until the anniversary of their birth, when they were considered to be recruited into the population.

Cohort growth curves were constructed from the length-age data. Mean total lengths of each age group in winter 1980–81 were compared between sites to determine whether individual growth was related to differences in flow and temperature at the two sites. Although this is an indirect measure of individual growth rates, it is indicative of growing conditions over the previous three years. Furthermore, owing to the positive correlation between total length and fecundity in fishes (Bagenal, 1978), total length in winter samples is a good indicator of growth constraints, which may reduce the number of young produced in the following spring.

Results

Ten benthic species were collected at each site from a total of 51 samples (27 at Mystery Cave and 24 at Forestville; table 10.4). The most abundant species at both sites was *E. flabellare*. The major differences between the benthic assemblages of the two sites were as follows: (1) *Cottus*

Table 10.4. Percent Frequency of Occurrence of Benthic Species in Riffle Samples at Mystery Cave and at Forestville

Species	Mystery Cave (%) (N = 27)	Forestville (%) (N = 24)
Campostoma anomalum	48.1	8.3
Nocomis biguttatus	44.4	4.2
Rhinichthys atratulus	66.7	45.8
R. cataractae	74.1	62.5
Catostomus commersoni	3.7	20.8
Etheostoma caeruleum	59.2	4.2
E. flabellare lineolatum	100.0	100.0
E. nigrum	92.6	91.7
Cottus bairdi	7.5	87.5

Table 10.5. Seasonal Mean Abundances (CPUE) and Coefficients of Variation (CV_a) of CPUE for the Most Abundant Fish Species at Mystery Cave and Forestville

Species	Season	Mystery Cave			Forestville		
		$\bar{x}$	CV_a %	N	$\bar{x}$	CV_a %	N
Etheostoma flabellare	Summer	33.6	69.0	9	34.1	98.4	7
	Winter	11.7	81.6	6	23.4	91.5	7
E. nigrum	Summer	7.8	77.1	9	2.5	90.3	7
	Winter	2.8	99.0	6	4.1	61.6	7
Cottus bairdi	Summer	—	—	—	3.2	94.9	7
	Winter	—	—	—	1.8	136.9	7

bairdi was abundant at Forestville and rare at Mystery Cave, and (2) *Etheostoma caeruleum* was abundant at Mystery Cave until June 1980 but was always rare at Forestville.

Relative Abundances

The comparison of relative abundances between sites was restricted to the most common species (darters and sculpin), for which the most reliable abundances were available. Abundances varied seasonally, with summer highs (June–August) and winter lows (September–March) resulting from the late-spring spawning period and perhaps from movement into adjoining pools in winter (fig. 10.1). Seasonal median abundances (CPUE) of *E. flabellare* were not significantly different between sites (Wilcoxon paired-sample test), for either summer ($P > 0.5$) or winter samples ($P > 0.05$; table 10.5). Winter *Etheostoma nigrum* abundances were not significantly different ($P > 0.50$), but this species had summer abundances that were significantly greater at Mystery Cave ($P = 0.05$).

In spite of these similarities, temporal variation in abundance differed between sites. For example, *E. flabellare* abundances at Mystery Cave were lowest in winter 1979 and highest in summer 1981. At Forestville, *E. flabellare* reached a maximum abundance in summer 1980 and a minimum in summer 1984. Spearman rank correlation coefficients based on comparisons of date-paired abundance estimates at each site were not significant for either summer or winter samples of *E. flabellare* or of *E. nigrum* (all $P > 0.50$; table 10.6). Because differences in the timing and success of reproduction might obscure covarying adult abundances, the correlations were recalculated with young-of-the-year (YOY) fish excluded from the abundance estimates. No significant correlations were obtained for either species in either season with YOY excluded (all $P > 0.50$; table 10.6). Thus the two species common at both sites did not covary in abundance between sites.

The populations of the three darter species at Mystery Cave did not covary over time, regardless of whether the analysis included YOY fish (table 10.7). Although none of

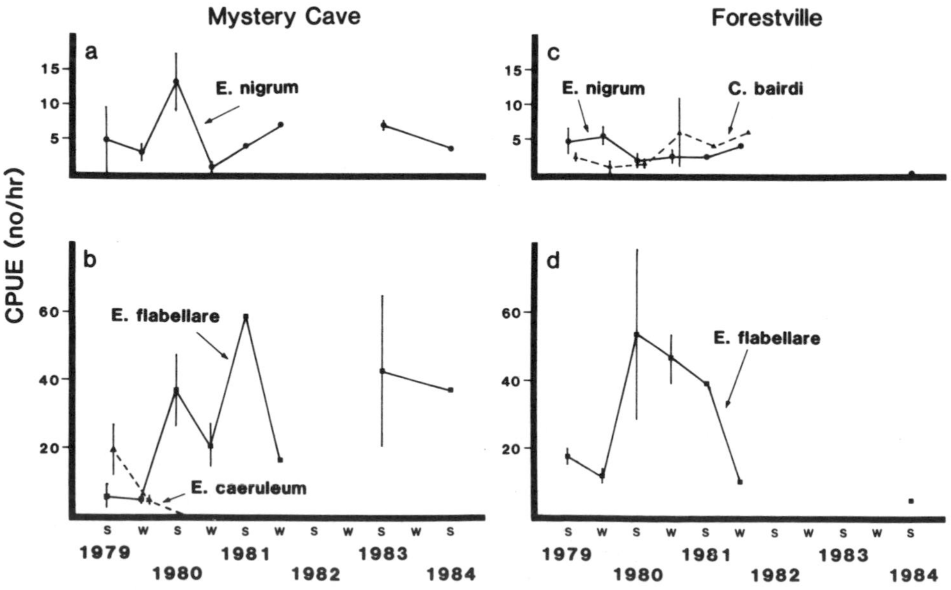

Fig. 10.1 Relative abundances (CPUE) of benthic fishes at Mystery Cave and Forestville, 1979–84. Means ± SE are plotted. Mystery Cave: a: *Etheostoma nigrum*; b: *E. flabellare* (solid line) and *E. caeruleum* (dashed line). Forestville: c: *E. nigrum* (solid line) and *Cottus bairdi* (dashed line); d: *E. flabellare*.

Table 10.6. Spearman Rank Correlation Coefficients for Between-Site Comparisons of Date-paired Abundances of Two Darter Species

Abundance	N	*Etheostoma flabellare* (NS)*	*E. nigrum* (NS)*
Total Abundance			
Summer samples	7	0.64	0.41
Winter samples	7	0.62	0.13
Adult Abundance			
Summer samples	7	0.43	0.63
Winter samples	7	0.21	0.39

*NS = $P > 0.10$.

Table 10.7. Spearman Rank Correlation Coefficients for Between-Species Comparisons of Date-paired Abundances at Each Site

Mystery Cave	N	*Etheostoma flabellare* –*E. nigrum*	*E. flabellare* –*E. caeruleum*	*E. caeruleum* –*E. nigrum*
Total abundance				
Summer	9	0.08 NS*	−0.27 NS	−0.50 NS
Winter	7	−0.30 NS	−0.69 NS	−0.21 NS
Adult abundance				
Summer	9	0.02 NS	−0.30 NS	−0.50 NS
Winter	7	0.24 NS	−0.60 NS	0.23 NS
Forestville	N	*E. flabellare* –*E. nigrum*	*E. flabellare* –*Cottus bairdi*	*C. bairdi* –*E. nigrum*
Total abundance				
Summer	7	0.75 ($P = 0.08$)	−0.65 NS	−0.40 NS
Winter	7	−0.89 ($P = 0.02$)	0.24 NS	−0.44 NS
Adult abundance				
Summer	7	0.37 NS	0.43 NS	0.58 NS
Winter	7	−0.32 NS	0.71 ($P = 0.10$)	0.04 NS

*NS = $P > 0.10$.

the rank correlation coefficients were statistically significant, the relationship between *E. flabellare* and *E. caeruleum* appeared to be negative, resulting from the decline of *E. caeruleum* after May 1980.

Total abundances of *E. flabellare* and *E. nigrum* at Forestville were positively correlated in summer samples ($r_s = 0.75, P = 0.08$) and negatively correlated in winter samples ($r_s = -0.89, P = 0.02$). However, these relationships were not significant when the analysis was applied to adult abundances, indicating that the correlations of total abundance resulted from variation of YOY abundance. Owing to the similar spawning habits of these two species, the positive correlation of summer abundances suggests that they are similarly affected by impediments to or enhancements of reproduction. The negative correlation between winter abundances of these two species may result from differences in habitat use in winter months. In particular, *E. nigrum* may leave riffle habitats for pools in extreme flow or cold conditions. *Etheostoma flabellare* and *C. bairdi* adult abundances were positively correlated in winter conditions, but no other correlations were significant (table 10.7).

Although the timing of abundance variations differed between sites, the magnitudes of variation were similar. The coefficients of variation (CV_a) for summer and winter samples of *E. flabellare* and *E. nigrum* at both sites and of *C. bairdi* at Forestville were high (all > 50%; table 10.5). The CV_a for the *E. caeruleum* population at Mystery Cave was not included in this analysis owing to its virtual extirpation after May 1980. There were no significant differences (all $P > 0.50$) of CV_a values between sites for either darter species in either season. Thus *E. flabellare* and *E. nigrum* population abundances were equally variable at the two sites. Furthermore, season-matched CV_a values were not significantly different between *E. flabellare* and *E. nigrum* at Mystery Cave ($P > 0.50$) and between the pairwise comparisons of *E. flabellare*, *E. nigrum*, and *C. bairdi* at Forestville (all $P > 0.50$).

At the beginning of this study *E. caeruleum* was more abundant than *E. flabellare* at Mystery Cave (fig. 10.1b), but by summer 1980 *E. caeruleum* was no longer present. The disappearance of *E. caeruleum* was quite sudden; the greatest abundances of *E. caeruleum* recorded were obtained in April and May 1980. Maximum abundance (42 fish/h) was recorded on 21 May, when fish were observed spawning over gravel substrate in the riffles. All fish were released after capture on this date to minimize interference with reproduction. I did not sample the population until after a severe storm on 28–30 May (18.4-cm rain at Preston, Minnesota) caused flashfloods throughout the Root River system. I collected only one *E. caeruleum* on 17–18 June, although I sampled for 2 h, during which time I captured 98 *E. flabellare* and 16 *E. nigrum*. I also sampled riffles downstream of the study area to determine whether the population had moved, but I failed to find any *E. caeruleum*. After the May 1980 flood I caught only 9 *E. caeruleum* in 7 of 19 samples at the Mystery Cave study riffles.

Population age structures

Etheostoma flabellare was the only species for which sample sizes were large enough to permit an estimate of age structure. Seven cohorts at Mystery Cave (year classes 1977–83) and five cohorts at Forestville (year classes 1976–80) were sampled at least once after having attained age I (fig. 10.2).

On the basis of chi-square analyses, the age structure of the *E. flabellare* populations differed significantly between years both at Mystery Cave ($\chi^2 = 29.62$, DF = 2, $P < 0.001$) and at Forestville ($\chi^2 = 37.18$, Df = 4, $P < 0.001$). The analysis of data from both sites was based on summer samples for the years 1979, 1980, and 1981. I also calculated the chi-square statistic for Mystery Cave data, including the 1983 and 1984 samples. Data from 1979 were excluded in this case to avoid bias caused by small expected cell values (Zar, 1974). The result was the same: age structure differed significantly between years ($\chi^2 = 112.28$, DF = 6, $P < 0.001$).

The variation in population abundance at both sites corres-

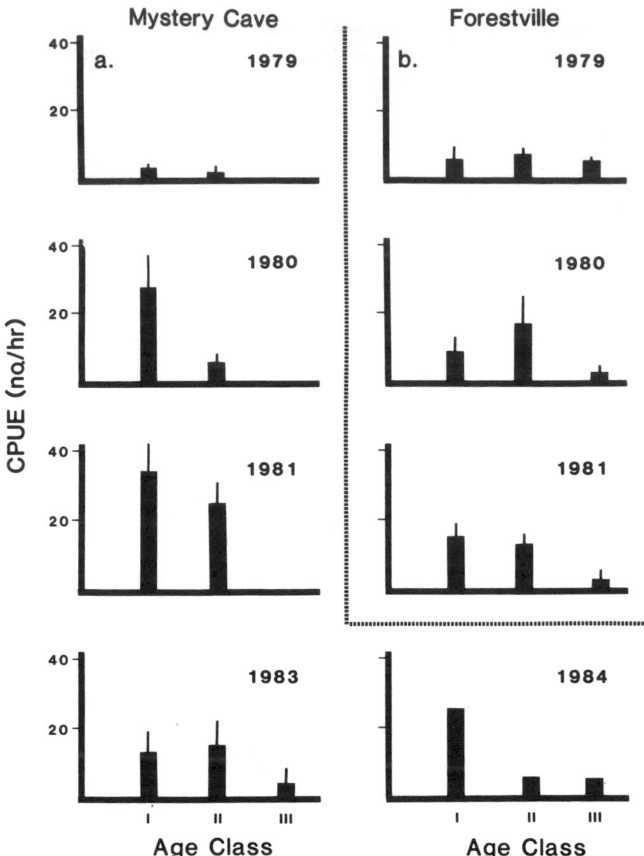

Fig. 10.2. Relative abundances (CPUE) of three adult age classes of *Etheostoma flabellare* at Mystery Cave (a) and at Forestville (b). Error bars = + 1 SE. In 1983 and 1984 data are available for only Mystery Cave.

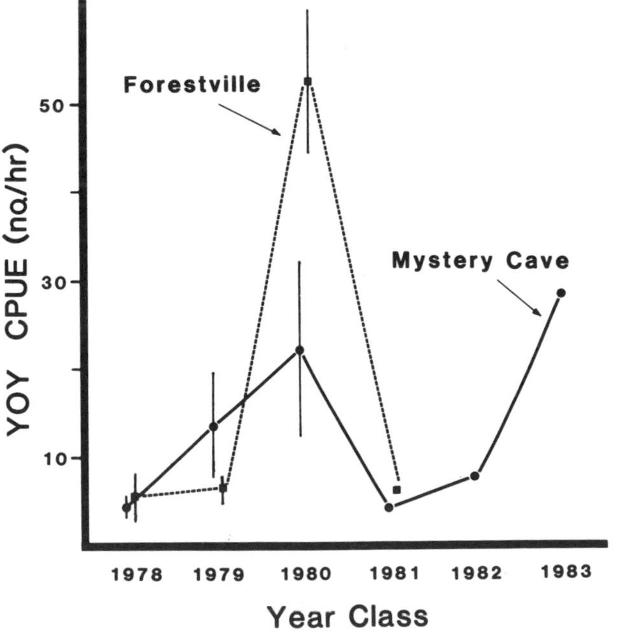

Fig. 10.3 Relative abundances (CPUE) of *Etheostoma flabellare* young-of-the-year (YOY) at Mystery Cave (solid line) and Forestville (dashed line). Means ± 1 SE are plotted.

ponded with variation in cohort size. The abundances of three year classes at Mystery Cave were relatively low (1977, 1978, 1982), and the 1976 class was absent from 1979 samples (even though it was present at Forestville; fig. 10.2). The 1979 and 1980 classes were the most abundant year classes at Mystery Cave. Their influence is apparent as high population abundances found in 1980 and 1981 (fig. 10.1b).

Variation in abundance of the five cohorts collected at Forestville was less extreme than at Mystery Cave (fig. 10.2b). None of the Forestville cohorts were as abundant as those sampled at Mystery Cave in 1979 and 1980. Furthermore, the two small year classes at Mystery Cave for which samples were collected at Forestville (1977 and 1978) were more abundant at Forestville. The 1978 cohort had a large influence on variation of abundance at Forestville and contributed to the 1980 maximum.

Recruitment

Variation in *E. flabellare* recruitment was high at both sites. At Forestville, one large year class (1980) accounted for virtually all of the variation; recruitment was relatively low and equal among the other three year classes (1978, 1979, 1981; fig. 10.3). The Mystery Cave population had three years of high recruitment (CPUE > 10 fish/h: 1979, 1980, 1983) and three years of low recruitment (1978, 1981, 1982). The highest recruitment occurred in 1980 at both sites. Young-of-the-year abundance in low recruitment years did not differ significantly between sites (Mann-Whitney *U*-test = 18, DF = 3, 11, $P > 0.20$), but the YOY abundance in the high recruitment year at Forestville was significantly greater than in the high recruitment years at Mystery Cave ($U = 74$, DF = 6, 14, $P < 0.01$).

For Mystery Cave data, the correlation between the abundance of a year class at age 0 and its abundance at age I was not significant ($r_s = 0.70$, $N = 5$, $P > 0.20$), nor was the correlation significant between age 0 and age II abundances ($r_s = 0.65$, $N = 4$, $P > 0.20$). In both cases the sample size was small, and the relationship was positive. Although the data are inconclusive, they suggest that the variation in recruitment may account for much of the variation in population density and in population age structure at Mystery Cave. The number of samples at Forestville was too small for testing similar comparisons.

Individual growth

The 1980 growing season for *E. flabellare* began in March and ended in October at both sites for all age groups except one (fig. 10.4). Age 0 fish at Forestville continued growing until November, although the Mystery Cave YOY ceased growing in September. Young-of-the-year fish grew in length more rapidly in the early spring growth period than adult fish, yet for all age groups the greatest increment of growth occurred in June–August.

Mean lengths of all three adult year classes were significantly different between sites. Fish in the adult year classes were longer at Forestville (1978 year class: $t = 3.761$, DF = 41, $P < 0.001$; 1979 year class: $t = 3.155$, DF = 76, $P < 0.005$), but juvenile fish (1980 year class) were longer at

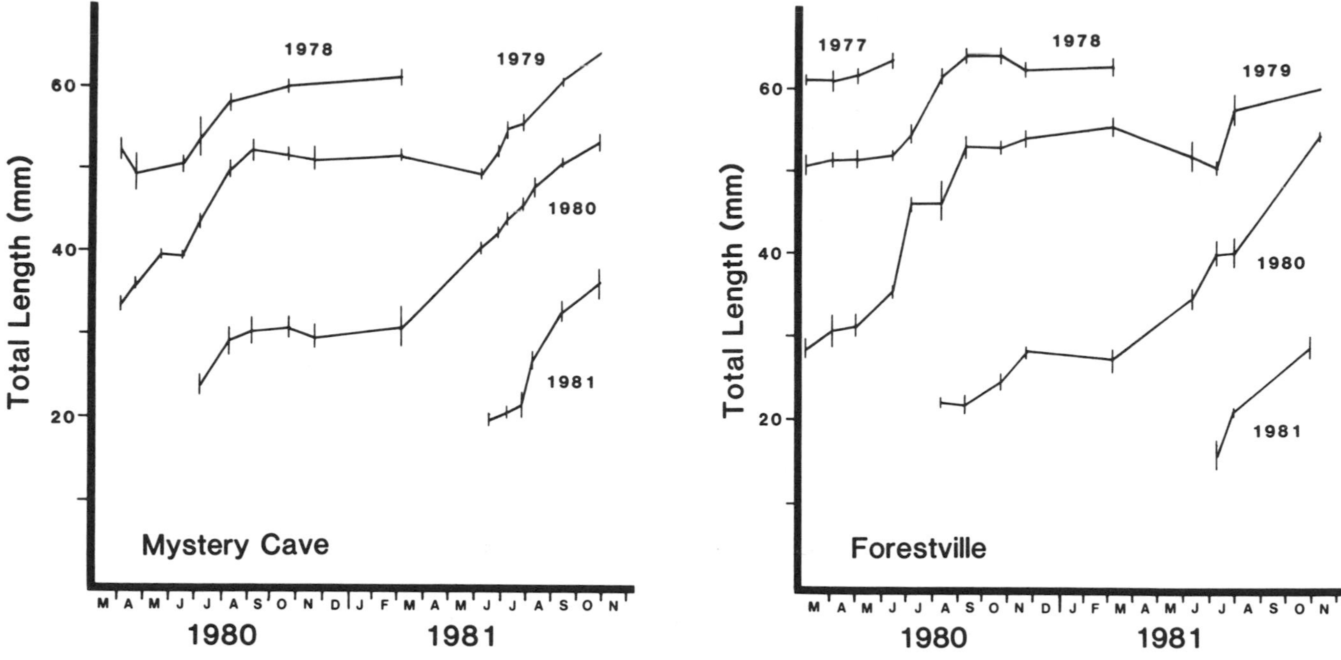

Fig. 10.4. Mean total length of *Etheostoma flabellare* year classes at Mystery Cave and Forestville. Error bars = ± 1 SE.

Mystery Cave (t = 2.252, DF = 109, $P < 0.05$). After the next growing season, however, the mean lengths of the 1980 year class were not significantly different between sites (t = 0.544, DF = 13, $P > 0.50$).

Discussion

Small benthic fishes that occupy riffle habitats are relatively sedentary and rarely move beyond one or two riffles (Reed, 1968; Ingersoll et al., 1984; Hill and Grossman, 1987). Consequently, I have assumed that characteristics of the darter and sculpin populations at the two study sites are determined primarily by recruitment, growth, and survivorship and much less by immigration and emigration.

Horwitz (1978) and Schlosser (1982b) hypothesized that fish populations in streams with variable discharge, particularly in headwater streams, are likely to be regulated more by local extinction-recolonization dynamics than by limitations of food and habitat resources or by interspecific interactions. Thus they predicted that populations in variable streams will exhibit a greater amplitude and frequency of variation in density and age structure than will populations in less fluctuating streams. Furthermore, since populations in variable streams rarely saturate their environment, they predicted that individuals will grow more rapidly than those in less variable streams.

Schlosser (1982a) found that the variation in reproductive success and age structure of feeding guilds was greater in a human-disturbed stream with more variable flow and habitat availability than a less variable, undisturbed stream. Within the undisturbed stream between-year differences in flow regime were correlated with between-year differences in reproductive success of some species, especially those with prolonged spawning periods.

Populations at both study sites on the South Branch Root River varied greatly in density and age structure, as predicted by Horwitz (1978) and Schlosser (1982a) for streams with highly variable discharge. However, the hypothesis that population densities would vary more in the more variable flow conditions at Mystery Cave was not substantiated. In fact, although between-site differences in abundance CV_a values were not significant for *E. flabellare* or for *E. nigrum*, the Forestville CV_a was greater than the Mystery Cave CV_a for three of the four species-season comparisons in table 10.5. A longer time period for the study and more equal sampling frequencies between sites would provide a more sensitive test of the hypothesis, yet high variability appears to be characteristic of populations at both sites.

The degree of variation in abundance caused by sampling error cannot be distinguished from other sources of error owing to the lack of sample replication. Some evidence suggests that the samples were biased on the basis of fish size. For example, of 18 transitions from age (X) to age (X + 1) for *E. flabellare* samples at both sites, eight transitions showed an increase in CPUE as the year class grew. This could be caused by an ontogenetic shift into the habitat from neighboring pools and/or size-biased sampling efficiencies favoring larger fish. Either type of bias would increase estimates of CPUE variance if recruitment varies between cohorts, as was found in this study; however, they would not influence the comparisons of variation in age structure, recruitment, or individual growth.

Age structure varied between years at both sites. The amount of between-year variation in age structure was similar between sites for the three years which were sampled with equal frequency at both sites (1979–81; fig. 10.2). However, the age structures for 1979–81 are quite different between sites. Age III fish were absent from Mystery Cave in all three years, yet no cohort failed to reach age III at Forestville. These results are consistent with the hypothesis that the more extreme environment will cause abbreviated age structures, owing to lower recruitment rates and/or greater adult mortality rates (Schlosser, 1982b).

Recruitment appeared to influence variation in cohort size primarily by generating a few large year classes. Recruitment failures (0 CPUE) did not occur, so even low recruitment years produced enough individuals that some survived to reproductive maturity (age II in these populations). Although correlations were not significant between abundance at age 0 and at age I and between age 0 and age II abundance at Mystery Cave, the positive r_s values are indicative that cohorts with high recruitment to age I remained abundant to the next age class. In other words, adult mortality did not compensate for higher recruitment. Rather, it appears that adult mortality was responsible for the abbreviated age structures at Mystery Cave, independent of recruitment. Once a cohort was recruited to age I, the likelihood that some individuals in the cohort would reach age III was greater at Forestville than at Mystery Cave, suggesting that adult mortality rates were greater at Mystery Cave, at least for the 1976-78 year classes.

This study illustrates several mechanisms that affect both recruitment and adult mortality. *Etheostoma flabellare* males guard nests in cavities under rocks during the spawning season (Winn, 1958). The larvae remain in the cavity after hatching and disperse to shallow stream margins after reaching 10–15 mm TL (Coon, 1982). *Etheostoma flabellare* YOY were abundant at Mystery Cave in June, 1981 but were scarce after a flashflood in early July. Capture rates of YOY in microhabitat traps decreased tenfold after the flood (Coon, 1982). The flood apparently occurred when the juvenile fish were particularly vulnerable. Juveniles had dispersed from the nests to shallow stream margins by late June, but the rise in discharge may have occurred too suddenly for them to find refuge in stream-shore vegetation. Alternatively, the sustained high discharge may have limited the significance of this habitat as refuge. The same flood had little effect on YOY abundance at Forestville, primarily owing to the later spawning period at Forestville. Few YOY had left the nest cavities before the flood.

Although no samples were collected in 1978, the low recruitment of YOY from the 1978 year class at Mystery Cave was evident in June 1979, perhaps owing to a similarly intense flood that occurred on 6 July 1978. Assuming that spawning phenology was similar in 1978 and 1981, *E. flabellare* YOY would have been as vulnerable to the 1978 flood as they apparently were in 1981.

Severe winters and flashfloods corresponded with high adult mortality of *E. flabellare* and *E. caeruleum*, respectively, at Mystery Cave. The winters of 1976–77, 1977–78, and 1978–79 were the most severe winters from 1976 to 1984. Sustained periods of extreme cold resulted in complete ice cover, supercooled water, and the formation of anchor ice at Mystery Cave. Ice never formed at Forestville, and water temperature at Forestville never dropped below 2° C. I found *E. flabellare* primarily in riffle habitats in less severe winter conditions, but *E. caeruleum* and *E. nigrum* appeared to overwinter in pools. Severe winter conditions may have caused the poor survival of adult *E. flabellare* from the 1976–78 year classes at Mystery Cave. The moderation of winter extremes by springs may also explain the greater survival of 1976–78 year classes at Forestville.

The disappearance of *E. caeruleum* from the Mystery Cave riffle sites in 1980 was apparently due to a flashflood that occurred during their spawning season. If so, an explanation is needed for the persistence of *E. flabellare* and *E. nigrum* populations that were spawning at the same time. Two aspects of *E. caeruleum* behavior make them more vulnerable to flash floods: (1) they spawn in open riffle habitats, in fast currents, and over sand-gravel substrates (Winn, 1958), and (2) they forage in exposed microhabitats, such as on the top surfaces of rocks (Paine et al., 1982; Schlosser and Toth, 1984). *Etheostoma flabellare* and *E. nigrum*, in contrast, spawn in cavities beneath rocks (Winn, 1958) and forage in more protected microhabitats (Paine et al., 1982; Schlosser and Toth, 1984). *Etheostoma caeruleum* may have been exposed to the full force of the flood, the suddenness of the flood preventing movement to more protected areas.

Thus the benthic fishes of these streams may be thought of as being disturbance specialists. Each species is vulnerable to environmental extremes, but the timing and the type of extremes may determine which species is most strongly affected in a given year. In addition to the flood and winter extremes described here, Schlosser and Toth (1984) found that drought affected an *E. caeruleum* population more than it affected the syntopic *E. flabellare* population. Drought does not affect these sites on the South Branch Root as severely as those in other midwestern streams, but intense storms in May–July capable of producing flashfloods occurred 12 times over a 30-y period (1951–81; Coon, 1982). These different responses to disturbances may explain why populations of *E. flabellare* and *E. nigrum* did not covary between or within sites.

The between-site differences in total length for equivalent age classes probably were caused by site-specific differences in water temperature. Spawning both begins and ends later at Forestville owing to the slower warming of the water noted earlier (Hubbs, 1985a). The earlier spawn and the warmer summer temperatures allow greater YOY growth rates at Mystery Cave. However, YOY growth proceeds later at Forestville, possibly owing to a delay in the onset of cold temperatures in autumn. By the end of their second growing season, individuals of the 1980 year class at the two sites were equal in size. Variation in discharge is probably no more important at Forestville than at Mystery Cave in affecting fish growth: at both sites *E. flabellare* populations do not reach densities at which food and/or microhabitat resources are likely to limit growth.

Although the two sites in this study differed in the amplitude of environmental variation, they were exposed to the same climatic extremes and thus the same frequency of environmental disturbance. Greater population differences might be expected between sites that differed in both the amplitude and the frequency of environmental extremes. For example, many springs in southeastern Minnesota and northeastern Iowa contain populations of *Cottus cognatus, C. bairdi,* or *E. flabellare*, but not combinations of these species (pers. obs.). Furthermore, *E. flabellare* populations in springs often have proportionately more age III and age IV fish than occur in the two South Branch Root River sites (pers. obs.). Lutterbie (1976) also found spring populations of *E. flabellare* in Wisconsin that contain proportionately more age III, age IV, and even age V individuals. Such observations support the hypothesis that the factors regulating stream-fish populations range over a gradient from variable, disturbance-regulated populations to stable populations regulated by resource limitation and interspecific interactions (Grossman et al., 1982; Schlosser, 1982a).[1]

[1]I am grateful to the members of my doctoral committee, P. Richerson, P. Moyle, and J. Underhill, for their support and assistance during the course of this study, and to friends too numerous to list who helped in field sampling. T. Finger, B. Goldowitz, C. Rabeni, and two anonymous reviewers provided valuable editorial advice. The data from 1979 through 1981 were included as part of a Ph.D. dissertation submitted to the Graduate Division, University of California—Davis. This project was supported by a National Science Foundation Predoctoral Fellowship and a UCD Chancellors' Fellowship to the author, two UCD Graduate Division Grants, the Luther College Biology Department, and Missouri Agricultural Experiment Station Project 188.

11. Response of Fishes to Flooding Regime in Lowland Hardwood Wetlands

Terry R. Finger and Elaine M. Stewart

Abstract

Larval, juvenile, and small adult fishes were sampled with activity traps in seasonally flooded lowland hardwood habitats in southeastern Missouri. In habitats with natural flooding regimes, fish-assemblage structure in a year with a wet spring (1981) was markedly different from the structure observed in the following dry year (1982). A shift from numerical dominance of early spring spawners (*Elassoma zonatum*, *Centrarchus macropterus*) in 1981 to dominance by late spring and summer spawners (*Fundulus dispar*,*Gambusia affinis*) in 1982 accompanied reduced spring flooding in 1982.

Comparison of these naturally flooded habitats with nearby sites where water levels are manipulated by man suggests, however, that there are limits to the amount of fluctuation in fish-assemblage structure related to natural variations in flooding. Manipulated sites were characterized by a very different assemblage structure dominated by juvenile *Micropterus salmoides* and *Ictalurus nebulosus* and essentially lacking several of the most abundant fishes of the natural areas.

In the last decade, the importance of seasonally flooded forests to fishes in tropical freshwaters has been elucidated. The strongly seasonal discharge pattern of many tropical river systems results in periodic inundation of large areas of low-elevation forested floodplain. Many fishes are known to undergo regular migrations to utilize these inundation forests as spawning, nursery, and foraging areas (Lowe-McConnell, 1975; Welcomme, 1979; Goulding, 1980).

Although inundation forests are most characteristic of low-gradient tropical systems, similar lowland hardwood wetlands occur in North America, particularly in the lower Mississippi Valley (Fredrickson, 1978; MacDonald et al., 1979). Like the tropical systems but smaller in scale, seasonal depositional floods also make these temperate habitats potentially valuable to fishes. Floods provide physically expanded habitat and high productivity because of nutrient pulses from floodwaters and the decomposition of leaf litter and other inundated allochthonous material (Crow and MacDonald, 1978; de la Cruz, 1978; Mitsch, 1978; van der Valk et al., 1978; Larson et al., 1981; Wharton et al., 1982; Wylie, 1985).

In North America several studies have examined fish use of the relatively narrow fringing floodplains of low-gradient rivers (Starrett, 1951; Guillory, 1979; Halyk and Balon, 1983; Ross and Baker, 1983), but little attention has been directed toward extensive flooded forests. Distribution of fishes in backwater lakes, bayous, and channel areas adjacent to seasonally inundated forests has been documented and used to infer the importance of lowland hardwood wetlands as spawning, nursery, and foraging areas for many species (Lambou, 1959; Bryan et al., 1974, 1975, 1976; Hall, 1979; Gallagher, 1979). Direct evidence of fish use of inundation forests, however, is very limited (Pardue et al., 1975), and no information exists on specific responses of fishes to the timing and duration of temperate forest flooding. In studies of fringing floodplains Starrett (1951) noted that changes in the abundance of several Cyprinidae were related to annual variation in flooding in an Iowa river. Ross and Baker (1983) found that the abundance of *Notropis texanus*, which they considered a flood-exploitative species, was positively related to spring discharge levels of a Mississippi stream over a six-year period. Whether such differential responses to flooding occur in fishes that utilize temperate inundation forests remains unknown.

As part of a study designed to document fish use of lowland hardwood wetlands in southeastern Missouri as spawning and nursery areas, we sampled larval, juvenile, and small adult fishes in seasonally flooded forest habitats during two years with very different precipitation and flooding patterns. Although flooding was sporadic in late winter and early spring of 1981, frequent heavy rains in mid- to late spring and summer resulted in widespread continual inundation (NOAA, 1981). In 1982 winter rains resulted in flooding in February, but the infrequency of heavy precipitation in spring and summer (NOAA, 1982) caused water levels to recede earlier than in 1981. Sampling in both years afforded us the opportunity to assess the response of fishes to different flooding regimes with particular reference to reproductive success. In this chapter we specifically seek to determine whether fish-assemblage structure was similar in two years of different flooding regimes and to relate any structural changes in the fish assemblage to differential responses to flooding by key species. To assess further the effects of flooding, we also compared these results to data from a nearby area where water levels and flooding regime are manipulated by man.

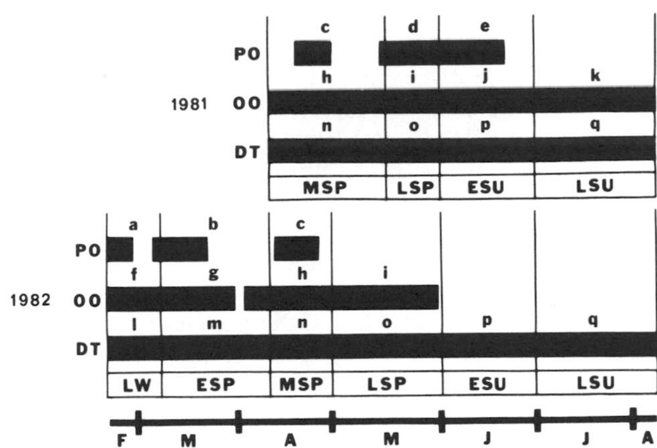

Fig. 11.1. Sampling dates for pin-oak (PO), overcup-oak (OO), and dead-timber (DT) habitats, 1981–82. Solid bars indicate when the sites were flooded. Lowercase letters above bars designate habitat- and season-specific sampling units (LW = late winter, ESP = early spring, MSP = mid-spring, LSP = late spring, ESU = early summer, LSU = late summer).

Study Area

The study was conducted at Mingo National Wildlife Refuge (NWR) and adjacent Duck Creek Wildlife Management Area (WMA), in southeastern Missouri. Although most of the original lowland hardwood wetlands in Missouri have been drained for agricultural purposes or are now characterized by modified flooding regimes (Korte and Fredrickson, 1977), sites selected on Mingo NWR have an approximately natural flooding pattern. In contrast, sites on Duck Creek WMA were in an area where water is impounded throughout winter, spring, and summer for use in flooding waterfowl management areas in fall.

Mean annual precipitation in the region is 114 cm, with greatest rainfall in spring (NOAA, 1982). Under the natural flooding regime on Mingo NWR, streams expand laterally in spring to inundate large contiguous areas of lowland hardwood forest. Water recedes slowly throughout the late spring and summer, although scattered areas remain semipermanently flooded where water is impounded by beaver. At individual sites, slight differences in elevation determine the depth and duration of flooding and the characteristic vegetation present (Bedinger, 1978; Fredrickson, 1978, 1979). Flooded sites of highest elevation are dominated by pin oak (*Quercus palustris*), which is tolerant of flooding when inundation averages 35–70 days/yr. Intermediate elevation sites are characterized by overcup oak (*Q. lyrata*), which can tolerate 110–145 days/y of flooding. Lowest elevation sites where water is impounded by beaver are continuously flooded in most years and are characterized by standing and fallen dead timber. Substrates in both the pin oak and overcup habitats have a thick litter of decomposing oak leaves, while substrates in dead timber areas are predominantly mud, with little or no leaf litter.

Sites on Duck Creek WMA were originally contiguous with those of Mingo NWR but are now separated by levees and drainage ditches. The two fish faunas thus had the same historical species pool but are now geographically isolated. Under the modified flooding regime at Duck Creek WMA there is relatively stable flooding of forest throughout spring and summer when water is impounded. Former pin-oak and overcup-oak sites in this area are shifting to a predominance of dead timber. The adjacent large central basin of the impoundment is permanently flooded.

Methods

Contiguous sites in pin-oak, overcup-oak, and dead-timber habitats on Mingo NWR were sampled from mid-April to early August in 1981 and from ice-out in late February to early August 1982. A dead timber site on Duck Creek WMA was also sampled from late April to late July 1982. For comparative purposes among sites and years, sampling dates were categorized into distinct seasons based on water temperature and vegetation phenology (fig. 11.1). Seasons were identical between years except that the mid-spring period was extended in 1981 because of below-average temperatures during May (NOAA, 1981).

Fish were collected with activity traps 15 × 30 × 15 cm constructed of clear acrylic sheet (Breder, 1960). Wings (15 × 45 cm) set at a 60° angle extended from the trap and created an entry slot 6 mm wide. Two grids 8 × 8 m were established at each sampling site, each consisting of nine potential trap locations 4 m apart. On each sampling date traps were placed at four randomly selected points on the grid. Each site was sampled for day (dawn to dusk) and night (dusk to dawn) periods approximately two times a week. Day and night samples were pooled for analysis, and all catch data were expressed as catch per unit effort (CPUE), where one unit of effort was one trap set for one day or night period. Because young-of-the-year and adult fishes may react quite differently to environmental perturbations (Rahel et al., 1984; Yant et al., 1984), larval, juvenile, and adult life-history stages were treated as separate taxa.

Trap contents were poured through a 425-μ sieve and preserved. Larval fish were identified with published keys (see Stewart, 1983, for list), from comparison with individuals reared in the laboratory (*Elassoma zonatum*), or by comparisons with descriptions of congeners (*Fundulus dispar*). Only 0.4% of all fish captured were excluded from the analyses because inadequate keys or poor specimen condition prevented their identification. Larval, juvenile, and adult life-history stages were separated with the standard terminology summarized in Kendall et al. (1984).

Overall differences in the Mingo fish-assemblage structure among years, seasons, and habitats were examined with principal-components analysis. Catch per unit effort data for each taxon were compiled for each sampling unit delineated in fig. 11.1. We excluded all taxa for which overall catch was less than 10 individuals to prevent very uncommon taxa from having a disproportionate effect. The resulting correlation matrix included the 16 most abundant taxa and 99.3% of the total catch (table 11.1), but because the number of taxa included can have a profound effect on structural analyses (e.g., Rahel et al., 1984; Matthews, 1986a), we repeated the calculations with the 14, 15, and 17 most abundant taxa. The results were nearly identical.

Results

Dynamics of Naturally Flooded Sites

Although 26 life-history stages of 19 species were captured on Mingo NWR, catches were dominated numerically by *E. zonatum*, *Gambusia affinis*, *Centrarchus macropterus*, and *F. dispar* (table 11.1). Collectively, the life-history stages of these species accounted for 93.9% of all individuals captured on Mingo, and, with the exception of larval and juvenile *F. dispar*, all used the seasonally flooded pin-oak and overcup-oak habitats during at least some period and may be considered flood-exploitative taxa (after Ross and Baker, 1983). Larval and juvenile *Esox americanus*, adult *Etheostoma gracile*, juvenile and adult *Lepomis symmetricus*, juvenile *Amia calva*, juvenile *Lepomis macrochirus*, and juvenile *Lepomis gulosus* also used seasonally flooded sites, but juvenile *Micropterus salmoides* and *Ictalurus nebulosus* and the remaining infrequently captured taxa were caught primarily in the semipermanently flooded dead timber.

There were marked differences in CPUE between years for

Table 11.1. Catch per Unit Effort of All Taxa Among Habitats on Mingo NWR, Years and Seasons Combined

Species	LHS[†]	Catch per Unit Effort			Total Number Caught
		Pin Oak	Overcup Oak	Dead Timber	
**Elassoma zonatum*	J	3.67	0.86	0.79	1,777
**Elassoma zonatum*	A	0.66	0.88	0.25	776
**Elassoma zonatum*	L	0.03	0.02	0.43	322
**Gambusia affinis*	A	0.24	0.26	0.15	294
**Centrarchus macropterus*	J	0.25	0.13	0.09	183
**Fundulus dispar*	A	0.39	0.08	0.08	177
**Fundulus dispar*	J	0	0	0.21	146
**Gambusia affinis*	J	0.01	0.15	0.08	142
**Fundulus dispar*	L	0	0	0.09	66
**Esox americanus*	J	0.04	0.05	0.04	64
**Ictalurus nebulosus*	J	0	0	0.07	49
**Micropterus salmoides*	J	0	< 0.01	0.05	37
**Etheostoma gracile*	A	0.01	0.03	0.01	26
**Lepomis symmetricus*	J	0.01	< 0.01	0.03	22
**Lepomis macrochirus*	J	0.01	< 0.01	0.02	15
**Amia calva*	J	0.04	0	0.01	12
Lepomis gulosus	J	< 0.01	< 0.01	0.01	8
Notemigonus crysoleucas	J	< 0.01	0	0.01	5
Lepomis symmetricus	A	0.01	0	< 0.01	4
Aphredoderus sayanus	J	0	< 0.01	< 0.01	3
Lepisosteus sp.	J	0	0	< 0.01	2
Erimyzon sucetta	J	0	0	< 0.01	2
Esox americanus	L	0	< 0.01	0	1
Notemigonus crysoleucas	A	0	0	< 0.01	1
Ictalurus natalis	J	0	0	< 0.01	1
Pomoxis nigromaculatus	J	0	0	< 0.01	1
Total number of trap days		208	528	712	

*Taxa used in the principal-components analysis.
[†]LHS = life-history stage: J = juvenile, A = adult, L = larva.

Table 11.2. Within-Habitat Comparisons of CPUE Between Years on Mingo NWR

Species	LHS[†]	Catch per Unit Effort					
		Pin Oak		Overcup Oak		Dead Timber	
	†	1981	1982	1981	1982	1981	1982
Lepisosteus sp.	J	—	—	—	—	0	0.01
Amia calva	J	0.25*	0	—	—	0.01	0
Esox americanus	L	—	—	0	0.01	—	—
Esox americanus	J	0.03	0.06	0	0.16*	0.04	0.06
Notemigonus crysoleucas	J	0.03	0	—	—	0.01	0
Erimyzon sucetta	J	—	—	—	—	< 0.01	< 0.01
Ictalurus natalis	J	—	—	—	—	< 0.01	0
Ictalurus nebulosus	J	—	—	—	—	0	0.18*
Aphredoderus sayanus	J	—	—	0.01	0	0.01	0
Fundulus dispar	L	—	—	—	—	0	0.24*
Fundulus dispar	J	—	—	—	—	0	0.54*
Fundulus dispar	A	0.03	0.08	0	0.05	< 0.01	0.20*
Gambusia affinis	J	—	—	0	0.24*	< 0.01	0.21*
Gambusia affinis	A	0	0.02	0	0.29*	0.01	0.39*
Centrarchus macropterus	J	0.44*	0	0.07*	0	0.19*	0.04
Elassoma zonatum	L	0.19*	0.02	0.01	0.06	0.95*	0.05
Elassoma zonatum	J	22.72*	0	2.23*	0.81	1.72*	0.19
Elassoma zonatum	A	0.25	1.0	0	0.68*	0.04	0.13
Lepomis gulosus	J	—	—	—	—	0	0.01
Lepomis macrochirus	J	0	0.02	—	—	0	0.04*
Lepomis symmetricus	J	—	—	0.01	0	< 0.01	0.06
Lepomis symmetricus	A	0	0.06	—	—	0	< 0.01
Micropterus salmoides	J	—	—	—	—	0	0.13*
Pomoxis nigromaculatus	J	—	—	—	—	< 0.01	0
Total number of trap days		32	48	96	144	296	272

Note: Comparisons are limited to times when a habitat was flooded and sampled in both years (see text and fig. 11.1).
*Significantly greater mean CPUE for the year (Mann-Whitney tests, $P < 0.05$).
[†]LHS = life-history stage: J = juvenile, A = adult, L = larva.

some taxa (table 11.2). Because sampling began later in 1981 than in 1982 and waters receded earlier in 1982 than in 1981 (fig. 11.1), statistical comparisons were limited to times when the same habitat was flooded and sampled during the same season in both years; i.e., mid-spring for pin-oak habitats, mid- to late spring for overcup-oak habitats, and mid-spring to late summer for dead-timber sites. In all habitats significantly more juvenile *E. zonatum* and *C. macropterus* were captured in 1981 than in 1982, as were larval *E. zonatum* in the pin-oak and dead-timber habitats. In contrast, all life-history stages of *F. dispar* had significantly greater CPUE in the dead-timber habitat in 1982 than in 1981, as did juvenile and adult *G. affinis* in the overcup-oak and dead-timber sites and adult *E. zonatum* in the overcup-oak habitat. Of the less frequently captured taxa, most significant differences in CPUE indicated greater catches in the dead-timber site in 1982 than in 1981. The significant differences between years for juvenile *A. calva* and *E. americanus* appeared to be the result of sporadic, concentrated catches (Stewart, 1983).

Principal component analysis of the catch data from all sampling units also exhibited distinct differences between years. In an ordination of the first two components (fig. 11.2), there was no overlap between the 1981 and 1982 clusters of sampling units, separation of years primarily along the second principal component (PC 2). Correlations of this component with the CPUE of each taxon suggested that differences between years were largely the result of greater catches of juvenile *E. zonatum* and *C. macropterus* in 1981 than in 1982 and greater catches of adult *E. zonatum* and *F. dispar* in 1982 than in 1981 (table 11.3). The significant correlations of PC 2 with *A. calva* and *E. gracile* were considered sampling artifacts. Sporadic catches were characteristic of juvenile *A. calva*, possibly because of schooling behavior (Doan, 1938), and *E. gracile* was captured only in 1982 because it utilized the sampled habitats exclusively in late winter and early spring, seasons that were not sampled in 1981 (Stewart, 1983).

The 1982 sampling units extended along the first principal component (PC 1) in a pattern that roughly corresponded to seasonal succession. PC 1 was significantly correlated with the CPUE of larval and juvenile *F. dispar*, juvenile and adult *G. affinis*, and juveniles of four infrequently captured taxa which appeared primarily in the dead timber in summer (table 11.3). Seasonal succession did not occur in 1981, largely because the most abundant taxa, larval and juvenile *E. zonatum* and juvenile *C. macropterus*, were present from the start of sampling and remained in the area.

These analyses suggest that differences in fish-assemblage structure between years were due largely to changes in the

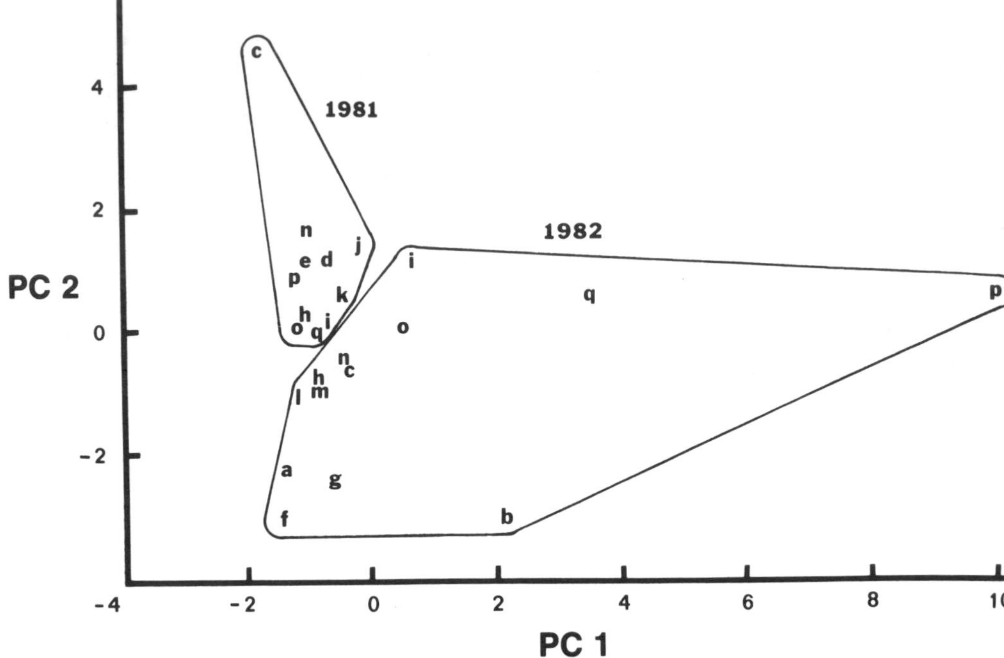

Fig. 11.2. Principal component ordination of CPUE correlation matrix. The letters indicate sampling units designated in Fig. 11.1.

Table 11.3. Correlations Between Sampling Unit CPUE and Scores of First Two Principal Components for Each Taxon

Species	LHS[†]	Correlation Coefficient	
		PC 1	PC 2
Amia calva	J	−0.17	0.61*
Esox americanus	J	0.29	0.40
Ictalurus nebulosus	J	0.88*	0.07
Fundulus dispar	L	0.76*	0.07
Fundulus dispar	J	0.87*	0.11
Fundulus dispar	A	0.40	−0.41*
Gambusia affinis	J	0.71*	0.28
Gambusia affinis	A	0.74*	−0.26
Centrarchus macropterus	J	−0.20	0.64*
Elassoma zonatum	L	−0.11	0.25
Elassoma zonatum	J	−0.19	0.65*
Elassoma zonatum	A	−0.16	0.77*
Lepomis macrochirus	J	0.93*	−0.10
Lepomis symmetricus	J	0.86*	−0.03
Micropterus salmoides	J	0.91*	0.09
Etheostoma gracile	A	−0.21	−0.60*
Cumulative percent variability explained		37.6	54.7

*Significant correlation ($P < 0.05$).
[†]LHS = life-history stage: J = juvenile, A = adult, L = larva.

abundance of the four most commonly caught species, *E. zonatum*, *C. macropterus*, *G. affinis*, and *F. dispar*. The overall dynamics of these species are summarized in fig. 11.3, where CPUE data are superimposed on the principal component ordination of fig. 11.2. Young-of-the-year *E. zonatum* were considerably more abundant in 1981 than in 1982, being present in all habitats in mid-spring and remaining through summer. Catches of *E. zonatum* in 1982 were largely adults, with highest densities occurring in late winter and early spring, seasons that were not sampled in 1981. Adults had left the area by early summer, presumably to move to nearby streams. Dynamics of juvenile *C. macropterus* were very similar to those of juvenile *E. zonatum*. *F. dispar* was captured almost exclusively in 1982; adults first utilized seasonally flooded areas in early spring, while larvae and juveniles appeared in the dead timber in last spring and early summer. CPUE of *G. affinis* was also greater in 1982 than in 1981, although differences between years were not as pronounced as in the other species. In 1982 adults used pin-oak and overcup-oak sites when they were flooded in spring and were found in the dead timber when the seasonal sites dried. Juveniles first appeared in late spring in the overcup-oak habitat and were also found in the dead timber in summer. In 1981 most juvenile and adult *G. affinis* were captured in the overcup-oak habitat, which remained flooded through summer.

Natural Versus Manipulated Area Comparisons

The Mingo NWR naturally flooded area and the manipulated site on Duck Creek WMA had very different CPUE for many taxa (table 11.4). Statistical comparisons were limited to the same habitat type (dead timber) and the same time period (mid-spring to late summer 1982). The Duck Creek WMA site had significantly greater CPUE for juvenile *M. salmoides* and *I. nebulosus* and was strikingly dominated by these taxa. In contrast, several of the most common taxa on

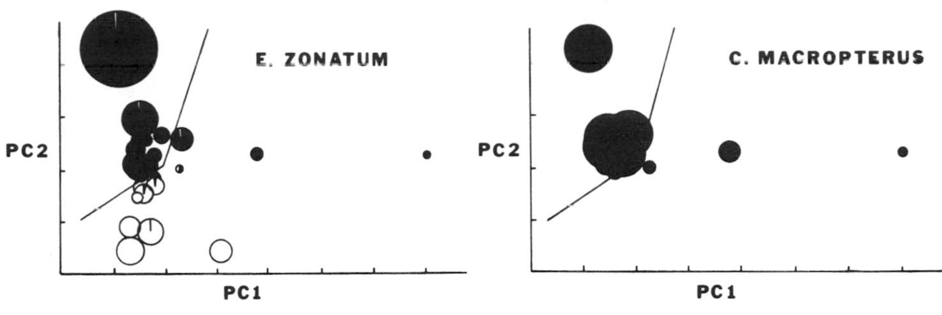

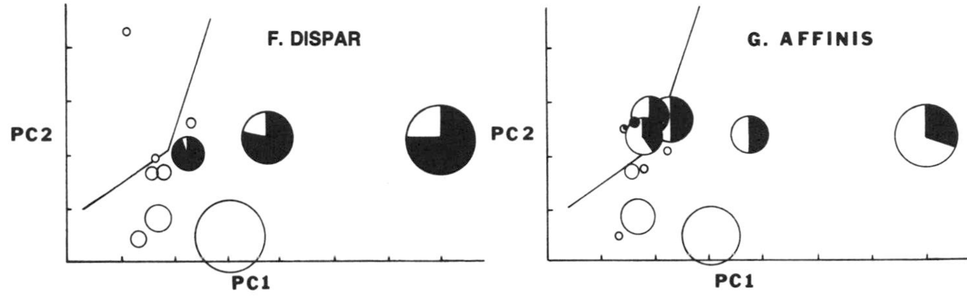

Fig. 11.3. Distribution of CPUE data in the principal component space of fig. 11.2 for the four most abundant species. The circle area is proportional to the relative CPUE in each sampling unit. The solid area within the circle indicates the proportion of catch composed of larvae and juveniles; the open area indicates the proportion of catch composed of adults. A line separates the 1981 and 1982 sampling units.

Table 11.4. Comparisons of CPUE Between Dead-Timber Areas on Mingo NWR and Duck Creek WMA

Species	LHS[†]	Catch per Unit Effort	
		Mingo NWR	Duck Creek WMA
Lepisosteus sp.	J	< 0.01	0
Amia calva	J	0	0.07
Esox americanus	J	0.06	0.01
Notemigonus crysoleucas	L	0	0.01*
Notemigonus crysoleucas	J	0	0.02*
Erimyzon sucetta	J	< 0.01	0
Ictalurus natalis	J	0	< 0.01
Ictalurus nebulosus	J	0.18	2.95*
Fundulus dispar	L	0.24*	0
Fundulus dispar	J	0.54*	0
Fundulus dispar	A	0.20*	0.11
Gambusia affinis	J	0.21*	0.06
Gambusia affinis	A	0.39*	0.12
Centrarchus macropterus	J	0.04	0.02
Elassoma zonatum	L	0.05*	0
Elassoma zonatum	J	0.19*	0
Elassoma zonatum	A	0.13*	0
Lepomis gulosus	J	0.01	< 0.01
Lepomis macrochirus	J	0.04	0.01
Lepomis symmetricus	J	0.06*	0
Lepomis symmetricus	A	< 0.01	0
Micropterus salmoides	J	0.13	2.21*
Pomoxis nigromaculatus	J	0	0.01
Number of trap days		272	208

Note: Comparisons are limited to mid-spring to late summer 1982, when both habitats were sampled concurrently.
*Significantly greater mean CPUE for the habitat (Mann-Whitney tests, $P < 0.05$).
[†]LHS = life-history stage: J = juvenile, A = adult, L = larva.

Mingo NWR, most notably all life-history stages of *E. zonatum*, were absent or captured in only low density on Duck Creek WMA.

Discussion

Our results indicate that the structure of the sampled fish assemblage on Mingo NWR was different in two years with different flooding regimes. The changes appear to be determined by the timing of flooding in relation to the spawning seasons of the respective species. Young-of-the-year *E. zonatum* and *C. macropterus* were considerably more abundant in 1981 than in 1982. In Missouri both these species spawn in early–mid-spring (Pflieger, 1975). In contrast, the species more common in 1982, *F. dispar* and *G. affinis*, spawn in late spring and summer. Flooding regimes of 1981 thus appeared to favor early-to-mid-spring spawners, while those of 1982 favored late-spring and summer spawners.

Although inundation was widespread and continuous in spring and summer of 1981, precipitation and thus availability of seasonally flooded sites was sporadic in late winter and early spring before sampling began (NOAA, 1981). Because seasonal sites were not flooded consistently during their spawning period in 1981, *E. zonatum* and *C. macropterus* appeared to spawn primarily in the dead timber and perhaps other permanent water nearby (Stewart, 1983). When the pin-oak and overcup-oak sites flooded in mid-spring, these nutrient-rich habitats were heavily utilized by juveniles of both species as nursery areas. In 1982 seasonally flooded sites were inundated earlier, and both species may have attempted to spawn there. Overall reproductive success was poor, however, possibly because many eggs, larvae, and juveniles were stranded when the habitats dried during mid- to late spring.

In 1982 adult *F. dispar* and *G. affinis* heavily utilized nutrient-rich seasonally flooded sites in early spring before spawning. Apparently this increased their energy available for spawning and resulted in good reproductive success. Although *F. dispar* appeared to spawn exclusively in the dead timber, *G. affinis* juveniles were found in the overcup-oak habitat shortly before it dried in late spring. Some *G. affinis* were undoubtedly stranded, as suggested above for *E. zonatum* and *C. macropterus*, but the prolonged spawning period of *G. affinis* (Krumholz, 1948) and possibly the mobility of the young of this live-bearer, seemed to result in good overall reproductive success in 1982, as evidenced by the relatively large number of juveniles found in the dead timber in summer. In 1981 seasonally flooded sites did not not become consistently inundated until mid-spring. Apparently this was too near the spawning time of *G. affinis* and *F. dispar* for adults to utilize the areas and realize significant gains in energy before spawning. Also, although the overcup-oak habitat remained inundated in 1981 and was thus available as a nursery area, by the time juveniles of the late-spawning species appeared, the site had been continually inundated for several weeks. It was probably not particularly nutrient-rich at this time because nutrients are rapidly released when lowland hardwood wetlands are initially flooded (Larson et al., 1981; Wylie, 1985). Thus, although most *G. affinis* captured in 1981 were in the overcup-oak habitat, reproduction appeared to be less successful in 1981 than in 1982.

The manipulation of flooding regimes on Duck Creek WMA appears to have altered fish-assemblage structure to a degree that exceeds natural variations. Because Duck Creek WMA and Mingo NWR historically had the same species pool, alterations in the flooding regime can be implicated in the low densities or absences of many flood-exploitative species and high densities of juvenile *M. salmoides* and *I. nebulosus* on Duck Creek WMA. Maintenance of relatively stable water levels on Duck Creek WMA has favored taxa that were essentially restricted to the dead-timber habitat on Mingo NWR, possibly through alteration of nutrient dynamics and resulting impacts on reproductive success and species interactions.

Our data are limited to two years and included only taxa susceptible to capture in activity traps. The findings do, however, suggest a mechanism by which environmental perturbations such as flooding may vary in their impact on the persistence of fish assemblage structure, a subject of considerable recent interest and debate (Grossman et al., 1982; Rahel et al., 1984; Yant et al., 1984; Herbold, 1984; Moyle and Vondracek, 1985; Ross et al., 1985; Matthews, 1986a). In our study the relative abundances of the sampled taxa, and hence fish-assemblage structure, changed in response to variation in the timing of annual flooding because the species had different spawning times. Similar differential responses by cyprinids in an Iowa river were observed by Starrett (1951). In contrast, Moyle and Vondracek (1985) found that, although absolute abundances of native species in a California stream changed in response to erosive flooding, relative abundances and thus assemblage structure did not change significantly because all these spring-spawning species reacted to disturbances in parallel. The impact of environmental perturbations on fish-assemblage structure should thus depend on the diversity of potential differential responses present in the assemblage.[1]

[1] We thank Leigh Frederickson and personnel at Gaylord Memorial Laboratory, Mingo National Wildlife Refuge, and Duck Creek Wildlife Management Area for assistance and for introducing us to the swamp. This research was supported by the Missouri Agricultural Experiment Station, Paul Wehmiller Fellowship, Edward K. Love Foundation, and Gaylord Memorial Laboratory. Contribution from the Missouri Agricultural Experiment Station Journal Series Number 10020.

12. Differential Selection by Flooding in Stream-Fish Communities of the Arid American Southwest

W. L. Minckley and Gary K. Mefee

Abstract

Nonnative fishes introduced into unregulated streams of arid, mountainous regions in Arizona and New Mexico are unable to resist flooding and are significantly reduced in numbers or destroyed. Native fishes show little if any response to such events; species composition and population sizes are similar before and following major floods. Differential responses reflect differences in evolutionary histories. Native faunal elements have long been subjected to vagaries of flashflooding in constrained channels and have capabilities to withstand such disturbances. Introduced alien fishes that evolved in mesic lowlands of other regions apparently do not.

Native ichthyofaunas of North America west of the Rocky Mountain axis are depauperate and unique, consisting largely of geographic relicts, monotypic genera, and endemic species (Miller, 1959). Relatively few fishes have become adapted to the natural rigors of aquatic systems in this region. The vast, rugged area between the Rockies and the Sierra Nevada, south of the Columbia and Klamath rivers and north of the U.S.-Mexico boundary, supports only about 75 species of native fishes; 43 (57%) of these are endemic to a single drainage, and 18 (21%) are at one locality each (Minckley et al., 1986). Although the area with which we are specifically concerned, Arizona and New Mexico west of the Continental Divide, has only 37 recognized species and subspecies, 4 are members of monotypic genera, and 14 (38%) are endemic (Minckley, 1973, 1985). Surviving species are (1) those that have evolved generalizations that promote remarkable resistance to extinction, (2) specialized inhabitants of long-existing habitats such as thermal springs or highly erosive streams, or (3) those suited for particular modes of life through preadaptation to factors such as high temperature or salinity (Hubbs, 1941; Miller, 1959, 1961; Deacon and Minckley, 1974; G. R. Smith, 1978, 1981; M. L. Smith, 1981; Minckley et al., 1986).

Habitat alteration and an influx of introduced fishes are resulting in reduction or extirpation of much of this native southwestern fauna (Miller, 1961 et seq.; Minckley and Deacon, 1968; Deacon, 1968, 1979; Miller and Pister, 1971; Minckley, 1973, 1985; Moyle, 1976a; Pister, 1974 et seq.; Soltz, 1979; Deacon et al., 1979; Williams, 1981; Meffe, 1983, 1985; Meffe et al., 1983; Rinne and Minckley, 1985; Williams et al., 1985). At least four species and six subspecies of fishes in six genera have become extinct in the last 40 years as a result of human-induced disturbance (Pister, 1981). Of 67 fishes in the United States listed as threatened or endangered, 45 (67.2%) live in arid zones (James E. Johnson, U.S. Fish and Wildlife Service, pers. comm.). The insular nature of the distributions of native desert fishes, with restricted ranges and few to no colonization pathways between populations (e.g., MacArthur, 1972), makes them particularly susceptible to local extinction.

On the other hand, more than 140 fish species have been successfully established outside their native ranges in North America for sport, forage, biological control, aquaculture, and hobby interests and by accident (Moyle, 1976b, 1985). We apply terminology for nonnative fishes recommended by Shafland and Lewis (1984) where appropriate; most of these in the American Southwest would be considered transplants, originating in the Mississippi or other mesic lowland drainages of the United States, but others are exotics from Eurasia, Central America, and Africa (Minckley, 1973; Moyle 1976a; Courtenay et al., 1984). The terms "introduced" or "nonnative" are applied to both these categories. Many of these animals have been dispersed by humans and thus are less restricted than native forms by natural or artificial barriers. As a result, southwestern stream-fish communities have been and are being transformed from native faunas to mixed native-nonnative associations, or in some cases to entirely introduced assemblages (Minckley, 1973, 1979a, 1982, 1985; Moyle and Nichols, 1973, 1974; Moyle,

1976a, b; Taylor et al., 1984; Marsh and Minckley, 1982, 1985; Moyle et al., in press).

Successful introductions are usually associated with construction of artificial habitats, particularly creation of lentic conditions in impoundments and regulation of rivers by dams that change violent, flood-prone systems to calm, mildly fluctuating lakes with stabilized downstream flows. Regulation of the Colorado and other western rivers not only reduces fluviatile habitats for native fishes but also enhances an amazing diversity of introduced groups, including clupeids, salmonids, cyprinids, catostomids, ictalurids, poeciliids, centrarchids, percichthyids, percids, and cichlids (Minckley, 1973, 1979a; Moyle, 1976a, b, in press). Mainstream impoundments and lesser lentic habitats, including recreational lakes and livestock ponds, also act as refuges for these fishes, from which they move both upstream and downstream.

Replacement of native species occurs most often and rapidly in impoundments. Moyle (1976b) noted that reservoirs are "hard on the native [California] fish fauna because they favor lake-adapted introduced species over native stream-adapted forms." Native Sacramento squawfish (*Ptychocheilus grandis*) and hardhead (*Mylopharodon conocephalus*) tend to "disappear from reservoirs after an initial five or ten years of abundance." He also noted a few native species that were enhanced by reservoirs, a situation not yet seen in the Colorado River system. With minor exceptions native fishes have not colonized Arizona impoundments. Certain markedly long-lived forms, razorback sucker (*Xyrauchen texanus*), bonytail chub (*Gila elegans*), and Colorado squawfish (*Ptychocheilus lucius*), persist for as long as 30 or more years without successful recruitment in reservoirs of the lower Colorado system and then decline toward local extinction (Miller, 1961; Minckley, 1983; McCarthy, 1986).

Variations on Trends of Species Replacement

Unlike predictable patterns in highly altered habitats, substantial variations exist both in extent and rapidity with which nonnative fishes replace indigenous forms in relatively natural southwestern drainages. Often environmental factors exclude introduced fishes and thus protect natural faunal elements. For example, temperatures greater than 36° C and dissolved oxygen less than 1 mg/l in some Nevada springs exclude nonnative forms but are tolerated by endemic springfishes (*Crenichthys baileyi, Crenichthys nevadae*) (Hubbs and Hettler, 1964; Hubbs et al., 1967; Deacon and Wilson, 1967; Courtenay et al., 1985). Similarly, moapa (*Moapa coriacea*) and desert dace (*Eremichthys acros*) live in water hot enough (more than 34° C) to be avoided by most introduced fishes (Hubbs and Miller, 1948; Nyquist, 1963; Deacon and Bradley, 1972). Desert pupfish (*Cyprinodon macularius*) were formerly abundant in the Salton Sea, California (Coleman, 1929; Cowles, 1934; Barlow, 1961), where they successfully occupied shore pools (Barlow, 1958a) in which salinities of 80 to 90 gm/l excluded other species. Their ova develop and hatch (with various rate and structural consequences) in salinities up to 70 gm/l, depending somewhat on temperature (Kinne, 1960; Kinne and Kinne, 1962a, b; Sweet and Kinne, 1964). Such extremes in salinities, as well as temperatures varying more than 20° C in a single day and to maxima greater than 38° C (Barlow, 1958a, b), until recently shielded the species from interactions with introduced forms. However, equally tolerant sailfin molly (*Poecilia latipinna*) and exotic cichlids (*Oreochromis* sp., *Tilapia zilli*) are now abundant. Desert pupfish have virtually disappeared (Crear and Haydock, 1971; Fisk, 1972; Schoenherr, 1979; Black, 1980) and are proposed to be listed as endangered (U.S. Department of the Interior, 1984).

More difficult to explain are situations where little or no replacement has occurred over decades in natural or seminatural streams, while dominance by introduced fishes was achieved in nearby regulated watercourses in only a few years. Natural flooding provides the most evidence for slowing or precluding establishment of aliens. Unique characteristics of stream segments also seem to affect species replacement. Native fishes persist in canyon-bound segments of both regulated and unregulated systems far longer than in other reaches. Species differences further exist, with river-adapted nonnative species enjoying more success than others.

We document that nonnative fishes that evolved under lowland, mesic conditions as a rule do poorly under natural southwestern flooding regimes and argue that this is due to fundamental differences in runoff patterns as contrasted with those of mesic lowlands. This phenomenon is attributed to differences in selective pressures associated with historic conditions of flooding over evolutionary time.

Contrasts in Flood Hydrology

Floods of southwestern arid lands differ qualitatively and quantitatively from those of lowland mesic regions owing to fundamental differences in geology, physiography, and climate (Hoyt and Langbein, 1955; Leopold et al., 1964; Fogel, 1981; Crosswhite and Crosswhite, 1982). The American Southwest is geologically active and mountainous, and watercourses are strongly influenced by local and regional relief. Watersheds are large, sparsely vegetated, and discretely divided, occupying steep valleys cut through uplifts and high plateaus. Precipitation is in the form of rainfall except at the highest elevations in winter and, although low in average amount, often falls as a few major storms a year.

High-intensity precipitation of summer monsoons can particularly result in abrupt and almost complete runoff into stream channels, increasing discharge by three or more orders of magnitude in seconds or minutes (Burkham, 1970, 1976a). A clearly defined frontal wave often leads a flash-flood, followed by high and variable discharges that last from a few minutes to several hours and rapidly subside. A channel is transformed almost instantaneously from a dry wash or intermittent stream to a torrent, returning to its former state almost as quickly (Ives, 1936; Wooley, 1946; Jahns, 1949; Lewis, 1963; Deacon and Minckley, 1974; Cooley et al., 1977; Harrell, 1978; Fisher and Minckley, 1978; Collins et al., 1981; Fisher et al., 1982). Geographically generalized and protracted winter precipitation results in scouring floods only when it is of unusual magnitude, as when augmented by warm rains melting snowpacks or falling on saturated land surfaces (Forbes, 1902; Olmstead, 1919; Burkham, 1970, 1976b).

Floods passing over impermeable bedrock and constrained by steep canyon walls cannot dissipate energy through overflow, infiltration, or straightening and widening of alluvial channels, and their destructiveness is amplified (Leopold and Maddock, 1955; Bull, 1979, 1981). Degradation and removal of terraces and mobilization and transport of large quantities of inorganic material, often of boulder size, are characteristic (Jahns, 1949; Kesseli and Beaty, 1959; Melton, 1965; Thomson and Schumann, 1968). Accompanying phenomena are transport of organic materials ranging from fine-ground detritus to mature riparian trees (Forbes, 1902; Rinne, 1975; Burkham, 1976b; Minckley and Clark, 1984; Minckley and Rinne, in press), sudden decreases in water temperature by 15° C or more (Deacon and Minckley, 1974), and rapid fluctuations in other physical and chemical parameters (Fisher and Minckley, 1978; Minckley, 1981; Rampe et al., 1985).

In contrast, most mesic watersheds have low relief, deep soils, and dense vegetative cover. Drainage channels meander, have low gradients, and are far less distinct, and broad floodplains extend laterally many times the widths of streams (Leopold, 1962). Floods are cumulative discharge events that take hours or days to peak and an equally long time to subside. Floodplain river lakes (Welcomme, 1979) or smaller pools (Halyk and Balon, 1983) are formed behind natural levees, in depressions, and in oxbows and serve as refugia for fishes escaping high discharges. Canyon and bedrock constraints are absent or minimal. High discharges spread and infiltrate with reduced energy over and into adjacent floodplains (Hoyt and Langbein, 1955; Leopold et al., 1964).

We chose for hydrologic comparison 5 unregulated Arizona streams and 10 streams of the Mississippi River basin. Data for each, including stream gradients, channel widths, and canyon profiles, were derived from appropriate U.S. Geological Survey topographic maps. The term *channel* denotes that part of the system scoured of perennial vegetation by flooding, while *floodplain* includes nonscoured alluvial fill (Burkham, 1972). *Stream* includes the channel portion occupied by water during modal discharge.

Gradients of southwestern streams are one to two orders of magnitude greater than in those of mesic lowlands (table 12.1). Overall relief is also far greater as a result of rugged terrain. Channel cross sections (fig. 12.1) illustrate the con-

Table 12.1. Geographic Relief of Some Mesic- and Arid-Zone (Arizona) Streams

Locality	Maximum Relief* (m)	Gradients (m/km)
Mesic zones:		
Mississippi River, near Saint Francisville, La.	4.6	0.03
White River, White River National Wildlife Refuge, Ark.	43.1	0.06
Saint Francis River, near Widener, Ark.	61.5	0.08
Mississippi River, Ky.	90.1	0.06
Licking River, near Visalis, Ky.	146.2	0.18
Marais des Cygnes River, near Ottawa, Kans.	270.8	0.52
Des Moines River, near Boone, Iowa	273.8	0.39
Wakarusa River, near Wakarusa, Kans.	292.3	0.84
Neosho River, near Neosho Falls, Kans.	292.3	0.52
Little Blue River, near Hanover, Kans.	360.0	0.51
Arid zones:		
Sycamore Creek, near Ft. McDowell, Ariz.	541.5	8.83
Salt River, above Lake Roosevelt, Ariz.	701.5	3.09
Aravaipa Creek, near Klondyke, Ariz.	873.2	14.58
Bonita Creek, near Gila River, Ariz.	1,009.2	8.67
Eagle Creek, near Morenci, Ariz.	1,156.9	5.14

*Maximum vertical distance from river surface at median discharge to highest adjacent terrain at area measured.

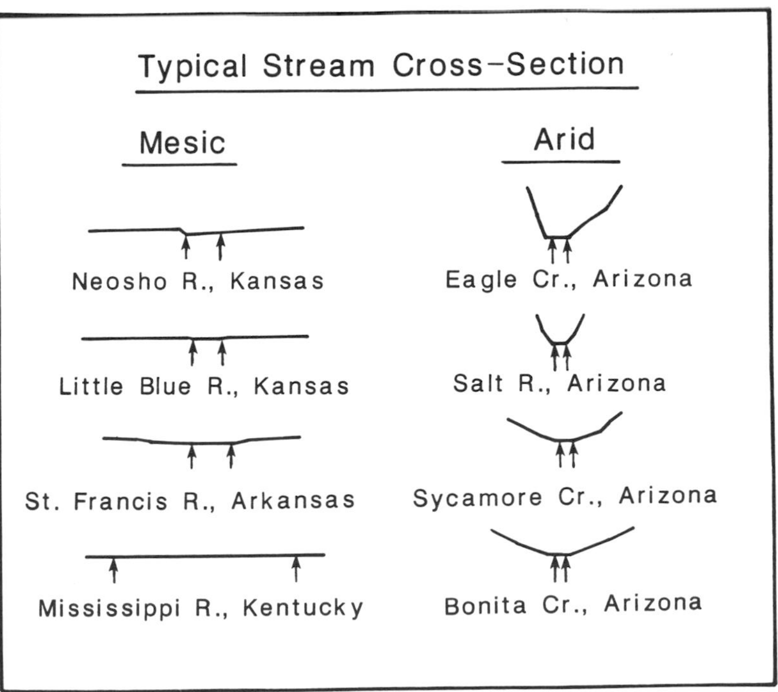

Figure 12.1. Representative channel cross sections from North American mesic and arid-zone streams; scales for the latter have been enlarged for clarity. Vertical notches indicate boundaries of channels.

Table 12.2. Summary of Gross Characteristics of Southwestern Arid-Land and Mesic Streams

Zone	Cross Section	Stream Gradient	Substrate	Competency	Flood Onset	Permanency	Available Refugia
Mesic zones	Generally unconstrained, broad floodplains	Low	Fine-grained, organic	Generally low	Slow—hours, days	Highest downstream	Floodplains, extensive interconnections with marshlands
Arid lands	Constrained by canyon walls	High	Coarse-grained, inorganic, or bedrock	Often high	Rapid—seconds, minutes	Highest in mid-reaches	Streamsides, eddies behind obstructions

strained nature of these systems, with an almost complete lack of floodplains, particularly in canyon-bound reaches. Other contrasts and a summary of discharge differences appear in table 12.2.

We also compared discharge patterns of several Arizona watercourses and three streams of the Suwannee River drainage of Florida and Georgia, the last chosen on the bases of "typical" mesic characteristics, similarity of watershed areas to Arizona systems, and record availability. Records for the following streams were examined (years of record and watershed areas in parentheses): Arizona—Santa Cruz River near Lochiel (1950–75; 213 km^2), Aravaipa Creek near Mammoth (1920, 1932–42, and 1967–75; 1,401 km^2), Gila River near Safford (1941–46 and 1957–65; 20,451 km^2); Florida—Santa Fe River near Graham (1971–81; 246 km^2), Santa Fe River at Worthington Springs (1971–81; 1,507 km^2), and Suwannee River at Ellaville (1971–81; 17,742 km^2). Data reported as mean instantaneous discharge per day in ft^3/sec were converted to m^3/sec. A set of these records is included as fig. 12.2 to illustrate seasonal patterns of flashflooding. Such means obviously tend to minimize peak flows, particularly in southwestern systems where floods are rapid and of short duration; a massive 10-min flow may be almost unrecognizable. The data are thus conservative with respect to discharge extremes.

Mean annual discharge patterns were developed by summing numbers of days at each discharge level on a log scale. For example, total days a stream flowed at or less than 0.003, 0.006, 0.009, . . . 0.03, 0.06, 0.09, . . . 0.3, 0.6, 0.9, . . . 3, 6, 9, . . . etc., m^3/sec were tallied. An index of total volume discharged was computed by multiplying number of days at a given discharge by the latter and summing over the period of record. Cumulative curves of number of days at each discharge level and total runoff (total water yield of the watershed per unit time) owing to a particular discharge were developed and contrasted for arid land and mesic watersheds of comparable size (fig. 12.3). The more widely two curves are separated, the greater the unevenness of discharge for a given watershed.

In aggregate these curves demonstrate a prevalence of high discharges producing most of the annual water yield in brief periods of time in southwestern systems, while low discharges produced a far greater proportion of total yield from mesic watersheds. For example, discharge 38% of the time was ≤ 0.03 m^3/sec in the Santa Cruz River, Arizona, which accounted for only ca. 0.5% of total water yield. Discharge ≤ 0.3 m^3/sec almost 84% of the time accounted for only 9% of the total. The upper 50% of total water yield occurred at greater than 7.5 m^3/sec in only 0.6% of the total time. In contrast, the two curves for Santa Fe River near Graham, Florida, are nearer together. The upper 50% of total water yield occurred in 9% of the time, 15 times greater than that necessary for an equivalent percentage of total yield in the arid-land system.

Selective Pressures on Riverine Fishes

It is reasonable to suspect from fundamental differences between arid-zone and lowland mesic streams that biotic elements are under contrasting hydrologic selection pressures. It is established that fishes of mesic drainages make use of inundated floodplains during floods, either to avoid

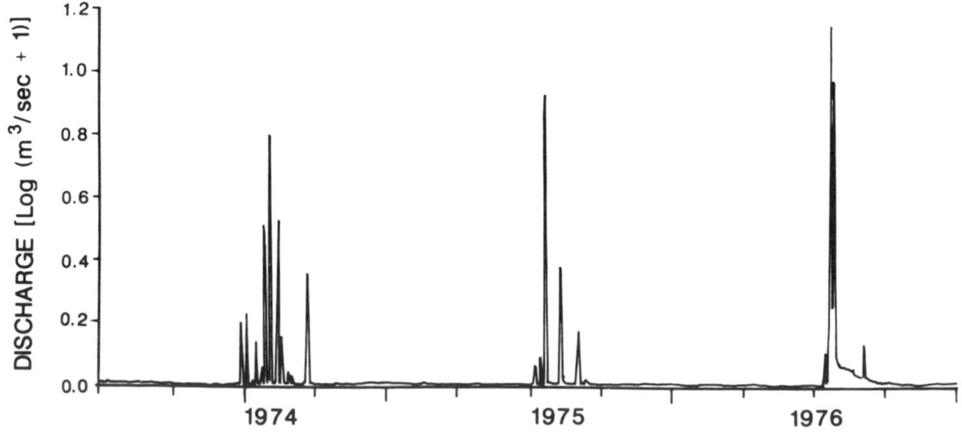

Figure 12.2. Discharge in the Santa Cruz River, Arizona, from 1974 through 1976. Data are daily instantaneous means and illustrate the seasonal and "flashy" nature of arid-land stream discharge.

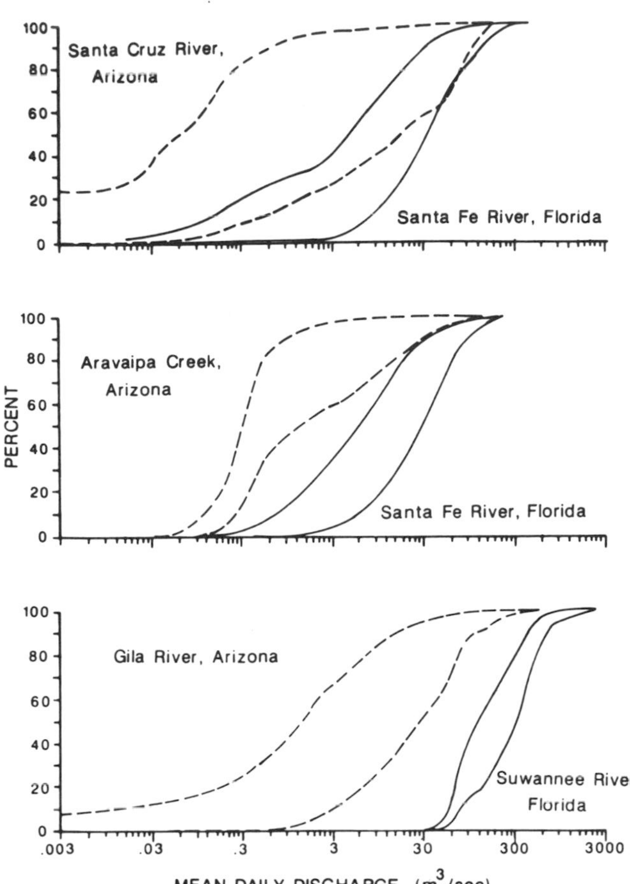

Figure 12.3. Cumulative discharge patterns for selected North American arid-land (dashed line) and mesic (solid line) streams of different discharges but similar watershed sizes. The lower curve for each watercourse is cumulative percentage of total yearly discharge owing to each daily discharge rate; the upper curve is cumulative total percentage time flowing at each daily discharge. Compiled from U.S. Geological Survey (published periodically). See text for further explanation.

physical conditions of the channel or for feeding, reproduction, and nursery areas (Guillory, 1979; Welcomme, 1979; Halyk and Balon, 1983; Ross and Baker, 1983). Even those fishes that remain in flooded channels and do not resist transport are merely moved to larger, more permanent, and perhaps more stable downstream habitats (Horton, 1945; Starrett, 1951; Strahler, 1957; Hynes, 1970; Horwitz, 1978; Vannote et al., 1980), which provide refuge during environmental extremes (Paloumpis, 1956, 1958). Strong selection for lowland mesic fishes to maintain position at discharges greater than the mode should therefore be minimal.

In contrast, arid-zone fishes often cannot avoid high discharges by movement onto floodplains, particularly in reaches constrained by bedrock canyons. Furthermore, there is evidence that native fishes concentrate in canyons in summer despite dangers of high water, presumably to avoid elevated water temperatures in shallower, unshaded segments (Siebert, 1980) and to take advantage of greater permanency in bedrock pools. It is sorely disadvantageous for these fishes to move or be carried downstream, as many arid land watercourses desiccate long before reaching master streams except in periods of major runoff (John, 1964; Deacon and Minckley, 1974; Constantz, 1981; Minckley, 1981; Minckley and Brown, 1982). High-volume, short-term floods produce downstream discharges for only a relatively few moments in time. Such spates percolate into coarse alluvial fans of smaller systems or finer-grained but extensive deposits of larger rivers. Infiltration coupled with spreading over terminal alluvial deposits or into saline waters of intermontane basins (Deacon and Minckley, 1974) and evapotranspiration that often exceeds 2 m/y cause floodwaters to disappear in minutes or hours (Burkham, 1976c). Fishes transported or swimming downstream are stranded and die. Substantial selection pressure must therefore exist for southwestern stream-dwelling organisms to maintain position during high discharges.

Apparent morphological adaptations of some fishes to swift and/or turbulent flow may reflect this phenomenon. Several cyprinids and catostomids that inhabit larger, severely flooding waters have depressed skulls and keeled or humped napes, huge buttressed fins, narrow caudal peduncles, slim bodies, and reduced scales, all of which tend to reduce drag and presumably improve swimming ability in fast and turbulent currents (Hubbs, 1941; Vogel, 1981; Minckley, 1973). Other aquatic animal groups in the region have comparable adaptations in morphology, behavior, and/or life-history characteristics (Bruns and Minckley, 1980; Gray, 1980, 1981; Fisher et al., 1982; Gray and Fisher, 1981; Jackson, 1984).

Flood Effects on Southwestern Fishes

Native fishes resist floods by maintaining position in or adjacent to channel habitats, persisting in microrefugia, or rapidly recolonizing if displaced. Nonnative fishes that evolved under regimes of mesic lowlands respond to flooding in their natural habitats by movement into floodplain or other refugia or downflow movement or transport. In erosive western streams the latter are frequently displaced and destroyed. Data supporting these claims are of three types: (1) a series of samples before and after major floods of known magnitudes that illustrate differential removal of alien fish species in Arizona and New Mexico streams, (2) detailed analyses of flood effects on two interacting Arizona fishes, one native and one transplanted, and (3) inferences from present distributional patterns of native and nonnative species elsewhere in the region.

Differential Effects of Flooding

Fish populations in seven unregulated and three regulated streams or stream reaches (fig. 12.4) were sampled before and after major floods in the period 1964 through summer 1985. Part of this information has been published or reported in agency documents (Barber and Minckley, 1966; Minckley and Clarkson, 1979; Minckley, 1981; Propst et al., 1985a, b), but a substantial proportion has not appeared elsewhere. Collections to be contrasted were chosen on the bases of (1) a substantial period (greater than six months) that did not

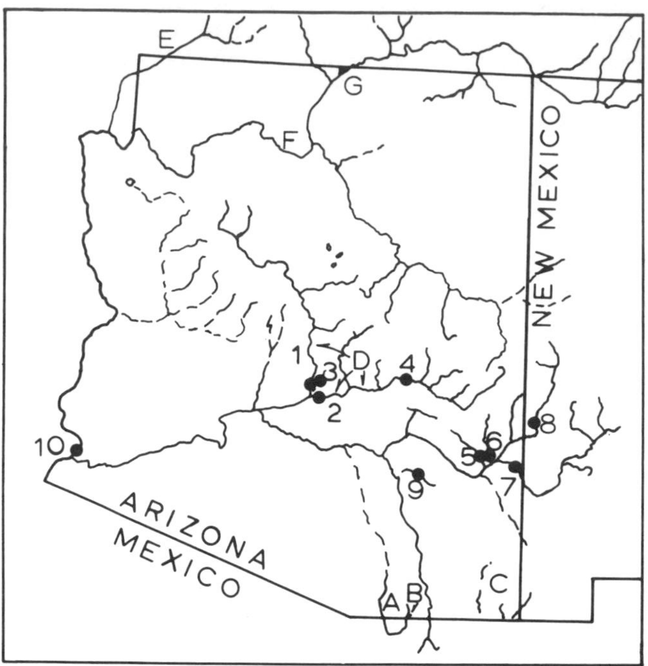

Figure 12.4. Map of Arizona and western New Mexico with major drainages. Sampling localities are 1: Verde River; 2: Salt River (regulated below controlling dams and above inflow of Verde River; 3: Sycamore Creek; 4: Salt River (unregulated, upstream from dams); 5: Bonita Creek; 6: Eagle Creek; 7: Gila River; 8: San Francisco River; 9: Aravaipa Creek; 10: lower Colorado River. Other localities mentioned in text include A: Santa Cruz River; B: Sharp Spring; C: Chiricahua Mountains; D: Salt and Verde river reservoirs; E: Virgin River; F: Grand Canyon of the Colorado River; G: Lake Powell.

include flooding before the first sample and (2) a short period of time (less than six weeks) between a flood event and a second sample from the same reach. Early examples (before 1975) were largely fortuitous in distribution relative to flooding, but for the past 10 years such events have been specifically evaluated for their faunal impacts. Floods were defined by their maximum instantaneous flows relative to mean discharges, as follows:

$$\text{Index of magnitude} = \frac{\text{Maximum instantaneous discharge}}{\text{Mean discharge}},$$

where maximum discharges for individual events and means over the period of record ending in 1982 were those given by U.S. Geological Survey records (published periodically). When an event was extended with multiple peaks, the largest was used for computation of an index of magnitude.

The largest unregulated streams are Salt River, Arizona, and Gila and San Francisco rivers, Arizona and New Mexico (in part Brown et al., 1981; Minckley, 1985), upstream from major water-control structures. Perennial, intermediate-size streams include Eagle and Aravaipa creeks, in Arizona (Minckley, 1979b, 1981; Silvey et al., 1984). The last two streams in the sample set are Bonita and Sycamore creeks, which are locally intermittent (Heindl and McCullough, 1961; Thomson and Schumann, 1968). All these watercourses are constrained by canyons through a substantial portion of their lengths. All support one or more native and introduced fishes. Regulated streams include the Salt and Verde rivers, in Arizona, downstream from impoundments, and the mainstream Colorado River, in Arizona-California (Minckley, 1979a, 1982, unpub. data; Marsh and Minckley, 1985).

Collections were by seines; gill, trammel, and hoop nets of various lengths and meshes; and electrofishing in all available habitats. Data for the Salt, Verde, and Colorado rivers are least reliable because of large habitat sizes. Pools greater than 10 m in depth and rapids with velocities greater than 1.5 m/sec defy effective sampling. Smaller streams were blocked and fishes removed and enumerated (Minckley, 1981). Fishes were identified (table 12.3) and released or preserved for later identification; representative specimens are in the Arizona State University Collection of Fishes. Samples before and after floods were compared for faunal composition and relative abundance. Terms for abundance when absolute numbers were not recorded in field notes were quantified for present purposes as follows: dominant = comprising 50% of a sample; abundant = 25%; common = 15%; scarce = 5%; and rare = 1%.

Fish faunas of canyon-bound reaches of unregulated streams invariably shifted from a mixture of native and nonnative species to predominantly, and in some instances exclusively, native forms after floods approaching or exceeding two orders of magnitude greater than mean discharge (table 12.3; fig. 12.5). Intermediate-size floods (those near one order of magnitude) depleted but rarely destroyed nonnative populations. Floods of less than one order of magnitude greater than mean discharge had no discernible effect on fish populations. Relationships between percentage increase in relative abundance of native species (declines in numbers of nonnative fishes) and declines in numbers of nonnative species were correlated with increasing magnitude of flooding; both are highly significant, while changes in native species with flood magnitude are not significant (fig. 12.5). Wider stream, channel, and/or floodplain segments often accumulate both native and nonnative fishes presumably displaced from canyons by major flooding, and the latter tend to persist in such places (Propst et al., 1985a). It is obvious from composition of samples taken before floods that drought periods and periods of "normal" flow separating flood events were characterized by increased incidence of nonnative fishes, resulting from reintroduction, redispersal, local reproduction by survivors, or other manner of appearance.

Among nonnative forms common carp (*Cyprinus carpio*) populations are substantially reduced by high-intensity flooding. This ubiquitous species is rarely abundant in unregulated systems, but large adults tend to be widespread. Red shiners (*Notropis lutrensis*) also are depleted or removed by flooding but rapidly reestablish substantial populations through survivors, reinvaders from protected habitats such as reservoirs, or direct reintroduction. Red shiners are aggressively spreading (or being spread), despite restrictions on their use as baitfish and the existence of substantial deter-

Table 12.3. Differential Effects of Floods of Contrasting Magnitudes on Native Versus Nonnative Fishes in Some Unregulated and Regulated Streams of Arizona and New Mexico

No. Pers. Obs.	Magnitude of Flood Maxima	Native Fishes				Introduced Fishes	
		No. Species		% Total Fauna		No. Species	
		Before	After	Before	After	Before	After
Unregulated Reaches							
Salt River above Roosevelt (mean discharge [69 yr] 24.7 m³/sec)							
2	5.9 ± 1.21 (4.2–9.5)	5.5 ± 0.29 (5–6)	5 ± 0.17 (4–6)	67.5 ± 8.50 (50–90)	68.8 ± 10.78 (50–95)	4.3 ± 0.48 (4–6)	5.3 ± 0.48 (4–6)
7	29.7 ± 8.60 (11.6–78)	4.7 ± 0.18 (4–5)	4.9 ± 0.26 (4–6)	67.9 ± 7.30 (40–95)	72.9 ± 6.97 (45–90)	4 ± 0.44 (2–5)	2.4 ± 0.48 (1–4)
2	106.2 ± 3.65 (103–110)	4.5 ± 0.50 (4–5)	4	72.5 ± 7.50 (65–80)	100	4 ± 0.44 (3–5)	0
Gila River Near Safford (mean discharge [58 yr] 12.8 m³/sec)							
1	5.6	3	3	20	25	7	8
5	30 ± 9.10 (11.6–47.8)	2.2 ± 0.37 (1–3)	2 ± 0.32 (1–3)	19 ± 2.45 (10–25)	64 ± 12.39 (30–95)	5.2 ± 0.37 (4–6)	4 ± 0.55 (3–6)
1	221	1	2	15	95	5	3
San Francisco River at Clifton (mean discharge [58 yr] 5.58 m³/sec)							
4	22.5 ± 8.60 (12.8 –48.2)	3 ± 0.41 (2–4)	3	21.4 ± 2.39 (15–25)	32.5 ± 5.95 (20–45)	5.5 ± 0.29 (5–6)	3.8 ± 0.85 (2–6)
1	284.9	4	3	25	95	6	1
Eagle Creek at Morenci Pump Station (mean discharge [38 yr] 1.45 m³/sec)							
3	5.7 ± 1.41 (3.7–8.4)	4 ± 0.58 (3–4)	3.7 ± 0.33 (3–5)	31.7 ± 4.41 (25–40)	33.3 ± 7.31 (20–45)	5.3 ± 0.33 (5–6)	6 ± 0.58 (5–7)
4	37.35 ± 12.27 (13.5–66)	3.8 ± 0.25 (3–5)	3.5 ± 0.29 (3–4)	36.3 ± 5.54 (30–50)	48.8 ± 9.87 (20–65)	5.8 ± 0.48 (5–7)	4 ± 0.91 (2–6)
1	479	4	5	35	100	4	0
Aravaipa Creek near mouth (mean discharge [27 yr] 0.85 m³/sec)							
4	6.6 ± 1.02 (4.8–9.4)	6.5 ± 0.29 (6–7)	6.5 ± 0.29 (6–7)	98.8 ± 1.25 (95–100)	100	0.3 (0–1)	0
5	49.9 ± 12.94 (14.6–78)	6.4 ± 0.24 (6–7)	6.2 ± 0.20 (6–7)	98.0 ± 1.22 (95–100)	100	0.2 (0–1)	0
3	358.5 ± 102.4 (185.6–540)	6.3 ± 0.33 (6–7)	6	96.7 ± 1.67 (95–99)	100	(0–1) (0–1)	0
1	1,999.2	7	7	99	100	1	0
Sycamore Creek near Fort McDowell (mean discharge [21 yr] 0.84 m³/sec)							
6	6.8 ± 1.08 (3.4–9.7)	1.5 ± 0.70 (1–3)	1.33 ± 0.21 (1–2)	87.5 ± 2.81 (75–95)	91.7 ± 2.47 (80–95)	1.5 ± 0.34 (1–3)	1.3 ± 0.21 (1–2)
3	39.3 ± 6.30 (30–51.3)	1.7 ± 0.67 (1–3)	1.7 ± 0.67 (1–3)	91.7 ± 3.33 (85–95)	99.33 ± 0.67 (98–100)	2 ± 0.58 (1–3)	0.3 (0–1)
4	397.7 ± 89.92 (174–504)	1.4 ± 0.24 (1–2)	1.6 ± 0.40 (1–3)	87 ± 2.63 (77–92)	99.2 ± 0.58 (97–100)	2.6 ± 0.24 (2–3)	0.6 (0–2)
Bonita Creek near mouth (estimated mean discharge [ungauged during study] 0.50 m³/sec)							
4	6.5 ± 1.40 (3.2–9.9)	4.3 ± 0.25 (4–5)	4.5 ± 0.29 (4–5)	68.3 ± 6.37 (60–75)	66.3 ± 6.25 (55–80)	4.3 ± 0.33 (4–5)	3.8 ± 0.63 (4–5)
4	62.5 ± 14.68 (24–90)	4.8 ± 0.25 (4–5)	4.3 ± 0.48 (4–5)	75 ± 2.35 (70–80)	93.3 ± 2.17 (85–100)	4.8 ± 0.25 (4–5)	2 ± 1 (1–5)
1	250	4	4	75	100	4	0
Regulated Reaches							
Salt River below Stewart Mountain Dam (mean discharge [52 yr] 26.2 m³/sec)							
5	3 ± 0.72 (1.6–5.8)	2.6 ± 0.24 (2–3)	2.8 ± 0.20 (2–3)	81.8 ± 2.60 (75–90)	84.6 ± 5.22 (70–95)	5 ± 0.32 (4–6)	4.8 ± 0.37 (4–6)
4	55.8 ± 14.3 (16–81.3)	2.3 ± 0.25 (2–3)	2.5 ± 0.29 (2–3)	72.5 ± 5.20 (60–85)	86.0 ± 4.56 (78–99)	7.5 ± 1.94 (5–13)	2.5 ± 2.10 (1–7)

Table 12.3. *Continued*

No. Pers. Obs.	Magnitude of Flood Maxima	Native Fishes No. Species Before	Native Fishes No. Species After	Native Fishes % Total Fauna Before	Native Fishes % Total Fauna After	Introduced Fishes No. Species Before	Introduced Fishes No. Species After
Verde River below Bartlett Dam (mean discharge [94 yr] 19.2 m³/sec)							
3	3.1 ± 0.89 (1.5–4.6)	3.7 ± 0.33 (3–4)	3.3 ± 0.33 (3–4)	61.7 ± 4.41 (55–70)	65 ± 0.86 (50–75)	6.7 ± 0.86 (5–8)	6.7 ± 1.67 (5–10)
1	149	3	4	65	97	11	3
Colorado River below Laguna Dam (mean discharge [12 yr] 9.10 m³/sec)							
1	>100[†]	1	1	1.3	0.5	17	15

Note: Means are followed by ± one standard error; ranges are in parentheses. See text for further explanation.

*Discharges in regulated reaches normally depend on releases to satisfy domestic, irrigation, and/or power-generation demands; maximum instantaneous discharges of higher magnitudes are from uncontrolled or emergency releases.

[†]Data are from two sampling periods (November 1982, February 1983) immediately before a high-discharge event and two periods (August and November 1983) following; information for May 1983, a time of transition from low to high discharges, was excluded (Marsh and Minckley, 1985).

rence in the form of dams, naturally or artifically dried channels, and other barriers. Both golden shiners (*Notemigonus crysoleucus*) and fathead minnows (*Pimephales promelas*) are typically removed by floods, and rarely reappear unless reintroduced. Catfishes, with the exception of flathead catfishes (*Pylodictis olivaris*), are depleted by large floods. The stream-adapted flathead is, however, rapidly expanding its range and populations, despite physical impacts of flooding, barriers, and other factors. Poeciliid fishes (*Gambusia affinis, Poecilia latipinna,* and others) are decimated by flooding. Their high reproductive potentials allow rapid recovery, especially by mosquitofish, if some survive or are reintroduced. Mosquitofish are widely used by public health agencies in the control of pestiferous insects and often are stocked immediately following high waters. Centrarchids (largemouth and smallmouth basses *[Micropterus salmoides, M. dolomieui]* and green and bluegill sunfishes *[Lepomis cyanellus, L. macrochirus]*) seem highly susceptible to displacement in Arizona streams (see also Schlosser, 1985). Smallmouth bass and green sunfish are in part stream-adapted, however, and usually reappear in a few weeks. Exotic cichlids introduced into unregulated streams have invariably disappeared (Minckley, 1973; Barrett, 1983). A number of common nonnative species with direct access to unregulated portions of one or more larger rivers have rarely or never been taken there, perhaps because of lack of flood resistance. Included are threadfin shad (*Dorosoma petenense*), buffalofishes (*Ictiobus bubalus, I. cyprinellus, I. niger*), redear sunfish (*L. microlophus*), black crappie (*Pomoxis nigromaculatus*), and yellow bass (*Morone mississippiensis*). Some are, however, displaced or disperse downflow through regulated stream reaches from reservoirs during major flooding into delivery and irrigation canals (Minckley, 1973; Marsh and Minckley,1982).

Depletions of native fishes, when they occurred, were in the most constrained streams or stream reaches, but no consistent patterns were evident. In no instance was a native species extirpated by high discharges, although differential displacement susceptibilities are undoubtedly reflected in recorded changes in species composition not reported here. Harrell (1978) similarly recorded some native west Texas species as more "flood-adapted" than others. When reductions in population sizes were detected, they typically involved relatively greater losses of young-of-the-year than adults, as has been reported elsewhere (John, 1963; Seegrist and Gard, 1972; Schlosser, 1982, 1985). One massive discharge in Sycamore Creek, Arizona, destroyed young and substantially reduced adults of longfin dace (*Agosia chrysogaster*) (Deacon and Minckley, 1974). Nonnative fishes were eliminated by that event. John (1963) recorded similar reductions in populations of speckled dace (*Rhinichthys osculus*) in streams of the Chiricahua Mountains, Arizona. A comparable flood in Eagle Creek in 1984–85 numerically reduced the entire native fauna of six species (in part, Propst et al.; 1985b), while a remarkably large flood in Aravaipa Creek in 1983 (almost 2,000 times mean discharge) had no discernible impacts on seven native fish species (D. A. Hendrickson, Arizona State University, pers. comm.). That stream is especially notable since no major changes in fish-community structure were demonstrable over a period of almost four decades for which data were available to Meffe and Minckley (1987), despite documented occurrences of many major floods.

Samples from regulated systems indicate relatively few or no changes in species composition of predominantly nonnative faunas as long as releases from upstream dams are of low, controlled volumes. However, emergency releases, some of which must have equaled flashflooding of the past, had major impacts in canyon-bound reaches of the Salt and Verde rivers (table 12.3) equivalent to those in unregulated systems. Native catostomids (*Catostomus insignis, Catostomus clarki*) and a few longfin dace remained. Nonnative forms were essentially destroyed, introduced fishes entrained from upstream impoundments were abundantly skewered on riparian trees, and a number of alien species formerly abundant in downstream wastewater ponds have not been found again (Minckley and Deacon, 1968; Minckley, 1973; Deacon and Minckley, 1974; Marsh and Minckley, 1982). On the other hand, similar emergency release of water into the lower Colorado River, which rose to flood over a locally broad valley, had little if any influence on nonnative or the single remaining native species (table 12.3).

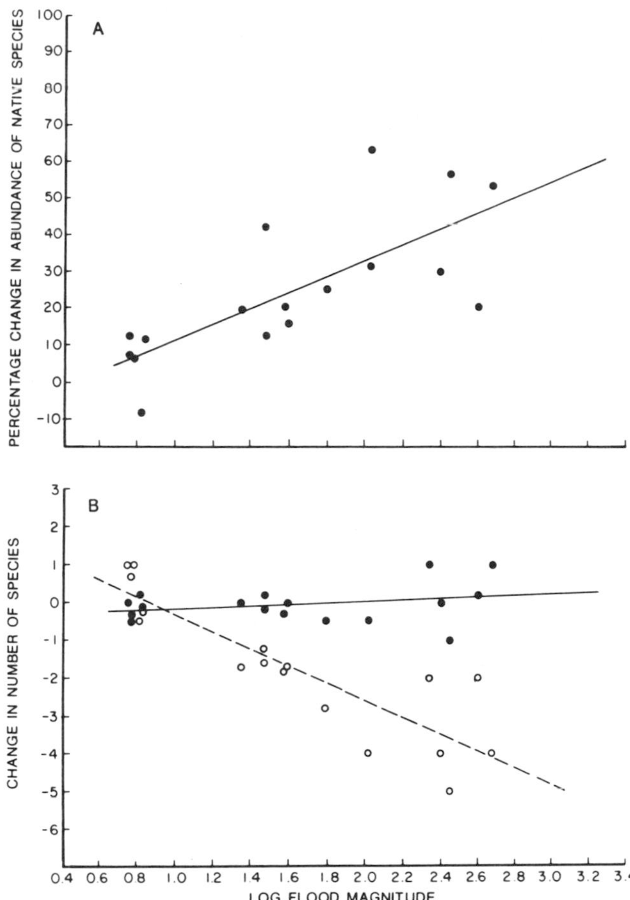

Figure 12.5 Change in percentage abundance of native fishes (transformed by arc sine square root) and change in number of native and introduced fish species as a function of log-transformed flood magnitude. Solid circles = native species; open circles = introduced forms. Percentage data are in part a result of arbitrary assignment of values to qualitative expressions for abundance (see text) and thus may reflect errors of 10% or more. Data for Aravaipa Creek (table 12.3) were excluded because of the consistently low occurrence of nonnative species in that system. Regression equations; (A) $Y = -10.319 + 21.62X$, $r = 0.773$, $P < 0.01$; (B) native: $Y = -0.0374 + 1.98X$, $r = 0.273$, $P > 0.05$ (NS); introduced: $Y = 1.952 - 2.275X$, $r = -0.873$, $P < 0.01$.

A Quantified Example

The most definitive example of maintenance of a native species through influences of flooding involves instances of coexistence of native Sonoran topminnows (*Poeciliopsis o. occidentalis*) and mosquitofish. The latter was transplanted to Arizona in the 1920s (Miller and Lowe, 1964) from an extensive natural range centered in the lower Mississippi River valley (Rosen and Bailey, 1963). Its regional colonization was accompanied by extirpation of topminnows through predation (Meffe, 1985). This pattern has been repeated throughout the United States range of the Sonoran topminnow, resulting in its endangered status (Minckley et al., 1977; Meffe et al., 1983; U.S. Fish and Wildlife Service, 1984).

Coexisting populations were studied in Sharp Spring, Arizona, from 1979 through 1983, and flood impacts were quantified (Meffe, 1984). The spring system consisted of 18 perennial pools connected by reticulate channels flowing through a 600-m reach of marshland within a moderately incised arroyo (Meffe et al., 1982). Approximately 2 km of intermittent pools and marshes below this section led to the Santa Cruz River floodplain.

Sampling with a variety of nets and seines was performed between August 1979 and early 1981. Adult fish were enumerated and released alive. Numbers of the two species were inversely related after prolonged low discharge (fig. 12.6*A*), and the numbers of topminnows declined as mosquitofish expanded their population. Fishes were again sampled in late July and September 1981 after a series of flashfloods, two of which were observed (Meffe, 1984) and at least one of which (not observed) scoured the system. Both species crowded along stream margins and in eddying currents until discharge crested during the first flood, but mosquitofish ventured into midstream at first signs of recession while discharge remained high and turbulent. Topminnows remained tightly along shorelines until discharge returned to preflood levels. Reductions in mosquitofish populations were greater than 98%, while topminnows suffered only a 75% decline (fig. 12.6*B*). Of the apparent loss of topminnows, thousands were found in newly filled pools a few hundred meters downstream, in position for recolonization of the permanent reach. Only three mosquitofish were collected from the downstream section, indicating that they were mostly transported from the habitat.

Behaviors of these two fishes were compared in a laboratory flume designed to provide water surges simulating flashflood conditions. Sonoran topminnows consistently maintained their positions in strong and pulsing currents by moving against walls of the flume. The behavior appeared genetic since it was well developed and effective in one-day-old individuals. By comparison, mosquitofish repeatedly failed; young fish in particular did not maintain position and were killed in the experimental system.

Distributional Inferences

Most native southwestern fishes persist in substantial numbers in streams that (1) are distant from human population centers or protected by Indian reservations or other reserves,

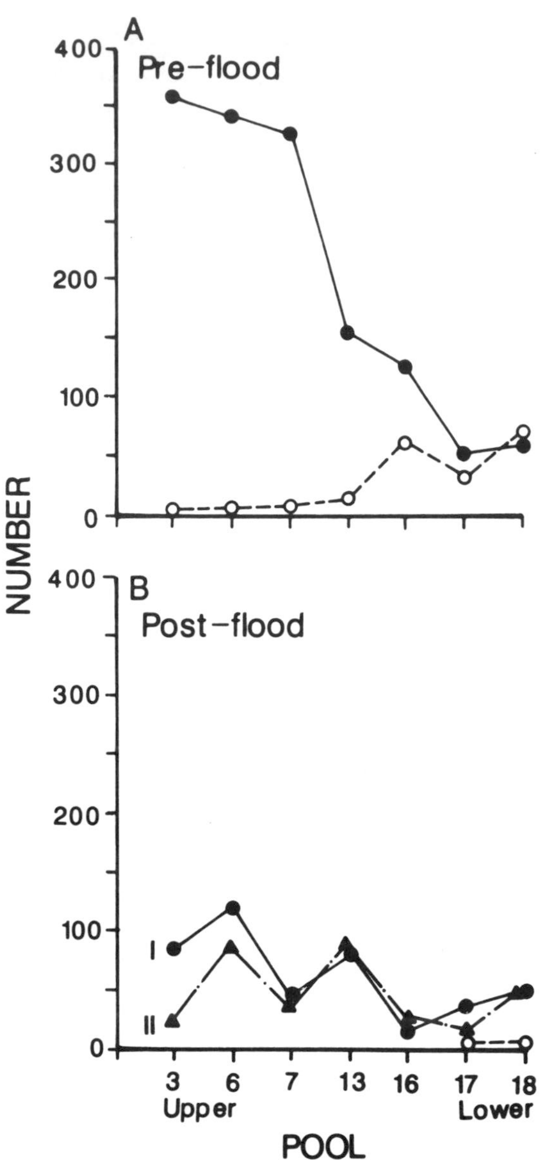

Fig. 12.6. Numbers of adult fishes (solid circles and triangles = native *Poeciliopsis occidentalis*; open circles = transplanted *Gambusia affinis*) captured in each of seven pools in Sharp Spring, Arizona, A, before, and B, after a series of major floods. Pools were numbered upstream to downstream. Consecutive roman numerals in B refer to two postflooding samples about five weeks apart. Modified from Meffe, 1984.

(2) act as delivery systems for water from montane watersheds and thus are unmodified because of their natural utility, and/or (3) are located in rugged terrain and thus are undisturbed because of poor access, tend to be precipitous, and are canyon-bound (Minckley, 1985). These patterns are discernible in Arizona and New Mexico, as well as in recent accounts of centers and patterns of abundance and persistence of native fishes elsewhere in the region.

Moyle and Nichols (1974) recorded abundant native minnows syntopic with scattered, large adults of green sunfish in unmodified streams of the Sierra Nevada foothills of California, whereas modified reaches were often dominated by the transplanted centrarchid. In the Virgin River, Arizona-Utah-Nevada, endangered woundfin (*Plagopterus argentissimus*) and other native cyprinoids are absent from or rare in modified downstream reaches, whereas the native fauna (two catostomids and four cyprinids, including woundfin) remains as recorded in the 1930s, and nonnative fishes are rare in canyon-bound, highly fluctuating, and often hot and saline middle portions of the stream (Cross, 1975; U.S. Fish and Wildlife Service, 1985).

This situation also obtains for fishes of special concern in the upper Colorado River basin. With the exception of Colorado squawfish, which still range widely (Miller et al., 1983a, b; Tyus, 1985), most are now restricted to habitat enclaves in reaches characterized by or associated with deep, swift water or other special conditions in canyons (Upper Colorado River Biological Subcommittee, 1984). Miller et al. (1982) summarized findings of the extensive Colorado River Fisheries Project in Utah and Colorado, reporting 10 native and 21 nonnative fish species upstream from Lake Powell. They commented on impacts of regulation in the system as follows:

> Sediment entering the rivers is accumulating in sand bars and filling the main river channel. There are now more silt/sand areas, braided channels, and aggradation of the main river channel with a reduction of deep runs, clear gravel/rubble areas, and the frequency and duration of overbank flows. A shallower, wider, and warmer river has resulted which fluctuates less seasonally but substantially more on a daily basis. These changes seem to benefit the introduced (exotic) fishes while having detrimental effects on the endemic endangered species. [Miller et al., 1982]

They specifically noted that humpback chub (*Gila cypha*) persisted in deep, canyon areas "too harsh for exotics." In the Colorado River itself Valdez et al. (1982a) found native fishes most abundant upstream and transplanted fishes dominant downstream in a 460-km reach. They forwarded no explanation for this pattern, but proximity to Lake Powell and a relatively greater number of backwater and eddy habitats almost certainly enhanced nonnative fishes in the lower reach, while the upper consisted largely of rapids, runs, and main-channel pools. Tyus et al. (1982) reported the Green River portion of the upper Colorado Basin dominated by transplanted species. However, they also observed that "endemic suckers and chubs were more common in canyon areas where exotics are less abundant. Although more stressful environmental conditions occur in canyons, these endemics appear to be more adapted to them." Comparisons of tributaries in the Gunnison and Dolores rivers corroborated conditions in the larger main stems (Valdez et al., 1982b). Both are modified and regulated, but the former far less so than the latter. Of all fishes taken, 88% in the Gunnison River and 27% in the Dolores River were native.

Conclusions

Declines in the Native Western Ichthyofauna

Native southwestern fishes have persisted in highly fluctuating and violently flooding river systems for millions of years (Minckley et al.,1986) and have obviously succeeded until recently at coping with the rigors of such hydrologic regimes. As pointed out by Minckley (1983), geologic changes have likely caused far more local and regional alterations in aquatic habitats than have human activities of the last century. Major differences are that humans altered these aquatic systems with remarkable rapidity, disallowing genetic adaptation, and that physical changes were accompanied by pressures from hordes of invading forms.

Losses of native fishes attributable in part to establishment of nonnative and exotic species have been noted and demonstrated in western North America for more than half a century (Miller, 1946, et seq.; Minckley, 1984; Moyle, 1984). Interactions identified in declines of native fish populations include competition, predation, reproductive inhibition, hybridization, associated parasites and disease, environmental effects, or any combination of the above (Moyle and Li, 1979; Li and Moyle, 1981; Schoenherr, 1977, 1981; Taylor et al., 1984; Welcomme, 1984; Moyle, 1985; Moyle et al., in press). Of these, the first two seem most important in southwestern waters, although the remainder have not been studied on an other than local basis (see in part Werner, 1980, 1984).

Role of Natural Flooding

It is clear that the more "natural" stream habitats support the greatest proportion of native fishes and that greater modifications lead to fewer native forms. Even in modified systems, reaches most similar to the original state (e.g., erosive, canyon-bound segments where higher flows of regulated streams cause conditions similar to those before modification) support the largest proportions of native forms.

It is further demonstrable that such generalizations apply to other life forms besides fishes. A parallel, for example, exists in relationships among "naturalness" of streams, riparian vegetation, and bird populations. Ornithologists have long regarded native riparian plant communities as essential to maintenance of diverse avifaunas in western North America (Carothers et al., 1974; Stevens et al., 1977). Invasion by exotic saltcedar (*Tamerix chinensis*) has a negative impact on population sizes of many riparian birds (Carothers, 1977; Cohan et al., 1978). Minckley and Clark (1982, 1984) pointed out that diverse native vegetation persists most luxuriantly in canyon segments of Arizona streams, especially in unregulated reaches, while nonnative saltcedar becomes dominant along regulated or otherwise modified segments

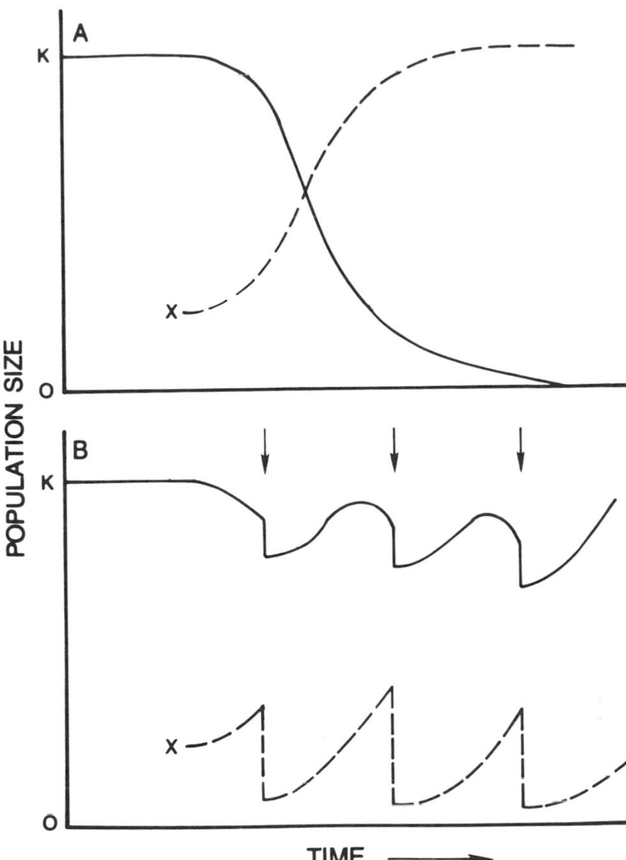

Fig. 12.7. Graphic model of suggested dynamic equilibrium between native and nonnative fishes in unregulated arid-land streams. A: In an artificial or regulated system native fishes (solid line) typically decline and disappear upon introduction (×) of nonnative fishes (dashed line). B: In a free-flooding system, native fishes similarly decline after nonnatives appear, but flooding (arrows) reduce the latter to levels that permit recovery of native fishes. During interflood periods, nonnative fishes again expand populations and ranges and negatively impact native species until the next flood. If flooding occurs frequently enough, long-term coexistence may occur. K = carrying capacity.

and on man-disturbed floodplains (Robinson, 1965; Haase, 1974; Horton, 1977).

Habitat changes that accrue from damming are profound (Simons, 1979), and certainly are far more complex and widespread than normally recognized. Because natural stream channels represent an average condition, tending toward a steady-state balance between supply and removal of water and sediments by adjustment of the geometry of the system itself (Chorley, 1962), alterations in amounts of water or quantity and quality of sediments elicit complex sequences of compensatory changes (Hendrickson and Minckley, 1985). A river channel represents the most efficient geometric form that can accommodate means and extremes of discharge occurring throughout its history (Curry, 1972). Thus water removal from the upper Colorado River basin results in aggradation of the middle portion of the system (Miller et al., 1982), removal of sediments by deposition in

Lake Powell results in degradation of sandbars and other alluvial deposits in Grand Canyon (Dolan et al., 1974), bottoms become armored by remaining larger gravel and boulders, while regulated flow allows even more accumulation of coarse sediments from tributaries that block the river and create greater rapids than before (Leopold, 1969; Dolan et al., 1974), and so on. All are compensatory waves of physical change resulting from alteration of dynamic equilibria (Chorley, 1962; Curry, 1972; Bull, 1979, 1981), and similarly dynamic waves pass through associated biological systems.

Floods maintain the unique nature of erosive western streams on which native biotas depend. Flooding furthermore alters fish-community structure by differential removal of lentic adapted nonnative species, forcing the system back toward a natural coevolved state and allowing lotic-adapted native species to persist. Differential capacities to persist in free-flooding southwestern streams have thus become important determinants of community structure, allowing persistence of native species that are otherwise eliminated by introduced predators and competitors. If floods occur with sufficient regularity, recovery of native species is permitted before they are driven to extinction, and a dynamic equilibrium of the two opposing faunas may be maintained (fig. 12.7). Such a cycle may continue if flooding is regular and strong. If floods are curtailed by damming, nonnative fishes typically increase in numbers to approach 100% of the fauna.

Implications for the Future

Implications of the apparent requirement for flooding to maintain native western fish faunas are critical to consider if indigenous species are to be perpetuated. Trends in rapidly developing arid lands are toward maximal exploition of water resources. Maintenance of any surface water at all, let alone a natural regime of annual discharge, may border on the impossible.

Attempts to accomplish this have involved estimations of minimum, maximum and "optimal" instream flows required to perpetuate fish and wildlife resources (Stalnaker and Arnette, 1976; Bovee and Milhous, 1978; Stalnaker, 1979; Bovee, 1981; Orth and Maughan, 1982). Data are generated for probability-of-use or preference curves, species by species for depths, current velocities, and substrate types (Bovee and Cochnauer, 1977; Orth et al., 1983). Such information is used in mathematical models that estimate volumes of discharge required to satisfy these preferences and allow the species to persist after streams are altered for human use. Instream flow techniques were developed primarily for salmonids (Bovee, 1978), and there are problems and concerns about their applicability to warmwater species (Orth and Maughan, 1982; Moyle and Baltz, 1985; Alley and Reed, in press). Such technology may succeed in streams where near-average flows produce a major proportion of water yield (e.g., mesic systems in fig. 12.3) and where fish faunas are adapted to that moderate regime as in mesic zones, but may fail in arid land systems. We do not discourage attempts to apply these techniques in our region but hesitate to accept that southwestern systems will respond with maintenance of indigenous faunas unless major floods are allowed.

We conclude that regulation of natural streams that includes an end to flooding will result in extirpation of native fish species adapted to what appears to humans to be a severe and unpredictable aquatic system. We recommend that managers dealing with endangered native faunas seek, define, and perpetuate naturalness in southwestern stream habitats despite their superficial appearances of violence and uninhabitability when in flood, rather than attempt to improve on nature through control and manipulation of discharge.[1]

[1]Data for this contribution were collected during projects funded by numerous private, state and federal sources, and we acknowledge them all. A large proportion of the samples was obtained by classes in aquatic sciences from Arizona State University, and their efforts are to be applauded. David L. Propst, of the New Mexico Department of Game and Fish, and Dean A. Hendrickson, of Arizona State University, provided unpublished information for the Gila River and Aravaipa Creek. This chapter was prepared while Minckley participated in an Interagency Personal Agreement appointment between Arizona State University and the U.S. Fish and Wildlife Service, Dexter National Fish Hatchery, Dexter, New Mexico, and Meffe was a Carr Postdoctoral Fellow in the Department of Zoology, University of Florida, Gainesville. Buddy L. Jensen and Sharon Coates, of Dexter National Fish Hatchery, are especially acknowledged for their support. David L. Galat, Paul C. Marsh, Peter B. Moyle, and an anonymous reviewer read, commented on, and improved the manuscript.

13. Seasonal Changes in the Thermal Preferences of Fantail *(Etheostoma flabellare)*, Rainbow *(E. caeruleum)*, and Greenside *(E. blennioides)* Darters

Ihor Hlohowskyj and Thomas E. Wissing

Abstract

Seasonal acute thermal preferences of fantail (*Etheostoma flabellare*), rainbow (*E. caeruleum*), and greenside (*E. blennioides*) darters were determined in the laboratory. Mean temperatures selected by the fantail darter ranged from 19° C in summer to 20.6° C in autumn. Median selected temperatures by this species ranged from 18.5° C in summer to 20.3° C in winter. The fantail darter, when compared with the other species, selected the widest range of temperatures in all seasons. With the exception of spring, mean and median selected temperatures for the rainbow darter were below 20° C in all seasons. Mean values for this species ranged from 18° C in autumn to 20.4° C in spring; median values ranged from 17.6° C in autumn to 19.3° C in winter. The greenside darter generally avoided temperatures below 18° C in all seasons and exhibited the highest mean (23.8° C) and median (25.4° C) values recorded for the three species. Intraspecifically, seasonal mean selected temperatures did not differ. However, mean selected temperatures for the greenside darter were significantly higher than those for fantail and rainbow darters in all seasons except autumn. In that season mean selected temperatures for greenside and fantail darters did not differ. Analysis of the temperature distribution data indicated acute thermal preferenda at or slightly below 20° C for fantail and rainbow darters and above 20° C for the greenside darter. Observed differences in selected temperatures of the three species suggest that the fantail and rainbow darters may be more thermally labile than the greenside darter and therefore less influenced by temperature in habitat selection.

Temperature is one of the major environmental factors governing reproduction (Marsh, 1980; Hubbs, 1985), predator avoidance (Coutant, 1973), feeding (Hathaway, 1927), and habitat selection (Stauffer et al., 1984) of freshwater fishes. Thermal environments in streams often vary considerably from those of lakes and ponds. For example, thermal stratification in the pelagic zones of lentic systems during summer can lead to vertical segregation of fish species (Dendy, 1945; Brandt, 1980; Brandt et al., 1980). Mean summer temperatures in streams usually increase in a downstream direction, thereby creating a longitudinal thermal gradient (Hynes, 1970; Whiteside and McNatt, 1972; Winger, 1981). The responses of stream fishes to thermal differences between headwater and downstream areas may be, in part, key elements in the description of their seasonal distributional patterns and habitat preferences (Stauffer et al., 1976; Calhoun et al., 1982; Maurakis and Woolcott, 1984).

Two types of measurements have generally been used to express thermal preferences of fishes: (1) acute thermal preference, which is strongly influenced by previous thermal acclimation (Reynolds and Casterlin, 1979), and (2) the final preferendum. The final preferendum is the "temperature around which all individuals will eventually congregate, regardless of their thermal experience, before being placed in the gradient" and "that temperature at which the preferred temperature is equal to the acclimation temperature" (Fry, 1947).

When presented with a temperature gradient, fishes will generally select and occupy a temperature range (i.e., thermal preferendum) at which physiological processes are maximized (Brett, 1971; Beitinger and Fitzpatrick, 1979). Hokanson (1977) noted that thermoregulatory behavior is a mechanism by which fish control their occupied temperature and optimize their physiological performance along a finite temperature gradient. Numerous studies of temperature preferences of freshwater fishes have shown that acute thermal preferenda vary with acclimation temperature, geographic area, and season, or are species-specific (Cherry et al., 1975; Stauffer et al., 1975; Mather et al., 1981; Cincotta and Stauffer, 1984; Inhat and Bulkley, 1984).

Darters of the genus *Etheostoma* (Pisces: Percidae) are common in streams of eastern North America. In streams of moderate size fantail (*Etheostoma flabellare*), greenside (*Etheostoma blennioides*), and rainbow (*Etheostoma caeruleum*) darters often occur sympatrically throughout the year. Unlike the rainbow and fantail darters, greenside darters are generally rare in or absent from shallow headwater streams. This species moves into headwater areas in late winter and early spring to spawn; soon thereafter it leaves these areas for downstream riffles and runs (Trautman, 1981; Winn, 1958). Trautman (1981) and Kuehne and Barbour (1983) reported that these three species frequently move downstream to larger and deeper pools in autumn, apparently to overwinter. The differences in longitudinal distributions during the summer months and the seasonal movements exhibited by these species may result partly from interspecific differences in thermal preferenda.

The temperature preferences of darters have been determined successfully by only a few investigators. Ingersoll and Claussen (1984) found that the riffle-dwelling fantail darter selected cooler temperatures than did the pool-dwelling johnny darter (*Etheostoma nigrum*). The observed differences in selected temperatures correlated well with the differences in the thermal regimes of riffles and pools. Hill and Matthews (1980) examined temperature selection by the orangethroat (*Etheostoma spectabile*) and orangebelly (*Etheostoma radiosum*) darters. They found that *E. spectabile* strongly selected lower temperatures than *E. radiosum*, suggesting that temperature could be a proximal cue guiding *E. spectabile* to the thermally stable spring runs that it often inhabits. The less precise temperature selection exhibited by *E. radiosum* coincided with the occurrence of this species in more thermally labile habitats.

The present study addressed the following questions: (1) Are there interspecific differences in the acute thermal preferenda of fantail, greenside, and rainbow darters? (2) Do the acute preferenda change seasonally?

Materials and Methods

Adult darters (mean standard length ±SD [mm]): fantail, 53.7 ± 5.5; rainbow 46.1 ± 4.1; greenside, 65.2 ± 5.6) were seined from Indian Creek (Butler County, Ohio) and Lost Creek (Miami County, Ohio) in January, April, July–August, and September–October 1983 and 1984. The streams and collection sites are described in Hlohowskyj and Wissing (1985). Water temperatures and oxygen concentrations were measured during each collection with a YSI Model 54 Oxygen Meter. Darters were returned to the laboratory and acclimated to a temperature of 20° (± 1.°) C for a minimum of two weeks (maximum of three). During acclimation, fish were held in 20-l glass aquaria provided with constant aeration and a 16 L:8D photoperiod and were fed frozen brine shrimp on alternate days. Although Javaid and Anderson (1967a) reported that starvation for as little as two days affected preferred temperature in salmonids, food was withheld from the darters for 48 h before testing to keep stomach contents consistent (Cherry et al., 1975).

All tests were conducted in a horizontal thermal gradient chamber (fig. 13.1). The chamber was constructed from a PVC pipe (184 cm long, 18 cm in diameter) split lengthwise with ends sealed with Plexiglas. Refrigeration for the cold end of the chamber was provided by a circulating refrigeration unit (Haake Model KT 33). Ethylene glycol was cooled to approximately −30° C in this unit, circulated through 3.2-mm diameter copper tubing coiled along the bottom of one-half of the gradient chamber and then returned to the refrigeration unit (Fig. 13.1). Heat for the warm end of the chamber was provided by a circulating heater (Polytemp Model 73). Warm water from a storage chamber was pumped through 3.2-mm diameter copper tubing coiled along the bottom of the warm section of the chamber. The cold and warm cooper coils overlapped by 20 cm in the center of the chamber. The copper tubing was wrapped tightly in plastic to prevent any possible toxic effects of the copper; both sets of tubes were then buried in quartz gravel (6.4 mm in diameter) to a depth of 3 cm. The usuable depth of the chamber, when filled with water, was 6 cm.

The gradient chamber was covered with safety glass to reduce heat exchange with the atmosphere. After the glass top was divided into 16 10-cm sections, a thermistor was attached at the midpoint of each section, so that the thermistor tips were positioned approximately 1 cm from the gravel substrate (fig. 13.1). Temperatures were monitored with a

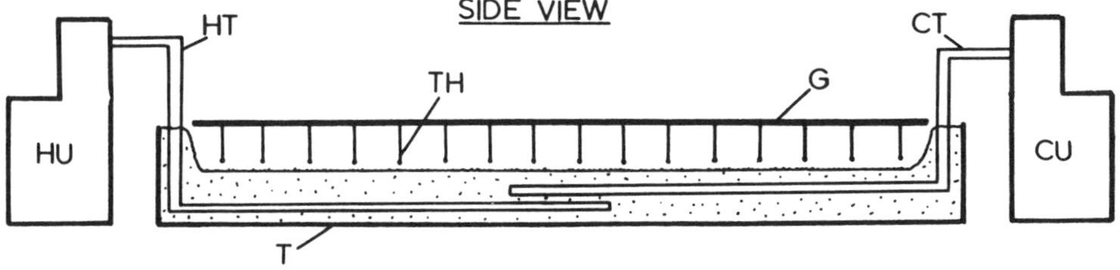

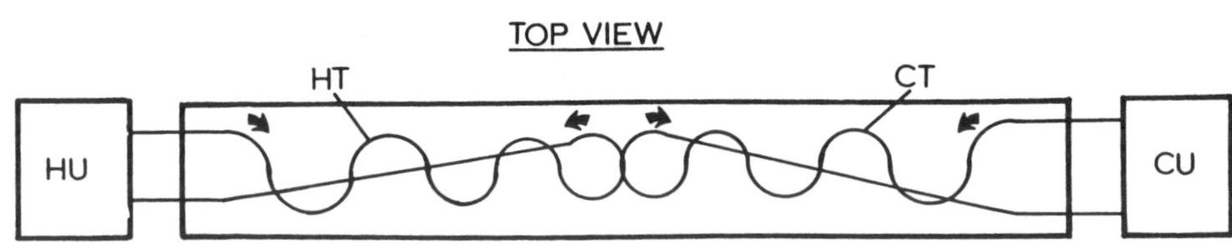

Fig. 13.1. Side- and top-view schematic drawings of the thermal gradient test chamber. Arrows indicate direction of coolant or heated water flow; the stipled area represents gravel. CU, cooling unit; HU, heating unit; G, glass cover; T, gradient tank; CT, cooling tubes; HT, heating tubes; TH, thermistor.

digital thermometer (Fluke Model 2100A) and a multipoint switch unit (Fluke Model 2150A). The design of the test chamber allowed for establishment of a relatively linear gradient of approximately 20° C (range = 10–30° C) within 2 h. Illumination was provided by four equally spaced 60-w light bulbs suspended approximately 50 cm above the test chamber. A mirror positioned along the back edge of the chamber aided in the observation of the fish.

To determine the acute temperature preferenda of darters, the gradient was established; three to four fish of a single species were then placed in the chamber at a point corresponding to the 20° C acclimation temperature (situated approximately in the middle of the gradient) and left undisturbed for 30 min. Ingersoll and Claussen (1984) examined thermal selection by fantail and johnny darters and reported no intraspecific interactions among fishes tested together ($N = 6$). In the present study no interaction among fishes tested together was observed. Positions of fish within the chamber were then recorded at 15-sec intervals for a period of 15 min. A fish was considered as being positioned within a specific 10-cm section of the gradient if more than 50% of the body length was observed in that section. The mean of these observations provided an estimate of the acute thermal preference for each test. Each test thus provided a single data point in the statistical analyses to avoid inflating the degrees of freedom (Mathur and Silver, 1980). Temperatures in the 10-cm sections of the gradient were recorded at the start of each test (immediately following the acclimation period) and at 5-min intervals thereafter. No attempt was made to distinguish between individuals or sexes in recording data; data for individuals not responding to the gradient were not included in analyses. Fish not responding to the gradient would remain motionless at the point of introduction into the chamber for the duration of the test or would immediately swim to a corner of the chamber and then remain motionless for the duration of the test. Of the fish tested in the gradient chamber, fewer than 10 failed to respond to the gradient.

Skewness was calculated by Pearson's coefficient of skewness (Ihnat and Bulkley, 1984). Calculated measures of central tendancy included the mean, median, and 80% modal range (the range of temperatures in which 80% of the observations were located). Distributions of fish in the test chamber in the absence of a gradient (controls) were also recorded and compared to a random distribution (equal number of observations in each 10-cm section) with the chi-square goodness-of-fit test (Sokal and Rolf, 1981). Mean selected temperatures were compared with Duncan's new multiple range test (Helwig and Council, 1979).

Results

Typical frequency distributions of darters in the experimental chamber in the absence of a thermal gradient (control distributions) are shown in fig. 13.2. All control distributions were significantly nonrandom and nonnormal (χ^2; $P < 0.01$), with fantail and rainbow darters showing some preference for the ends of the chamber, owing, perhaps, to the darters seeking cover.

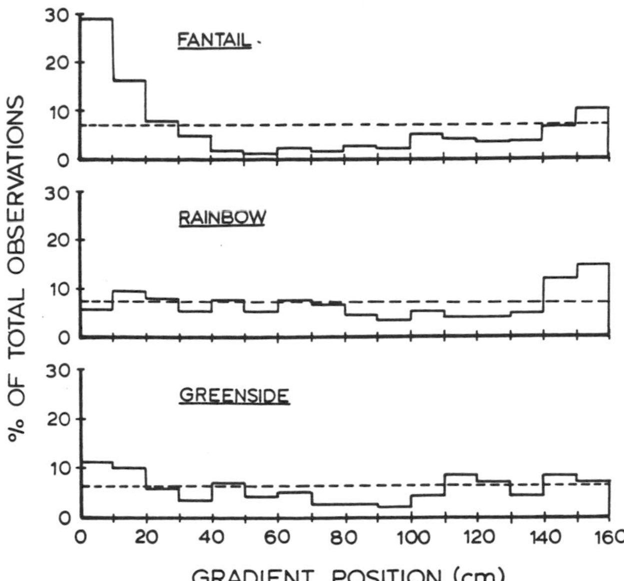

Fig. 13.2. Typical distributions of fantail (*Etheostoma flabellare*), rainbow (*E. caeruleum*), and greenside (*E. blennioides*) darters in the experimental chamber in the absence of a thermal gradient. Dashed line represents a random distribution (even number of observations in each 10-cm section). In the presence of a gradient the left end of the chamber will be "hot."

The entire frequency distributions of selected temperatures (as recommended by Richards et al., 1977) are portrayed in fig. 13.3. The observed distributions of the three species in all seasons were significantly nonnormal (χ^2; $P < 0.01$), with skewness ranging from +0.90 to −1.48; they were also significantly different from the distributions exhibited by the control fish (χ^2; $P < 0.01$)

Most of the temperatures selected by the fantail darter were below 20° C in summer and autumn; in winter and spring the selected temperatures were about equally distributed around 20° C (fig. 13.3). Mean and median selected temperatures for the fantail darter were lowest in summer. Mean temperatures ranged from 19.0° C in summer to 20.6° C in autumn and did not differ significantly ($P > 0.05$) (table 13.1). The median values ranged from 18.5° C in summer to 20.3° C in winter. The 80% modal ranges of the selected temperatures for this species were greatest in autumn and spring; the smallest modal range occurred in summer. When compared with the other darters, the fantail darter selected the widest range of temperatures in all seasons (fig. 13.3).

With the exception of spring, mean temperatures selected by the rainbow darter were below 20° C in all seasons (table 13.1). Mean values ranged from 18° C in autumn to 20.4° C in spring and were not significantly different; the median selected temperatures ranged from 17.6° C in autumn to 19.1° C in spring. The smallest 80° modal ranges for the rainbow darter were recorded in summer and spring; the largest range occurred in winter (table 13.1). There was no significant difference in mean selected temperature between fantail and rainbow darters in any season.

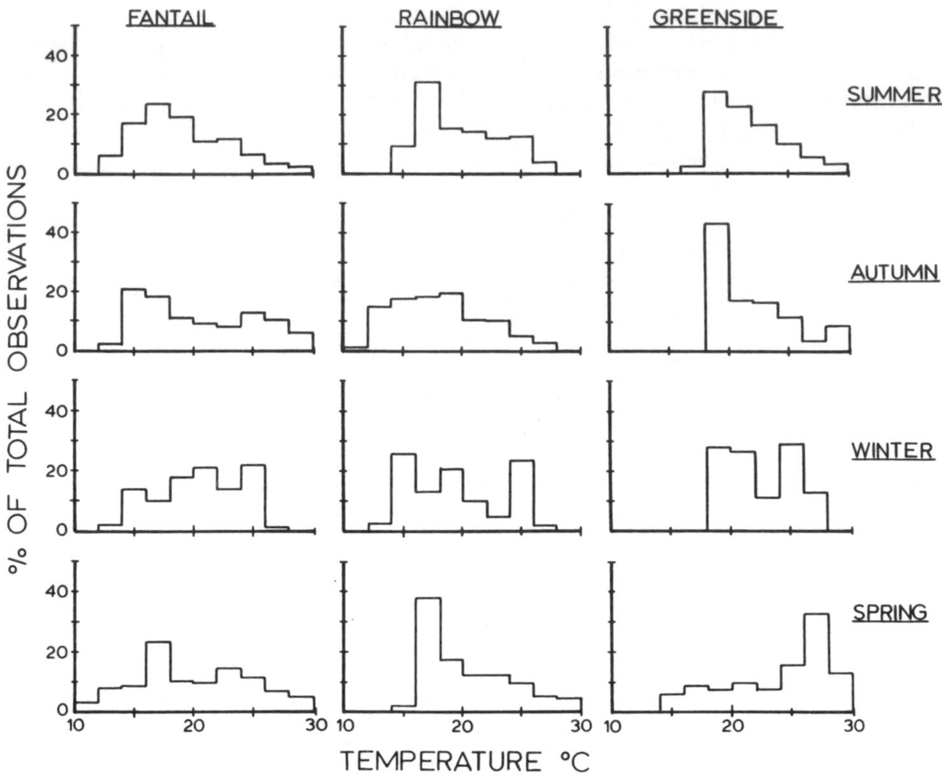

Fig. 13.3 Seasonal distributions of 20° C–acclimated fantail (*Etheostoma flabellare*), rainbow (*E. caeruleum*), and greenside (*E. blennioides*) darters in the test chamber in the presence of a 10°–30° C thermal gradient.

Table 13.1 Mean (± SE), Median, 80% Modal Range, and Skewness of the Observed Temperatures Selected Seasonally by Greenside (*Etheostoma blennioides*), Rainbow (*E. caeruleum*), and Fantail (*E. flabellare*) Darters Acclimated at 20° C

Season and Species	N*	N†	Mean‡			Median	80% Modal Range	Skewness
Summer								
Greenside	23	6	21.4	(±0.39)	B	20.5	18.4–25.7	+0.52
Rainbow	16	4	19.8	(±0.68)	A	18.8	16.0–24.4	+0.83
Fantail	12	3	19.0	(±0.29)	A	18.5	14.5–24.4	+0.84
Autumn								
Greenside	12	4	21.5	(±0.90)	B	20.1	18.8–27.6	+0.73
Rainbow	15	5	18.0	(±1.22)	A	17.6	13.2–23.8	−0.05
Fantail	40	10	20.6	(±0.19)	AB	19.6	14.8–27.6	+1.02
Winter								
Greenside	12	4	22.8	(±1.04)	B	21.7	19.2–26.2	−1.08
Rainbow	16	5	19.5	(±0.84)	A	19.3	14.5–25.6	−1.48
Fantail	13	4	20.4	(±0.67)	A	20.3	15.0–25.4	−0.30
Spring								
Greenside	20	5	23.8	(±0.81)	B	25.4	16.9–28.3	−0.31
Rainbow	8	2	20.4	(±0.17)	A	19.1	17.2–25.7	+0.90
Fantail	30	8	19.8	(±0.44)	A	19.5	13.5–26.3	+0.59

*Total number of fish tested.
†Total number of tests.
‡Mean values followed by identical letters do not differ significantly at $P < 0.05$ (Duncan's new multiple-range test).

In contrast to fantail and rainbow darters, greenside darters did not select temperatures below 14° C in any season (fig. 13.3). This species generally avoided temperatures below 18° C (fig. 13.3); in fact, no individuals selected temperatures below 18° C in autumn and winter. In spring and summer only a small percentage (14% and 3%, respectively) of the observations were below this temperature.

The greenside darter exhibited the highest mean and median selected temperatures of the three species examined. Although mean selected temperatures for the greenside darter did not differ seasonally, values for this species were significantly greater ($P < 0.05$) than those for fantail and rainbow darters in all seasons except autumn (table 13.1). In this season mean values for greenside and fantail darters did not differ. Means for the greenside darter ranged from 21.4° C in summer to 23.8° C in spring, and the median values ranged from 20.1° C in autumn to 25.4° C in spring (table 13.1). With the exception of spring, this species also had the smallest 80% modal ranges recorded for any of the three species.

Discussion

The final preferendum, as noted earlier, is that temperature at which the acclimation temperature and the selected temperature are equal (Fry, 1947). Below this point selected temperatures will be greater than the acclimation temperature; above this point selected temperatures will be less than the acclimation temperature. Examination of the data in the present study shows fantail and rainbow darters to exhibit mean and median selected temperatures at or below the 20° C acclimation temperature. In contrast, the mean and median temperatures selected by the greenside darter are greater than the acclimation temperature. These data suggest final temperature preferenda at or slightly below 20° C for rainbow and fantail darters, and somewhere above 20° C for the greenside darter.

In the present study the greenside darter rarely selected a temperature less than 18° C in any season. Differences in the acute thermal preferenda of the three darter species and the general avoidance of temperatures less than 18° C by the greenside darter may have an important influence on the distributions of these forms. The greenside darter occurs throughout eastern North America. Northward it is found as far as the Lake Saint Clair drainage of southwestern Ontario and is absent from much of the upper Great Lakes and Midwest (i.e., Iowa, Minnesota, Wisconsin, northern Illinois, and Michigan) (Scott and Crossman, 1973). Rainbow and fantail darters, however, have ranges extending into the upper Great Lakes and upper Midwest and as far north as the Canadian tributaries of the upper Saint Lawrence River system in southern Quebec (Scott and Crossman, 1973). These dissimilarities in northward distribution may result from differences in the final temperature preferenda of the three species. Stuaffer et al. (1984) found that the final preferred temperatures of the creek chub (*Semotilus atromaculatus*), fall fish (*Semotilus corporalis*), and pearl dace (*Semotilus margarita*) coincided with the thermal regimes of their geographic ranges and a river system in which they occurred sympatrically.

Examination of the southern limits of the geographic ranges of the rainbow, fantail, and greenside darters reveals patterns in distribution that appear to contradict the presumed relationship between thermal preferenda and the northern limits of distribution of these species. The ranges of the fantail and rainbow darters, with lower acute thermal preferenda than those of the greenside darter, extend farther south (into the Gulf states) than the range of the greenside darter (Scott and Crossman, 1973).

In the present study examination of the frequency distributions of selected temperatures shows that fantail and rainbow darters occupied a wider range of temperatures in the thermal gradient than the greenside darter. Hlohowskyj and Wissing (1985) reported a higher thermal tolerance (CTM) for the fantail and rainbow darters than for the greenside darter and an increased capacity of the rainbow darter to adjust CTMax in response to changing temperatures. Matthews and Styron (1981) reported the fantail darter to be very tolerant of extreme temperature fluctuations. These data suggest that the fantail and rainbow darters, though having lower acute thermal preferenda than the greenside darter, may be more thermally labile, not only in temperature preferences but also in temperature tolerances.

A unimodal response by a fish species in a thermal gradient implies that active temperature selection has occurred, the modal preferendum comprising a specific "search image" (Reynolds, 1977). On the other hand, a bimodal or board response to a thermal gradient indicates that a species does not actively seek a particular thermal regime but moves merely to avoid adverse conditions (Reynolds, 1977). In the present study examination of the distributions of selected temperatures revealed a strongly unimodal response (except in winter) by the greenside darter. The fantail and rainbow darters, however, exhibited broad unimodal or weakly bimodal distributions. These distributions suggest that the greenside darter is more of a thermal "specialist." In contrast, the fantail and rainbow darters appear to be thermal "generalists" and, therefore, potentially less sensitive to temperature.

Autumn and spring temperatures in small midwestern streams are highly variable, often exhibiting rapid and sharp fluctuations. Thus it may be disadvantageous for fishes in these habitats to be very precise in selecting temperatures, particularly in autumn and spring, when temperatures change most rapidly. Examination of the 80% modal temperature ranges derived from this study showed that the fantail darter, which is generally a year-round inhabitant of headwater areas, had the widest ranges (except in winter) recorded for the three species. It also showed high upper limits for the 80% modal ranges recorded in autumn and spring. The greenside darter, which enters headwater riffles in spring to spawn, exhibited its widest 80% modal range and highest upper limit (28.3° C) for the modal range at that time. The rainbow darter, which is another common inhabitant of headwaters throughout much of the year, exhibited a large 80% modal range in autumn and its highest upper limit for this range in spring. These patterns may indicate shifts in thermal preferences and thermal tolerances in response to the rapid and unpredictable fluctuations in temperature that occur during the spring and autumn months. Hlohowskyj and

Wissing (1985) reported fantail, rainbow, and greenside darters to have an increased capacity to adjust temperature tolerance (CTM) in response to changing temperatures in autumn and spring.

The fantail, rainbow, and greenside darters are often found in sympatry in mainstream areas of many Ohio streams. Greenside darters, however, are generally absent from the headwater areas of these systems throughout much of the year. The differences in longitudinal distribution among the darters may result in part from the differences in thermal preference and tolerances to variable environmental conditions. Fishes occupying headwater areas are presumably more tolerant of fluctuating environmental conditions than are mainstream forms (Thompson and Hunt, 1930; Metcalf, 1959; Harrel et al., 1967). Matthews and Styron (1981) compared several headwater fishes (including the fantail darter) with mainstream forms for tolerance of abrupt changes in dissolved oxygen, temperature, and pH and found the headwater forms to be more tolerant than those restricted to more environmentally stable mainstream areas. Hlohowskyj and Wissing (1985) reported a greater thermal tolerance (CTM) for fantail and rainbow darters than for greenside darters and an increased capacity of the rainbow darter to adjust CTM in response to changing temperature. Hlohowskyj and Wissing (in press) also found the greenside darter to be less tolerant of low dissolved oxygen levels than rainbow and fantail darters. The results of these studies suggest that the absence of greenside darters from headwater areas may be due to a lower tolerance in this species of fluctuating and extreme environmental conditions. In summer months mean stream temperature often increases, and stream temperature variability decreases, with increasing stream order (Hynes, 1970; Allan, 1969; Whiteside and McNatt, 1972). The higher acute thermal preferendum observed for the greenside darter in the present study may act to restrict this species to the more thermally stable mainstream areas.

[1] We would like to thank Robert L. Schaeffer for his assistance with the statistical analyses. Dennis L. Claussen is gratefully acknowledged for the use of various laboratory instrumentation, and also for his helpful suggestions for the design of the gradient chamber. Finally, we would like to thank William J. Matthews and two anonymous reviewers for their constructive criticisms of an earlier draft of this paper.

14. Physicochemical Tolerance and Selectivity of Stream Fishes as Related to Their Geographic Ranges and Local Distributions

William J. Matthews

Abstract

Zoogeographic and local distributions of North American stream fishes are a product of many biotic and abiotic phenomena, including physicochemical limiting factors. A large number of studies have addressed temperature or oxygen tolerance of fishes or preferences of fishes in physicochemical gradients, but review of the literature does not clearly show the extent to which tolerances or preferences of fishes directly relate to their distributional ecology. I asked whether a combination of tolerances and "selectivities" (as opposed to preference) comprise the strategies of fishes for coping with harsh environments and tested for the existence of adaptive "types" in harsh versus benign habitats. Among 12 species of *Notropis* those adapted for harsh, prairie stream habitats had greater tolerance for hypoxia and high temperatures and were more selective in oxygen gradients than were congeners from physically benign upland streams. Within one prairie-margin watershed, species persistently occurring farther into the harsh headwaters had greater tolerance for hypoxia than species successful only in the lower, more benign parts of the watershed. Intraspecifically, two widespread species tested in my laboratory showed markedly different patterns in local thermal tolerance. One (*Notropis lutrensis*) had no significant differences in tolerance among populations but exhibited marked variation in thermal selectivity across its range. The results are interpreted with respect to the hypothetical "types" of adaptation for physicochemically harsh environments. Overall, there was good correspondence between the ability of species to cope with harsh conditions in the laboratory and their distribution in naturally harsh environments, an observation reinforcing the concept that physical factors as well as biotic phenomena shape composition of stream-fish assemblages.

In the last 15 years there has been a marked increase in quantitative ecological studies of stream fishes, emphasizing biotic interactions, resource partitioning, equilibrium versus nonequilibrium community models, and the role of mechanical phenomena such as floods in regulating community ecology. This interest in community ecology should not exclude the potential influence of physicochemical factors on the structure of fish assemblages. The premise that differential responses (even of closely related fishes) to physicochemical stress can set bounds to geographic ranges of species or influence composition of local assemblages allows testable hypotheses about distributional ecology.

Probably no one factor pervasively regulates most stream-fish assemblages across the markedly varying streams of North America. However, effects of physical stress may be important in the hierarchy of regulating factors. Streams in North America vary widely with regard to potential stress for fishes. Within many North American streams there is also longitudinal variation in potential physical stress. Distributions of fish both within and among streams may relate to the responses of the fishes to temperature, oxygen, or other physicochemical factors. For freshwater fish, Echelle et al. (1972a), Heins and Clemmer (1975), Kushlan (1976), Harrell (1978), Matthews and Hill (1979a, 1980), Matthews and Maness (1979), Moyle and Li (1979), and Matthews and Styron (1981) have demonstrated strong influence of physicochemical factors on zoogeographic or local distribution patterns. Herein I further develop that concept, based on new data and on the large literature on ectotherm biology.

In North America there are two trenchantly different kinds of streams: (1) "benign" habitats in which neither physicochemical extremes (e.g., annual maxima/minima) nor rates or change (e.g., diel) impose stress on fishes and (2) "harsh" habitats in which absolute extremes, diel fluctuations, or unpredictable schedules of change cause potentially stressful or lethal conditions for fishes at least occasionally. Fish of "harsh" environments should have capabilities for surviving physicochemical stress that exceed those of fish in benign habitats.

In this research I consider "tolerance" as the relative

ability of fish to survive acute stress and "selectivity" as the relative breadth of distribution of a fish population in an environmental gradient (rather than "selection" or "preference," both of which refer to the absolute location on an environmental gradient at which the peak of distribution occurs). While tolerance may set ultimate limits on microhabitat or range space available to fishes, selectivity may determine patterns in their use of microhabitat space within the local habitat or geographic range and thus influence foraging strategies, physiological efficiencies, or overlap among species or resource axes. Tolerance and selectivity (or "selection") of fishes have often been investigated separately, but I ask whether a combination of tolerance and selectivity forms the strategy of fish for coping with harsh environments and propose that these factors should be investigated jointly.

This study evaluates temperature and oxygen tolerance and selectivity of freshwater fishes from streams of the Midwest. Temperature is pervasive in its effects on aquatic organisms (Hutchison, 1976). Small fish have internal body temperatures that approximate external water temperatures; thus profound changes in physiology accompany environmental temperature changes (Crawshaw, 1979). Death occurs quickly outside tolerance limits. Direct death of freshwater fishes from thermal stress has been documented in natural habitats (Bailey, 1955; Tramer, 1978), and Matthews et al. (1982) found evidence of natural heat death of stream fishes at temperatures approximating their tolerance limits in the laboratory. Dissolved oxygen is critical to fish survival, although some species can tolerate limited anoxia. In Great Plains streams local oxygen concentrations become low enough to stress or kill fish (Davis, 1975; Oklahoma State Dept. Health, 1977; U.S. Geological Survey, 1978).

Review of Previous Research

Fish have received much attention from physiological ecologists, providing a broad background for testable hypotheses. As ectotherms in aquatic habitats, fish have a relatively discernible physicochemical history; measurement of environmental conditions in their habitat provides an estimate of the regime to which fish are exposed. While it is clear that fish can follow physicochemical gradients (Matthews and Hill, 1979a), they cannot generally escape gross environmental changes as easily as other ectotherms. Fish are often active near their limits of tolerance (Reynolds and Casterlin, 1979); thus even slight differences in tolerances may provide major selective advantages (Matthews and Maness, 1979, Matthews and Styron, 1981). Finally, tolerance or selectivity of fishes often corresponds with characteristics of their environments (Hill, 1968, 1969, 1970, 1971; Hill et al., 1973, 1975, 1978; Matthews and Hill, 1977, 1979a, b, 1980; Ultsch et al., 1978).

Interspecific Patterns of Tolerance and Selectivity

Relationships exist between latitudinal distributions of some ectotherms and their physiological tolerances (Moore, 1949; Snyder and Weathers, 1975). Trends relating tolerances or preferences of fish to conditions typical of their habitats are indicated by Hart (1952), Brett (1956), Ferguson (1958), Gee et al. (1978), Kowalski et al. (1978), and Ingersoll and Claussen (1984); however, none of these studies focused on harsh, abruptly fluctuating environments. A few studies involving a limited number of fish species show good correspondence between laboratory tolerance or selectivity and success in harsh environments (Hagen, 1964; John, 1964; Lowe et al., 1967; Cross and Cavin, 1971; McFarlane et al., 1976). Among *Drosophila* (Levins, 1969), amphibians (Hutchison, 1961; Brattstrom, 1968), and lizards (Licht et al., 1966a; Kour and Hutchison, 1970) ranges in thermal tolerance related roughly to environmental temperatures encountered by different species.

The literature does not, however, make clear the extent to which finer details of ectotherm distributions correspond to their tolerance of selectivity characteristics. Some studies have even suggested a lack of correspondence between the physicochemical milieu of the habitat and tolerance or selectivity of ectotherms. Brown and Feldmeth (1971) found thermal tolerances of closely related pupfish unrelated to differences in their thermal environments; however, Hirshfield et al. (1980) subsequently found differences among some of those populations. Hutchison (1961), Licht et al. (1966a, b), and Dawson (1967) found some interspecific thermal tolerance-preference differences among ectotherms that correspond more to phylogenetic relationships than to physicochemical characteristics of their habitats.

Other studies have provided important base-line information on fish tolerance or selection but have compared species that were (1) only distantly related, (2) from similar habitats, or (3) from distinctly different latitudes (Hart, 1952; Black, 1953; Brett, 1956; Ferguson, 1958; Cherry et al., 1975, 1977; Stauffer et al., 1976; Reynolds and Casterlin, 1976; Cvancara et al., 1977; Kowalski et al., 1978). Finally, comparisons of tolerance or selectivity among species on the basis of different studies may be inconclusive because of differences in acclimation or test conditions which can markedly affect results (Hutchison, 1976; Reynolds and Casterlin, 1979). Although many previous studies provide information on tolerance or preferences of fishes or other ectotherms, they do not adequately test for the existence of combined tolerance-selectivity strategies or for the relationship between such strategies and comparative distributions of species on harsh-benign habitat gradients.

Intraspecific Patterns of Tolerance and Selectivity

Within a genetically malleable ectotherm species, change in tolerance-selectivity strategies of populations in novel environments could facilitate dispersal into different kinds of habitats, permitting successful colonization of harsh environments or comprising an important incipient stage in speciation. At the other extreme, some fish species may have genetically fixed tolerance or selectivity and successfully colonize only a limited range of habitat types. Some laboratory studies (e.g., Winkler, 1979) and the abrupt border of the ranges of many fish species (e.g., at the edges of uplands) suggest that this explanation could account for extant distributions of some species.

Some investigations have shown differences in tolerance or preference (considered separately) among populations of a fish species (Huets, 1947; Hubbs and Armstrong, 1962; Hubbs, 1964; Otto, 1973; Hall et al., 1978; Matthews and Styron, 1981; Calhoun et al., 1982; Feminella and Matthews, 1984; King et al., 1985), and two papers report heritability of physiological tolerance within different strains of a species (Robinson et al., 1976; Swarts et al., 1978). For amphibians, Brattstrom (1968), Cupp and Brodie (1972), Miller and Packard (1974, 1977), and Hoppe (1978) showed differences in tolerances of populations that corresponded to differences in environmental conditions. Other intraspecific studies have produced contradictory results. Hart (1952), McCauley (1958), Hutchison (1961), and Spellerberg (1973) found intraspecific differences in thermal tolerance of some species but not of others. Others have found little difference in temperature selection among populations despite physicochemical differences in their environments, suggesting that thermal responses are relatively fixed in some species (Reynolds and Casterlin, 1979; Beitinger and Fitzpatrick, 1979; Winkler, 1979; Calhoun et al., 1981; Matthews, 1986b). The literature is thus contradictory, providing no clear indication of the prevalence of intraspecific differences in tolerance-selectivity strategies among populations that occupy contrasting environments.

Hypothetical Tolerance-Selectivity Strategies

Levins (1968, 1969) provided a theoretical and empirical background, suggesting that (1) organisms exposed to great environmental variation within generations may exhibit broad tolerance for adverse conditions through physiological flexibility and (2) organisms having strong habitat selectivity may exhibit decreased limits of tolerance. On the basis of Levins's generalizations, Mayr (1966, pp. 414–15), and a review of the literature, I hypothesized three tolerance-selectivity patterns of fish in harsh versus benign environments:

Type 1: Fishes in harsh, fluctuating habitats might evolve very wide limits of tolerance and be relatively nonselective within physicochemical gradients. A type 1 animal could move freely within a physicochemically heterogeneous habitat or could adopt sit-and-wait habitat use to wait out severe conditions. Although using the available habitat widely, this animal might sacrifice precise tracking of physicochemical conditions that could optimize physiological performance.

Type 2: Alternatively, fishes in harsh environments might, through evolutionary trade-off, have less width of tolerance but be more acutely selective than type 1 animals and more closely track optimal physicochemical conditions. A type 2 animal might sacrifice some of its total use of space in a harsh, heterogeneous environment or migrate more often during severe periods in return for improving its immediate physicochemical surroundings and potentially optimizing physiological performance.

Type 3: In contrast to fishes in harsh environments, those in benign environments (where they are never exposed to physical stress) might have narrower limits of tolerance and also have less selectivity in habitat use, showing less capacity to avoid stressful microhabitat conditions. Questions designed to test these hypothetical relationships between tolerance-selectivity of fishes, harshness of their environments, and their distributions are:

1. Do fish species occupying harsh habitats (on a broad geographic scale) exhibit different tolerance-selectivity strategies than those of benign habitats? If so, do species of harsh environments correspond to tolerance-selectivity types 1 or 2? Do closely related species in benign environments exhibit type 3?
2. Within a watershed does tolerance-selectivity of various species coincide with longitudinal differences in their distributions and to headwaters-to-mainstream differences in environmental harshness?
3. Within widely distributed fish species do populations differ intraspecifically in tolerance-selectivity corresponding to differences in environmental harshness of their habitats?

Interspecific comparisons seek patterns in tolerance-selectivity among species that relate to extant habitats, while intraspecific patterns relate to the dispersal potential of a species and thus to the manner in which fish faunas can become established. Question 2 applies tolerance-selectivity to the phenomenon of longitudinal zonation of fishes, which has been documented in North America since Shelford (1911). Headwaters of streams that are not spring-fed are often intermittent and environmentally harsh and fluctuating relative to larger tributaries and mainstreams (Starrett, 1950; Neel, 1951; Metcalf, 1959; Whiteside and McNatt, 1972). Such intermittent headwaters are characterized by a limited number of species that have been presumed to be highly tolerant of harsh conditions (Thompson and Hunt, 1930; Burton and Odum, 1945; Starrett, 1950), and Matthews and Styron (1981) found significantly greater temperature, oxygen, and pH tolerance of a headwaters species than of congeneric or confamilial mainstream taxa.

Interspecific Differences Versus Geographic Ranges of Species

Various streams in Arkansas contrast markedly in environmental harshness. Large creeks and rivers of the Ozark, Ouachita, and Arbuckle (southern Oklahoma) uplands are characterized by diverse fish communities, strong permanent flow, relatively constant physicochemical conditions that remain within limits of tolerance for fish, and a paucity of physicochemical gradients within localities (Pflieger, 1971; Robison and Harp, 1971; Matthews and Harp, 1974). Although temperature fluctuates seasonally in these upland mainstreams, diel temperature variation is minimal owing to the influence of cool springs or shading by riparian forest.

In sharp contrast to the uplands, many streams of the southwestern Great Plains are wide and shallow, with much variation in discharge. Sluggish flow, direct insolation, and photosynthesis combine to produce harsh diel and annual physicochemical fluctuations, with extremes approaching or exceeding limits of tolerance for many fish species (Matthews and Maness, 1979; Matthews et al., 1982b).

Hefley (1937) described one such river as follows: "Probably no more ecologically dynamic region exists: the seasonal, diurnal, and yearly fluctuations of meteorological factors are great and sudden; the course of the river changes with each succeeding rain and the shifting sand . . . is constantly being moved by wind and water." Daily thermal fluctuations of 10–13° C are common in these streams in summer (Matthews, 1977; Echelle et al., 1972b), far exceeding typical diel temperature changes in upland mainstreams. In addition to fluctuating temporally, streams of the Great Plains often exhibit harsh spatial physicochemical gradients, for example, between mainstreams and backwaters (Matthews, 1977). Reports of the earliest explorers (Metcalf, 1966) indicate that extant physical conditions in streams of the Great Plains are not the result of recent cultural impacts. Water quality records of the U.S. Geological Survey support the assumption of trenchant differences between streams of uplands and plains.

By the end of the Wisconsin glaciation fish species of the central highlands and the southern Great Plains were distributed much as they are now (Metcalf, 1966; Pflieger, 1971). I thus assumed in this research that the species have occupied sharply constrasting habitats similar to those they now occupy for a long enough period of time to be adapted for their environments (cf. Brown and Feldmeth [1971], who suggest lack of thermal adaptation by fish in such a length of time).

Tolerance and selectivity of 12 *Notropis* (Cyprinidae) species in Arkansas and Oklahoma were compared. As a family, Cyprinidae is eurythermal, with species occupying varied thermal environments (Magnuson et al., 1979). However, numerous abundant species are found only in uplands, while others are abundant only in streams of the Great Plains. A few cyprinid species are successful in both plains and uplands, with populations that occupy sharply different environments. In this research I considered a priori two groups of *Notropis*, based on Miller and Robison (1973), Buchanan (1973), Pflieger (1975), Lee et al. (1980), and several hundred fish collections I have made in Arkansas and Oklahoma since 1972. One group, including *Notropis lutrensis*, *Notropis girardi*, *Notropis bairdi*, *Notropis stramineus*, *Notropis atherinoides*, and *Notropis venustus*, I considered "prairie stream" species. They are all common or abundant in harsh stream habitats in central or western Oklahoma, although *N. venustus* is also present in clear upland streams, for example, in the Edwards Plateau of Texas; and *N. atherinoides* is lost from local assemblages of prairie mainstreams in harsh years (Matthews and Maness, 1979). The other group, *Notropis pilsbryi*, *Notropis nubilis*, *Notropis boops*, *Notropis chrysocephalus*, *Notropis rubellus*, and *Notropis umbratilis*, includes species either wholly restricted to clear upland streams or most successful in those habitats. None are typical of harsh streams of the prairie, although *N. umbratilis* occupies some upland-prairie ecotone habitats.

Methods

Adult fishes were collected by seining, transported in sealed containers to the laboratory, and acclimated in 210-l aquaria in a controlled environment room a minimum of two weeks before thermal tests and one week before oxygen tests. Acclimation to homogeneous conditions is necessary for comparison of tolerance-selectivity among fish from various locations: otherwise, differences in recent environmental conditions can cause spurious variation (Hutchison, 1976). Additionally, if fish were tested immediately after capture, individuals from two localities could differ in tolerance or selectivity simply because one environment cycled thermally more than the other (Feldmeth et al., 1974; Crawshaw, 1975; Hutchison and Maness, 1979).

Thermal tolerance was evaluated by standard CTM (critical thermal maximum) methods described by Hutchison (1961) and applied to fish by Otto (1973), Kowalski et al. (1978), Matthews and Maness (1979), and many other investigators, using actual equipment and procedures of Feminella and Matthews (1984). In CTM tests fish were heated at a rate of 1° C/min from ambient so that deep body temperatures followed temperature of water in the test chamber; but fish did not have time to begin acclimation to the higher temperature, which can complicate interpretations (Hutchison, 1976). The endpoint of CTM tests was final loss of equilibrium (Feminella and Matthews, 1984). All tolerance tests were carried out between 0830 and 1530 h, no species being tested entirely within any small part of the day. In tests of oxygen tolerance, fish were transferred to aerated 210-l aquaria or 20-l polypropylene containers and left undisturbed for 24 h so that activity levels or oxygen consumption increases owing to handling (Fry, 1957) could subside. Oxygen concentration in the container was then lowered from ambient to 0.8 ppm over approximately 2 h (Gee et al., 1978) by replacement of ambient water with deoxygenated water from a degassing column (Hicks and Dewitt, 1970). After oxygen concentration reached 0.8 ppm, it was held as near constant as possible, and the number of fish exhibiting loss of equilibrium at discrete time intervals was recorded.

Tests for selectivity of fish in physicochemical gradients focused on the breadth of their dispersal in laboratory gradient chambers measuring 180 cm long × 9 cm wide, with water 3.5 cm deep. The thermal gradient (following Javaid and Anderson, 1967b) was established by introducing cold water from an aerated reservoir at one end. As the water moved slowly through the chamber (about 20 min residence time, thus very low current speeds and no rheotaxis of fish), it was heated by a bank of heat lamps positioned beneath the chamber and individually controlled by rheostats. After some trial and error, positioning of the rheostats was left unchanged, and the apparatus was turned on and off by unplugging the rheostats from the electrical source, producing very similar gradient conditions from one day to the next. Four chambers positioned side by side were used simultaneously in all tests.

For oxygen gradients the same chambers were used, modified by the addition of rigid plastic tubes about 2 mm in diameter along the other sides of each unit. These tubes were drilled with very small holes to permit inflow of oxygenated water from a reservoir. To establish an oxygen gradient, deoxygenated water in the primary source reservoir was pumped into the "upstream" end of the chamber as in thermal gradient tests. At the same time well-oxygenated water was introduced through the lateral plastic tubes, producing a gradual increase in oxygen content of water in the chamber as it moved from the upstream, deoxygenated end to the downstream end. All gradients consisted of realistic ranges of temperature and oxygen that could be encountered by fish in the field.

Following Richards et al. (1977), fish were tested in groups of five in each chamber. Fish were held in the test chambers (with usual flow of water and with temperature, oxygen concentrations, and pH matching their acclimation conditions) for 30 min before the establishment of a gradient. Once the desired gradient was established, positions of fish were recorded every minute for the next hour. Acute tests of up to 2-h duration are recommended for determining responses of fish to a gradient without confounding interpretation owing to onset of acclimation to available conditions within the gradient itself (Richards et al., 1977; Reynolds and Casterlin, 1979).

In the selectivity tests the interest is on differences in acuity of selection (or avoidance) between species, not on the actual values of temperature or oxygen selected. For visual recording of fish positions the gradient chamber was divided into 33 equal increments, and selectivity within the chambers was analyzed and is reported herein in those units for both oxygen and temperature tests. Table 14.1 provides conversion of numbered locations in chambers to measured values of temperature or oxygen. "Selectivity" as used henceforth is based on the concept of a thermal "niche" (or oxygen "niche," as appropriate) defined by Magnuson et al. (1979). They considered the thermal "niche" of a fish in a gradient chamber (with intolerable conditions at both ends) to consist of the part of the gradient including 66% of the distribution of the test fish, centered on the median of their distribution and including 33% of the distribution on either side of the median. In the present tests (warm weather only; similar cold weather tests are described elsewhere) the gradients were adjusted in the laboratory to provide realistic conditions for fish for the time of year. Thus in these "summer" tests fish were offered a thermal gradient ranging from about 15° C (no possible stress) to 37° C (potential stress at one of the chambers only). To describe "selectivity," I have modified the concept of Magnuson et al. (1979) in a one-tailed manner and determined the position in each gradient above which (toward the "good" end) 83% of the positions of fish were recorded. This comprises the median of Magnuson et al. plus the entire 50% below the median (in the acceptable part of the gradient), plus 33% of fish distribution above the median (toward the unacceptable part of the gradient). The result of an entire gradient run is thus reduced to a single number: that location bounding 83% of the fish away from a potential stress. This procedure is highly conservative relative to the comments of Mathur and Silver (1980) about inflated numbers of data points in gradient tests with fishes. In oxygen gradients a similar single value for "selectivity" was determined, that is, that position in the chambers that included 83% of the fish positions toward the "good" end and away from the hypoxic region of the apparatus.

Table 14.1. Temperature and Dissolved Oxygen Values in Gradient Chambers, Interspecific Tests, Summer 1981 and 1982

Parameter		Segment				
		31	24	17	10	3
Dissolved oxygen (ppm)						
(*N* = 36) 1982	Mean	8.57	7.40	6.16	3.32	1.35
	SD	0.62	0.58	0.48	0.71	0.41
Temperature (° C)						
(*N* = 40) 1982	Mean	35.22	31.10	25.09	19.05	14.44
	SD	1.02	1.36	2.58	2.18	1.42
(*N* = 58) 1981	Mean	35.07	31.34	24.66	19.27	14.72
	SD	0.65	1.05	1.62	1.37	0.54

*Entire gradient comprises 33 segments; values measured at five specified segment numbers.

Results

Thermal tolerances (CTMs) differed significantly among all *Notropis* species tested (table 14.2); means ranged from 32.99° C (*N. pilsbryi*) to 36.41° C (*N. lutrensis*). An a priori *F*-test (Sokal and Rohlf, 1969) indicated that *Notropis* species of the predefined "prairie" group have higher thermal tolerance than those of the "upland" group (table 14.2). Thermal selectivity differed significantly among all species (table 14.2), but a priori comparison of prairie and upland groups was nonsignificant (table 14.2). Table 14.3 summarizes the results of tolerance and selectivity of species. Comparison of each species to the overall mean for the 11 species indicates that all but one of the *Notropis* that are successful in harsh prairie stream environments have "high" tolerance for elevated temperatures. The exception is *N. atherinoides*, which, as noted earlier (Matthews and Maness, 1979) is not successful in (disappears from) river mainstreams in particularly hot summers. With the exception of *N. umbratilis*, all the upland species showed poor capacity to cope with high temperature, suggesting that relative differences in thermal tolerance among *Notropis* may indeed relate to their range limits into the semi-arid, hot Southwest. Note that *N. umbratilis*, although classified a priori as an "upland" taxon, does indeed occupy relatively low-gradient streams in some parts of its range, for example, northern Missouri (Pflieger, 1975).

Thus a direct relationship existed between thermal tolerance and geographic distribution of the 11 *Notropis* species, but there was no such pattern for thermal selectivity. Four of the five prairie *Notropis* species showed little avoidance of high thermal conditions (tables 14.2 and 14.3); thus I must conclude that their strategy for coping with thermally harsh environments depends more on tolerance than on acute avoidance of hot microhabitats. Within the hypothetical tolerance-selectivity types for temperature, the most successful taxa in prairie streams thus tend to be type 1, and those of uplands are more type 2 or type 3 (table 14.3).

There were marked differences between the upland and prairie *Notropis* with respect to tolerance of hypoxia. In tests lasting 8.5–10.0 with oxygen concentrations held 0.2–0.9 ppm, four of the five prairie *Notropis* species showed good survivorship (33–84%). In contrast, none of the upland species exhibited more than 5% survival, and all individuals of four species died. The capacity to tolerate low oxygen con-

Table 14.2. Temperature and Oxygen Tolerance and Selectivity of *Notropis* Species from Prairie Versus Upland Streams in Oklahoma and Arkansas

Habitat Type and Species	CTM(° C)	Thermal Selectivity	% Surviving 0.2–0.9 ppm DO: 8.5- and 10-h Tests	% Surviving 0.2–0.9 ppm DO: 35-h Test	Oxygen Selectivity: 1982	Oxygen Selectivity: 1982
Plains–prairie						
Notropis lutrensis	36.41 (86)(1.30)	18.2 (17)(6.4)	84.2 (19)	20.8 (24)	13.1 (7)(7.3)	22.5 (6)(3)
N. girardi	35.92 (42)(1.15)	19.9 (7)(3.5)	65 (20)	17.3 (23)	21 (3)(3)	18 (3)(4)
N. stramineus	36.13 (28)(0.64)	18.9 (7)(4.3)	54.2 (24)	0 (28)	19.2 (5)(7.5)	—
N. venustus	35.89 (35)(1.25)	12.1 (7)(4.6)	0 (16)	0 (11)	23.8 (5)(3.4)	26.7 (3)(0.6)
N. atherinoides	34.47 (26)(1.23)	19.4 (7)(3.9)	33 (15)	14.8 (27)	23.7 (4)(4)	24.7 (3)(0.6)
Uplands						
N. boops	34.98 (65)(0.87)	18.9 (15)(5.9)	5 (20)	0 (42)	26.3 (6)(2.3)	27.2 (9)(1.6)
N. umbratilis	35.52 (15)(0.37)	13.2 (3)(4.0)	0 (10)	0 (33)	26.0 (3)(2.0)	—
N. rubellus	34.56 (35)(1.03)	21.3 (6)(1.2)	0 (1)	0 (35)	20.3 (3)(5.1)	30.0 (3)(1.0)
N. chrysocephalus	34.52 (33)(1.04)	15.3 (6)(6.5)	0 (18)	0 (22)	25.3 (3)(4.5)	27.0 (3)(3.0)
N. nubilis	34.56 (46)(0.68)	19.2 (6)(2.8)	0 (11)	0 (25)	25.3 (3)(1.5)	26.7 (3)(0.05)
N. pilsbryi	32.99 (28)(1.42)	15.4 (5)(3)	4.3 (23)	9 (22)	25.3 (3)(2.9)	25.0 (3)(3.6)
Overall differences (F_s) (one-way ANOVA)	33.64*	4.06[†]	—	—	3.75[†]	5.55[†]
A priori test (F_s) of upland versus prairie groups	189.04	0.016 NS	—	—	155.36*	22.20*
Mean of species' means	35.09	17.44	22.3	5.6	22.7	25.3

Note: Values for selectivity = number of gradient units encompassing 83% of all fish, as described in the text. For each kind of test the mean is given, with *N* and standard deviation below the mean in parentheses. In selectivity tests *N* = number of test runs, not number of individual fish tested; tabular mean value in selectivity tests = number of gradient segments (from "good" end) including 83% of recorded fish positions. Localities of collections available from author on request.

*$P < 0.001$.

[†]$P < 0.01$.

ditions is clearly better developed in the prairie taxa (table 14.3). The prairie species also exhibited significantly sharper avoidance of low oxygen conditions (tables 14.2 and 14.3). The low end of the oxygen gradient averaged 1.35 ppm in 1982 and 2.34 ppm in 1981. In both years the taxa (for example, *N. lutrensis* and *N. girardi*) that are most successful in prairie stream environments exhibited the greatest avoidance of low oxygen concentrations (table 14.2). None of the upland species, which are rarely if ever exposed naturally to hypoxia, exhibited acute avoidance of low oxygen concentrations. The results suggest that *Notropis* species of harsh prairie environments would be more tolerant if trapped in hypoxid conditions, for example, isolated pools, and are also better able to avoid such conditions across microhabitat gradients (= a combination of types 1 and 2). The mechanisms by which successful *Notropis* in harsh environments cope with environmental stress thus include high temperature and oxygen tolerance and acute avoidance of poor oxygen conditions relative to their upland congeners. A direct correspondence between those capabilities and the penetration or success of *Notropis* into prairie environments is suggested.

Interspecific Differences Versus Local Distribution of Species

Brier Creek is a small, prairie-margin stream in Marshall County, Oklahoma. The headwaters are intermittent, arising from pasture runoff, and often dewater for long reaches in dry, hot summers. In all years they represent a harsh environment for fishes. During August 1982 temperature recorders showed average diel fluctuations of 9–10° C in headwater pools and an average daily maximum of 32.6° C. In this same period early-morning oxygen concentration in 10 of 11 headwaters pools was 0.4–2 ppm. Approximately 10 km downstream at mid-reach in Brier Creek the stream is more deeply incised, canopy shades some of the creek, and cool

Table 14.3. Classification of Prairie and Upland *Notropis* Species by Tolerance and Selectivity, Based on Their Outcome Relative to the Mean of All Species' Means for Each Characteristic (see Table 14.1)

Habitat and species	Thermal Tolerance	Thermal Selectivity	Adaptive Type	Oxygen Tolerance	Oxygen Selectivity	Adaptive Type
Prairie						
Notropis lutrensis	High	Nonselective	1	High	Selective	1 and 2
N. girardi	High	Nonselective	1	High	Selective	1 and 2
N. stramineus	High	Nonselective	1	High	Selective	1 and 2
N. venustus	High	Selective	1 and 2	Low	Nonselective	3
N. atherinoides	Low	Nonselective	3	High	Moderately selective	1
Uplands						
N. boops	Low	Nonselective	3	Low	Nonselective	3
N. umbratilis	High	Selective	1 and 2	Low	Nonselective	3
N. rubellus	Low	Nonselective	3	Low	Moderately selective	2 and 3
N. chrysocephalus	Low	Selective	2	Low	Nonselective	3
N. nubilis	Low	Nonselective	3	Low	Nonselective	3
N. pilsbryi	Low	Selective	2	Low	Nonselective	3
Significant difference between prairie and upland species?	Yes	No		Yes	Yes	

seep springs provide permanent water and (in all but driest summers) continuous flow. During August 1982 temperature recorders showed average daily fluctuations of only 1.2° C in a pool in this mid-reach and an average daily maximum temperature of 24.2° C. Oxygen depletion does not to my knowledge occur in mid-reach pools of Brier Creek.

The distribution of fishes in Brier Creek is well known from surveys of five fixed stations since 1969 (Smith and Powell, 1971; Ross et al., 1985). Although we have found some changes in community composition across time at these stations (Ross et al., 1985), there are consistently a distinct, depauperate headwaters fauna and a more speciose fauna at mid-reach and in the lower part of the watershed near its confluence with Lake Texoma. On the basis of our collecting records (Ross et al., 1985) and those of Smith and Powell (1971) for the summers of 1969, 1976, and 1981, I calculated the mean longitudinal position of the common species of Brier Creek from station 2, the most upstream site, to station 6, the most downstream site, for comparison with physicochemical tolerance and selectivity of the species. Following procedures identical to those previously described, temperature and oxygen tolerance-selectivity of numerous Brier Creek species were determined in the laboratory.

Results

Eight Brier Creek species showed no significant difference in oxygen selectivity (table 14.4). Thermal selectivity differed significantly among species but was not related to longitudinal position of fish in the stream (table 14.4). There was no significant correlation between mean CTM of individual species and their mean longitudinal distribution in Brier Creek (table 14.4). Ten of 11 Brier Creek fish species exhibited high tolerance of thermal stress (table 14.4), relative to CTM values (table 14.2) for prairie versus upland *Notropis* species. Only one Brier Creek species, a darter, *Percina macrolepida*, exhibited a markedly low CTM. This species is found in Brier Creek only in downstream stations with permanent water and without thermal stress. Thus virtually all of the fish species successful in mid-reach and upper Brier Creek have high tolerance for harsh thermal conditions; as a result there is no significant correlation between CTM and position in the watershed (table 14.4). We documented very high temperatures for fish (39° C) in drying mid-reach pools in 1980; death of fish from thermal stress occurred at that time (Matthews et al., 1982b). Although such conditions are unusual in the mid-reach of Brier Creek in human chronology, perhaps thermal stress prevails often enough in ecological time that all the common species throughout Brier Creek are adapted for potentially harsh thermal conditions.

In contrast to selectivity results and to results for CTM, none of which showed a significant correspondence to longitudinal position of fish in Brier Creek, there was a significant positive correlation ($r_s = 0.64$; $P < 0.05$) between percent survival in low oxygen (less than 1 ppm) for 8.5–10 h and the longitudinal position of 12 species in Brier Creek. Although virtually all the species are adapted for high temperature, perhaps only those capable of surviving periods of hypoxia can persist in the headwaters. This outcome is consistent with the very low environmental oxygen concentrations in most of the headwater pools that I examined in late summer.

The fishes of Brier Creek also exhibited a significant relationship between oxygen tolerance and successful colonization of a lengthy reach of desiccated and rewatered

Table 14.4. Temperature and Oxygen Tolerance and Selectivity Among Fish Species of Brier Creek, Marshall County, Oklahoma

Species	Rank Order in Distribution Upstream	CTM (° C)	Thermal Selectivity	% Surviving 3 Days < 1 ppm) Oxygen	Oxygen Selectivity
Lepomis cyanellus	1	36.50 (44)(0.51)	30.8 (4)(3.4)	100 (18)	26 (6)(3.3)
Lepomis humilis	2	37.17 (15)(0.72)	21 (4)(3.5)	80 (4)	26.6 (5)(1.8)
Campostoma anomalum	3	35.51 (30)(0.98)	24 (4)(3.7)	67 (9)	24 (4)(4.8)
Lepomis macrochirus	4	36.78 (15)(0.39)	—	73 (11)	—
Notropis lutrensis	5	36.66 (30)(0.83)	23.7 (9)(4.6)	100 (19)	19.6 (9)(6.7)
Notropis boops	6	35.51 (15)(0.56)	27.7 (6)(4.9)	24 (17)	20 (4)(10.3)
Lepomis megalotis	7	36.48 (19)(0.70)	20.8 (4)(5.1)	100 (14)	22.3 (3)(5.9)
Etheostoma spectabile	8	35.78 (20)(0.67)	—	0 (12)	—
Fundulus notatus	9	36.75 (15)(1.32)	27.3 (4)(5.2)	57 (14)	21.7 (3)(2.5)
Notropis venustus	10	35.51 (30)(0.95)	22 (4)(5.9)	40 (10)	21.8 (5)(1.8)
Percina macrolepida	11	31.53 (15)(1.72)	—	—	
Overall differences, (one-way ANOVA)		—	$F_s = 3.24$ $P < 0.05$	—	F_s (log trans.) $= 1.58$ NS
Rank correlation with longitudinal position in creek		$r_s = 0.38$ NS	$r_s = 0.35$ NS	$r_s = 0.64$ $P < 0.05$	—

Note: For each test the mean is given, with N and (as appropriate) standard deviation in parentheses. For selectivity tests, N = number of trials, not number of fish; tabled mean selectivity = number of gradient segments including 83% of distribution.

Table 14.5. Catch of Fish in a Recently Rewatered Reach of Brier Creek, Oklahoma, 1983

Species	3 March	18 April	12 May	20 June	12 July	16 Aug.	18 Aug.	2 Sept.	4 Sept.
**Campostoma anomalum*	4	10	23	35	20	8	8		
Etheostoma spectabile		2	1						
**Lepomis cyanellus*		2	2	30	68	207	195	48	No fish
Notropis boops		4	8		1		1		
**Notropis lutrensis*		4	7	1	3	5	6		
Notropis crysoleucas		1			1				
**Pimephales promelas*			1	15	1		1		
**Micropterus salmoides*				10	33	47	33		
**Lepomis megalotis*				10		16	9		
Lepomis humilis					1	1			
Fundulus notatus					1	1	3		

*Successful colonists.

headwaters. In a late-summer–autumn drought in 1982, a 1.5-km reach of Brier Creek at our station 2 was completely dewatered. This reach of stream remained dewatered until March 1983, when several heavy rains flooded the creek. From then until June 1983 there were continuous water connections between the formerly dewatered reach and the nearest persistent pools of water upstream and downstream. From 3 March 1983 to 4 September 1983 I made monthly collections with small meshed seines in a 350-m reach of Brier Creek at and downstream from station 2 (table 14.5). Fish were identified in the field and then released. After initial rewatering, 1983 also proved to be a harsh year in Brier Creek headwaters; by July there was no further flow between pools. On 4 September only one pool remained; no fish were alive therein. Thus during 1983 it was possible to follow in detail the recolonization of fish into the rewatered reach, the appearance of young-of-the-year of the species, and the sequence of the demise of species as the reach again dewatered (table 14.5). In table 14.5, I arbitrarily designated some species as ''successful colonists'' (asterisked). Those species (1) arrived in substantial numbers from elsewhere in the creek, (2) spawned successfully within the rewatered reach, (3) showed good survival during late-summer drought, or (4) exhibited some combination of 1–3. In contrast, the ''nonsuccessful colonists'' appeared only in low numbers or showed no evidence of reproductive success in the reach.

The successful colonists showed no particular capacity for thermal selectivity (table 14.4), one species (*Lepomis megalotis*) being relatively selective, two (*N. lutrensis* and *Campostoma anomalum*) showing average selectivity, and one showing the least thermal selectivity of any Brier Creek species (Lepomis cyanellus). Apparently, as in broad geographic comparisons, there is little relationship between thermal selectivity and successful colonization of harsh headwater reaches of Brier Creek. Mean CTMs for successful and nonsuccessful colonists were virtually identical, 36.3° C and 36.2° C, respectively. However, the successful colonists of Brier Creek exhibited an overall survival of 93% in low oxygen in the laboratory (table 14.4), whereas the other species exhibited only 46% survival. Thus both on a wide geographic scale for one genus (*Notropis*) and among several families and genera in one small creek there was a distinct link between the ability to survive hypoxia and the distribution of fish species in harsh environments.

Intraspecific Differences Versus Habitats Occupied by Widespread Species

We have evaluated intraspecific variation in thermal tolerance within two common fish species of the Midwest. Populations of *Etheostoma spectabile* (orangethroat darter) from four distinctly different thermal habitats were found by Feminella and Matthews (1984) to have significantly different CTMs, suggesting directional selection for local habitats. This species is widespread in upland and prairie-margin stream environments of the Midwest, occupying somewhat harsher habitats than many congeners that are restricted to benign upland streams. Of the four populations one from a cool, constant temperature spring run had the lowest mean CTM. One from a sharply fluctuating thermal environment exhibited the highest mean CTM, and two populations from intermediately harsh natural habitats had intermediate CTM values. Echelle et al. (1976) demonstrated that *E. spectabile* populations are often isolated, with much local genetic differentiation. Plasticity of the genome appears to be reflected in malleability of limits of thermal tolerance, agreeing with the ''labile'' view of thermal physiology (Hertz et al., 1983) and potentially explaining some of the capacity of this species to occupy a wide variety of thermally differing environments.

In contrast to *E. spectabile*, 18 populations of *Notropis lutrensis* collected from north Kansas to south Texas in May–June 1983 showed no significant difference in mean CTM (Matthews, 1986b). All CTM means were within 0.35° C of 36° C. Such invariance in population mean CTM was surprising in light of the wide range of thermal conditions occupied by the species across this north-south gradient of more than 1,100 km and also in view of a demonstrated change in CTM of *N. lutrensis* populations exposed less than 50 y to an artificially altered thermal regime (King et al., 1985).

Thermal selectivity of *E. spectabile* from the four populations has not been evaluated, but in 2–17 June 1983 I compared thermal selectivity among 14 of the 18 *N. lutrensis* populations for which CTM had been determined. There was a very significant difference among populations (F_s = 6.741; $p < 0.01$) and a pattern of markedly more acute selectivity in populations from six adjacent north-south drainages (Kansas-Oklahoma) than in others farther north or south (fig. 14.1). There is no obvious explanation for the pattern. It does not follow major basin affinities. For example, *N. lutrensis* from Rattlesnake Creek, Kansas, was much more selective than the population from the Arkansas River, of which Rattlesnake Creek is a tributary (fig. 14.1).

Thermal selectivity was not significantly correlated ($r = -0.042$) with mean CTMs for the 14 populations; that is, there was no trade-off between the two characteristics. For example, in the four streams having *N. lutrensis* with most acute selectivity in the thermal gradients (Rattlesnake Creek, Ninnescah River, Chikaskia River, and Salt Fork of the Arkansas River; fig. 14.1) some of the larger (albeit nonsignificant) differences existed in mean CTMs. Apparently, unless the results are unknown artifacts of some laboratory procedure, populations of *N. lutrensis*, while essentially ''static'' (Hertz et al, 1983) in thermal tolerance, may be quite ''labile'' with respect to thermal selectivity.

Empirical Fit of the Hypothetical Model?

How well do the results of these empirical laboratory tests fit the predictions of the hypothetical adaptive types with regard to physicochemical tolerance and selectivity of fishes in various environments? At the scale of zoogeographic range limits, species of *Notropis* that are successful in harsh prairie streams had high tolerance for temperature and oxygen stress. One ''prairie'' form (*N. atherinoides*) showed considerably lower thermal tolerance than did other species of

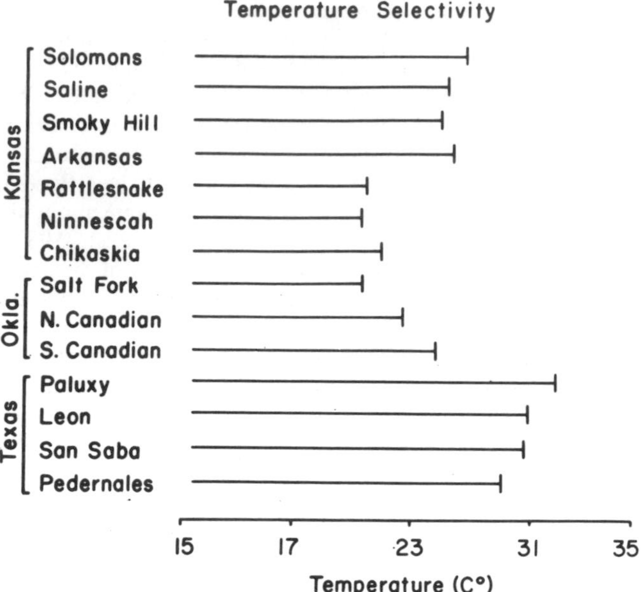

Figure 14.1. Temperature selectivity of *Notropis lutrensis* from streams in Kansas, Oklahoma, and Texas in June 1983, with data from four to six test runs per species pooled. For each species the horizontal line, ending at the vertical bar, represents the location of 83% of the recorded positions of fish, from the "benign" left end (about 15° C). To the right of the position of the vertical bar, in the "harsh" (about 35° C) end of the gradient chamber, only 17% of the population occurred.

this a priori designated group, but it is the species most often lost from prairie stream assemblages in hot summers. *Notropis umbratilis*, classified as an "upland" species, showed considerable tolerance for physicochemical stress. Note that in some parts of its range it does occupy prairie habitats that are likely to be hot or fluctuating at times. The most restricted upland species (*N. pilsbyri* and *N. nubilis*) and the species most distinctly successful in harsh environments (*N. lutrensis*, *N. girardi*, and *N. stramineus*) showed sharp differences in both temperature and oxygen tolerance. Thermal selectivity did not differ significantly between upland and prairie taxa, but the prairie taxa were significantly more selective than upland species in oxygen gradients. Overall, the results show generally good support for type 1 adaptation (high tolerance) in prairie forms, but several of those taxa adapted to harsh environments also showed acute selectivity (type 2) in oxygen gradients. For those species adaptation should be considered an overall combination of types 1 and 2. Virtually none of the species exhibited a pure type 2 adaptation, that is, narrow tolerance limits but acute selectivity or avoidance of poor conditions. Although some prairie forms exhibit acute selectivity (this study; Matthews and Hill, 1979a), it is clear that an innate tolerance of harsh conditions is requisite for consistent success of fish in prairie environments. I thus reject, at least for these *Notropis*, the existence of a purely type 2 species in harsh environments.

At the within-watershed level, interspecific differences in thermal tolerance, thermal selectivity, and oxygen selectivity were not related to longitudinal distribution of fishes across a gradient of physicochemical harshness from headwaters to mainstream. However, there was a correspondence between oxygen tolerance of species and their (1) longitudinal distribution in the watershed and (2) ability to successfully recolonize a rewatered reach of stream. These results suggest that oxygen tolerance of stream fishes may deserve more study and support the conclusion of Matthews and Styron (1981) that tolerance plays a role in longitudinal distribution of fishes in some streams.

At the intraspecific level *E. spectabile* appears to be quite adaptable with respect to thermal tolerance; this adaptability may enhance its colonization of new or novel environments. In contrast, *N. lutrensis*, probably the most abundant and widespread fish species of the Great Plains, showed little difference in thermal tolerance among populations, yet a curious variation in thermal selectivity, the significance of which is still unknown. The finding of similar mean thermal tolerances in *N. lutrensis* populations across a wide part of its range, that is, the finding of "static" tolerance limits in a *Notropis* species, is consistent with the known fact that numerous *Notropis* species have sharp range boundaries at upland-prairie junctions. If further investigation shows the "static" condition prevalent in many *Notropis* species, we may conclude that fixed thermal limits (or oxygen limits etc.) do indeed play limiting roles in distribution patterns within the genus.

Thus at both local and zoogeographic scales the reults of this study suggest agreement between the responses of closely related or of coexisting fish species to physicochemical stress and the distribution of species across the earth's surface. The results reinforce concepts of Smith and Powell (1971) and others, suggesting that harshness of the environment may help sort species into assemblages and thus that the composition of stream-fish assemblages is not solely the product of biotic interactions or community regulation. At times, particularly in environmentally stable periods, biotic interactions likely fine-tune composition of fish communities. However, the degree to which individual species' responses to physicochemical conditions, presumably important in harsh environments, regulate composition of fish assemblages is largely unresolved.[1]

[1]In particular, I thank Loren G. Hill for a decade of strong support for this research and for many discussions and ideas on responses of fish to water-quality phenomena. Others who have contributed much to my thinking about these concepts have been Victor Hutchison and Anthony Echelle; however, any errors of logic are entirely my own. For assistance in the field and/or laboratory I am grateful to Hank Bart, David Edds, Stewart Jacks, David McNeely, Vernon Miner, Bradley O'Neal, Stephanie Contreras Osburn, Scott Schellhaass, and Bruce Wagner. Vernon Miner was an excellent "tinkerer" without whom I would probably never have gotten the gradient chambers to work in the first place. Al Schwartzkopf provided much help with statistics, and Susan Kelso cheerfully typed and retyped the manuscript. This research was supported by a National Science Foundation Grant BSR-8023659.

15. Living Among Predators: The Response of a Stream Minnow to the Hazard of Predation

Douglas F. Fraser, Debra A. DiMattia, and James D. Duncan

Abstract

In a field stream young creek chubs, *Semotilus atromaculatus,* avoided locations containing predatory adult creek chubs. However, they took risks because avoidance of hazardous places was never complete. Aquarium experiments, designed to assay for the behavior of juvenile chubs toward the hazards of predation by adult chubs at different densities of food, showed that in bright light young chubs responded to attacks by rapid escape accompanied by a temporary suspension of feeding. They responded to hazards to about the same degree, regardless of density of food, confirming an earlier study in which it was found that young chubs adjusted their response to hazard but did not take proportionately greater risks when the rewards were greater (Cerri and Fraser, 1983). In dim light chubs shifted to an avoiding response by decreasing foraging and increasing use of a refuge. Predatory attacks in these circumstances usually caused a cessation of foraging. Behavior toward predation hazard was not affected by the size/age of the young chubs. The field and aquaria studies indicated that chubs made trade-offs when confronted with predation hazards. Suggestions for future work include using the behavioral assay for comparative studies involving individuals from habitats that differ in predation hazards.

Most animals experience predation hazards when actively foraging. If predators and prey live in proximity to one another and use the same habitat patches, circumstances may arise in which the need to forage conflicts with the need to avoid predation (Sih, 1980). Energetically profitable patches may also be dangerous (Gilliam, 1982). How do prey make trade-offs when faced with such conflicts? While it is clear that predators can influence patterns of habitat use (Fraser and Cerri, 1982; Grubb and Greenwald, 1982; Sih, 1982; Power, 1983, 1984; Power and Matthews, 1983; Stamps, 1983), less is known about the ability of foragers to facultatively balance foraging and predation avoidance when these needs conflict. Because the balancing of conflicting demands can affect microhabitat selection and habitat use patterns, this question has attracted considerable attention (Stein and Magnuson, 1976; Milinski and Heller, 1978; Sih, 1980; Caraco et al., 1980; Cerri and Fraser, 1983; Werner et al., 1983; Kotler, 1984; Dill and Fraser, 1984; Holmes, 1984).

The pools of small headwater streams present such conflicts to fish whose activities are restricted to pools, semi-isolated by intervening riffles. Under these circumstances young creek chubs, *Semotilus atromaculatus,* are faced with the hazard of predation from adults that are facultatively piscivorous (Fraser and Sise, 1980). Fraser and Cerri (1982) recently showed that young creek chubs avoided locations in an artificial field stream that contained adult chubs, although the strength of the avoidance response was dependent on the time of day and the presence of physical structure in the habitat. These findings suggested that predation hazard could play an important role in controlling patterns of habitat use among juvenile minnows and that use patterns should be further investigated from that standpoint.

Accordingly, in this chapter we report the findings of a field study that used a natural stream to address the question: do young chubs avoid predatory adults, and is the response ameliorated by time of day and physical structure, as was the case for chubs tested in an artificial stream (Fraser and Cerri, 1982)? We further studied the response to predation hazard by using a new method for assaying individual fish for their behavior toward predation hazards (Fraser and Huntingford, 1986). We asked: (1) Given that young chubs are found in the same stream locations as adults, how great a risk will a young chub take, and to what extent is the response to predation hazard dependent on the size/age of the fish? (2) To what extent is the response to predation hazard dependent on light levels?

Methods

Experiments in Natural Stream: Response to Predation Hazard

Fraser and Cerri (1982) predicted that (1) young chubs would avoid locations, e.g., pools, that contained piscivorous adults, and (2) the strength of the avoidance would diminish in bright light and in the presence of physical structure in the pool. To test these predictions in the field, we chose a small headwater stream of low gradient, 12 m/km, at Cranberry Lake, Saint Lawrence County, New York. We selected a section of stream 20 m long containing a series of four pools (surface area 3.7–5.1 m^2, $\bar{x}$ = 4.5 m^2; maximum depth 22–25 cm, $\bar{x}$ = 23 cm), each separated by an intervening riffle. We added stones to the riffles to ensure that there were no small pools that could provide a refuge for fish within the riffle. We screened the experimental section at the upstream and downstream ends with 2-mm mesh wire screen. In addition to screening the ends, we screened each pool with 13-mm^2 mesh screen, a size small enough to confine adult chubs while permitting the juveniles unimpeded access to each pool; we observed that they readily passed through. We selected a single pool, the second downstream (pool 2), as the treatment pool in which we manipulated predator density and structure. The experimental protocol was similar to that used by Fraser and Cerri (1982). We counted the number of juvenile chubs in the treatment pool, without (control) and with predators, at two levels of structure and in daylight and darkness.

After removing all native fish from the study area, we stocked 72 juvenile chubs at a density of 18 per pool. The juveniles were drawn from a community holding tank containing about 100 fish. Because the entire experiment took 10 weeks to complete, juveniles had to be replenished at regular invervals to make up for losses and to make adjustments for growth during the period. We kept the juveniles within a size range that the adult chubs could eat, 30–57 mm total length. The mean total length of juveniles throughout the period was 44 mm. Our general procedure was to allow them 24 h to acclimate before the first sampling. Afterward we seined each pool, starting with the downstream pool, until no fish were caught on successive seinings. Although only the data from pool 2 were used in the final analysis, we seined all pools to be able to account for losses, which were replenished daily. After each daily sampling, the seined fish were returned to mix in the community tank before restocking of another 72 fish. Our recapture success was almost always above 90%.

Predators and Structure

Six adult chubs were stocked in pool 2. They were drawn randomly from a community pool of 66 adult chubs, $\bar{x} \pm 1$ SE = 138.9 ± 2.5 mm total length, range 119–165 mm. To monitor predation, we periodically killed 2–3 adult chubs (total = 33) and determined whether their stomachs contained prey fish. We also compared the daily loss rate of juveniles in the predator and control treatments. We manipulated physical structure in pool 2 by adding seven rocks (each about 7 cm in diameter) and two logs, 0.15 m in diameter × 1 m long. These were organized into piles at one side of the pool.

Sampling

Each treatment was sampled once daily for 6 days. Daytime replicates were sampled between 1100 h and 1400 h; nighttime replicates, between 2030 h and 2300 h. The eight treatments (six replications each) were done during the period 8 July–27 September 1982. Although 48 days were required to complete the eight treatments, delays were encountered as when heavy rains forced us to remove experimental fish and the blocking screens.

The six control replicates (no predator) were alternated with the experimental replicates for all the nighttime treatments. However, of the four daytime treatments (structure–no predator, structure–predator, no structure–no predator, no structure–predator), the latter two were run sequentially with the no–predator controls done first. Although predators and prey were restocked from the community holding tanks in each replicate, the lack of interspersion of treatments over time increased the possibility of temporal correlation of successive replicates. Thus the predator effects in the last treatment may have been spurious (see "Discussion" below).

Analysis

Our design called for counting prey in the test pool, with and without predators (control). The tests were run at two times of day (light and dark), and with and without rock and wood structures in the test pool. Thus the design was a 2 (predators) × 2 (time) × 2 (structure) factorial. The predator effect was analyzed by comparing the number of prey in the test pool when predators were absent with the number when they were present, at each time and level of structure. We used the Mann-Whitney *U*-test (two-tailed), α = 0.05, for these comparisons. To test for interactions among the three factors, we used a multidimensional contingency table analysis (MDCTA; procedural details in Fraser and Emmons, 1984). Because the analysis of multidimensional contingency tables increases the probability of making a type 1 statistical error (Sokal and Rohlf, 1981), we set the rejection level at α = 0.01.

Laboratory Experiments: Response to Predation Hazard

Because we often found young chubs in predator locations, both in the artificial and in the natural streams, we designed a laboratory experiment to assess the feeding response of young chubs when in the presence of predatory adults. We assessed response to predation hazard by means of a factorial experiment in which predator and food density were varied in a test compartment of a 75-l aquarium (29 × 29 × 75 cm). We gave each fish a choice between foraging in the test compartment containing a combination of food and predators and a safe refuge without food. We monitored the number of bites taken for five minutes and the amount of time that the fish spent hiding in the refuge.

Juvenile chubs were seined from local streams and kept in a community tank at room temperature and were fed commercially prepared flake food. The test aquarium was divided into two compartments by an opaque partition. The upper half of the vertical partition was cut to provide a rectangular opening (8 × 10 cm), screened with 13-mm^2 mesh to permit the small prey fish, but not the predator, to pass through. The smaller of the two compartments (one-third of the tank) was designated the refuge. Food and predator densities (0, 1) were manipulated in the larger compartment. A test period lasted 5 min, during which the number of bites taken in each minute interval and the amount of time spent in the refuge were recorded. Subjects were chosen arbitrarily from a community tank. At the beginning of a trial the subject was taken from the community tank and placed in the refuge side. The 5-min test period began when the subject crossed to the test side. Subjects were starved for 24 h before testing. We used live adult chubs, 125–145 mm total length, as predators in preliminary tests, but because individuals varied greatly in activity (some chased the prey, while others occasionally ambushed them), we found that a model predator made of wood carved in the likeness of an adult chub was preferable. The model was attached to the end of a metal rod that was attached to a long handle. The experimenter could maneuver the model through the water from behind a screen, without being seen by the fish. In the predator treatments the model was made to chase the fish (duration 2 sec), once each minute at the beginning of the minute interval. In the preliminary tests with live adult chubs we found that, on the average, they chased the small fish at about this frequency and duration. Commercial flake food, cut into 1-mm^2 bits, was added to the flow of an aquarium pump that carried them into the water column. Depending on the specific test (see below), three densities of food were used: 15, 30, and 60 flakes/5 min. We created dusk conditions by dimming the light to the point at which the experimenter could just see the flakes in the water column. The dim-light condition (53 lux) was provided by a single 15-w incandescent bulb suspended 1 m above the tank. Bright light (538 lux) was provided by ceiling-level fluorescent bulbs.

Analysis of Aquarium Experiments

The tests were replicated 10 times using a different individual for each trial. Therefore, it was appropriate to analyze the factorial experiments by means of a three-way analysis of variance, $\alpha = 0.05$.

Ontogenetic Response to Predation Hazard at Different Light Levels

We investigated the response to hazard by three size/age classes of chub (size/age relationships given in Fraser, 1983): size 1 : 20–31 mm total length ($\bar{x} \pm 1$ S E = 27 ± 4.5); size 2, 32–50 mm total length ($\bar{x} \pm$ S E = 42.4 ± 6.1; and size 3, 51–76 mm total length ($\bar{x} \pm$ S E = 65.2 ± 13.4).

We tested different size/age classes in bright and dim light conditions and in the presence and absence of the model predator. Two separate experiments were done, one at the low food level (15 flakes/5 min), using all three size/age classes, and one at the high food level (60 flakes/5 min), using sizes 1 and 2.

Assay for Behavioral Response to the Hazard of Predation

We used a single size/age class of chub, size 2, to assay for response to the hazard of predation at all three densities of food. These tests were performed in bright and dim light in the presence and absence of the model predator.

Results

Experiments in Natural Stream

When all treatments are combined, the prey showed a significant reduction in the use of the pool with predators ($P <$ 0.001, fig. 15.1, bottom panel). Figure 15.1 shows that in darkness predators significantly reduced the probability of finding prey in the test pool, regardless of the level of structures ($P < 0.01$). However, in daylight predators had an effect when structure was present ($P < 0.01$), but not when it was absent ($P > 0.05$). The latter result is consistent with the MDCTA in that the third-order interaction was significant (P = 0.0002): if structure is considered, the predator effect depended on time of day. The MDCTA showed that none of

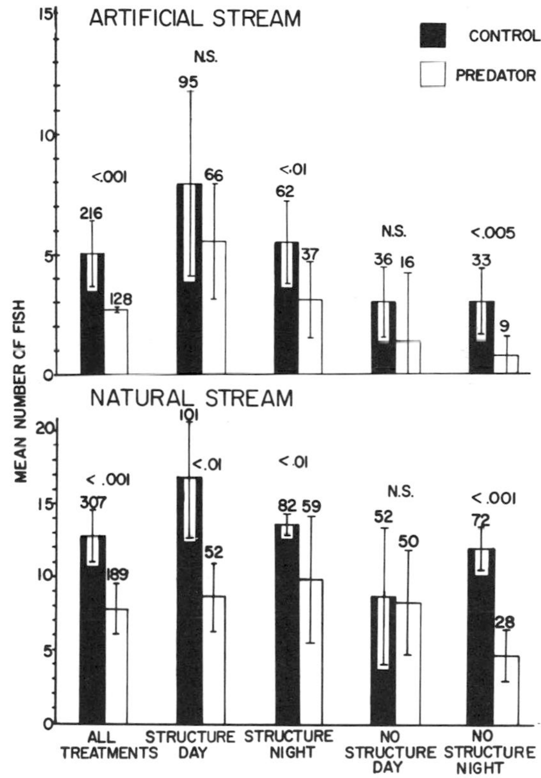

Fig. 15.1. Mean number of juvenile creek chubs in predator (treatment) compartments of the artificial stream (top) and pool containing predators in the natural stream (bottom). Vertical lines are 2 SE. Numbers above vertical lines are total numbers of fish found in the treatment compartments or pool. The *p* value is the result of the Mann Whitney *U*-test comparing the predator treatment with the control (no predator) (data from artificial stream from Fraser and Cerri 1982, Copyright © 1982 by the Ecological Society of America, reprinted by permission).

the second-order interactions was significant (structure × predator: $P = 0.56$; time of day × predator: $P = 0.65$). The lack of second-order interactions involving predators indicates that the predator effect did not depend on time of day alone or level of structure alone.

Predation

Prey losses were no greater when predators were present than when they were absent ($P > 0.05$, ANOVA); in both we lost an average of 3 fish/day. However, predators did occasionally catch prey: 6 of 33 stomachs contained a single juvenile chub.

Aquarium Experiments: Ontogenetic Response to Predation Hazard at Different Light Levels

The smaller prey spent significantly more time in the refuge than did the larger prey, both when food levels were low (fig. 15.2, table 15.1) and when they were high (fig. 15.3, table 15.1). Generally this was true in both bright and dim light. However, the interaction between predator and prey size/age was not significant at either food level, indicating that the tendency of smaller prey to spend more time in the refuge than did larger prey was independent of the presence or absence of the predator. Similarly, the size/age of the prey was not dependent on light levels in affecting time in refuge.

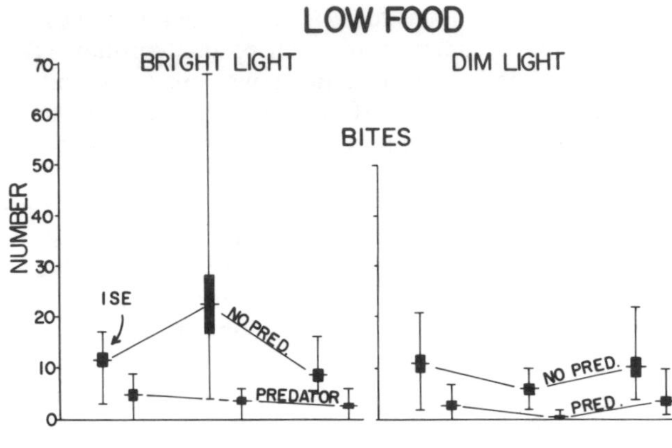

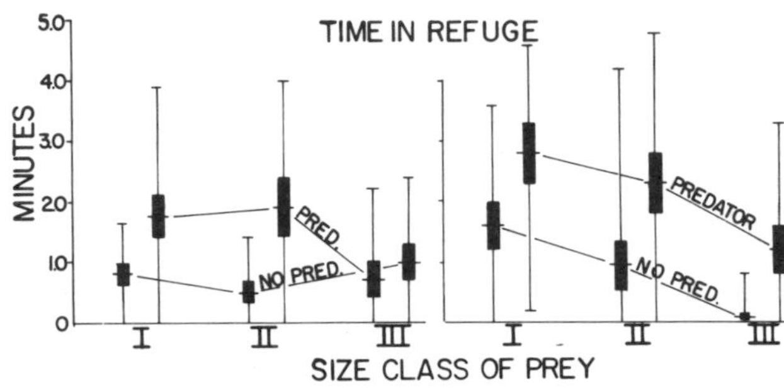

Fig. 15.2. Average number of bites taken in feeding compartment (top) and time spent in refuge (bottom) by three size/age classes of juvenile chubs in the presence and absence of model predator. Range, mean, and 1 SE (bars) are shown.

Table 15.1. Analysis of Variance for Response to Predation Hazard

Ontogenetic Response: Design Is Light × Size/Age × Predator Density				
	Low Food		High Food	
	Bites	Time in Refuge	Bites	Time in Refuge
Source of variation	*F*	*F*	*F*	*F*
Light (*L*)	8.2*	2.9	87.3†	1.4
Size/age (*S*)	0.8	7.6‡	28.5†	11.6*
Predator (*P*)	60.9†	22.0†	77.2†	29.3†
$L \times S$	8.6*	2.5	45.8†	1.1
$L \times P$	3	1.3	9.7†	0.1
$S \times P$	2.5	1.9	20.4†	2.9
$L \times S \times P$	4.3‡	1.3	15.1†	0.2
Response of Size 2 Chubs: Design Is Light × Food × Predator Density				
Source of Variation				
Light (*L*)	106.2†	2.2		
Food (*F*)	19.6†	0.3		
Predator (*P*)	94.0†	51.8†		
$L \times F$	9.4†	0		
$L \times P$	22.6†	0.3		
$F \times P$	3.6	1.6		
$L \times F \times P$	1.033	0.1		

*$P < 0.01$.
† $P < 0.001$.
‡ $P < 0.05$.

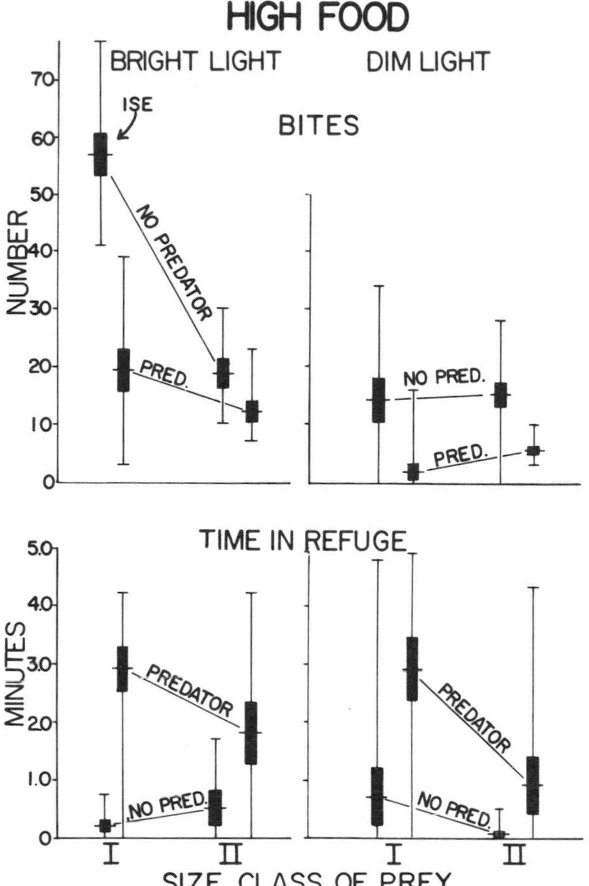

Fig. 15.3. Average number of bites taken in feeding compartment (top) and time spent in refuge (bottom) by two size/age classes of juvenile chubs in the presence and absence of a model predator. Range, mean, and 1 SE (bars) are shown.

Smaller prey took the same number of bites as larger prey in low food (fig. 15.2, table 15.1), but in high food they took more bites in bright light (fig. 15.3, table 15.1). All prey took significantly fewer bites in the presence of the predator. In the "low-food" treatment the predator effect was the same for all size/age classes of prey, in both bright and dim light (light × size/age, predator × size/age interactions not significant; (table 15.1), but in "high-food" treatments these interactions were significant (fig. 15.3, table 15.1): the smaller prey took more bites than did the larger prey but reduced feeding in dim light (significant light × size/age interaction). Further, the predator caused a greater reduction in bites among the smaller size/age classes than they did in the larger one (significant prey × size/age interaction).

Response of Size 2 Minnows to Light, Predators and Food Density

Figure 15.4 shows that the presence of the predator significantly affected the response of the size 2 chub in both bright and dim light. They took significantly fewer bites and spent significantly more time in the refuge when the predator was present (table 15.1). However, they also dramatically decreased feeding in the dim-light condition, even when predators were absent, and the effect of the predators was to cause most of the prey to stop feeding (fig. 15.4). Although light levels affected the number of bites taken, they had no effect on time in refuge (table 15.1). Among the interaction effects, the food-predator and three-way interactions were not significant.

Discussion

Experiments in Natural Stream

The main effects of predators, time, and structure in the natural stream were remarkably similar to those for the artificial streams (Fraser and Cerri, 1982). However, two notable differences occurred. First, the two-way interactions (predators × time of day) were significant in the artificial streams, where prey avoided predators only at night, but not in the natural stream, where they avoided predators in both day and night. Pieces of pipe were used as cover in the artificial stream, but not in the natural stream. Predators hiding in the pipes by day may not have been visible to the prey. Second, in the natural stream predators had a significant effect in the structure-day treatment, but not in the artificial stream. This result must be treated with caution, because, as noted above (see "Methods"), replicates involving the structure treatments (daytime) were not interspersed over time; the six predator replicates followed the six control replicates. Be-

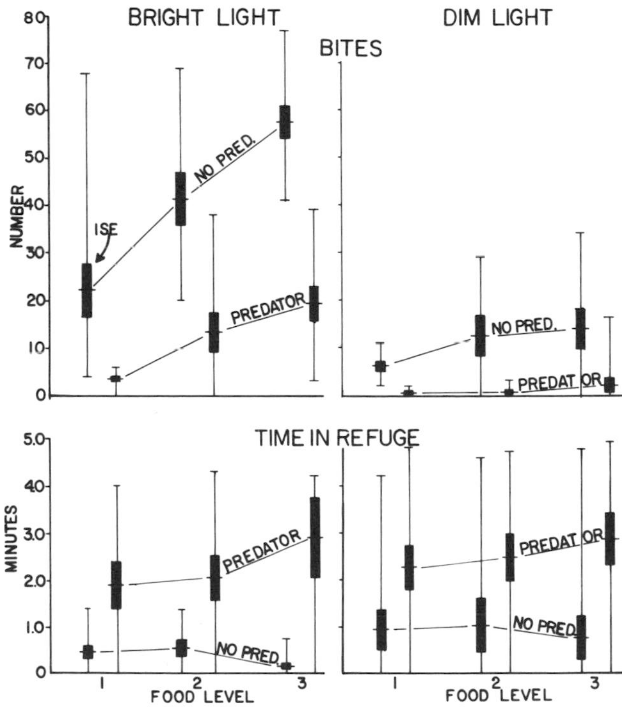

Fig. 15.4. Average number of bites taken in feeding compartment (top) and time spent in refuge (bottom) by size 2 chubs in relation to food density in the presence and absence of model predator. Range, mean, and 1 SE (bars) are shown.

cause it is possible that environmental conditions may have been different at these times, the predator effect could have been spurious.

In the natural stream prey avoided predators to about the same extent regardless of the amount of structure in the treatment pool, while in the artificial stream the level of structure made a difference. The lack of a structure-predator interaction in the natural stream seems reasonable in that there were many places for the small chubs to hide. Addition of structure to the treatment pool did not have as large an effect as it did in the artificial stream.

Helfman (1978) pointed out that juveniles and predatory adults living in temperate lakes may be less separated in space than in marine environments, suggesting that cannibalism may be of importance in affecting community structure in those communities. Fraser and Sise (1980) and the present study have shown that juvenile creek chubs, using pools of headwater streams, may be in close proximity to adults; they were often found together in the same pools. Although the pool use patterns of the young chubs were clearly affected by the predators, these studies have shown that the prey did not always avoid predation hazard by foraging only in safe locations. The aquarium experiments (see below) assess behavior toward predation hazard under different environmental conditions.

How Large a Risk Will a Minnow Take?

Fraser and Huntingford (1986) have recognized four nominal prey responses when predators are spatially near: (1) ignore hazard and eat maximally at all levels of food (risk-reckless), (2) avoid hazard and eat minimally or not at all (risk-avoiding), (3) reduce feeding by the same amount at each level of food (risk-adjusting), and (4) reduce feeding at low levels of food but accept a greater risk when food levels are high (risk-balancing).

The aquarium experiments showed that juvenile creek chubs did not risk-balance; they did not increase proportionately their exploitation level in high food; rather they reduced it by the same amount at each level. Therefore, they may be known as risk adjusters. This finding closely parallels the results of Cerri and Fraser (1983), who found that young creek chubs did not risk-balance when tested in the artificial stream. Dill and Fraser (1984) obtained a similar result with juvenile coho salmon (*Oncorhynchus kisutch*). When tested in an aquarium, juvenile cohos did not take greater risks (travel farther) to obtain the largest flies after exposure to a predator.

Milinski (1985) challenged the findings of Cerri and Fraser (1983), because hunger was not tightly controlled. While this was not possible in the setting of the seminatural, artificial stream, it was possible to do so in the aquarium experiments. Thus it is interesting that the results of the two experiments were similar. If the fish did not take greater risks to enter high-food locations in the artificial field stream because their hunger levels were diminished by being able to find food in low-food locations, we believe it is unlikely that they would take proportionately greater risks in the natural stream, where they could be expected to find some food even in relatively low-food patches. Contrary to Milinski (1985), the evidence presented to date indicates that these fish do not balance conflicting demands (sensu Sih,1980; Cerri and Fraser, 1983). However, this does not mean that they do not take into account predation hazard when foraging; rather, it means that they always respond similarly to hazard, their response being independent of food level. In the aquaria young chubs responded to attacks by suspending feeding for several seconds and remaining motionless. They occasionally swam into the refuge, but regardless of the escape response, they almost always commenced feeding soon after the threat had passed. On the other hand, attacks in dim light usually caused the fish to cease feeding and move into the refuge. In dim light juvenile chubs shifted their response from risk-adjusting to risk-avoiding.

We believe that the behavior of the chubs toward hazard reflects the fact that in headwater streams they live among relatively weak predators and can avoid predation by feeding during safe periods, i.e., in bright light. When attacked, they can elude the predator by executing a rapid escape. We predict that in habitats that contain strong predators, such as bass (Centrarchidae) or pike (Esocidae), small, vulnerable fish are strong risk avoiders.

Ontogenetic Response

Vulnerability to predation by other fish should be inversely related to size. As a fish grows, it should respond less to the same predation hazard. However, as an individual grows, it may actually become more cautious, because vulnerability to other kinds of predators, e.g., birds, may increase. Like many other fish (Helfman, 1981), during the day adult chubs are more wary than younger fish. Gilliam (1982) and Werner and Gilliam (1984) have recently considered how fish may make foraging and patch-use decisions under predation hazard. On theoretical grounds they predicted that, given a choice of two microhabitats, e.g., pools, juveniles should choose the one with the lowest ratio of mortality rate to growth rate, implying that they can make a trade-off and that they are neither risk-reckless nor risk-avoiding. The result for adults is rather similar, but compared with juveniles adults generally require a substantially greater gain in growth accompanied by some decrease in mortality before they will shift from a situation in which mortality is already low; i.e., they shift later than juveniles. Thus adult chubs may be relatively more risk-avoiding than juveniles, and the response to risk lies on a continuum from risk-adjusting to risk-avoiding. Our data support this in that when food levels were high size 3 fish reduced their foraging in bright light even though they were capable of eating more (fig. 15.3). Although adult chubs are crepuscular feeders (Cerri, 1983), the larger prey did not increase their feeding rate over the smaller ones in dim light, but they spent less time in the refuge in light, even under predation threat.

Future Directions

Two directions for future work are suggested: (1) response to risk and (2) behavioral responses to predation hazard. Because the cost of avoiding predators may be high, e.g., lost foraging time, the strength of the behavioral response should be adjusted to the degree of hazard (Stein, 1979). Thus we predict that behavior toward predation hazard should reflect the severity of that hazard: fish from locations with high predation hazard should be relatively more risk-avoiding than ones from places with low hazard. Two types of comparisons ought to be useful in testing this prediction: (1) within species, comparisons of individuals from habitats of different predation hazard (e.g., Seghers, 1974) and (2) comparisons of individuals from different taxa occupying habitats of contrasting predation hazard. Response to different types of predation hazard, e.g., piscivorous fish versus birds, would also be of interest. The behavioral responses to predation hazard described in this chapter should have meaning for the process of microhabitat selection; i.e., we need to know to what extent choices made by the fish affect their growth and mortality rates. Werner and Gilliam (1984) discussed the trade-off between foraging and avoiding predators in terms of size-distributed populations where foraging rates and vulnerability to predators are known to depend on body size. Predictions of microhabitat selection (= pool use patterns) and hence response to predation hazard in these circumstances depend on knowing to what extent growth and mortality rates affect microhabitat selection. For example, a fish that increases its growth rate at the cost of exposing itself to higher predation hazard may decrease its vulnerability to predators at a later time because it is larger. Therefore, experiments that manipulate and measure mortality and growth rates in alternative microhabitats, e.g., pools, are needed.[1]

[1]We thank Edward E. Emmons and Elaina Tuttle for help in the field. The experiments in the natural stream were conducted on the lands of the State University of New York at Syracuse, Cranberry Lake Campus, and we thank its director, Rainer Brocke, for his support. We thank James F. Gilliam, Hiram W. Li, and Roy A. Stein for their critiques of the manuscript. The research was supported by a grant from the National Science Foundation, DEB-8116001.

16. Grazing Fishes as Components of North American Stream Ecosystems: Effects of *Campostoma anomalum*

William J. Matthews, Arthur J. Stewart, and Mary E. Power

Abstract

Algivorous fishes in North American streams have been largely overlooked by ecologists. Our work indicates that a widespread and abundant grazing minnow (*Campostoma anomalum*) can strongly influence distribution or standing crop of attached algae in streams; they thus have the potential to significantly impact biological processes fundamental to stream ecosystems. Studies of this species in a southcentral Oklahoma prairie-margin stream (Brier Creek) showed that: (1) *Campostoma* can control the pool-to-pool distribution of algae, and (2) the presence of predators (*Micropterus*) influences the distribution of *Campostoma*. Other streams in the Ozark and Ouachita uplifts in Oklahoma and Arkansas showed very different patterns of bass-*Campostoma*-algae distributions. In Ozark and Ouachita streams, *Campostoma* were larger, more abundant, and foraged more freely than in Brier Creek. Grazing by *Campostoma* in Ozark and Ouachita streams appears to have a strong influence on the kinds and standing crops of attached algae. We review the distribution of other potentially important algivorous North American stream fishes and outline certain interactions between grazing fishes and other ecosystem components that a priori are likely to be important.

Recent reviews and conceptual syntheses of stream ecology (Vannote et al., 1980; Barnes and Minshall, 1983; Fontaine and Bartell, 1983) have illuminated the historical dichotomy between those stream ecologists who study fishes and those who do not. These important publications include only two chapters specifically addressing stream fishes, plus a few basic statements about longitudinal distribution patterns of fish in streams. Much contemporary literature in stream ecology ignores the fact that large, active, and abundant fishes may play important roles in system-level processes in streams. Most authors have failed to consider the role that herbivorous fishes can potentially play in influencing the distribution or standing crops of periphyton, the sites or rates of primary production, or the processing of organic matter, as observed for grazing or scraping invertebrates by Cummins (1978), Gregory (1983), and McAuliffe (1984).

Important interactions occur between grazing fishes and their plant "prey" in marine habitats such as reefs (Lobel, 1980; Montgomery, 1980; Montgomery et al., 1980; Sammarco, 1983; Meyer and Schultz, 1985), sea-grass beds (Weinstein et al., 1982), intertidal zones (Lubchenco, 1982; Miller, 1982), and tropical freshwaters (Lowe-McConnell, 1975; Goulding, 1980; Power, 1983, 1984b). Hynes (1970) described much of the basic ecology of stream fishes but included little information on the ecology of grazing fishes. Several studies have suggested the importance of carnivorous or detritivorous fishes at the ecosystem level in North Temperate waters (Juday et al., 1932; Hall, 1972; Rickey et al., 1975; Durbin et al., 1979). Nevertheless, native grazing fishes have remained largely ignored as components of temperate stream ecosystems; most studies of organic-matter processing continue to focus on activities of invertbrates, fungi, or bacteria.

At least 42 species of stream fish in North America are largely herbivorous; 24 of these species feed predominantly by grazing attached algae (Lee et al., 1980). Several species (e.g., *Cyprinodon* spp. and *Gila* spp.) occur only in spring or sinkhole systems in the western United States. However, these restricted species are often abundant where they occur and can rival invertebrates as consumers of attached algae or higher plants. Some large, abundant catostomids that are primarily herbivorous (e.g., *Catostomus santannae*, which occurs in four river systems of southern California) can comprise a large part of the biomass of certain western streams.

Many species of algivorous minnows occur in the eastern half of the United States. Some, such as *Notropis pilsbryi* and *Notropis cerasinus*, occasionally have large quantities of filamentous algae in their guts (Matthews et al., 1979; Surat et al., 1982), although in such cases algae likely are consumed incidentally with aquatic insects. Others, such as *Notropis nubilus*, *Phoxinus erythrogaster*, and *Phoxinus cumberlandensis*, feed almost exclusively on algae, which they scrape from the surfaces of rocks. Several of these minnows are among the most abundant fish species in their respective habitats.

The most abundant and widespread algivorous minnows in eastern and central North America are in the genus *Campostoma*. *Campostoma anomalum* ranges across more than half of North America (Burr, 1980a). *Campostoma oligolepis* occurs in the uplands of the Midwest and in the Tennessee River and Mobile Bay drainages, and *Campostoma pauciradii* is found in eastern Gulf Coast drainages (Burr and Cashner, 1983). *Campostoma anomalum* is a large minnow (to 230 mm [SL]) that can be extremely abundant in small or medium-size streams, sometimes dominating the fish community numerically and on the basis of biomass (cf. Lennon and Parker, 1960; Beets, 1979). In one pool (about 100 m long) in an Ozark stream, for example, our snorkeling surveys have provided estimates of more than 5,000 *C. anomalum*, many more than 120 mm total length.

In this chapter we summarize our studies of the ecology of *C. anomalum* and attached algae in streams of the Midwest. We recapitulate studies involving interactions between the grazer and its food and describe a three-trophic-level interaction in which predators (bass) control distributions of *Campostoma* and, indirectly, attached algae. We also present new data providing a broader view of predator-*Campostoma*-algae relationships in several midwestern streams and offer explanations for differences in the patterns observed in different stream systems. Finally, we speculate from preliminary data about the ecological significance of *Campostoma* (and other grazing fishes) in North Temperate stream ecosystems.

Campostoma Anomalum in Brier Creek, Oklahoma

Brier Creek, in south-central Oklahoma, is a small prairie-margin stream of the Red River drainage. A 1-km mid-reach section consisting of a series of 14 pools and their attendant riffles contains a substantial number of *Campostoma anomalum*; this section of stream serves as the site for studies by our research group.

Power and Matthews (1983) noted that *Campostoma* influenced standing crops of attached algae in this stream reach. Four of the 14 sequential pools in the study site contained large schools (50–400 individuals) of *Campostoma* and lacked large predatory fishes. These "*Campostoma* pools" were essentially devoid of algae except along shallow pool margins. Nine other pools lacked *Campostoma* and contained 3–8 large (> 70 mm SL) largemouth (*Micropterus salmoides*) or spotted (*Micropterus punctulatus*) bass. All these "bass pools" had prominent growths of filamentous green algae (primarily *Spirogyra* sp. and *Rhizoclonium* sp.). Bass and *Campostoma* co-occurred in only one relatively large pool. Bass occupied deeper areas of the pool, and *Campostoma* occupied shallower areas. Within this pool attached algae occurred in deep areas where bass patrolled but not in shallow areas occupied by *Campostoma*. As far as we know, this was the first indication in a freshwater stream that piscivorous fish could influence distribution of a smaller herbivorous fish, which in turn influenced the distribution of attached algae.

We (Power and Matthews, 1983) transferred various algae-covered substrates from bass pools to a *Campostoma* pool to assess short-term grazing impacts of *Campostoma*. *Campostoma* immediately swarmed to and actively fed on all these new algae-covered substrates but virtually ignored bare control cobbles relocated within the same pool. Algal biomass on the transferred substrates was dramatically and rapidly reduced; in 24 h ash-free dry weight of algae on the cobbles was < 25% of its initial value.

In the initial study we also showed that bass could alter the use of habitat by *Campostoma*. Algae-covered substrates were again transferred into a *Campostoma* pool, and these substrates were actively grazed by these minnows. A largemouth bass (300 mm SL) was then tethered near the algae-covered rock with a line attached to its lower jaw. Over the next four days the tethered bass effectively "guarded" the transferred algae-covered cobbles; similar cobbles placed 1.3 m away were grazed frequently by *Campostoma*.

Five other snorkeling surveys of fish in the Brier Creek study reach were made in 1983. The occurrence (presence-absence) of bass and *Campostoma* in the 14 pools was inversely related in all but one of these censuses (Power et al., 1985). Bass and *Campostoma* co-occurred in more than 2 of the 14 pools on only two occasions—after major floods. In late summer and in both autumns of the study algae and *Campstoma* were inversely distributed in the pools. However, during spring some algae (predominantly *Spirogyra*) accumulated despite grazing by *Campostoma* and became conspicuous in most pools.

Algae were also intermittently scoured from most stream substrates by large floods. During and immediately after periods of high discharge, then, algal standing crop may have little relation to distribution of grazers (cf. Fisher et al., 1982; Power and Stewart, in press). However, during extended periods without floods (i.e., "normal" low-flow regimes), grazing by *Campostoma* in Brier Creek establishes a clear and recurrent pattern: there is a markedly lower standing crop of algae in Brier Creek "*Campostoma*" pools than in pools that lack *Campostoma*.

Grazing by *Campostoma* can apparently regulate standing crops of attached algae, even when *Campostoma* densities are somewhat less than normal. In autumn 1983 a pool containing bass and large quantities of attached algae was split longitudinally by a plastic fence, and we removed the bass and all large sunfish by electroshocking (Power et al., 1985). We stocked *Campostoma* on one side of the pool (at a density slightly less than that found in most *Campostoma* pools) and left the other side of the pool (and another, nonmanipulated *Campostoma* pool) as a control. Over the next five weeks attached algae on the *Campostoma* side of the pool declined rapidly and remained low for the duration of the experiment. On the side of the pool lacking *Campostoma*, a bloom of algae (largely *Spirogyra*) occurred. During the experiment filamentous green algae were conspicuous in other pools of the reach that lacked *Campostoma*, but not in pools containing *Campostoma*.

Two other experiments in 1983 and in 1984 evaluated the impacts of predators (largemouth bass) on the distribution and use of habitat by *Campostoma*. In these experiments (Power et al., 1985) we added largemouth bass to a pool containing a school of *Campostoma*. In both experiments addition of bass resulted in immediate changes in habitat used by *Campostoma*: some emigrated from the pool, and others moved to shallow-water areas near the margin of the pool. *Campostoma* remaining in the pool after bass were added spent significantly less time feeding and more time hiding among cobbles than they did in the pool before bass were added. Substantial regrowth of attached algae occurred one to two weeks after addition of bass in both experiments.

Collectively, our observations and experiments in Brier Creek indicate that during periods of normal flow (1) *Campostoma* can regulate standing crops and distribution of attached algae and (2) bass can influence distribution of *Campostoma*, both within and among pools. The results from the Brier Creek study suggested two broader questions: First, are the patterns evident in Brier Creek typical of those in other stream systems in the Midwest? Second, does grazing by *Campostoma* have predictable effects on stream algae and stream ecosystem processes? We address these questions below.

Stream Surveys of Bass-*Campstoma*-Algae

In September 1983 and in June–July 1984 we quantified distribution of bass, *Campostoma*, and algae in two Ozark uplift streams and in a stream in the Ouachita Mountains of LeFlore County, Oklahoma (table 16.1). In April 1984 we conducted a similar survey in Brushy Creek (Johnston County, Oklahoma), and in July 1984, we surveyed Tyner Creek (Adair County, Oklahoma). In all of the surveys Matthews snorkeled slowly upstream through each pool, recording numbers of *Campostoma* and numbers and species of *Micropterus*; sizes of all bass were estimated to the nearest inch total length (TL). Algal height and composition were determined by Stewart and Power (September 1983–April 1984), who used methods described in Power and Matthews (1983). In July 1984 algae were asssessed more rapidly by scan surveys. In each pool numbers of invertebrates were estimated by having one person spend 10 minutes picking organisms from all available kinds of substrates with forceps.

In Brushy and Tyner Creeks (table 16.2) so few bass were present that these streams appear to represent *Campostoma* distribution in essentially predator-free environments. In these two streams *Campostoma* were present in relatively low numbers but were widely distributed in almost all pools. One exception was that no *Campstoma* occurred in the four most densely shaded pools of Tyner Creek where substrates on the stream bed were virtually devoid of algae. In all other surveyed pools at least thin, slick coatings of epilithic diatoms occurred on submersed rocks. In the four canopied pools of Tyner Creek rocks were not even slippery to the touch, suggesting that *Campostoma* may avoid areas of extremely low primary productivity.

One Ozark stream (War Eagle Creek) and the Ouachita Mountain stream (Big Eagle Creek; table 16.2). had intermediate densities of bass (*Micropterus* > 150 mm TL in 17–50% of all pools; some pools had as many as 8 bass). In these two streams, however, *Campostoma* were present in virtually all pools, including those with bass (table 16.2). The second Ozark uplift stream (Baron Fork, in northeast Oklahoma) had the largest number of bass per pool that we observed in these stream surveys (table 16.1). Despite the presence of 20 or more bass in some Baron Fork pools, however, *Campostoma* remained abundant. Even a brief inspection of table 16.1 shows that the strong "Brier Creek type" of pool-to-pool complementarity of bass and *Campostoma* does not occur in streams we surveyed in the Ozark and Ouachita mountains; there bass and *Campostoma* distributions among pools were independent ($\chi^2 = 0.942$; $P = 0.33$; 2×2 contingency analysis). Of 86 pools surveyed outside Brier Creek, *Campostoma* occurred without bass in 51 pools but co-occurred with bass (> 150 mm TL) in 29 pools.

At least three factors could account for the lack of a bass-*Campostoma* complementarity pattern in streams of the Ozark and Ouachita uplands: (1) pool size, (2) ease of movement across riffles between pools, and (3) aspects involving prey size and/or predator capabilities. Some Ozark-Ouachita stream pools may simply be too large to be effectively patrolled even by several bass. In larger Ozark pools bass often occupied deeper portions of the pool, while schools of *Campostoma* remained near the substrate on gravel slopes at distances > 1m from larger bass.

Riffles connecting Ozark pools are deep (often 10–15 cm) compared to those in Brier Creek (2–4 cm). Hence most riffles in Brier Creek can preclude movement of large fish like bass at normal flow; but *Campostoma* and bass can readily traverse most riffles in the Ozark-Ouachita streams. Formation and maintenance of bass-*Campostoma* complementarity in Brier Creek may therefore depend in part on restricted movement of fish between pools (which allows time for attrition of *Campostoma*) or on more frequent pool-to-pool movement of prey (*Campostoma*) than of predators (bass).

The specific type of predator and size of prey may also influence bass-*Campostoma* interactions in Ozark streams. Most bass in Ozark and Ouachita streams are smallmouth bass (*Micropterus dolomieui*) (table 16.1), which have relatively smaller mouths than largemouth bass. Additionally, smallmouth bass typically eat crayfish more often than fish (Lewis and Helms, 1964; Carlander, 1977), although they do feed on a variety of minnows (Scott and Crossman, 1973). In this context it may also be important that *Campostoma* in virtually all the Ozark and Ouachita streams are larger than those in Brier Creek. To date we have used nondestructive census methods and thus lack precise length-frequency data for *Campostoma* in these streams. However, the same individual (Matthews) has made all snorkeling observations, standardizing the estimates to a large degree. *Campostoma* larger than 150 mm TL are very rare in Brier Creek; the largest individuals we have collected there are about 125 mm TL. In Ozark streams schools of *Campostoma* (often 100–500 individuals) frequently consist of individuals 125–150

Table 16.1. Numbers of *Campostoma* (Minnows), Bass (by Size, Class, TL), and Invertebrates in Pools of Streams in Oklahoma and Arkansas

Stream (Date)	Pool													
Taxa	1	2	3	4	5	6	7	8	9	10	11	12	13	14
Brushy Creek (April 1984)														
Campostoma	0	9	19	58	17	10	19	30	32	82	5	1	9	
SMB* 150–250 mm														
SMB≥250 mm														
LMB[†]≥150 mm	1			1										
Invertebrates	18	32	31	39	20	‡	24	22	20	39	21	53	‡	
Tyner Creek (July 1984)														
Campostoma	540	110	13	104	23	17	0	0	0	0	23			
SMB 150–250 mm		1									1			
SMB ≥250 mm														
LMB ≥150 mm														
Invertebrates	25	16	21	11	25	13	32	33	‡	‡	‡			
War Eagle Creek (September 1983)														
Campostoma	630	0	800	503	3,000	500								
SMB 150–250 mm						6								
SMB ≥250 mm														
LMB ≥150 mm														
Invertebrates	‡	‡	‡	‡	‡	‡								
War Eagle Creek (June 1984)														
Campostoma	210	33	22	202	210	1,820	120	765	310	25	109	655	254	
SMB* 150–250 mm				3		2						2		
SMB ≥250 mm				4								1		
LMB† ≥150 mm														
Invertebrates	9	10	8	14	11	6	13	17	9	11	12	6	19	
Big Eagle Creek (September 1984)														
Campostoma	112	70	50	50	60	550								
SMB 150–250 mm	3				6	1								
SMB ≥250 mm	2				2									
LMB ≥150 mm														
Invertebrates	51	48	30	45	41	51								
Big Eagle Creek (July 1984)														
Campostoma	186	60	36	50	277	370	105	88	44	250	58	19	37	23
SMB 150–250 mm	3				7	2					2			1
SMB ≥250 mm					1									
LMB ≥150 mm														
Invertebrates	9	13	‡	12	37	27	21	31	29	35	25	‡	30	‡

Note: Numbers of invertebrates = numbers of individuals collected in 10 minutes of picking with forceps by one investigator.
*SMB = smallmouth bass.
[†] = largemouth bass.
[‡]No invertebrate sample taken.

Table 16.1. *Continued*

Stream (Date)	Pool													
Taxa	1	2	3	4	5	6	7	8	9	10	11	12	13	14
Baron Fork (September 1983)														
Campostoma	800	1,000	500	232	2,450	800	50	5,350	3,000					
SMB* ≥150–250 mm		7	3	1	38		6	20	17					
SMB ≥250 mm					6			7						
LMB[†] ≥150 mm					2									
Invertebrates	76	95	107	111	136	134	70	99	91					
Baron Fork (July 1984)														
Campostoma	1,003	1,000	350	1	1,920	1,020	550	16	1,195	120	76	1,490	385	1,220
SMB 150–250 mm +					13	6	5	2	14			5		1
SMB ≥250 mm					8	1								
LMB ≥150 mm														
Invertebrates	7	19	18	44	19	46	30	32	42	20	33	25	30	35

mm TL, and specimens as large as 160–175 mm are not uncommon. Smallmouth bass, therefore, may be less effective predators on the large *Campostoma* in Ozark streams than are largemouth bass that prey on *Campostoma* in Brier Creek. In feeding experiments (April 1985) medium-sized smallmouth bass (ca. 250 mm TL readily ate *Campostoma* as large as those typical for Brier Creek.

Campostoma Behavior

Regardless of the ultimate causes, *Campostoma* in Ozark streams occur in most pools, where large individuals move and feed with little apparent restriction by predators. Understanding the feeding ecology of *Campostoma* permits greater insight into the potential consequences of such unrestricted grazing.

Campostoma typically feed in large schools, even at temperatures as low as 7° C (table 16.2). In Brier Creek pools with slow flow of water, *Campostoma* school when undisturbed. They browse substrates, but schools move little. In larger pools and in shallow areas of Baron Fork pools where flow is greater, schools of *Campostoma* exhibit a distinct pattern of grazing and movement. A school of about 200–500 individuals, for example, often grazes on algae attached to cobble or gravel. Individuals are typically about 10 cm apart, and most orient upstream. The school as a discrete unit often grazes in a given area for 1–2.5 min; members of the school then cease feeding in unison, drift 3–5 m downstream, and resume grazing. A series of such grazing-drifting sequences continues until the school is displaced a considerable distance downstream. Eventually fish in the school move upstream, and the entire grazing-drifting sequence is initiated again.

The pattern is not always as consistent as described; sometimes *Campostoma* schools browse upstream into the current or show little net movement. However, repeated observations suggest that (1) the schools have discrete grazing patterns, (2) schools graze relatively large areas each day, and (3) within-pool grazing movements may depend on pool size, depth, and water velocity. The extent to which *Campostoma* grazing and movement depend on availability of algae or on predators, or what cues influence their behavior, remains unknown.

Campostoma have distinct feeding modes that appear to be influenced by availability of particular types of food. The most common feeding mode in Brier Creek, where *Campostoma* often forage in deposits of detritus or on epiphytes growing on *Chara*, is "nipping"; this mode is similar to that described for *Poecilia* (Dussault and Kramer, 1978). In nipping, *Campostoma* incline their bodies at about 45° to the substrate and take small, rapid bites. At times several individuals may take turns nipping at one small location on the substrate, suggesting that they are selective and that they receive foraging cues from each other. Detritus in Brier Creek "*Campostoma* pools" contains few high-quality food items (intact algal cells), and these pools also have a low algal standing crop. In such conditions selectivity would be beneficial.

"Swiping" is the most common feeding mode displayed by *Campostoma* in Ozark streams. This mode is used to detach blue-green and diatomaceous algae growing as dense, 1- to 2-mm-thick felts on rock surfaces. In swiping, *Campostoma* position themselves above the substrate, hold their bodies rigid, manuever with rapid pectoral fin beats, and then strike the algae suddenly with sharp sideways thrusts of the head so that the cartilaginous lower jaw scrapes algae from

Table 16.2. Feeding Rates of *Campostoma**

Date	Temp. (°C)	Location	SL (mm)	$\bar{x}$	SE	N[†]
Nov. 1982	17	Brier Creek	50–60	16.7	1.5	28
Nov. 1982	17	Brier Creek	50–60	8.9	1.9	21
Dec. 1982	7	Brier Creek	50–60	11.2	2.1	10
Nov. 1982	10	Baron Fork	50–130	15.2	3.1	17
June 1984	25	Brier Creek	40–80	10.8	2.3	35

*Bites per minute.
[†]Number of individual fish observed and timed.

the rocks. This feeding mode is physically more vigorous than nipping. Swiping leaves distinct grazing scars on rock, wood, or leaf substrates (Matthews et al., 1986). Often a fish makes two "swipes" in rapid succession, leaving a pair of grazing scars. Grazing scars are common where schools of *Campostoma* have fed.

A third grazing mode, "shoveling," is used by *Campostoma* when they feed on algae attached to large, smooth rock surfaces. In shoveling, *Campostoma* push their lower jaws against the substrate and swim forward, removing algae en route. *Campostoma* feeding in this manner make grazing trails several cm long; these trails are readily distinguished from the more meandering trails left by snails. Kraatz (1923) observed similar behavior of *Campostoma* feeding on diatomaceous mats on aquarium walls.

When grazing on blue-green algal felts, *Campostoma* do not remove algae down to the bare rock surface. Microscopic examination of typical scars indicates that the fish remove only the upper layers of algae and on epialgal layer of mucilaginous material heavily invested with bacteria. A thin film of algae (about 10% of the pregrazed crop) typically remains within the scars.

The grazing scars left by *Campostoma* often cover much of the available rock substrates where schools have recently worked. We (Matthews et al., 1986) quantified the number and sizes of grazing scars left by *Campostoma* in a pool with bedrock substrate and predominantly blue-green algal felts (Tyner Creek, Oklahoma). At depths of 10 to 59 cm the number of grazing scars attributable to *Campostoma* averaged 1,800 per m^2; these data included numerous sites in water < 20 cm deep, where there were few or no scars. At depths > 40 cm we found $> 5{,}000$ grazing scars per m^2. The size of individual scars was highly variable but averaged 0.57 cm^2 ($N = 90$). Thus across all depths in this part of Tyner Creek about 10% of the submersed substrate area exhibited evidence of grazing by *Campostoma*. In deeper areas with $>$ 5,000 scars per m^2, as much as 28.5% of surface areas of substrate was, on average, recently grazed.

Consequences of Herbivory by *Campostoma*

Huge schools of *Campostoma*, some containing thousands of individuals, are common in some Ozark streams. Such streams show evidence of intense grazing by *Campostoma*; the grazing scars produced by these minnows often coalesce, covering most of the surface area of heavily grazed substrates. In Baron Fork of the Illinois River, *Campostoma* are extremely abundant, and the standing crop of algae is consistently low. Epilithic communities of algae in this stream are primarily slick, dark-colored blue-green felts 1–2 mm thick. Although thin, these felts are highly productive (0.6 g $0_2/m^2/h$; Stewart, unpub. data), suggesting that the relatively low standing crop of algae (108–325 g dry weight/m^2) is more likely the result of biomass removal by grazing than of low rates of algal growth (cf. Gregory, 1983). On the basis of our censuses and observations to date, *Campostoma* appear to be the major herbivores in this and many other Ozark Mountain streams. What are the ecological consequences of intense herbivory by stream fishes?

Consequences of Herbivory by *Campostoma* to algae

In October 1984 we incubated glazed ceramic tiles in Fiberglas troughs in Baron Fork. The troughs permitted substantial through-flow of water but excluded *Campostoma*, snails, and crayfish. Chironomids gained access to the tiles, but their characteristic grazing pattern (a circular area cleared around their point of attachment) permitted areas they affected to be readily identified. In the stream outside the troughs, where *Campostoma* grazed heavily, the typical algal flora consisted of a 1- to 2-mm-thick felt of epilithic blue-green algae (largely *Calothrix*, *Phormidium* and *Oscillatoria* spp.). Tiles incubated within the troughs rapidly developed a diatomaceous flora dominated by *Melosira*, *Cymbella* and *Synedra* spp. (Power et al., unpub. data). When these tiles were moved to the stream bed, they were actively grazed by *Campostoma*; the diatoms turfs were within weeks replaced by blue-green felts. Conversely, natural felt-covered slate substrates transferred from the stream bed into the troughs were overgrown by diatoms within 4–10 days. *Campostoma* finally gained access to the ends of the troughs (because of sagging of the ends) and grazed on algae growing on the tiles. These grazed tiles also developed blue-green felts, thereby ruling out "trough effects" as a cause of differences noted for substrates exposed to and protected from grazing by *Campostoma*. These results show that (1) grazing by *Campostoma* can maintain low standing crops of algae on rocks of Ozark streams, and (2) grazing by *Campostoma* alters taxonomic composition of the algal community that develops.

That herbivory by *Campostoma* has the potential to regulate standing crops or kinds of stream algae during much of the year is suggested by all of our studies in Brier Creek and in streams of the Ozark region. Because grazing by *Campostoma* typically removes mainly the algal overstory, light and nutrients are more available to algae remaining within the grazing scars. Moderate intensities of grazing by *Campostoma* therefore stimulate primary productivity per unit algal biomass. Additionally, microscopic examination of *Campostoma* feces shows that some fraction of the ingested algae pass successfully through the gut and remain viable. Although we have some data suggesting that epiphytic diatoms suffer greater mortality than their filamentous green algal hosts in passage through the alimentary canal of *Campostoma*, additional data are needed before we can determine the consequence to algae of passing through the gut of *Campostoma*. *Campostoma* could conceivably benefit some filamentous algae (e.g., *Rhizoclonium*) by "stripping" them of encrusting epiphytes (cf. Lubchenco, 1983).

Campostoma feces contain both "regenerated" nutrients and viable algae; the feces accumulate in large quantities in deeper areas of all Brier Creek "*Campostoma* pools," and are reworked frequently by *Campostoma* when algae are scarce. Nutrient translocation as a result of fish activity is important in reef systems (c.f. Meyer and Helfman, 1983; Meyer and Schultz, 1985) and has been shown to be important in freshwater streams (Hall, 1972; Durbin et al., 1979). The significance of the accumulation of *Campostoma* feces to the ecology of algae that are not consumed or to those that are consumed but survive gut passage remains unknown.

To date we know little about relationships between *Campostoma* and the spatial distribution of algal biomass and productivity. In a tropical stream Power (1983, 1984) showed that densities of grazing catfish tracked algal productivity; catfish were seven times more dense in sunlit pools, where primary productivity was 6–7 times higher than in dark pools. Our data from Tyner Creek suggest that *Campostoma* are absent where extensive canopy cover limits algal growth. Although removal of algae by grazing and subsequent recovery of algae in previously grazed areas undoubtedly affects the way stream habitat is used by *Campostoma* and other stream algivores, data addressing these aspects are still unavailable; much remains to be learned about dynamics of grazing fishes and the distributions of algae in North American streams.

Consequences to Other Stream Biota

Periphyton communities provide refugia for a variety of invertebrates (Cuker, 1983), and removal of erect or foliose algae has important consequences to stream invertebrates. We found relatively similar numbers of invertebrates in pools with few or many *Campostoma* in the Ozark and Ouachita streams we surveyed (table 16.1), but the scale of our observations or our collecting techniques may have been inadequate to detect differences. Herbivory by *Campostoma* might influence stream invertebrates in two ways: first, grazing by *Campostoma* alters the standing crop and growth forms of algae and so alters the types or amounts of food or shelter available to grazing invertebrates; second, *Campostoma* could promote downstream drift of stream invertebrates if their disturbance of algae and rock substrates causes invertebrates to enter the water column. If *Campostoma* remove algae that harbors invertebrates or increases their emigration, a given stream reach may support fewer invertebrates and, therefore, be a less profitable place for insectivorous minnows to forage. Our snorkeling observations suggest that stream reaches containing many *Campostoma* have a lower diversity of other small fishes (compared to typical stream segments not dominated by *Campostoma*), but additional data in a range of stream types are needed to evaluate quantitatively the impact of high densities of *Campostoma* on fish-community structure.

Positive interactions between *Campostoma* and other fishes could also exist. For example, our snorkeling observations in numerous Ozark streams reveal that *Campostoma* and *Notropis pilsbryi* often occur in the same pools, in very close proximity or actually intermixed. Feeding opportunities for *N. pilsbryi* may be improved by the grazing activities of *Campostoma*, the former consuming invertebrates made available in the water column by grazing activities of the latter.

Consequences to the Stream Ecosystem

Grazing by *Campostoma* initiates a cascade of effects apparent at both large and small spatial scales. At the whole-stream level these effects can be expected to include large-scale changes in patterns of nutrient uptake, regeneration, and downstream transport; changes in overall rates of primary production and in the sites and rates of decomposition; and increases (or decreases, depending on flow regimes) in the degree of spatial heterogeneity of various biotic processes. We offer here speculations about the possible range and types of processes and conditions that herbivory by *Campostoma* may initiate and mantain in stream ecosystems.

Our observations and experiments imply that in Ozark streams such as Baron Fork schools of *Campostoma* generate and maintain "grazing lawns" (sensu McNaughton, 1984), much as herds of ungulates do on the Serengeti grasslands. The algal lawns maintained by *Campostoma* in Ozark streams consist largely of tightly attached blue-green algae (notably *Calothrix*) that have prostrate growth forms; like grasses, *Calothrix* has a "basal meristem" (most cell divisions occur just above the basal heterocyst; B. Whitton, University of Durham, England; pers. comm. with Stewart). This spatial "growth refuge" allows *Calothrix* to persist despite intense grazing by *Campostoma*. The *Calothrix* lawn that forms in response to grazing by *Campostoma* can be expected to alter large-scale nitrogen cycling characteristics of the stream, for *Calothrix* fixes N_2, while diatoms (which flourish when *Campostoma* are excluded) do not. Because many blue-green algae can fix N_2 and because nitrogen content of food is sometimes an important determinant of food quality for herbivorous invertebrates (Ward and Cummins, 1979) and fish (Horn et al., 1982; Horn and Neighbors, 1984), *Campostoma* may indirectly influence growth rates or use of space by other stream algivores such as crayfish, snails, and aquatic insects (see also Hart, 1985; McAuliffe, 1984).

Changes in algal community composition owing to grazing by *Campostoma* may also have consequences to the cycling of nitrogen and carbon at very small spatial scales. Microscopic examination of the blue-green algal communities dominating when *Campostoma* were present showed that many bacteria were attached to the mucilaginous sheaths of *Calothrix*; diatoms dominating when *Campostoma* were excluded supported visibly fewer bacteria. Jones and Stewart (1969) found that *Calothrix scopulorum* released combined nitgrogen compounds that were readily assimilated by various fungi and bacteria; other filamentous blue-greens do so also (Paerl, 1978). We do not yet know the extent to which bacteria influence nutrient and energy fluxes in Baron Fork, but Cole (1982), Newbold et al., (1983), and Currie and Kalff (1984) show that this possibility should not be overlooked.

The effects of *Campostoma* on nutrient cycling may change seasonally. In early spring, for example, *Campostoma* often grazed on bedrock substrates in shallow, fast-flowing areas of Brier Creek; these substrates supported visually uniform thin layers of attached diatoms dominated by species of *Synedra*, *Gomphonema*, and *Cymbella*. *Campostoma* feces were displaced from three areas by water currents and accumulated downstream in crevices and deeper pockets in microdepositional zones. Water level and velocity in Brier Creek decline in summer, and most riffles become so shallow that *Campostoma* no longer feed there. *Campostoma* then graze almost exclusively in deeper areas of pools; and owing to lack of downstream transport, their feces accumulate where feeding occurs. Over larger spatial scales herbivory by these minnows in summer lowers spatial heterogeneity of algae within pools ("*Campostoma* pools" are uniformly low in algae) but increases heterogeneity of algal biomass (and possibly growth) between pools ("*Campostoma pools*" versus "bass pools"). By late summer most "*Campostoma* pools" are so nearly devoid of algae that bare substrates predominate in sites that are frequently grazed; bare sites will alter sediment-water exchange characteristics for most nutrients (cf. Mulholland et al., 1983).

When primary productivity is nutrient-limited and the rate of regeneration of nutrients from *Campostoma* feces is low, sustained grazing may gradually lower productivity and distort normal patterns of nutrient spiraling in streams by converting nutrients into inaccessible forms. Conversely, if algae are nutrient-limited and regeneration of nutrients from *Campostoma* feces proceeds rapidly, moderate grazing may increase productivity by favoring algae with higher rates of turnover (see also Mulholland et al., 1983; and Hom, 1982). In streams where algae are not nutrient-limited, grazing by *Campostoma* could increase primary productivity by removing algal "overstories" that reduce light to understory communities or by altering feeding behavior of other algivores. Conversely, they may decrease total productivity on an areal basis if they remove excessive quantities of algal biomass or if they promote the development of algal lawns comprised of species with lower productivity but which persist by virtue of having polar cell division (such as *Gloeotrichia* or *Calothrix*). In general, intense grazing by *Campostoma* will alter spatial distributions and relative intensities of biotic (algae and bacteria) and abiotic (exposed sediment) processes controlling nutrient uptake and release. The consequences of such changes to nutrient-spiraling characteristics at very large spatial scales (km reaches) remain unknown.

In the arguments above, a very fundamental question remains unanswered: How much of the ecological theory generated from studies of grazers in low-vectored terrestrial or lake systems (cf. Noy-Meir, 1975; McNaughton, 1979, 1984; McNaughton et al., 1982; Caughley and Lawton, 1981) can be applied directly to grazing processes in streams that include some factors that are strongly vectored by the flow of water? In aquatic ecosystems many of the obvious ecological consequences of grazing are immediately nutrient-related, because nutrient availability limits productivity in aquatic ecosystems more often than in terrestrial ecosystems (cf. Ricklefs, 1979). Nutrients released by stream herbivores can be effectively carried away from sites of nutrient uptake by the flow of water.

In summary, our studies to date suggest that *Campostoma*, as abundant, active algivores, may strongly influence a variety of very basic processes in North American streams. As yet we have investigated only a few aspects of the ecology of *Campostoma* in detail; other features about its ecology for which we have only preliminary data further suggest its potential influence in biotic communities and in stream ecosystems. Our work has focused on a single species of large herbivorous minnow, but many other abundant or widespread fish taxa may play similarly important roles in streams throughout the United States. We hope that ichthyologists and stream ecologists in general will be stimulated to consider in more detail the potential significance of grazing fishes in various stream ecosystems.[1]

[1] We thank Bret Harvey, Beth Goldowitz, Larry Greenberg, Sheila Wiseman, Stephanie Contreras, Arlene Stapleton, Scott Matthews, and Tom Heger for help in the field or laboratory and Bob Cashner, Bill Dietrich, and Steve Threlkeld for helpful discussions at various phases in our work. We are particularly grateful to the Parrish family, Marshall County, Oklahoma, for access to field sites, and to Phill and Donna Bright and the staff of Camp Egan, Oklahoma, for many courtesies. Susan Kelso typed innumerable drafts of the manuscript. This research was supported initially by a visiting investigator award to Matthews and Power from the Department of Zoology, University of Oklahoma, and has been funded since October 1983 by the National Science Foundation (BSR-8307014).

17. The Importance of Phylogenetic Constraints in Comparisons of Morphological Structure Among Fish Assemblages

Richard E. Strauss

Abstract

Morphological approaches to the study of community relationships are based on the premise that morphological differences among organisms reflect in large part their ecological relationships and that morphological "space" can be mapped onto ecological "space." Although morphological characteristics have been used to account for aspects of foraging and habitat use, phylogenetic effects of form diversity on the repeatability of morphological patterns of variation among communities are unknown. The morphological structures of several North and South American freshwater fish assemblages were compared to assess the dependence of morphological congruence on taxonomic similarity. Correlations of morphological patterns are high (> 0.7) for geographically proximate assemblages, but for comparisons between North and South American assemblages the average correlation is 0.20. The density at which species are "packed" into morphospace, and thus the average similarity between species, is independent of the number of species present; within assemblages, therefore, total size-independent morphological variation is highly dependent on species diversity.

Hypotheses about patterns in natural communities, their structure and composition, are at the center of current ecological debate (Cody and Diamond, 1975; Wiens and Rotenberry, 1980a; Anderson et al., 1981; Strong, 1983; Salt, 1984; Strong et al., 1984). Important questions are the extent to which competitive interactions pattern the observed ecological and morphological relationships of species within communities, and to what degree the ecological functions (niches) of members can be predicted from their morphological characteristics. The assumption of strong correspondence between niche and morphology (that is, that morphological "space" maps directly onto ecological "space"; Hutchinson, 1968; Ricklefs and Travis, 1980) is critical to many community studies. For example, several researchers have compared patterns of morphological structure among communities (Ricklefs and O'Rourke, 1975; Findley, 1973, 1976; Gatz, 1979b; Ricklefs and Travis, 1980; Ricklefs et al., 1981) or expressed relative niche characteristics in terms of morphological differences among species (Hespenheide, 1973; Gatz, 1979a). Yet congruence between morphology and ecology is seldom tested directly (Felley, 1984; Miles and Ricklefs, 1984).

It is evident that morphological characteristics can be used to predict aspects of foraging behavior and habitat use (Flanagan, 1981; Gatz, 1979b, 1981; Findley and Black, 1983; Miles and Ricklefs, 1984). However, a considerable amount of residual morphological variation in many communities cannot be related directly to ecological variables (Weins and Rotenberry, 1980b; Felley, 1984), reducing the predictability of morphological relationships in one assemblage from those observed in another. An additional confounding factor is faunal composition: if the historical pool of taxonomic "morphotypes" has been very different for two assemblages—that is, if the communities being compared are comprised of species derived from sets of independent evolutionary lineages—then the resulting morphological patterns could differ profoundly. How might morphological structure be affected, for example, when characins are "substituted" (in a historical sense) for cyprinids? Two possibilities are (1) that ecological (e.g., hydrodynamic, foraging) factors are so important in sorting out sets of coexisting species that the major patterns of variation remain relatively stable among communities, irrespective of the actual species present, or (2) that differences in body form among major evolutionary lineages are large enough to override small-scale, localized ecological pressures, so that, for example, North American stream-fish communities might be structured very differently from corresponding South American communities. In the latter case some degree of correspondence in major patterns of morphological variation might be evident once phylogenetic constraints (taxonomic similarities) have been taken into account.

Table 17.1. Localities and Their Taxonomic Composition*

Locality		Number of Families	Number of Genera	Number of Species	Number of Individuals	Collection No. Sites	Collection Area[†]
1. Little Fishing Creek, Pennsylvania	PA	8	19	28	176	6	12 km
2. Yellow Breeches Creek, Pennsylvania	PA	6	15	23	138	4	14 km
3. Lake Opinicon, Ontario	ON	8	14	16	114	5	8 km^2
4. Big Sandy Creek, Texas	TX	8	16	30	186	3	12 km
5. Martis Creek, California	CA	5	9	12	78	4	3 km
6. Río Paraná, Paraguay	PY	9	31	38	240	5	16 km
7. Río Aquidabán, Paraguay	PY	5	21	24	158	5	24 km
8. Composite		22	22	22	290		

*Taxa are given in the Appendix.
[†]Sampled length of stream or surface area of lake.

To explore such questions in detail, I initiated a study of morphological variation among freshwater fish assemblages collected from a variety of climatic regions and having varying degrees of taxonomic similarity to one another. Specifically, the study was designed to answer the following questions: (1) What are the major patterns of variation, independent of ontogenetic effects on body form, among fishes in stream assemblages? (2) Are patterns of variation consistent among assemblages from different habitats? (3) Is degree of concordance dependent on faunal composition? If so, at what taxonomic level? (4) Is the overall level of similarity, the degree to which species are "packed" into morphological space, dependent on the number or composition of species present? And does packing density differ for temperate versus subtropical habitats?

Materials and Methods

Localities and Taxonomic Composition

Localities were chosen to represent differing habitats and taxonomic assemblages (table 17.1). Assemblages were represented by series of fish collections taken within a limited region (less than 25 km linear extent) of the watershed. Localities and associated collections were selected from three different sources: personal records, selected literature records, and museum expedition records.

The two Pennsylvania localities (PA) were extensively sampled in 1978–79; all specimens were deposited in the Pennsylvania State University research collections. Lake Opinicon, Ontario (ON; Keast and Webb, 1966; Keast, 1978b), Big Sandy Creek, Texas (TX; Evans and Noble, 1979, stations 3–5), and Martis Creek, California (CA; Moyle and Vondracek, 1985) had been surveyed by the authors cited. On the basis of their species lists and descriptions, I located collections in the University of Michigan Museum of Zoology (UMMZ) that corresponded as nearly as possible to the cited geographical locations and that had been collected in similar habitat, especially lake versus stream (similar studies that lacked corresponding UMMZ collections were disregarded). These collections were considered to be representative of the described assemblages, under the reasonable assumption that intraspecific geographic variation is negligible in relation to ontogenetic and interspecific variation. The two Paraguayan (PY) localities were selected from a large survey conducted by the UMMZ Paraguayan Expedition of 1979. All specimens examined were taken directly from those collections.

Because the North American and the Paraguayan assemblages had virtually no faunal overlap, a composite sample was assembled by pooling data on one species from each of 22 families represented in the study (see Appendix). Species were chosen to maximize taxonomic overlap among localities. In several analyses of morphological structure this composite was treated as an independent assemblage, though the data comprising it were replicated from the other samples.

Measures of taxonomic similarity (S) among assemblages were based on Dice's (= Sorenson's) index, $S = 2N_c/(N_1 + N_2)$, where N_1 and N_2 are the numbers of taxa in two assemblages and N_c is the number held in common. The index ranges from 0 to 1 and is linearly proportional to the proportion of shared taxa (Cheetham and Hazel, 1969). Indices were computed separately for species, genera, and families; the three values were averaged to give a composite measure of taxonomic similarity. This procedure diminishes the effect of taking at face value the names and ranks assigned to taxa, particularly for South American groups taxonomic treatments of which have been uneven in scope and quality.

Cluster analyses of assemblages in relation to taxonomic structure were performed on the 1's complements of similarity values ($D = 1 - S = [N_1 + N_2 - 2N_c]/[N_1 + N_2]$) using the UPGMA clustering algorithm (Sneath and Sokal, 1973).

Description of Morphology

The biological reliability of any morphological study is critically dependent on how form and form differences are quantified and analyzed (Strauss and Bookstein, 1982; Bookstein et al., 1985). The geometric and statistical methods used in this study were chosen (1) to provide a fairly complete morphological description of each species, unbiased by prior functional expectations; (2) to encompass sets of functionally analogous anatomical reference points (= landmarks); (3) to explicitly include information on ontogenetic (allometric) variation; and (4) to allow forms to be archived and reconstructed.

Species in each assemblage were represented by 5–12 specimens, deliberately chosen to give the largest size range possible (from 1:1.5 to 1:17, smallest:largest standard lengths). All species were used except for several extreme phenotypes: anguillids, synbranchids, gymnotids, and rhamphichthyids. Data consisted entirely of mensural characters (distances measured with respect to anatomical landmarks). Specimens were photographed in lateral aspect, with accompanying metric scale, with the use of small insect-mounting pins to locate midsagittal landmarks (e.g., anus, supraoccipital crest) that could not easily be seen from lateral view. Landmarks (fig. 17.1) were marked on each photograph and digitized as Cartesian coordinates. Euclidean distances were subsequently computed between pairs of scaled landmark coordinates; distances were selected to form "trusses" (fig. 17.1A; Strauss and Bookstein, 1982) and additional combinations of measurements in lateral projection (fig. 17.1B). Auxiliary measurements of body width, taken with digital calipers into a computer file, were used to approximate a triangulation in dorsal projection (fig. 17.1C); bilateral measurements were averaged before analysis. Body-width measurements and distances across the abdomen were selected to be minimally affected by variation in volume of gas bladder, gut, or ovaries. The resulting data set adequately describes the major features of external body form, including body proportions and relative sizes and positions of mouth, eye, head, and fins. It omits information about complex fin shapes; degree of separation of dorsal fins; adipose fins, barbels, and other specialized appendages; and internal anatomy.

Morphological Space

Analyses are based on the positions of specimens in a multidimensional morphological hyperspace (morphospace) the axes of which are logarithms of the 54 mensural characters. The logarithmic transformation linearizes allometries, standardizes variance, and produces a scale-invariant covariance matrix (Bookstein et al., 1985).

Ontogenetic size variation was explicitly included as a major factor by an examinination of secondary size-independent patterns of variation with respect to multivariate size factors. This procedure takes into consideration the substantial changes in form that occur during growth. It also negates the necessity of arbitrarily limiting size ranges to "adults."

The full morphospace was reduced by means of principal component analysis (PCA) of the covariance matrix (Bookstein et al., 1985). Use of the covariance matrix preserves allometries and leaves the geometric space undistorted, so that Euclidean distances based on original log measurements and on principal component scores are identical. Because of the large size ranges within and among species, the first component was in all cases a strong size vector, accounting for $> 72\%$ of the total variance within assemblages and $> 97\%$ of the variance within species, with consistently positive loadings. The first five components always accounted for $> 98\%$ of the variance among species; thus the sixth and subsequent components were disregarded for multivariate comparisons (but not for calculation of nearest-neighbor distances). For size-free comparisons among assemblages, sheared principal components (Humphries et al., 1981; Bookstein et al., 1985) were computed by regressing out the pooled within-group size factor (PC 1) while maintaining the group centroids. Sheared components are very stable discriminant axes that are unaffected by differences in mean size among groups.

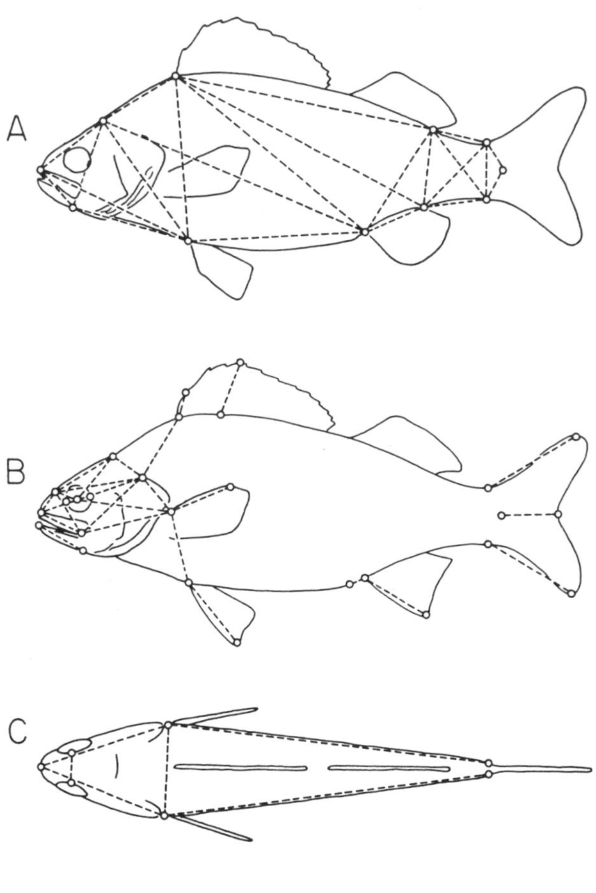

Fig. 17.1. The set of 56 mensural characters used for morphometric analyses. Anatomical landmarks are indicated by open circles; distance measures, by dotted lines. A: Midsagittal truss measures. B: Auxiliary measures in lateral projection. C: Auxiliary measures in dorsal projection.

Assessment of pairwise congruence of morphological variation among assemblages was based on shared principal component analyses. For each pairwise comparison the data for two assemblages were pooled, PCs were extracted, and PC 1 was sheared (regressed) from components 2–5. Within this reduced size-free space, loadings can be represented as vector correlations (directional cosines; Wright, 1954), estimated for each mensural character by its correlations with projection scores across individuals (fig. 17.3). The correlation between assemblages for each character is the cosine of the angle between corresponding vectors. Mean character correlation was estimated by standardizing all character correlations between assemblages with arc sine transformations (Sokal and Rohlf, 1981) and reconverting the mean value across characters with an inverse arc sine transformation.

Species-packing analyses were based on PCAs performed separately for each assemblage. Size-independent nearest-neighbor distances (NNDs) were computed within the reduced ($n-1$, for n characters) PC space from which the first component had been sheared. Distributions of NNDs were compared against random models using the method of Donnelly (1978) and Sinclair (1985).

Results

Similarity in Faunal Composition Among Assemblages

The two PA and two PY assemblages were initially intended to be pairs of "replicates" sampled from within major drainage basins. The PA samples are similar at all three taxonomic levels (table 17.2), except for the presence of ictalurids and a cyprinodont at Little Fishing Creek and for several substitutions of congeneric species. The Paraguayan assemblages are much less similar to one another than is the PA pair owing to the presence of a diverse collection of catfishes at the Río Paraná locality. The ON, TX, and CA groups share intermediate numbers of taxa at all taxonomic levels. The CA assemblage, which is small and has a high degree of endemism (Moyle and Vondracek, 1985), is the most dissimilar among the North American assemblages. As expected, there is almost no faunal overlap between the Paraguayan and the North American groups; Río Paraná and Little Sandy Creek

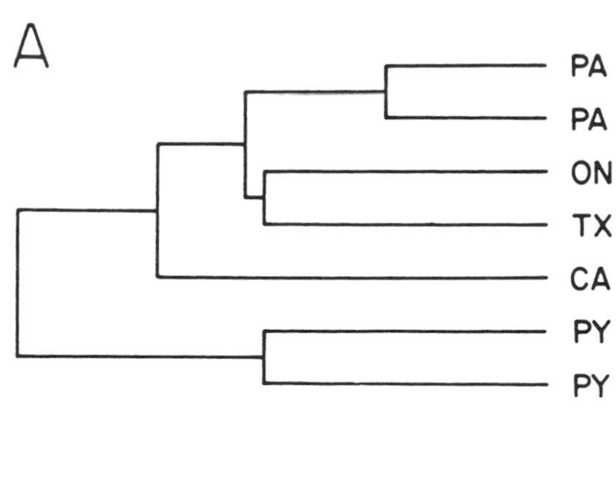

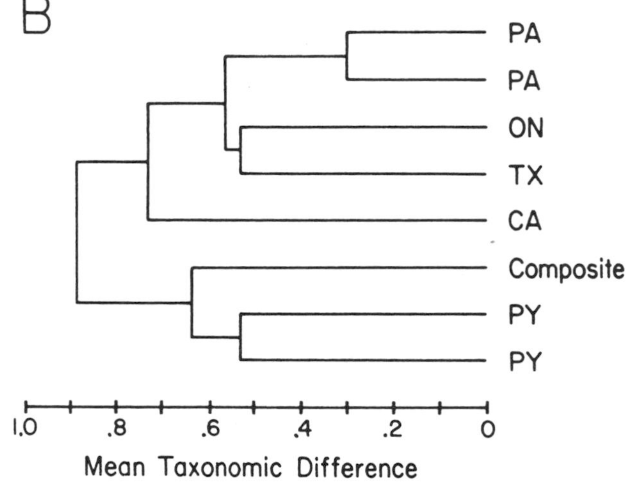

Fig. 17.2. Dendrograms of assemblages clustered by taxonomic dissimilarity, excluding (A) and including (B) the composite sample. Locality abbreviations are given in table 17.1.

Table 17.2. Numbers of Species, Genera, and Families Shared Among Assemblages (Above Diagonal), and Associated Measures of Taxonomic Similarity (Below Diagonal)

Locality	1 PA	2 PA	3 ON	4 TX	5 CA	6 PY	7 PY	8 Composite
1. PA	—	17, 12, 5	7, 8, 6	3, 10, 7	0, 4, 4	0, 0, 0	0, 0, 0	6, 7, 8
2. PA	0.70	—	5, 6, 3	2, 6, 4	1, 5, 5	0, 0, 0	0, 0, 0	5, 6, 6
3. ON	0.52	0.39	—	3, 8, 6	0, 1, 2	0, 0, 0	0, 0, 0	6, 8, 8
4. TX	0.52	0.35	0.47	—	1, 1, 3	0, 0, 1	0, 0, 0	1, 7, 8
5. CA	0.30	0.46	0.13	0.20	—	0, 0, 0	0, 0, 0	1, 4, 5
6. PY	0.00	0.00	0.00	0.04	0.00	—	9, 13, 4	8, 8, 9
7. PY	0.00	0.00	0.00	0.00	0.00	0.45	—	5, 5, 5
8. Composite	0.37	0.32	0.43	0.31	0.23	0.38	0.27	—

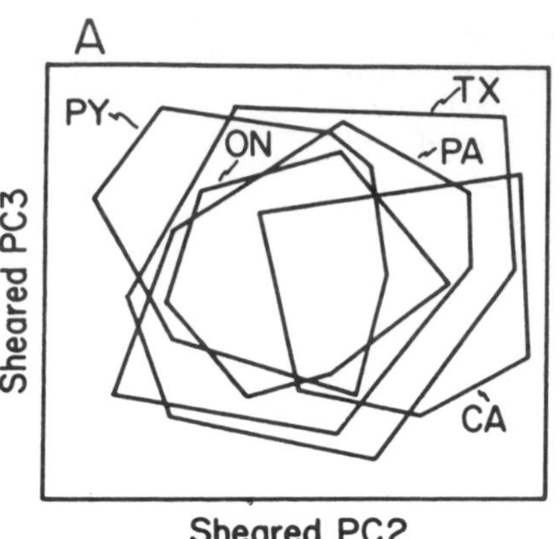

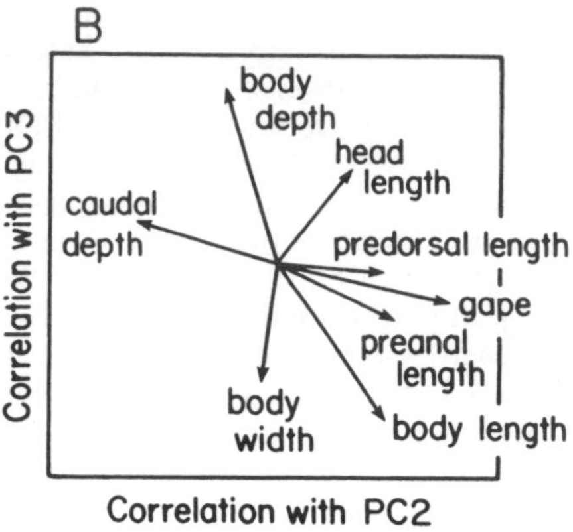

Fig.17.3. A: Scatterplot of projections of all specimens within the plane of the second and third sheared (size-independent) principal components, based on 54 mensural characters. Convex polygons enclose all points within corresponding assemblages; pairs of assemblages from PA and PY have been combined. B: Selected character vectors portraying correlations of characters with the corresponding principal components of panel A.

possess a single but different poeciliid each. Dendograms of the assemblages (fig. 17.2) provide an overall assessment of taxonomic similarity.

Congruence of Morphological Distribution

All assemblages overlap considerably in morphological space, and no pairwise combinations of localities could be discriminated (fig. 17.3). However, species are not distributed evenly or randomly within assemblages; observed distributions of nearest-neighbor distances indicate that species are significantly clustered, with NNDs both longer and shorter than expected based on random models.

Comparisons of assemblages in the sheared PC space of fig. 17.3 are meaningful only to the extent that the within-assemblage size vectors (within-group PC 1 axes) are parallel within the full morphological space (Humphries et al., 1981). Pairwise correlations among size vectors are all > 0.90 (table 17.3), indicating that PC 1 as a multivariate measure of body size is highly consistent across species and assemblages.

Mean character vectors within the sheared PC space (fig. 17.3B) characterize the major size-independent trends in body form within and among assemblages. At a given body size species vary from elongated forms (lower right of fig. 17.3B) with relatively wide body, posteriorly displaced medial fins, and wide oral gape, to deep-bodied, narrow forms (upper left). Size of the head and associated cephalic features (snout length, eye diameter, posterior displacement of pectoral fin, etc.) are more or less independent of this morphocline. These and other associated trends are generally consistent with the major shape variations observed by Flanagan (1981) for marine reef fishes. Note that these are average character correlations across all assemblages; as described below, the trends within any particular assemblage deviate from these to some extent.

Patterns of Species Packing

The average morphological "density" of species within assemblages, as indicated by mean nearest-neighbor distance (NND), is not a function of number of species (fig. 17.4A). Species in diverse assemblages are neither more nor less similar than species in depauperate ones. The slight nonsignificant trend of decreasing distance with increasing number in fig. 17.4A is due to the influence of the two Paraguayan assemblages, which have slightly smaller (but not significantly different) mean NNDs from those of the North American assemblages. However, when total occupied morphological space (that is, total size-independent variance subsumed) is examined as a function of diversity (fig. 17.4B) there is a significant positive relationship, indicating that the total space occupied (total variance) increases in proportion to the number of species present. Again, the Paraguayan species are relatively more similar to one another than are the North American species. For example, the Río Paraná assemblage, with 38 species, has approximately the same total variance as a PA assemblage having 28 species; and the Río Aquidabán, with 24 species, has about the same variance as Lake Opinicon, with only 16 species.

Table 17.3. Pairwise Correlations Among Size Vectors (Within-Assemblage PC 1) (Above Diagonal) and Among Sets of Character Vectors (Below Diagonal)

Locality	1 PA	2 PA	3 ON	4 TX	5 CA	6 PY	7 PY
1. PA	—	0.99	0.97	0.96	0.96	0.93	0.93
2. PA	0.77	—	0.97	0.96	0.96	0.95	0.95
3. ON	0.44	0.42	—	0.98	0.96	0.94	0.94
4. TX	0.63	0.49	0.73	—	0.96	0.93	0.94
5. CA	0.37	0.71	0.28	0.24	—	0.91	0.91
6. PY	0.32	0.25	0.19	0.20	0.07	—	0.98
7. PY	0.28	0.17	0.16	0.34	0.26	0.44	—

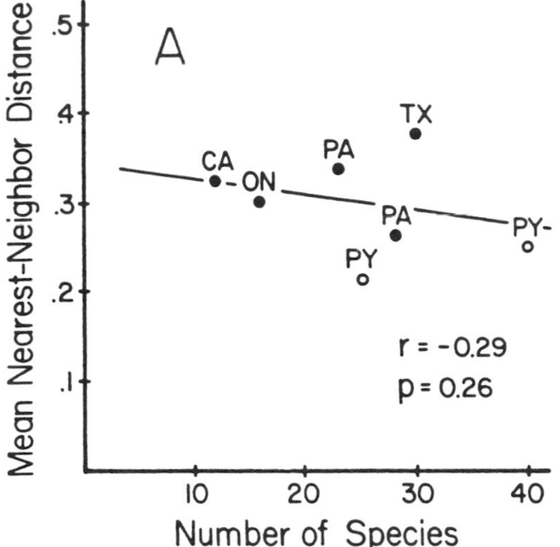

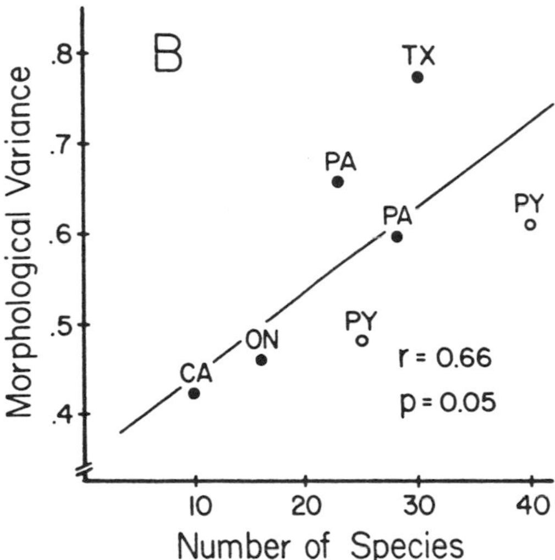

Fig. 17.4. Scatterplots of (A) mean nearest-neighbor distances and (B) total size-independent morphological variance as functions of number of species within each assemblage. Variance is expressed as a percentage of total size-independent variance among all assemblages. Solid circles = North American localities; open circles = South American localities. The expected grand-mean NND for randomly distributed points would be 0.51; observed values are significantly less than expected, indicating aggregation.

Distributions of NNDs are significantly nonrandom ($P << 0.01$) for all assemblages and indicate clustering within morphospace with respect to random models. This nonrandomness could be due to phylogenetic patterning, in that confamilial and congeneric species might be expected to aggregate and to be distant from less closely related species (Gatz, 1979a). To examine this possibility, NND distributions were determined for cyprinids in the two PA assemblages and for characids in the two PY assemblages; of the families studied, these were the only ones having sufficient numbers of species for comparison. In all four cases NND distributions were not significantly different from random (though somewhat overdispersed), indicating that the morphospace aggregations do correspond to taxonomic groupings at the family level.

Congruence of Morphological Structure

Mean character correlations, estimated among all possible pairs of assemblages (table 17.3), range from 0.77 between the two PA localities to a nonsignificant 0.07 between the CA and Río Paraná (PY) assemblages. The high congruence between the PA "replicates" is not surprising; if two such localities had exactly the same species composition, their patterns of morphological variation should be identical except for minor differences owing to geographic variation. However, there is no prior expectation for correlations between North American and South American assemblages, which actually range from 0.07 (CA-PY) to 0.34 (TX-PY) with a mean correlation of 0.20. Such low correlations seem to indicate that phylogenetic differences among component species are more important than ecological constraints in determining overall patterns of morphological structure.

Moreover, the effect of taxonomic similarity is clinal rather than discrete. The linear relationship between mean character correlation and taxonomic similarity (fig. 17.5) is highly significant ($r = 0.82, t = 7.3, df = 26, P << 0.01$). Thus assemblages having intermediate levels of taxonomic similarity are also intermediate in morphological congruence. The regression function, when extrapolated to the case of identical faunal composition ($S = 1$), gives a pre-

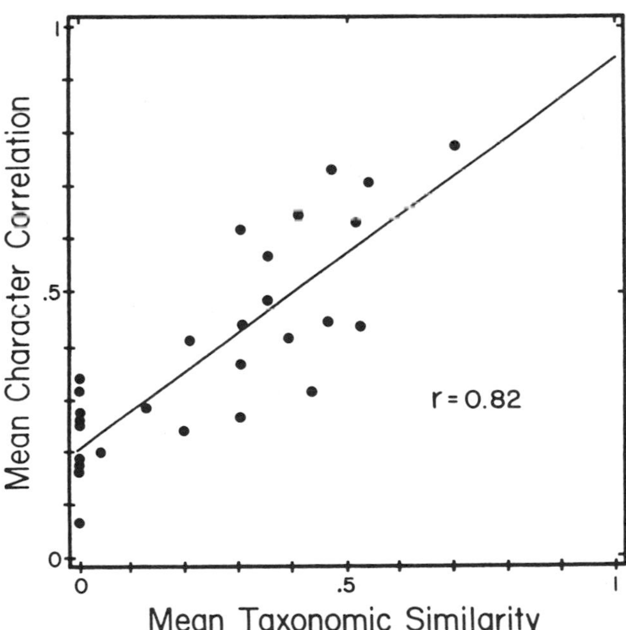

Fig. 17.5. Scatterplot of morphological congruence as a function of taxonomic similarity for all pairs of assemblages, including the composite. Each point represents one assemblage pair. The regression line assumes independent residuals; observed residual correlations were statistically negligible.

dicted mean character correlation not significantly different from the expected 1. The predicted mean correlation of 0.20 for complete taxonomic dissimilarity is a measure of the amount of congruence expected from ecological constraints acting alone.

Discussion

Morphological approaches to descriptive analyses of community relationships are based on the premise that morphological features of organisms reflect in large part their ecological relationships, or at least that morphological analyses may reveal patterns of structure that require explanation in the context of ecological and evolutionary theory (Ricklefs and Travis, 1980; Douglas, chap. 18). The concept of morphological structure within a community or assemblage has had a dual context in the literature, being used in some cases to indicate the spatial patterns of species within the morphospace, particularly in terms of distances between species and overlap among groups of species, and in other cases to indicate patterns of variation among morphological characters. Because convergence in body form and other features seems to be widespread among fishes in both freshwater and marine habitats (at least at a gross morphological level), it might seem likely that the ecological interactions that sort out coexisting combinations of species may structure assemblages in predictable ways, even if a one-for-one replacement of species in different habitats does not occur (Schlosser, 1982a).

The results of this study, however, suggest that the ability to predict patterns of variation among communities is limited by the degree to which the component species have been derived from a common evolutionary and biogeographic background. Thus a serious methodological problem concerns the scale of sampling. Population sizes and degrees of ecological overlap among species may vary widely both spatially and temporally, and the detection of repeatable patterns may be a critical function of the scale on which ecological processes act, particularly in relation to magnitudes of gene flow among populations inhabiting different communities and experiencing varying combinations of predators, prey, competitors, and physical-habitat characteristics. Nevertheless, these results should serve as a caveat for the comparative study of ecomorphological patterns. When the communities chosen for study lie within the same biogeographic or faunal region, a high degree of concordance is to be expected (e.g., Gatz, 1979a, 1981).

Schoener (1974) originally suggested that the total amount of "niche space" occupied by an assemblage of coexisting species should enlarge as the number of extant species increases, because additional species may utilize previously unused aspects of the available ecological resources. This hypothesis has been tested indirectly by a number of investigators using morphological analysis (e.g., Karr and James, 1975; Findley, 1973, 1976; Ricklefs and O'Rourke, 1975; Gatz, 1979a; Ricklefs and Travis, 1980; Ricklefs et al., 1981; Findley and Black, 1983). Their results, and those of this study, have generally supported Schoener's hypothesis that the "core" of the community space, consisting of relatively unspecialized species, is ecologically saturated and that species are added to a community in secondary or novel directions. An alternative explanation is that the ecological conditions of less diverse communities are favorable only to generalist species (Ricklefs and Travis, 1980); however, the continuous relationship between total morphological variance and species number, demonstrated in this study, would argue against a hypothesis invoking response to harsh or variable environments as a general controlling mechanism. A possible mechanism for the assemblage of freshwater fishes into specific habitats is the sorting out from the regional source pool of species (both specialized and unspecialized) that can coexist in the short term, with minor subsequent modification following from competitive ecological interaction.

These findings are complementary to those of Mayden (chap. 26) in demonstrating that an understanding of the history of a community is an important prerequisite to assessing the degree to which morphological features have been molded by competition or other ecological interactions (see also Brooks, 1985). In the absence of detailed knowledge about the phylogenetic relationships of component taxa and the geological history of the regions under study, it is impossible to judge the extent to which extant communities have resulted from recent coevolutionary processes versus the chance assemblage of historically available species. In such cases assessment of faunal similarity will at least provide a rough estimate of the amount of morphological congruence expected among assemblages in the absence of adaptive modifications.

In summary, the hydrodynamic and competitive constraints imposed by the aquatic environment do not necessarily lead to morphological similarity among assemblages by way of evolutionary convergence, at least with regard to patterns of variation among species. The teleost "morphotype" seems to be sufficiently flexible that morphological structure need not be highly constrained in similar ways in different habitats. Instead, each characteristic body form exploits the aquatic environment somewhat differently in terms of its own morphological and ecological design, and resultant differences among species (in magnitude and direction) are highly variable. Thus phylogenetic patterns of form diversity are responsible both for consistency among different fish assemblages within the same biogeographic regions and for noncongruence among assemblages having little faunal similarity.[1]

[1]The University of Michigan Morphometrics Study Group served as the forum in which much of my philosophy about biological form and geometric morphometry was developed, and I am grateful to the participants: F. L. Bookstein, B. Chernoff, R. L. Elder, J. M. Humphries, and G. R. Smith. I thank E. L. Cooper for use of the PSU collections, and R. R. Miller, G. R. Smith, and W. L. Fink for use of the UMMZ collections. Critical comments by M. E. Douglas, M. A. Houck, and G. D. Schnell substantially improved the manuscript. National Science Foundation grant BSR-8307719 provided financial support.

Appendix

Families and Species of Fishes Included
in the Present Study

1.
Little Fishing Creek, Pennsylvania (PA). Esocidae: *Esox niger*. Cyprinidae: *Campostoma anomalum, Cyprinus carpio, Exoglossum maxillingua, Notemigonus crysoleucas, Notropis amoenus, N. cornutus, N. hudsonius, N. procne, N. spilopterus, Pimephales notatus, Rhinichthys atratulus, R. cataractae, Semotilus atromaculatus, S. corporalis*. Catostomidae: *Catostomus commersoni, Erimyzon oblongus, Hypentelium nigricans*. Ictaluridae: *Ictalurus nebulosus, Noturus insignis*. Cyprinodontidae: *Fundulus diaphanus*. Centrarchidae: *Ambloplites rupestris, Lepomis auritus, L. gibbosus, L. macrochirus*. Percidae: *Etheostoma olmstedi, E. zonale*. Cottidae: *Cottus cognatus*.

2.
Yellow Breeches Creek, Pennsylvania (PA). Salmonidae: *Salmo trutta*. Cyprinidae: *Campostoma anomalum, Exoglossum maxillingua, Notropis cornutus, N. hudsonius, N. procne, N. rubellus, N. spilopterus, Pimephales notatus, Rhinichthys atratulus, R. cataractae, Semotilus atromaculatus, S. corporalis*. Catostomidae: *Catostomus commersoni, Hypentelium nigricans*. Centrarchidae: *Ambloplites rupestris, Lepomis gibbosus, L. macrochirus, Micropterus dolomieui, M. salmoides*. Percidae: *Etheostoma olmstedi, Percina peltata*. Cottidae: *Cottus bairdi*.

3.
Lake Opinicon, Ontario (ON). Umbridae: *Umbra limi*. Esocidae: *Esox lucius*. Cyprinidae: *Notemigonus crysoleucas, Notropis heterodon, Pimephales notatus*. Ictaluridae: *Ictalurus natalis, I. nebulosus*. Cyprinodontidae: *Fundulus diaphanus*. Atherinidae: *Labidesthes sicculus*. Centrarchidae: *Ambloplites rupestris, Lepomis gibbosus, L. macrochirus, Micropterus salmoides, Pomoxis nigromaculatus*. Percidae: *Perca flavescens, Percina caprodes*.

4.
Big Sandy Creek, Texas (TX). Esocidae: *Esox americanus*. Cyprinidae: *Notemigonus crysoleucas, Notropis amnis, N. atrocaudalis, N. buchanani, N. emiliae, N. fumeus, N. umbratilis, N. venustus, N. volucellus, Pimephales vigilax, Semotilus atromaculatus*. Catostomidae: *Erimyzon oblongus, Minytrema melanops, Moxostoma poecilurum*. Ictaluridae: *Ictalurus melas, I. natalis, Noturus nocturnus*. Cyprinodontidae: *Fundulus notatus, F. olivaceus*. Poeciliidae: *Gambusia affinis*. Centrarchidae: *Lepomis cyanellus, L. gulosus, L. humilis, L. microlophus, L. megalotis, L. punctatus, Micropterus salmoides*. Percidae: *Etheostoma chlorosomum, Percina sciera*.

5.
Martis Creek, California (CA). Salmonidae: *Prosopium williamsoni, Salmo clarki, S. gairdneri, S. trutta, Salvelinus fontinalis*. Cyprinidae: *Gila bicolor, Rhinichthys osculus, Richardsonius egregius*. Catostomidae: *Catostomus platyrhynchus, C. tahoensis*. Centrarchidae: *Lepomis cyanellus*. Cottidae: *Cottus beldingi*.

6.
Río Paraná, Paraguay (PY). Characidae: *Apareiodon affinis, Aphyocharax dentatus, Astyanax bimaculatus, A. fasciatus, A. scabripinnis, Bryconamericus iheringi, B. stramineus, Chirodon notomelas, Holoshesthes pequira, Hyphessobrycon* cf *melanopleurus, Moenkhausia intermedia, Oligosarcus jenynsi, Roeboides descalvadensis, R. prognathous, Salminus maxillosus*. Anostomidae: *Abramites solarii, Leoporinus* sp., *Prochilodus reticulatus*. Hemiodontidae: *Characidium fasciatum, Hemiodus orthonops*. Aspredinidae: *Bunocephalus coracoideus*. Doradidae: *Trachydoras paraguayensis*. Pimelodidae: *Hemisorubim platyrhynchus, Heptapturus mustelinus, Iheringichthys westermanni, Pimelodella gracilis, Pimelodus maculatus, P.* sp., *Rhamdia quelen*. Loricariidae: *Ancistrus cirrhosus, Hypostomus strigaticeps, Loricaria* cf *catamarcensis, Loricaria labialis, Otocinclus vittatus*. Poeciliidae: *Phalloceros caudimaculatus*. Cichlidae: *Cichlasoma facetum, Crenicichla iguasseunsis, Crenicichla lepidota*.

7.
Río Aquidabán, Paraguay (PY). Characidae: *Acestrorhynchus lacustris, Aphyocharax dentatus, Astyanax bimaculatus, A. fasciatus, A. lineatus, Bryconamericus ihringi, Cheirodon piaba, Curimata nitens, Deuterodon acanthogaster, Holoshesthes pequira, Hoplias malabaricus, Hyphessobrycon leutkeni, Moenkhausia intermedia, M. sanctaefilimenae, Psellogrammus kennedyi, Xenurobrycon macropus*. Hemiodontidae: *Characidium fasciatum*. Loricariidae: *Ancistrus cirrhosus, Cochliodon cochliodon, Hypostomus boulengeri, Loricaria parva*. Callichthyidae: *Corydoras aeneus*. Cichlidae: *Cichlasoma bimaculatum, Crenicichla lepidota*.

8.
Composite assemblage. Salmonidae: *Salmo trutta*. Umbridae: *Umbra limi*. Esocidae: *Esox niger*. Characidae: *Astyanax bimaculatus*. Anostomidae: *Abramites solarii*. Hemiodontidae: *Characidium fasciatum*. Cyprinidae: *Notropis hudsonius*. Catostomidae: *Catostomus commersoni*. Ictaluridae: *Ictalurus nebulosus*. Aspredinidae: *Bunocephalus coracoideus*. Doradidae: *Trachydoras paraguayensis*. Pimelodidae: *Pimelodella gracilis*. Loricariidae: *Ancistrus cirrhosus*. Callichthyidae: *Corydoras aeneus*. Cyprinodontidae: *Fundulus diaphanus*. Poeciliidae: *Gambusia affinis*. Atherinidae: *Labidesthes sicculus*. Centrarchidae: *Lepomis gibbosus*. Percidae: *Percina caprodes*. Cichlidae: *Crenicichla lepidota*. Cottidae: *Cottus bairdi*.

18. An Ecomorphological Analysis of Niche Packing and Niche Dispersion in Stream-Fish Clades

Michael Edward Douglas

Abstract

Niche width and niche dispersion are defined morphologically and analyzed multivariately in two large clades of stream fishes (the sunfish, genus *Lepomis*, and the minnows, genus *Notropis*). Overall, body size (principal component 1) and body shape (subsequent components sheared against PC1) are partitioned from the log-transformed data and compared between clades to assess the importance of these parameters in structuring the ecological niche. Results of these analyses are used to derive morphological competition coefficients between coexisting species of each clade (e.g., coefficients based on size and shape, independently). Ecological relationships are then hypothesized from these coefficients. For instance, minnows are phenotypically less variable in both size and shape parameters than are sunfish and are much more tightly packed in morphospace. Minnows thus appear to be niche specialists that deflect interspecific competition through habitat partitioning. Sunfish, on the other hand, display phenotypic niche diversification primarily on the basis of shape rather than size; they appear to be niche generalists that rapidly shift foraging sites in the absence of congenitors.

The theory that biological communities are structured through competition and the coevolution of competing forms is an ecological tenet widely accepted but recently criticized (Connor and Simberloff, 1979; Strong et al., 1979; Gatz, 1979a; Wiens and Rotenberry, 1980b; Connell, 1980; Simberloff, 1983). An important aspect of this inquiry is the hypothesis that ecological functioning of community members can be predicted by their morphological properties. If this hypothesis is validated, community structure would be based not on random associations of species but rather on the adaptation of forms for specific niches. Critical tests have been performed to evaluate the ecomorphological hypothesis, and results confirm the existence of a statistically significant relationship between the phenotype of an organism and the ecological niche it occupies (W. J. Matthews and M. E. Douglas, unpub. data). Here I explore how niche width, niche dispersion, and competitive interactions between constituent species of stream fish clades can be morphologically defined. I also examine how niche parameters between component species are affected by obvious differences in phenotypic size and shape. The focus of this report is on two genera of freshwater fishes that are, in both numbers of individuals and species, ubiquitous to most stream-fish assemblages. Results from these analyses can be generalized to accommodate other aggregations of fishes and may provide a mechanism by which competitive and coevolutionary hypotheses can be tested within other communities of organisms as well.

Two different perspectives are involved in the morphological analysis of stream-fish communities. One compares the form and constituency of species found in separate communities (as in Strauss, 1986), while the second (Gatz, 1979a, b; Douglas and Avise, 1982) evaluates large clades that comprise most stream-fish communities. The first perspective examines distributions of taxa within morphospace, while the second evaluates trends of variation among taxa in morphospace (R. Strauss, pers. comm.). This report is based on the second perspective.

The Ecomorphological Approach

Philosophy

By virtue of its evolutionary history, the phenotype of a species possesses a particular functional ecological role that is averaged across selective pressures in diverse environments. This ecological role permits the phenotype either to exist or not to exist within particular community assemblages, depending on coexisting predators, competitors, prey, and combinations thereof. From the ecomorphological perspective patterns of resource partitioning among closely related forms can be clarified within a clade or community by a thorough analysis of the phenotype alone. The strong positive relationship between phenotypic form and ecological functioning has been demonstrated (Van Valen, 1965; Hespenheide, 1973; Matthews and Douglas, unpub. data) and repeatedly employed by researchers to evaluate niche width and community structure in a diverse array of organisms (Schoener, 1965, 1975; Willson, 1969; Grant, 1971; Pianka, 1973; Karr and James, 1975; Cody and Mooney, 1979; Gatz, 1979a, b; Ricklefs and Travis, 1980).

Weaknesses of the Ecomorphological Approach

There are several inherent weaknesses in the ecomorphological evaluation of community structure. The phenotype, for instance, does not respond to environmental conditions, which fluctuate over the life-span of the organism. However, physiological and behavioral characteristics do show such a response. The phenotype instead averages out the effects of environmental variability in space and time, while behavioral and physiological characteristics are more finely tuned to local conditions and hence show greater fluctuations (Ricklefs and Travis, 1980). Morphological measurements are thus more indicative of general ecological patterns than are phsyiological and behavioral characteristics and can thus be employed in the analysis of clade or community structure.

Morphological measurement may also contain varying amounts of ecological information about the niche relationships of individual species, and inferences are frequently drawn from a few select (albeit important) variables, while others are excluded. For example, trophic structures are excellent indicators of resource partitioning among species yet frequently convey little usable information about habitat segregation, which is clearly the most important ecological factor for partitioning species (Schoener, 1974; Werner, et al., 1977; Felley and Felley, 1986). Yet it is the phenotype of the organism that evolves, not individual characters.

However, most of these disadvantages can be readily addressed (see below), and those that cannot are counterbalanced by the relative ease and objectivity of obtaining ecomorphological measurements and by the availability of replicates and samples.

Overall Body Size

Size discrepancies between species and the interplay between overall body size and size-related shape are also influential in the segregation of species. From an ecological and an analytical standpoint, however, these topics are difficult to deal with. Quantitative genetic studies on a variety of organisms have shown that body size is moderately to highly heritable (often as high as 50%; Atchley, 1982; H. B. Shaffer, pers. comm.). Not only is body size pleiotropically related to virtually all other loci in the genome (Wright, 1968; Atchley et al., 1981), but it is fundamentally involved in the evolutionary tracking of environmental variability (Bryant, 1977). Body size is also believed to be a major component of niche segregation among closely related species (Wilson, 1975). Yet many biologists still view overall body size as a nuisance factor that must somehow be removed from data before "true" systematic or ecological relationships can be determined.

Methodologies for removing size from a morphological data set are technically diverse and occasionally baffling to the uninitiated. Jolicoeur and Mosimann (1963) proposed that the first principal component of log-transformed measurements be used as an estimate of overall body size between study forms. However, no intrinsic notion of overall body size is built into a PC analysis, and there is no guarantee that the first component will turn out to be a suitable estimate of size. A PC analysis simply guarantees that the first principal component will be a linear combination of those variables that possess maximum variance. If many coefficients are negative on the first component of log-transformed morphological data or if all coefficients are positive but vary greatly in magnitude (Gould, 1967), "data-derived" size measure like the first component should be passed over and a specific size measure employed instead (Mosimann and Malley, 1979).

Even if PC analysis gives a first component that can be satisfactorily interpreted as a size variable, generalizations about size and shape variation may still be difficult to formulate because the relative importance of each type of morphological variation has only recently been elucidated. Atchley (1983) demonstrated that size (regardless of how it was defined) possessed heritability values greater than those estimated for his shape measures. Size obviously has important ecological and genetic considerations. Hence removing it from a data set should be to evaluate size variation relative to shape variation, not because size is a form of biological static that must be filtered from an analysis.

Ecophenotypic Methodology

To overcome the problem of extracting ecological information from one or a few characteristics, multivariate morphometric techniques are used to evaluate large suites of trophic and habitat-related characteristics collected across a variety of species. By applying ordination and distance analyses to the morphological data matrix, species can then be arrayed within an n-dimensional phenetic space analogous to the n-dimensional Hutchinsonian niche (see Sneath and Sokal, 1973, for details of analyses). Distances between species (average taxonomic, minimum, Mahalanobis, etc.) are derived within this multidimensional space, and a "species × species" triangular matrix of $n(n-1)/2$ comparisons (one between every species pair) is produced. The alignment of species in hyperspace (e.g., their degree of phenetic packing) and the total amount of phenetic space occupied by a clade or community (e.g., its dispersion) are obtainable from this matrix and, more importantly, translatable into statistics of niche packing and clade or community hypervolume.

In addition, a quantitative assessment of the competitive relationships between species in a clade or community can be derived through the use of a community matrix (Vandemeer, 1969, 1972), the pairwise elements of which represent the levels of competitive interactions between species pairs. These elements can be derived from morphological data through the use of a competition equation first formulated by

MacArthur (1972) and later adapted for use with phenetic data by Findley (1976).

In this report ordination, distance, and shape analyses are used to investigate the structure of two diverse clades of freshwater fishes, the sunfishes (Centrarchidae; *Lepomis*) and the minnows (Cyprinidae; *Notropis*). By first shearing overall body size from the log-transformed data matrix (Humphreys et al., 1981), the importance of size and shape in structuring these clades and in determining competitive interactions between their coexisting species can then be performed.

Analyzing Trends in Variability Between Stream-Fish Genera

The genus *Notropis* is by far the most species-rich group of fishes in North America, with well over 100 species described. By comparison, *Lepomis* is species-poor, with 11 living species. Both genera are of similar geologic age, dating from the Pliocene or the Miocene-Pliocene boundary. Members of both genera are restricted to and have evolved on the North American continent. Available evidence argues that living *Notropis* have experienced many more speciational events in their recent evolutionary history than have *Lepomis*. Has species proliferation in the minnows been associated with an accelerated pace of morphological differentiation? Douglas and Avise (1982) employed several multivariate statistical procedures to analyze more than 26,000 individual morphological measurements in 11 species of sunfishes and 37 species of minnows (selected primarily on availability of specimens but representing a diverse array of species groups; see Douglas and Avise, 1982). The results of their tests showed that in spite of an accelerated pace of species proliferation North American minnows are no more differentiated from one another morphologically than are sunfishes (see fig. 18.1). The patterns of morphological diversity in minnows and sunfishes, and their species packing in morphospace should suggest means by which component clades of stream fishes are structured over evolutionary time.

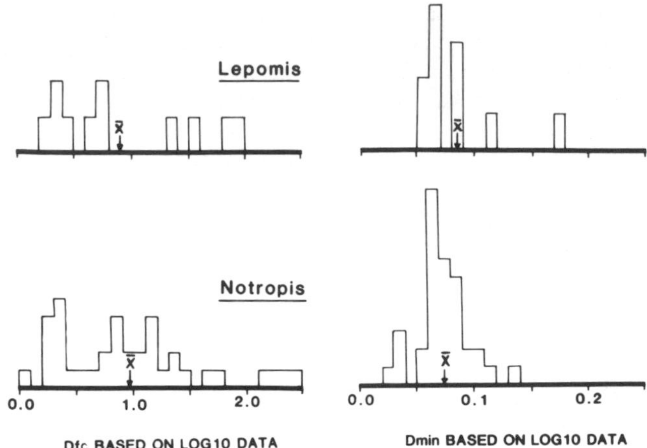

Fig. 18.1. Histograms of phenetic dispersion (Dfc: Mahalanobis distances) and phenetic packing (Dmin: minimum taxonomic distances) separating species of *Notropis* and *Lepomis*. Distances were calculated from $\log_{10}$ transformed data, which contains both size and shape components.

Methods and Materials

The analyses in this chapter are based on 10 individuals each of all 11 species of *Lepomis* and 37 species of *Notropis*. Diversity within *Notropis* was maintained by selecting species from each subgenus and species group in the phylad. Adults were selected so as to maximize the range of body sizes within each species. Study species were arrayed in a morphological space defined by the common logarithm (base 10) of the 50 measurements (Douglas and Avise, 1982; see app. 1 in Douglas, 1978, for the known or inferred ecological properties of these measurements). Principal components were calculated for each genus on the basis of the covariance matrix of the log-transformed data (Dixon, 1983). Principal components are linear combinations of logarithmic values; hence they represent logarithms of the products and ratios of measurements and thereby reflect the allometry of size and shape inherent in the data (Ricklefs et al., 1983). Since a range of adult sizes was selected within each species, the first principal component should demonstrate between-species (rather than within-species) size. Sheared principal components analysis (Humphries et al., 1981) was then applied to the pooled, log-transformed data matrix of each genus so that overall body size could be extracted as a factor separating species. The usual procedure in this technique is to shear the pooled, within-group PC 1 against PC 2 to generate a size-free shape vector. However, I also sheared components 3 and 4 against the size component so that my end product was not a shape vector consisting of one sheared component but rather a shape matrix of three such components (cf. Strauss, 1986). I included PC 4 in the shearing process even though it had an eigenvalue equal to 0.85. I also retained the first principal component for use in subsequent analyses.

Thus each genus was placed in a phenetic space whose geometric dimensions were (1) the logarithms of the 50 measurements, (2) the shape coefficients (PCs 2–4) derived from a sheared principal component analysis of log-transformed data, and (3) a size vector composed of PC 1 coefficients also derived from the covariance matrix of log-transformed data. I calculated the volume of morphological space occupied by each clade first on the basis of sizes and shapes of constituent species and then body shapes and body sizes separately. Other, similar analyses have also arrayed a variety of organisms within community morphospace (birds—Karr and James, 1975; Mosimann and James, 1979; Ricklefs and Travis, 1980; lizards—Ricklefs et al., 1981; bats—Findley, 1976, 1983; rodents—Smart, 1978). Gatz (1979a, b), Douglas and Avise (1982) and Matthews and Douglas (unpub. data) performed similar analyses with stream-fish communities.

For each genus the average taxonomic and Mahalanobis distances among the species were calculated from the three matrices, and the following information was extracted: (1) for each species the minimum distance from its nearest neighbor in the genus (e.g., Dmin; Rohlf et al., 1980), (2) for each genus the mean value of the distance matrices, (3) the distance separating each species from the centroid of the genus (e.g., Dfc; the Mahalanobis distance separating each *Lepomis* and *Notropis* from an "average" sunfish or minnow, with the use of program BMDP4M of Dixon, 1983), (4) for each species the average amount of morphological overlap, e.g., am = $\exp(-[d]^2/2[s_1 + s_2])$, where d is the taxonomic distance separating two species, s_1 is the mean variance for the first species, and s_2 is the mean variance of the second species (Findley, 1976). Step 4 is an attempt to use in the multivariate case a univariate model derived by MacArthur (1972). An am near 1 suggests quite similar morphologies and hence sharp competition; a value near 0 indicates little overlap. Computations in step 4 were performed with Proc Matrix of the Statistical Analysis System (SAS Inst., 1982). Morphological competition coefficients were then summed and averaged for each genus.

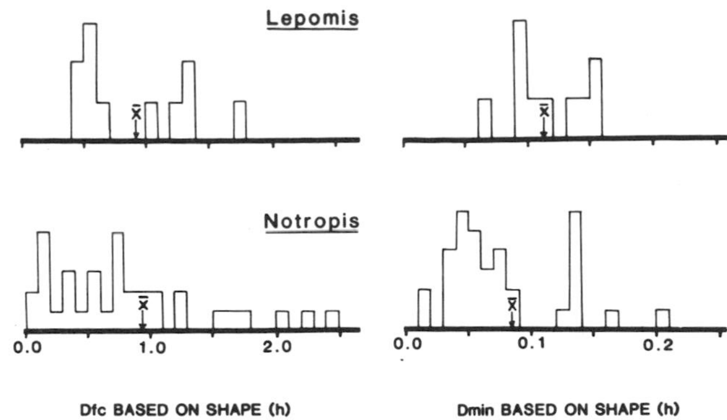

Fig. 18.2. Histograms of phenetic dispersion (Dfc: Mahalanobis distances) and phenetic packing (Dmin: minimum taxonomic distances) that separate species of *Notropis* and *Lepomis*. Distances were calculated from sheared principal component coefficients (e.g., shape-related coefficients only).

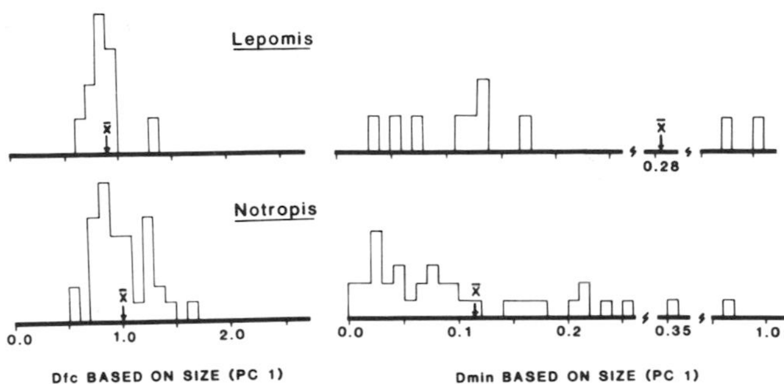

Fig. 18.3. Histograms of penetic dispersion (Dfc: Mahalanobis distances) and phenetic packing (Dmin: minimum taxonomic distances) that separate species of *Notropis* and *Lepomis*. Distances were calculated from coefficients derived from the first (c.g., size-related) principal component.

Results

Principal Component Analysis

Character coefficients for each PC are not presented here but are available from the author. The first component is clearly size-related, with coefficients large and of positive sign; the same percent variance is explained by this PC in each genus. Size variations among species may thus be relatively similar within both groups. Components 2 and 3 explain considerably less variance, and each is interpreted as a shape vector. *Lepomis* has approximately 40% more characters loading on the second component than does *Notropis*. Morphological shape may play a more important role in niche diversification of sunfishes than of minnows. The second component for sunfishes may be interpreted as a fin-head factor (and is thus habitat-related). In minnows only head characters define the second component. The third component in both groups is a trophic component, with the same three characters predominating. Sunfishes also have intestine length and length of lower jaw involved with component 3; for minnows a fin character (anal fin base) and a raker characteristic (the distance between adjacent raker bases) load heavily onto this component.

Packing and Dispersion of Species

Phenetic packing (Dmin) and phenetic dispersion (Dfc) based on log transformed data (e.g., size and shape together) are presented for each genus in fig. 18.1. The balanced distributions of Dmin suggest that within each genus the majority of species are relatively close to their nearest neighbor. *Notropis* has a relatively smaller mean and spread of values ($\bar{x}$ = 0.73; range = 0.12 distance units) than does *Lepomis* ($\bar{x}$ = 0.84; range = 0.18). The distribution of Dfc values is slightly skewed to the left in each genus, suggesting that most species are relatively close to their respective phenetic centroids ($\bar{x}$ = 0.90 and 0.97 for sunfish and minnows, respectively) with fewer species relatively distant from the centroid (e.g., Dfc > 2). Both genera obviously fill the same phenetic hypervolume. The relatively equal dispersion of Dfc values in each genus is further underscored by the fact that 66% of the *Lepomis* species and 50% of the *Notropis* species fall at or below the mean.

Phenetic packing and dispersion based on shape alone are presented for each genus in fig. 18.2. Most minnow species are packed rather tightly within their shape hypervolume (70% less than or equal to the mean of 0.83), while sunfishes are relatively more dispersed ($\bar{x}$ = 1.23). Shape differences apparently provide greater diversity within sunfishes. Both genera possess congruent shape centroids (mean Dfcs = 0.91 and 0.97), but more minnow species reflect "identical" shape morphologies (e.g., Dfc < 0.75) than do sunfish. Fewer minnow species exceed the typical or average minnow shape. Sunfishes, however, are equally dispersed about the mean; fewer species show congruence with the "ideal" sunfish morphology.

The analysis of species packing and dispersion based on size alone tells a similar story within each clade. Most minnows are of an identical small size (mean Dfc = 0.11; fig. 18.3), with fewer relatively large forms (e.g., Dmin > 0.2). Approximately 70% of the minnow Dmin values are at or below the mean. Sunfishes, however, display a much greater range of size variation, with two species (e.g., *Lepomis marginatus* and *Lepomis symmetricus*) quite distant from the nine remaining sunfishes. Yet the "size" centroid is virtually identical in each genus (mean Dfc = 0.99 and 1.00), suggesting that both sunfishes and minnows maintain a "typical" size for their respective body forms. Size variations among species (based on the amount of morphological variance explained by the first component) appear similar within each genus.

Morphological Overlap

Average competition coefficients for *Lepomis* and *Notropis*, based on $\log_{10}$ (e.g., size and shape) data, are 0.010 and 0.224, respectively. Average competition coefficients based on shape only are 0.223 and 0.342 respectively.

Discussion

The number of species living together in a community at equilibrium depends on several associated parameters: the niche widths of the species (e.g., the range of resources used), their niche overlap (e.g., the tolerable amount of similarity in their resource use), and the total range of resources used by the entire clade or community (MacArthur, 1972). Each of these parameters is discussed with regard to the results obtained in this study. Although *Notropis* and *Lepomis* are dissimilar in the size of their respective phylads and in their positions in the food chain, each clade fills the same phenetic hypervolume (Dfc; fig. 18.1). Both also show identical niche dispersion about their faunal centroids (Dmin; fig. 18.1). When both size and shape are considered, most *Lepomis* and *Notropis* species resemble the "average" or "typical" sunfish and minnow morphology, respectively. However, phenetic niches are more tighly packed in *Notropis* (fig. 18.1). These results suggest that most minnow species may have closely limited niche space while several have broader niches. Niche width in *Notropis* would then be comparable to that found in lizards (Pianka, 1973) and bats (Findley, 1976). Sunfishes, however, seem to display a broader niche width on the average, with more species standing apart from the "typical" sunfish ground plan.

On the basis of the character coefficients for PC 2, shape appears to be more important in the morphological definition of sunfishes. The 11 species of sunfishes are as dispersed from their faunal centroid as are the 37 species of minnows (Dmin; fig. 18.2). Within their shape hypervolume, minnows are densely packed (Dfc; fig. 18.2), with a paucity of distant forms. While minnows show a greater range of niche packing and dispersion values, mean values in each matrix are less than or equal to those of the sunfishes. Thus, on average, minnows maintain a basic shape with few exceptions, while sunfishes are well dispersed within their shape hypervolume. Fewer sunfishes show congruence with an "ideal" sunfish form.

Size seems less important in separating sunfishes, although the group as a whole shows a greater spread of variation than minnows, which display, on average, a similar small size with fewer large forms. However, both genera again fill the same basic size hypervolume. Minnows are simply much more packed, while sunfishes are much more dispersed.

Niche overlap in each genus was evaluated with the use of competition coefficient modified for morphometric data. When both genera were evaluated over all 50 morphometric characters (which thus included a strong size component; *Notropis* demonstrated a greater mean competition coefficient than *Lepomis* (am = 0.22 versus 0.01, respectively, with 0.21 distance units separating the genera). When both genera were evaluated on the basis of shape alone, each showed elevated competition coefficients (although minnows still reflected substantially greater values; am = 0.36 versus 0.23, respectively, with 0.13 distance units separating the genera). If minnows do compete among themselves, it is because numerous forms possess similar sizes and shapes. Sunfishes, on the other hand, show greater dissimilarities in shape (and, to a lesser degree, size) which could alleviate competitive interactions. In short, minnows are phenotypically less variable in both size and shape parameters than are sunfishes and hence are more tightly packed in morphological space. Sunfishes, on the other hand, reveal niche diversification primarily on the basis of shape. Yet how do these results translate into the ecology of each clade?

The genus *Notropis* consists of a large array of coexisting forms that coalesce into large, multispecific aggregations in nature, with individual species effectively stratifying the water column into zones (Mendelson, 1975; Gorman, 1986). These species then utilize the trophic resources within the zone to which they are restricted. However, diets of minnow species frequently show considerable prey overlap (Starrett, 1950; Keast and Webb, 1966), with most species making use of prey that shifts seasonally in abundance and in periods of occurrence within seasons. In single-species assemblages, minnows should theoretically forage within the richest part of the environment. As species are added to the community, diets should remain as wide as possible; however, foraging habitat should condense so that most minnows become habitat specialists yet remain trophic generalists (Hespenheide, 1975). My morphological results support this scenario. Minnows, for instance, are found to be morphologically condensed about species means, permitting many forms to be packed within the *Notropis* hyperspace. Although the similarities shown in size and shape predict a modest level of interspecific competition, minnows apparently deflect these interactions through consistent habitat partitioning (Felley and Felley, 1986). Minnows should thus be considered niche specialists, an ecological role that juxtaposes well with their rapid and speciose evolution (Avise, 1977a; Douglas and Avise, 1982).

The genus *Lepomis*, by contrast, is a species-depauperate clade. Quantitative differences in feeding morphology and in head shape allow considerable trophic variability between species (Keast and Webb, 1966; Mullan and Applegate, 1970; Etnier, 1971). The gibbose body plan and fin arrangement enable sunfishes to maneuver and "water-hang" in quite southern reservoirs and slow-moving streams that provide historical habitat for these forms. Sunfishes also possess considerable niche plasticity in that open-water forms (e.g., *Lepomis macrochirus*) and benthic feeding forms (*Lepomis gibbosus*) readily shift to littoral-zone foraging in the absence of congeneric competition (primarily *Lepomis cyanellus*; Werner and Hall, 1976b). The adaptative significance of niche plasticity in sunfishes apparently stems from seasonal patterns of resource abundance. Congeneric species converge on similar resources during the spring flush and diverge as resources dwindle again in late summer. However, the pattern of convergence-divergence is much more apparent in sunfishes and runs from cladocera–large odonates in bluegill to small aquatic insects–large-shelled gastropods in pumpkin seed (Werner et al., 1977). While ecological segegration in both genera is primarily by habitat, sunfishes are pliable enough to shift foraging sites rapidly in the absence of congenitors, whereas minnows apparently are not. Again, morphological analyses substantiate ecological characteristics. Sunfishes fill the same size phenetic hypervolume as minnows, yet species means are widely dispersed in the former but condensed in the latter. Dispersion in sunfish is primarily by shape (Dfc), with mophological shape distances much greater, on the average, than those of minnows. Interspecific size apparently does much less to diversify niches in sunfish (Dfc; fig. 18.2). Interestingly enough, while elevated shape distances prevent competition in sunfishes, similarities in the overall sunfish-body plan (Dmin; fig. 18.2) apparently permit interspecific niche shifting in the absence of congeneric competition.

In conclusion, niche packing, dispersion, and congeneric niche shifting in sunfishes and minnows can be hypothesized from the morphological definition of MacArthur's (1972) competition coefficient. These parameters can be translated into ecological terms of niche overlap and species packing through the use of distance and ordination analyses. Multivariate analyses of morphological characteristics in these fishes can provide predictions about the form and maintenance of their community structure, with species interrelationships partitioned into those mediated by size and by shape similarities, respectively.

Analyses such as these are not an alternative or a challenge to field investigations. Instead, ecomorphological studies are a useful mechanism for defining ecological problems, establishing alternative hypotheses, and formulating critical tests, as advocated by Platt (1964).

19. Ecological and Evolutionary Implications of Phenotypic Plasticity of Swim-Bladder Volume and Lift in Stream Environments

John H. Gee

Abstract

Stream fishes derive lift primarily from the swim bladder and/or hydrodynamic sources. The former provides the greatest amount of lift with the least drag in still waters; the latter are more efficient when fish are swimming against strong currents. Stream fishes encounter variation in water velocity and under some conditions change the relative amounts of lift from both sources so that total lift is optimal and the most efficient source is utilized. Much of the regulation comes from adjusting swim-bladder volume, which is increased in still water and decreased in current.

The extent and rate at which this behavioral plasticity in swim-bladder volume takes place is described in several species. Comparisons between physoclistous and physostomous species show many similarities. Developmental plasticity in swim-bladder morphology is shown in laboratory experiments with two species. Those reared all their lives in current develop smaller swim bladders than those reared in still water. Such phenotypic plasticity is adaptive in stream environments where considerable variation in water velocity occurs within a fish's lifetime. It indirectly allows fishes to expand their distributions and to occupy different environments, exposing individuals to different selective pressures and thereby setting the stage for genetic differentiation.

Water flow is the dominant environmental variable in stream communities. In streams fishes must resist the downstream force of water currents to maintain local populations. In addition water flow influences a number of other stream variables, including dissolved O_2, turbidity, substrate particle size, development of aquatic vegetation, and food availability, that directly affect stream fishes. Velocity varies in time and space, commonly from 0 to 2 m/sec^{-1}, and changes over time can occur rapidly and are often unpredictable.

Many fishes permanently reside in streams while other species complete only a portion of their life cycle there. To maintain permanent populations, or to survive and reproduce, fishes must hold position with an efficient expenditure of energy. To do so, pelagic fishes at neutral buoyancy must swim against the current; benthic fishes must develop frictional forces between the body and the substrate (negative buoyancy). As stream fishes encounter variations in water velocity, they must alter swimming behavior (pelagic species) and frictional forces (benthic species) and regulate lift derived from different sources.

This chapter describes two primary sources of lift used by stream fishes and the conditions under which they are best utilized. I review information on how stream fishes regulate total lift by altering swim-bladder volume and summarize information on the rate and extent of such alterations. The ecological and evolutionary significance of this phenotypic plasticity of swim-bladder volume in stream environments is discussed.

Phenotypic plasticity is a characteristic of an individual and permits adaptation to environmental variables occurring within its life-span. It can be either behavioral, where features can be changed in a relatively short time and the change is reversible, or developmental, where changes occur over the individual's life-span and are irreversible (Birch, 1960).

Sources of Lift and Their Relative Importance

Control of lift to offset weight in water is most important for stream fishes. Such control permits pelagic species to hold position at depth and permits efficient locomotion by both pelagic and benthic species. Lift can be derived from gas inclusions (usually a swim-bladder), hydrodynamic forces, lipids, and low-density tissues and fluids (Gee, 1983). The last function best in marine waters, where accumulations of salt-free fluids in the body provide lift, and reduction of muscle and skeletal tissues reduces weight. Lipids are inappropriate in streams because their excessive bulk adds considerably to drag when water currents are encountered. Gas inclusions and hydrodynamic lift are common sources of lift in stream fishes (Gee, 1983). Lift from both sources potentially can be altered rapidly: swim-bladder lift by altering swim-bladder volume, hydrodynamic lift by altering swimming speed, angle of attack, or fin geometry. However, there is a most important distinction to be made between these two sources of lift. Gas inclusions provide the greatest amount of lift with the least amount of drag at slow swimming speeds. At fast speeds hydrodynamic lift becomes more efficient (Alexander, 1972, 1977).

When fishes encounter an increase in water velocity, they increase swimming speed, thereby holding position. In this process hydrodynamic lift is often developed, increasing total lift from all sources above the optimal required to offset weight. The opposite occurs as fish reduce swimming speed in response to decreasing water velocity. As a result, adapting to variations in velocity requires constant adjustment and control of total lift from all sources, as well as generation of as much of the required amount of lift as possible from the most economical source. Therefore, stream fishes typically lower swim-bladder volume (lift) in response to increased water velocities and make more use of hydrodynamic lift generated from swimming. In response to slower currents or still water, the more economical swim-bladder lift is increased, compensating for loss of hydrodynamic life caused by the reduction in swimming speed.

Relative Amounts of Swim-Bladder and Hydrodynamic Lift and Mechanisms of Their Adjustment

Swim-bladder lift can be expressed in terms of swim-bladder volume (ml) in the intact fish divided by weight of the gas-free-fish in water (g). Neutral buoyancy is attained at 1.0 ml/g^{-1} because 1 ml of atomospheric gases at a given depth of water will support a weight of 1 g. Thus this measure gives the proportion of the fish's weight in water that is supported by swim-bladder lift. The procedures for measuring swim-bladder volume in an intact fish and related variables are given by Chiasson and Gee (1983). The relative contributions of swim-bladder and hydrodynamic lift can be determined for a pelagic fish holding vertical position because the total amount of lift from both sources must equal 1 ml/g^{-1}. Hydrodynamic lift as a proportion of total lift can be obtained by subtraction once swim-bladder lift is measured. This cannot be done in benthic fishes, for it is difficult to distinguish between the weight of the body supported by hydrodynamic lift and that supported by the substrate.

Pelagic stream fishes adapted to still water typically generate 85% or more of the lift required to support their weight in water from the swim bladder (Gee, 1968, 1970; Gee and Gee, 1976; Gee et al., 1974). In currents these fishes typically reduce swim-bladder volume to generate 20 to 65% of their total lift from hydrodynamic sources with the remainder from the swim bladder. Benthic species possessing a swim bladder generate a variable amount of swim-bladder lift in still water and show considerable reductions in swim-bladder lift when currents are encountered.

Swim-bladder volume (lift) can be altered in several ways. Physostomes can gulp and spit gases to and from the swim bladder via the pneumatic duct. Physoclists and some physostomes can secrete or resorb gases readily to and from the swim bladder. Both can make limited adjustments by altering internal pressure of swim-bladder gases by relaxing or contracting muscles within the swim-bladder wall. Spitting or gulping gas is rapid but does not appear to be a precise way of changing volume (Stewart and Gee, 1981). Secretion and resorption are slower but more precise. Adjusting internal pressure is rapid and precise, but the extent of change is limited. *Pimephales promelas* uses all three of these mechanisms. It makes significant changes in internal pressure when altering swim-bladder volume (Gee, 1977). When it is increasing swim-bladder volume in response to a reduction of water velocity, it uses a combination of gulping and secretion, doubling swim-bladder size in 12 h (Stewart and Gee, 1981). By using two or more of these mechanisms, it can exploit the advantages of each.

Fishes acclimated to still water and then exposed to a strong water velocity increase swimming speed, maintaining position, but in doing so create excess lift. To remain in the same general portion of the stream, they must either reduce swim-bladder or hydrodynamic lift rapidly or move to nearby areas of reduced current. As will be shown, few species can reduce swim-bladder volume rapidly, and hydrodynamic compensation involves an increase in drag. Berezay and Gee (1978) and Stewart and Gee (1981) found that fish acclimated to still water and then exposed and confined to water currents swam with a negative angle of attack, decreasing hydrodynamic lift, but at the expense of additional drag. As swim-bladder lift was gradually reduced, the angle of attack gradually returned to horizontal. In this way hydrodynamic lift replaced swim-bladder lift as swim-bladder volume decreased. Fish could temporarily reduce hydrodynamic lift at the expense of drag during short bursts of accelerated swimming, as when moving upstream through a section of rapids. Selecting a different habitat to avoid increased velocities must be viewed as a solution to a very short period of increased velocity because fishes forced from their normal habitat may experience difficulty in locating food, mates, or nesting resources and may be unable to defend territories and nest sites.

Benthic species may modify body position and alter swimming or fin movements in increasing water velocities to counteract increased hydrodynamic lift. I am not aware of any such studies on stream fishes, but certainly the subject would be interesting and challenging. The investigations on the reactions of plaice to water currents and the hydrodynamics of such reactions by Arnold (1969) and Arnold and Weihs (1978) would provide a useful starting place.

Fishes acclimated to fast water velocities and then exposed to still water lose hydrodynamic lift as swimming speed is reduced. As a result, total lift generated does not support the weight of the body in water. Here fish can either gulp air at the surface (physostomes), swim with a positive angle of attack generating hydrodynamic lift, or rest on the bottom, secrete gas, and regain an appropriate lift. *Pimephales pro-*

Table 19.1. Extent of Adjustment of Swim-bladder Lift by Physostomes and Physoclists Between Still Water and Water Current (25–45 cm sec^{-1})

Taxa	Fork Length (mm)	Mean Swim-Bladder Lift (ml/g^{-1})[a]		
		Still	Current	Difference[b] (% of Still-Water Lift)
Physostomes				
Order Salmoniformes				
Esox lucius	45–116	0.95	1.28	0.33 (35)
Salmo gairdneri	63– 79	0.93	0.39	0.54 (58)
S. salar[c]	86–150	0.78	0.42	0.36 (46)
Salvelinus fontinalis[d]	93–170	0.74	0.61	0.13 (18)
Order Cypriniformes				
Catostomus commersoni	42–125	0.85	0.49	0.36 (42)
Moxostoma macrolepidotum	48–113	0.93	0.57	0.36 (39)
Semotilus atromaculatus[e]	151–224	0.99	0.53	0.46 (46)
Notropis cornutus	77–111	0.79	0.46	0.33 (42)
N. blennius	23– 41	0.94	0.61	0.33 (35)
N. volucellus	48– 74	1.02	0.82	0.20 (20)
Pimephales promelas[f]	20– 30	0.98	0.85	0.13 (13)
	31– 40	1.01	0.70	0.31 (31)
	41– 50	0.98	0.65	0.33 (34)
	51– 84	0.91	0.51	0.40 (44)
Hybognathus hankinsoni	55– 74	0.89	0.71	0.16 (18)
Rhinichthys atratulus[g]	39– 62	0.99	0.63	0.36 (36)
R. cataractae[h]	31– 44	0.87	0.30	0.57 (66)
Ictalurus punctatus	287–382	0.85	0.75	0.10 (12) (NS)
I. melas[i]	25– 34	1.00	0.68	0.32 (32)
	60– 80	0.86	0.65	0.21 (24)
	180–200	0.79	0.78	0.01 (1) (NS)
Noturus flavus	112–205	0.49	0.24	0.25 (51)
N. gyrinus[i]	28– 36	1.10	0.80	0.30 (27)
	50– 65	0.90	0.69	0.21 (23)
	75– 90	0.86	0.69	0.17 (20)
Physoclists				
Order Percopsiformes				
Percopsis omiscomaycus	35–101	1.02	0.84	0.18 (18)
Order Gasterosteiformes				
Culaea inconstans[j]	50– 60	0.93	0.37	0.56 (60)
Pungitius pungitius[j]	50– 60	0.88	0.14	0.74 (84)
Order Perciformes				
Ambloplites rupestris	26– 46	1.05	0.87	0.18 (17)
Aplodinotus grunniens	155–208	1.10	0.91	0.19 (17)
Perca flavescens	31– 68	0.98	0.50	0.48 (49)
Stizostedion vitreum	106–126	0.97	0.72	0.25 (26)
Percina maculata[k]	51– 60	0.76	0.03	0.73 (96)
P. shumardi[k]	36– 50	0.44	0.04	0.40 (91)
P. caprodes[k]	51– 70	0.56	0.07	0.49 (88)

Source: From Gee et al., 1974, except where noted.
[a]Mean lift values (N = 6 or more) represent the proportion of body weight in water supported by swim-bladder lift.
[b]All differences between still water and water current are significant ($P < 0.05$; t-test) except where indicated (NS).
[c]Neave et al., 1966.
[d]Saunders, 1965.
[e]Berezay and Gee, 1978.
[f]Gee, 1977.
[g]Gee, 1970.
[h]Gee, 1968.
[i]Machniak and Gee, 1975.
[j]B. J. Beaver, unpub. data.
[k]H. Cavadias, unpub. data.

melas, when exposed to still water after living in strong currents, swim with a positive angle of attack, gulp air at the surface, and secrete gas into the swim bladder. Gulping air contributes an average of 58% of the increase in juveniles and 79% in adults (Stewart and Gee, 1981). As swim-bladder volume is increased, the angle of attack gradually approaches horizontal as swim-bladder lift replaces hydrodynamic lift.

Behavioral Plasticity of Swim-Bladder Volume: Extent and Rate of Adjustment

Because of the benefits of regulating the amount and sources of lift following a change in water velocity, one would expect natural selection to favor the ability to alter swim-bladder volume over an extensive range and to accomplish the change as rapidly as possible. Typically temperate stream fishes reduce swim-bladder volume (lift) on the average of 36% for physostomes and 53% for physoclists. Such changes take place when fish adapt to strong water velocities (40–50 cm/s^{-1}) after acclimation to still water (table 19.1). All species examined (except *Esox lucius*) responded in this way and were capable of at least a 12% reduction of swim-bladder lift. Pelagic species adjust over high values of swim-bladder lift; benthic species, over lower values. The maximum and minimum amount of swim-bladder lift as well as the extent of adjustment varies within and among species and relates to the velocity of water encountered in nature and its variation.

The rate at which fishes alter swim-bladder lift in response to changes in water velocity is variable, particularly among physostomes. *Salmo gairdneri* complete an extensive adjustment in less than 1 h; *Noturus gyrinus* make a moderate adjustment but over 8 days (table 19.2). Within a species smaller-size groups adjust faster than larger ones. Surprisingly, physostomes, which can spit gas from the swim bladder, reduce volumes during all phases of the decrease at similar rates as physoclists (table 19.2).

Table 19.2. Rate of Change of Swim-Bladder Lift When Fish Acclimated to Still Water Are Exposed to Current or When Acclimated to Current and Exposed to Still Water[a]

Species	Fork Length (mm)	Change in Swim-Bladder Lift on Exposure to					
		Current			Still water		
		Loss of Lift (mlg^{-1})	Time Required (h)	Rate of Change[a] (mlg^{-1})	Gain in Lift (mlg^{-1})	Time Required (h)	Rate of Change (mlg^{-1})
Physostomes							
Order Salmoniformes							
Salmo gairdneri[b]	64–89	0.44	0.75	58.67	0.54	0.42	129.83
	64–98[c]				−0.20	116	−0.17
S. salar[d]	86–150	0.25	24	1.04			
Order Cypriniformes							
Pimephales promelas[e]	20–30	0.23	12	1.92	0.19	3	6.33
	20–30[c]				0.19	6	3.17
	47–63	0.43	24	1.79	0.41	24	1.71
	47–63[c]				0.40	48	0.83
Rhinichthys cataractae[f]	20–50	0.68	96	0.71	0.55	24	2.29
	20–50[c]				0.58	48	1.21
R. atratulus[g]	39–62	0.32	132	0.24	0.35	84	0.42
Noturus gyrinus[h]	24–41	0.25	96	0.26	0.22	96	0.23
	44–59	0.15	192	0.08	0.15	192	0.08
	61–101	0.13	192	0.07	0.14	192	0.07
Physoclists							
Order Gasterosteiformes							
Culaea inconstans[i]	54–65	0.75	168	0.45	0.68	48	1.42
Pungitius pungitius[i]	50–58	0.84	96	0.88	0.72	48	1.50
Order Perciformes							
Percina maculata[i]	41–50	0.66	48	1.38	0.68	48	1.42
P. shumardi[k]	56–71	0.67	96	0.70	0.78	96	0.81
P. caprodes[k]	81–101	0.62	48	1.29	0.65	48	1.35

[a]Rates shown are × 100. The time required to make the change was determined by repeated sampling of fish in either still water or current until adjustment was completed.
[b]Gee, unpub. data.
[c]Physostomes exposed to still water without surface access.
[d]Neave et al., 1966.
[e]Gee, 1977.
[f]Gee, 1968.
[g]Gee, 1970.
[h]Machniak and Gee, 1976.
[i]B. J. Beaver, unpub. data.
[j]H. Cavadias, unpub. data.
[k]H. Balesic, unpub. data.

Comparison of physostomes with and without surface access shows the former to increase swim bladder much more rapidly than the latter, indicating that gulping air at the surface plays a role in inflation. Some physostomes (table 19.2) with surface access increased swim-bladder lift more rapidly than physoclists, although *R. atratulus* and *N. gyrinus* were considerably slower. *Salmo gairdneri* was unable to increase swim-bladder lift without surface access, indicating a limited ability (if any) to secrete gases into the swim bladder. Some physostomes (*P. promelas*, *R. cataractae*) without surface access were able to increase swim-bladder lift at a similar rate as physoclists (table 19.2).

With their ability to gulp and spit gases to and from the swim bladder, physostomes are surprisingly slow at altering swim-bladder volume. Apart from *S. gairdneri*, adjustments require at least several hours. Why should physostomes be so slow? Excluding salmonids, all species studied were ostariophysans. Their swim bladder responds to pressure variation caused by the passage of sound waves through water. These vibrations are passed from the swim bladder to the inner ear via the Weberian apparatus. Rapid changes in swim-bladder volume would probably interfere with this sensory function of the swim bladder.

For the Weberian apparatus to function, changes in volume of the anterior sac of the swim bladder must be kept within a certain range (Alexander, 1961, 1966). This sac is composed of a tunica externa and a tunica interna that are only loosely connected, allowing independent movement. The tunica interna is elastic, while the tunica externa is not extensible to sudden changes in volume. It is, however, elastic and viscous and is slowly extensible to forces generated over time. The tunica externa has a slit along the dorsal surface, and if the anterior sac were to suddenly expand or contract, the slit would either open or close and then slowly return to its original size. The Weberian apparatus attaches to the edges of the slit. Its structure is such that if there are sudden and extensive increases in volume, increasing the size of the slit, ligaments connecting the Weberian apparatus would become slack. Sudden decreases in volume reducing the size of the slit would produce slackness of ligaments connecting the Weberian apparatus to the tunica externa. This loss of tension would disrupt the sensory function of the swim bladder and would be corrected only slowly over time. However, slight or slow changes in volume could be compensated by the viscoelastic properties of the tunica externa. As a result, change in swim-bladder volume of the Ostariophysi are slow, allowing continuous functioning of the swim bladder in a sensory role.

Developmental Plasticity of Swim-Bladder Lift

Information on developmental plasticity is limited to two species of *Rhinichthys*. Gee (1972) found that within the genus *Rhinichthys* there were differences within and among populations of the same species in length and volume of the swim bladder that were correlated to evironment occupied. Fishes from fast-flowing waters possessed swim bladders that were shorter and of smaller volume than those from still waters. Such variations could not be explained by behavioral plasticity of adjusting swim-bladder volume.

Gee (1974) tested the hypothesis that developmental plasticity accounted for this extreme variation in swim-bladder morphology that affects volume and, ultimately, lift. The hypothesis was tested on *R. atratulus* (stream population) and *R. cataractae* (lake and stream populations). These fishes were captured as fry and reared in the laboratory to adult size under two treatments, still water and strong current. Individuals from both treatments were tested in still water and current to compare swim-bladder length and volume and weight of tissues between treatments. Fishes reared in still water possessed swim bladders that were significantly longer and composed of a greater weight of tissue than those reared in currents (Gee, 1974). The former attained a greater volume in both still water and current testing conditions than did the latter. These data support the hypothesis that developmental plasticity in swim-bladder morphology accounts for a major portion of the variation.

Ecological and Evolutionary Significance

Phenotypic plasticity provides the ability not only to adapt to sudden changes in the environment but also to occupy a variety of habitats. Streams and rivers appear stable over the short term, but over long periods of time they seldom remain permanent. Floods, movements of the earth's crust, erosion, rock slides, and the activities of man and other animals alter the course and direction of lotic environments, often changing the stream environment dramatically. Opportunities for expanding distributions within and between drainage systems are great, given sufficient time. Phenotypic plasticity, indirectly provides the potential for individuals to expand ranges and exploit new environments. If it is followed by isolation and exposure to different selective pressures, the stage is set for genetic differentiation. As a result, phenotypic plasticity of swim-bladder morphology has strong ecological and evolutionary implications.[1]

[1] I thank R. Ratynski, B. J. Beaver, and H. Cavadias for constructive comments on the manuscript. The Natural Sciences and Engineering Research Council of Canada provided support for the project. B. J. Beaver and H. Cavadias made available to me portions of their unpublished data.

20. Historic Changes in Fish Communities and Aquatic Habitats in Plains Streams of Kansas

Frank B. Cross and Randall E. Moss

Abstract

Most fishes native to Plains streams have wide distributions in eastern North America. Species richness declines from east to west as aridity increases; taxonomic diversity also decreases, with a few minnows and fewer killifishes becoming increasingly dominant westward. Subordinate to that trend, the fauna contains distinguishable communities characteristic of (1) large streams with erratically variable flow, sandy substrate, and high levels of turbidity and dissolved solids, (2) prairie ponds, marshes, and small streams that are clear and relatively stable, sustained by high water tables, and (3) residual pools of highly intermittent streams.

The first community is most distinctive, including several endemic species with sensory and reproductive adaptations to extreme turbidity and widely fluctuating discharge. The second community includes relic populations of species whose occurrence in the Great Plains is traceable to glacial climates. The third community consists of four or five exceedingly widespread, nearly ubiquitous species. Historically the small-stream community in Kansas was extirpated or reduced in complexity soon after settlement of the western plains in the last quarter of the nineteenth century. Dominant species of the turbid-river community persisted longer, but many declined precipitously in 1950–80 coincident with receding water tables in the west and regulated flows in the east (following impoundment of nearly all rivers in the region). The endemic riverine fauna was largely replaced by sight-feeding planktivores and piscivores adapted to lentic habitats and clear, moderate flow. Several plains species that were common 30 years ago are now seriously threatened.

A review of geologic events that determined the habitats for fishes in plains streams may aid in the understanding of the composition and distribution of the regional fish fauna and the changes that have taken place in historic times. The region is flat because it evolved beneath shallow seas whose final recession occurred in late Cretaceous time. The plains are arid owing to their midcontinental location and to the rain shadow established by the Rocky Mountains, elevated in orogenic episodes extending from late Cretaceous through Miocene times. Massive sedimentary strata that accumulated beneath Pennsylvanian, Permian, and Cretaceous seas were tilted sharply upward. Erosion of this sedimentary overburden on the mountain slopes gradually filled the broad lowland trough east of the Rockies, culminating in Tertiary deposition of the coalescent series of alluvial fans known as the Ogallala Formation. This deep, porous bed of sand and gravel blankets the Great Plains from South Dakota to Texas and influences riverine habitats and plains fish communities to the present day.

Pleistocene climatic oscillations affected the region in several ways. Ice advances altered drainage patterns, enabling dispersal across the plains of fishes now characteristic of cooler, wetter regions in the eastern Mississippi and Great Lakes drainages. Intense winds redistributed surface sands and silt that were often deposited transverse to the river valleys. These aeolian deposits augmented and extended the unconsolidated, porous alluvial outwash; the Sand Hills of Nebraska, for example, were formed by Pleistocene periglacial winds (Wright, 1970). Increased precipitation and runoff during glacial intervals saturated the Ogallala sediments, raising the water table to the land surface by the onset of Holocene time.

Ensuing aridity made the western plains exceedingly erosible. Maximal erosion occurs where annual precipitation is 25–40 cm, annual runoff is approximately 1.5 cm, and rainfall occurs mainly in brief, intense storms (Leopold et al., 1964)—conditions definitive of Recent climates in the Great Plains.

This combination of edaphic and climatic circumstances accounts for the habitat characteristics of plains streams before Euro-American settlement. Rivers with mountain headwaters, such as the Platte and the Arkansas, formed wide, shallow channels as they crossed the plains. Peak flows cut away the erosible banks and drove sand downstream along straight channels, redepositing it as transverse, dune like shoals at nearly uniform intervals along the river's course. This process extended the channel form and habitat conditions of the western plains far downstream along the Missouri mainstream into the Mississippi River and along the Arkansas River into western Arkansas. During high flows generated by snowmelt, the largest rivers were "losing" streams as they crossed the western plains because much of their volume infiltrated the coarse alluvium along their valleys, sustaining shallow water tables. At other times they were "gaining" streams as water seeped back into their channels from the continuous alluvial aquifer (McLaughlin, 1943; Tomelleri, 1984). Conceptually, in our view, the riverbed acted as a sand filter with a back-flushing mechanism as pore pressure reversed during high and low flows.

The rivers were extremely turbid during high flows owing to their erosible watersheds and scouring of their beds and banks. They remained turbid during low flows owing to erosional additions from tributaries carrying runoff from isolated storms in their vast drainage basins. Currents in the shallow channels kept fine particles in suspension, and back flushing in the riverbeds may also have contributed to the sediment during low flows. The riverbeds retained their sandy texture because subsurface flows made them semibuoyant, producing loose "quicksands" that inhibited crossings by early travelers despite the rivers' shallow depths. During low flows in summer, water temperatures often exceeded 30° C (Burns, 1975) owing to exposure of the barren, unshaded riverbed; and salinity was high owing to high rates of evaporation and natural intrusions of salt- and gypsum-laden groundwaters into some streams.

Faunal Associations

These harsh environmental conditions caused the Recent fish fauna to diminish in species richness and taxonomic diversity westward along plains drainages (McAllister et al., 1986; Cross et al., 1986a). A few cyprinids and fewer cyprinodontids become increasingly dominant as aridity increases. Subordinate to that primary trend, three distinct habitat types and associated fish communities are recognizable in the fauna as it existed at the time of Euro-American settlement.

1. Channels of fluctuating, shallow streams with shifting sand beds. Diagnostic fishes are *Scaphirhynchus albus*, *Hiodon alosoides*, *Hybopsis gracilis*, *Hybopsis meeki*, *Hybopsis gelida*, three subspecies of *Hybopsis aestivalis*, *Notropis oxyrhynchus*, *Notropis shumardi*, *Notropis potteri*, *Notropis buccula*, *Notropis bairdi*, *Notropis girardi*, *Hybognathus argyritis*, *Hybognathus placitus*, *Cyprinodon rubrofluviatilis*, and *Fundulus zebrinus*. Ranges of these species are nearly confined to plains rivers of the type described above (fig. 20.1A–C). These species represent the only truly distinctive regional fauna. Other species that occur, sometimes abundantly, in plains streams are more widely distributed in other regions and other habitats (e.g., *Notropis atherinoides*, *Notropis lutrensis*, *Notropis stramineus*, *Carpiodes carpio*, *Ictalurus punctatus*, *Lepomis cyanellus*).

2. Clear brooks, ponds, and marshes sustained by springs and seeps. Habitats are mostly lentic, often supporting macrophytes, and substrates are often overlain by organic sediment and detritus. Where flow occurs, gradients are low, and flow velocities are moderate over substrates of sand and small gravel. Species found in such habitats on the plains are *Semotilus atromaculatus*, *Semotilus margarita*, *Phoxinus erythrogaster*, *Phoxinus eos*, *Phoxinus neogaeus*, *Couesius plumbeus*, *Nocomis biguttatus*, *Notropis cornutus*, *Notropis heterolepis*, *Notropis topeka*, *Fundulus sciadicus*, *Etheostoma cragini*, *Etheostoma exile*, and *Etheostoma spectabile*. Most of these occur on the plains as scattered communities that vary latitudinally in species composition, presumably as glacial relics. All except *N. topeka*, *F. sciadicus* and *E. cragini* are more abundant in regions other than the Great Plains.

3. Residual pools of highly intermittent streams, dependent on runoff not supplemented by springs. Principal fishes in such streams (*N. lutrensis*, *Pimephales promelas*, *Ictalurus melas*, *L. cyanellus*) are widely distributed geographically and occur broadly in habitats other than this type, although they are often abundant in intermittent streams. Our discussion focuses on the historic record in Kansas of fishes and habitats in the first three categories.

Arkansas River in Southwestern Kansas

Of 54 species believed to be native to the Arkansas River and its southwestern tributaries, 36 species had been reported there by 1891 (Girard, 1857; Cragin, 1885; Gilbert, 1885, 1886; Jordan, 1891). Subsequent collections date from the 1920s but are most extensive since 1950. We surveyed the area in 1979–83, making collections at 46 sites. In this chapter we emphasize changes along the Arkansas mainstream because of their severity.

Among 19 fishes reported from the western part of the basin before 1900, several occur mainly in small spring-fed streams: *P. erythrogaster*, *Phenocobius mirabilis*, *N. topeka*, *Campostoma anomalum*, *E. cragini*, and *E. spectabile*. Three of these (table 20.1) were recorded from a "brook" at Garden City, Finney County, adjacent to the Arkansas mainstream. None of the three has since been found in this part of the Arkansas Valley, although all three still inhabit headwaters of tributaries south of the mainstream. In the eastern part of the basin Jordan (1891) listed 26 species from the Arkansas River at Wichita, but we suspect that the collection was aggregated from nearby tributaries as well. It included 10 species characteristic of small streams with semipermanent flow: *P. mirabilis*, *Notropis umbratilis*, *Notropis camurus*, *N. topeka*, *N. heterolepis*, *Pimephales notatus*, *C. anomalum*, *Lepomis megalotis*, *Percina caprodes*, and *E. spectabile*. The records of *N. heterolepis* and *N. topeka* are noteworthy because neither has since been taken in this area. Fossil records of early Pleistocene age exist for *N. heterolepis* in Meade County, Kansas (Cimarron drainage about 280 km southwest of Wichita), and *N. topeka* still occurs in tributaries of Neosho River (Arkansas drainage) northeast of

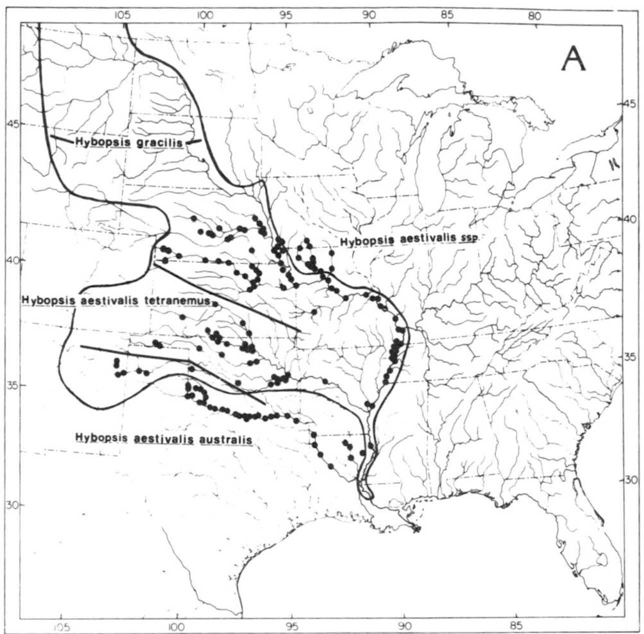

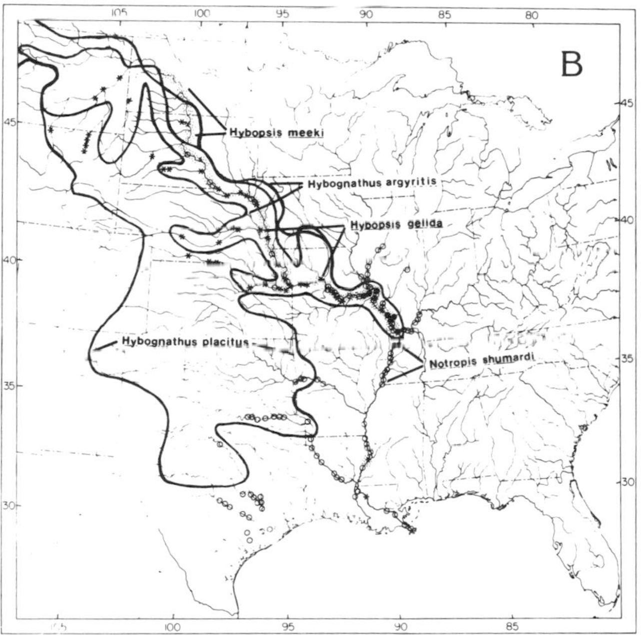

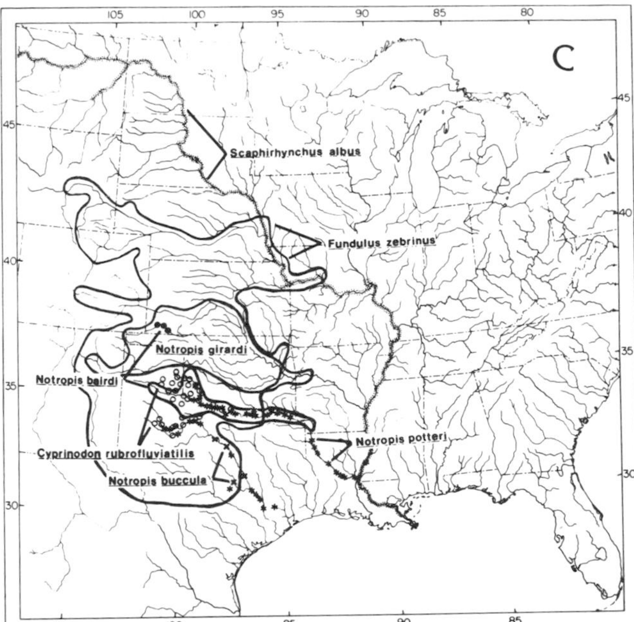

Fig. 20.1. A–C. Native ranges of fishes exemplary of the turbid-river community in the central plains. Species ranges were modified from Lee et al. (1980): C. R. Gilbert (pp. 178, 236, 242, 268, 297, 308), R. E. Jenkins (pp. 185, 191), S. T. Kucas (p. 186), D. S. Lee (p. 43), W. L. Minckley (p. 501), W. L. Pflieger (p. 174), and R. K. Wallace (p. 180). *Fundulus zebrinus* was modified from Poss and Miller (1983).

Wichita. All the remaining species persist in tributaries of the Arkansas River near Wichita, and some have been taken recently in the mainstream as strays. If Jordan's (1891) records are accepted as evidence that these species did occur in or adjacent to the Arkansas River, their habitats must have consisted of persistent pools sustained by the water table in low swales and joined to the river by shallow runs, possibly similar to the brook seined by Cragin (1885) at Garden City. Wedel (1970) and Tomelleri (1984) cite other evidence for such habitats along the Arkansas Valley. In any case, the earliest change notable in the regional fauna involved reductions in the ranges of some species that usually inhabit pools of small, clear, spring-fed streams.

Table 20.1. Native Fishes Reported in or Adjacent to the Arkansas River, Colorado Line to Garden City, Kansas, with Last Dates of Collection in That Reach

Date	Species
1885	*Phoxinus erythrogaster*
	Etheostoma cragini
	E. spectabile
1952	*Hybopsis aestivalis*
	Notropis girardi
1958	*Carpiodes carpio*
1964	*Hybognathus placitus*
1973	*Hybopsis gracilis*
	Catostomus commersoni
	Ictalurus punctatus
	I. melas
	Lepomis cyanellus
	L. humilis
1979–80 (extant)	*Phenacobius mirabilis*
	Notropis lutrensis
	N. stramineus
	Pimephales promelas
	Campostoma anomalum
	Fundulus zebrinus

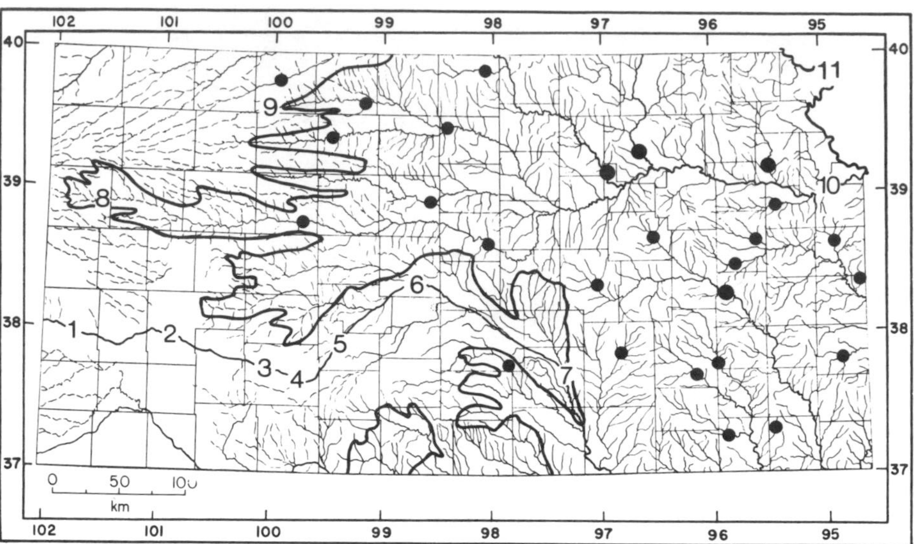

Fig. 20.2. Localities cited in this report. Arkansas River: (1) Syracuse, (2) Garden City, (3) Dodge City, (4) Ford, (5) Kinsley, (6) Great Bend, (7) Wichita. Kansas River basin: (8) Smoky Hill River at Wallace, (9) North Fork Solomon River at Lenora, (10) lower Kansas River, Lawrence to mouth. Missouri River: (11) near Saint Joseph. The heavy line marks the eastern edge of continuous alluvial sand and loess, inclusive of the Ogallala Formation and approximately coextensive with major regional aquifers. Disks = locations of mainstream impoundments.

All fishes characteristic of the fluctuating, sandy river habitat (three species of *Hybopsis*, *Hybognathus placitus*, and *F. zebrinus* represent the Arkansas River component) were recorded from the mainstream before 1900. *Notropis girardi* is exceptional; although endemic to the western Arkansas basin, it was not recognized until a later date (Hubbs and Ortenburger, 1929). This group of species persisted in the Arkansas mainstream when our first collections were made in the 1950s. *Hybopsis gracilis* remained common in the western part of the channel; it has never been reported downstream from Ford (fig. 20.2). *Hybopsis aestivalis* occurred along the full length of the mainstream but was captured most often in the lower part of the basin. *Notropis girardi* occurred throughout the mainstream. Numbers of *N. girardi* recorded from sites seined in 1952 diminished from west to east, a trend that reversed in later years when *N. girardi* occurred abundantly in the lower mainstream but disappeared from the western reaches of the channel, as did *H. aestivalis* (Table 20.1). *Hybognathus placitus* was abundant throughout the mainstream during the 1950s, and *F. zebrinus* inhabited the entire mainstream, most abundantly at western localities. Populations of all these species have declined precipitously. Despite intensive collecting in the mid-1970s by personnel of the Kansas Fish and Game Commission and by us in 1979–83, *H. gracilis* was not found anywhere in southwestern Kansas; it formerly occurred in the Cimarron and Arkansas rivers. *Hybopsis aestivalis* is represented by a single recent specimen, captured in one of many collections downstream from Wichita by personnel of Wichita State University in 1983–84. *Notropis girardi* has disappeared from the Arkansas mainstream. Although earlier collections sometimes yielded hundreds of specimens (281 as recently as 1967, in KU 12192, from Oxford, Sumner County), this species has been taken recently at only two sites in the Cimarron River, where it represented less than 1% and 8%, respectively, of the fishes captured in 1983. *Hybognathus placitus* was found at only one of 20 sites along the Arkansas River in 1979–83; it comprised less than 1% of fishes seined at that site. *Fundulus zebrinus* remains widely distributed, but its abundance in 1983 was below that recorded in previous years.

Declining populations of the species named above are associated with declining rates of discharge and changes in channel characteristics of the Arkansas River. These changes result from (1) diversion of surface flows for irrigation of cropland, which has occurred for more than a century, (2) impoundments and land-use practices, which have progressively modified the natural-flow regime, especially during the past 40 years, and (3) extensive mining of groundwater for irrigation, which has significantly lowered the water table in southwestern Kansas during the past 20 years. Discharge records from gauging stations at Syracuse, near the Colorado state line, and Dodge City are plotted in figs. 20.3–20.5. Before 1942 flows greater than 28.3 m^3/s and less than 0.17 m^3/s occurred with equal frequency (10% of the time) at Syracuse (fig. 20.3). The steep incline of the flow duration curve for that period is typical of widely fluctuating plains rivers in their natural state.

Beginning in 1942, John Martin Reservoir, on the Arkansas River in eastern Colorado, modified the flow regime by retaining water during high flows to meet later irrigation needs. The initial effect (1943–65) was moderation of the extremes of discharge, as is usual following impoundment. Flows of 10% frequency dropped from 28 m^3/s to 12.7 m^3/s. Flows of 75% frequency increased from 0.48 to 1.76 m^3/s, and flows of 90% and 95% frequency approximately doubled (fig. 20.3). Extreme reduction in total discharge did not occur until the final period (1977–82), following expanded irrigation from wells. The incline of the duration curve for 1977–82 nearly parallels that for 1904–42, but the discharge rate at each level of frequency is only one-fourth to one-tenth that in the original period.

Changes in the seasonal patterns of flow at Syracuse are shown in Fig. 20.4. Extreme levels of discharge frequency (10% and 95%) were selected for this analsyis and plotted monthly over the four periods of record. In 1904–42 fluctuation was greatest in summer, when high flows exceeded 85 m^3/s and low flows were less than 0.08 m^3/s. The curves

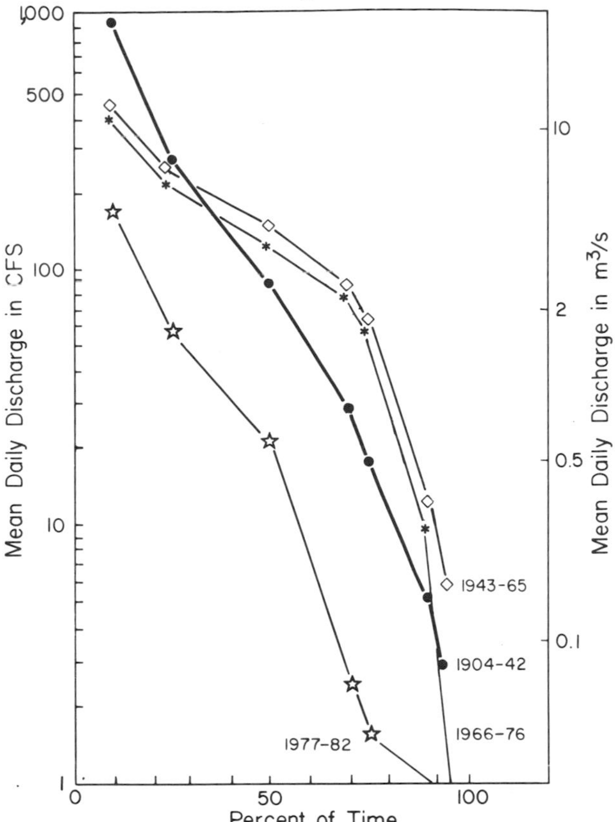

Fig. 20.3. Flow duration in the Arkansas River at Syracuse, Hamilton County, Kansas. Rates of discharge exceeded 10, 25, 50, 70, 75, 90, and 95 percent of the time are plotted for four successive periods. Lines intersecting abscissa indicate flow less than 1 cfs. Data from gauging-station records of U.S. Geological Survey.

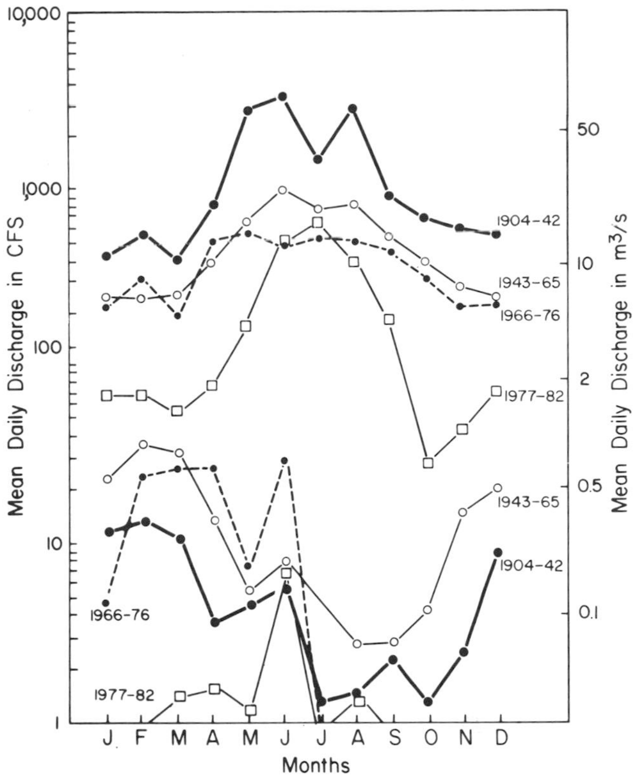

Fig. 20.4. Historic changes in the flow of the Arkansas River at Syracuse, Kansas, summarized from gauging-station records of the U.S. Geological Survey for four successive periods. Upper set of four lines = daily discharge rates exceeded 10% of time in each month; lower four lines = discharge rates exceeded 95% of time.

converged in winter, when flow was least variable. The initial effect of impoundment upstream was amelioration of the extremes in all months—10% and 95% frequency curves for 1943–65 parallel but lie within those of the initial period. In the final period (1977–82) the high-flow curve reflects sustained reduction in the volume of discharge but retains the original seasonal configuration. The low-flow curve, however, is an inversion of the original form. Some flow remains during the irrigation season, but in fall and winter the river is often dry.

Downstream from Syracuse summer discharge rates are depressed more severely. At Dodge City flow now exceeds 0.028 m^3/s only 10% of the time (fig. 20.5). Actually the riverbed is dry along a 160-km reach from Lakin (Kearny County) to Ford, except for local discharge from municipalities along its course (e.g., Garden City, Cimarron, and Dodge City). Where recovery begins near Ford, channel width declined from 324 m in 1825 (Sibley in Gregg, 1952) to about 162 m in 1905, 100 m in 1940 (Tomelleri, 1984), and 2 m in 1983 (Cross et al., 1985). The riverbanks were nearly devoid of trees in 1825, but fringe forest now shades the channel at Ford.

Thus the Arkansas River now has a second "headwater region" within the reach between Dodge City and Great Bend (Barton County). Table 20.2 shows the transition in faunal composition through that reach. It lists the predominant species and their proportional abundance at sites successively farther downstream from the origin of surface water, as recorded by R. Clarke of Emporia State University, in 1980 and by our survey in 1983. In each instance numerical dominance shifted progressively from *P. promelas* to *Gambusia affinis* (an introduced species) to *N. lutrensis*—and, in our more extended series, to *N. stramineus* and *F. zebrinus*. Only the last three species were formerly common in the Arkansas mainstream. At one of these sites (Kinsley), C. L. Hubbs and L. P. Schultz caught only two of the same species (*N. stramineus* and *F. zebrinus*) in 1926, and *F. zebrinus* was dominant (84% of total catch, assuming that numbers of specimens cataloged into the University of Michigan Museum of Zoology reflect the numbers of each species actually seined).

Flow in the Arkansas River now increases rapidly from Great Bend downstream, owing to influx from tributaries and from municipalities (such as Hutchinson and Wichita) that derive their water supplies largely from wells in the alluvial aquifer. Gauging stations downstream from Wichita reveal little change in discharge rates during the periods of record (fig. 20.6). However, various water-quality attributes and channel characteristics must now differ from those prevalent when flow came mainly from sources in the Rocky Mountains and western plains rather than from local sources as it does now.

Twenty-six species were collected in 1983 at Oxford (downstream from Wichita), a greater number than in previ-

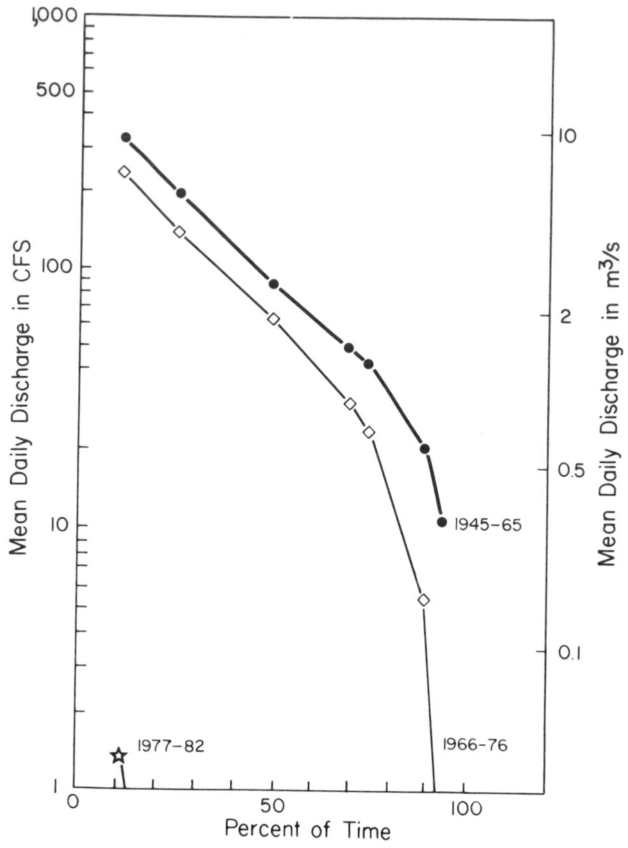

Fig. 20.5. Flow duration in the Arkansas River at Dodge City, Ford County, Kansas, in three successive periods. See Fig. 20.3 for further explanation.

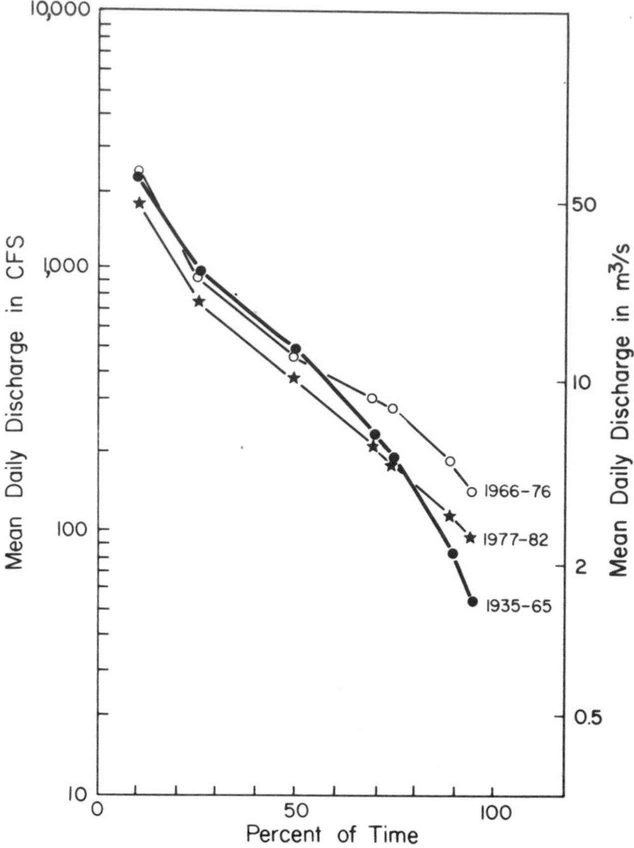

Fig. 20.6. Flow duration in the Arkansas River at Wichita, Sedgwick County, Kansas, in three successive periods.

ous collections at this site. The predominant fishes in 1983 were *N. lutrensis*, *Dorosoma cepedianum*, *N. stramineus*, *N. atherinoides*, and *Pimephales vigilax*. Five kinds of centrarchids, *Morone chrysops*, and such typically clear-water fishes as *Notemigonus crysoleucas*, *P. notatus*, *Pimephales tenellus*, *C. anomalum*, *G. affinis*, and *Labidesthes sicculus* were also represented in the 1983 collection. In contrast, all *Hybopsis* spp. and *N. girardi* were absent in 1983. *Hybognathus placitus* comprised less than 1% of fishes collected, and *F. zebrinus* less than 4% of the total catch.

Table 20.2. Relative Abundances (% Total Catch) of Prevalent Species at Successive Collection Sites Downstream from Origin of Surface Water, Arkansas River, by Clarke (1980) and Cross (1983)

Date and Species	Collection Site					
1980	Howell	Dodge City	Fort Dodge	Kinsley	Larned	Dundee
Pimephales promelas	87	2	7	2	<1	7
Gambusia affinis	1	91	85	1	0	0
Notropis lutrensis	6	0	5	71	69	33
N. stramineus	1	0	2	16	18	23
Fundulus zebrinus	1	4	1	2	9	3
1983	Cimarron	Ford	Kinsley	Dundee	Sterling	
Pimephales promelas	100	1	11	3	11	
Gambusia affinis	0	74	10	9	1	
Notropis lutrensis	0	18	58	7	17	
N. stramineus	0	5	5	60	47	
Fundulus zebrinus	0	0	0	9	21	

Western Kansas River Basin

The principal streams in the western Kansas River basin are the Republican, Solomon, Saline, and Smoky Hill rivers. None of these streams reaches the Rocky Mountains; all have headwaters in the Ogallala Formation, where their base flows originate as small springs and diffuse seepage. Records of fishes in these streams are available from the periods 1871–85 (including collections by O. P. Hay, 1887), 1910–12 and 1934–35 (Breukelman, 1940), 1950–63 (Metcalf, 1966), 1965–66 (Summerfelt, 1967), 1974–75 (faunal survey reports of Kansas Fish and Game Commission), 1978–79 (collections by O. T. and W. Gorman), and 1985 (two collections by J. T. Collins). Table 20.3 lists fishes reported by Hay (1887) and their subsequent fates at two sites—the Smoky Hill River, near Fort Wallace, Wallace County; and the North Fork of Solomon River at Lenora, Norton County (fig. 20.2). Hay's species list from Wallace was compared with collections taken in a 45 km reach of the Smoky Hill River from Sharon Springs, Wallace County, to Russell Springs, Logan County, and two collections from Rose Creek, a principal tributary of the Smoky Hill near Wallace. Collections compared with Hay's Lenora list were obtained in a 16-km reach of the North Fork Solomon River extending from Lenora downstream to Edmond in south-central Norton County. Only four species not reported by Hay (1887) have been captured at these sites: *Cyprinus carpio*, *Ictalurus natalis*, *Micropterus salmoides*, and *Lepomis macrochirus*. Their occurrences stem from introductions.

Most of the species recorded near Wallace and Lenora inhabit pools of small, relatively clear streams. Many require patches of rocky or gravelly substrate for reproduction, but none is an obligatory riffle inhabitant. Species confined to persistent, swift riffles are notably absent in all periods. Absent also are species characteristic of large pools and riverine habitats, apart from the introduced fishes mentioned, which were captured in the period 1950–61.

We attribute the loss of diversity evident in the chronologic series of records (table 20.3) to reduced seepage flow into the Smoky Hill and Solomon rivers. Few stream-gauging stations exist in the immediate area; there are none on the Smoky Hill near Wallace. The most pertinent data available (Jordan, 1979) are summarized here. Records for Rose Creek exist for the period 1946–53. During that time the stream never dried, mean daily discharge averaged 0.13 m^3/s, and flows greater than 0.18 m^3/s occurred less than 10% of the time. The values indicate a stream sustained by small but nearly constant springs and seeps. Discharge records in the North Fork of Smoky Hill River about 24 km northeast of Wallace are available for 1948–53 and 1960–76. This station recorded zero flows on an average of 45 days/year in 1948–53, 156 days/year in 1960–67, and 238 days/year in 1968–76. In 1976 flow occurred on only 14 days, and the highest mean daily rate was 0.014 m^3/s. Flow in the North Fork Solomon River is gauged approximately 65 km downstream from Lenora. Only slight reduction in discharge is evident at that site during the period of record (1953–76).

Numerous direct observations confirm an eastward (downstream) retreat of the origins of flow and reductions of annual discharge in these streams. Cross and Metcalf (unpub. data) found significant flows in the Smoky Hill River and Rose Creek near Wallace in June 1958 and August 1961, respectively. Flow increased downstream to Russell Springs approximately 38 km east of Wallace. Summerfelt (1967) reported flow of 0.56 m^3/s in the Smoky Hill River at Russell Springs in July 1965, but the stream bed was dry there in June 1966. Personnel of the Kansas Fish and Game Commission reported flow of 0.25 m^3/s in Rose Creek in February 1975 but only isolated pools in the Smoky Hill River at Russell Springs in May 1975. These sites were dry when they were visited by O. T. Gorman in the summers of 1978 and 1979. In the North Fork Solomon River, springs maintained a stream 5 m wide 32 km upstream from Lenora in June 1963 (Metcalf, 1966), but that site was dry in November 1974 (Kansas Fish and Game survey reports). Gradual, eastward recession of flow in the North Fork Solomon River is indicated also by the species composition of collections made in this reach in 1958–85. Neither Cross (in 1958) nor Metcalf (in 1963) found *E. spectabile*, a headwater species, at the Lenora site; however, Metcalf found the species 32 km upstream from Lenora, at the site that dried before 1974. *Etheostoma spectabile* occurred in all collections at Lenora (1978, 1985) and Edmond (1974, 1985), 16 km downstream from Lenora. *Notropis lutrensis* and *N. stramineus* occurred in all collections at Lenora before 1985 but were captured only at Edmond in May 1985. With these exceptions collections made in the Lenora–Edmond reach in 1974, 1978, and 1985 are identical in composition, consisting of *S. atromaculatus*, *P. promelas*, *C. anomalum*, *F. zebrinus*, and *E. spectabile*. These species represent 31% of the species recorded at Lenora by Hay in 1885.

Table 20.3. Fishes Reported in 1885 from the Smoky Hill River at Wallace, Kansas, and/or North Fork of the Solomon River at Lenora, Kansas, by Hay (1887)*

Species	Status
Phoxinus erythrogaster *Nocomis biguttatus* *Notropis heterolepis* *N. topeka* *N. umbratilis* *Etheostoma nigrum*	Not subsequently captured; disappeared before 1935.
Notropis cornutus *Hybognathus hankinsoni* *Pimephales notatus* *Catostomus commersoni*	Last captured in 1950–58; disappeared before 1961.
Phenacobius mirabilis *Hybognathus placitus* *Ictalurus melas* *Noturus flavus* *Lepomis cyanellus* *L. humilis*	Last captured in 1961–74; disappeared before 1978.
Semotilus atromaculatus *Notropis lutrensis*† *N. stramineus*† *Pimephales promelas* *Campostoma anomalum* *Fundulus zebrinus* *Etheostoma spectabile*	Recorded at Lenora in 1978–85.

*Species are grouped according to the sequence of their extirpation, on the basis of subsequent collections from the sites.
†Not found in 1985.

The sequence in which species were lost from the Wallace and Lenora sites (table 20.3) seems consistent with expectations based on their present geographic distributions and ecological preferences. *Notropis heterolepis* was at the southwestern limit of its Holocene range and must have been on the verge of extirpation in 1885, since it was represented in Hay's collection only in hybrid form (with *Hybognathus hankinsoni*, as identified by Hubbs, 1951). Those two species as well as *P. erythrogaster* and *N. biguttatus* are characteristic, in this region, of cool spring-fed streams stable enough to sustain beds of macrophytes. Of the six species extirpated before 1935, only *N. topeka* now persists in the Kansas River basin west of the Flint Hills area (in Willow Creek, another tributary to the Smoky Hill River).

The second group of species—*N. cornutus*, *Hybognathus hankinsoni*, *P. notatus*, and *Catostomus commersoni*–likewise inhabits clear pools of streams sustained by springs. High temperatures coupled with reduced summer flows may account for their extirpation. It is noteworthy that these species survived 70 years of agricultural development in the area, including the most intense drought of record (the dust bowl of the 1930s) before disappearing. Among fishes in the third group last captured in the period 1961–74, *P. mirabilis* and *Noturus flavus* are most dependent on continuous flow; *H. placitus* is most common in large, sandy streams; and *Ictalurus* and the two *Lepomis* species are the only fishes that attain moderately large size.

Agricultural land use explains the gradual desiccation of streams in this area. Precipitation patterns do not account for it. Jordan (1982) analyzed rainfall-runoff relationships in northwestern Kansas based on precipitation and stream discharge records extending through water year 1978. He attributed approximately one-third of the decrease in stream flows to groundwater withdrawals for irrigation, two-thirds "to farming practices that increase infiltration rates and evapotranspiration and to ponds and terraces that increase the evaporation from water surfaces."

Lower Kansas River

Records from the Kansas River at Lawrence date from 1875, but most nineteenth-century reports concerned large fishes of economic interest. *Acipenser fulvescens* has not been reported since 1900, *Lota lota* since 1906. Both probably occurred as vagrants from the Missouri River. Several extant fishes declined significantly before our records began in 1951 (table 20.4), based on newspaper reports, photographs, and interviews with commercial fishermen. One cyprinid, *Notropis shumardi*, disappeared in the first half of the century.

Since 1951 we have seined the Kansas River frequently, usually several times a year. Electrofishing has been used occasionally, and angling catches have been monitored casually. The composite record indicates that several species decreased from 1951 to 1983, whereas others increased greatly (table 20.4). *Scaphirhynchus albus* and *F. zebrinus* have not been recorded since 1953. The former probably migrated into the lower Kansas River from Missouri River; the latter dispersed downstream from the western part of the basin. *Hybopsis gracilis* was last recorded in 1959, *H. meeki* in 1969. *Hybopsis aestivalis*, *Hybognathus placitus*, and *H. argyritis* were among the 10 most common fishes at Lawrence in the 1950s but are now relatively rare.

From 1979 to 1981 we sampled fishes 9 or 10 months each year at 14 sites along a 24-km reach of the lower Kansas River, using seines, electrofishing, and trammel nets (Cross et al., 1982). Totals of 10 *Hybopsis aestivalis*, 3 *H. gelida*, 39 *Hybognathus placitus*, and 21 *H. argyritis* were captured. Of the barbeled chubs only *Hybopsis storeriana* remained common (645 were taken). Other minnows were far more abundant: *N. lutrensis* (70,521), *N. stramineus* (21,300), *N. atherinoides* (3,122), and *P. vigilax* (2,105). The last species had not been recorded in the Kansas River basin before 1976; within five years of its initial capture at Lawrence, *P. vigilax* had dispersed along 275 km of the Kansas River and become

Table 20.4. Fishes Whose Abundance in the Lower Kansas River (Lawrence, Douglas County, to the Mouth) Has Clearly Changed in the Periods Indicated*

Decreased before 1950	Decreased in 1950–80	Increased in 1950–80
Acipenser fulvescens	*Scaphirhynchus albus*	*Dorosoma cepedianum*
Hiodon alosoides	*Hybopsis gracilis*	*Notropis blennius*
Anguilla rostrata	*H. meeki*	*N. lutrensis*
Notropis shumardi	*H. gelida*	*N. stramineus*
Ictiobus spp.	*H. aestivalis*	*Pimephales vigilax*
Ictalurus furcatus	*Pimephales promelas*	*Carpiodes cyprinus*
Lota lota	*Hybognathus placitus*	*C. carpio*
	H. argyritis	*Morone chrysops*
	Ictalurus melas	*Micropterus salmoides*
	Fundulus zebrinus	*Lepomis macrochirus*
		Pomoxis annularis
		P. nigromaculatus
		Aplodinotus grunniens

*Additional species, never recorded in the Kansas River before 1965, are now taken there occasionally: *Alosa chrysochloris, Notropis rubellus, Noturus exilis, Lepomis megalotis, Stizostedion vitreum, Percina caprodes, Etheostoma spectabile*.

the third- or fourth-ranking minnow there (Cross and Haslouer, 1984). Other fishes abundant at sites surveyed in 1979–81 were *Carpiodes carpio* (8,683), *D. cepedianum* (2,187), *I. punctatus* (1,081), and *Aplodinotus grunniens* (637). *Morone chrysops* (163), *Lepomis macrochirus* (332), and *Pomoxis annularis* (301) were more numerous than *Hybognathus* spp. and *Hybopsis* spp. (except *H. storeriana*).

Species that increased are mostly widespread in the eastern Mississippi basin as well as westward. Many are pelagic; most are relatively large-eyed and presumably feed visually. Most species that decreased are confined to plains rivers and are adapted to their shallow, turbid conditions by being benthic and by extreme development of chemosensory tissues (Moore, 1950) that substitute for vision in food location.

The changes in species abundance accelerated after completion of the reservoir system that now controls flow in all major tributaries of the Kansas River (fig. 20.2). The total time span of closure of the 18 impoundments in the system in 1946–75, most being constructed in 1950–67. Rates of discharge were moderated, turbidity declined about 67% (Simons et al., 1984; table 20.5), and phytoplankton density increased approximately tenfold (table 20.6). The character of the substrate has changed from loose and "quick" to firm and stable (Cross, unpub. data). Shoals formed by long, transverse dunes no longer occur, and shallow bars seldom develop ripples of slowly moving sand.

Table 20.5. Annual Discharge–Suspended Sediment Relationships in the Lower Kansas River Before and After Completion of the Reservoir System in the Basin

Water Year	Water Yield in Million Acre-Ft. (Million m^3)	Suspended Sediment Yield in Million Tons (Billion kg)	Ratio
1958	6.76 (8,338)	29.30 (26.58)	1:4.3
1959	4.99 (6,155)	19.68 (17.85)	1:3.9
1961	6.74 (8,313)	28.68 (26.02)	1:4.3
	$\bar{x}$ = 6.16 (7,602)	$\bar{x}$ = 25.89 (23.48)	$\bar{x}$ = 1:4.17
1978	6.26 (7,721)	7.03 (6.38)	1:1.1
1979	6.59 (8,128)	10.28 (9.33)	1:1.6
1980	4.60 (5,674)	8.18 (7.42)	1:1.8
	$\bar{x}$ = 5.82 (7,174) (94%)	$\bar{x}$ = 8.50 (7.71) (33%)	$\bar{x}$ = 1:1.5 (36%)

Source: Data from Bonner Springs–DeSoto, Kansas, gauging station.

Table 20.6. Quantitative Phytoplankton Records, Kansas and Missouri Rivers

River, and Reach (Source)	Date (No. Sites)	Cells/ml*
Kansas River		
Topeka, Lawrence (Damann, 1951)	1950, June–July (3)	383
Western tributaries (Damann, 1951)	1950, August (8)	349
Bonner Springs–Kansas City (Cross et al., 1982)	1979–80, June–Aug. (28)	4,205
Missouri River		
State of Missouri (Berner, 1951)	1945, April–Oct. (11)	67†
Montana—mouth (Damann, 1951)	1950, June–Aug. (27)	460
Nebraska City–Kansas City (Damann, 1951)	1950, June (4)	50
St. Joseph–Kansas City (Walter, 1971)	1968, Oct.–Nov. —	1,300–2,000
St. Joseph—Kansas City (Krakowiecki, 1972)	1972, summer (8)	3,000
Cooper Station, Nebraska (Reetz, 1982)	1974–77, April–Oct. (28 mo. samples)	2,000–5,000
St. Joseph USGS, 1982	1980–81, Nov.–Sept. (7)	28,000

*Means of all sample counts.
†Net plankton per liter; all other counts from unfiltered samples, ml basis.

Missouri River

Fishes characteristic of the unmodified Missouri River were as follows (asterisks denote species whose ranges are confined to turbid rivers west of the Mississippi): *Scaphirhynchus albus**, *Scaphirhynchus platorynchus*, *Lepisosteus platostomus*, *Hiodon alosoides*, *Hybopsis aestivalis*, *H. gelida**, *H. gracilis**, *H. meeki**, *H. storeriana*, *Notropis atherinoides*, *Notropis blennius*, *N. shumardi*, *N. lutrensis*, *N. stramineus*, *Hybognathus argyritis**, *H. placitus**, *Ictiobus cyprinellus*, *Carpiodes carpio*, *Ictalurus furcatus*, *I. punctatus*, *Pylodictis olivaris*, *Stizostedion canadense*, and *Aplodinotus grunniens*. We captured all these species by seining the reach bordering Kansas in the 1950s and early 1960s (in brief collections at eight sites), or specimens of them were obtained from commercial fishermen in that period.

In 1977 and 1978 we made 96 collections at eight sites in a 22-km reach of the Missouri River upstream from Saint Joseph, Missouri (fig. 20.2). The samples comprised 13,512 fish of 44 species, captured by seines, hoop nets, and electrofishing. The most abundant species and numbers of each were *H. placitus* (3,716), *N. lutrensis* (2,585), *N. atherinoides* (1,597), *P. promelas* (1,106), *N. blennius* (736), *D. cepedianum* (559), *N. stramineus* (506), *H. storeriana* (447), *Carpiodes carpio* (419), *H. argyritis* (382), *A. grunniens* (331), *I. punctatus* (177), *H. alosoides* (111), *Cyprinus carpio* (109), and *S. canadense* (108).

Scaphirhynchus albus, *H. aestivalis*, *H. meeki*, and *N. shumardi* were absent from those collections. *Hybopsis gelida* was represented by one specimen, *H. gracilis* by two specimens, and *F. zebrinus* by seven. Populations of those fishes, formerly common in the Missouri River, have been decimated in the last two decades. Several fishes atypical of the natural Missouri River fauna greatly exceeded the entire group of species in numbers caught (e.g., *M. chrysops*, *L. macrochirus*, *Pomoxis* spp.).

Hesse et al. (1982) reported similar results based on extensive samples from the Missouri mainstream in Nebraska in 1971–77. Of 57 species recorded, the nine most abundant, on the basis of five collecting methods, were (in declining order) *D. cepedianum*, *H. alosoides*, *Cyprinus carpio*, *Hybognathus argyritis*, *Hybopsis storeriana*, *N. atherinoides*, *N. blennius*, *Carpiodes carpio*, and *A. grunniens*. Based exclusively on seine samples, the rank order of abundance was *D. cepedianum*, *H. argyritis*, *H. placitus*, *H. storeriana*, *N. atherinoides*, *N. lutrensis*, *N. stramineus*, *N. blennius*, *Notropis dorsalis*, *Carpiodes carpio*, and *I. punctatus*. Hesse et al. (1982) found no *S. albus*, *H. meeki*, or *N. shumardi*, one *H. gelida*, and three *F. zebrinus*. On the other hand, their catch included *Esox lucius*, *Morone americana*, *M. chrysops*, nine species of centrachids, and four species of percids, a group unexpected in the natural Missouri fauna.

Changes in fish habitats in the Missouri River result from flood-control and navigational developments. The 107 major reservoirs on the upper mainstream and its principal tributaries, constructed in the period 1937–75, have stabilized flows and reduced turbidity in the free-flowing section of the river from the South Dakota–Nebraska state line to its mouth. Suspended sediment loads have declined 80% at Omaha and approximately 67% at Saint Joseph (Slizeski et al., 1982; Cross and Huggins, 1975). Secchi disk readings at our sites near Saint Joseph in 1977–78 were most often 10 to 43 cm, whereas readings of less than 5 cm were formerly common (Berner, 1951). The stabilized flows facilitated confinement of the wide, shallow, braided channel to a uniformly narrow, deep channel of trapezoidal form by means of wing dikes and revetments (Slizeski et al., 1982). Planktonic organisms (table 20.6), mostly transported downstream from impoundments, have increased dramatically.

Discussion

Distinctive small-stream and turbid-river fish communities probably occurred in close proximity before settlement of western Kansas in the late nineteenth century. Cragin (1885) reported seven species typical of small streams from a brook at Garden City, and only one species (*H. gracilis*) from the adjacent Arkansas River. As recently as 1926, Hubbs and Schultz (field notes and collection records of the University of Michigan Museum of Zoology, communicated to Cross by R. M. Bailey) recorded five native riverine species from the Arkansas mainstream at Kinsley and seven creek species from a floodplain tributary there. Only two (*N. stramineus* and *L. cyanellus*) were taken at both sites. In the western Kansas River basin, only the small-stream community inhabited streams that cut headward into the Ogallala alluvial outwash, but turbid-river fishes replaced those species as the channels became aggraded downstream.

Little endemism existed in the small-stream community. Most species in that group range widely over eastern North America, where they inhabit clear pools of spring-fed streams. Some of those species disappeared as agrarian development began in the river valleys. The sequence of their decline affords evidence on their relative tolerance of unstable water levels, loss of aquatic vegetation, and increasing temperatures and turbidity. *Phoxinus erythrogaster*, *Nocomis biguttatus*, *Notropis heterolepis*, *N. topeka*, *N. umbratilis*, *N. cornutus*. *H. hankinsoni*, and *Etheostoma* spp. were among the first to disappear from the Kansas high plains. Those fishes as a group, at the latitude of Kansas, are limited to streams that remain cool owing to spring influx. High oxygen concentrations are associated with these conditions. Most spawn briefly in May or June. Species that have persisted in western Kansas (e.g., *S. atromaculatus*, *N. lutrensis*, *N. stramineus*, *P. promelas*, *C. anomalum*, *F. zebrinus*) tolerate variable flows, temperatures, and turbidities. They spawn in early spring (March) before evapotranspiration reduces groundwater influx (*Semotilus* and *Campostoma*) or reproduce repeatedly during late spring and summer.

Fishes characteristic of widely fluctuating, turbid, sandy streams persisted through several decades of intensive agricultural development. Conceivably increased erosion from cultivated lands enhanced their abundance following settlement, although high rates of erosion were naturally prevalent on the western plains (Leopold et al., 1964). Many of those species were endemic to plains streams, except where their habitats and ranges were protracted eastward in the channels of rivers that transported large amounts of silt and sand downstream (fig. 20.1A–C). In varying degrees those species share adaptations to high turbidity, shallow flow, and molar effects of shifting sand (Hubbs, 1940; Moore, 1950; Davis and Miller, 1967): small eyes and optic lobes, hyperdeveloped cutaneous sense organs and facial lobes of the brain, thickened integument, crowded or embedded scales, benthic habit, and, in some instances, enlarged lateral line canals. The limited information available on food habits of these species suggests a considerable dependence on allochthonous material, either terrestrial insects or particulate organic matter. The reproductive mode is not known for most of these fishes, owing in part to difficulty of observation in their turbid habitats. Some, perhaps most, spawn pelagically during floods at whatever time the first abrupt increase in flow occurs in late spring or summer. *Hybopsis aestivalis tetranemus* and *N. girardi* are known to synchronize spawning with flood flows (Bottrell et al., 1964; Moore, 1944). That mode seems peculiarly adaptive to plains rivers. Floods normally occurred annually, even in drought years, but at inconstant intervals. Strong flows suspended buoyant eggs, partly protecting them from molar action of sand moving continuously along the riverbed, and floods maximized available habitat and food supplies for developing young through organic matter that washed into the stream and concentrated there as water levels receded.

An alternative reproductive mode common in plains fishes is prolonged spawning. Most fishes known to spawn in this way (*H. storeriana*, *N. atherinoides*, *N. lutrensis*, *N. stramineus*, *P. promelas*, *F. zebrinus*, *I. melas*, *L. cyanellus* and *Lepomis humilis*) have less extreme sensory adaptations to turbid rivers, and their ranges are not confined to such streams.

Modified flow regimes have greatly altered the composition of the riverine community in the past two decades.

Species most highly adapted, morphologically and behaviorally, to plains rivers have been decimated, whereas fishes less specifically adapted to fluctuating, turbid rivers have increased. In the Arkansas River basin diversion of surface water and groundwater withdrawals for irrigation largely account for these changes; impoundments in Colorado and Oklahoma are important secondarily. In the Kansas River drainage and the Missouri River, impoundments are the primary cause of faunal change, supplemented by agricultural practices that diminish runoff. Fishes dependent on floods to trigger spawning disappeared as flooding was reduced or eliminated. Without extreme annual fluctuation in discharge, many of the river channels have become narrower and more uniform in depth. Substrates have become firm, rather than loose and continuously shifting. Reduced turbidity and elevated plankton populations in discharge from reservoirs favor sight-feeding fishes, including game fishes (largely piscivorous) introduced into impoundments. Of the barbeled minnows only *H. storeriana*, which locates prey visually (Davis and Miller, 1967), remains common in the lower Kansas and middle Missouri rivers.

Other fishes indigenous to plains rivers that have sustained or increased their former abundance are *D. cepedianum*, *N. lutrensis*, *N. stramineus*, *Carpiodes carpio*, all centrarchids, and *A. grunniens*. Several fishes not native to these rivers are now established there at various levels of abundance: *Alosa chrysochloris*, *Notropis rubellus*, *P. vigilax*, *Noturus exilis*, *M. chrysops*, *Morone saxatilis*, *L. megalotis*, *Pomoxis nigromaculatus*, *Stizostedion vitreum*, and *P. caprodes*.

The result is opposite to trends described by Trautman (1957, 1981) in Ohio, where clear-water fishes have often been replaced by species tolerant of more turbid conditions. In Kansas the predominant turbid-river fishes are being eliminated by the combination of dewatered channels in the west and stabilized flows in the east, leading to their replacement by planktivores and piscivores characteristic of clearer, deeper streams of the eastern United States.[1]

[1] We thank Paul R. Jordan, of the U.S. Geological Survey, Lawrence, Kansas, for aid in obtaining hydrologic records and Michael Bronoski, of the Kansas City District Office, and Rick Hunter, of the Tulsa District Office, U.S. Corps of Engineers, for information on dates of reservoir closures and other assistance. Ken Brunson, Joseph T. Collins, Scott Campbell, Robert Clarke, Donald A. Distler, Owen T. Gorman, Wendy Gorman, Kelly Irwin, Stuart Leon, John Snell, and David Wiseman provided collecting assistance or information about recent collections on which this report is based. Some of these collections were facilitated by contracts with the U.S. Corps of Engineers, the U.S. Fish and Wildlife Service, and the Kansas Fish and Game Commission (University of Kansas numbers 4652, 4929, and 5400, respectively). J. D. Stewart, R. M. Bailey, C. H. Hocutt, P. R. Jordan, and D. C. Heins reviewed the manuscript and offered useful suggestions.

21. Changes in the Fish Fauna of the Lower Missouri River, 1940–1983

William L. Pflieger and Timothy B. Grace

Abstract

The presettlement Missouri River was characterized by high turbidity, wide seasonal fluctuations in flow, and a wide, braided channel that was in a constant state of change. Construction of an extensive system of dikes, revetments, levees, and upstream reservoirs since 1900 has restricted the lower river to a single narrow, deep, swift channel. The turbidity and sediment load have been reduced, and the natural-flow regimen has been modified. Fish species that have increased in abundance in response to these changes are mostly pelagic planktivores and sight-feeding carnivores: skipjack herring, *Alosa chrysochloris*; gizzard shad, *Dorosoma cepedianum*; white bass, *Morone chrysops*; bluegill, *Lepomis macrochirus*; white crappie, *Pomoxis annularis*; emerald shiner, *Notropis atherinoides*; river shiner, *Notropis blennius*; and red shiner, *Notropis lutrensis*. Several exotics (rainbow smelt, *Osmerus mordax*; grass carp, *Ctenopharyngodon idella*; silver carp, *Hypophthalmichthys molitrix*; common carp, *Cyprinus carpio*; and striped bass, *Morone saxatilis*) occur in the river, but all except the common carp are uncommon. Two species specialized for life in the presettlement Missouri River (pallid sturgeon, *Scaphirhynchus albus*, and flathead chub, *Hybopsis gracilis*) have declined in abundance and could be extirpated from the lower river if trends continue. Other species that were similarly specialized (speckled chub, *Hybopsis aestivalis*; sturgeon chub, *Hybopsis gelida*; and sicklefin chub, *Hybopsis meeki*) have not declined. Changes in the river appear to have favored the dispersal of tributary species, including Ozark minnow (*Notropis nubilus*), spotted bass (*Micropterus punctulatus*), and longear sunfish (*Lepomis megalotis*).

The Missouri River is one of the principal streams of the Mississippi Valley, draining about one-sixth of the continental United States (fig. 21.1). In presettlement times it was one of the most turbid large streams on the North American continent. It also was subject to wide seasonal fluctuations in volume of flow. Bank erosion was continuous, and the configuration of the river channel changed with every flood. This rigorous environment supported a limited but distinctive assemblage of fishes, including species that were restricted to the Missouri River and the Mississippi River below its confluence with the Missouri or species that had a limited distribution in other plains streams where conditions like those in the Missouri River prevailed.

Since 1900 the channel of the lower 1,175 km of the Missouri River has been drastically altered to facilitate navigation. These changes involved losses of channel length and water area and the conversion of a wide, shallow stream with numerous channels, islands, and bars to a single narrow, deep, swift channel (Funk and Robinson, 1974). Reservoirs have impounded or otherwise modified 1,954 km of the upper Missouri River. They have changed the natural-flow regimen and measurably reduced the turbidity and sediment load to the mouth of the river (Neel et al., 1963; Jordan, 1968). Pollution of the river by organic wastes, pesticides, heavy metals, and heated water have also affected the river environment (Whitley and Campbell, 1974; Ford, 1982).

The presettlement fish fauna of the Missouri River is not well known, but a few early records are available (Jordan and Meek, 1885; Meek, 1892). Benson (1968) reviewed changes in fish populations of the impounded upper Missouri River. Other workers have studied the postimpoundment fish fauna of the river immediately downstream from the lowermost reservoir (Walberg et al., 1971; Schmulbach et al., 1975; Kallemeyn and Novotny, 1977). The impacts of nuclear power generation on fishes and other aquatic life were investigated by Hesse et al. (1982). Fisher (1962) made the first extensive survey of fishes in the lower Missouri River (Iowa-Missouri border to mouth) in 1945. In 1962 and 1963 author Pflieger conducted another survey. In 1982 and 1983 we obtained collections from stations at or near those sampled by Fisher and Pflieger. For this report these three series of collections, obtained at approximately 20-year intervals and supplemented by scattered collections obtained in other years, are analyzed to describe changes in the fish fauna of the lower Missouri River during the period 1940–83.

Changes in the River Environment

Modification of the Missouri River channel to facilitate navigation has been a federal responsibility since 1884 (Funk and Robinson, 1974). Snag removal was the principal activity until 1900. After that, channel deepening and bank stabilization received increasing emphasis. Establishment of a navigation channel 1.8 m deep and 61 m wide between Kansas City and the mouth of the river was authorized by Congress in 1912. By 1945 the project limit had been extended upriver to Sioux City, Iowa, and the authorized dimensions of the channel were increased to a depth of 2.7 m and a width of 91 m.

In 1972, when the Missouri River navigation and stabilization project was nearly complete, Funk and Robinson (1974) calculated that the length of the river between Rulo, Nebraska, and its mouth had been reduced by 8% and the water surface area had been reduced by 50%. The stabilized width of the river ranges from 180 m at Sioux City to 330 m at the mouth (Anonymous, 1976). These changes were accomplished by the construction of a system of dikes and revetments that eliminated side channels through the accretion of islands to the adjacent shore. Since 1974 some side channels have been restored, and habitat diversity has been increased by notching dikes or otherwise modifying channel structures (Burke and Robinson, 1979). The navigation and stabilization project also called for the construction of 2,415 km of levees along the river between Sioux City and the mouth. By 1976, 87 of 150 levee units were completed (Anonymous, 1976). These levees, in combination with the narrowing of the river channel, have increased the water stage at any given discharge. Thus if the maximum discharge of record that occurred in 1951 had occurred in 1979, the river stage below Kansas City would have been 0.9 m higher (Burke and Robinson, 1979).

Between 1938 and 1963 six large reservoirs having a storage capacity approximately equal to the average three-year flow at Sioux City (Whitley and Campbell, 1974) were constructed on the upper Missouri River (fig. 21.1). These reservoirs impound 1,435 km of the river and have a combined capacity of 9.38×10^{10} m^3 at full pool. Although the reservoirs were not fully operational until about 1970, measurable effects on the flow regimen, sediment load, and turbidity of the river were evident by 1955 (Neel et al., 1963; Jordan, 1968). These changes are detectable, but with diminishing effect all the way to the mouth of the river. Turbidity measurements obtained from the Missouri River at the Saint Louis, Missouri, water-treatment facility demonstrate these effects (fig. 21.2). These measurements suggest that Fort Peck Lake, the most upstream of these reservoirs and the first to become operational, had no measurable effect on turbidity in the lower river. However, a nearly fourfold decline is evident over the period from 1930 to the present, the most abrupt decline occurring in the 1950s as additional reservoirs became operational. Sediment loads in the Missouri River at Hermann, Missouri, were reduced by about one-third after the reservoir system became fully operational (Ford, 1982).

Mean monthly discharge data from the U.S. Geological Survey gauging station near Boonville, Missouri, demonstrate the effect of these reservoirs on flow regimen (fig. 21.3). Before impoundment (1926–52) there were wide seasonal fluctuations in discharge, with peak discharges generally in April and June. Water-level fluctuations after the reservoirs became fully operational (1966–83) were more

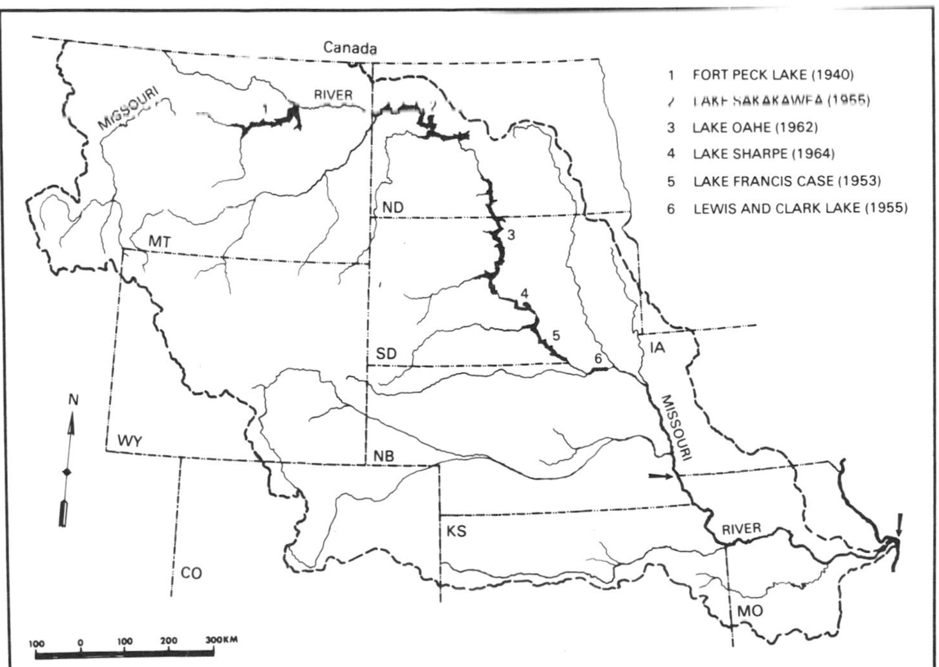

Fig. 21.1. The Missouri River basin and the study area (between arrows).

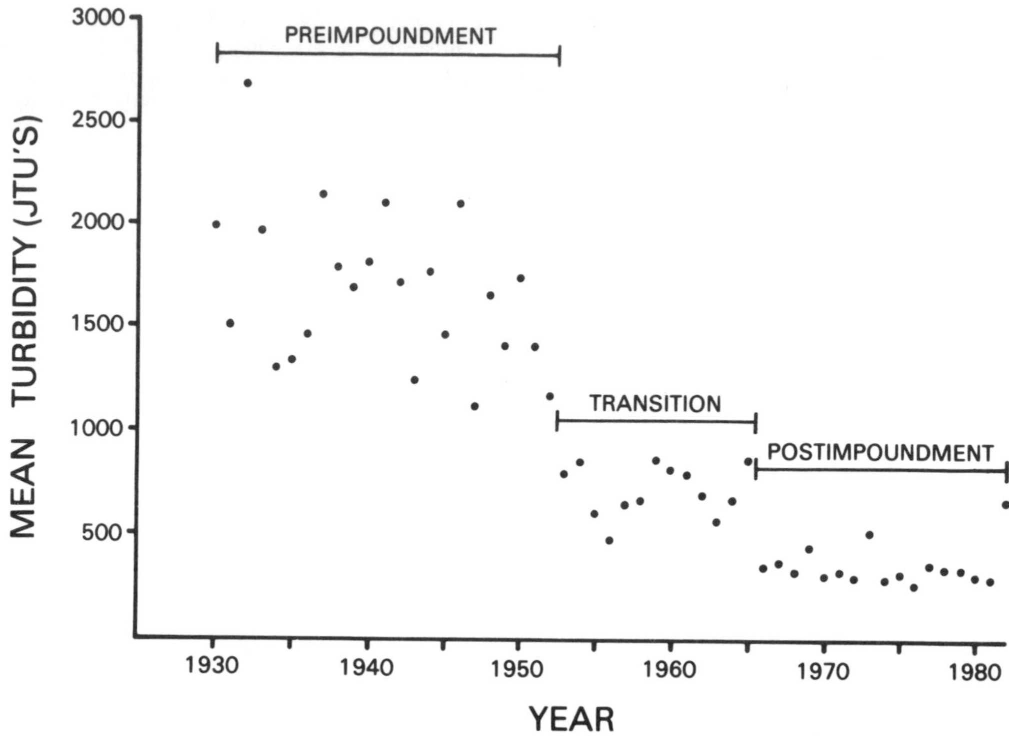

Fig. 21.2. Mean annual turbidities (JTU's) of the Missouri River, determined from daily measurements at the Saint Louis water-treatment facility.

gradual and of a lesser magnitude. During the period when the reservoirs were filling (1953–65), mean discharges were less for any given month than they have been since the reservoir system became operational. Water-management objectives for the reservoir system call for releases to the lower river in the range of 850–1,000 m^3/sec during the navigation season (mid-March to mid-November), and 420–570 m^3/sec during the remainder of the year (Anonymous, 1976). Higher releases occur in years of above-average inflow into the reservoir system. The degree of control over river flow is reduced downstream from the reservoirs owing to inflow from tributaries. The lower tributaries contribute an additional 420–570 m^3 to the Missouri River when they are not in flood during the navigation season.

The slope of the lower Missouri River averages 0.017%, a relatively high value for so large a stream, and the current in the main channel is quite swift. Current velocities in mid-channel are about 1.2–2.1 m/sec during the navigation season (Anonymous, 1976).

Pollution of the Missouri River by organic wastes from towns, packing houses, and stockyards was evident by the early 1900s and continued to increase as populations grew

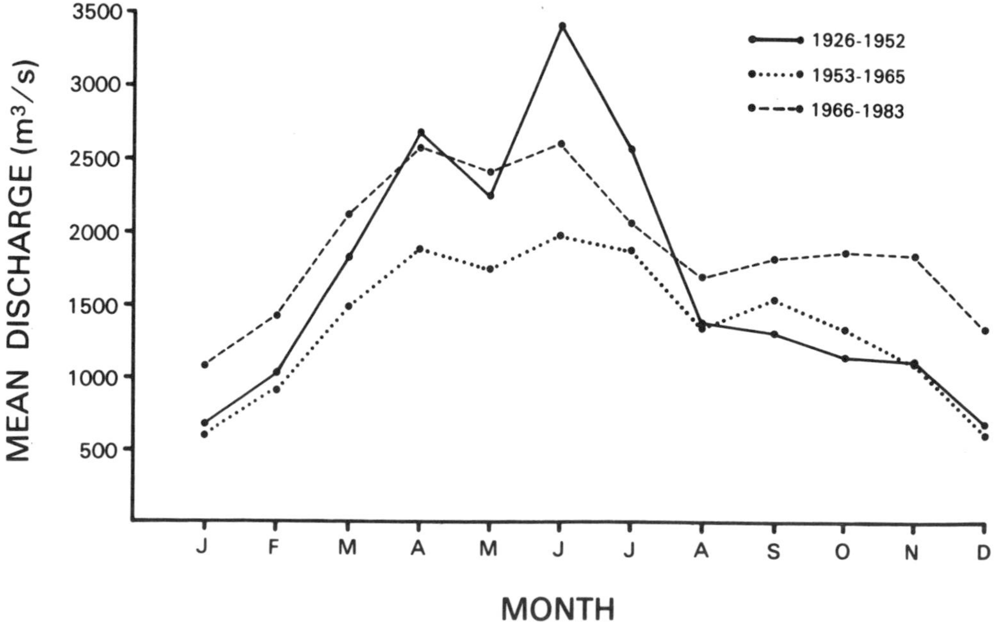

Fig. 21.3. Mean monthly discharges (m^3/s) of the Missouri River, determined from daily measurements at the USGS gauging station at Boonville, Missouri.

and additional industries were established along the river (Whitley and Campbell, 1974). Dissolved oxygen concentrations as low as 2.8 mg/l were recorded at Boonville, Missouri, in 1950; and a massive fish kill attributed to almost complete deoxygenation of the river occurred in 1964 (Ford, 1982). The establishment of primary and secondary sewage-treatment facilities in towns along the river in the 1960s and 1970s, coupled with flow augmentation by upstream reservoirs during the navigation season, have alleviated these problems.

The increased manufacture and use of pesticides and other chemical compounds in the Missouri Basin is a major water-quality concern along the river today. Sampling in the 1970s revealed the presence of 10 heavy metals, 3 pesticides, and 2 volatile organic compounds identified as water pollutants (Ford, 1982). The discharge of heated water and the impingement of larval fishes on the intake screens of several coal-fired and nuclear power plants now in operation along the Missouri River also result in degradation of environmental conditions and mortality among fishes in affected reaches (Hesse et al., 1982).

Methods and Materials

The study reach extends from the Iowa-Missouri border for 885 km to the river mouth (fig. 21.1). To analyze longitudinal changes in the fish fauna, we divided the study area into three sections (fig. 21.4): an upper section extending for 295 km downstream from the Iowa-Missouri border to the mouth of the Kansas River, a middle section extending downstream for another 380 km to the mouth of the Osage River, and a lower section extending another 210 km to the river mouth.

Most of the collections used in this analysis were made in 1945, 1963, and 1982. Because collections made in other years were also used, we defined three sampling periods: period A, 1940–45; period B, 1962–72; and period C, 1978–83. Most collections were made during the warmer months of the year (late March to early November), primarily from July to October. One C-period station was seined 11 times between July 1982 and October 1983 as part of a separate study of sand-island use by Missouri River fishes. Only collections from the 10 September 1982 sampling were used in our computations so that data from that station would be comparable with those from other C-period stations.

For purposes of this study a "station" is loosely defined as a river reach encompassing several kilometers of river, selected to adequately represent all available habitats. Although most sampling was done within the river channel, we also collected in backwaters and the lower reaches of tributaries that were directly influenced by water levels in the main channel at the time the collection was made. However, Fisher (1962) obtained some samples in tributaries as much as 3.2 km from the river at points that were only occasionally influenced by backwater from the river. For our analysis we excluded certain species he designated as having been collected only from tributaries and did not include the large numbers of four other species (creek chub, *Semotilus atro-*

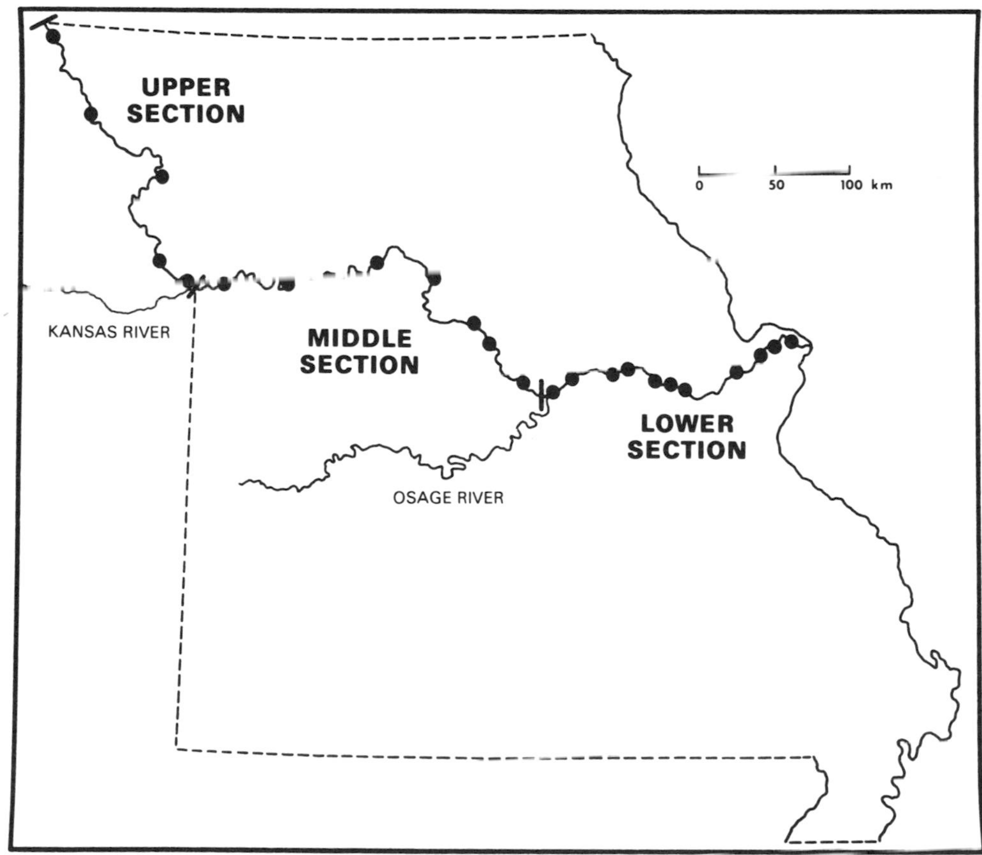

Fig. 21.4. Stations on the lower Missouri River. Some locality symbols represent two or more closely approximated stations.

Table 21.1. Percent Composition by Number of Large (≥ 150 mm TL) and Small (< 150 mm TL) Fishes in Missouri River Collections from Three Time Periods*

Species	Composition by number		
	Period A (1940–45)	Period B (1962–72)	Period C (1978–83)
Large			
Chestnut lamprey (*Ichthyomyzon castaneus*)	Trace	0.2	1.2
Shovelnose sturgeon (*Scaphirhynchus platorynchus*)	0.1	0.8	0.1
Pallid sturgeon (*S. albus*)	0.1	—	—
Shortnose gar (*Lepisosteus platostomus*)	2.0	3.1	1.9
American eel (*Anguilla rostrata*)	—	—	0.1
Skipjack herring (*Alosa chrysochloris*)	—	0.1	Trace
Gizzard shad (*Dorosoma cepedianum*)	8.8	26.7	31.8
Goldeye (*Hiodon alosoides*)	0.7	2.8	1.2
Mooneye (*H. tergisus*)	4.0	0.2	—
Common carp (*Cyprinus carpio*)	34.9	12.9	5.9
River carpsucker (*Carpiodes carpio*)	18.4	18.2	4.8
Bigmouth buffalo (*Ictiobus cyprinellus*)	4.2	0.7	0.4
Black bullhead (*Ictalurus melas*)	4.9	0.1	—
Channel catfish (*I. punctatus*)	9.1	7.1	30.8
Flathead catfish (*Pylodictis olivaris*)	1.8	1.2	0.8
White bass (*Morone chrysops*)	—	4.2	1.0
Striped bass (*M. saxatilis*)	—	—	Trace
Bluegill (*Lepomis macrochirus*)	0.7	2.1	4.1
Spotted bass (*Micropterus punctulatus*)	—	Trace	0.3
White crappie (*Pomoxis annularis*)	0.8	2.5	1.9
Sauger (*Stizostedion canadense*)	0.1	1.6	0.5
Freshwater drum (*Aplodinotus grunniens*)	5.0	8.6	10.6
Small			
Rainbow smelt (*Osmerus mordax*)	—	—	0.1
Western silvery minnow (*Hybognathus argyritis*)	6.4	6.9	2.7
Plains minnow (*Hybognathus placitus*)	56.0	31.7	35.6
Speckled chub (*Hybopsis aestivalis*)	0.2	2.5	4.7
Sturgeon chub (H. gelida)	0.1	0.2	0.8
Flathead chub (H. gracilis)	31.0	8.1	1.1
Sicklefin chub (H. meeki)	0.7	2.1	2.8
Silver chub (H. storeriana)	1.0	8.1	3.8
Emerald shiner (*Notropis atherinoides*)	0.1	22.1	28.5
River shiner (*N. blennius*)	Trace	4.6	7.7
Ghost shiner (*N. buchanani*)	0.2	0.7	0.9
Red shiner (*N. lutrensis*)	3.4	7.7	8.2
Sand shiner (*N. stramineus*)	Trace	2.8	1.8
Mimic shiner (*N. volucellus*)	—	0.8	0.6
Bluntnose minnow (*Pimephales notatus*)	Trace	0.1	1.3
Fathead minnow (*P. promelas*)	0.3	0.2	1.0
Mosquitofish (*Gambusia affinis*)	0.3		0.2

*Only species discussed in the text are included.

maculatus; bigmouth shiner, *Notropis dorsalis*; central stoneroller, *Campostoma anomalum*; and white sucker, *Catostomus commersoni*) that almost certainly were from the tributaries. Fisher (1962) did not identify carpsuckers (*Carpiodes*) to species, so we treated them as river carpsucker, *Carpiodes carpio*. He also did not distinguish between the mimic shiner (*Notropis volucellus*) and the ghost shiner (*Notropis buchanani*), and we treated these specimens as ghost shiners.

A-period samples are available from 12 stations. Eleven of these were sampled by Fisher (1962) in 1945. He used hoop nets of 64-mm mesh and 25-mm mesh with mouths 1.2 m in diameter, a 64-mm mesh trammel net 91.4 m × 1.5 m, a 25-mm mesh seine 137.2 m × 2.4 m, and a 6.4-mm mesh seine 4.6 m × 1.8 m. Four A-period stations (including three of those sampled by Fisher) were sampled in 1940 and 1941 by G. V. Harry, who used a bag seine of unknown specifications.

Fifteen B-period stations were sampled by Pflieger in 1962 and 1963, using a 6.4-mm mesh seine 7.6 m × 2.4 m. Some stations were also sampled with a 5.1-mm mesh seine 22.9 m × 2.4 m. Most small fishes were preserved for subsequent identification and counting except that a few times only large random samples were kept. Most large fishes were counted and released, but in some instances only an indication of abundance was recorded. In subsequent years (1964–72) collections were made at four stations (including one sampled previously by Pflieger). All of these were seined, but two were also sampled with a boat-mounted electroshocker. One of these was also sampled with hoop nets and gill nets.

Thirteen C-period stations were sampled in 1982 with a seine identical to that used in 1962 and 1963 and a boat-mounted electroshocker with pulsed direct current. One additional station was sampled with an electroshocker and rotenone in 1978. All fishes in C-period samples were counted and released in the field or were preserved for subsequent identification and counting.

The common and scientific names used in this paper are those recommended by Robins et al. (1980). Common names are used throughout the report. The scientific names for most species are in table 21.1. The scientific names of species not listed in the table appear the first time the species is referred to in the text. To promote uniformity in the computation of relative abundance, we divided the species into "large" species (adults commonly ⩾ 150 mm TL), and "small" species (adults < 150 mm TL). Small species are adequately represented only in samples made with the 6.4-mm mesh seines, and large species are adequately represented only in samples obtained with other gear. The 6.4-mm mesh seines were invariably used at all stations and in all time periods; however, there was considerable variability in the other kinds of gear used (particularly between time periods). Therefore, the small-fish samples may be better in portraying changes in the fish fauna than the large-fish samples. Missouri River commercial fishermen have been required to report their harvest each year since 1945, and we used these reports as additional documentation for the trends shown for some species

Results

Chronological Changes in the Fauna

When tributary species recorded by Fisher (1962) are excluded, 55 species occurred in A-period collections. Fisher (1962) reported an additional three species (lake sturgeon, *Acipenser fulvescens*; American eel, *Anguilla rostrata*; and burbot, *Lota lota*) caught by fishermen. Common carp and carpsuckers (probably river carpsuckers) occurred at nearly all stations and together comprised 53.3% by number of large fishes (table 21.1). Other common large species were, in descending order of abundance: channel catfish, gizzard shad, freshwater drum, black bullhead, bigmouth buffalo, mooneye, shortnose gar, and flathead catfish. Most mooneye (95%) and black bullhead (70%) were from single stations, and the black bullhead may have been from a tributary collection. River sturgeons (*Scaphirhynchus*) were rare in Fisher's collections, but 4 of 13 specimens (31%) were identified as the pallid sturgeon.

The small-fish fauna in A-period collections was dominated by minnows (Cyprinidae), with western silvery minnows and plains minnows (*Hybognathus*) and chubs *Hybopsis*) comprising 95.4% by number of all small fishes. The plains minnow and flathead chub were by far the most abundant species. The only common *Notropis* was the red shiner.

B-period collections included 67 species, an increase of 12 over A-period collections. Three species not in the survey collections (lake sturgeon, pallid sturgeon, and grass carp, *Ctenopharyngodon idella*) were identified in the catches of fishermen. Most species recorded in B-period but not in A-period collections were rare, occurring as single individuals at one or two stations. Three species (skipjack herring, grass carp, and white bass) apparently were added to the fauna after 1945. Cross and Huggins (1975) reviewed records for the skipjack herring in the Missouri Basin and stated that the earliest documented record was 1954. Pflieger (1978) found that the grass carp first appeared in the Missouri River commercial harvest in 1971. Walberg et al. (1971) reported that the white bass was introduced into Lewis and Clark Lake on the upper Missouri River in 1959. In our collections it occurred at more than one-third of B-period stations and comprised 4.2% by number of all large fishes.

Large fishes were not well represented in most B-period collections, but it appears that there were changes in the relative abundances of several species (table 21.1, fig. 21.5). Of the species listed as common in A-period collections, the gizzard shad apparently increased and the common carp and bigmouth buffalo declined substantially in B period collections. Five other species (goldeye, bluegill, white crappie, sauger, and freshwater drum) may also have increased.

One of the most notable changes in the small-fish fauna was the increasing prominence of shiners (*Notropis*). The emerald shiner showed the biggest increase over A-period collections; substantial increases were also evident in the river shiner, red shiner, and sand shiner (fig. 21.6). Substantial declines occurred in relative abundance of the plains minnow and flathead chub, while four other species of chubs (speckled chub, sturgeon chub, sicklefin chub, and silver chub) showed slight to substantial increases.

C-period collections included 65 species, nearly as many as in B-period collections. Many of the changes in relative abundances evident in C-period collections appeared to be continuations of trends noted previously in comparing A-period and B-period collections. Thus among large fishes the common carp and bigmouth buffalo continued to decline; and the gizzard shad, bluegill, and freshwater drum showed further increases (table 21.1, fig. 21.5). The goldeye, skipjack herring, white bass, white crappie, and sauger were more common in C-period than in A-period collections but did not register a further increase over B-period collections. Notable changes in the relative abundance of large fishes in C-period compared to B-period were a substantial increase in the channel catfish and a decline in the river carpsucker.

The striped bass was first stocked in Lake of the Ozarks, on the Osage River, in 1967. The first specimens (N = 4, 107–21 mm TL) from the Missouri River were taken from impingement screens of the Labadie Power Plant, Franklin County, and Sibley Power Plant, Jackson County, in 1975 and 1976. An adult female measuring 808 mm TL of the 1968-year class was captured by a commercial fisherman near Easley, Boone County, in 1976. In the 1982 survey an

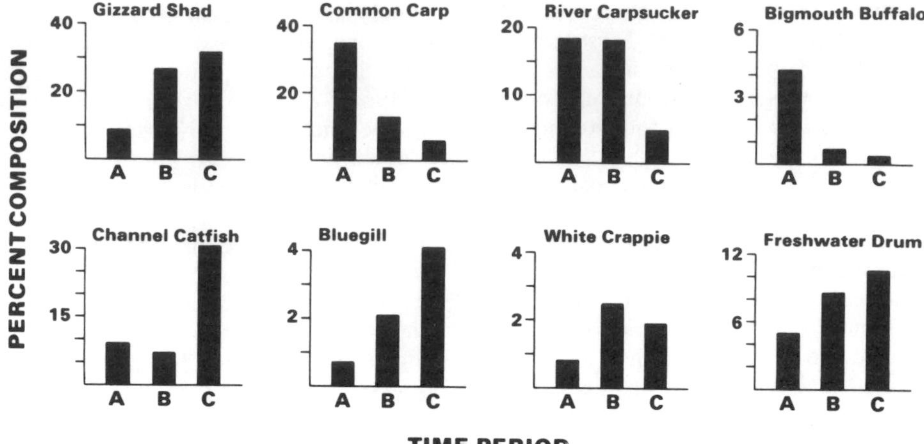

Fig. 21.5. Percent composition by number of selected large-fish species in Missouri River collections from three time periods: A, 1940–45; B, 1962–72; C, 1978–83.

adult striped bass 286 mm TL was collected near Lexington, Lafayette County; and two specimens 70 mm and 83 mm TL were seined near Easley.

Shiners (*Notropis*) comprised 47.9% by number of all small fishes in C-period collections, compared to 39.5% for B-period samples. Most shiners that showed an increase in B-period collections over A-period collections increased further or remained essentially unchanged in C-period collections (fig. 21.6). The sand shiner declined but was still far more abundant than in A-period collections. Three species of chubs (sicklefin chub, speckled chub, and sturgeon chub) showed a further increase in C-period collections, but the silver chub declined. The flathead chub continued to decline. The plains minnow increased slightly but remained well below A-period levels, and the western silvery minnow declined substantially. The mosquitofish occurred with greater frequency in C-period collections than in those from earlier time periods and appeared to have extended its range 600 km upstream since 1945.

The rainbow smelt was introduced as a forage fish into Lake Sakakawea, North Dakota, in 1976 (Cross et al., 1986). The first specimens known to us from the lower Missouri River were collected near Kansas City by P. J. Jeffries, Jr., on 26 October 1978. Other reports of rainbow smelt from the lower Missouri River include 119 specimens from impingement screens of the Iatan Power Plant, Platte County, in 1980 (Geo-Marine, Inc., 1981) and 100 specimens from near Reform, Callaway County, in 1980 and 1981 (T. C. See, pers. comm.). Eight specimens of rainbow smelt occurred in our 1982 survey collections from stations near Saint Joseph, Leavenworth, and Glasgow. An additional 490 specimens were seined near Easley between 10 November 1982 and 23 March 1983.

Harvest statistics for commercial fishes provide additional information concerning trends in the abundance of certain species in the Missouri River since 1945 (fig. 21.7). These statistics are in general agreement with the trends indicated by our survey data for some species but not for others. Thus

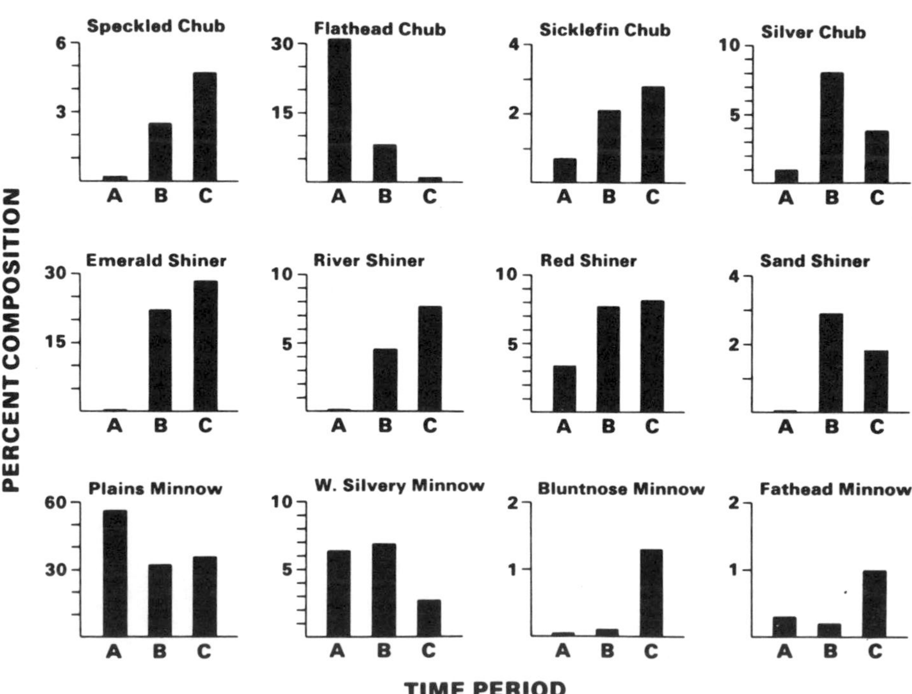

Fig. 21.6. Percent composition by number of selected small-fish species in Missouri River collections from three time periods: A, 1940–45; B, 1962–72; C, 1978–83.

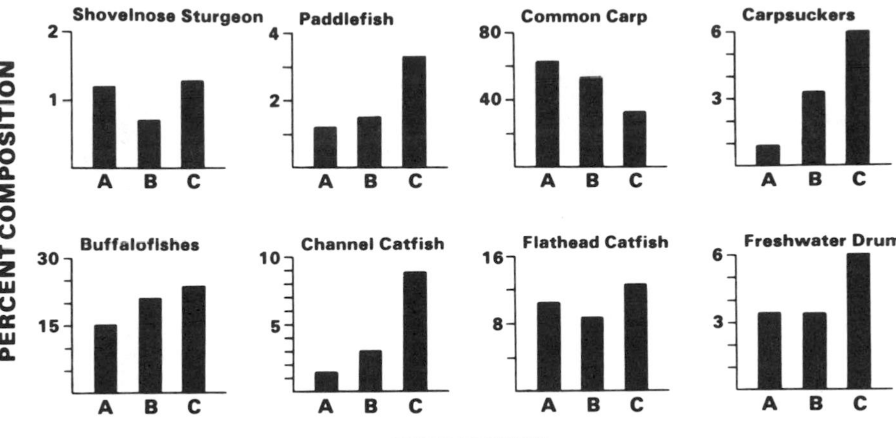

Fig. 21.7. Percent composition by weight of selected fish species in the reported commercial harvest from the lower Missouri River during three time periods: A, 1945–49; B, 1962–66; C, 1978–83.

both sets of data suggest a consistent decline in the common carp and an increase in the channel catfish and freshwater drum. On the other hand, the survey data suggest a decline in carpsuckers (*Carpiodes*) and buffalofishes (*Ictiobus*), whereas the commercial-fisheries statistics suggest an increase in carpsuckers and no significant change in buffalofishes. The inconsistency in buffalofishes may result because they are more vulnerable to capture by the nets used by fishermen and by Fisher (1962) than to the electrofishing gear used in obtaining most B-period and C-period survey collections of large fishes. This explanation does not hold for carpsuckers, however, because our observations lead us to believe that they are readily sampled with electrofishing gear.

Commercial-fishery statistics provide the principal evidence available to us concerning trends in the abundance of the grass carp. The harvest of this species has increased each year since it was first reported in 1971, and in 1983 it comprised 1.7% of the total reported commercial harvest. In August 1984 we found 78 young-of-the-year grass carp (79–133 mm SL) in a dried-up overflow pool of the Missouri River near Easley. These specimens provide the first substantial evidence for natural reproduction of this species in the river.

In July 1982 a commercial fisherman captured a silver carp (*Hypophthalmichthys molitrix*) weighing 3.6 kg in the Missouri River near Mokane, Callaway County. This large eurasian cyprinid is being propagated and stocked on a limited basis in Missouri and surrounding states.

River sturgeons comprised a small but consistent proportion of the commercial fishes harvest throughout the period of record (fig. 21.7). Carlson et al. (1985) examined 1,806 river sturgeons from the Missouri River in 1978 and 1979, and only five (0.3%) were pallid sturgeon. Of potentially greater significance was that four other specimens were hybrids between this species and the shovelnose sturgeon. The ratio of pallid sturgeon to shovelnose sturgeon indicated by their study is substantially lower than that found by Fisher (1962).

Many of the differences in species composition among sampling periods involved rare species that seem to occur in the river only as stragglers from tributary streams and other nearby habitats. Species judged to be stragglers occurred more frequently in B-period and C-period collections than in A-period collections. Thus of 26 species designated as stragglers, 5 occurred only in B-period collections (smallmouth bass, *Micropterus dolomieui*; largescale stoneroller, *Campostoma oligolepis*; Mississippi silvery minnow, *Hybognathus nuchalis*; rosyface shiner, *Notropis rubellus*; and johnny darter, *Etheostoma nigrum*), 7 occurred only in C-period collections (shorthead redhorse, *Moxostoma macrolepidotum*; rock bass, *Ambloplites rupestris*; golden shiner, *Notemigonus crysoleucas*; bigeye shiner, *Notropis boops*; southern redbelly dace, *Phoxinus erythrogaster*; brook silverside, *Labidesthes sicculus*; and slenderhead darter, *Percina phoxocephala*), and 8 occurred only in B-period and C-period collections (quillback, *Carpiodes cyprinus*; spotted bass, *Micropterus punctulatus*; brassy minnow, *Hybognathus hankinsoni*; gravel chub, *Hybopsis x-punctata*; Ozark minnow, *Notropis nubilus*; spotfin shiner, *Notropis spilopterus*; redfin shiner, *Notropis umbratilis*; and logperch, *Percina caprodes*). Two species (white sucker, *Catostomus commersoni* and yellow bullhead, *Ictalurus natalis*) occurred only in A-period collections, and 3 species (golden redhorse, *Moxostoma erythrurum*; central stoneroller, *Campostoma anomalum*; and creek chub, *Semotilus atromaculatus*) occurred only in A-period and B-period collections.

Differences in the Fish Fauna Between River Sections

Pflieger (1971) noted a striking hiatus in the distribution of the river shiner in the Missouri River. In 1963 collections this species was common at the mouth of the Missouri River but was not encountered in any other collection below Lexington, 518 km upstream. From Lexington upstream it occurred at every station sampled and comprised 6% by number of all fishes in the samples. Pflieger (1971) noted that Fisher (1962) recorded this species only above Kansas City, suggesting that the pattern had persisted for at least 20 years. We found that this pattern was still evident in 1982 and documented other comparable examples (figs. 21.8 and 21.9) Species that appeared to increase upstream include shortnose gar, white bass, bluegill, freshwater drum, plains minnow, emerald shiner, and fathead minnow. A number of species exhibit the opposite trend, being most abundant in the

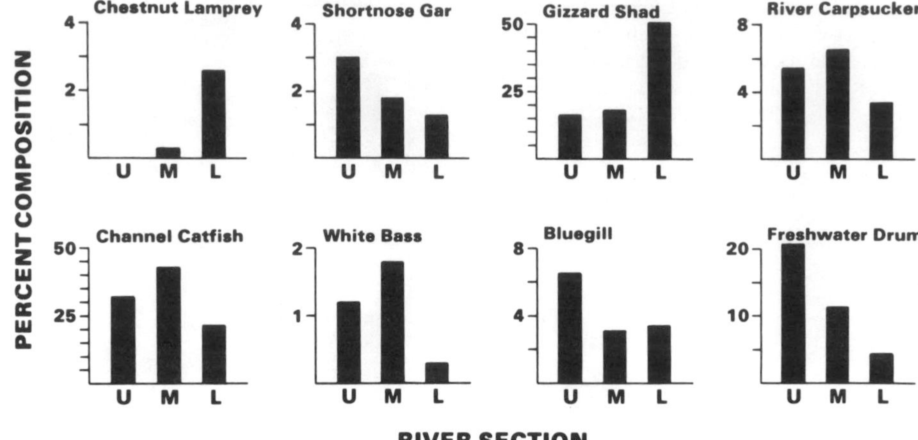

Fig. 21.8. Percent composition by number of selected large-fish species in collections from three sections of the lower Missouri River, 1978–83 (C period): U, upper; M, middle; L, lower.

lower section and descreasing in relative abundance upstream. These include chestnut lamprey, gizzard shad, speckled chub, sturgeon chub, sicklefin chub, mimic shiner, and bluntnose minnow.

Patterns are also evident in the occurrence of species judged to be stragglers in the river. Of the 26 species designated as stragglers, 14 were recorded only in the lower river section (rock bass; longear sunfish, *Lepomis megalotis*; spotted bass; largescale stoneroller; Mississippi silvery minnow; gravel chub; bigeye shiner; Ozark minnow; rosyface shiner; spotfin shiner; southern redbelly dace; brook silverside; johnny darter; and slenderhead darter), and an additional three species (white sucker, redfin shiner, and logperch) were recorded only in the middle and lower sections. The middle and upper sections had one straggler each not recorded in any other river section (smallmouth bass and brassy minnow, respectively) and shared one species (bigmouth shiner).

Variations in Species Richness and Diversity Indices

When collections from different time periods were compared, slight but consistent differences were evident in species richness (number of species per station) and diversity indices (Shannon, 1948; table 21.2). Values for C-period stations were invariably higher than those for A-period stations, while those for B-period stations were generally intermediate. Species richness for all species was lower for B-period than for A-period stations in the upper and lower river sections, but this was an artifact. Only seines were used in sampling the B-period stations, while other gear more effective in sampling large fishes was used in sampling the A-period and C-period stations. This inconsistency is not evident when only small species are compared.

Slight but consistent differences were also evident when different stream sections were compared. Within a given time period species richness and diversity indices were invariably lowest in the upper section and were generally intermediate between other river sections in the middle section. Again the results for B-period stations were inconsistent, primarily because some stations in the middle section were sampled over a longer time period and with gear more effective in collecting large fishes.

The differences indicated in diversity appear to involve the evenness component as well as the number of species component of the diversity equation. This is indicated by the fact that three species (plains minnow, flathead chub, and western silvery minnow) comprised 93.4% by number of all small fishes in A-period collections, while the three most abundant small species comprised only 61.9% of the B-period collections and 72.3% of the C-period collections.

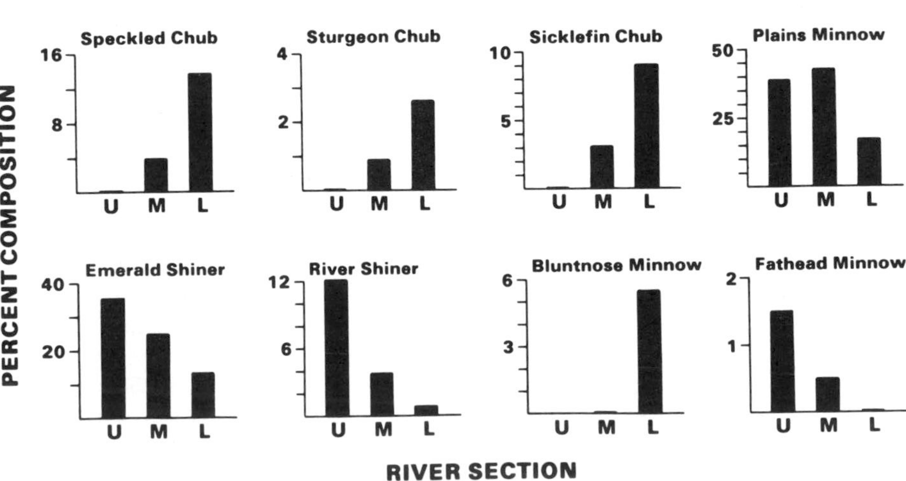

Fig. 21.9. Percent composition by number of selected small-fish species in collections from three sections of the lower Missouri River, 1978–83 (C period): U, upper; M, middle; L, lower.

Table 21.2. Species Richness and Diversity Indices for Collections from the Missouri River

Time Period and River Section	All Species						Small Species					
	Number of Species/Station			Shannon Diversity Index			Number of Species/Station			Shannon Diversity Index		
	N	$\bar{x}$	SE	*N*	$\bar{x}$	SE	*N*	$\bar{x}$	SE	*N*	$\bar{x}$	SE
Period A (1940–45)												
Upper section	3	23.3	2.19	2	2.20	0.325	3	9.0	1.00	2	1.45	0.016
Middle section	6	23.5	1.89	6	2.45	0.294	6	9.2	1.11	6	1.45	0.230
Lower section	2	32.5	6.50	2	2.85	0.179	2	10.0	1.00	2	1.34	0.028
All sections	11	25.1	1.80	10	2.48	0.192	11	9.3	0.65	10	1.43	0.134
Period B (1962–72)												
Upper section	7	16.6	1.36	7	2.33	0.144	7	11.0	0.38	7	2.04	0.235
Middle section	5	29.8	4.70	3	3.52	0.275	5	13.6	0.93	3	2.66	0.111
Lower section	6	23.8	2.76	6	2.97	0.095	6	14.3	1.38	6	2.59	0.078
All sections	18	22.7	2.04	16	2.79	0.142	18	12.8	0.63	16	2.36	0.128
Period C (1978–83)												
Upper section	4	30.0	0.82	4	2.83	0.132	4	12.5	1.19	4	2.04	0.155
Middle section	4	30.8	0.88	4	3.27	0.149	4	13.0	1.15	4	2.28	0.160
Lower section	6	35.3	1.91	6	3.61	0.216	6	15.3	0.92	6	2.83	0.135
All sections	14	32.5	1.13	14	3.29	0.129	14	13.9	0.68	14	2.43	0.120

Discussion

Under presettlement conditions, the Missouri River supported a relatively limited fauna comprised of species adapted for life in an environment characterized by persistent high turbidity, wide seasonal fluctuations in flow and temperature, and an unstable sand-silt substrate. The more distinctive species in this fauna were pallid sturgeon, western silvery minnow, plains minnow, flathead chub, sturgeon chub, and sicklefin chub. Early collectors (Jordan and Meek, 1885; Meek, 1892) recorded about 28 species in the river near Saint Joseph, Missouri, and Sioux City, Iowa. In the first thorough survey of fishes in the lower river Fisher (1962) recorded 55 species, including all those listed by earlier workers. The general composition of the fauna may not have changed substantially by 1945, but meager evidence suggests that there were changes in relative abundance. Carpsuckers, listed as rare by Meek (1892), were abundant in Fisher's collections; and the sturgeon chub, listed as abundant by early workers, was uncommon in Fisher's collections. The common carp may have been present in the Missouri River by the late 1800s, but it was not recorded. In 1945 it was by far the most abundant large fish in Fisher's collections.

Surveys made at approximately 20-year intervals since 1940 provide documentation for an increase in the number of species and substantial changes in relative abundances. Species that became established in the river or became more abundant are mostly pelagic planktivores and sight-feeding carnivores: skipjack herring, gizzard shad, white bass, bluegill, white crappie, emerald shiner, river shiner, and red shiner. These changes are probably related to decreased turbidity and changes in flow regimens following construction of upstream reservoirs. Moderation of extreme fluctuations in dissolved oxygen resulting from reductions in organic pollutants in recent decades could also have been a factor in the increased species richness. Since many of the species listed above are far more abundant in the upstream reservoirs than they were in the unimpounded river, escapement from the reservoirs could also be a factor in maintenance of populations in the lower river. Five species (white bass, bluegill, freshwater drum, emerald shiner, and river shiner) became progressively more abundant upstream in the study reach, a distribution pattern that would be expected if the reservoirs were their source. However, the gizzard shad was most abundant in the lower section, and the skipjack herring does not occur in the upstream reservoirs. Downstream populations of the rainbow smelt must be maintained entirely by escapement from the reservoirs, as indicated by marked seasonal patterns in abundance and its intolerance for normal summer temperatures that prevail in the lower river.

The pallid sturgeon and flathead chub, two of the species adapted for life in the presettlement Missouri River, have declined markedly in abundance. Perhaps the decline of the pallid sturgeon resulted from competition with the closely related shovelnose sturgeon, which is still abundant in the river. Competition is indicated by increased frequency of hybridization between them. Reduced habitat diversity related to channelization and to reductions in turbidity and sediment load that favor the more adaptable shovelnose sturgeon may no longer permit survival of two sturgeon species with similar requirements in the Missouri River. Competition may also have been a factor in the decline of the flathead chub. Davis and Miller (1967) compared brain patterns and gustatory structures in chubs and concluded that the flathead chub was a generalist. They noted that Olund and Cross (1961) found that this species feeds primarily on terrestrial insects and surmised that the insects were obtained from the water surface by sight feeding. This habit might bring the flathead chub into direct competition with the shiners that are now much more abundant in the river. Increased predation could also be a factor in the decline of the flathead chub. This midwater species evolved in an environment where sight-feeding predators were scarce, and it might not possess effective mechanisms for avoiding predation.

Other chubs (speckled chub, sturgeon chub, and sicklefin chub) that are specialized for life in turbid plains streams (Davis and Miller, 1967) have fared better than the flathead chub. These species have increased in abundance in the middle and lower sections of our study area during the last 40 years. Habitat for them (open channels with swift current and firm substrate) has actually been increased by channelization. This habitat is sparsely inhabited by most other fishes, largely isolating the chubs from potential competitors and predators. Their close association with the substrate may also result in their being less vulnerable to predation than the midwater flathead chub. The lower Missouri River may be the last stronghold for the sturgeon chub and sicklefin chub. They were rare in C-period samples from the upper section of our study area and were not recorded in recent collections from the upper impounded river or tailwaters below the most downstream reservoir (Benson, 1968; Walberg et al., 1971; Schmulbach et al., 1975; Kallemeyn and Novotny, 1977). They have been reported in recent collections from the upper Missouri River basin (Elser et al., 1980; Owen et al., 1981) but appear to be uncommon and localized in distribution.

The two common species of silvery minnows (western silvery minnow and plains minnow) declined in relative abundance over the period of record. These species typically occur in silty backwaters and probably subsist largely on organically rich mud and ooze like the related Mississippi silvery minnow (Forbes and Richardson, 1908). Silty backwaters became less prevalent as the river was channelized and its sediment load was reduced. The bluntnose minnow and fathead minnow, two minnows with rather similar food habits, may not have become sufficiently abundant in the river to offer significant competition to the silvery minnows. Cross (1967) noted the similarity in food habits between the plains minnow and the river carpsucker. He suggested that they were ecological counterparts, the river carpsucker occurring in deeper water. Our C-period collections indicate an abrupt decline in abundance of the river carpsucker, perhaps indicating that silvery minnows and carpsuckers have responded similarly to changes in the river environment. However, commercial-fisheries statistics suggest that river carpsucker has not declined.

Enrichment of the Missouri River fish fauna has resulted in part from accidental and intentional introductions by man. The rainbow smelt and the white bass were introduced as forage and game fish, respectively, in reservoirs on the upper river. The latter species occurred naturally in the Mississippi River and perhaps invaded the lower Missouri River from that source. The grass carp became established in the Missouri River by escapement of specimens stocked in ponds and reservoirs throughout the Mississippi Valley. The success of this phytophagous species in the Missouri River is surprising, considering the virtual absence of aquatic plants in the river. Populations in the river are not being maintained by movement from tributaries, judging by the paucity of records of grass carp in tributaries of the lower Missouri River. The discovery of numerous young in overflow waters of the river provides evidence that river populations are self-sustaining. Striped bass specimens found in the Missouri River may have escaped from reservoirs on tributaries but may also result from reproduction in the river, as indicated by the presence of small specimens.

Enrichment of the Missouri River fish fauna has also included increased frequency of species that are stragglers from tributaries. This increased frequency is particularly evident in the lower and middle sections and involves species characteristic of clear upland streams that border these river sections. The presettlement Missouri River may have been a substantial barrier to dispersal of these species, and their increased frequency in recent collections suggests that the river is now less of a barrier. Some of the stragglers appear to have capitalized on changes in the river environment to increase their range in the lower basin. Spotted bass were restricted to the Osage River drainage in the early 1940s, but had become established in the following additional tributaries of the lower Missouri River by the indicated years: Moreau River, 1958; Gasconade River, 1966; Auxvasse Creek, 1980; Cedar Creek and Moniteau Creek, 1984. Since 1975 the longear sunfish has extended its range to include Moniteau Creek, Bonne Femme Creek, Splice Creek, and Jamerson Creek. The Ozark minnow became established in the Moreau River sometime between 1965 and 1979.

A decline in relative abundance of the common carp, as indicated by survey collections and commercial-fisheries statistics, may be related to the establishment of more intensive waste treatment by towns discharging effluents into the river. The tolerance of this species for various pollutants and its concentration at points where sewage entered a river were noted by Sigler (1958). We have also observed concentrations of this species below sewage outfalls. Low levels of dissolved oxygen appear to favor the common carp over some other species in lakes subject to winterkill (Moyle and Clothier, 1959). The reduction in organic wastes and amelioration of the oxygen sags that formerly accompanied rising water levels on the Missouri River may have reduced the food supply for the common carp and changed its competitive relationships with other species less tolerant of low dissolved oxygen.

We cannot definitely ascribe any changes in the fish fauna of the Missouri River to thermal discharges by power plants. The spread of mosquitofish for nearly 600 km upstream in the river in recent decades could be due in part to heated effluents providing winter refuges. However, this species also seems to be extending its range into streams not affected by thermal effluents. We find that the threadfin shad (*Dorosoma petenense*) has extended its range 450 km northward in the Mississippi River since 1963 and suspect that thermal effluents may have been a factor in this extension.

The public works projects responsible for most of the principal environmental changes described in this report are essentially complete. The trends in fish species abundance set in motion by these changes will probably continue until a new equilibrium is reached, but it is difficult to predict the magnitude or duration of these continuing trends. It seems likely that the pallid sturgeon and possibly also the flathead chub will disappear from the lower river. The abundance of other species that are in decline may stabilize at levels short of complete extirpation. The grass carp may continue to increase but will probably not become a dominant species in the fauna because of a limited food source. The planktivorous silver carp may have greater success if it is able to reproduce, considering the abundance of other planktivores in the river. Another large planktivorous cyprinid, the bighead carp (*Aristichthys nobilis*), is present at several locations with potential access to the Missouri River and may also become established in the future.

The scenario outlined above assumes no further drastic alterations in the river environment. However, additional demands that may be placed on water resources of the Missouri River in the future could render these predictions moot. Proposals for water-resource development that are of particular concern include the diversion of water for irrigation to other basins and the use of water for coal gasification and transport.[1]

[1] Funds for this study were provided by the National Marine Fisheries Service, National Oceanic and Atmospheric Administration. John W. Robinson made data available on the harvest of commercial fishes. Don Rea and Loyd A. Waite provided turbidity and discharge data, respectively. Otto F. Fajen, Mark D. Hansen, Philip J. Jeffries, Frank Putz, John W. Robinson, Thomas C. See, and Philip L. Wampler provided locality records for several species. Frank B. Cross, William H. Dieffenbach, John W. Robinson, Thomas R. Russell, and Norman P. Stucky reviewed the manuscript and provided useful suggestions. Kenneth D. West assisted in the field, and Holly V. Wheeler sorted small-fish collections. We thank all of these individuals for their important contributions.

22. Changes in the Fauna of the Little River Drainage, Southeastern Oklahoma, 1948–1955 to 1981–1982: A Test of the Hypothesis of Environmental Degradation

D. Allen Rutherford, Anthony A. Echelle, and O. Eugene Maughan

Abstract

Despite more than 15 years of intensive silvicultural activity, including clear-cutting, in the Little River drainage of southeastern Oklahoma, there is little evidence of extinction or addition of stream fishes. However, a comparison of collections made in 1948–55 and 1981–82 from the same 44 localities indicates a pattern of change in faunal structure that, before the analysis, was an expected corollary to human-induced faunal change: species that occur both in Little River and in plains streams of western Oklahoma show little evidence of change in frequency of occurrence since 1948–55, while, as a group, species restricted to eastern Oklahoma appear to have declined. The former group of species is presumed to have generally greater tolerance to environmental extremes, while the latter should have less tolerance. Intensive forestry activity is the only conspicuous human activity that is closely associated with the indicated faunal change.

Declines in the occurrences of fish species in the central United States have been documented in numerous studies (Trautman,, 1939; Black, 1949; Minckley and Cross, 1959; Larimore and Smith, 1963; Smith, 1971; Trautman and Gartman, 1974; Pflieger, 1975; Cross et al., 1983). These declines typically are attributed to anthropogenic environmental changes and are often accompanied by increased occurrence of species considered more tolerant of environmental disturbance.

In this chapter we present an analysis of differences in the fish fauna of the Little River of southeastern Oklahoma between two intervals of time separated by 25 years. In those 25 years the terrestrial environment was greatly altered by clear-cutting forestry practices, and our purpose was to determine whether there have been any associated changes in the fish fauna. Comparison of collections made in our 1981–82 survey of the Little River drainage with those in the same area in 1948–55 (Reeves, 1953, Finnell et al., 1956) suggests that some species declined in occurrence while others increased and that there have been changes in indices of community structure.

Any two ichthyofaunal surveys made by different workers at times separated by two and a half decades are likely to show changes. Such changes may be due to any or all of three hypothetical causes: (1) human-related environmental change, (2) natural fluctuations in faunal structure, or (3) sampling bias. In our analysis we cannot completely eliminate hypotheses 2 and 3; on the other hand, these hypotheses do not provide easily seen corollaries regarding qualitative faunal changes. However, since intense human activity would generally cause a decline in environmental quality for natural faunas, hypothesis 1 produces the following corollary: species with greater tolerances to environmental extremes should increase in occurrence while those with lesser tolerances should decrease. By tolerance we refer to persistence of the species in the face of environmental extremes, by whatever means, e.g., behavioral and reproductive attributes, not just physiological tolerances.

To examine the expected corollary to human-related change, we looked for trends among changes in occurrence of two groups of fishes in the Little River drainage: (1) those occurring westward into plains streams of Oklahoma and (2) those restricted to the eastern half of the state. In general those fishes that can tolerate plains streams should have the greater tolerances to environmental extremes (cf. Matthews, Chap. 14).

Species of plains streams are exposed to widely fluctuating variables such as salinity, oxygen concentrations, temperature, and water flow (Hubbs and Hettler, 1959; Cross, 1967; Echelle et al., 1972; Matthews and Hill, 1980) and natural die-offs are probably relatively common, especially during harsh periods such as droughts accompanied by high temperatures (e.g., Matthews et al., 1982b). In contrast, conditions in streams of the forested area east of the plains environment are more stable and less harsh (Cross, 1967; Ross et al., 1985). Thus species restricted to eastern Oklahoma should be less tolerant of environmental extremes than would those occurring in plains streams. On that assumption we examine the null hypothesis that changes in the Little River drainage fish fauna are not related to the assumed tolerances of the species. This allows potential falsification of the hypothesis that the observed changes are due to human activities.

Study Area

The Little River drains about 5,700 km^2 in LeFlore, Pushmataha, and McCurtain counties of southeastern Oklahoma. The system has three major components, the Little River proper and two major tributaries, Glover Creek and Mountain Fork River. The Little River flows in Oklahoma for about 241 km and then 129 km in Arkansas to its confluence with the Red River. Two large, artificial reservoirs occur in the Oklahoma portion of the drainage, Broken Bow Reservoir (1,952 km^2, impounded in 1968) and Pine Creek Reservoir (1,644 km^2, impounded in 1969).

The headwaters of the drainage lie in the Kiamichi and Ouachita mountains, where the typical streams are small and clear and have rocky bottoms and steep gradients. The lower sections of the river pass through lowlands where streams are sluggish and bordered by swampy areas. The upper and middle reaches of the Little River flow through mixed pine/deciduous forest used primarily for silvicultural activities. There are few farms, communities, or other developments that might affect the fish fauna.

The human population in the three-county area of the Little River drainage (McCurtain, Pushmataha, and LeFlore) grew 15% (from 35,276 to 40,698) between 1950 and 1980 (Peach and Pool, 1965a, b; Dikeman and Earley, 1982). Much if not all of this growth was in the larger urban centers (Peach and Pool, 1965a, b). In the Little River system the larger urban centers (Broken Bow and Idabel) are in the lowlands and are downstream of or well removed from all locations used in our analysis of frequencies of occurrence.

Poor soil quality has ensured continuously low agricultural activity in the Little River drainage. In fact, total area devoted to farmlands has declined from 444,316 ha in 1950 (Peach et al., 1965) to 405,754 ha in 1978 (Dikeman and Earley, 1982). Altered farming practices (e.g., increased fertilizer application) could cause changes in the fish fauna despite reduced farmland. However, water analyses at a number of sites do not indicate an increase in nutrient inputs (B. Burks, pers. comm.).

Commercial forestry in southeastern Oklahoma began around 1910 with selective cutting of pine, cypress, and oak (Honess, 1923). Selective cutting continued to be the dominant forestry method until the 1960s, when intensive silvicultural activities were initiated, including clear-cutting and extensive dirt and gravel road building. At present, more than 16,200 ha are clear-cut each year, and since 1970 an extensive network of more than 6,400 km of new logging roads has been constructed in southeastern Oklahoma (Oklahoma State Dept. Agric., 1982). This kind of activity is especially intense in the Little River drainage.

Weather conditions were generally similar in 1948–55 and 1981–82. Average annual rainfall across nine weather stations over the Little River drainage was 115.8 cm in 1948–55 and 113.3 cm in 1981–82. Average annual temperatures for these periods were 17.3° C and 16.3° C, respectively (U.S. Weather Bureau, 1948–55; National Oceanic and Atmospheric Administration, 1975–82).

Methods and Materials

Data Collection

The data for 1948–55 were taken from 91 collection localities reported by Reeves (1953) and 62 reported by Finnell et al. (1956). Reeves's collections were made with seines and/or gill nets in August 1948, 1950, and 1951 by George A. Moore and his students, including J. D. Reeves. Collections reported by Finnell et al. were made with seines or rotenone in July–August 1955.

In July–September 1981 and 1982 we sampled fishes at 156 localities in the Little River drainage, 44 of which were also sampled by Reeves (1955) or Finnell et al. (1956) or both. Of the sites sampled in the two earlier surveys, 98 were not included in our survey for one or another of three reasons: (1) they were nonstream sites (oxbows, stock ponds), (2) they had been inundated by reservoir construction, or (3) they could not be located from the available descriptions.

Each sample area extended from the first available riffle (usually downstream from the access bridge) downstream to the next riffle or, if no second riffle was encountered, to a point about 100 m downstream. Sampling consisted of 45–60 min of electroshocking (AC generator, 220 v, 12 amp; hand-held electrodes) followed by intensive seining of all available microhabitats. Seining was done with either a 1.2-m × 3.7-m seine with 3.2-mm Ace mesh or a 1.8-m × 9.1-m seine with 4.8-mm Ace mesh or both. All fish were preserved in 10% Formalin and returned to the laboratory for identification.

Each collection locality was scored for six environmental variables that are not likely to have changed significantly since 1948–55. This allows examination of changes in the fish fauna relative to the physical environment in a situation where we have no information on past environmental conditions.

The six variables recorded were (1) maximum stream width, based on on-site measurements, (2) elevation, (3) stream gradient, (4) stream order (5) distance from the headwater terminus of the stream (variables 2–5 based on U.S. Geological Survey maps), and (6) soil type (taken from U.S. Soil Conservation Service maps). Strahler's (1957) method was used for determining stream order. Soil type was scored as follows: 1 = clay, 2 = silt loam, 3 = loam, 4 = fine sandy loam, 5 = sandy-gravelly loam, 6 = gravelly loam.

Data Analysis

Frequencies of occurrence of each species in the two periods (early and recent) were compared on the basis of presence in or absence from collections. The original data matrix will be available in D. A. Rutherford's Ph.D. dissertation (in prep.,

Oklahoma State University). Chi-square analysis of 2 × 2 contingency tables (α = 0.05) were used to test the null hypothesis of no difference between recent and early collections in the presence or absence of species. In these analyses only species occurring in a combined total of 10 or more recent or early collections (hereafter referred to as "common" species; those in fewer than 10 collections are termed "rare") were included. Fisher's exact test was used for contingency table analysis in cases where expected frequency in one or more cells was less than 5. Data for the 1948–55 collections made by gill netting or with rotenone were eliminated from this analysis. This approach allowed direct comparison of 44 early seine collections with recent seine and electroshocking collections from the same locations (fig. 22.1).

Small cyprinids and other small, nectonic fishes are generally more susceptible to seining than to electroshocking, and our seining efforts may have been less intensive than those in 1948–55. However, we attempted to sample all available microhabitats at each site, and during the electroshocking effort we tried to preserve as many cyprinids and other small fishes as possible. Furthermore, all analyses are based only on the presence or absence of species, and the weighting of a single specimen equaled that of a large number of specimens of one species.

Our use of electroshocking and the absence of this method from the 1948–55 collecting effort might produce a bias toward higher frequencies of occurrence of larger, more mobile fishes (centrarchids, catfishes, suckers) in our collections. However, of the five members of this group that showed statistically significant deviations from the early frequencies, two were less common in recent than in earlier collections. This would not be predicted on the basis of more efficient sampling in the recent efforts.

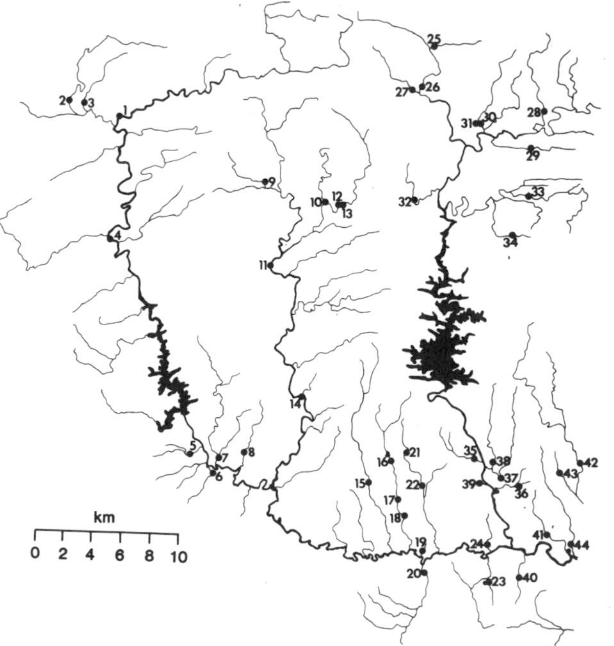

Fig. 22.1. Locations of 44 sites in the Little River drainage where fish collections were made in 1948–55 and in 1981–82.

To help in the search for sampling bias relevant to our study of widespread and restricted species, we divided into two groups all fishes taken at the 44 localities sampled in both 1948–55 and 1981–82. From our experience we placed gars, bowfins, shad, suckers, catfishes (except *Noturus nocturnus*), and centrarchids in a group we considered more susceptible to capture by electroshocking than by seining. All other species were considered more susceptible to seining; these included species that, in general, are smaller than the members of the other group and tend to be less affected by electroshock (e.g., minnows, darters, pirate perch, pigmy sunfish, brook silverside). Chi-square tests of contingency between membership in the two groups and of increase or decrease in frequency of occurrence from 1948–55 to 1981–82 revealed no significant relationship in separate analyses of the common (χ^2 = 1.1) and rare species (1.2), nor for the common and rare species considered together (2.1).

As an indication of environmental tolerance we rated each species on the basis of whether or not it is a common inhabitant of plains streams in the Red River drainage of western Oklahoma. We used contingency chi-square analysis (α = 0.05) to test for independence between increased or decreased frequency of occurrence and whether species have widespread or restricted distributions.

To help in the examination of patterns of change in community structure, the simple matching coefficient of similarity (Sneath and Sokal, 1973) in presence or absence of species was computed, separately for the recent and the early data sets, for all pairwise combinations of collections. With the Mantel test (Sokal, 1979) we then tested for covariance between recent and early matrices. If patterns of relative similarity among sites are similar in the matrices of recent and early collections, the Mantel test produces a significantly positive test statistic (= positive covariation), while if the matrices differ in pattern of relative similarity, the test statistic is either nonsignificant (no covariation) or significantly negative (negative covariation). Significant negative values suggest an overall tendency toward reversed patterns in which similarities that are high for the early collections are low for the recent collections and vice versa.

With the simple matching coefficient and the Mantel test we also compared the recent and early species-by-species matrices of similarity of presence or absence across the 44 sites. This allows insight into the possible changes in pairwise species associations.

Patterns of covariation between the matrices of community similarity and a matrix of environmental dissimilarity at the collection sites were also examined with the Mantel test. Environmental dissimilarity was computed as Euclidean distance based on the six environmental variables described earlier.

Computations of similarity coefficients included only common species as defined above. Similarity coefficients and Mantel tests were computed, with, respectively, NT-SYS (Numerical Taxonomy System, a multivariate computer program developed by F. J. Rohlf, J. Kishpaugh, and R. Bartcher) and GEOVAR (a series of computer programs written by D. M. Mallis, State University of New York at Stony Brook).

Results

Drainage-Wide Presence or Absence

Totals of 96 and 74 species, respectively, were taken from the 153 collections in 1948–55 and 156 in 1981–82. All species in the recent collections were also present in the early collections, with three exceptions: *Hybognathus hayi, Erimyzon sucetta,* and *Etheostoma collettei*. These species were recognized only rather recently as occurring in Oklahoma (Miller and Robison, 1973; Matthews and Robison, 1982; Rutherford et al., 1985). Two of these, *Erimyzon sucetta* and *Etheostoma collettei*, were present but misidentified in early collections from the area. It is possible, but not verified, that *H. hayi* was also present but confused with *H. nuchalis*.

In 1982–83 we failed to collect 25 species taken in the earlier collections. Most of these species were lowland forms inhabiting marshes or large waters, which were not well represented in our collections. Our collections on class field trips or communications with others (C. Hubbs, W. J. Matthews, J. Pigg) revealed that most of these fishes still occurred in the Little River drainage in 1981–82. However, we are aware of no recent Little River collections of *Polyodon spathula, Alosa* spp., *Hiodon* spp., *Moxostoma carinatum, Hybognathus nuchalis*, or *Ictalurus nebulosus*. Most of these species were rare in the early collections and their absence from recent collections probably reflects our restricted collecting effort in the larger waters. Reeves (1955) reported the only known record, a single specimen, of *Notropis pilsbryi* from the Little River drainage. Presumably this was a stray, or perhaps a released baitfish.

In regular sampling from the Little River drainage over the past eight years, J. Pigg (pers. comm.) collected the following species, which were absent from both the early and our recent collections: *Ichthyomyzon gagei, Notropis buchanani, N. lutrensis, Ictalurus furcatus, Menidia beryllina, Morone mississippiensis, Percina shumardi,* and *P. macrolepida*. Also in 1983, Miller (1984) collected the first specimens of *Notropis hubbsi* known from the Little River. All these species are rare in the Little River system. Finally, the recently described *Notropis snelsoni* (Robison, 1985) brings the ichthyofaunal total for the Little River system to 109 species from 20 families.

Frequency of Occurrence

A total of 70 fish species were taken in collections from the 44 sites analyzed for frequency of occurrence of species in 1981–82 versus 1948–55. Thirty-five (50%) of these species were less frequent and 26 (37%) were more frequent in the recent collections; 9 (13%) were equally frequent in both series of collections. We placed each common species (occurring in a combined total of 10 or more recent and early collections) in one of four groups on the basis of microhabitat preference and our subjective assessment of their susceptibility to capture by seining; recent occurrence was then plotted against historical occurrence (fig. 22.2).

Nine of the 15 "small easily seinable fishes," a group composed primarily of cyprinids, were less frequent in the 1981–82 collections than in those taken in 1948–55 collections (fig. 22.2A) Three species, *Notropis whipplei, N. atrocaudalis*, and *Pimephales notatus*, showed statistically significant decreases in frequency. No member of this group was significantly more frequent in recent collections.

Six of the nine "large nectonic pool-dwelling" fishes, primarily centrarchids, were more frequent in the recent than in the early collections. The increases of two of these, *Lepomis cyanellus* and *L. punctatus*, were statistically significant (fig. 22.2B). One species, *Micropterus punctulatus*, was significantly less frequent in the recent collections.

Of three "large bottom-dwelling" fishes, one (*Ictalurus natalis*) was significantly more frequent in the 1981–82 collections, and a second (*Moxostoma erythrurum*) was significantly less frequent (fig. 22.2C). Two of the four "small riffle-dwelling" fishes (*Noturus nocturnus* and *Etheostoma spectabile*) were significantly more frequent in recent collections (fig. 22.2D).

There was a nonrandom association between the change in frequency (+ or −) of a species in recent versus early collections and wide distribution of the species versus restriction to eastern Oklahoma (table 22.1). Species that were equally frequent or more frequent in the 1981–82 collections were about evenly divided between widespread species and restricted species, whereas those occurring less frequently in recent collections tended to be those with restricted distributions. This relationship was statistically significant for all species considered together and for the common species, but not for the rare species alone.

All five common species showing statistically significant reductions in occurrence are restricted to the eastern half of Oklahoma. In contrast, four of the five common species showing statistically significant increases in occurrence either are widespread throughout Oklahoma (*Ictalurus natalis, Lepomis cyanellus*) or are more widely distributed and occur farther westward than their congeners in our study (*Noturus nocturnus, Etheostoma spectabile*); the fifth species, *Lepomis punctatus*, is a lowland form restricted to eastern Oklahoma.

Table 22.1. Contingency Table to Test the Hypothesis That Changes in Frequency of Occurrence of Fish Species in Recent Versus Early Collections Are Not Associated with Distribution of the Species

Change in Occurrence	Distribution			
	Widespread		Restricted	
	Common*	Rare	Common	Rare
Increase or no change	9	7	8	11
Decrease	0	6	14	17
Significance	Common Species† $P = 0.002$	Rare Species $\chi = 0.46$ NS	All Species $\chi^2 = 6.63$ $P < 0.01$	

*Common = occurrence at 10 or more of the early and/or recent collections; rare = less than 10 occurrences.
†Fisher's exact probability.

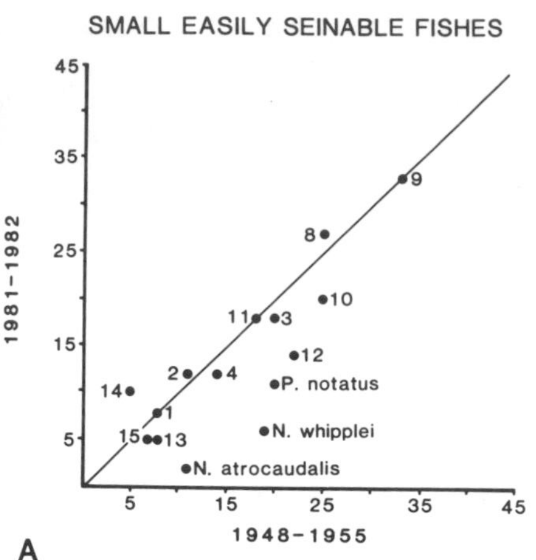

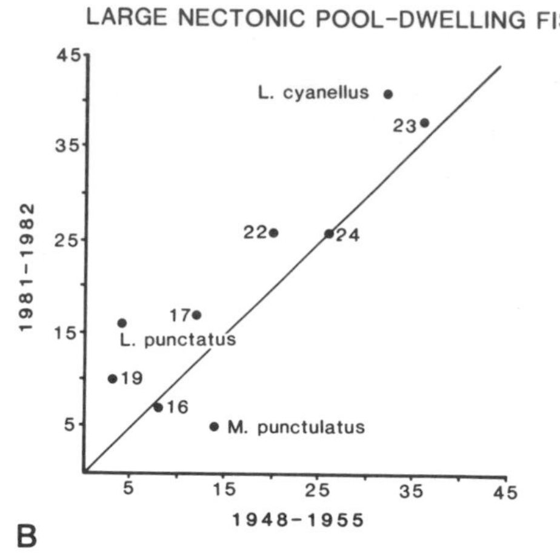

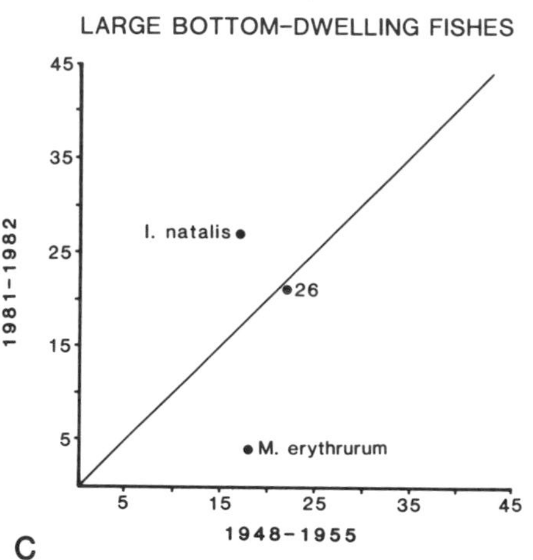

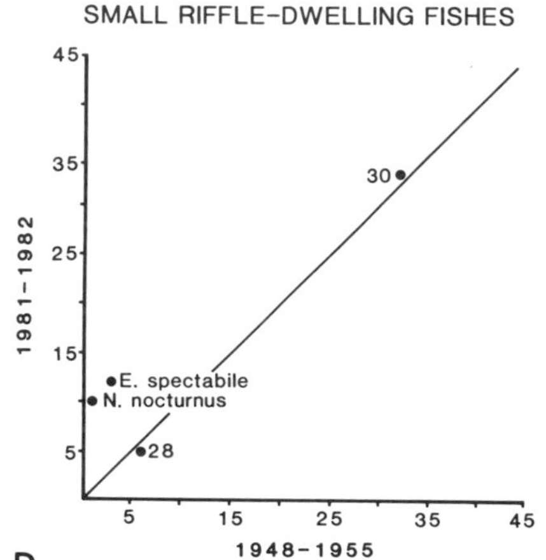

Fig. 22.2. Common fish species, grouped by general microhabitat preference, in collections from 1948–55 and 1981–82. Numbers asssociated with points show the species identification number. Points identified with names represent species that showed statistically significant changes. The diagonal line represents equal frequency in the two data sets. Numbers on figures represent species as follows: 1—*Notemigonus crysoleucas*, 2—*Notropis sp.* (mostly *snelsoni*, but may include some *fumens*), 3—*N. umbratilis*, 4—*N. chrysocephalus*, 5—*N. whipplei*, 6—*N. atrocaudalis*, 7—*Pimephales notatus*, 8—*Notropis boops*, 9—*Campostoma anomalum*, 10—*Fundulus notatus*, 11—*Gambusia affinis*, 12—*Labidesthes sicculus*, 13—*Etheostoma gracile*, 14—*Aphredoderus sayanus*, 15—*Elassoma zonatum*, 16—*Micropterus dolomieui*, 17—*Micropterus salmoides*, 18—*M. punctulatus*, 19—*Lepomis gulosus*, 20—*L. cyanellus*, 21—*L. punctatus*, 22—*L. macrochirus*, 23—*L. megalotis*, 24—*Esox americanus*, 25—*Moxostoma erythrurum*, 26—*Erimyzon oblongus*, 27—*Ictalurus natalis*, 28—*Percina sciera*, 29—*Etheostoma spectabile*, 30—*E. radiosum*.

Pairwise Species Associations

The Mantel test comparing recent and early matrices of pairwise similarities of occurrence among species revealed significant positive covariation between the two matrices when all 31 common species were included in the analysis ($t = +8.93$, $P < 0.001$) and when only those 22 species restricted to eastern Oklahoma were considered ($t = +2.03$, $P < 0.05$). The test involving the nine widespread species alone revealed positive, albeit nonsignificant, covariation between recent and early matrices ($t = +1.07$, $P < 0.05$). The Mantel estimate is relatively crude for matrices as small as our 9 × 9 matrix of similarity among widespread species (Sokal and Wartenberg, 1983); thus the nonsignificant t value is suspect.

Community Similarities

The Mantel test comparing early and recent matrices of similarity among collections produced a nonsignificant, negative test statistic for the matrices based on all 31 common species ($t = -0.986$, $P > 0.05$). This suggests that the 1981–82 pattern of similarities among local communities is not predictable from the pattern of similarities present in 1948–55. However, when the widespread species and those restricted to eastern Oklahoma are analyzed separately, an interesting difference emerges: the widespread species show significant positive covariation ($t = +3.08$, $P < 0.005$), while the restricted species show a significant negative relationship ($t = -2.09$, $P < 0.05$). The occurrences of widespread species apparently have not changed significantly, and the lack of predictability from 1948–55 to 1981–82 seems due to changes in occurrences of restricted species. The contingency analysis of occurrence (table 22.1) and plots of recent versus early occurrence onto maps of the drainage indicate that these changes primarily result from a drainage-wide decline in occurrence of restricted species and not from any localized patterns of change.

Environment Versus Community Similarity

Mantel tests of congruence between the matrix of environmental dissimilarity among collection sites and matrices of community similarity showed significant negative covariation in all six cases ($P < 0.005$; three analyses each for early and recent data —the 31 common species, the 22 restricted species, and the 9 widespread species). Thus community similarities are somewhat predictable from the environmental features we examined.

Both the early data set and the recent data set show higher covariance with environmental similarity for those species restricted to eastern Oklahoma than for the more widely distributed species ($t = -6.73$ and -3.59 for early collections; -4.48 and -2.91 for recent collections). Thus the occurrences of widespread species may be less tightly related to the environmental variables we measured than are occurrences of the species restricted to eastern Oklahoma. This direct comparison of t values is valid because the early and recent matrices are the same size.

Discussion

There is no compelling evidence for extinctions or invasions of new species in the Little River system since 1948–55. Thus the present species list is probably representative of the natural fauna of the drainage. However, frequency of occurrence of individual species and indices of community similarity suggest that the faunal structure is different from that in 1948–55.

The results of our comparison of 1948–55 and 1981–82 collections agree with the expected corollary to human-induced faunal changes: (1) Little River species that also occur in the plains environment of western Oklahoma seem to have undergone little overall decline in frequency of occurrence, while species restricted to eastern Oklahoma appear to have declined; and (2) statistically significant changes in patterns of interlocality community similarity have occurred between the early and recent collections, and these seem centered in the decline in occurrence of those species restricted to eastern Oklahoma. As argued previously in this chapter, these observations are consistent with the hypothesis that human activities have caused environmental changes that favor species with greater tolerance of environmental extremes.

The small sizes and distribution of urban centers relative to our collection localities and the generally sparse population and declining agricultural activity of the area suggest that these factors cannot explain the changes we observed. Regarding other anthropogenic factors, the most conspicuous changes in the Little River watershed in the period from 1948–55 to 1981–82 have resulted from commercial forestry and reservoir construction

Reservoir construction and associated alterations in downstream flow and thermal regimes obviously can have direct effects on occurrences of stream fishes (Mundy and Boschung, 1981; see Wagner, 1984, for an example in Little River). However, such effects probably do not explain the changes we observed. None of the 44 collection sites used in our analysis of frequency of occurrence were from reservoirs, and all were from smaller streams well outside the direct influence of reservoirs. Echelle and Schnell (1976) suggested that dispersal of generalist species from reservoirs into tributary streams might cause faunal shifts of the kind indicated by our survey. However, such effects would be most pronounced in waters near the reservoir, and, because of the positions of our collection sites (fig. 22.1) we doubt that this has been an important factor.

The decade and a half of intensive clear-cutting (and associated activities—e.g., road building) that began in the 1960s remains as the one conspicuous anthropogenic factor that might explain the apparent faunal changes that have occurred since 1948–55. We are aware of no previous attempt to document the effects of forestry activities on a warmwater system as large as the Little River of southeastern Oklahoma. Most studies either have dealt with coldwater faunas or have attempted to compare "experimental" and "control" stretches of stream for short-term effects on community structure (e.g., Boschung and O'Neil, 1981).

Comparisons such as the one described herein of drainage-wide surveys separated by long periods of time are fraught with problems, including (1) lack of rigid control of sampling differences, (2) the possibility that observed differences are part of an unknown, normal cycle that is intrinsic to the fauna itself, (3) the possibility that subtle climatic change is causing faunal change, and (4) the possibility that faunal change is a synergistic result of a poorly understood interaction of different factors. Nonetheless, such comparisons typically represent the only avenue of investigation that can provide empirical insight into the possible long-term effects of a given environmental perturbation. In the case of Little River fishes the apparent changes are of a type that is consistent with expectations based on anthropogenic effects, and forestry practices seem to be the only intensive human activity that is closely associated with the change.

[1]We thank Bruce Wagner, David Edds, Alice F. Echelle, and the members of the Oklahoma Cooperative Fisheries Research Unit for technical support; M. E. Douglas for help with data analysis; and W. J. Matthews for valuable suggestions. Financial support was provided by the Environmental Protection Agency, the U.S. Fish and Wildlife Service, the Oklahoma Department of Wildlife Conservation, and Oklahoma State University. Although the research was funded partly by the U.S. Environmental Protection Agency, it has not been subjected to the agency's peer and administrative review and does not necessarily reflect the views of the agency.

23. Physical Factors and the Distribution and Abundance of Fishes in the Upper Tombigbee River System of Alabama and Mississippi, with Emphasis on the Tennessee-Tombigbee Waterway

Herbert Boschung

Abstract

The effects of the physical factors of the environment on the distribution and abundance of fishes in the upper Tombigbee River system were assessed on the basis of approximately 77,300 specimens in 362 collections from 209 stations. A total of 119 species of fishes is known to occur in the study area.

Species composition differs among five physiographic districts, and fishes generally show a linear change in occurrence from higher to lower elevations. Data from baseline studies are compared with data following construction of the Tennessee-Tombigbee Waterway. Correlation analysis relative to abundance and stream order is used to define riverine and fluentine species. The riverine species are most vulnerable to alterations of the river environment. Fluentine species are vulnerable to the extent that lower-order streams are inundated.

Various factors affect the distribution of stream fishes. Shelford (1911), for example, related the distribution of fishes to the geological aging of stream beds, and Thompson and Hunt (1930) ascribed the number of fish species at a locality to the size of the drainage area. Trautman (1942) and Huet (1959) defined faunal regions and predicted species distributions on the basis of stream gradient and width. Sheldon (1968) showed that succession took the form of additions to the headwater assemblages and that the number of species in any area was corrrelated with stream depth. Gilbert (1980) discussed the geography of fishes relative to stream gradients. The Horton (1945) stream classification, as modified by Strahler (1954, 1957), was employed by Kuehne (1962), who described the fish fauna of Kentucky streams; Boschung (1973), Boschung and Jandebeur (1974), Jandebeur (1975), and Mundy and Boschung (1981) used the modified system to explain fish distributions as an aid to predicting the effects of impoundments and channelization on stream fishes. An in-depth review of physical characteristics of streams is given by Winger (1981).

The primary purpose of this chapter is to quantify and to discuss some physical factors that influence the distribution of fishes within a major river system. The physical factors considered herein include natural factors, i.e., physiography, elevation, and stream order, as well as a recent insult to the natural integrity of the upper Tombigbee River, the Tennessee-Tombigbee Waterway (TTW). The upper Tombigbee River system served well for this endeavor because (1) it occupies five physiographic districts, (2) it has been disturbed recently by impoundment and channelization, and (3) it encompasses seven stream orders and an elevational differential of about 170 meters. In addition, the system's rich ichthyofauna has been well sampled.

Study Area

The upper Tombigbee River system lies entirely within the Coastal Plain Province and is separated from the Highland Rim and Cumberland Plateau by a narrow transition zone, the Fall Line. Before the construction of the Tennessee-Tombigbee Waterway, flow of the upper Tombigbee River showed high annual variation. For the years of record, 1938–78, the minimum and maximum flows at Aliceville, Alabama, were 4.67 m^3/s and 4,700 m^3/sec. The substratum was either mud, silt, sand, gravel, rubble, or a combination of these. There was a great diversity of habitat, ranging from stagnant backwaters to very swift chutes.

The river is now modified for navigation. From its confluence with the Black Warrior River at Demopolis, Alabama, to Bay Springs Lock and Dam on Pickwick Pool, on the Tennessee River, the upper Tombigbee has a minimum depth and width of 2.7 m and 91 m, respectively. There are four locks and dams between Demopolis, Alabama, and Aberdeen, Mississippi, and five locks between Aberdeen and the Tennessee River. The resulting impoundments inundated approximately 650 km^2 of land. Thirty-five cutoffs have been dredged to shorten the navigational channel, resulting in relatively stagnant bendways. Above Columbus the waterway is essentially a perched canal that is crisscrossed by the meandering river. The canal connects with Pickwick Pool at an elevation of approximately 125 m above sea level.

Physiography

The brief descriptions of the physiographic districts given herein were compiled from works of Adams et al. (1926), Caldwell (1969), Fenneman (1938), Murray (1961), Stephenson and Monroe (1940), and Thornbury (1965).

Fall Line Hills

The Fall Line Hills have a maximum width of 80 km and an area of 12,491 km^2. The headwaters of the Buttahatchee and Sipsey rivers, major tributaries of the Tombigbee, are deeply entrenched and provide habitat similar to that of the upland streams of the Cumberland Plateau. The streams in the Fall Line Hills, generally flowing from northeast to southwest, are typically of moderate gradient, sandy bottoms, and gravel riffles between pools. Water flows continuously throughout the year, and aquatic vegetation is abundant (fig. 24.1).

Black Belt

This district, 7,716 km^2 in area, is 32 to 40 km wide throughout Alabama and Mississippi. The topography contrasts sharply with that of the Fall Line Hills. Gently rolling hills of low relief are developed upon Mooresville and Demopolis Formations of the Selma Group of Cretaceous age. The upper Tombigbee River parallels the eastern edge of the Black Belt in Mississippi, but after entering Alabama the river dissects the Black Belt before it meets the Black Warrior River to form the lower Tombigbee. The streams are typically entrenched, and only the large ones have a permanent flow. They usually originate in the sandy-hills region on either side of the Black Belt, where groundwater is available. The streams are susceptible to flash flooding owing to the low permeability of the chalk substrate.

Pontotoc Ridge

Pontotoc Ridge is a narrow physiographic district of 1,891 km^2, consisting of hills that form the drainage divide between the northwesternmost part of the Tombigbee system and the tributaries of the Mississippi River. Its greatest width in the upper Tombigbee watershed is about 12 km. The Pontotoc Ridge is developed upon Cretaceous sediments of the Ripley Formation, the highest sand unit of the Cretaceous sediments in Alabama and Mississippi. In some areas the ridge is fragmented by streams flowing out of the Flatwoods district that lies to the west. The common elevation is between 150 and 180 m.

Flatwoods

This physiographic district is 8 to 13 km wide and occupies 2,163 km^2. Its sediments are Porters Creek Clay of Paleocene age, and the topographic character is very similar to that of the Black Belt. Where the two meet at the southern apex of Pontotoc Ridge, the Flatwoods and the Black Belt are almost inseparable as physiographic units. The clays of the Flatwoods, like the chalk of the Black Belt, are relatively impervious to water, causing rapid runoff and subsequent erosion. The permanent streams usually originate in the adjacent hill regions. Intermittent streams are characterized by isolated pools where the substrate is mud or gravel and the vegetation is sparse.

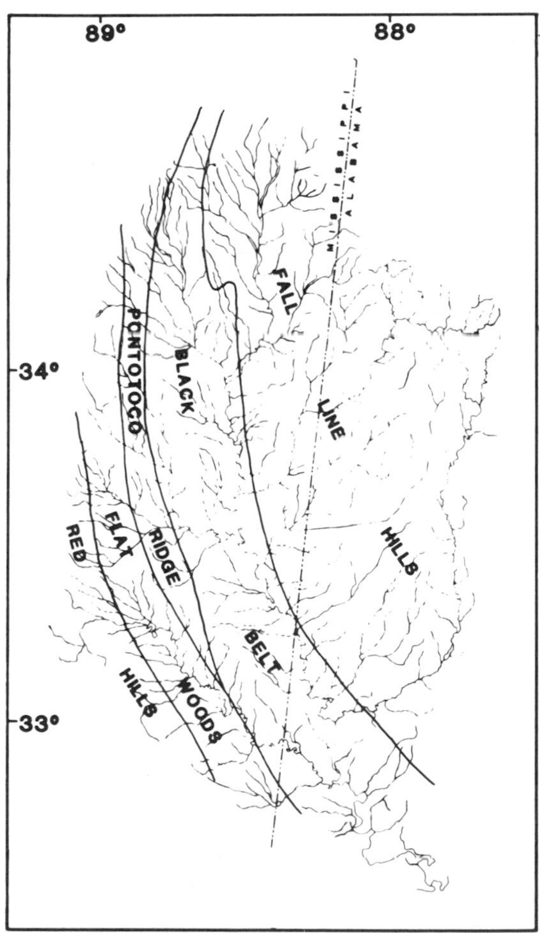

Fig. 23.1. Physiographic districts of the upper Tombigbee River system.

Red Hills

The Red Hills district, only 953 km^2, lies in the southwest edge of the upper Tombigbee watershed. The hills reach elevations of 180 m and tower about 90 m above the Flatwoods district on the east. The Red Hills district is developed upon sandy sediments of the Wilcox Group of Eocene age. Most of the Red Hills streams flow eastward from an escarpment and then through the Flatwoods to the Black Belt.

Upper Tombigbee River Proper

Although the river proper (that part of the upper Tombigbee below Mackey Creek) is entirely within the Black Belt district and its bed traverses substrates of several geological ages, it is given the status of a physiographic district for the purpose of discussion in this chapter. Sixth- and seventh-order streams are defined as upper Tombigbee River proper for the purpose of discussing the effects of physiography.

Materials and Methods

The data base for the quantitative aspects of the paper consists of 77,300 specimens from 362 collections made at 209 stations throughout the upper Tombigbee River system: (1) 25,360 specimens collected from 90 stations, 1964–68, notably by Caldwell (1969); (2) 41,937 specimens collected from 119 stations, 1971–72, throughout the upper Tombigbee River system (Boschung, 1973); and (3) 10,023 specimens from 72 stations collected in 1983 in the system between Demopolis, Alabama, and Columbus, Mississippi (Boschung, 1984). All these specimens are housed in the University of Alabama Ichthyological Collection (UAIC). Details of collection methods and sampling effort are given in the papers cited above.

Similarity between groups was measured by Sorenson's Similarity Index, $S = 2C/A + B$, where C is the number of species in common, A is the number of species in one group, and B is the number of species in the other group. A more quantitative comparison can be made by using overlap as described by Pianka (1974a). Overlap ranges from 0 for no similarity to 1 for total similarity. Relative abundance was determined by $R = n/N$, where n is the number of individuals representing the species and N is the total number of individuals in the collection.

The product-moment correlation coefficient, r, (Sokal and Rohlf, 1981) between stream order (independent variable) and relative abundance of a species (dependent variable) was determined for each species that occurred 12 times or more or whose relative abundance was greater than 1%. A significant ($P < 0.05$) positive correlation coefficient indicated that the species in question increases in relative abundance with stream order. This shows that the species is more abundant in large streams and less abundant in small streams. Species positively correlated with stream order are called riverine species. A significant negative correlation coefficient indicates that the species is more abundant in small streams. Species in this category are called "fluentine" species (*fluentine* is derived from the Latin *fluere*, "to flow," and the suffix *ine*, from Middle English indicating "of," "pertaining to," or "belonging." Species found in abundance independent of stream order are classified as ubiquitous or cosmopolitan. Stream orders were determined from U.S. Geological Survey 7.5-minute topographic maps, scale 1:24,000.

Results and Discussion

Species Richness

Based on the collections cited above and on collections of Kelly (1975), Timmons et al. (1982), and Pierson and Schultz (1984), the species richness (number of species) of the upper Tombigbee River system stands at 119 (table 23.1). This number is derived for the most part from actual collections; questionable literature records are not included. For example, there is no evidence that *Hypentelium nigricans*, reported by Cook (1959), occurs in the upper Tombigbee system. Nor does the list contain *Etheostoma gracile*, since there is no evidence indicating its occurrence since it was reported by Collett (1962). Remaining on the list but very questionable are *Scaphirhynchus* sp.cf. *platorynchus*, which was last collected in 1953 (Chermock, 1955), and *Notropis chalybaeus*, a species that if present, as indicated by Smith-Vaniz (1968), has escaped our nets. New to the list since the impoundment of the river, but not necessarily a result of it, are *Notropis lutrensis* (Timmons et al., 1982), *Ictalurus nebulosus*, *Lepomis marginatus*, and *Micropterus dolomieui*.

Physiography, Distribution, and Relative Abundance

Species composition was most similar between the river proper and the Fall Line Hills and least similar between the river proper and the Pontotoc Ridge district (table 23.2). Similarity between species of the Fall Line Hills (84 species) and all other physiographic districts combined (70 excluding the river species) was 0.779. Similarity between the river proper (98 species) and all other physiographic districts combined (90 species) was 0.788. That species composition differs among physiographic districts probably is due to differences in habitats; but this is not necessarily so, because Matthews (1982) gives evidence that physically similar adjacent watersheds may differ considerably in species of cyprinids, cyprinodontids, and atherinids.

Twenty-two species were restricted to the river proper, and seven (indicated by an asterisk) are poorly represented in collections and are considered rare in the upper Tombigbee system: *Scaphirhynchus* sp. cf. *platorynchus**, *Polyodon spathula**, *Lepisosteus oculatus*, *L. spatula**, *Alosa alabamae**, *Alosa chrysochloris*, *Dorosoma petenense*, *Hiodon tergisus*, *Hybopsis aestivalis*, *Notropis candidus*, *Notropis edwardraneyi*, *Carpiodes cyprinus*, *Cycleptus elongatus**, *Ictiobus bubalus*, *Moxostoma carinatum*, *Ictalurus furcatus*, *Noturus munitus*, *Strongylura marina*, *Morone saxatilis**, *Ammocrypta asprella*, *Percina lenticula**, and *Stizostedion vitreum*.

Twenty-six species occurred in only one physiographic

Table 23.1. Annotated List of Fish Species Known to Occur in the Upper Tombigbee River System of Alabama and Mississippi[a]

Ichthyomyzon castaneus	*N. baileyi*	*M. poecilurum*	*L. punctatus*
I. gagei	*N. bellus*	*Ictalurus furcatus*	*Micropterus dolomieui*[l]
Lampetra aepyptera	*N. callistius*	*I. melas*	*M. punctulatus*
Scaphirhynchus sp. cf. *platornychus*[b]	*N. candidus*[f]	*I. natalis*	*M. salmoides*[m]
	N. chalybaeus	*I. nebulosus*[h]	*Pomoxis annularis*
Polydon spathula	*N. chrysocephalus*	*I. punctatus*	*P. nigromaculatus*
Lepisosteus oculatus	*N. edwardraneyi*	*Noturus funebris*	*Ammocrypta asprella*
L. osseus	*N. emiliae*	*N. gyrinus*	*A. beani*
L. spatula[c]	*N. lutrensis*[g]	*N. leptacanthus*	*A. meridiana*[n]
Amia calva	*N. maculatus*	*N. munitus*	*Etheostoma chlorosomum*
Anguilla rostrata	*N. stilbius*	*N. nocturnus*	*E. fusiforme*
Alosa alabamae	*N. texanus*	*Pylodictis olivaris*	*E. histrio*
A. chrysochloris	*N. venustus*	*Aphredoderos sayanus*	*E. nigrum*
Dorosoma cepedianum	*N. volucellus*	*Strongylura marina*	*E. parvipinne*
D. petenense	*N. welaka*	*Fundulus notatus*	*E. proeliare*
Hiodon tergisus	*Notropis* sp. cf. *longirostris*	*F. notti*	*E. rupestre*
Esox americanus	*Pimephales notatus*	*F. olivaceus*	*E. stigmaeum*
E. niger	*P. vigilax*	*Gambusia affinis*	*E. swaini*
Campostoma oligolepis[d]	*Semotilus atromaculatus*	*Labidesthes sicculus*	*E. whipplei*
Carassius auratus	*Carpiodes cyprinus*	*Morone saxatilis* × *M. chrysops*[i]	*E. zoniferum*
Cyprinus carpio	*C. velifer*	*Ambloplites ariommus*[j]	*Etheostoma (Ulocentra)* sp.
Ericymba buccata	*Cycleptus elongatus*	*Centrarchus macropterus*	*Percina lenticula*
Hybognathus hayi	*Erimyzon oblongus*	*Elassoma zonatum*	*P. maculata*
H. nuchalis	*E. sucetta*	*Lepomis cyanellus*	*P. nigrofasciata*
Hybopsis aestivalis	*E. tenuis*	*L. gulosus*	*P. sciera*
H. storeriana	*Hypentelium etowanum*	*L. humilis*	*P. shumardi*
H. winchelli[e]	*Ictiobus bubalus*	*L. macrochirus*	*P. vigil*[o]
Nocomis leptocephalus	*Minytrema melanops*	*L. marginatus*[k]	*Percina* cf. *caprodes*[p]
Notemigonus crysoleucas	*Moxostoma carinatum*	*L. megalotis*	*Stizostedion v. vitreum*
Notropis atherinoides	*M. erythrurum*	*L. microlophus*	*Aplodinotus grunniens*

[a] The list includes introduced and undescribed species.
[b] An undescribed species last collected in the upper Tombigbee in 1953 (Chermock, 1955).
[c] Observed in the upper Tombigbee River above Demopolis Lock and Dam (M. F. Mettee, pers. comm.). A coastal species, it probably no longer occurs there.
[d] *Campostoma anomalum* is not the stoneroller of the Mobile basin, as previously thought (Burr and Cashner, 1983).
[e] Clemmer (1971) recognizes *Hypbosis winchelli* as a full species, not a subspecies of *H. amblops*.
[f] Described by Suttkus (1980), replaces *Notropis shumardi* in the Mobile basin.
[g] Recently introduced in Alabama (Timmons et al., 1982).
[h] Recorded for first time in the upper Tombigbee by Timmons et al. (1982).
[i] Hybrids of *Morone saxatilis* and *M. chrysops* were introduced in the upper Tombigbee in 1982.
[j] Long regarded as a subspecies of *Ambloplites rupestre*, *A. ariommus* was elevated to full species status by Cashner and Suttkus (1977).
[k] *Lepomis marginatus* appeared in upper Tombigbee post-TTW (Timmons et al., 1982).
[l] Introduced in Bull Mountain Creek by Mississippi Department of Wildlife Conservation (Malcolm Pierson, pers. comm.).
[m] *Micropterus salmoides floridanus* was introduced in the upper Tombigbee in 1980 (Jerry Moss, pers. comm.).
[n] Replaces *Ammocrypta vivax* in the Mobile basin (Williams, 1975).
[o] Replaces *Percina ouachitae* and/or *P. uranidea* in the Mobile basin (Suttkus, 1985).
[p] A species being described by Bruce Thompson to replace *Percina caprodes* in the upper Tombigbee.

Table 23.2. Similarity of Species Between the Physiographic Districts in the Upper Tombigbee River System*

Physiographic District (No. Species)	I	II	III	IV	V	VI
I. Fall Line Hills (84)	—	0.727	0.432	0.641	0.559	0.758
II. Black Belt (59)		—	0.628	0.699	0.581	0.675
III. Pontotoc Ridge (27)			—	0.620	0.525	0.416
IV. Flatwoods (44)				—	0.718	0.549
V. Red Hills (34)					—	0.454
VI. River proper[†] (98)						—
Total no. of species = 112						

*Data base from Caldwell (1969) and Boschung (1973).
[†]Before construction of the Tennessee-Tombigbee Waterway.

district, 25 in two, 18 in three, 15 in four, 13 in five, and the following 15 species in all six districts: *Hybognathus nuchalis*, *Notemigonus crysoleucas*, *Notropis bellus*, *Notropis emiliae*, *Notropis venustus*, *Notropis* sp. cf. *longirostris*, *Pimephales vigilax*, *Semotilus atromaculatus*, *Noturus gyrinus*, *Gambusia affinis*, *Lepomis cyanellus*, *Lepomis megalotis*, *Micropterus salmoides*, *Etheostoma nigrum*, and *Etheostoma proeliare*.

Distribution of Fishes Relative to Elevation

Fishes are distributed by elevation and generally show a linear change in occurrence and abundance from higher to lower elevations (table 23.3). Forty percent of the species occurred at all elevations. Only two species, *Ericymba buccata* and *Etheostoma parvipinne*, were absent below the 90-m contour, and 20% of the fish fauna were never found above 60 m. Although no negative correlation between elevation and stream order (a function of physiography) was determined, one would have to assume that it exists. Since

Table 23.3 Similarity of Species Composition in the Upper Tombigbee River System Relative to Elevational Categories*

Elevation (Meters Above Sea Level)	< 60	61–90	91–120	121–150+
< 60	—			
61–90	0.851	—		
91–120	0.679	0.791	—	
121–150+	0.611	0.727	0.907	—

*Data base from Boschung (1973).

stream order is generally related to elevation, streams at high elevations in the upper Tombigbee system are small streams, but small streams are not necessarily at higher elevation.

The Tennessee-Tombigbee Waterway as a Physical Factor

Base-line studies were conducted in the upper Tombigbee system by Caldwell (1969) and Boschung (1973) before the construction of the TTW (the period herein referred to as pre-TTW). Another study, following completion of the waterway between Demopolis, Alabama, and Columbus, Mississippi, was made in 1983 (Boschung, 1984) as an attempt to assess the effects of the TTW on the distribution and abundance of fishes (post-TTW). To duplicate the pre-TTW collections precisely, the post-TTW collections were made in the same places and on the same dates with few exceptions.

Relative to species richness for the entire system, post-TTW gains have partly offset losses (table 23.4). The balance is not expected to persist, for certain riverine species will be extirpated through loss of habitat. Table 23.4 gives a summary of the species-richness data and provides similarity and overlap indices for comparing pre- and post-TTW species lists.

If we consider only those species whose relative abundance was 1% or more, we see no overall change, pre- versus post-TTW, in species richness and similarity (table 23.5). Overlap indices depend on numbers of individuals as well as numbers of species. The tributary species were little affected by the waterway. Less abundant riverine species account for the discrepancies in richness, similarity, and overlap. Of the 31 species of greatest relative abundance, pre- versus post-TTW, 7 gained and 24 lost in absolute abundance, and 19 gained and 12 lost in relative abundance (table 23.6).

Table 23.4. Upper Tombigbee River System Fishes in Terms of Species Richness (Number of Species) Pre– Versus Post–Tennessee-Tombigbee Waterway

Areas	Number of Species				
	Pre-TTW	Post-TTW	C*	S[†]	O[‡]
All tributaries of study area (N = 89 species)	79	84	74	0.908	0.894
River proper (N = 84 species)	81	44	41	0.656	0.240
Tributaries and river proper combined (N = 105)	101	98	94	0.945	0.668

*C = species in common.
[†]S = similarity index.
[‡]O = overlap.

Table 23.5. Species Richness (Number of Species) of Upper Tombigbee River System Fishes, Pre– versus Post–Tennessee-Tombigbee Waterway for Those Species Whose Relative Abundance was 1% or More

Areas	Number of Species				
	Pre-TTW	Post-TTW	C*	S[†]	O[‡]
All tributaries of study area (N = 19 species)	17	19	17	0.944	0.902
River proper (N = 22 species)	22	14	14	0.778	0.176
Tributaries and river combined (N = 22)	22	22	22	1.000	0.659

*C = species in common.
[†]S = similarity index.
[‡]O = overlap.

Percina vigil showed a threefold increase in relative abundance post- versus pre-TTW, by moving from primarily a river habitat into the larger tributaries (fig. 23.2). This indicates that the fish was extirpated from the main channel as a result of the impoundment of the river and that it is successful in the large tributaries. *Ammocrypta meridiana* showed a similar but somewhat less conspicuous pattern of distribution. The distribution of *Hybognathus nuchalis* indicates that it is facing extirpation in the upper Tombigbee as it did in the Tennessee River following impoundment (Etnier et al., 1979). Although it occurred 4 times in the river proper and 26 times elsewhere in pre-TTW collections, the river proper was the place of its greatest success. Post-TTW distribution (fig. 23.3) and abundances indicate that the river is essential to part of the species' life cycle.

Riverine fishes require various habitats within the river. As pointed out by Mundy and Boschung (1981), the sign (+) of the correlation coefficient between stream order and relative abundance is not sufficient evidence of enhancement or vulnerability of species. Both *Aplodinotus grunniens* and *Ammocrypta asprella* are riverine species, but the former species increased after impoundment of the river, whereas the latter was vulnerable to the point of apparent extirpation. *Hybopsis aestivalis* and *Notorus munitus*, also riverine species, are expected to survive the TTW by moving into the larger tributaries. Certain river species of low frequency of occurrence increased greatly in numbers under post-TTW conditions. The relative abundance of *Lepisosteus osseus* increased 1160%; *Amia calva*, 3322%; *Cyprinus carpio*, 2622%; *Ictiobus bubalus*, 2520%; and *Ictalurus furcatus*, 5450%.

Relative to distribution and frequency of occurrence, similarity indices show in a quantitative way changes or shifts in stations occupied by each species. The larger the similarity index, the less the change in distribution from one time period to the other; or the larger the S, the greater the similarity of distribution, pre- versus post-TTW. Seventy-

Table 23.6. Species Whose Relative Abundances Were Greater Than 1% Either Pre– or Post–Tennessee-Tombigbee Waterway or Both, and the Percentage Change Post- Versus Pre-TTW

Species	Percent Relative Abundance		Percent Change
	Pre-TTW	Post-TTW	
*Dorosoma cepedianum**	0.41	3.70	+802
*D. petenense**	0.75	1.31	+75
*Hybognathus nuchalis**	1.38	0.96	−30
*H. hayi**	4.34	0.48	−89
*Hybopsis aestivalis**	7.00	0.01	−99
*H. storeriana**	2.12	0.07	−97
Notropis baileyi	3.18	5.07	+59
N. bellus	7.66	8.90	+16
*N. candidus**	1.48	0.95	−36
N. chrysocephalus	3.57	3.78	+6
*N. edwardraneyi**	3.31	0.14	−96
N. texanus	3.04	6.06	+99
N. venustus	22.62	6.53	−71
N. sp. cf. *longirostris*	2.06	2.81	+36
Pimephales notatus	3.07	2.85	−7
P. vigilax	5.02	5.00	−<1
Semotilus atromaculatus	2.00	0.60	−70
*Ictiobus bubalus**	0.07	1.84	+2,528
*Ictalurus furcatus**	0.02	1.11	+5,450
*I. punctatus**	1.26	1.02	−19
Fundulus olivaceus	1.18	2.31	+95
Gambusia affinis	2.05	4.23	+106
Lepomis cyanellus	0.42	2.41	+474
L. macrochirus	1.39	6.69	+381
L. megalotis	2.07	4.68	+126
Micropterus salmoides	2.53	1.65	−35
*Pomoxis annularis**	0.31	1.02	+229
Etheostoma nigrum	0.77	1.27	+65
E. rupestre	1.09	1.60	+47
E. stigmaeum	0.94	1.32	+40
*Aplodinotus grunniens**	0.51	1.69	+231

*Species usually associated with higher-order streams.

one stations were sampled in each time period of the pre- versus post-TTW study. Some species were collected so infrequently that chance alone could account for similarity (or dissimilarity).

The net change in the river fish fauna was marked. Seventeen species previously known in the upper Tombigbee River proper could not be accounted for in any of the post-TTW collections: *Alosa alabamae, Hiodon tergisus, Campostoma oligolepis, Notropis baileyi, Notropis bellus, Notropis volucellus, Semotilus atromaculatus, Hypentelium etowanum, Noturus munitus, Noturus nocturnus, Etheostoma histrio, Etheostoma nigrum, Etheostoma rupestre, Ammocrypta asprella, Ammocrypta beani, Percina nigrofasciata*, and *Percina vigil*. Several others may be added to the list of losses as the impoundments age. Consideration of the typical habitat of each of these species helps explain why it is unlikely that they can survive the impoundments of the TTW.

The 101 species collected in the study area pre-TTW were represented by 31,183 specimens, whereas the 98 post-TTW species were represented by only 10,023 specimens. The large difference in total abundance, pre- versus post-TTW, was due primarily to the paucity of individuals taken from the river post-TTW. Fifty-seven percent of the pre-TTW specimens were collected in the river, and 43% were collected in tributaries. In post-TTW collections the percentages of river and tributary specimens were 25% and 75%, respectively. These data are summarized in table 23.7.

The species that account for most of the reduction in abundance in the river are *Hybognathus hayi, Hybopsis aestivalis, Notropis edwardraneyi, Notropis venustus, Pimephales vigilax*, and *Noturus munitus*. These six species alone accounted for 12,901 (73%) of all pre-TTW river specimens, whereas in post-TTW collections they were represented by only 375 specimens, or 14.3% of the total post-TTW river specimens. *Pimephales vigilax* accounted for 81.5% of the total number of individuals of the six species.

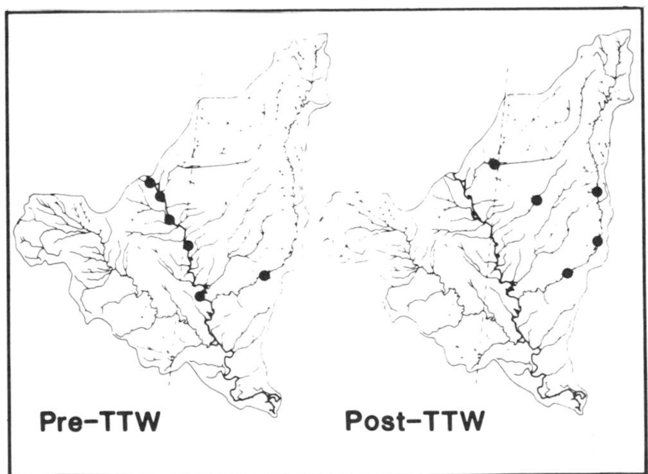

Fig. 23.2. Distribution of *Percina vigil* in the upper Tombigbee River system between Demopolis, Alabama, and Columbus, Mississippi, pre- versus post-TTW.

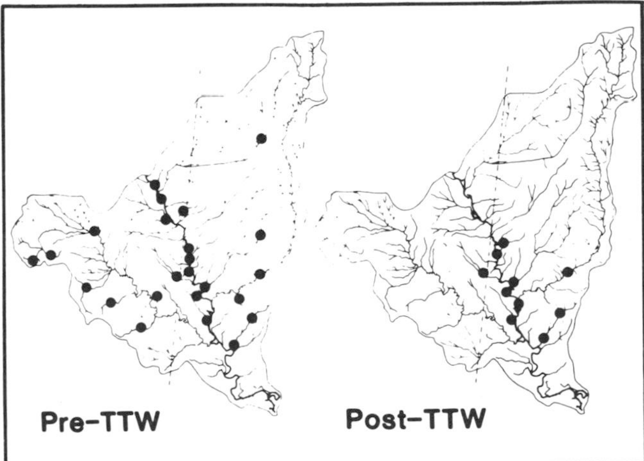

Fig. 23.3. Distribution of *Hybognathus nuchalis* in the upper Tombigbee River system between Demopolis, Alabama, and Columbus, Mississippi, pre- versus post-TTW.

Table 23.7. Upper Tombigbee River System Fishes, Pre– Versus Post–Tennessee-Tombigbee Waterway

Group	Period	1[a]	2[b]	3[c]	4[d]	5[e]
All tributaries	Pre-TTW	79	13,482	64	43.2	32.7
	Post-TTW	84	7,532	36	75.1	18.3
	Total	89	21,014	100	—	51.0
River	Pre-TTW	81	17,701	88	56.8	43.0
	Post-TTW	44	2,491	12	24.8	6.0
	Total	84	20,192	100	—	49.0
Entire area	Pre-TTW	101	31,183	76	100.0	75.7
	Post-TTW	98	10,023	24	100.0	24.3
	Total	106	41,206	100	—	100.0

[a]Number of species.
[b]Number of specimens.
[c]Percentage of specimens of group.
[d]Percentage of all specimens in time period.
[d]Percentage of all specimens in both time periods.

A number of factors could account for great fluctuations in abundance in the river and tributary species, such as spawning success, development and survival of young to adulthood, and availability of food. These factors are environmentally influenced, but, in addition, the fishes of the river found their habitats altered drastically and irreversibly. Some species face extirpation or extinction; others have shown, in a relatively short time, great increases in relative abundance.

In some communities four species groups are discernible: groups of species that occur frequently and in large numbers, those that occur frequently but in small numbers, those that occur infrequently and in large numbers, and those that occur infrequently and in small numbers (O'Neil et al., 1981). Table 23.8 shows the results of this categorization of upper Tombigbee system fish specimens and compares pre- and post-TTW groups.

As expected, the species of low frequency and small relative abundance dominated. Species of low frequency of occurrence and large relative abundance had no similarity, pre- versus post-TTW. This category was made up of river species. The pre-TTW river species were *Hybognathus hayi, Hybopsis aestivalis, Hybopsis storeriana, Notropis candidus, N. edwardraneyi,* and *Ictalurus punctatus*. Post-TTW river species were *Dorosoma petenense* and *Ictiobus bubalus*. Here again is an example of the marked effect the TTW had on fishes of sixth- and seventh-order streams.

As discussed by Boschung (1973) and Mundy and Boschung (1981), correlation analysis of relative abundance and stream order indicate that two groups of fishes are present in the upper Tombigbee River system that may be characterized by their concentrations of population in small-order (1–4) or large-order (6–7) streams. Those species positively correlated with stream order are the riverine species, and those negatively correlated with stream order are the fluentine ones. A third group, the cosmopolitan species, are those whose centers of distribution are not defined in terms of stream order; they are usually found in varying numbers in all orders of streams.

The preferred habitat of any species of fish within a river system is defined as the area of greatest abundance. For species characterized as riverine, the number will be the greatest in the larger streams of the river system, with the maxima occurring in collections from the largest streams in the river system. In general, riverine species are those most drastically affected by alterations of the river environment; however, this generalization must be qualified.

As was pointed out by Mundy (1973), functional definitions of fish groups based solely on adult occurrence criteria have severe limitations on their utility in matters of prediction of environmental consequences for fishes of a project such as the TTW. Even though adults and juveniles of a species may spend their entire nonreproductive lives in a well-defined aquatic area such as a reservoir or large river, they may leave the area to return to small streams to spawn. In this event destruction of the habitat of the adults by inundation may have no consequences on the population density of the species as a whole; adult fishes are characteristically more tolerant of extremes of physiochemical parameters than are their eggs and larvae. If the system is not altered in a fashion that will cause the upper and lower lethal limits of any critical physiochemical parameter to occur on a widespread basis, the population of most species will be able to maintain themselves somewhere within the system. The problem is to define those species that are dependent on the river as their sole vehicle of existence.

The reproductive aspect notwithstanding, sufficient data are available to define those riverine species that are vulnerable to inundation and channelization of the riverine environment. Those species that never occur beyond the confines of sixth- and seventh-order streams must be assumed to use the river for all aspects of their existence inclusive of reproduction. Aside from the vulnerable group, there are those species that use the slack-water microenvironment of the river for reproduction; impoundment will expand these environments, not destroy them. Therefore, fishes that will be eliminated or decimated by the TTW are those riverine species that inhabit the swift-moving portions of sixth- and seventh-order streams.

By definition, fluentine species of fishes have small-sized streams as their center of distribution. Small streams are tributary either directly or indirectly to transitional streams (fifth order) or rivers. Small streams in the upper Tombigbee River system are orders 1–4. Fluentine species are common in all permanent fluentine streams (orders 2–4), maximum numbers occurring in the largest fluentine environments of the system (order 4 in the upper Tombigbee system). Fluentine species are vulnerable to the TTW only to the extent that order 1–4 streams are inundated. The fluentine species are displaced and reduced in numbers in proportion to the inundation of the fluentine environment. Presumably fluentine species are unable to reproduce in a reservoir environment.

Cosmopolitan species of fishes have no well-defined center of distribution, and they occur to some extent in all permanent streams in the upper Tombigbee system and are at times relatively large components of a given sample of fishes. They appear to be limited by factors related to the

Table 23.8. Upper Tombigbee River System Fishes: Species List According to Frequency of Occurrence and Relative Abundance, Pre– Versus Post–Tennessee-Tombigbee Waterway*

Pre-TTW	Post-TTW
Species of High Frequency of Occurrence and High Relative Abundance	
Hybognathus nuchalis	*Dorosoma cepedianum*
Notropis baileyi	*Notropis baileyi*
N. bellus	*N. bellus*
N. chrysocephalus	*N. chrysocephalus*
N. texanus	*N. texanus*
N. venustus	*N. venustus*
N. sp. cf. *longirostris*	*N.* sp. cf. *longirostris*
Pimephales notatus	*Pimephales notatus*
P. vigilax	*P. vigilax*
Semotilus atromaculatus	*Ictalurus furcatus*
Fundulus olivaceus	*I. punctatus*
Gambusia affinis	*Fundulus olivaceus*
Lepomis macrochirus	*Gambusia affinis*
L. megalotis	*Lepomis cyanellus*
Micropterus salmoides	*L. macrochirus*
Etheostoma rupestre	*L. megalotis*
	Micropterus salmoides
	Pomoxis annularis
Similarity between groups = 0.7368	*Etheostoma nigrum*
	E. stigmaeum
	Aplodinotus grunniens
Species of High Frequency of Occurrence and Low Relative Abundance	
Lepisosteus osseus	*Lepisosteus oculatus*
Dorosoma cepedianum	*Esox americanus*
Esox americanus	*Campostoma anomalum*
E. niger	*Ericymba bucatta*
Campostoma anomalum	*Hybognathus nuchalis*
Ericymba bucatta	*Nocomis leptocephalus*
Nocomis leptocephalus	*Notemigonus crysoleucas*
Notemigonus crysoleucas	*Notropis emiliae*
Notropis emiliae	*N. stilbius*
N. stilbius	*Minytrema melanops*
Erimyzon oblongus	*Noturus leptacanthus*
Hypentelium etowanum	*Pylodictis olivaris*
Moxostoma erythrurum	*Fundulus notatus*
M. poecilurum	*Lepomis gulosus*
Noturus gyrinus	*L. microlophus*
N. leptacanthus	*Etheostoma chlorosomum*
Fundulus notatus	*E. swaini*
Elassoma zonatum	*E. whipplei*
Lepomis cyanellus	*E. (Ulocentra)* sp.
L. microlophus	*Percina nigrofasciata*
L. punctatus	
Micropterus punctulatus	
Etheostoma chlorosomum	
E. nigrum	Similarity between groups = 0.5185
E. proeliare	
E. stigmaeum	
E. swaini	
E. whipplei	
E. (Ulocentra) sp.	
Ammocrypta meridiana	
Percina nigrofasciata	
P. sciera	
Aplodinotus grunniens	
Species of Low Frequency of Occurrence and High Relative Abundance	
Hybognathus hayi	*Dorosoma petenense*
Hybopsis aestivalis	*Ictiobus bubalus*
H. storeriana	
Notropis candidus	Similarity between groups = 0.0000
N. edwardraneyi	
Ictalurus punctatus	
Species of Low Frequency of Occurrence and Low Relative Abundance	
Ichthyomyzon gagei	*Lampetra aepyptera*
Lampetra aepyptera	*Lepisosteus osseus*
Lepisosteus oculatus	*Amia calva*
Amia calva	*Alosa chrysochloris*
Alosa alabamae	*Esox niger*
A. chrysochloris	*Cyprinus carpio*
Dorosoma petenense	*Hybognathus hayi*
Hiodon tergisus	*Hybopsis aestivalis*
Cyprinus carpio	*H. storeriana*
Hybopsis winchelli	*H. winchelli*
Notropis atherinoides	*Notropis atherinoides*
N. chalybaeus	*N. callistius*
N. volucellus	*N. candidus*
N. welaka	*N. chalybaeus*
Carpiodes cyprinus	*N. edwardraneyi*
C. velifer	*N. maculatus*
Erimyzon sucetta	*N. volucellus*
Erimyzon tenuis	*Semotilus atromaculatus*
Ictiobus bubalus	*Carpiodes cyprinus*
Minytrema melanops	*C. velifer*
Moxostoma carinatum	*Erimyzon oblongus*
Ictalurus furcatus	*E. sucetta*
I. melas	*E. tenuis*
I. natalis	*Hypentelium etowanum*
Noturus funebris	*Moxostoma erythrurum*
N. munitus	*M. poecilurum*
N. nocturnus	*Ictalurus melas*
Pylodictis olivaris	*I. natalis*
Aphredoderus sayanus	*Noturus funebris*
Strongylura marina	*N. gyrinus*
Labidesthes sicculus	*N. nocturnus*
Ambloplites ariommus	*Aphredoderus sayanus*
Centrarchus macropterus	*Labidesthes sicculus*
Lepomis gulosus	*Fundulus notti*
L. humilis	*Morone saxatilis* × *M. chrysops*
Pomoxis annularis	*Amplopites ariommus*
P. nigromaculatus	*Centrarchus macropterus*
Ammocrypta asprella	*Elassoma zonatum*
A. beani	*Lepomis humilis*
Etheostoma histrio	*L. marginatus*
E. parvipinne	*L. punctatus*
Percina caprodes	*Micropterus punctulatus*
P. maculata	*Pomoxis nigromaculatus*
P. vigil	*Ammocrypta beani*
P. shumardi	*A. meridiana*
Stizostedion vitreum	*Etheostoma histrio*
	E. parvipinne
	E. proeliare
	Percina caprodes
	P. maculata
	P. vigil
Similarity between groups = 0.6000	*P. sciera*
	P. shumardi
	Stizostedion vitreum

*Frequency of occurrence of 10% or more is high; relative abundance of 1% or more is high.

population dynamics of sympatric fluentine and riverine species and not directly by the availability of resources as fluentine and riverine species likely are. Therefore, the populations of cosmopolitan species are altered by the TTW in a manner proportional to the alteration of populations of fluentine and riverine species.[1]

[1]I thank Richard D. Caldwell for the use of data from his dissertation and Phillip R. Mundy for his contributions to the analysis of pre-TTW data. Financial support provided by the U.S. Corps of Engineers, Mobile District, in 1972 (contract No. DACW01-72-C-0009) and in 1983 (contract No. DACW01-83-C-0044) was essential to the project; Jack C. Mallory was my liaison. Maurice Mettee and Patrick O'Neil made helpful suggestions regarding the manuscript in its early stages, to which were added valuable criticisms by Steven T. Ross and David C. Heins. My wife, Elaine, read the manuscript in its stages of development.

24. Factors Influencing Changes in Fish Assemblages of Pacific Northwest Streams

Hiram W. Li, Carl B. Schreck, Carl E. Bond, and Eric Rexstad

Abstract

Recent structural alterations to watersheds of the Pacific Northwest have changed the ecological setting for fish assemblages. Dams have acted as physical zoogeographic barriers and may have increased the importance of fish diseases both as zoogeographic barriers and as mechanisms structuring fish assemblages. The impoundments favor the establishment of exotic, temperate mesotherms and eurytherms from the Midwest. Forestry, grazing, and bank-stablization practices have changed the morphology of watersheds and diminished the role of large woody debris and riparian vegetation, which are important regulators of physical change and stream metabolism. Fishing has depleted juvenile *Oncorhynchus tshawytscha*, a formerly very abundant fish in large tributaries of major watersheds, and certain other species no longer support commercial fisheries. Harvesting of salmonids has led to a significant reduction of nutrient input to nutrient-poor stream complexes. Stock depletion has given rise to hatcheries that now produce fish that are different genetically from the ancestral populations.

Recent debate has rekindled interest in the nature of fish taxocene structures in streams (Moyle and Li, 1979; Grossman et al., 1982; Herbold, 1984; Rahel et al., 1984; Yant et al., 1984). The heart of the controversy is whether the fish fauna is the result of independent physiological responses to physical gradients by each species or the result of biological interactions. If the composition of the fish assemblage is relatively constant through time, it is deterministically governed, and biological interactions are important mechanisms determining its structure (Grossman et al., 1982). We will argue that the problems of temporal and spatial scaling will affect the interpretation of variations in relative composition of fish assemblages. The problem of scale is linked with anthropogenic change and the difficulties in separating its confounding influences from natural, periodic disturbances. The goal of this chapter is to recount the forces that have changed faunal composition in the Pacific Northwest and to relate them to the current controversy.

Faunal Characteristics in Relationship to Spatial Scale

Connell and Sousa (1983) have made us more aware that scaling is important when we are examining the stability of populations and communities. Their criteria state that the area of study must encompass the home ranges of the organisms throughout their life cycles and through at least one complete generation. For river systems such as those of the Pacific Northwest, any investigation of assemblage dynamics requires that entire basins be considered the unit of study. Approximately 40% of the native fish fauna is anadromous, and a high degree of potadromy is exhibited by various species (Moring et al., 1981). Anadromous fishes can be found in the Snake and Columbia rivers throughout the entire year, migrating upstream to spawn or downstream to the sea (Allen et al., 1976; Northwest Power Planning Council, 1981; Everest and Sedell, 1983).

The suggestion that the river basin is the most meaningful spatial unit in which to study fish communities is theoretically supported by the River Continuum Concept (RCC) of Vannote et al. (1980) and the hierarchical stream structure proposed by Warren and Liss (1983). We believe that these frameworks can explain the distribution of fish guilds as they do functional groups of insects. For instance, the distribution of chiselmouth (*Acrocheilus alutaceus*), an herbivorous minnow, corresponds well with stream order as predicted by RCC (D. R. Lassuy, unpub. data; fig. 24.1).

Figure 24.2 displays native fishes along a continuum of a generalized Pacific Northwest river system. Much of this information was derived from the computerized data base of the Department of Fisheries and Wildlife, Oregon State University, which has stored collection records since 1900 that

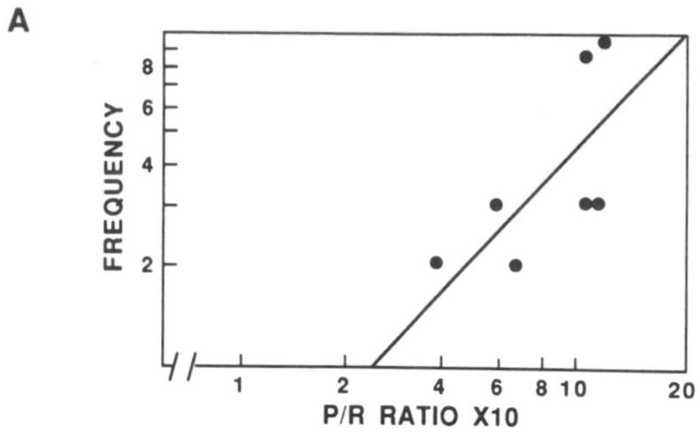

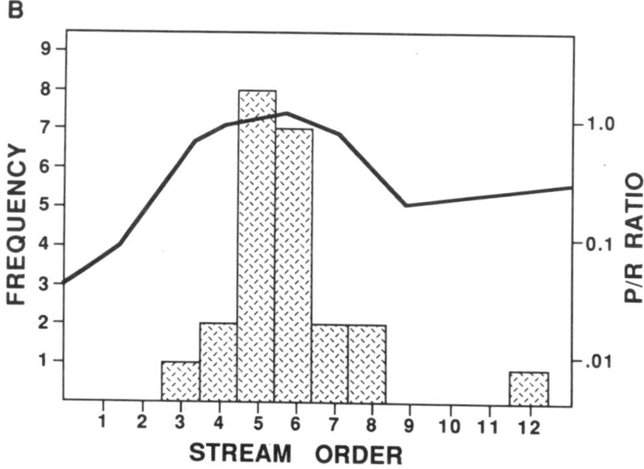

Fig. 24.1. A: Frequency of occurrence of chiselmouth plotted against the P/R (productivity/respiration) ratio. The solid line is the theoretical distribution of P/R ratios by Vannote et al. (1980). B: Frequency of occurrence of chiselmouth by stream order. The solid line is the theoretical distribution of *P/R* ratios by Vannote et al. (1980).

are highly oriented toward an Oregonian perspective. However, the shared species pool of Pacific Northwest river systems is substantial (Miller, 1958; Reimers and Bond, 1967; McPhail, 1967; McPhail and Lindsey, 1970; Moyle, 1976). From this figure one observes that the fauna was composed mostly of salmonids and cottids, which constituted 39–50% and 20–30%, respectively, of the fishes collected from 1900 to the mid-1940s. Figure 24.2 is analogous to a canonical function with three important physical factors: gradient, temperature, and stream size. In general, species are added to the system as gradient lessens and as water temperature rises and stream size increases. Temperate stenotherms are physiologically most efficient at temperatures < 20° C (Hokanson, 1977) and are found, therefore, primarily in lower-order streams. Temperate mesotherms and temperate eurytherms form larger fractions of the fauna when water temperatures increase. Hence, some species replacement may occur as a result of physiological specialization for temperature. For instance, mountain suckers (*Catostomus platyrhynchus*) and longnose suckers (*Catostomus catostomus* are gradually replaced by the bridgelip sucker (*Catostomus columbianus*) and the largescale sucker (*Catostomus macrocheilus*) as the gradient becomes less steep, and water temperatures increase. The mountain sucker and the longnose sucker are stenotherms; the bridgelip sucker, a mesotherm; and the largescale sucker, a eurytherm. The pattern of down stream species addition also follows a trophic gradient consistent with the RCC; surface insect feeders are found in the headwaters, followed by small benthic invertebrate feeders, herbivore-detritivores, omnivores, and large invertebrate-piscivores in higher-order streams.

The impacts of interactions among native fishes on distributional patterns are highly localized, resulting primarily in shifts in microhabitat use. The presence of torrent sculpin (*Cottus rhotheus*) alters habitat choice by the reticulate sculpin (*Cottus perplexus*) and the Piute sculpin (*Cottus beldingi*; Finger, 1982). Numerous studies have documented interactions among various species of salmonids that cause shifts in microhabitat use (Lister and Genoe, 1970; Andrusak and Northcote, 1971; Schultz and Northcote, 1972; Stein et al., 1972; Everest and Chapman, 1972; Allee, 1974; Glova, 1978). Competitive dominance plays a major role in microhabitat use where several salmonid species are found locally. Coho salmon (*Oncorhynchus kistuch*) is the most aggressive species, followed in order by steelhead trout (*Salmo gairdneri*), cutthroat trout (*Salmo clarki*), and chinook salmon (*Oncorhynchus tshawytscha*).

Impacts of Fishing

Before commercial fishing, the dominant fish in the Columbia River was the summer run of chinook salmon. By 1889–90 this run was badly depleted, and the fishery shifted to the spring and fall runs of chinook salmon, steelhead trout, sockeye salmon *Oncorhynchus nerka*), coho salmon, and chum salmon (*Oncorhynchus keta*), in order of importance. By 1975 the total catch of chinook salmon had dropped eightfold from historical peaks, coho salmon by tenfold, and steelhead trout and chum salmon by one hundredfold. Sockeye salmon were no longer capable of supporting commercial fishing (Allen et al., 1976). Sturgeon stocks were also overfished. The catch was 2,500,000 kg in 1895 and declined to 36,000 kg in 1934 (Craig and Hacker, 1940).

Overharvest of anadromous salmonids has had several ecological impacts. The overharvest of salmonid stocks denied a substantial amount of nutrients to the Columbia system. The diminution of nutrients destined for natal streams can be appreciated by the pattern of nutrient loss to the fishery (fig. 24.3). Salmonids actively transport nutrients against a gradient when they migrate from the relatively nutrient-rich ocean environment to relatively poor-nutrient headwater stream systems (Nikolskii, 1969). We calculate that the amount of nutrients in a spawning adult population is roughly four times that of seaward-migrating juveniles from the same stream. Nitrates and phosphates are rapidly sequestered by the periphyton during the height of carcass decomposition. Decaying carcasses can elevate primary production tenfold (Richey et al., 1975). Bacterial heterotrophy is also stimulated and hastens decomposition of leaf litter, thereby enriching the food base for shredder insects (Durbin

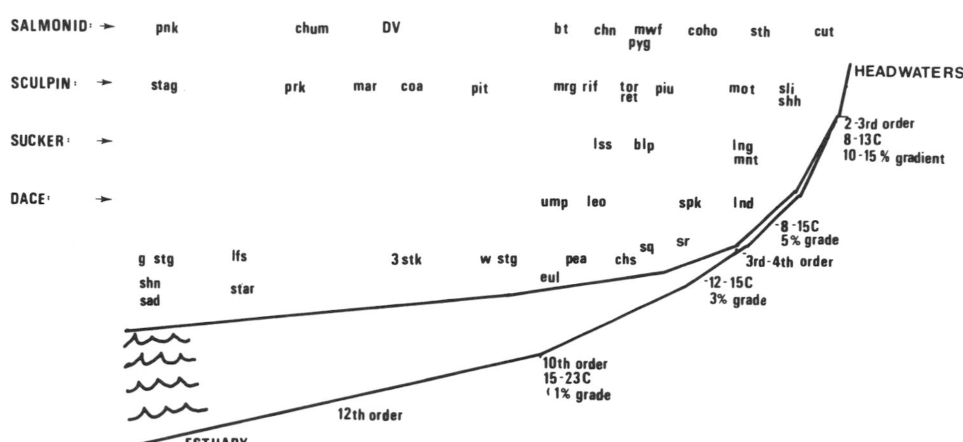

Fig. 24.2. Generalized distribution of selected native fishes along a river continuum of the Pacific Northwest. bt = bull trout, blp = bridgelip sucker, chum = chum salmon, chn = chinook salmon, chs = chiselmouth, coa = coast-range sculpin, cut = cutthroat trout, coho = coho salmon, DV = Dolly Varden, eul = eulachon, g stg = green sturgeon, leo = leopard dace, lfs = longfin smelt, lng = longnose sucker, lnd = longnose dace, lss = largescale sucker, mar = marbled sculpin, mnt = mountain sucker, mot = mottled sculpin, mrg = margined sculpin, mwf = mountain white-fish, pea = peamouth, pit = pit sculpin, piu = piute sculpin, pnk = pink salmon, prk = prickly sculpin, pyg = pygmy whitefish, ret = reticulate sculpin, rif = riffle sculpin, sad = saddleback gunnel, shh = shorthead sculpin, shn = shiner perch, sli = slimy sculpin, spk = speckled dace, sq = squaw-fish, sr = sandroller, stag = staghorn sculpin, star = starry flounder, sth = steelhead, 3 stk = three-spined stickleback, tor = torrent sculpin, ump = umpqua dace, w stg = white sturgeon.

et al., 1979). The loss of nutrients consequent to depletion of the stocks must have had profound impacts on the trophic system, and greater competition among species may have been one consequence.

We have attempted to mitigate for decreased natural production through hatchery supplementation. Hatcheries significantly contributed to salmonid production during the mid-1960s (Allen et al., 1976; Raymond, 1979; Northwest Power Planning Council, 1981). Runs of coho salmon entering the lower Columbia River increased from 72,000 fish in 1960 to 2,606,000 in 1970. It is debatable whether hatcheries will continue to produce well over the long term because the percentage of fish returning to hatcheries has decreased (Gunsolus, 1978).

Studies of different salmonids show that hatcheries profoundly change stock gene pools (Kincaid, 1976; Allendorf and Phelps, 1980; Ryman and Stahl, 1980). Hatchery coho salmon are distinguishable from wild stocks irrespective of geographic origin, on the basis of electrophoretic, morphological, and life-history characteristics; moreover, the progeny of wild fish reared in hatcheries differ from those reared in the wild (Hjort and Schreck, 1982). Reisenbichler and McIntyre (1977) found that growth and survival of juvenile steelhead trout to a migratory status is best in wild × wild progeny, intermediate in wild × hatchery progeny, and worst in offspring of hatchery fish. Hatchery practices have significantly altered run timing in coastal steelhead trout (Peterson, 1978).

Hatchery fishes behave differently from those reared in the wild. Their behavioral repertoire is more limited and is disruptive to wild inhabitants (G. Glova, pers. comm.). Territories of resident salmonids may be swamped by introductions of hatchery fish, which forces them to leave preferred microhabitats (Stein et al., 1972).

Impacts of Dams

There are now more than 100 high dams within the Columbia River basin. From the first recorded construction in 1850, numbers of dams grew exponentially through the 1960s. They have primarily had an impact on the system by inundating spawning areas and blocking migration runs. The dams have changed river conditions to increase migration difficulty for anadromous fishes, possibly increase the role of fish disease as a zoogeographic barrier, and favor exotic fishes to the detriment of native fishes.

Dams as Physical Barriers

The demise of the "June Hogs," large chinook salmon that once migrated into the upper basin of the Columbia River, is attributed to the lack of fish ladders at Grand Coulee Dam (Chaney, 1978). More than 50% of the basin is now blocked by dams. Counts at existing fish ladders indicate that white sturgeon appear to be declining in the Snake River system

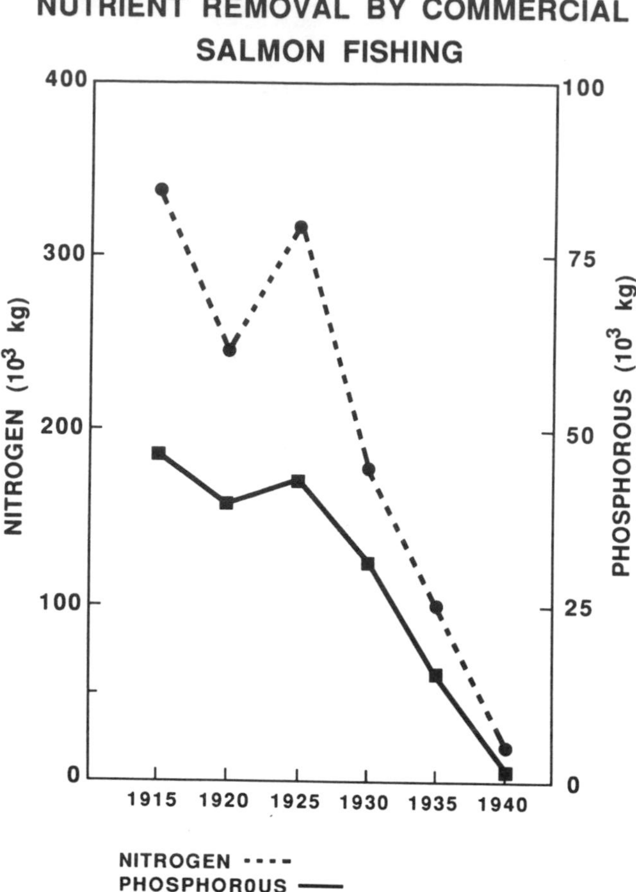

Fig. 24.3. Nutrients removed by commercial harvest of salmonids, 1915–45. Annual harvest by the aboriginal Indian fishery, estimated to be 8 million kg, was discounted (Craig and Hacker, 1940). Conversion values of Bull and Mackay (1976) were used to calculate nitrogen and phosphorus values from biomass of the catch.

(Coon et al., 1977). There are 8,000 to 12,000 white sturgeon between Lower Granite Dam and Hells Canyon Dam, but they are growing slower now than formerly, apparently because new dams are trapping nutrients upstream. Runs of lampreys are declining both in the Sanke Basin and in the mid-Columbia, again presumably because of the dams (Coon et al., 1977; J. Mullan, unpub. data). Splash dams used by the timber industry to store logs for drives downstream blocked substantial amounts of spawning area of coastal streams in Oregon and Washington, estimated to be as much as 60 percent in some areas (Wendler and Deschamps, 1955; Sedell and Luchessa, 1982).

Changes in discharge patterns have changed the timing and increased the duration of migrations by salmonid smolts two- to threefold in the Columbia River system because the fish are no longer aided by the fast currents that were once present (Raymond, 1979). The mortality of juvenile salmonids varies inversely with discharge through each dam: 5% at high levels of spill and 15% at low levels of spill (Northwest Power Planning Council, 1981). During the 1973 drought losses at each dam may have reached 45 percent. Buchanan et al. (1981) suggest that northern squawfish (*Ptychocheilus oregonensis*) may concentrate in large numbers at dams to feed on migrating juvenile salmonids. Gas-bubble diseases are no longer a problem in the Columbia River because corrective ''flip-lip'' structures have been installed at dams (Raymond, 1979).

Dams and Fish Diseases

Fish diseases have always been a potent force in structuring fish assemblages in the Pacific Northwest. For instance, 14 million fish of three species succumbed to an epizootic of *Flexibacter columnaris* in Klamath Lake, Oregon (Rohovec and Fryer, 1979). Native fishes differ in susceptibility to these diseases because of differential immunity and because the virulence of endemic diseases is temperature-dependent. *Flexibacter columnaris* becomes virulent to salmonids at temperatures above 10° C; however, catostomids and cyprinids are relatively unaffected at temperatures below 20° C (Becker and Fugihara, 1978). Infectious hematopoietic necrosis is responsible for epizootics in sockeye salmon, chinook salmon, and steelhead trout when temperatures rise above 15° C, but coho salmon are immune. *Ceratomyxa shasta* affects various species differently (Sanders et al., 1970). Infected coho salmon show an increasing susceptibility as temperature rises: mortality below 10° C is 2% at most, 22% at 15° C, and 84% at 20.5° C. In contrast, mortality of infected juvenile steelhead trout can be as high as 80% and is independent of temperature.

The distribution of *C. shasta* is well known, and its role as a zoogeographic barrier has been documented (Sanders et al., 1970; Hoffmaster, 1985). Chinook salmon and steelhead trout that evolved in drainages with *Ceratomyxa* are less susceptible than are fishes that evolved in its absence (Zinn et al., 1977; Buchanan et al., 1983). Immunity to some of these diseases has a heritable basis. Suzumoto et al. (1977) and Winter et al. (1980) showed that resistance to bacterial kidney disease is correlatable to the genotype for transferrin in coho salmon. Transferrin may limit endogenous iron by binding it and making it unavailable for bacterial use.

Disease problems may have been exacerbated by the installation of dams on the Columbia River. Becker and Fugihara (1978) concluded that fish ladders were epicenters for epizootic outbreaks of *F. columnaris*. They suggested that relatively unaffected resident species such as that large scale sucker inhabit the fish ladders and disperse spores that infect migrating adult salmonids. Chinook salmon of the summer run are severely infected because of a lack of immunity and because they migrate when water temperature is high and disease most virulent. Spring chinook, in contrast, are relatively unaffected because they migrate when the water is cold.

Ratliff (1983) found that the hypolimnions of reservoirs now harbor dense concentrations of *Ceratomyxa shasta*. Spores from carcasses of infected fish lodge and age in the reservoir mud, becoming infective when temperatures rise. He speculated that diseased carcasses are retained to a greater degree because of dams.

Table 24.1. Classification of Selected Native Freshwater Fishes of the Pacific Northwest According to Hokanson's (1977) Thermal Guilds (Stenotherms, Mesotherms, Eurytherms) and Trophic Guilds, Maximum Mandible Length, Maximum Total Length, and Maximum Age*

Species	Age	Trophic (Primary Prey)								Jaw:TL Ratio	TL (mm)	Jaw (mm)
		S	*M*	*B*	Plt.	Det.	Mic.	Mac.	Fish			
Stenotherms												
Lampetra richardsoni	Ammocoete			*c*	*d*	*X*	*x*					
L. ayresi	Ammocoete			*c*	*d*	*X*	*x*					
Cottus beldingi	4			*c*				x		0.035	60	2.0
C. marginatus	?			*c*				x		0.039	60	2.5
C. bairdi	5			*c*				*x*	YOY	0.029	130	3.7
C. cognatus	4			*c*				*x*	YOY	0.045	80	3.8
C. gulosus	4			*c*				*x*	YOY	0.049	90	4.2
C. confusus	4			*c*				*x*		0.046	100	4.7
C. aleuticus	4			*c*				*a*		0.067	80	5.1
C. rhotheus	6			*c*				*X*	*x*	0.056	150	8.5
Catostomus catostomus	14			*c*	*D*	*x*	*x*	*x*				
C. platyrhynchus	9			*c*	*D*	*x*	*x*	*x*				
Lota lota	10		*c*	*C*				*x*	*X*	0.035	790	27.9
Spirinchus thaleichthys	3		*c*	*C*				*Z*		0.087	110	9.7
Thaleichthys pacificus	4		*c*	*C*				*Z*		0.092	200	18.4
Steelhead	5	*c*	*c*	*C*				*x*		0.072	790	56.7
Steelhead	Juvenile	*c*	*C*	*c*				*x*		0.436	50–130	2.2–5.7
Oncorhynchus nerka	Juvenile	*c*	*C*	*c*				*z*		0.682	50–130	3.1–8.9
Salmo gairdneri	4	*c*	*C*	*c*				*x*		0.081	300	24.7
Salvelinus confluentus	7	*c*	*C*	*c*				*x*	*X*	0.071	720	51.7
O. kisutch	Juvenile	*C*	*c*	*c*				*x*		0.102	50–130	5.1–13.3
O. tshawytscha	Juvenile	*C*	*c*	*c*				*x*		0.110	50–130	5.5–14.2
Salmo clarki clarki	6	*C*	*c*	*c*				*X*	*x*	0.079	430	34.2
Mesotherms												
Cottus perplexus	6			*c*				*A*	*x*	0.040	70	2.8
Novumbra hubbsi	?			*c*				*X*	*x*	0.052	70	3.4
C. asper	7			*c*				*X*	*x*	0.038	130	5.1
Rhinichthys cataractae	5			*c*				*x*		0.033	160	5.2
R. falcatus	5			*c*				*x*		0.051	120	6.2
Percopsis transmontana	?			*c*				*x*	*x*	0.083	80	6.3
Mylocheilus caurinus	9			*c*				*x*	YOY	0.021	340	7.3
Acipenser transmontanus	82			*c*	*x*	*x*	*x*	*X*	*x*	0.038	3660	139.1
A. medirostris	?			*c*	*x*	*x*	*x*	*X*	*x*	0.025	2300	57.5
Catostomus columbianus	17			*c*	*D*			*x*			430	
Lampetra tridentata	Ammocoete			*c*	*x*		*X*	*x*				
Eurytherms												
Rhinichthys osculus	3			*c*				*x*		0.030	70	2.0
Acrocheilus alutaceus	6			*c*	*D*			*x*			300	
Catostomus macrocheilus	11			*c*	*D*	*x*	*x*	*x*			600	
Couesius plumbeus	5		*c*	*C*	*P*			*Z*	*x*	0.037	230	8.3
Ptychocheilus oregonensis	19	*c*	*c*	*C*				*x*	*x*	0.082	740	60.1
Gasterosteus aculeatus		*c*	*C*	*c*				*x*		0.070	80	5.6
Richardsonius balteatus	5	*c*	*C*	*c*				*x*		0.044	180	7.8
Hybopsis crameri	?	*c*	*C*	*c*			*X*			0.034	70	2.3
Gila bicolor	7	*c*	*C*	*c*	*X*		*X*		YOY	0.050	410	20.7

*Age = maximum life span; *S* = surface feeder; *M* = midwater feeder; *B* = bottom feeder; Plt. = plant; Det. = detritus; Mic. = microinvertebrate; Mac = macroinvertebrate; Jaw = maximum mandible length; TL = maximum total length; *c* = location in the water column; *d* = diatom; *x* = feeds on entire array within prey class; YOY = young-of-the-year; *z* = zooplankton; *a* = aquatic insect; *p* = phytoplankton. Capital letters denote dominant mode.

Table 24.2. Classification of Fishes Introduced into the Pacific Northwest According to Hokanson's (1977) Thermal Guilds (Stenotherms, Mesotherms, Eurytherms), Trophic Guilds, and Maximum Mandible Length, Maximum Total Length, and Maximum Age*

Species	Age	Trophic (Primary Prey)								Jaw:TL Ratio	TL (mm)	Jaw (mm)
		S	*M*	*B*	Plt.	Det.	Mic.	Mac.	Fish			
Stenotherms												
Coregonus clupeaformis	10		*c*	*C*				*X*	*x*	0.018	610	10.8
Salvelinus fontinalis	5	*c*	*C*	*c*				*X*	*x*	0.079	410	32.4
Salmo trutta	9	*c*	*C*	*c*				*x*	*x*	0.117	550	63.9
Mesotherms												
Stizostedion vitreum vitreum	10		*c*	*C*				*x*	*X*	0.064	760	48.9
Morone saxatilis	9		*C*	*c*					*x*	0.061	760	46.4
Esox americanus vermiculatus	7		*C*					*x*	*X*	0.075	360	26.8
Perca flavescens	7	*c*	*C*	*c*				*Z*	*x*	0.045	330	15.1
Micropterus dolomieui	10	*c*	*c*	*C*				*x*	*x*	0.066	470	31.2
Eurytherms												
Noturus gyrinus	2?			*C*				*x*		0.106	90	9.4
Ictalurus punctatus	40			*C*				*d*	*x*	0.04	860	15.9
I. nebulosus	7			*C*	*x*	*x*	*x*	*X*	*x*	0.053	360	18.7
Tinca tinca	?			*C*	*x*			*X*		0.036	610	22.0
Ictalurus natalis	5			*C*	*x*	*x*	*x*	*D*	*x*	0.052	430	22.3
I. melas	6			*C*	*x*			*X*		0.074	460	33.7
Cyprinus carpio	15			*C*	*x*	*x*	*x*	*X*		0.048	710	33.9
Pylodictus olivaris	19			*C*				*d*	*X*	0.049	1040	50.9
Carrassius auratus	20?		*c*	*C*	*P*	*x*	*x*			0.057	250	14.4
Ambloplites rupestris	7		*c*	*C*				*x*	*x*	0.072	290	21.1
Lepomis gibbosus	6		*C*	*c*				*X*	YOY	0.04	180	7.2
L. cyanellus	7		*C*	*c*				*x*	*x*	0.071	130	9.1
L. gulosus	7		*C*	*c*				*X*	*x*	0.071	250	18.1
L. macrochirus	9	*c*	*C*	*c*				*Z*	YOY	0.045	150	6.9
Pomoxis nigromaculatus	9	*c*	*C*	*c*				*z*	*x*	0.481	300	14.4
P. annularis	10	*c*	*C*	*c*				*z*	*x*	0.051	330	16.8
Micropterus salmoides	14	*c*	*C*	*c*				*x*	*X*	0.071	510	36.3
Gambusia affinis	1.25	*C*	*c*					*x*		0.064	60	4.1

*Age = maximum life span; *S* = surface feeder; *M* = midwater feeder; *B* = bottom feeder; Plt. = plant; Det. = detritus; Mic. = microinvertebrate; Mac. = macroinvertebrate; Jaw = maximum mandible length; TL = maximum total length; *c* = location in the water column; *x* = feeds on entire array within prey class; *d* = diatom; *P* = phytoplankton; YOY = young-of-the-year; *z* = zooplankton. Capital letters denote dominant mode.

Dams and Exotic Species

Dams have created conditions that favor warmwater fishes, largely introduced from the Midwest. This has greatly increased the numbers of piscivorous fishes and greatly increased the risk of predation to the native fauna in the Columbia River. This was judged from an index of predatory capability (Maximum jaw size; tables 24.1, and 24.2) and dietary studies (Wydoski and Whitney, 1979; Hjort et al., 1981; Bennett et al., 1983; Stainbrook, 1982; Gray et al., 1984; Maule and Horton, 1984).

Before the introduction of exotic predators, most predation affected young-of-the-year fishes (fig. 24.4). Bull trout (*Salvelinus confluentus*), cutthroat trout, and burbot (*Lota lota*) are native fishes most able to prey on adult fishes in coldwater streams of the Columbia basin. The northern squawfish was probably the most abundant large predator in warmwater streams, although the omnivorous white sturgeon (*Ascipenser transmontanus*) was and is able to ingest large prey on occasion. Consequently, being a large species served to reduce chances of predation. Fish larger than 200 mm were seldomly preyed on, and most predation pressure was probably exerted on the young-of-the-year.

Food-web patterns changed after the introduction of warmwater game fishes (fig. 24.5). Sculpins, cyprinids, and catostomids are subject to more predation because large size no longer confers immunity from predation. Only the squawfish among the native fauna is known to prey to any extent on exotic fishes, and its diet overlaps substantially with that of exotic species, suggesting that competition for food is possible.

Walleyes (*Stizostedion vitreum vitreum*) have recently invaded the lower Columbia River from the reservoir of Grand Coulee Dam, where they are now extremely abundant (Harper et al., 1980; Hjort et al., 1981; Nigro et al., 1981). Growth rates of walleyes in the mid- and lower Columbia are comparable to the highest published values, suggesting that rapid population growth may soon follow (Maule and Horton, 1985). This fish is a large, schooling predator, unlike any in the native fauna. Its impact on juvenile salmonids

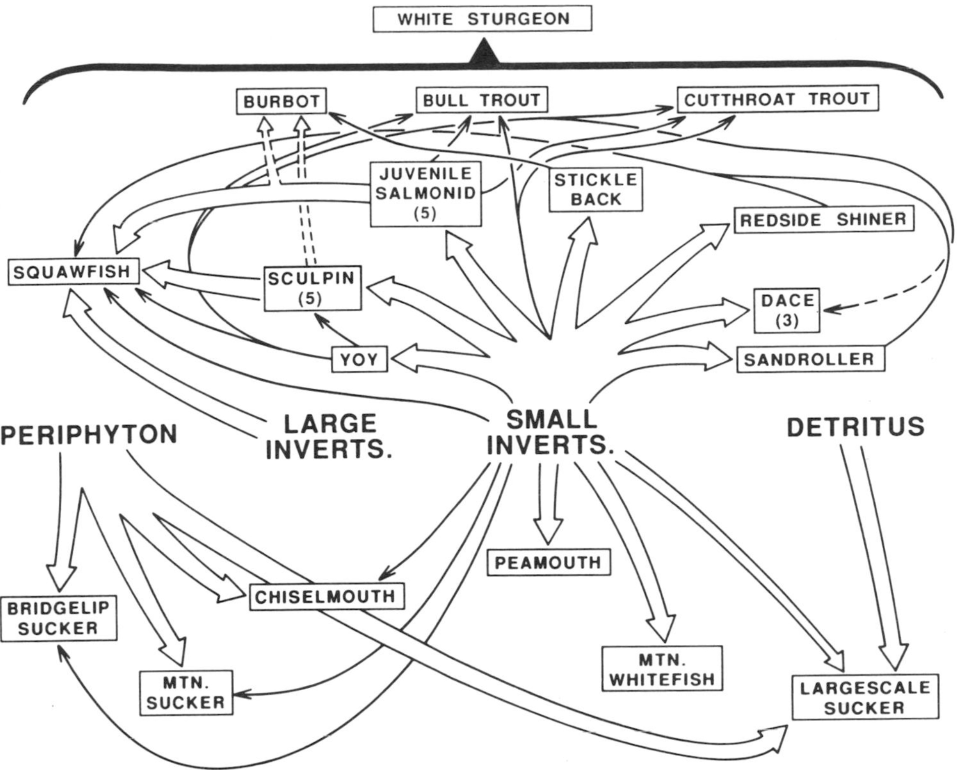

Fig. 24.4. Hypothetical food web of the middle and lower Columbia River before 1800. The width of the trophic link represents the relative importance of prey to the predator. Dashed arrows denote the assumption that burbot preys mostly in deep lakes within the drainage. Sturgeon is capable of eating anything.

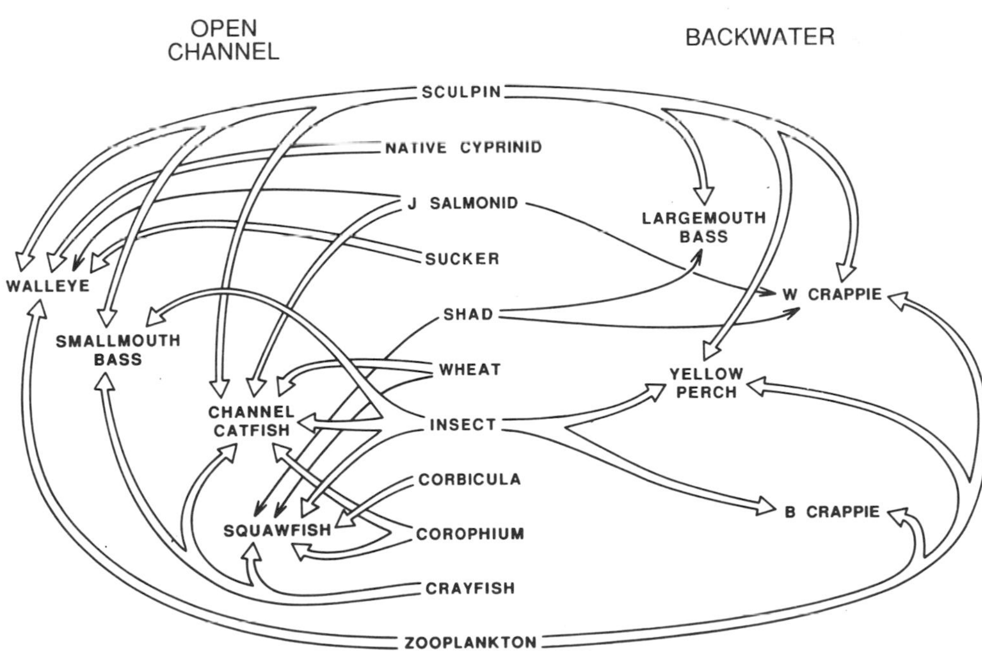

Fig. 24.5. Major changes in the food web of the middle and lower Columbia River ca. 1888–1983.

Table 24.3. Exotic Fishes as a Percent of the Total Catch per Unit Effort (CPUE), as a Fraction of the Total Species Assemblage (No.) Exotics/No. Total), and the Common Name of the Most Abundant Species and Its Ranking of Abundance in the Entire Assemblage (in Parentheses)

Area Sampled*	Seines			Gill Nets		
	Percent Exotics, CPUE	No. Exotics/ Total No.	Highest-ranked Exotic	Percent Exotics, CPUE	No. Exotics/ Total No.	Highest-ranked Exotic
Upper Columbia River						
Grand Coulee Dam	53	7/11	Yellow perch (1)	54	7/15	Walleye (1)
Hanford Reach						
Km 605–13	0	0/9	None	5	1/11	Carp (7)
Km 557–66	< 1	1/9	Yellow perch (9)	6	3/13	Yellow perch (7)
Snake River						
Ice Harbor Dam	65	10/17	Centrarchids (1, 2, 3)	62	7/14	Carp (1)
Lower Monumental Dam	86	7/11	Yellow perch (1)	41	9/17	Carp (2)
Little Goose Dam	63	12/18	White crappie (1)	40	10/20	Yellow perch (2)
Lower Granite Dam	75	5/9	Brown bullhead (1)	24	9/16	Yellow perch (4)
Mainstem Columbia River						
John Day Dam	63	13/27	Black crappie (2)	36	11/23	Yellow perch (1)

Sources: Gray and Dauble (1977), Harper et al. (1980), Hjort et al. (1981), Nigro et al. (1981), Bennett et al. (1983).
*All areas except those in the Hanford Reach are reservoirs.

could be great because of the potential for density-depensatory predator-prey interactions.

The impact of dam-related habitat changes and exotic introductions on fish assemblages of the Columbia Basin is shown in table 24.3. Note the difference between the reservoir assemblages and that of the Hanford Reach, the last free-flowing reach above Bonneville and below Priest Rapids Dams. Few exotics inhabit the Hanford Reach, a seminatural stretch of the Columbia River. However, exotic species have become dominant elements in reservoir assemblages. For example, walleye and yellow perch were twice as numerous as the next most abundant species in gill-net catches and seine hauls at Grand Coulee Reservoir. The overall pattern is that the fish fauna now resembles faunas found in the Midwest.

Impacts on Riparian Habitats

Essentially, the impact of logging, stream channelization, and grazing are similar. As the watershed becomes physically less complex, it loses its buffering capacity to retain runoff, trap and retain organic and inorganic material, and provide cover to protect fish from physical injury during floods (Bustard and Narver, 1975a, b; Tschaplinski and Hartman, 1983; Rodnick, 1983; Bottom et al., 1985; Cederholm and Peterson, 1985).

Stands of old-growth (450–to–500-year-old) Douglas fir (*Pseudotsuga menziesii*) and western hemlock (*Tsuga heterophylla*) once dominated watersheds west of the Cascade Mountains, shaping stream morphology and development as well as influencing trophic input: primary productivity versus organic detritus (Swanson et al., 1982). Forestry practices have disrupted these regulatory processes of the old-growth conifer forest and have simplified the physical structure of watershed by changing the amount of large woody debris in streams. Beaver dams function like large woody debris in watersheds and are important in creating habitats for coho salmon (Everest and Sedell, 1983). They act as retention devices and receive nutrient input from the beavers but do not impede fish movement during high flows (C. Dahm and J. Sedell, in prep.). Destruction of beaver dams is one of the reasons why habitat for coho is now more limited in coastal streams of Oregon (Bottom et al., 1985).

Removal of the forest canopy by logging can influence changes in the faunal assemblage through temperature-mediated effects on competitive ability and differential disease resistance of various species. Reeves (1985) found that at temperatures of 19–22° C redside shiners (*Richardsonius balteatus*) displace juvenile steelhead trout through exploitation competition for food resources: at temperatures of 12–15° C juvenile steelhead trout dominate redside shiners through aggressive challenges. Infection from *Flexibacter columnaris* led to high mortality among the less competitive species at those temperature ranges; however, the dominant competitor was relatively unaffected. In contrast, the production of aquatic insects and cutthroat trout dramatically increases as a result of the increase in sunlight entering stream reaches affected by clear-cut timber harvests in smaller, colder, higher-gradient streams (Hawkins et al., 1982; Hawkins et al., 1983; Murphy and Hall, 1981; Murphy et al., 1981).

Overgrazing riparian vegetation in the dry interior east of the Cascade Range causes higher water temperatures, greater stream-bank erosion, loss of spawning habitat, and deleterious changes in stream-channel structure (Hall and Baker, 1982; Bottom et al., 1985). Porosity of the soils decrease, and stream banks slump because of trampling; streams may become intermittent because of these changes (Winegar, 1977).

Bank-stablization practices reduce the amount of riparian vegetation, especially large trees. It causes another negative

Fig. 24.6. Changes in the Willamette River floodplain caused by revetments. Open circles along the 1967 river channel indicate location of revetments.

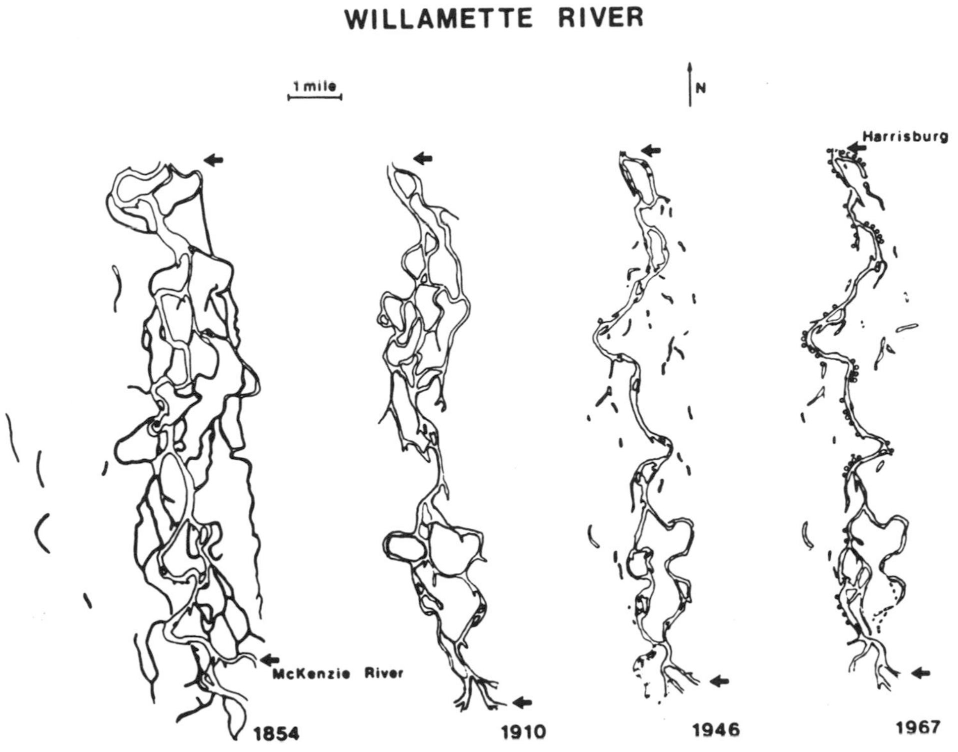

impact: the hydraulic energy is redirected from lateral scour to downcutting. Since the first installation of a revetment in the Willamette River in 1888, there has been a tremendous loss of secondary side channels, backwaters, and oxbows (fig. 24.6)—important habitat for juvenile salmonids and the Oregon chub (*Hybopsis crameri*), a species now uncommon in the Willamette drainage. Revetments are poor habitat for most larval and postlarval fishes (Li et al., 1984). Five specimens appear to benefit from revetments: prickly sculpin (*Cottus asper*), redside shiners, northern squawfish, largescale suckers, and chiselmouths (Hjort et al., 1984; Li et al., 1984). The first three of these species are attracted by high densities of invertebrate prey living in the interstices. Chiselmouths and a largescale suckers graze on diatoms, and stone revetments provide good substrate for periphyton.

Discussion

The fauna of the Pacific Northwest was probably adapted to invade and exploit new or recently disturbed environments. Massive tectonic movements, volcanic eruptions, huge landslides (up to 5.4 km^2), large-scale glacial movement, and massive floods shaped several basins. This was especially characteristic of the Columbia basin, where some of the largest floods on record have occurred. It is estimated that 6 to 40 floods caused by the fracturing of ice dams occurred during a period 19,000–12,000 years ago. Each flood released an estimated 22 km^3 of water at a rate of 2.3 km^3/h for 40 h (Spranger, 1984). This may explain why much of the fish fauna is either anadromous or euryhaline. The ability to recolonize was clearly important. These events suggest that we should expect a fauna that has evolved primarily in response to physical gradients rather than to biological interactions. However, biological interactions are important in patterns of interactive segregation among salmonids and sculpins, and diseases can influence community assemblages. Certain disturbances have predictable outcomes. For example, a characteristic fauna results from the installation of stone revetments. It is evident, therefore, that both stochastic and deterministic forces shape the stream assemblages of Pacific Northwest streams, but their relative roles are unknown.

The streams of the Pacific Northwest, especially streams of the Columbia basin, operate very differently now from the way they once did because of all the man-made disturbances. Many of these perturbations caused secondary impacts (e.g., dams and fish disease, dams and exotic species). These disturbances have affected the fauna basinwide. Commercial fishing with gill nets at the mouth of the Columbia River affected nutrient inputs to oligotrophic streams of the upper basin. Logging of the upper watershed effected changes in species composition by limiting recruitment of young. This means that a basinwide perspective is needed to understand assemblage structure of this region. It also means that one must be very cautious about extrapolating present species assemblages to issues concerning regulation of assemblage or community structures.

Biological communities respond to disturbance as resetting mechanisms. Wiens (1984) suggests that the frequency of disturbances shapes the characteristics of natural communities so that they can be aligned on an equilibrium-nonequilibrium gradient. If disturbances are frequent and severe, the environment will be unsaturated, and therefore biological interactions may be relatively insignificant (Wiens, 1984). Biased conclusions may result from a study that uses stability measures in stream systems from the Pacific Northwest. A species assemblage that may otherwise behave like an equilibrium community may mimic a nonequililbrium community as it responds to anthropogenic perturbations.

It is inappropriate to use time-series data from a single stream, even a relatively undisturbed one, to examine whether or not fish assemblages are stable in Pacific Northwest streams. A substantial proportion of the fauna is migratory, inhabiting different parts of a drainage during different life-history stages. The presence or absence of a species in a single stream may not be due entirely to physiological responses to shifting physical gradients but may be governed by biological events elsewhere in the basin. For example, a small year class of fish may be decimated by predators before it migrates into the study area. A species may spawn in an ecologically similar stream lower in the drainage that its natal stream because an oxygen block to migration resulted from failure of an overtaxed sewage treatment plant at the time of migration. The absence of a species is therefore an artifact of man's activities. When fish assemblages are viewed from the perspective of drainages rather than stream reaches, patterns appear less random because a reach is more homogeneous physically than are streams of different orders within a watershed. Large physical gradients between stream orders separate those fishes specialized for headwater environments from those better adapted for larger streams (see Matthews, chap. 14). Habitat use by stream fishes at the reach level may be plastic and dependent on spatiotemporal variability in habitat availability, which suggests that habitat electivity studies are needed (Angermier, chap. 7).

Connell and Sousa (1983) recommend a minimum time of one generation needed for stability analyses of populations. It is more difficult to choose a time span for communities. Should the generation time of the longest-lived species, such as the white sturgeon, be chosen? Should it be the life span of chinook salmon, the dominant species in the basin? Perhaps the time scale for the entire stream community should be adjusted to successional patterns of riparian vegetation, because the stream and its valley are an ecological unit (Hynes, 1975). Minimally, the time scale may be in the order of decades before noticeable recovery from anthropogenic disturbance is observed. Two examples follow: Dramatic improvement of habitat and shifts in species composition have been noticed in stream reaches of eastern Oregon 10 years after the use of fencing to limit cattle grazing near stream banks (see Hall and Baker, 1982). The riparian vegetation has not yet fully matured, and further changes can be expected following this time period. Native fishes now inhabit portions of the Willamette River not inhabited 35 years ago because minimum standards for dissolved oxygen were set in 1947, and the river has recovered from pollution from domestic and industrial sources (Hjort et al., 1984).

Can one determine how assemblages or communities are regulated in the Pacific Northwest? We think so, but it will require many approaches because of the problems outlined previously. It should be obvious that a historical perspective is important to the understanding of stream systems. We need to reconstruct, at least in part, how the system evolved. Mayden (chap. 26) argues persuasively that one needs to examine the zoogeographical record before interpreting present-day distributional patterns of the fauna. We need to establish how the stream systems we are studying have been affected by man (Sedell and Luchessa, 1982; Minshall et al., 1985). Some of this can be done through examination of historical records (past and present comparisons), while effects of other alterations can be examined through appropriate field comparisons. Biologists in the Pacific Northwest can use management agency experiments in stream rehabilitation as an approach to study factors affecting stream assemblages. Long-term surveys carefully designed along appropriate spatial and temporal scales will always be important, but studies that incorporate analyses of morphological and physiological limitations will provide a useful framework for generating null hypotheses concerning the influence of biological interactions on assemblage structure (see Matthews, chap. 14). Appropriate experiments that address the effects of biological processes on community structure should then be applied to test these hypotheses. Biological interactions are often limited to studies of predation and competition; the impacts of diseases, parasites, and symbionts are often overlooked. Stream systems from various regions may operate differently because they are on different evolutionary paths, and we must be cautious about generalizing findings from a particular system to all streams.[1]

[1] We thank S. Gregory, J. Hall, R. Hughes, D. Lassuy, J. Li, J. Rohovec, and J. Sedell for sharing their insights concerning the ecology of Pacific Northwest streams. R. Hughes, J. Sedell, and O. Garman read previous drafts of the manuscript. E. Li drafted the illustrations. Any errors are the responsibility of the authors.

25. Rarity: Patterns and Consequences for Stream Fishes

Andrew L. Sheldon

Abstract

Absolute numbers of individuals influence the genetic structure of populations, risk of extinction and strength of within- and between-species interactions. In Owego Creek, New York, most species were uncommon, and abundances spanned six orders of magnitude. The largest population was > 100,000 individuals (age 1 or older). The median population size was 1,100, and populations of seven species were < 100. Most rare species were peripheral individuals from populations centered downstream, but two rare species were of limited distribution and vulnerable to local extinction. The implications of rarity and stream geometry for extinction above impoundments are illustrated with these data. Dominance-diversity curves were linear for sections with few species and sigmoid (approximately lognormal) for more diverse assemblages. The lognormal and, less effectively, the logseries distributions fit abundance patterns of stream fishes. Species-area (discharge) curves and lognormal theory are used to predict small populations (hundreds) of the rarest species in large rivers with diverse faunas and to predict extinctions as drainage systems are fragmented into isolated sections.

"*. . . rarity is the attribute of a vast number of species in all classes, in all countries.*"

—CHARLES DARWIN, *The Origin of Species*, 1859.

Rarity, with its attendant risks of genetic impoverishment or extinctions, is a central concern of conservation biologists (Soulé and Wilcox, 1980; Frankel and Soulé, 1981; Schonewald-Cox et al., 1983). Through its effect on the relative likelihood of intra- or interspecific encounters, rarity must also influence the evolution and dynamics of competitive and social interactions in natural communities. Although Darwin's insight and subsequent developments in the ecology of rarity and species-abundance relationships arose without much concern for fishes, the consensus (Deacon et al., 1979) that some stream fishes are rare and endangered and the meager representation of some species in collections (e.g., Shepard and Burr, 1984; Robison and Harp, 1985) suggest that fishes fit the pattern identified by Darwin. If so, mathematical descriptions of species-abundance relationships (Preston, 1962a, b; Williams, 1964; May, 1975) and the rudiments of a theory of commonness and rarity (Hanski, 1982a, b 1985; Taylor and Woiwod, 1982; Brown, 1984) should have descriptive and predictive utility in studies of assemblages of stream fishes. In this chapter I present quantitative data on abundances in communities of moderate richness and show that these patterns are concordant with observation and theory derived from other taxa. I then use the theory to make speculative predictions concerning the diverse fish faunas of larger streams for which quantitative data are lacking.

A Case Study

The headwaters of Owego Creek, in central New York (see Sheldon 1966, 1968, for description), contain a typical assemblage of Susquehanna drainage fishes (Denoncourt and Cooper, 1975). Quantitative collections (N = 115) from stream sections isolated with block seines were made with multiple runs of an AC electrofisher (Lennon and Parker, 1955) The sampling design and estimators follow Cochran (1953) and are detailed in Sheldon (1966). The stream was divided into six sections (geographic strata) within which 170-m subsections (clusters) were allocated randomly. Clusters were mapped, and each discrete pool, riffle, or run was assigned to one of four depth categories (habitat strata). Units to be sampled were randomly allocated from available habitats within each cluster. Population estimates (excluding YOY) and their variances were derived for successive levels of aggregation. Estimates for all fish species in each of six

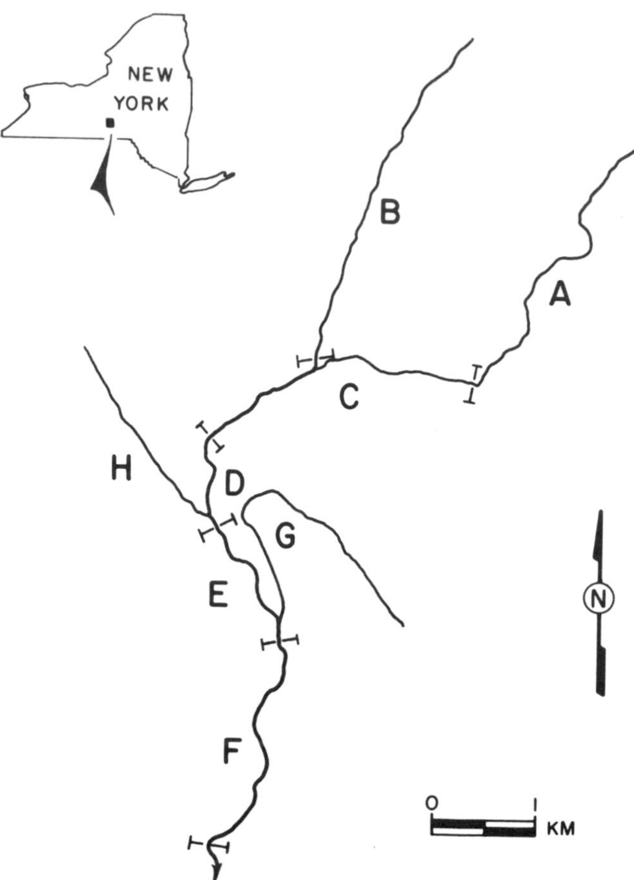

Fig. 25.1. Owego Creek, New York, with section boundaries.

sections (A–F, fig. 25.1) are shown in fig. 25.2, and species totals are summarized in table 25.1. Sections G and H (see fig. 25.1), which are small or intermittent were not sampled.

Figure 25.2 presents abundances as dominance-diversity curves (log number versus ranked abundance). Whittaker (1972) showed that such curves are often linear for assemblages with few species (e.g., sections A, B) and typically approach the strongly sigmoid pattern of section F in species-rich systems. Thus fish communities show parallels with plants, birds, and other taxa. The logarithmic form conveniently accommodates the great range of population sizes found in all sections and in the total (table 25.1), where abundances span six orders of magnitude. The overwhelming dominance of *Cottus bairdi* ($\hat{N}$ = 105,000) contrasts vividly with the median population size of 1,100 and the seven species with estimated populations < 100 individuals.

Most of the small populations consisted of peripheral individuals from populations centered downstream from the study area; two did not. *Clinostomus elongatus* ($\hat{N}$ = 198) and *Cottus cognatus* ($\hat{N}$ = 12) were rare, were confined to the middle sections of the area, and may have faced local extinction. At least a few *Clinostomus* occurred in sections G and H, which were not sampled quantitatively, and the sculpin may also have been present. Nonetheless, these species existed in precariously small populations.

Fig. 25.2. Population estimates by stream sections for Owego Creek fishes. Population totals (≥ age 1) are given ± 1 SE.

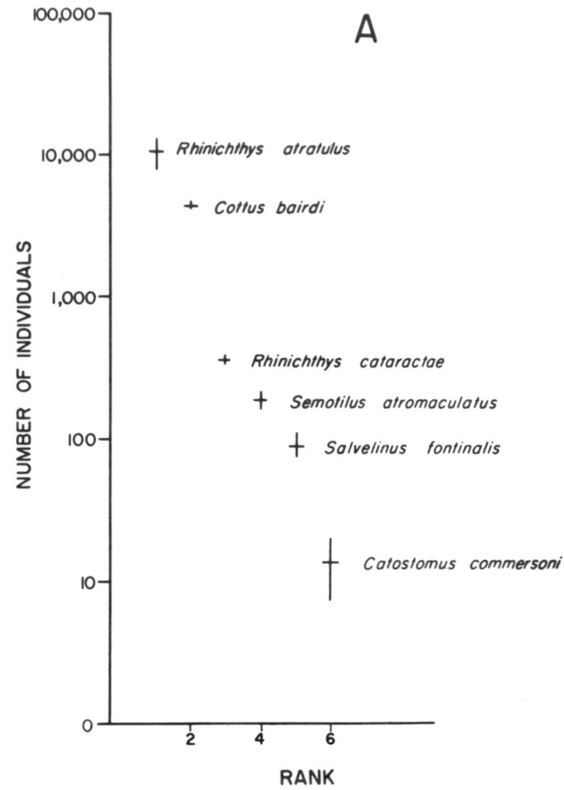

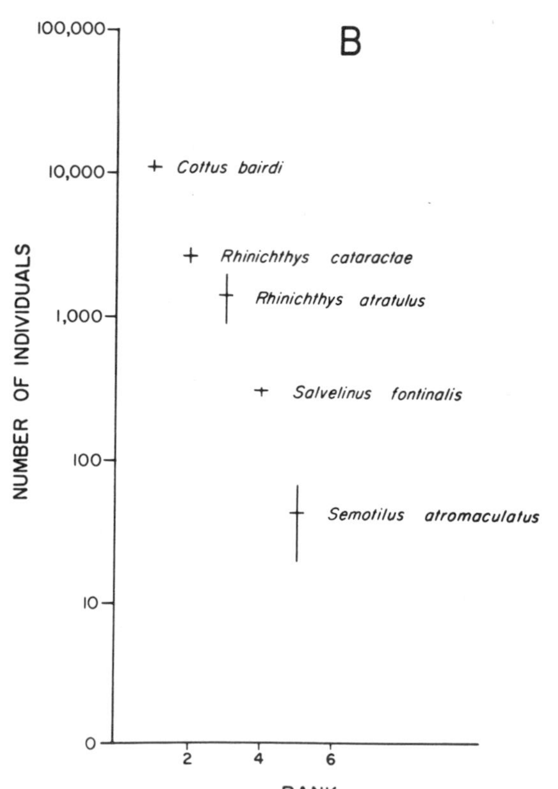

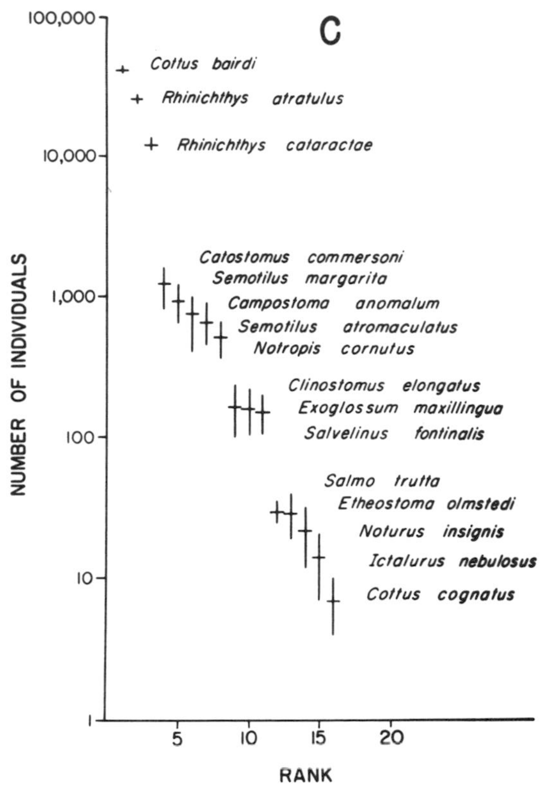

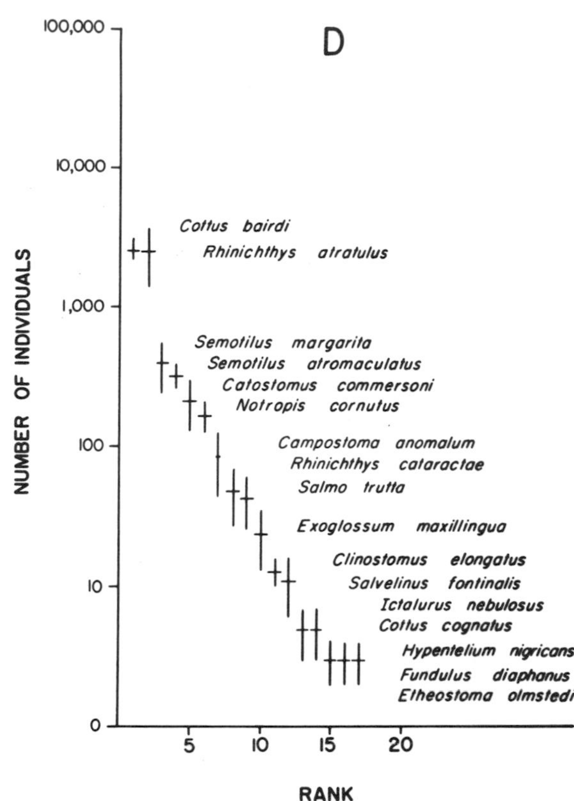

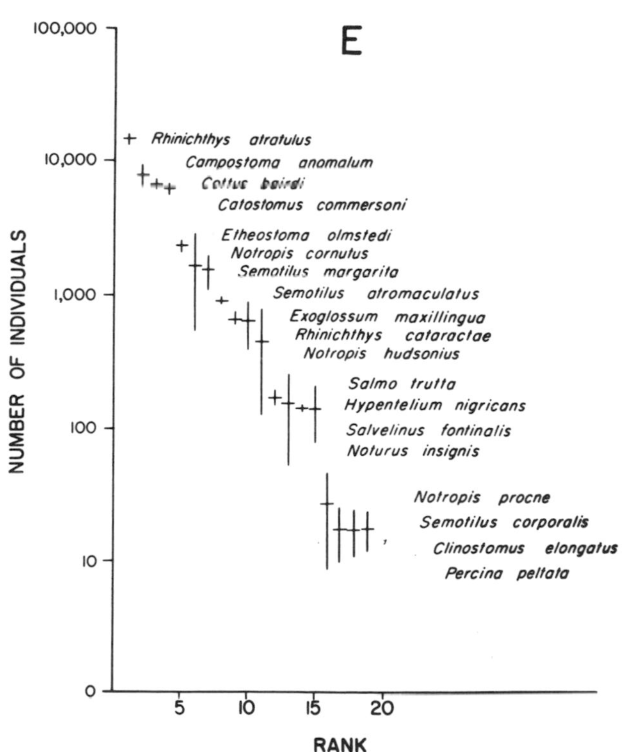

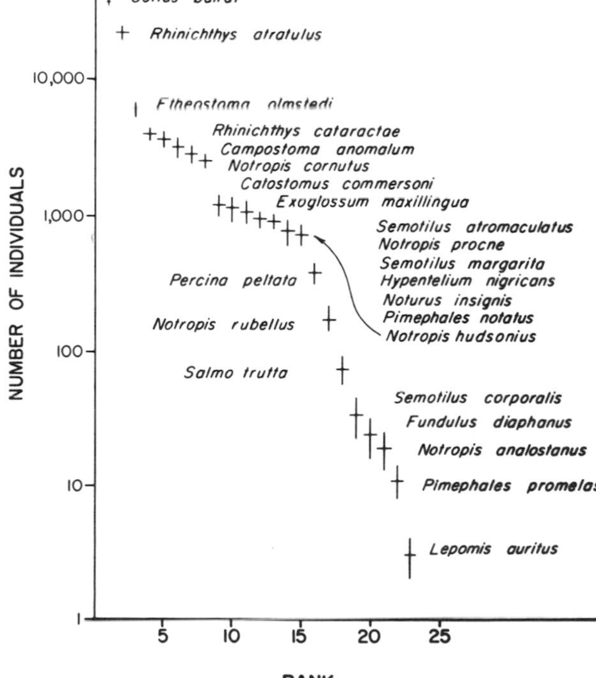

Fig. 25.2. *Continued*

Table 25.1. Estimated Total Populations in Logarithmic Abundance Classes for Sections A–F (Fig, 25.1), Owego Creek, New York

Abundance	Species
> 100,000	*Cottus bairdi*
10,001–100,000	*Rhinichthys atratulus* *R. cataractae* *Campostoma anomalum* *Catostomus commersoni*
1,001–10,000	*Etheostoma olmstedi* *Notropis cornutus* *Semotilus margarita* *Exoglossum maxillingua* *Semotilus atromaculatus* *N. hudsonius* *N. procne* *Hypentelium nigricans* *Noturus insignis*
101–1,000	*Pimephales notatus* *Salvelinus fontinalis* *Percina peltata* *Salmo trutta* *Clinostomus elongatus* *Notropis rubellus*
11–100	*Semotilus corporalis* *Fundulus diaphanus* *Notropis analostanus* *Ictalurus nebulosus* *Cottus cognatus* *Pimephales promelas*
≤10	*Lepomis auritus*

The role of immigration in maintaining small populations (the "rescue effect" of Brown and Kodric-Brown [1977]; see also Watkinson [1985]) or elevating local diversity ("mass effect" of Shmida and Wilson [1985]) has not been investigated in fish communities. However, a simple numerical exercise (fig. 25.3) illustrates potential consequences of isolation by barriers such as reservoirs. Arbitrarily selecting $N < 100$ as leading to extinction within a finite time and imagining a reservoir that rose ever higher until only the headwaters of Owego Creek remained shows that isolation and diminution of available habitat would reduce species richness from that observed in the open system by about 25–35% at each step in the process. Actually, this is a conservative guess since at least some of the preimpoundment populations would have been maintained above the assumed critical size by immigration. Countering the hypothesized decrease is the possibility that some species might increase in a reservoir and extend their distribution upstream as described by Ruhr (1956), Erman (1973), and Crisp et al. (1984). Probably most stream fishes would not thrive in reservoirs (Mahon and Ferguson, 1981), so this potentially important effect is not considered here. Such impoundment effects are another demonstration of the importance of source areas and immigration and deserve more attention than they have received.

In summary, absolute numbers of most species in Owego Creek were small. At least a few species were so rare that local extinction was a distinct possibility, and more would face this risk if the system were isolated from the rest of the drainage.

Generalization and Extrapolation

Data like those for Owego Creek do not exist for larger streams that, especially in the southeastern United States, support rich faunas and numerous uncommon species. An indirect and speculative approach is used here to predict patterns of abundance, diversity, and risk of extinction.

Three mathematical models have been used to summarize species-abundance relationships. The random breakage, or "broken stick," model of MacArthur (1957) is simple to fit and serves as a useful null model. King (1964) claimed satisfactory fit of the model to some data on fishes. The log series (Williams, 1964) graduates data from some large collections very well and has desirable mathematical properties. The lognormal distribution (Preston, 1962a, b) is the most cumbersome to use. However, if one is willing to make additional assumptions, the parameters of the lognormal are interrelated in a fixed fashion that allows predictions to be made.

Fit to these models (fig 25.4) was tested against the combined data from a series of collections (Boschung and O'Neil, 1981) from a short section of Barbaree Creek, Alabama. The Owego Creek data, which are expansions of samples rather than complete collections, are less suitable for this purpose since additional rare species would have been detected in a collection as large as the estimated total population. Numerical procedures follow MacArthur (1957; ran-

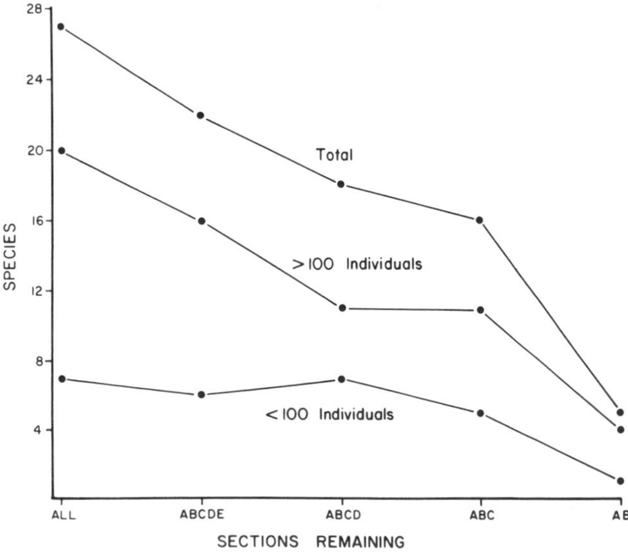

Fig. 25.3. Hypothetical consequences on diversity and population sizes of sequential elimination of sections of Owego Creek.

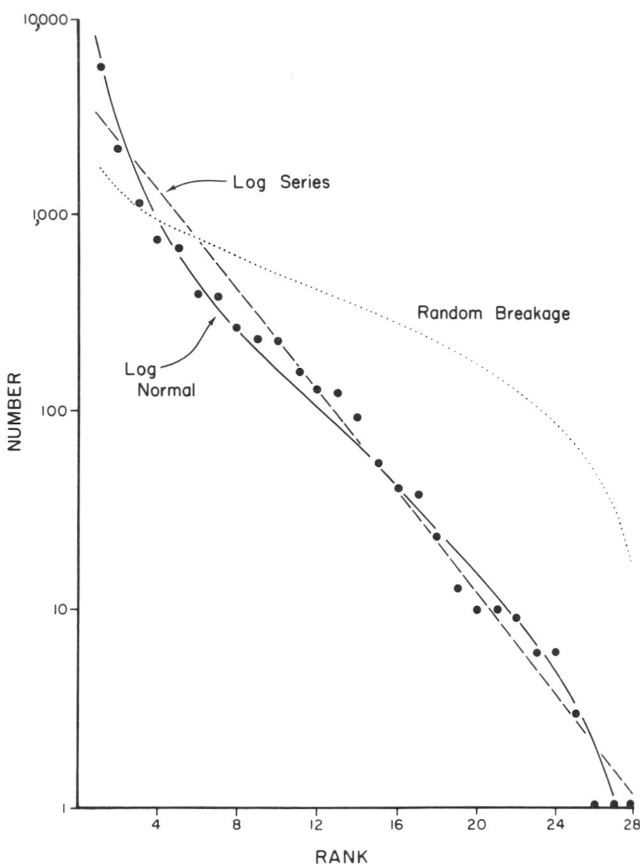

Fig. 25.4. Fit of species-abundance models to the data of Boschung and O'Neil (1981) from Barbaree Creek, Alabama.

dom breakage), Williams (1964; log series), Preston (1962a, b; lognormal), and Pielou (1975; lognormal). The random-breakage model, with its relatively even distribution of abundances, is totally inadequate to describe these data, whereas the log series, based on the same single parameter (individuals/species), captures much of the information in the dominance-diversity curve. However, the lognormal, which includes the variance as a second parameter, has the smallest residual error and the appropriate sigmoid shape. The Owego Creek data (fig. 25.2) also approximate this form that is characteristic of lognormal distributions of abundances (Whittaker, 1972). From these limited data, and by analogy with results for other taxa, the lognormal distribution provides a good description of abundance patterns in fish communities; and the log series runs a close second.

Preston (1962a, b) reviewed a large body of data and concluded that, not only was the lognormal the model of choice, but a particular set of parameters defined one lognormal distribution, which he termed canonical. Although he (Preston, 1980) recently described and analyzed major departures from the canonical form, many data sets agree with the canonical lognormal. May (1975) claimed that the canonical parameters are a consequence of the central limit theorem and that the canonical distribution is an expected or average lognormal. Sugihara (1980) showed that lognormal parameters approach the canonical values more closely than would be expected from statistical arguments alone and proposed an explanatory model to account for this convergence. Empirical, statistical, and theoretical evidence supports the generality of the canonical lognormal distribution. The virtue of the canonical form is a fixed relationship between N (total number of individuals in the universe of concern), S (number of species) and m (population size of the rarest species) (Preston, 1962a, b). The canonical assumption is used here, for lack of better, to explore expected patterns of rarity, diversity, and extinction in a species-rich system. Neither lognormality nor the canonical variant is accepted by all ecologists as a reasonable approximation of reality. The theory does provide semiquantitative predictions that highlight problems in the conservation of stream fishes and requisite data for better understanding and management.

Table 25.2 Area, Discharge,* and Number of Fish Species in the Duck and Tennessee Rivers

Stream Characteristics	Duck River	Tennessee River
No. species (S)	140	215
Area (A), km^2	6,650	104,580
Discharge (Q), m^3 sec^{-1}	115	1,815

*U.S. Geological Survey (1979).

The Duck River, in central Tennessee, is the exemplar, although enough approximations are made so that some portions of the analysis approach the hypothetical. D. Etnier (pers. comm.) and associates have collected 140 fish species from the Duck River. This is a large fraction of the native fauna (Stauffer et al., 1982) of the entire Tennessee drainage, of which the Duck River is a part (table 25.2).

Species-abundance models provide some insight into the problem of scarcity of species in collections. Collector's curves (Pielou, 1975) relate the number of species observed to the number of (randomly selected) individuals examined. See Engen (1979; random breakage), Williams (1964; logseries), and Preston (1962a, b; lognormal) for procedures. Except for the unrealistic random-breakage model, collections exceeding 100,000 individuals would be required to detect the rarest species in faunas as diverse as those of the Duck or the Tennessee (fig. 25.5). As shown below, the fauna of the Duck is a sample of that of the Tennessee rather than an isolate; thus the expected curve will be intermediate. Since real collectors take batches from particular habitats rather than randomly selected individuals over all habitats but compensate by attempting to collect from all available habitats, the theoretical curves will not be observed in practice. For the truly rare and unpredictable species, however, the theoretical curves should provide reasonable predictions at large sample size.

Closely related to collector's or species-individual curves are species-area curves, which may be treated as empirically determined relationships (Connor and McCoy, 1979) or derived from the canonical lognormal model (Preston, 1962a, b). The usual form

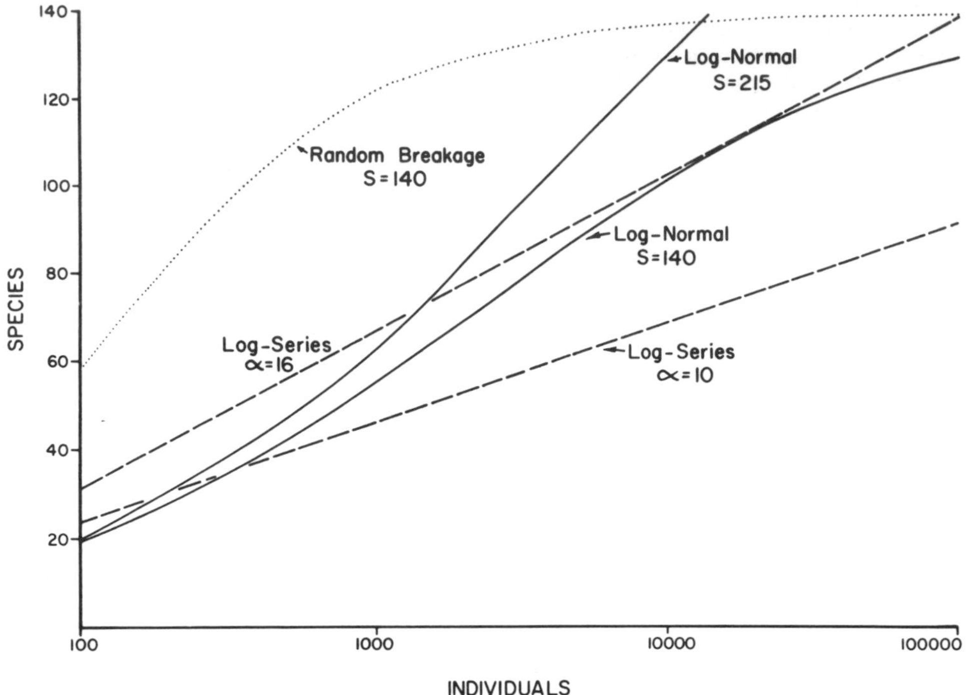

Fig. 25.5. Species-individual (collector's) curves for the Duck (S = 140) and Tennessee (S = 215) rivers. The log series-diversity parameters ∝, which must be estimated from the number of individuals and species in a real collection, were selected to illustrate position and shape of the log-series relationship.

$$S = cA^z, \qquad (25.1)$$

where S = number of species, A = area, z = dimensionless coefficient and c = constant, is linear in logarithmic form

$$\log S = \log c + z \log A. \qquad (25.2)$$

On theoretical grounds Preston (1962a, b) argued that $z \approx 0.27$ if the collections are true isolates with abundances distributed in canonical lognormal fashion. This prediction is supported by observation on insular biota with z lying between 0.20 and 0.30 (MacArthur and Wilson, 1967). In contrast, collections that are samples from within isolates have z values in the 0.12–0.20 range. We can ask whether the fishes of the Duck River are a true self-contained isolate or a sample of the Tennessee River fauna. Livingstone et al. (1982) substituted stream discharge for watershed area to correct for differences in runoff and their procedure is followed here. Then

$$\frac{S_1}{S_2} = \left(\frac{Q_1}{Q_2}\right)^z, \qquad (25.3)$$

where S_1 and S_2 are the number of species in drainages 1 and 2 and Q_1 and Q_2 are mean discharges in the same drainages. Substituting discharge and species richness values from table 25.2 in eq. 25.3 yields z = 0.155 characteristic of samples rather than isolates. Livingstone et al. (1982) obtained z = 0.30 for independent African rivers. Species-discharge relationships are comparable to the more conventional species-area curves. A test of the estimate of z for the Duck-Tennessee contrast is provided if one assumes that the Tennessee River samples the still larger fauna of the Mississippi system. Substituting z = 0.155, Q and S for the Tennessee (table 25.1), and Q = 17,545 m^3sec^{-1} for the Mississippi (Czaya, 1981) yields S = 305, which compares very well with the 280-300 species total given by Moyle and Cech (1982).

We can ask what would happen if the fauna of the Duck River were severed from the rest of the Mississippi drainage. Taking S = 300 for the Mississippi system and accepting z = 0.27 as a best guess for isolates yields $\hat{S}$ = 77 (eq. 25.3), which implies that the Duck River is overstocked by about 60 species that are presently maintained by immigration but would disappear if interchanges with the larger system were blocked. This prediction is not immediately testable, but since the Duck and its smaller confluent the Buffalo River now enter Kentucky Lake, a huge mainstem reservoir on the Tennessee River, the stage is set for extinctions. Presumably riverine fishes can pass through or persist in the reservoir, but isolation must take a toll (Harris, 1984; Wilcox and Murphy, 1985).

The species-area formulation says nothing explicit about rarity. However, the usual explanation for low z values in areas with free exchange with their surroundings is the presence of a few individuals of species straying from other habitats or of species (e.g., large carnivores) existing in low densities (MacArthur and Wilson, 1967). Without sustaining immigration these species will probably disappear. The canonical lognormal provides an exploratory tool with which to estimate population sizes under the scenario of isolation of presently interconnected rivers. If the Duck River were isolated, could it maintain its present richness, and how abundant would the least common species be? Preston's (1962a, b) formula relating N (total individuals), S (number of species), and m (population size of rarest species) was solved to

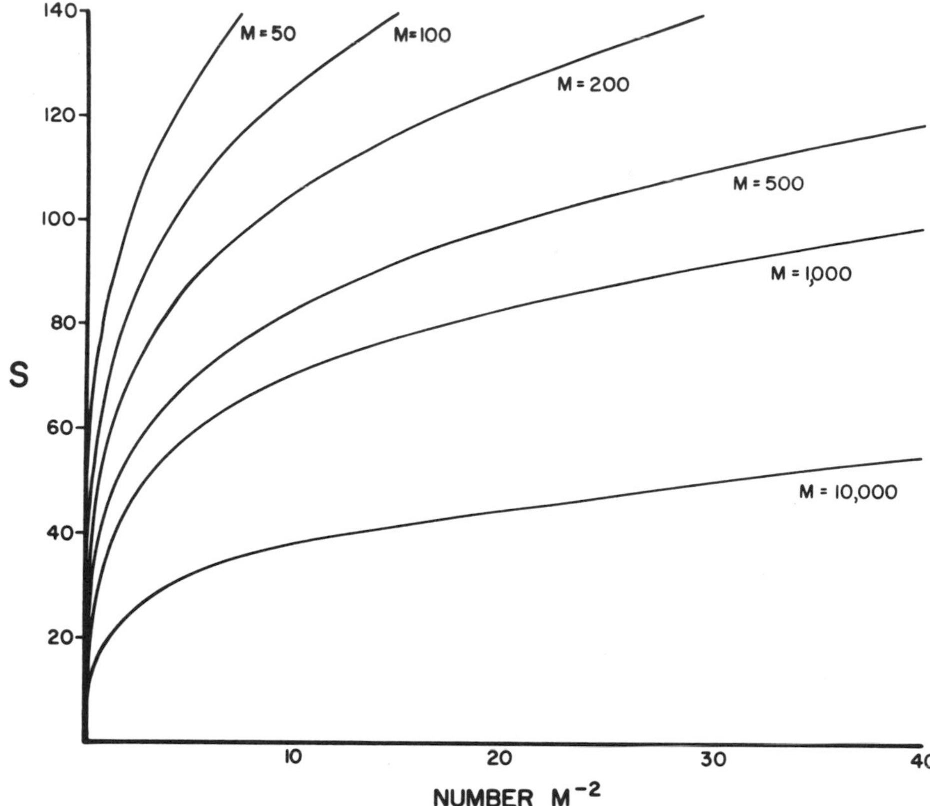

Fig. 25.6. Theoretical relationships of *S* (number of species), population density and minimum population size (*m*) under the canonical lognormal hypothesis for a river system (e.g., Duck River, Tennessee) of estimated area 6.65 × $10^7 m^2$.

estimate *m*. Since *m* is derived from a logarithmic regression, rests on the assumption of canonical lognormality, and involves a quantity from the extreme tail of a probability distribution, the estimates are informed guesses and not much more. Nonetheless, they provide order-of-magnitude hints about abundances and species richness. For the Duck River, $S = 140$ was determined directly (table 25.2); but $\hat{N}$ required a series of approximations. The surface area of all streams in the Duck drainage was estimated as 1% (Naiman, 1983) of basin area (table 25.2). If density is taken as 4 m^{-2} (approximate mean for Owego Creek, Sheldon, unpub. data), the total population of the Duck River is 2.7 × 10^8 fish. For this combination of *N* and *S*, $m = 27$. Is this a viable population? No one knows. A more general solution (fig. 25.6) shows, for a canonical isolate the size of the Duck system, $S > 100$ is possible only with high densities or small values of *m*. In my judgment these are impossible conditions to sustain. The species-discharge analysis suggested an equilibrium fauna of 80 species for an isolated Duck River. At this richness and these realistic densities (2–10 m^{-2}), minimum population sizes between 100 and 500 seem more reasonable. In the absence of data on density and absolute population sizes, reasonableness is the only criterion available. The analysis suggests that some fish species may number in the hundreds and that the fragmentation of river systems will cause extinctions and a catastrophic decline in diversity.

Discussion

Rarity is more nearly a fact than an evil, although extinction and previous rarity are inextricably linked. As Darwin noted, most species are rare, and stream fishes provide no surprises except in the small absolute population sizes (hundreds) observed or predicted. Such populations are vulnerable to natural accidents and human-caused alterations of habitat. Over the short run the conservation aspects should be paramount. The analysis attempted here, however, implies that maintenance of local populations and suitable habitat may not be enough. If the theory-in-the-large of canonical lognormal distributions is a valid approximation of reality, fragmentation of drainage networks by dams, pollution, and channelization projects will take an enormous toll on the diverse fish faunas of heavily impacted rivers such as the Tennessee.

A general theory of rarity of fishes has not yet been developed. In particular, the interactions of spatial patchiness and local density need to be explored, and temporal fluctuations must be considered in any discussion of rarity (Harper, 1981; Rabinowitz, 1981). A quantitative assessment of distribution and abundance in a large river system would contribute to ecological theory and the conservation of evolutionary diversity.[1]

[1]Gene Christman and DeWayne Williams prepared the figures. Two helpful reviewers identified some especially soft spots in the speculative discussion. Final preparation of the manuscript was supported by the University of Montana sabbatical program and by the Savannah River Ecology Laboratory, operated by the University of Georgia for the U.S. Department of Energy under contract No. DE-AC09-76-SR00819.

26. Historical Ecology and North American Highland Fishes: A Research Program in Community Ecology

Richard L. Mayden

Abstract

Historical ecology is a complementary approach to evolutionary ecology and supplies the much-needed historical framework for areas of ecology concerned with revealing historical patterns. Without some form of historical perspective it is very difficult to determine whether contemporary ecological coexistence is the direct result of present-day communities or of inheritance from coexisting ancestors. Phylogenetic relationships of taxa must be applied to any questions concerned with biogeography, the age of a community or its structuring, sympatric speciation, ecological shifts, behavioral shifts, parasite-host interactions, or any hypothesized "adaptive change." One must provide a historical control for the experiment. Here the control is a hypothesis of descent with modification, a historical null hypothesis.

In the present example the methods and philosophy of historical ecology have permitted answers to many questions about Central Highland fish communities that until now have been inaccessible. The faunas are ancient (predating the Pleistocene glaciation) and, after more geological data are available, they may be found to be surprisingly old. I have also provided a robust explanation to the question why species display only certain, predictable distributions and why only certain species associations exist. I cannot at this time answer questions concerning the evolution of ecological traits and their correlation with speciation events, owing to a lack of comparable and detailed ecological data for these communities. This chapter does, however, outline a research program that will permit them to be addressed efficiently.

The mechanics of ecological communities and their composition and structure have been the subject of considerable attention and debate. Although several processes have been viewed as instrumental (e.g., predation, parasitism, competition, climate, chance dispersals, nutrient availability), one, competition, has attracted considerable attention. The evolutionary significance of interspecific competition in organizing communities of organisms was recently challenged by Wiens (1977). This viewpoint is also held by others and supported by arguments of Conner and Simberloff (1979), Strong et al. (1979), Connell (1980), Lawton and Strong (1981), Simberloff (1982, 1983), Strong (1983), Walter et al. (1984), and others (see Strong et al., 1984). The importance of interspecific competition, however, has been defended by Schoener (1982, 1984b) and others (see Strong et al., 1984). Controversies such as these are considered by some to be a waste of time, energy, and paper. However, they help in our understanding of the processes and mechanisms involved in the observed pattern(s).

Previous discussions of evolutionary ecology have ignored one facet of organismal biology that I think should have been of considerable interest and importance in these controversies, that is, the genealogical histories of the organisms. What is the role of speciation and cladogenesis in community organization? What proportion of the ecologies of these organisms being studied in great detail may be explained in terms of their ancestry and not in terms of the contemporary community of coexisting species?

These questions are historical in nature and require historical data for the fishes and the geographic areas inhabited by them. As noted by Brooks (1985) for parasite-host associations, questions such as these are better addressed under the philosophy and methods of historical ecology. This area of ecology represents the union of systematics and ecology and differs from evolutionary ecology primarily in its ability to derive direct estimates of history through the use of phylogenetic systematics. Evolutionary ecology, on the other hand, differs from historical ecology primarily because genealogies of organisms are not considered, and estimates of history are at best indirect. Under this approach the number of species in a community, the geographic range of a species, and specificity of ecological interactions are generally thought to be positively correlated with the age of the species or community. The greater the diversity in a community, the older its estimated age; the larger the range of a species, the older it is estimated to be; and with time ecological interactions become increasingly more complex (Brooks, 1985). Using the approach of historical ecology, no such assumptions are required. All of the above questions and even more specific questions may be answered directly for an entire community or characteristics.

Thus the primary purpose of this chapter is to illustrate the importance of historical data (e.g., phylogenies) in explaining community organization. Three major sets of information are necessary for exploring and testing hypotheses in this field. These are (1) faunal composition of the region, (2) phylogenetic data for the species, and (3) geological history of the region. Gathering such information is a considerable task, but each is necessary in pursuing community ecology. Below I discuss each of these required data sets in reference to existing communities of fishes inhabiting the Central Highland streams of eastern North America. Further, I illustrate how this research program can provide a methodology that will permit, for the first time, direct answers to historical questions in ecology.

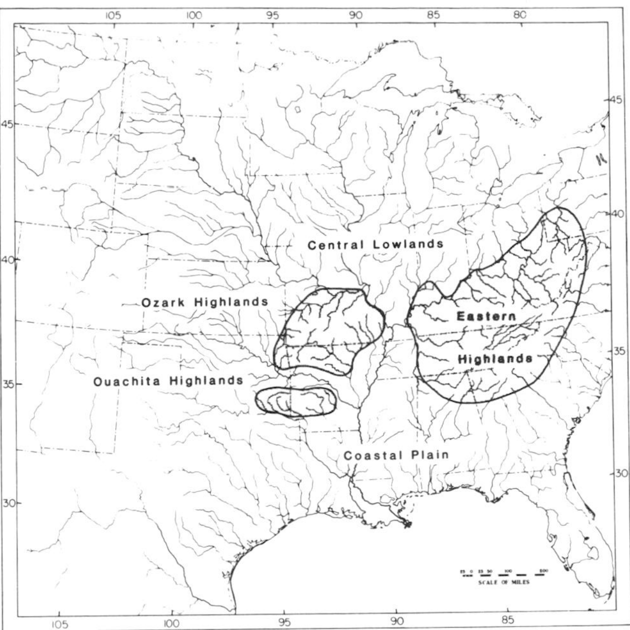

Fig. 26.1. Highland areas of eastern North America and surrounding lowlands. The Ouachita and Ozark highlands form the Interior Highlands biogeographic track. These areas and portions of the Eastern Highlands drained by the Ohio, Cumberland, and Tennessee rivers form the Central Highlands track.

Central Highland Fish Communities

For years many biologists have noted an interesting faunal distribution in eastern North America, replicated by several groups of organisms. Closely related species or populations of the same species are found in areas of highland topography east and west of the Mississippi River (fig. 26.1; Mayden, 1987, fig. 3). Many species of the Ouachita Highlands have their closest relatives in the Ozark Highlands, and these species in turn have their closest relatives in the Eastern Highlands. The three regions combined form the Central Highlands biogeographic track (Mayden, 1985a). Fish communities of these areas are distinctive and diverse, with several endemic species. The Central Highlands fish communities have attracted the attention of ecologists (Matthews, 1982; Gorman, 1983) and icthyologists (see Hocutt and Wiley, 1986), who have been concerned with community organization and have used these communities as laboratories. Several interesting questions can be formulated for these isolated communities concerning the age of the fauna and species associations and the mechanisms behind the evolution of particular life-history traits that ensure successful coexistence. Until recently evolutionary ecology appeared most appropriate to answer such questions. However, the existing research protocol is inadequate. Questions such as these are historical and necessitate historical data for the fishes and geographic regions inhabited by them. Historical ecology supplies the needed historical framework in which to answer these questions.

Geological History

The Central Highlands as defined by Mayden (1985a) and Wiley and Mayden (1985) includes three uplifted and disjunct regions separated by intervening lowlands (fig. 26.1). The regions include the Ouachita Mountains, the Ozark Plateaus, and the Eastern Highlands. The Eastern Highlands, the largest of the three, are drained by the Tennessee, Cumberland, and Ohio (portions) rivers; the upper Mobile Bay; and the headwaters of some Atlantic Slope drainages. This region includes the Interior Low Plateau, Ridge, and Valley, and Blue Ridge provinces (Thornbury, 1965). The Ozark Plateaus are drained by northward-flowing tributaries of the lower Missouri River, the White River system, and portions of the lower Arkansas River system. The Ouachita Mountains are drained by the Ouachita River system and the Kiamichi and Little rivers of the Red River system. All three regions are at least Eocene in age and are characterized by clear, cool, high-gradient streams, although there are exceptions in some areas.

All three regions are separated by lowland habitats atypical of highland species. Between the Eastern and Ozark highlands spans the floodplain of the Mississippi River, the glaciated Central Lowlands Province, and the Coastal Plains Province. Lowland areas of the Arkansas River narrowly separate the Ozark and Ouachita highlands (fig. 26.1). These regions were once continuous, however, and formed a large, expansive highland region inclusive of areas north and east of the Ozark and Eastern highlands in the central Lowlands Province (Dowling, 1956; Quinn, 1958; Pflieger, 1971; Mayden, 1985a, 1987; Wiley and Mayden, 1985). These observations are supported by geological as well as faunal data.

Before the Pleistocene, highland topography and presumably highland streams were widespread north of the existing Central Highlands over much of the eastern Central Lowlands. Most of this highland topography was obliterated by glacial materials with the advance of glaciers in the Pleistocene (Cross et al., 1986). Early in the Pleistocene two isolated highland areas were formed through the fracturing of the widespread contiguous region by glacial advance into a western Interior Highlands and the Eastern Highland region (see Mayden, 1985a, fig. 5B). Later the continuous Interior Highland was split into the northern Ozark Plateaus and southern Ouachita Mountains with the development of the ancestral Arkansas River (Quinn, 1958; see Mayden, 1985a, fig. 5C). This presumably occurred before the Sangamon interglacial that followed the "Wisconsin" glacial advance (Quinn, 1958; Mayden, 1985a).

Rivers draining the preglacial Central Lowlands presumably had characteristics similar to those draining existing highlands to the south (Pflieger, 1971; Mayden, 1985a). This hypothesis is supported by the Tertiary geomorphic history of much of the region, which paralleled that of the existing Central Highlands (Thornbury, 1965). Further, the disjunct nature of many "highland" fishes north of the highlands, in the glaciated Central Lowlands, supports the hypothesis of a more widespread distribution in the past (Mayden, 1987, fig. 3; Pflieger, 1971; Mayden, 1985a; Wiley and Mayden, 1985). Thus before the Pleistocene there were widespread highland topography and biota in eastern North America encompassing the presently recognized highland areas and regions to the north in the Central Lowlands. The present "highland islands," therefore, represent Pleistocene fragments of an older biota and geologic formation. Drainage patterns of this region were different before the Pleistocene and have changed, in some places considerably, since that time. The drainage history of the Central Highlands and adjacent regions is summarized and documented in Hocutt and Wiley (1986).

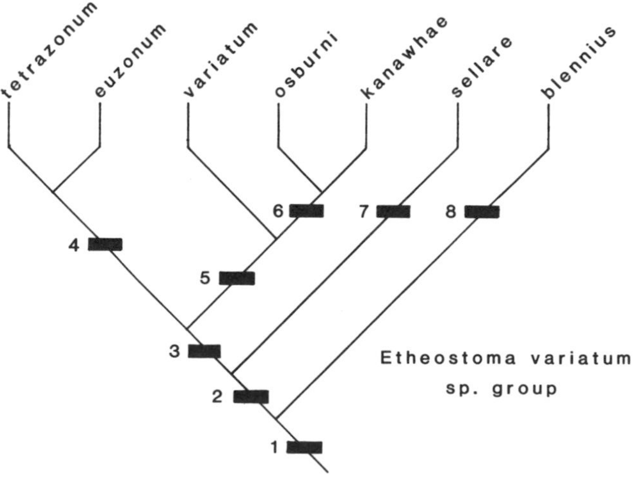

Fig. 26.2. Phylogenetic relationships of species in the *Etheostoma variatum* species group (Wiley and Mayden, 1985).

Faunal Composition

The icthyofaunas of streams draining the Central Highlands are some of the most diverse in North America. The three regions are also distinctive, each with a number of endemic species. Faunas of the regions have been reviewed by Pflieger (1971), Buchanan (1973), Clay (1975), Burr (1980b), Starnes and Etnier (1986), Burr and Page (1986), Cross et al. (1986), and Mayden (1985a) and require only summarization here.

Each of the highland regions is characterized by a number of endemic fishes distributed throughout most of the region or restricted to single drainages within them. *Erimystax monacha, Erimystax insignis, Nocomis effusus, Notropis leuciodus, Phenacobius uranops, Noturus elegans, Etheostoma cinereum, Etheostoma kennicotti*, and *Etheostoma rufilineatum* are examples of Eastern Highland endemics distributed throughout much of the region, delimiting the highlands. *Etheostoma punctulatum* and *Notropis greenei* of the Ozark Plateaus and *Etheostoma radiosum* of the Ouachita Mountains are found throughout most of their respective areas of endemism.

Within each region internally endemic species are numerous and in many instances, where relationships are known, form monophyletic groups with other species whose composite distributions also delimit regions of endemism. Within the Ouachita Mountains seven additional endemic species are presently known, including *Notropis perpallidus, Notropis snelsoni, Noturus lachneri, Noturus taylori, Etheostoma pallididorsum, Percina pantherina*, and *Percina* sp. cf. *nasuta*. Fourteen additional species are known only from streams within the Ozark Plateaus. These include *Notropis ozarcanus, Notropis zonatus, Noturus albater, Noturus flavater, Ambylopsis rosae, Ambloplites constellatus, Etheostoma euzonum, Etheostoma juliae, Etheostoma moorei, Etheostoma nianguae, Etheostoma tetrazonum, Percina cymatotaenia*, and *Percina nasuta*. The fauna of the Eastern Highlands is the most diverse, with at least 52 endemic species in addition to those listed above. Represented here is *Erimystax cahni, Nocomis platyrhynchus, Notropis scabriceps, Notropis spectrunculus, Phenacobius crassilabrum, Phenacobius teretulus, Phoxinus cumberlandensis, Moxostoma atripinne, Noturus baileyi, Noturus flavipinnis, Noturus staunali, Noturus trautmani, Amblyopsis spelaea, Chologaster agassizi, Speoplatyrhinus poulsoni, Fundulus albolineatus, Fundulus julisia, Etheostoma acuticeps, Etheostoma aquali, Etheostoma atripinne, Etheostoma baileyi, Etheostoma barbouri, Etheostoma barrenense, Etheostoma bellum, Etheostoma blennius, Etheostoma boschungi, Etheostoma chlorobranchium, Etheostoma duryi, Etheostoma etnieri, Etheostoma jessiae, Etheostoma kanawhae, Etheostoma luteovinctum, Etheostoma meadiae, Etheostoma microlepidum, Etheostoma obeyense, Etheostoma olivaceum, Etheostoma osburni, Etheostoma rafinesque, Etheostoma sagitta, Etheostoma simoterum, Etheostoma smithi, Etheostoma squamiceps, Etheostoma striatulum, Etheostoma swannanoa, Etheostoma tuscumbia, Etheostoma virgatum, Percina aurantiaca, Percina burtoni, Percina gymnocephala, Percina oxyrhynchus, Percina squamata*, and *Percina tanasi*. It is a long list but that would be predicted since this region is the largest. The list is not, however, complete since undescribed species are still known from this region. Also, it includes only those species found in the Ohio, Cumberland, and Tennessee rivers. Close relatives of some of these taxa are known from this highland region but are also known from the upper Mobile Bay, other Gulf of Mexico drainages, or some Atlantic Slope drainages.

At a higher geographic level, some species are shared exclusively between two of the three regions or between all three. *Notropis telescopus, Notropis galacturus*, and *Typhlichthys subterraneus* occur only in the Eastern and Ozark highlands and *Pimephales tenellus, Nocomis asper*, and *Notropis pilsbryi* are shared by the Ozark and Ouachita highlands. No species share a Ouachita and Eastern highland distribution. Unlike the list of endemics above, this list of species is not long. However, given the phylogenetic relationships of endemics and shared species (next section), the list is much longer and more robust.

Many typical highland species fit a different, yet very informative pattern. These species are characteristic of one or more highland regions but have disjunct populations north of the highlands in the glaciated Central Lowlands. Species found in all highland regions and with northern populations include *Campostoma anomalum, Notropis boops, Notropis rubellus, Notropis whipplei, Noturus eleutherus, Hypentelium nigricans, Moxostoma carinatum, Moxostoma duquesnei, Moxostoma erythrurum, Fundulus catenatus, Etheostoma blennioides, Etheostoma zonale* (exclusive of *Etheostoma lynceum*), *Percina copelandi*, and *Percina phoxocephala*. At least 18 species occur in the Ozark and Eastern highlands and have northern populations, including *Ichthyomyzon fossor, Lampetra appendix, Campostoma oligolepis, Hybopsis amblops, Phoxinus erythrogaster, Catostomus commersoni, Lacochila lacera, Moxostoma anisurum* (typical race), *Noturus exilis, Noturus flavus, Ambloplites rupestris, Etheostoma caeruleum, Etheostoma flabellare, Percina evides*, and *Cottus carolinae*.

In addition to these species, another series of species is found in only one of the regions and also has northern disjunctions. At least 12 species are found in the Eastern Highlands and the Central Lowlands, including *Ichthyomyzon bdellium, Ichthyomyzon greeleyi, Nocomis platyrhynchus, Notropis ardens, Notropis ariommus, Notropis photogenis, Rhinichthys atratulus, Ammocrypta pellucida, Etheostoma camurum, Etheostoma maculatum, Etheostoma tippecanoe*, and *Percina macrocephala*. Ozark species are few, including *Nocomis bigutattus, Notropis nubilus*, and perhaps *Etheostoma microperca*. No species are shared exclusively between the Ouachitas and the Central Lowlands.

The above species represent a considerable proportion of the diverse eastern North American highland fish communities, all being either endemic to one or more of the regions or found in one or more of the regions as well as in the northern glaciated regions. Thus these fishes are consistent with the hypothesis of Mayden (1985a) and Wiley and Mayden (1985) that much of the diversity present today existed before the Pleistocene in a much more widespread eastern North American highland fish fauna. A composite map of highland endemic clades and species with their disjunct northern populations and relatives or populations on the Atlantic or Gulf slopes, illustrating the effect of the combined glaciers and their associated processes on the pre-Pleistocene biota, appears in Mayden (1987). Similar patterns were observed by Ross and Ricker (1971) for plecopterans and by Johnson (1978) for unionid mussels.

As in any other community, a portion of the species inhabiting the Central Highlands is uninformative biogeographically and ecologically in the sense of community organization. These species are in the fauna because they are widespread geographically over most of eastern North America and have diverse habitat requirements. I follow Nelson and Platnick (1978) in considering these to be shared-primitive species biogeographically and of limited use in this analysis. This may not be true, however, for all examples. Whatever the case, these wide-ranging species are not informative here but may be informative at a higher level in the analysis (e.g., the derivation of the eastern North American fish fauna). Species with widespread distributions inclusive of the Central Highlands include *Lepisosteus osseus, Notropis atherinoides, Notropis umbratilis, Notropis volucellus, Pimephales notatus, Pimephales promelas, Pimephales vigilax, Semotilus atromaculatus, Minitrema melanops, Noturus nocturnus, Fundulus notatus, Fundulus olivaceus, Gambusia affinis, Lepomis cyanellus, Lepomis gulosus, Lepomis macrochirus, Lepomis megalotis, Lepomis microlophus*, and *Micropterus punctulatus*.

Thus in review of the "typical" Central Highlands fish fauna, the vast majority of the species represented here are endemic to one or more of the regions or occur in one or more of the regions and the northern Central Lowlands. By comparison, very few species are from the adjacent Coastal Plain Province or from neighboring drainage systems not included in the Mississippi River basin.

Phylogenetic Relationships of Central Highland Fishes

Given the high degree of endemism within each of the highland regions and the few exclusively shared species, historical patterns of the three regions, whether they are biogeographical or ecological, are not obvious without a historical perspective. Exploring historical questions in evolution or ecology requires a methodological framework based on revealing history. Phylogenetic systematics as outlined by Hennig (1966) and Wiley (1981) is presently the most robust technique available to infer historical connections (genealogies) between species. Under this method, closest relatives can be determined and history inferred.

Once species relationships are resolved, closest relatives are believed to have shared a common ancestor, and this common ancestor more than likely had a distribution equal to or nearly the same as that of its two or more descendants. At least two warnings are attached to this general statement. First, the relationships presented are hypotheses, just like any other testable statements made in biology, and may be falsified or corroborated. Second, the ancestor may not have had a summary distribution equal to the distribution of its descendants. There may have been dispersal by the ancestor or the descendants. Like the first concern, however, dispersal can be tested. A species owes its distribution either to evolution in the region presently occupied or to dispersal from another region where it presumably evolved. Testing for historical dispersal is a difficult task, to say the least. However, given that geographic patterns of species and interrelationships are available, species that are alien to the core pattern(s) may represent dispersal events. The point here is that the dispersal explanation for a distribution must be a conclusion and not an assumption.

Unfortunately, only a portion of the highlands fauna has been studied systematically. Many species have been thoroughly studied for variation, and some hypotheses concerning their relationships to other species have been proposed. Some of these statements, however, are not formulated with the use of phylogenetics and therefore are not considered here. Statements of relationship included below include only those for which share-derived character justifications have been provided.

Use of existing interrelationships of species provides evidence that much of the existing highland fish fauna represents the remnants of a once widespread highland biota fractured by midcontinental glaciers during the Pleistocene. An apparently smaller group of species from the Ouachita Highlands fits different tracks inclusive of surrounding lowland regions or adjacent drainages (Mayden, 1985a). Relationships of several highland species remain to be resolved; but if the present sample is representative, this latter category represents a much smaller class of species presently forming the highland communities. Below I present in abbreviated fashion our present understanding of relationships of Central Highland fishes.

Etheostoma Variatum Species Group. Seven species are included in this monophyletic group: *Etheostoma blennius, Etheostoma sellare, Etheostoma variatum, E. kanawhae, E. osburni, E. tetrazonum*, and *E. euzonum* (fig. 26.2). The first and the last five species occur in the Central Highlands and represent one of the most nearly complete historical pictures of the region. *Etheostoma sellare* is endemic to the Susquahanna River of the Atlantic slope. Relationships of species in this group have been examined by Wiley and Mayden (1985).

Etheostoma euzonum of the White River is the sister to *E. tetrazonum* of the lower Missouri River. These two species from the sister group to *E. variatum* plus *E. kanawhae* and *E. osburni* of the upper Ohio River. *Etheostoma sellare* of the East Coast forms the sister group of these five species, and *E. blennius* of the Tennessee River is the sister group of all other species. None of these taxa or their close relatives occurs in the Ouachita Highlands.

This group appears to be of considerable age, one that existed before the Pleistocene and whose present distribution is a direct result of habitat modification in the Central Lowlands (Mayden, 1985a; Wiley and Mayden, 1985). Although the age of this clade is uncertain, the existence of a member east of the Appalachians and two species above the Kanawha Falls suggests that the group is quite old. The present existence of species in the various Central Highland regions has a simple, historical explanation involving only the preexisting widespread and diverse highland biota and its subsequent fracturing by glaciation.

Subgenus Ozarka of Etheostoma. Five species are included in this group: *Etheostoma trisella, E. boschungi, E. punctulatum, E. cragini*, and *E. pallididorsum*. Relationships are presented in Mayden (1985a). *Etheostoma trisella* is sister to other members of the group and supports an early Tennessee–Mobile Bay drainage connection. *Etheostoma boschungi* is sister to the western members of the clade. Within the Interior Highlands, *E. punctulatum* is sister to *E. cragini* and *E. pallididorsum*. Thus the evolutionary history of this group is consistent with the geological history of the Central Highlands (Mayden, 1985a). In this group the most recent speciation event, *E. pallididorsum–E. cragini*, corresponds to the most recent geological event, the fracturing of the Interior Highlands by the Arkansas River. The sister relationship between *E. boschungi* and western members may correspond to the earlier division of the Central Highlands by glaciation, or it may be older. The age of *E. trisella* and other *Ozarka* members may date to the Miocene, when a possible connection existed between the upper Tennessee River and the Mobile Bay drainage. It is not clear that glaciation had anything to do with cladogenesis of this group. Pleistocene events probably restricted preexisting diversity in this group and enhanced extinction, especially in the northern Eastern Highlands. Although highlands existed in this region before the Pleistocene and still do today, no members of this subgenus are known from the Cumberland and Ohio rivers. The possibility of extinction in this group is supported by area cladogram anomalies. *Etheostoma boschungi* corresponds to *E. blennius* of the *E. variatum* group. The Interior Highlands *Ozarka* correspond to *E. tetrazonum–E. euzonum*, but the *E. variatum–E. kanawhae–E. osburi* analog is missing in *Ozarka*. Thus the sister relationship between *E. boschungi* and western members of *Ozarka* may not be an actual sister-group relationship but only an apparent relationship owing to extinction (Mayden, 1986).

Genus Erimystax. This genus forms the sister group to the genus *Phenacobius* (fig. 26.3). With the exception of the possible sister-group relationship between *Erimystax insignis* and *Erimystax dissimilis*, species relationships in the subgenus are unresolved. This group will be significant in the establishment of the history of the highland regions and their communities. Some species are widespread, and some are endemic to one or more regions. These species are, however, consistent with the preglacial speciation hypothesis. This is readily apparent since several species of this group and one species of the sister clade, *Phenacobius*, experienced the Pleistocene events fracturing the highlands. Even within *Erimystax* both *E. dissimilis* and *Erimystax x-punctata* share a widespread Central Highlands distribution.

Genus Phenacobius. Relationships of these five species are presented in figure 26.3. *Phenocobius mirabilis* is the sister species to the remaining members of this group and the most widespread geographically. It occurs in some western Gulf Coast drainages, the upper and middle Red and Arkansas rivers, the Missouri and Ohio rivers, and the upper Mississippi. It is common throughout the glaciated Central Lowlands but is largely absent from the highland areas. *Phenacobius teretulus* is endemic to the New River and forms the

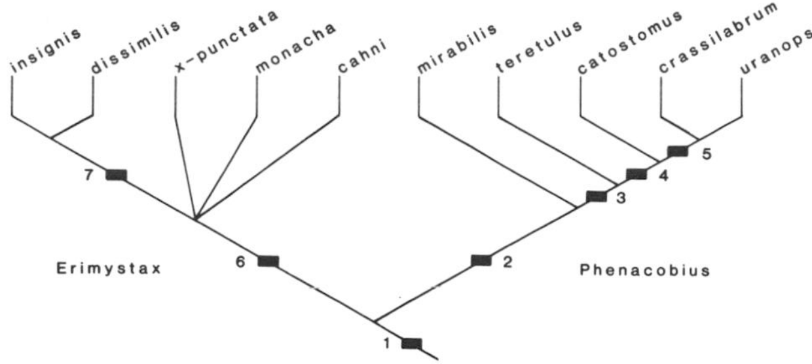

Fig. 26.3. Phylogenetic relationships of species in the genera *Phenacobius* and *Erimystax*. Characters are as follows: (1) narrow caudal skeleton, high vertebral numbers, and enlarged papillae on pectoral fins; (2) maxillary barbel reduced; dentary, maxillary, and premaxillary very heavy; pectoral fin tuberculation pattern (Mayden, 1985b); (3) anterior neck of urohyal with short anterior arms and mesial processes; (4) palatine with anterior and posterior processes surrounding preethmoid; (5) pharyngeal pad of basioccipital narrow and not expanded into large plate; metapterygoid-hyomandibular articular surface on metapterygoid with cartilage ventrally and bone dorsally; palatine very broad mesially with a bridge connecting anterior and posterior processes; (6) barbel stellate; number of vertebrae increased; basihyal elongate; (7) distinct lateral blotches along flanks. For additional discussion of these characters see Mayden (1985b).

sister group to the remaining species. *Phenacobius catostomus* is a Mobile Bay endemic and is the sister to *P. uranops–P. crassilabrum*, supporting the Tennessee–Mobile Bay connection. *Phenacobius uranops* and *P. crassilabrum* are sister species, the latter of the upper Tennessee and the former sporadically distributed in the Green, Cumberland, and Tennessee rivers. No Ozark or Ouachita representatives are known from this group.

Notropis zonatus–N. coccogenis Species Groups. Species relationships were resolved for this group by Buth (1979a). *Notropis zonatus* and *N. pilsbryi* are sister species and sister to the group *Notropis cerasinus* plus the sister species *Notropis coccogenis–Notropis zonistius*. *Notropis zonatus* and *N. pilsbryi* are Interior Highland endemics. *Notropis cerasinus* is endemic to the Atlantic Coast, *N. coccogenis* to the Tennessee River and some upper Atlantic Slope drainages. *Notropis zonistius* occurs in the Apalachicola, upper Savannah, and Altamaha rivers. The Mobile Bay connection is absent from this group, but a Gulf Coast–Tennessee connection predates the Central Highlands vicariance. Like the subgenus *Ozarka*, the *E. variatum–E. kanawhae–E. osburni* analog of this group is missing. Thus extinction of preexisting taxa in the Ohio and Cumberland rivers through glaciation may have occurred, and the *N. zonatus* and *N. coccogenis* clades may in fact represent apparent sister groups (Mayden, 1986).

Notropis leuciodus Species Group. *Notropis leuciodus* of the Tennessee, Cumberland, and upper Green rivers is most closely related to *N. nubilus* (fig. 26.4). *Notropis chrosomus* is endemic to the Mobile Bay drainage and is the sister to these two species. The disjunct distribution of *N. nubilus* (fig. 26.4) is significant. Populations of this species are found in the Ozark Plateaus and in the upper Mississippi River—all regions near the unglaciated region. This distribution and the fact that *N. nubilus* has the unique and derived condition in *Notropis* of a coiled gut supports a preglaciation vicariance of the *N. nubilus–N. leuciodus* ancestor. Like other Central Highland species, populations of the *N. nubilus* survived in the unglaciated refugium (Mayden, 1985a). The sister-group relationship between *N. chrosomus* and the other two species is also significant. Given the ancestor-descendant relationships, the Mobile Bay event had to precede the *N. nubilus–N. leuciodus* speciation event. If the Central Highlands split occurred before the Pleistocene, the Mobile Bay connection must be older.

Notropis telescopus Species Group. Species relationships for this group were presented by Coburn (1982). *Notropis telescopus*, the oldest member of the group is found in the Ozark Plateaus and the Cumberland and Tennessee rivers of the Eastern Highlands. *Notropis ariommus* forms the sister group to the two Atlantic Slope highland species *Notropis semperasper* and *Notropis scepticus* and is sporadically distributed in the Ohio, Cumberland, and Tennessee rivers of the Eastern Highlands. North of the Cumberland and Tennessee rivers the distribution consists of several isolated populations in the glaciated Central Lowlands. If the event responsible for the transfer of the ancestor to *N. scepticus* and *N. semperasper* to the Atlantic Slope corresponds to the same event in the *N. coccogenis* species group, the age of the speciation event for *N. telescopus* must predate the Pleistocene.

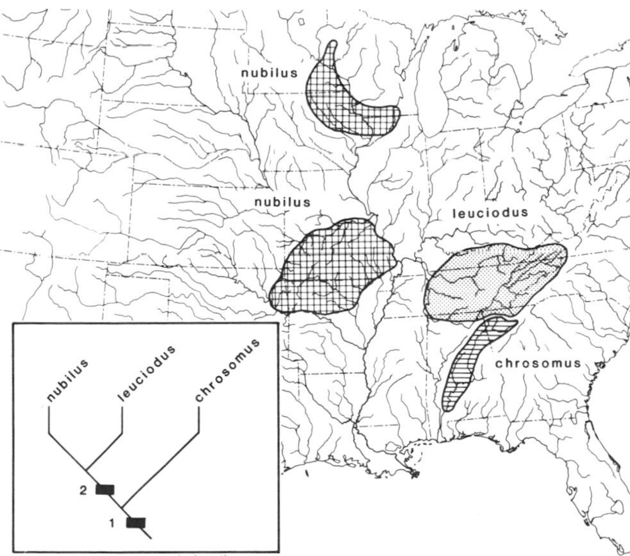

Fig. 26.4. Distributions and phylogenetic relationships of species in the *Notropis leuciodus* species group. Characters are as follows: (1) breeding colors iridescent and very bright reds and oranges; dorsolateral scale pigment pattern heavily scalloped; (2) iridescent predorsal stripe of live specimens dashed, not solid.

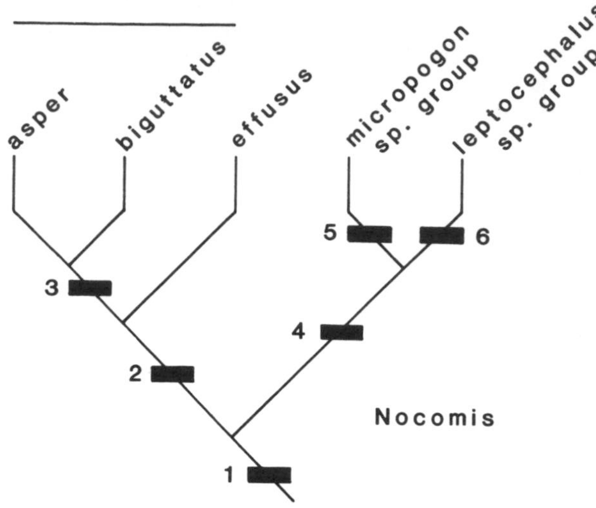

Fig. 26.5. Phylogenetic relationships of some species in the genus *Nocomis*. Characters are as follows: (1) light postocular spot; breeding males construct unique mound nests by carrying stones in mouth; (2) red postocular spot developed; lateral band developed; (3) well-developed and consistent red postocular spot; strongly developed lateral band; (4) swollen nuptial crest developed; head tubercles with laterally directed tips; loss of minor tooth row on pharyngeal arch, teeth 4-4; dorsal head tubercles large; body tubercles lost; (5) tubercles developed on lacrymal; tubercles developed on snout; (6) extremely large head tubercles; intestine whorled. Some data from Lachner and Jenkins (1971a, b).

Subgenus Swainia of Percina. Species relationships of these five species were presented by Mayden (1985a). *Percina phoxocephala* is the most widespread geographically and forms the sister to the other four species. Its distribution is similar to that of *Phenacobius mirabilis,* but with no Gulf Coast populations. *Percina nasuta* is endemic to the Ozark Plateaus and is the sister to *Percina* sp.cf. *nasuta* of the Ouachita Highlands. *Percina oxyrhyncha* and *P. squamata* are sister species, the former found in the southern tributaries of the upper Ohio and the latter an upper Cumberland and Tennessee river endemic. The biogeography of this group is consistent with a pre-Pleistocene origin of the species and is discussed by Mayden (1985a).

Nocomis biguttatus Species Group. Three species groups of *Nocomis* have been diagnosed, of which *N. biguttatus* group contains three species (fig. 26.5). *Nocomis asper* is restricted to the Interior Highlands, and *N. effusus* occurs in the Green, Cumberland, and Duck rivers. *Nocomis biguttatus* is widespread in the northern glaciated Central Lowlands, parapatric with *N. asper* in the Interior Highlands, and generally present only in the northern tributaries of the Ohio River. It is absent from the Cumberland and Tennessee rivers. Relationships in this group suggest an early divergence of *N. effusus* from the common ancestor of *N. biguttatus* and *N. asper,* similar to the *E. variatum* species group of *Etheostoma* as well as other groups.

The combined distributions of the three species groups of *Nocomis* cover all of eastern North America. Their distributions, together with species relationships, suggest that this genus is quite old, especially since the *N. biguttatus* group and *Nocomis micropogon* of the *N. micropogon* group both inhabit the Central Highlands and were presumably subjected to the same geological factors (e.g., Pleistocene glaciation) of the regions. Thus, both groups must have existed in the region before the Pleistocene.

Notropis spectrunculus Species Group. *Notropis spectrunculus* is endemic to the upper Tennessee river, and *N. ozarcanus* is endemic to the Ozark Plateaus. The distribution and relationships of the undescribed third species are presently unknown, although it apparently occurs in the Cumberland and Tennessee rivers and is sympatric with *N. spectrunculus* in the latter (D.A. Etnier, pers. comm.). These three species form a monophyletic group (fig. 26.6) and are related to *Notropis maculatus, Notropis volucellus, Notropis emiliae,* and *Notropis heterolepis*.

Notropis venustus Species Group. *Notropis venustus* and *N. galacturus* are included in this group (fig. 26.7). *Notropis galacturus* occurs in the Ozark Plateaus and the Cumberland and Tennessee rivers of the Eastern Highlands. *Notropis venustus* is widespread throughout the Coastal Plain Province from northern Florida to west Texas. The age of this speciation event presumably dates to the uplift of the Central Highlands.

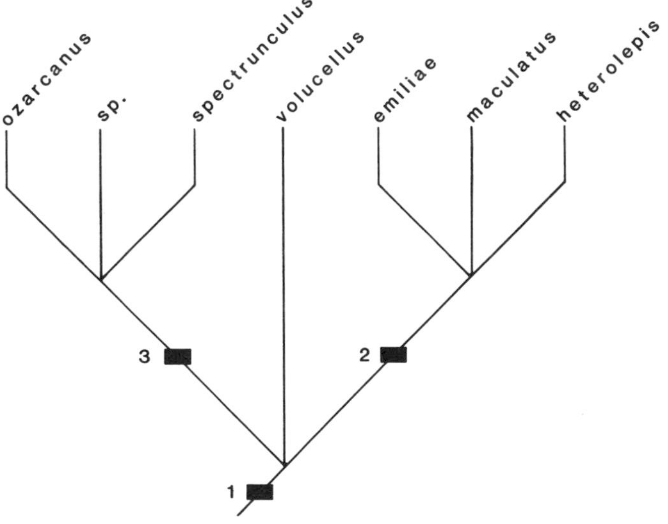

Fig. 26.6. Phylogenetic relationships between seven species of *Notropis*. Some species are found in the Central Highlands. Characters are as follows: (1) palatine with an extremely long maxillary process; (2) pharyngeal pad of basioccipital very narrow and without laterally directed processes; (3) body very slender; pigment patterns on scales in strongly developed cross-hatched pattern; leading ray of pectoral fin of breeding males with two rows of large, erect tubercles.

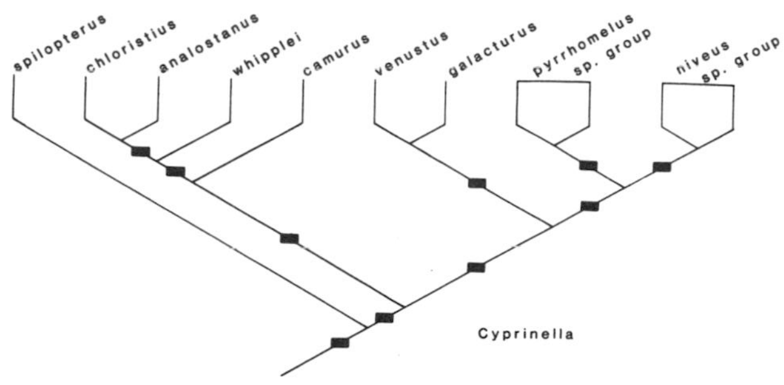

Fig. 26.7. Phylogenetic relationships of the *Notropis whipplei* clade of the subgenus *Cyprinella*. Characters and justifications are presented by Mayden (1985b).

Subgenus Litocara of Etheostoma. Relationships of the two species in this group are described by Kuehne and Bailey (1961) and Page and Whitt (1973). *Etheostoma nianguae* is endemic to the Ozarks, and *E. sagitta* occurs in the East. Although this species pair is consistent with a preglacial speciation event, extinctions have apparently played a major role in determining their widely disjunct distributions. Whether these species are actual or apparent sister species remains unresolved (Mayden, 1987).

Subgenus Odontopholis of Percina. Relationships of these two species are described by Page (1974, 1981). Like the *E. nianguae* species group, this clade has suffered from a considerable amount of extinction. *Percina cymatotaenia* is endemic to the northern Ozarks, and *Percina* sp. cf. *cymatotaenia* occurs in the Ohio River in Kentucky.

Etheostoma maculatum Species Group. Relationships in this group are unresolved, but monophyly was suggested by Williams and Etnier (1982). *Etheostoma moorei* is the only representative in the Interior Highlands; all others, except *Etheostoma rubrum*, are in the Eastern Highlands and northern glaciated Central Lowlands. *Etheostoma rubrum* is endemic to the Bayou Pierre drainage, a direct tributary of the Mississippi River in the Coastal Plain Province of Mississippi. Species relationships in this group will be very informative for the history of the highland regions.

Subgenus Ericosma of Percina. Two species are included here, *Percina evides* and *Percina palmaris*. Monophyly of this clade is discussed by Page and Whitt (1973) and Page (1974, 1976). *Percina evides* is a widespread highland species with several disjunct relict populations in the northern glaciated Central Lowlands. *Percina palmaris* is endemic to the upper Mobile Bay drainage. This clade represents an example of the former Tennessee–Mobile Bay connection.

Etheostoma tippecanoe Species Group. Two species are included in this group, *Etheostoma tippecanoe* and *Etheostoma jordani*. Both species share a reduced body size and the loss of horizontal lateral stripes. The distribution of *E. tippecanoe* is discontinuous. Several disjunct populations are found in the Tennessee, Duck, Cumberland, and Ohio rivers, inclusive of the glaciated Central Lowlands. *Etheostoma jordani* is a Mobile Bay endemic and supports a historic connection between this system and the Tennessee River.

Notropis xaenocephalus Species Group. The sister relationship between *Notropis boops* and *Notropis xaenocephalus* was described by Swift (1970) and Burr and Dimmick (1983). *Notropis boops* occurs in all highland regions, as well as to the north in the Central Lowlands. *Notropis xaenocephalus* is a Mobile Bay endemic. This species pair further supports a previous connection of this system with the Tennessee River.

Subgenus Imostoma of Percina. Five species are included in this subgenus, *Percina shumardi, Percina vigil* (Suttkus, 1985), *Percina uranidea, Percina tanasi*, and *Percina antesella* (Page, 1981). The last four species have well-developed dorsal saddles and are hypothesized to form a monophyletic group. *Percina vigil* is a Coastal Plain species, and *P. uranidea* occurs in the Interior Highlands and in the lower Wabash River. *Percina tanasi* is an upper Tennessee River endemic, and *P. antesella* is found only in the upper Mobile Bay. Relationships among these saddle-backed species are not fully resolved, but Etnier (1976) considered *P. uranidea* and *P. tanasi* to be sister species and *P. antesella* to be the sister of the two. If so, this group further supports an early Tennessee–Mobile Bay connection and a later Central Highlands vicariance.

Genus Hypentelium. Included in this genus are the species *Hypentelium nigricans, Hypentelium etowanum*, and *Hypentelium roanokense*. *Hypentelium nigricans* and *H. etowanum* are considered sister species (Lee et al., 1980, references therein). Combined distributions of these species cover most of eastern North America. *Hypentelium nigricans* is widespread, occurring in the Interior Highlands; the upper Mississippi, Ohio, Cumberland, Tennessee, and upper Atlantic Slope rivers; and some Gulf Coast drainages. The other two species are restricted in distribution, *H. etowanum* to Mobile Bay and *H. roanokense* to the Roanoke River. Relationships in this group support the Tennessee–Mobile Bay connection *(H. etowanum)* and a northern Atlantic Slope connection *(H. roanokense)*. The Central Highlands vicariance remains unnoticed, however, for no significant anagenesis has been noted between populations of *H. nigricans*.

Fundulus catenatus Species Group. Five species are included in this group (Wiley, 1986; Williams and Etnier, 1982). *Fundulus catenatus* occurs in all highland regions and to the north. *Fundulus stellifer*, the closest relative of *F. catenatus*, is found in the Mobile Bay drainage and the upper Chattahoochee River. Two species, *F. albolineatus* and *F. julisia*, are known from only a few localities in the Tennessee drainage. *Fundulus rathbuni*, sister to all other members of the subgenus, is an Atlantic Slope endemic. The sister-group relationship between *F. catenatus* and *F. stellifer* supports the Mobile Bay–Tennessee connection, which presumably occurred after the speciation events resulting in *F. julisia* and *F. albolineatus*.

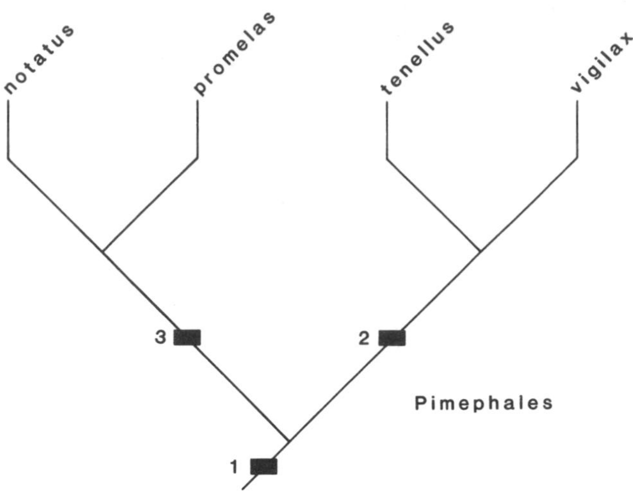

Fig. 26.8. Phylogenetic relationships of species in the genus *Pimephales*. Characters are as follows: (1) eggs clustered on the undersides of rocks; breeding males with three rows of enlarged tubercles clustered on snout; second dorsal fin ray short and separate from third ray; (2) posterior ascending process on metapterygoid high and broad; dentary flattened; anterior wing of hyomandibular very broad and notched; (3) pharyngeal pad on basioccipital flattened and round.

Genus Pimephales. Four species are included in this genus (fig. 26.8). All are widespread geographically except *Pimephales tenellus*, which is endemic to the Interior Highlands in the Arkansas River and the Ouachita Mountains. The closest relative to *P. tenellus* is the sympatric *P. vigilax*. *Pimphales vigilax* is unique among closest relatives of other highland endemics in being found in all highland regions as well as the Central Lowlands and Coastal Plain provinces.

Other Highland Species. In addition to species groups listed above, some single species have a Central Highlands distribution supporting a widespread pre-Pleistocene biota. Included here are *Typhlichthys subterraneus*, *L. lacera*, *E. blennioides*, *E. zonale* (exclusive of *E. lynceum*), and *C. carolinae*. Further, several additional species have distributions that not only support the Central Highlands biota but support the Tennessee–Mobile Bay connection. *Icthyomyzon castaneus*, *Lampetra aepyptera*, *Acipenser fulvescens*, *Scaphirhynchus* sp. cf. *platyorynchus*, *Campostoma oligolepis*, *Hemitremia flammea*, *Nocomis micropogon*, *Notropis ardens*, *Notropis chrysocephalus*, *Notropis lirus*, *N. whipplei*, *M. duquesnei*, *M. erythrurum*, *T. subterraneus*, and *Cottus carolinae* have populations in both river drainages. These species, especially the larger river forms, together with the numerous taxa mentioned in earlier accounts, are strongly suggestive of a connection between the upper Mobile Bay basin and the Tennessee River drainage. This connection is further supported by mussel faunas of these systems (J.D. Williams, pers. comm.).

Species Ecologies

Relatively little is known of the ecologies of Central Highland fishes. Several authors working with state, river, or stream surveys (some listed above) have described gross habitat parameters of many of these fishes and have summarized the existing ecological literature of each. Most of the literature deals with autecological studies of the genera *Notropis, Pimephales, Noturus* (reviewed by Mayden, 1983; Mayden and Walsh, 1984), and *Etheostoma* and *Percina* (reviewed by Page, 1983). These studies are invaluable but have concentrated on single-species ecological parameters, not communities. Because of the independent and temporally extended nature of these research efforts, comparisons between regions are difficult. The only available studies on fish-community structure in the Central Highlands are those by Matthews (1982) and Gorman (1983), both dealing only with Ozark species. We have no comparable data for other highland fishes. Unfortunately, this particular area of research in community ecology of fishes has been overlooked.

Comparative Biogeography

The biogeography of the Central Highlands fishes was discussed in detail by Wiley and Mayden (1985) and Mayden (1985a, 1987) and is only summarized here. Species relationships and distributions support one consistent generalized track inclusive of the upper Mobile Bay, the Eastern Highlands, and the Interior Highlands (fig. 26.1; Mayden, 1987, fig. 3). Other, less frequently observed patterns occur but are shared by only single or a few species (Mayden, 1985a; Wiley and Mayden, 1985). These patterns are not discussed here. Within the Central Highlands track, an Eastern Highlands track, an Interior Highlands track, an Ozark Highlands track, and a Ouachita Highlands track can be recognized.

The temporal sequence of the tracks is fairly consistent between clades. The oldest event is the connection between Mobile Bay and the Tennessee River. Although much controversy exists over this connection (see Starnes and Etnier, 1986), it would seem unusual, given the number of taxa sharing this pattern, that such a connection did not exist. On the basis of geological and faunal data some authors have hypothesized an ancient Appalachian River connecting the upper Tennessee River and the Mobile Bay drainage. This river was later captured by the lower Tennessee at Waldens Gorge, forming the present drainage pattern. Others have denied the existence of such a connection. Whatever the case, faunal data for fishes are fairly conclusive for a previous river connection between these two drainages. Furthermore, the presence of the large river species in the upper Mobile Bay basin, some of which do not occur in any other Gulf Coast drainages, together with their large river-habitat requirements, suggests that the connection must have been semipermanent and that the river must have been fairly large.

The next sequence of major events in the Central Highlands track was the separation of the Tennessee River system from the Teays and Interior Highlands drainages. Minimally, this was followed by a Teays and Interior Highlands–

northwestern Central Lowlands vicariance and later with a north-south Interior Highlands split by the Arkansas River. Unfortunately, dates for most of these geological events are unknown at this time, but future research in these areas may provide answers.

Discussion

Several interesting and realistic questions in historical ecology can be posed for the Central Highland fish communities. Why do the species in the Central Highlands have the geographic distributions that they have? Why do we find only certain ecological species associations in these regions? Why do the species possess certain ecological traits; and if these traits differ between species, under what conditions did they evolve? How and when did these associations and traits emerge? Do ecological changes keep pace with speciation events? In terms of community ecology, are the faunas in each of the highland regions a composite of species and/or closest relatives from surrounding regions, or is there a single nonrandom historical pattern that may explain the composition? Further, are the ecologies of species in each region the direct result of interactions with associated species in each community, or is there an irreducible historical factor of ancestory involved?

Age of the Highland Fauna

Through the use of phylogenies of several clades of highland fishes and the geology of the region, we can employ historical ecology to answer the first three research questions above. Furthermore, we can determine whether highland faunas and ecological associations in these communities are the result of dispersal or nonrandom historical events.

Species relationships and distributions and the geology of the Central Highlands suggest that (1) the fauna is old and was once more widespread geographically than at present (Mayden, 1985a; Wiley and Mayden, 1985), (2) closest relatives are only rarely sympatric, and (3) most clades fit a single, consistent historically determined geographic pattern. The age of the Central Highlands fauna can realistically be dated to before the Pleistocene and perhaps well before that once additional geological data are available. Species relationships and distributions alone, however, suggest that the fauna of the Central Highlands is older than the Pleistocene. Relationships in the *N. leuciodus* clade argue strongly for a pre-Pleistocene origin of these species (fig. 26.4), given the Mobile Bay–Tennessee River connection and the two disjunct populations of *N. nubilus*. The sister-group relationship for species of fishes and crayfishes between the Ozark and Ouachita highlands dates the most recently evolved species of these groups minimally to the Sangamon interglacial (Mayden, 1985a; Wiley and Mayden, 1985). Further, the replicated patterns of Central Highland disjunctions and the Mobile Bay–Tennessee connection of more than one species in the groups *Percina, Etheostoma, Nocomis, Notropis, Erimystax,* and *Phenacobius* demonstrate pre-Pleistocene origins of these clades. For example, within the subgenus *Cyprinella* of *Notropis* alone, three species (*Notropis spilopterus, N. whipplei,* and *N. galacturus*), all more closely related to other members of the clade (fig. 26.7) and from basal stems in the clade, were affected by glacial processes. If the vicariant event responsible for the disjunct populations of *N. galacturus* was the Pleistocene, the speciation event responsible for the origins of *N. galacturus* and *N. venustus* must be older, as is also true for the speciation events for *N. spilopterus* and *N. whipplei*. Further, the widespread sympatry between the *Notropis cornutus, N. coccogenis,* and *N. zonatus* species groups in the subgenus *Luxilus* and between the highland species *N. spectrunculus* and *N. ozarcanus* and their closest relatives (fig. 26.6), *N. volucellus* and *N. heterolepis*, demonstrates that these clades, all with distributions congruent with many other highland species of presumably equal age, are quite old. These patterns could be possible only if these clades existed before the Pleistocene.

Closer age estimates for these and other clades will be possible when more reliable dates exist for key geological events. If dates become available for the Kanawha Falls and the northern and central Appalachian vicariant events, ages of some clades may become available. For example, if one were to hypothesize that the formation of the Kanawha Falls led to the vicariance of the ancestor of *E. osburni* and *E. kanawhae* in the New River and *E. variatum* in the Ohio (Teays) River, all other cladogenetic events in this group, with the possible exception of the *E. tetrazonum–E. euzonum* species pair, had to predate this event (fig. 26.2). If a reliable date were available for the vicariant event that led to the separation of *N. coccogenis* in the Tennessee River and *N. zonistius* in the Chattahoochee River, one could confidently conclude that the speciation event responsible for the evolution of the *N. coccogenis* and *N. zonatus* species groups preceeded this event. Even though these dates are not always available, it is apparent that the fauna of the Central Highlands is older than the Pleistocene. This is adequately supported by the *N. leuciodus* species group, the Interior Highlands vicariance event, and several taxa shared across the Tennessee–Mobile Bay divide, a connection Miocene in origin or older (Starnes and Etnier, 1986).

Thus with the use of historical ecology we now have partly answered the first two research questions concerning the age of the faunas and species distributions. The faunas are older than the Pleistocene and are very likely much older. Further, species have their present distributions because they are the remnants of an ancestral widespread fauna. We can now turn to our third research question, addressing contemporary species associations, and see how historical ecology can be applied.

Species Associations

Fish species in the Central Highlands are found in one or more of the isolated highland areas because they evolved either in a specific region or in some other place and dispersed into the highlands. These two models of community formation form the fundamental differences between vicariance biogeography and island biogeography, respectively. In all likelihood, however, most faunas and their component ecological associations are not derived strictly from one or the other modes but are composites of both. Because these two modes are fundamentally different and have different evolutionary and ecological predictions of community structure, it is important to separate the two processes on a species-by-species basis. Partitioning diversity into species conforming to each of these two classes will be instrumental in determining the underlying mechanisms of community ecology of this region and perhaps others.

Since we cannot go back into time to observe ancestral biotas, the placement of a species in the "dispersal" and "vicariance" groups requires phylogentic hypotheses of organisms inhabiting the regions. Lineages that demonstrate historical constraints of distribution (vicariance) will correspond to the same or nearly the same interrelationships of regions inhabited by their component species (e.g., generalized biogeographic tracks are formed). Thus species of communities with duplicate phylogenies and area cladograms are said to have historically determined associations. On the other hand, species that evolved elsewhere and dispersed into the community will presumably illustrate a new and different pattern of geographic relationships. One must be careful, however, in that unique distribution patterns may also represent more ancient vicariant patterns, not recent dispersal (Platnick and Nelson, 1978).

Species distributions and relationships and our knowledge of the geological history of the highlands reveal that the existence of species in any one community is usually the direct result of the fracturing of a once widespread and diverse highland biota into several isolated communities. Instances of individual species dispersal into the highland communities, with subsequent competition and adaptive shifts in ecology, need not be hypothesized. Species evolved in their respective regions before the Pleistocene disruption and presently exist in communities of historically determined associations. At this time only a few instances of dispersal into a highland region seem possible. *Etheostoma radiosum, P. pantherina, N. lachneri, N. taylori,* and *N. perpallidus* are candidates for possible dispersal into the Ouachita Mountains (Mayden, 1985a), as well as *Fundulus sciadicus* into the Ozarks. The Ouachita endemics may, however, represent older vicariant events similar to examples provided by Platnick and Nelson (1978), not dispersal (Mayden, 1985a). Closest relatives of these species surround the highlands.

Given the antiquity of the fauna, the Pleistocene fragmentation of this fauna, and the predominant pattern of historically determined species associations, the most parsimonious explanation for the reason species are found together in any one of the regions is not the competitive interactions in the contemporary communities, as is frequently proposed for community structuring. Species exist in these isolated regions because they occurred there for millions of years as part of a larger fauna. If competition or any other ecological processes were instrumental in this community composition, their involvement would have been much earlier, when the highlands were continuous and more widespread. There is no reason to assume that the community structuring is a continuous and/or ongoing process. Furthermore, if a proximal ecological process were causally involved, the test for speciation driven by competition, predation, parasitism, or any other process responsible for divergent life history traits would be difficult with the existing research protocol. With historical data provided in the research program of historical ecology, such tests are possible. An appropriate test would involve inspection of the ecologies of nearest relatives of these species to determine if ecologies of species in question evolved in the community being examined.

Ecological Attributes of Species and Their Evolution

Knowing when ecological associations originated and when and under what conditions life-history characteristics of a particular species evolved is of utmost importance to our understanding of community structure. Above I have examined the probable age of the Central Highland communities and the length of the predominantly historically determined species associations, both of which are quite old. At least for minnow species in the Ozarks, we know that ecological differences exist between species and may be maintained even in the absence of other species (Gorman, 1983). However, we do not know the relative importance of "ecological pressures" involved in the origin or maintenance of these differences. Nor do we know when and under what conditions these differences evolved. In evolutionary ecology competition is frequently assumed to exist between extant species of a community. Further, not infrequently, a hypothetical process such as this is labeled as the factor responsible for the emergence of the divergent life-history traits of species. This uniformitarian viewpoint is not implicit in historical ecology (Brooks, 1985).

The origins of particular life-history traits of a species are theoretically varied and fall into three basic categories. A trait may be retained from an ancestral species and thus be the result of inheritance. Alternatively, it may result from a speciation event, or it may develop within the range of a species after the speciation event. In addition, species associations may be due to dispersal into a community from outside or may result from historical community associations fractured into smaller communities and thus inherited through vicariance (e.g., communities of the separate highland areas in the Central Highlands track).

Before one can make the statement that the successful existence of a particular species association is the result of competition, predation, or any other ecological interaction resulting in "adaptive" ecological shifts, one must determine the evolution of the trait and the origin of the species association to document that the shift occurred in the community, not earlier in the history of the clade or outside the community. Brooks (1985) outlined four scenarios for contemporary ecological associations. Examples used were derived from host-parasite associations but are analogous to the area-species relationships seen in the Central Highlands. Pertinent to determining which association exists are how and when the association took place and when the ecological traits of a species evolved, as outlined above. All four depend on determining whether the associations are the result of vicariance or dispersal and whether the ecologies are primitive or derived. Generally only the last category contains species of concern to most community ecologists interested in extrinsic ecological factors influencing community formation and structure, that is, species whose ecologies are the direct result of ancestral and contemporary interactions. Yet seldom are species or communities examined thoroughly enough to determine whether particular associations fit into this category. In the Central Highland communities an ecologist interested in uncovering factors responsible for the evolution of ecological traits should be interested in species with derived ecologies that are the result of contemporary associations, not ecologies whose explanations are historical (or inherited from common ancestors). These too are interesting questions, but their answers are at a different level of universality. The only detailed ecological study available for fishes of the Central Highlands was done by Gorman (1983), whose work was restricted to minnows in the Ozark region. Thus it is impossible at this time to test the origins of the particular life-history traits observed in those minnows. We lack the necessary detailed habitat partitioning data for closest relatives of these taxa. However, the research protocol of historical ecology will allow us to address the last three questions outlined above and obtain direct estimates of history.

A major difference between historical ecology and evolutionary ecology is that historical ecology cannot be studied by examining a single community. We also need to examine communities containing close relatives of those species in the community of interest, which serve as "historical controls" or historical (i.e., evolutionary) null hypotheses. These additional communities allow us to determine which ecological associations and traits are historically determined and thus of only minor interest in evolutionary ecology.

As an example, we may examine habitat partitioning between hypothetical species in four communities found in areas I–IV (fig. 26.9A). Areas I–III are highland areas, and area IV is outside the region. One may substitute species *A* and *X* for any two species examined by Gorman (1983) for an approximation of findings. In the simplest case we can compare two congruent clades (fig. 26.9C), both demonstrating historical congruence in species and area relationships. Species relationships in this instance are based on morphological or biochemical data. Also, like the Central Highland fishes, no colonization through dispersal need be invoked. These species are intended to mirror highland taxa as closely as possible.

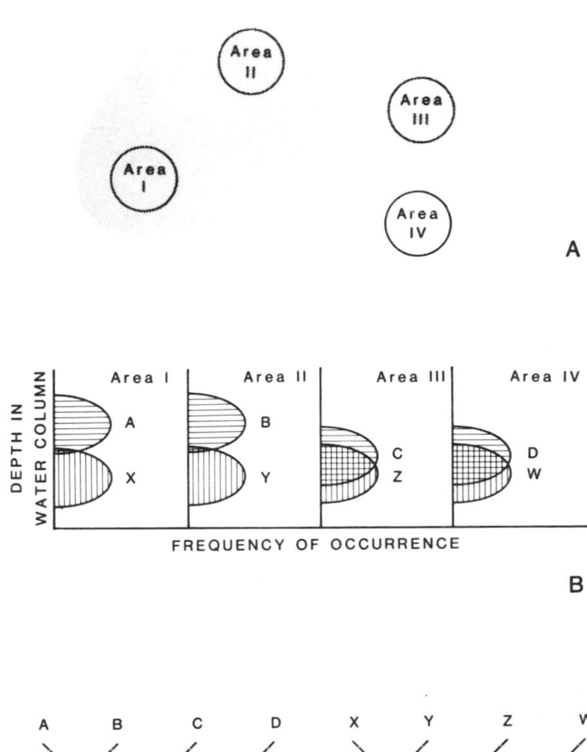

Fig. 26.9. Example of an inherited habitat shift in two clades of fishes. A: Four different fish communities. Areas below stippled region are highland in characteristic and are remnants of a once widespread highland biota distributed as indicated by the stippled area. B: resource partitioning, as measured by depth in water column occupied by a species, for species *A–D* and *X–W*, all inhabiting areas I–IV, respectively. C: Phylogenetic relationships of clades *A–D* and *X–W*, based on nonecological data, illustrating congruence of species and area relationships. The open box represents the time of origin of unique resource space utilization for species *A* and *B*. In this instance it was in the ancestor of these taxa.

Species *A* and *X* inhabit area I; species *B* and *Y*, area II, and so on. Patterns of resource partitioning for these hypothetical species are also provided (fig. 26.9B). In area I species *A* and *X* have almost no overlap in the water column and perhaps in other resources. Most ecological studies stop at this point and may interpret these data, two distinct habitat traits of these species, as evidence of former disruptive selection through competition. This is one point at which evolutionary ecology and historical ecology differ. Historical ecology claims that to make such a statement one would need to examine ecologies of closest relatives of both taxa, which in this case are species *B* and *Y* in area II. If appropriate data are available for *B* and *Y*, we can determine whether these traits are inherited ecologies or whether they indeed represent ecological shifts in community I. In this instance we see that species *B* and *Y* in area II, the closest relatives of *A* and *X*, respectively, also illustrate minimal space overlap. Thus the observed minimal resource overlap observed in area I must not have had its origin in this community. If we examine the next-closest relatives, we see that in this instance *A* and *B* have ecologies different from that of *C* but that *X*, *Y*, and *Z* have similar ecologies. Thus in this instance it is more parsimonious to hypothesize that the shift occurred in their ancestor. Further, if competition were instrumental in the origin of this pattern, the explanation would be in an ancestral community, not in areas I and II. Species in these areas inherited these particular life-history traits. Competition in these particular communities may, however, be very important in fine-tuning or maintaining these differences but perhaps it was not involved in their origins.

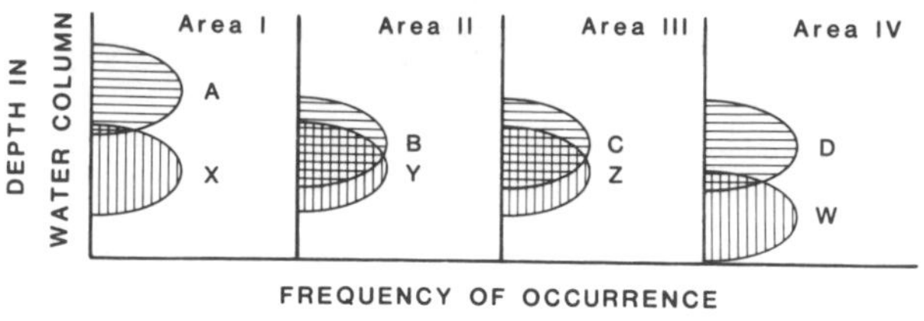

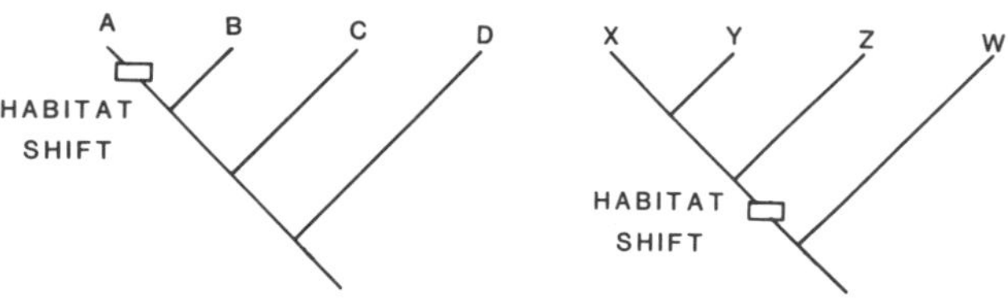

Fig. 26.10. Example of habitat shift in two clades of hypothetical fishes. Area designations refer to fig. 26.9. Open boxes represent origins of unique ecological life-history traits, here the area occupied in the water column. In clade *A–D* the shift may be due to contemporary species associations. In clade *X–Z* and *W* the shift occurred in an ancestral community containing the ancestor to the species *X–Z*.

Turning now to a second instance (fig. 26.10) in which contemporary associations may be involved in an ecological shift, we again examine species *A* and *X* in area I. In this example species *Y* in area II has the same habitat association as its closest relative, species *X*. Species *B*, however, has a different habitat association from that of its closest relative, species *A*. Given the present example, one can say only two things: (1) the explanation for the habitat associations in the species *X* and *Y* may lie in the common ancestor of these taxa and is a shared primitive ecology, and (2) species *A* and *B* have different habitat associations. We cannot say at this time which has the derived ecology and is thus indicative of evolution of ecological traits owing to species association. To determine which of the two traits represents a new evolutionary innovation, we must examine the next-closest relatives in area III. In this community we see that the habitat of *C* is the same as that of *B* but different from that of *A*. Species *A* then has the derived ecology, and its association with species *X* in area I may be responsible for the observed differences. Species *B* and *C* and species *X*, *Y*, and *Z* share retained-primitive ecologies inherited from their respective common ancestors. No explanations are required for the observations of these ecologies in the single communities of I, II, or III, other than a historical retention.

This technique can be used at an even higher level, the origin of the widespread highland fauna. In this example species *X*, *Y*, and *Z* have similar habitat parameters that are different from those of sister group *W*. Species *B* and *C* (and modified *A*) share the same ecology with sister group *D*. Here dispersal or vicariance would have to be determined by use of multiple phylogenies of species and areas. The origin of the derived ecology in the ancestor of *X-Y-Z* could also be determined by employing these phylogenies and reconstructed ecologies of ancestors.

To substantiate further whether species *A* shifted ecologically owing to a competitive association with species *X* or any other species, one may wish to do species-exclusion experiments or locate populations of species *A* outside the range of *X*. In the Central Highlands some actual examples are available. Several species in the Interior and Eastern highlands are found in the glaciated Central Lowlands without typical highland-species associations. The *N. leuciodus* species group is a perfect example. If the ecologies of the northern populations of *A (N. nubilus)* are the same as those of species *B (N. leuciodus)* and *C (N. chrosomus)*, but different from southern populations of *A (N. nubilus)*, one may have a strong case for an Ozark species association driving an ecological shift. Only with these kinds of data can one justify scenarios of historical species associations leading to present-day coexistence.[1]

[1]I wish to thank Daniel Brooks, Brooks Burr, Linda Dryden, Darrel Frost, Robert Holt, Tom Titus, Kim Woellter, and E.O. Wiley for reading and commenting on an earlier version of this paper. I also wish to thank the reviewers and editors of this symposium for comments that improved this publication.

27. Analysis of Factors Associated with Intraspecific Variation in Propagule Size of a Stream-Dwelling Fish

David C. Heins and John A. Baker

Abstract

We examined egg sizes in *Notropis venustus*, the blacktail shiner, from 16 populations in river systems along the northern Gulf of Mexico from eastern Texas to northwestern Florida. Egg size was not related to female size within populations. However, egg size was significantly correlated with female size among populations and among all females, showing that populations with larger adult females had larger eggs. No trade-off between egg size and observed clutch size was shown within any population, among populations, or among all females. However, comparisons of mean egg size with predicted clutch size (at 60 mm standard length) among populations did suggest a trade-off. Egg diameter, egg weight, or both were significantly correlated with gonadosomatic index in 11 populations. These relationships were nonsignificant for mean values among populations and significant but weak among all females.

Individual females produced eggs of a relatively consistent size, but mean egg size varied significantly both among females within populations and among populations. Principal components and regression analyses showed that egg size was most closely associated with mean annual runoff, larger eggs occurring in populations in regions with higher runoff.

The recent renewal of theoretical and empirical interest in intraspecific variation in propagule size began when Capinera (1979) rejected earlier notions that propagule size (energy expenditure per offspring) and individual fitness were positively correlated (Smith and Fretwell, 1974; Smith, 1975), at least for insects and plants. Instead, Capinera proposed a model in which differences in individual quality (fitness) associated with propagule size and time are a function of the environment. Variations in fitness of propagules result from an interaction of propagule size and environment, and the optimal propagule size changes with concomitant changes in environmental factors. In doing so, Capinera began a challenge to the notion of an optimum propagule size.

Capinera's paper was followed by a series of studies of within- and among-female intrapopulation variability in egg sizes of amphibians which resulted in the conclusion that the concept of an optimum egg size was difficult to support (Kaplan, 1980; Crump, 1981, 1984; Kaplan and Cooper, 1984). Mann and Mills (1979) speculated that variability in egg size among fishes may result in a reduction of competition for food resources among larvae and a selective advantage for variation in egg size. Marsh (1984) considered the possibility of an absence of an optimum egg size in relation to among-female variation in the orangethroat darter.

Notwithstanding the doubts about the notion of an optimum size, propagule size and its variation are considered to be genotypic and phenotypic adaptations to a heterogeneous environment. For example, Harper et al. (1970) conclude that seed sizes reflect "complex adaptive compromises," and Capinera (1979) states that, although propagule size appears to be hereditary, "the process involved may not be narrowly genetic." In this respect Crump (1981) found a "range of egg size, rather than one optimal egg size" in each of two contrasting environments. Further, there may be selection for developmental "coin-flipping" mechanisms to produce random variation in propagule size (Kaplan and Cooper, 1984).

Streams present a wide range of environments in which factors potentially affecting propagule size and its variability show great latitude. Therefore, we examined the structure of variation in egg size in a stream-dwelling fish in relation to variations in chemical and physical factors. We selected *Notropis venustus*, the blacktail shiner, because it is a widespread, eurytopic species which shows some taxonomic differentiation, with three subspecies currently recognized.

Propagule Size: A Chronology of the Theory

Parental investment per offspring is related to reproductive effort, but these phenomena may be considered individually. A given optimum level of reproductive effort invested in propagules as energetic resources may be partitioned among a few large propagules or many small ones. The ultimate and proximal factors that determine this allocation and the biological mechanisms they influence are complex. Questions about these phenomena represent a basis for understanding some of the major issues in life-history evolution.

Using concepts similar to those presented by Lack (1948), Svardson (1949) first gave theoretical consideration to the trade-off between egg size and egg number. He theorized that there might be selective forces which operate in opposition to those which must lead to high fecundity. However, this could occur only if there were advantages to the larger larva which would result from a larger egg. Citing evidence that larger eggs produce larger larvae with greater growth after hatching, he concluded that offspring resulting from larger eggs have better chances for survival in the face of intraspecific competition for food.

Williams (1966) considered food resources, predation, and "other loss" to be potentially important in determining the optimum egg size–egg number relationship. He viewed the problem in terms of a maximal return on the parental investment in the offspring. If surviving offspring do not grow fast enough to bring about a net increase in their total mass as their numbers decrease, the parental investment in the subsequent generation will be poor. Fewer, larger offspring would be favored where resources are scarce or where predation pressure is high for small eggs or young. Conversely, a larger number of smaller young would be favored when food resources are abundant and predation risks are low.

Smith and Fretwell (1974) developed graphical and mathematical models to demonstrate the relationships among parental fitness, energetic investment in individual progeny, and offspring fitness. Their models involved several assumptions: (1) parents have finite energetic resources available at a given time for reproductive effort, (2) there is an inverse relationship between the number of offspring parents can produce and the amount of energy allocated to (= size of) each offspring, (3) there is a minimal requirement of energy for offspring to be viable, (4) the fitness of individual offspring increases as the energetic investment per individual increases, and (5) there is a point at which an increased investment per individual results in a declining increase in fitness. The concept of an optimum offspring size was inherent in their models, resulting from the latter two assumptions. Smith (1975) used the same graphical model to discuss the basis of selection of optimal seed size in response to density-independent physical factors. Shaffer and Gadgil (1975) used a similar fitness-investment curve to consider optimal energy investment per seed as affected by competition.

Brockelman (1975) used a slightly modified form of the offspring fitness-parental resource investment curve of Smith and Fretwell (1974) to examine the effects of intraspecific competition, mortality rate, and predictability of food resources on optimal resource investment per offspring. He assumed that "optimal allocation corresponds to . . . 'optimal offspring fitness.' " Brockelman's analysis focused on competition, and he developed the idea that greater optimal investments per individual should result from interference competition for resources that can be hoarded or contested and where individual success is a function of size, strength, or learning. However, these selective forces acting through competition and population size should be opposed by mortality from predation or harsh physical conditions which would reduce population size and competition. Brockelman also thought that where food resources were unpredictable and fell below the optimal level per offspring there should be an "attrition of enough young to maintain the optimal level per individual." Under conditions of exploitative competition where no optimal resource level exists, little investment per offspring should result.

Wilbur (1977) also considered the optimal balance between offspring size and number, believing that allocation of resources was a function of competition, predation, and environmental uncertainty. He modeled the balance between size and number of propagules by finding the combination of the two variables that maximized survival of offspring to the time of the independence from parental resources. The optimum was determined by the shape of the relationship between propagule survival and weight.

Capinera (1979), as discussed above, argued that there was not necessarily a direct, positive correlation between propagule size and fitness. Capinera also concluded that phenotypic variability in propagule size, although relatively conservative, allows production of at least some offspring which are able to cope with the vicissitudes of the environment. The selective advantage of this strategy is that by producing offspring of variable size the survival of some offspring is more likely. Kaplan (1980), Crump (1981, 1984), and Kaplan and Cooper (1984) support Capinera's ideas.

Kaplan and Cooper (1984) developed a model to explain the developmental basis for the interclutch variability in egg size that has been observed in amphibians. The phenomenon, which they call "adaptive coin-flipping," involves a "chance device" that produces random variation in egg size in response to "environmental variation or developmental noise." They discuss evidence for the genetic nature of this poorly canalized developmental mechanism and for the superiority of this strategy in a temporally heterogeneous environment.

The *r*- *K*-selection and stochastic, bet-hedging theories also address the question of egg size among a suite of life history traits. Both models predict the occurrence of two alternative suites of traits, the "accepted scheme" of Stearns (1977). However, they predict these alternative associations as a result of somewhat different selective factors. The *r*- *K*-selection theory predicts that small propagule size will evolve when the environment is variable and/or unpredictable; however, the bet-hedging viewpoint predicts the evolution of a small egg size where adult mortality is variable (Stearns, 1976, 1977).

A number of issues now confront the evolutionist. One is the concept of an optimum egg size vis-à-vis the observed intrapopulation variability in egg size. Questions about the biological mechanisms which operate to determine egg size are related to this issue and to others such as the adaptive nature of variation in egg size. Consideration of the adaptive significance of phenotypic plasticity and genetically based

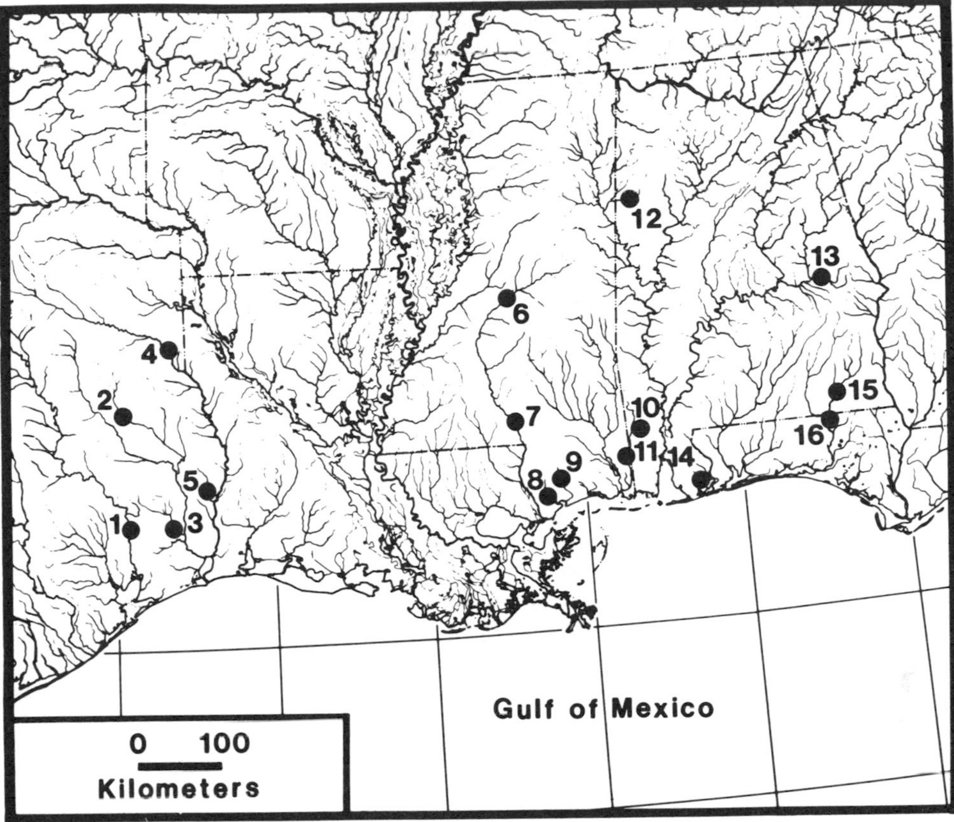

Fig. 27.1 Distribution of 16 sampling localities for populations of *Notropis venustus* in the southern United States: (1) Trinity River, (2) Angelina River, (3) Village Creek, (4) Sabine River, (5) Big Cow Creek, (6) Pearl River near Coal Bluff, (7) Pearl River near Columbia, (8) Catahoula Creek, (9) Wolf River, (10) Puppy Creek, (11) Escatawpa River, (12) Luxapalila River, (13) Uphapee Creek, (14) Blackwater River, (15) Choctawhatchee River near Clayhatchee, (16) Choctawhatchee River near Pittman.

variation in egg size raises even further questions about the ecological factors involved and their roles in determining egg size. The selective factors which may be involved, other than food resources and competition, have been given little consideration. This is true of theoretical studies, but it is particularly true of empirical studies on fishes which we consider later.

Materials and Methods

We examined female *N. venustus* from 16 populations in river systems along the northern Gulf of Mexico from eastern Texas to northwestern Florida. Each of the three subspecies (Gibbs, 1957) was included. To minimize the effect, if any, of seasonal variation in egg size, we restricted the period of our collections as much as possible, making all collections 2–18 June 1984. Exact locations for the collecting sites (fig. 27.1) are available from the authors.

Specimens were preserved in 10% formalin and stored in 50% isopropyl alcohol. When available, 10 reproductively mature females containing at least 10 mature eggs were randomly selected from each collection. We classified female maturity according to the criteria of Heins and Rabito (1986). However, females containing unovulated ripe eggs were excluded from our analyses. Ova were judged to be mature if they were opaque and cream to yellow in color, were in the follicles, and did not have vitelline membranes clearly separated from the yolk mass, and if their size distribution did not overlap that of the smaller, immature eggs.

Both ovaries were removed from each female, and all mature ova were extracted and counted to determine clutch size. Ten mature ova were randomly selected for estimation of mean egg diameter. Because preserved ova were not spherical, diameters of individual ova were estimated by averaging measurements of the largest and smallest dimensions. Measurements were made to the nearest 0.05 mm with the use of an ocular micrometer in a dissecting microscope. Each specimen was measured to the nearest 0.1 mm standard length (SL). Mature ova, immature ova with ovarian tissue, and eviscerated females were dried separately to constant weight at 100–105° C and weighed to the nearest 0.001 g. Ovaries and ova were stored in 25% isopropyl alcohol until drying. Mean mature egg weight was determined for each female by dividing the total dry weight of the mature eggs by the total number of mature eggs. A gonadosomatic index (GSI) was calculated by dividing the total ovary dry weight by the dry weight of the eviscerated specimen. Specimens that were not sacrificed for our study were deposited in the Florida State Museum at the University of Florida.

Streamflow and water-quality data were obtained for the nearest gauging or water-quality station. These data were taken from published U.S. Geological Survey records, where available. Water-quality data for the Pearl River were obtained from unpublished records provided by the Mississippi Bureau of Pollution Control. All data for the Blackwater River were estimated from published records for the nearest watershed (Styx River) that was similar. Environmental variables included upstream drainage area, mean annual discharge, coefficient of variation in discharge, gradient, stream width, runoff, pH, alkalinity, specific conductance, and total dissolved solids (TDS). Because specific conductance and TDS showed a highly significant correlation ($r = 0.982, N = 16, P \leq 0.001$), we included only TDS in our analyses. Streamflow regimes do not exhibit strongly marked seasonal differences in the streams we sampled; thus we believe our annual values properly represent the conditions experienced by the eggs, larvae, or fry. Further, *N. venustus* has a prolonged breeding season (March–October; Heins and Dorsett, 1986); and small young-of-the-year may be present during much of the year.

Relationships between egg size and other life-history traits were examined by correlational analyses at three different levels: among females within each population, among populations using population mean values, and among pooled females from all collections. Differences in mean egg diameter were assessed both for individual females within populations and also among the 16 populations using a nested analysis of variance. The relationships among female reproductive traits and environmental variables were examined by means of a principal-components analysis (PCA; Gorsuch, 1974) followed by rotation to simple structure according to the varimax criterion. In a similar manner the environmental variables alone were subjected to a PCA and rotated to simple structure. The purpose of this procedure was twofold: (1) to reduce, if possible, the number of variables to be used in subsequent multiple regression analyses of egg size (diameter and weight) on environmental variables and (2) to produce uncorrelated variables (components) for use in the regression analyses. For the second PCA factor scores were computed for each population on each component and regressed against egg diameter and egg weight. Stepwise multiple regression of female traits on the individual environmental variables was performed to test for the best set of predictor variables. An "all possible regressions" approach was also used to examine the proportion of total variance explained by the best single-variable and multiple-variable models. Statistics were computed using the Statistical Analysis System (SAS; SAS Institute, 1982) and Statistical Package for the Social Sciences (SPSS; Nie et al., 1975; Hull and Nie, 1981) program packages.

Results

Relationships Between Egg Size and Other Life-History Traits

Mean female egg diameter was not correlated ($P > 0.05$) with female size (SL or weight) in any population. Mean egg weight was not significantly correlated ($P > 0.05$) with SL in any population but was significantly correlated with female weight in two of the 16 populations, the Choctawhatchee River near Pittman ($r = 0.639$, $N = 10$, $P < 0.05$) and Catahoula Creek ($r = -0.658, N = 10, P < 0.05$). Among populations, mean egg size (both diameter and weight) and mean female size (both SL and weight) showed significant correlations for each of the four possible combinations of the variables ($r = 0.591$–$0.784, N = 16, P < 0.05$). Among all females both egg diameter and egg weight were significantly correlated with SL and female weight, respectively ($r = 0.428$–$0.592, N = 154, P < 0.0001$). However, the coefficients of determination showed that there was a wide range in the strength of these relationships.

Observed clutch size was not correlated with egg diameter ($r = -0.499$–0.590, $P > 0.05$) or egg weight ($r = -0.602$–0.597, $P > 0.05$) in any population, among populations ($r = 0.080, -0.013$, respectively; $N = 16$; $P > 0.05$), or when females were pooled ($r = 0.148, 0.100$, respectively; $N = 154$; $P > 0.05$). However, populations differed in the sizes of females available in our samples, and linear regressions of clutch size on SL were highly significant ($r = 0.857$–0.980, $P < 0.01$) for 15 of the 16 populations. One population (Catahoula Creek) had a moderate correlation ($r = 0.525, N = 10, P > 0.05$), presumably because of a small range of female sizes in our sample. Analysis of covariance showed that there were no significant differences ($F = 0.92$; $df = 15{,}139$; $P > 0.05$) in the slopes of the regression lines describing the relationships between clutch size and SL in each of the populations. Since most samples contained females 55–65 mm SL, we calculated the predicted clutch size for a 60-mm SL female in each population by using the common slope and respective intercepts. Among populations, predicted clutch size was significantly correlated with mean egg weight ($r = -0.502, N = 16, P < 0.05$) but not with mean egg diameter ($r = -0.469, N = 16, P > 0.05$). Nevertheless, this latter relationship is in the same direction as the first and is close to significance.

Among females in each of 11 populations, GSI and mean egg diameter, mean egg weight, or both were significantly correlated (table 27.1). Among populations, mean egg diameter and mean egg weight were not correlated with mean GSI

Table 27.1. Correlations of Mean Egg Diameter and Mean Egg Weight with Gonadosomatic Index (GSI) in Populations of *Notropis Venustus*

Population Number	*N*	GSI and Diameter	GSI and Weight
1	10	0.515	0.524
2	9	0.580	0.683*
3	10	0.381	0.377
4	10	0.864†	0.822†
5	10	0.830†	0.889†
6	10	−0.023	0.843†
7	10	0.225	0.258
8	10	0.458	0.384
9	10	0.865†	0.848†
10	10	0.681*	0.663*
11	10	0.693*	0.680*
12	10	0.658*	0.681*
13	7	0.473	0.606
14	10	0.775†	0.826*
15	8	0.921†	0.956†
16	10	0.845†	0.815†

*$P < 0.05$.
†$P < 0.01$. All other correlations are nonsignificant.

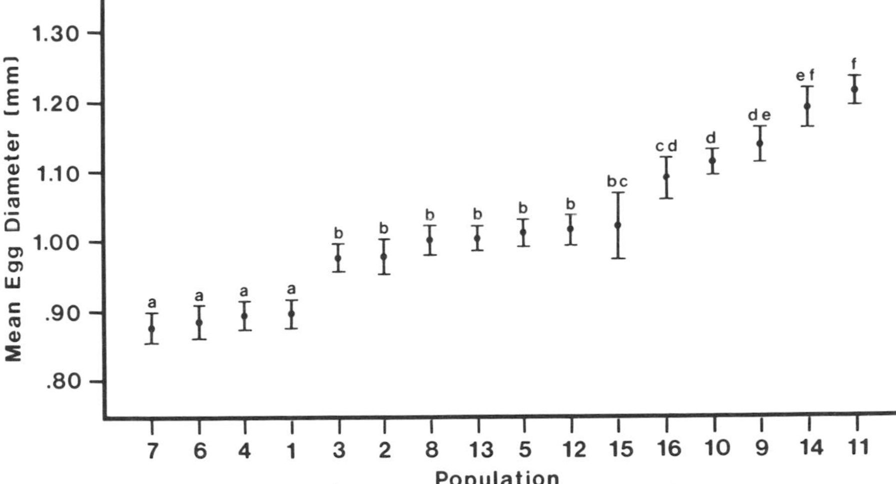

Fig. 27.2 Means of egg diameters (± 1 SE) for populations of *Notropis venustus* arranged in ascending order. Population numbers are those identified in fig. 27.1. Means sharing the same superscripted letter are not significantly different. ($P > 0.05$), as tested by Duncan's New Multiple Range Test.

($r = 0.306, 0.134$, respectively; $N = 16; P > 0.05$). Among pooled females, mean egg diameter and GSI were significantly correlated ($r = 0.318, N = 154, P < 0.05$), as were mean egg weight and GSI ($r = 0.299, N = 154, P < 0.05$). However, the low coefficients of determination ($r^2 = 0.10$, 0.09, respectively) show that predicting egg size from GSI would not be meaningful overall. GSI was correlated with female size (SL and/or weight) in three populations. In the Escatawpa River population there were significant correlations with both SL ($r = 0.627, N = 10, P < 0.05$) and female weight ($r = 0.666, N = 10, P < 0.05$). GSI was significantly correlated with SL ($r = 0.709, N = 8, P < 0.05$) in the Choctawhatchee River near Clayhatchee population and with female weight ($r = 0.653, N = 10, P < 0.05$) in the Village Creek population.

Intraspecific Variation in Egg Size

In 15 of 16 populations mean egg diameter and mean egg weight were highly correlated ($P < 0.01$), as correlation coefficients ranged from 0.925 to 0.989. Mean egg diameter and mean egg weight were not significantly correlated in the Pearl River near Coal Bluff population ($r = -0.024, N = 10, P > 0.05$). Within each population there were significant differences in mean egg diameter among the females ($P < 0.0001$ for all sites). However, individual females produced eggs of a relatively consistent size, as the mean individual coefficient of variation in egg diameter (0.036 to 0.053) was always less than the population coefficient of variation (0.060 to 0.131). There also were significant differences ($F = 19.21$; $df = 15{,}138$; $P < 0.0001$) in mean egg diameter among the populations (fig. 27.2). Mean egg weight showed the same patterns of among-female and among-population differences as mean egg diameter, but the magnitude of the differences was greater because the weight of an egg is an exponential function of its diameter. For example, the difference in mean egg diameter between populations having the smallest and largest eggs respectively was 38%. This translated to a nearly threefold increase (292%) in mean egg weight. No observed variations could be attributed to subspecific differentiation.

Relationships Among Reproductive Traits and Environmental Variables

The first PCA including both environmental variables (table 27.2) and female reproductive traits (table 27.3) produced four components with eigenvalues greater than 1 that explained 81.1% of the total variance (table 27.4). The rotated loadings for component I indicated that runoff, pH, TDS, and egg size (diameter and weight) comprised a closely related group of variables. Runoff was significantly ($P < 0.05$) correlated with egg diameter ($r = 0.824, N = 16$; fig. 27.3) and egg weight ($r = 0.844, N = 16$). TDS and pH showed significant ($P < 0.05$) negative correlations with egg diameter ($r = -0.609, -0.761$, respectively) and egg weight ($r = -0.595, -0.744$, respectively). Based on coefficients of variation for the three female reproductive traits, component II showed that variability existed in egg diameter and egg weight which was not adequately explained by the measured environmental variables. The environmental variable loading most strongly was the coefficient of variation of mean annual discharge. However, it was only moderately loaded and was significantly correlated only with the coefficient of variation for egg diameter ($r = -0.554, N = 16, P < 0.05$). Component III was clearly one of stream size, loading heavily on drainage area, mean annual discharge, gradient, and stream width. No female reproductive traits were associated with this component. Component IV included GSI, the coefficient of variation for GSI, and alkalinity. Both GSI ($r = -0.721, N = 16$) and its coefficient of variation ($r = -0.577, N = 16$) showed a significant ($P < 0.05$) negative correlation with alkalinity.

The second PCA of environmental variables produced three components with eigenvalues greater than 1, which accounted for 76.3% of the variance (table 27.4). The inclusion of the fourth component (eigenvalue = 0.82) increased the total variance accounted for to 85.4%. The rotated loading pattern showed components (in parentheses) with the following compositions: (I) stream size, including drainage area, discharge, and width; (II) TDS and variability in discharge; (III) runoff, pH, and TDS; and (IV) gradient and alkalinity. Of these four components, only component III was significantly correlated with egg diameter ($r = -0.735$,

Table 27.2. Environmental Variables for Populations of *Notropis Venustus*

No.	Drainage Area (km^2)	Mean Annual Discharge (m^3/sec)	Coefficient of Variation, Discharge	Gradient (m/km)	Width (m)	Mean Annual Runoff (cm)	pH	Total Alkalinity (mg/l)	Specific Conductance (μmho/cm)	Total Dissolved Solids (mg/l)
1	44,512	203	1.39	0.10	46	14	7.4	103	314	180
2	4,144	34	1.44	0.16	17	26	6.6	18	161	95
3	2,236	21	1.74	0.14	20	30	6.6	10	110	70
4	9,047	70	1.57	0.17	21	24	6.8	34	235	130
5	332	3	1.60	0.50	17	30	6.9	35	206	120
6	3,486	56	1.47	0.25	53	50	6.8	40	100	70
7	11,637	190	1.50	0.17	91	45	6.8	39	125	80
8	401	9	1.15	0.13	18	55	5.7	18	40	30
9	798	19	1.17	0.25	15	75	6.0	14	35	28
10	75	1	1.60	1.25	6	67	5.4	4	143	90
11	1,440	40	1.50	0.34	26	88	5.2	10	32	21
12	624	9	1.06	0.80	20	47	6.6	14	33	22
13	855	12	1.46	0.76	23	46	7.0	35	67	41
14	156	5	1.36	0.19	18	76	5.6	9	23	18
15	1,769	27	1.03	0.27	38	48	6.9	25	35	23
16	8,311	136	0.90	0.15	61	55	6.8	36	93	51

Table 27.3. Population Means for Female Traits for Populations of *Notropis Venustus**

No.	SL (mm)	Weight (g)	Mature Egg Number	Mean Egg Diameter (mm)	Mean Egg Weight μ	GSI	Number of Females
1	54.1	0.59	336	0.895	115	0.101	10
	(1.8)	(0.08)	(45)	(0.020)	(8)	(0.005)	
2	55.3	0.69	376	0.976	150	0.121	9
	(2.9)	(0.10)	(74)	(0.025)	(13)	(0.012)	
3	63.9	1.26	401	0.975	151	0.066	10
	(3.3)	(0.22)	(95)	(0.020)	(11)	(0.005)	
4	56.2	0.57	285	0.893	111	0.080	10
	(1.1)	(0.03)	(18)	(0.021)	(10)	(0.005)	
5	60.7	0.94	323	1.010	171	0.084	10
	(2.8)	(0.14)	(39)	(0.019)	(9)	(0.009)	
6	48.9	0.42	214	0.885	113	0.080	10
	(1.7)	(0.06)	(28)	(0.024)	(9)	(0.005)	
7	44.5	0.30	140	0.876	108	0.075	10
	(1.8)	(0.04)	(23)	(0.022)	(9)	(0.008)	
8	60.3	0.77	230	1.000	155	0.063	10
	(0.9)	(0.03)	(22)	(0.021)	(9)	(0.005)	
9	61.4	0.70	200	1.136	254	0.097	10
	(1.6)	(0.06)	(18)	(0.025)	(16)	(0.008)	
10	67.2	0.98	263	1.111	217	0.080	10
	(2.2)	(0.12)	(28)	(0.018)	(12)	(0.007)	
11	62.3	0.89	215	1.212	315	0.100	10
	(2.1)	(0.09)	(42)	(0.020)	(16)	(0.009	
12	67.5	1.08	436	1.014	161	0.105	10
	(1.7)	(0.12)	(44)	(0.022)	(12)	(0.006)	
13	57.5	0.57	287	1.002	175	0.119	7
	(1.9)	(0.06)	(36)	(0.018)	(14)	(0.014)	
14	81.5	1.81	343	1.188	284	0.074	10
	(2.5)	(0.23)	(47)	(0.029)	(26)	(0.007)	
15	61.6	0.92	294	1.020	182	0.084	8
	(3.5)	(0.20)	(97)	(0.048)	(25)	(0.015)	
16	68.9	1.24	457	1.088	211	0.108	10
	(3.5)	(0.20)	(82)	(0.030)	(18)	(0.008)	

*Standard deviations are given in parentheses.

Table 27.4. Rotated Component Loadings from Principal Components Analyses for Populations of *Notropis Venustus*

Environmental Variable or Female Trait	Environmental Variables—Female Traits				Environmental Variables			
	Component				Component			
	I	II	III	IV	I	II	III	IV
Drainage area	0.41	−0.14	0.79	−0.09	0.68	0.29	0.45	0.21
Discharge	0.28	0.06	0.93	0.02	0.95	0.07	0.26	0.08
Discharge variability	0.45	−0.59	−0.25	−0.24	−0.12	0.88	0.04	−0.03
Gradient	−0.16	−0.43	−0.45	0.34	−0.36	0.29	−0.32	−0.59
Runoff	−0.94	−0.04	−0.14	−0.09	−0.11	−0.24	−0.94	0.04
Width	0.14	0.37	0.73	0.09	0.89	−0.23	0.07	−0.03
pH	0.74	0.30	0.34	0.24	0.32	−0.11	0.86	−0.09
Alkalinity	−0.21	0.13	0.06	−0.89	−0.04	0.08	−0.23	0.89
Total dissolved solids	0.75	−0.37	0.34	−0.05	0.32	0.67	0.61	−0.01
Egg diameter	−0.90	−0.13	−0.23	−0.12				
Egg-diameter variability	0.08	0.96	0.11	−0.01				
Egg weight	−0.90	−0.13	−0.17	−0.15				
Egg-weight variability	0.19	0.90	0.02	−0.16				
GSI	0.11	−0.16	0.22	0.85				
GSI variability	0.05	0.40	−0.26	0.69				

$N = 16, P < 0.01$) and egg weight ($r = -0.754, N = 16, P < 0.01$), a result consistent with the pattern of variable loadings seen in the first PCA.

The stepwise multiple regression of egg diameter on all environmental variables showed that runoff was the only significant predictor ($F = 29.79$; $df = 1{,}14$; $P < 0.0001$), explaining 68% of the variation. The "all possible regressions" approach indicated that runoff and mean annual discharge provided the best two-variable model, although the addition of discharge increased the variance explained by only 4% over runoff alone. A model incorporating runoff, discharge, alkalinity, and drainage area accounted for nearly 78% of the egg-diameter variance. All higher models increased the R^2 only very slightly.

Discussion

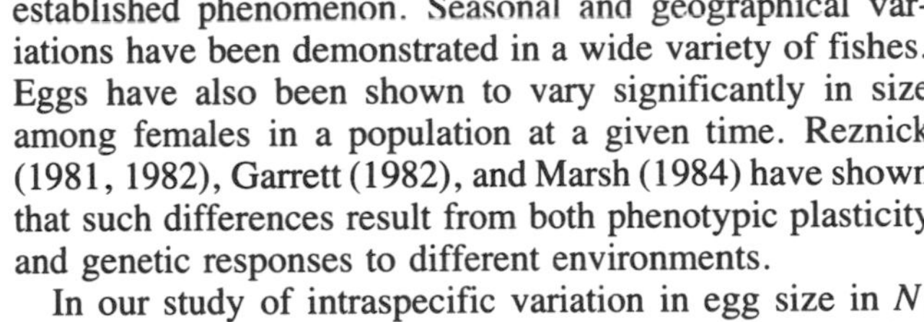

Intraspecific variation in egg sizes of fishes is a well-established phenomenon. Seasonal and geographical variations have been demonstrated in a wide variety of fishes. Eggs have also been shown to vary significantly in size among females in a population at a given time. Reznick (1981, 1982), Garrett (1982), and Marsh (1984) have shown that such differences result from both phenotypic plasticity and genetic responses to different environments.

In our study of intraspecific variation in egg size in *N. venustus*, we found egg size to be unrelated to female size within populations. However, there was a positive correlation between egg size and female size among populations and

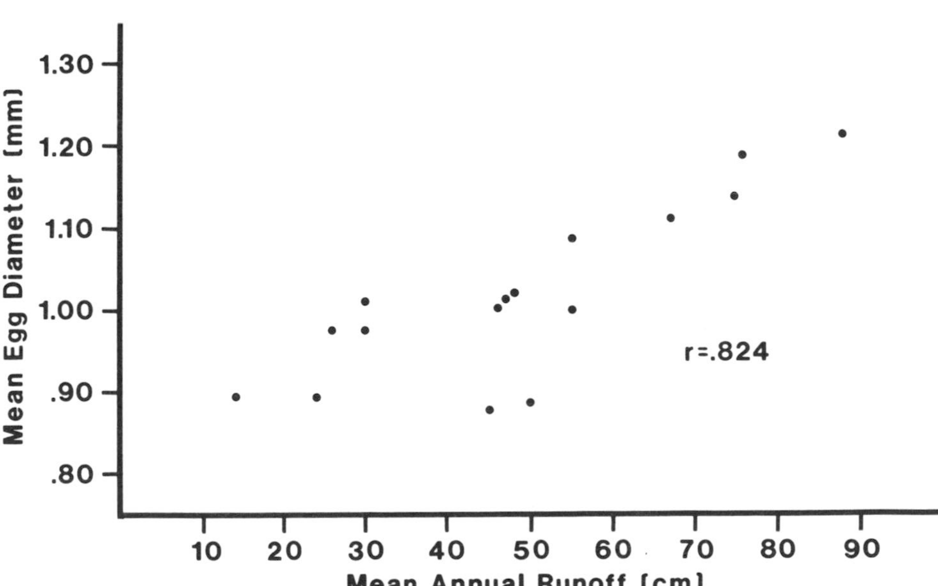

Fig. 27.3. Mean annual runoff versus mean mature egg diameter for populations of *Notropis venustus*.

also among pooled females, showing that populations with larger adult females had larger eggs. This relationship fits with the "accepted scheme" of covariation among suites of life-history traits (Stearns, 1977) and also appears to occur within and among other *Notropis* (Heins, 1979).

Our analyses suggested a weak reciprocal relationship (trade-off) between egg size and predicted clutch size, but results based on observed clutch sizes did not show a trade-off. In terms of the maximum number of eggs which a female may produce, this type of relationship on which much theory is based presumably must exist. However, the high degree of variation in clutch size in our data seems to obscure this relationship, since we did not select for specimens with maximum ovarian masses (i.e., maximum fecundities).

While at a given time individual females of *N. venustus* produce ova of a relatively consistent size, there is significant variation in mean egg size among females in a population. As discussed above, the latter type of variation has been cited by other authors as part of the evidence that the notion of an optimum egg size cannot be supported, and our data support the no-optimum hypothesis.

The intraspecific geographical variation we observed in egg size showed the strongest relationship to stream runoff, with larger eggs occurring in regions with greater runoff (fig. 27.4). However, our analyses indicated that some biological consequence of pH and TDS (or conductivity) may oppose the effects of runoff to a slight degree. Heins (1979) also observed variations in life history traits, including egg size, in *Notropis longirostris* which showed a relationship with streamflow. We know of no published data on the effects of pH or TDS on egg size in fishes; however, the relationships we observed may involve differences in fertility or productivity of the respective environments.

The variability we observed in egg size among populations showed a negative relationship with variation in mean annual discharge, but the relationship was weak. Further, one or more other aspects of streamflow or its variability may be involved, such as the absolute difference between high and low flows or the frequency of streamflows exceeding some critical level.

Larger eggs may have a selective advantage in streams with greater annual runoff if the following conditions pertain: (1) streamflow operates as a density-independent force of mortality on eggs, larvae, or fry; (2) the degree of mortality is related to the amount of streamflow, other conditions being equal; (3) genetically based qualitative differences in egg size result in differences in size, growth rate, strength, or susceptibility to damage for eggs, larvae, or fry which result in greater survivorship for offspring originating from larger eggs. The operative factor may not be runoff per se. Greater runoff may be indicative of a larger number of rainfall events and/or longer or heavier rainfalls which could produce streamflows that kill a small portion of or decimate a recent spawn or spawns, depending on the vulnerability of the propagules or young.

Data on qualitative characteristics of hatchlings from larger eggs are not always consistent, suggesting that progeny from larger eggs generally, but not always, are larger, grow faster, and show greater survivorship (cf. Capinera, 1979). Studies on a number of species have shown that larger eggs normally produce larger larvae (Gray, 1928; Brown, 1957; Blaxter and Hempel, 1963, 1966; de Ciechomski, 1966; Bilton, 1971; Fowler, 1972; Gall, 1974; Reagan and Conley, 1977; Wallace and Aasjord, 1984; Marsh, 1986).

Data on other qualitative characteristics are less consistent. Blaxter and Hempel (1963), Bagenal (1969), Wal-

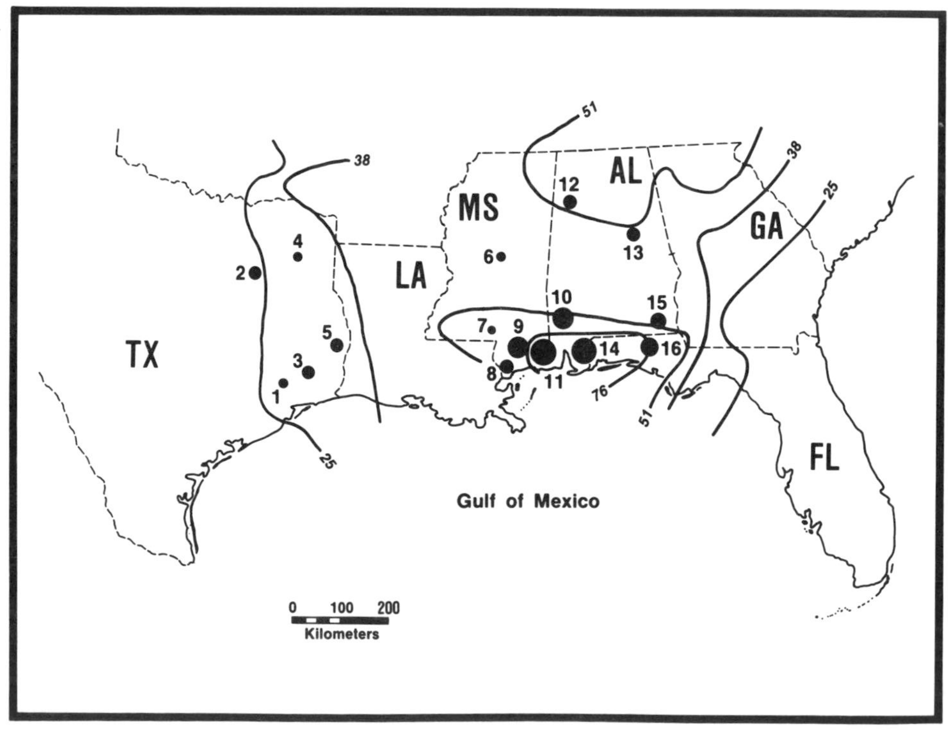

Fig. 27.4. Geographic variation in mean mature ovum diameter for *Notropis venustus* in relation to mean annual stream runoff (cm) in the southern United States. For purposes of illustration the mean diameters were divided into eight size groups using fig. 27.2 as a guide, and the size groups are shown by dots of different diameters. After Geraghty et al. (1973), by permission.

lace and Aasjord (1984), and Marsh (1986) observed that hatchlings from larger eggs show greater survivorship under different test conditions. However, de Ciechomski (1966) did not find an influence of egg size on survival, and Fowler (1972) found that larger eggs and fry and fingerlings from larger eggs of chinook salmon had higher mortalities. Other studies (Gray, 1928; Gall, 1974; Wallace and Aasjord, 1984) have shown that the larger larvae originating from larger eggs grow faster. Brown (1946), however, concluded that larger brown trout fry grew faster than smaller ones because of the effect of size hierarchy, not alevin weight. Wallace and Aasjord (1984) found that larger alevins of arctic charr from larger ova began to feed first, which they associated with a greater growth weight and hence the maintenance of a greater size by the larger alevins during early growth. Fowler (1972) reported that larger chinook salmon fry from larger ova maintained their greater size during early rearing.

Bilton (1971) found a significant positive correlation between egg size and the size of three-month sockeye salmon fry, but his correlations for nine-month fingerlings were not as strong. Regan and Conley (1977) found that when they fed channel catfish to satiation the initial size differences they observed to be associated with larger eggs at 30 days disappeared within 60 days. Marsh (1986) reported that starved orangethroat darter hatchlings from larger eggs grew faster and were larger at starvation than those from smaller eggs, but hatchlings that were fed showed no differences in growth rates with egg size.

The results of these studies suggest that the effect of egg size on offspring survival may be influenced by the amount of food available, time after hatching, or both. Other factors such as temperature (Marsh, 1986) may also be involved. In his review on the development of eggs and larvae Blaxter (1969) asserted that "larger larvae may be expected to be stronger, better swimmers, less susceptible to damage, and less liable to predation."

In previous studies the selective advantages of intraspecific geographical variation in egg size in fishes have been largely attributed to biotic factors with little consideration given to abiotic factors. Hubbs and Delco (1960), Hubbs and Johnson (1961), Scott (1962), McFadden et al. (1965), and Hubbs (1967) have argued in terms of the relative degree of intraspecific competition, following the ideas of Svardson (1949). Hempel and Blaxter (1967) related what they considered to be genetically based geographical differences in egg sizes to available larval food resources and predation pressure. Reznick and Endler (1982) showed that geographic variation in offspring size in guppies was related to differences in predation. Mann and Mills (1979) considered the possibility that predation was involved in the fecundity and egg-size differences in plaice observed by other authors who discounted food availability as a factor. Heins (1979) proposed that streamflow might have acted as a selective factor to determine life-history traits in populations of *N. longirostris*, including egg sizes, and Garrett (1982) suggested that differences in egg sizes of Pecos pupfish populations might be genetic adaptations to different ranges of variation in local physicochemical factors. Solemdal (1967) and C. F. Hubbs (pers. comm.) found salinity to be important in phenotypic plasticity in the sizes of flounder and silverside eggs, respectively.

The geographic variation we have observed in egg size in *N. venustus* may be the result of both genotypic and phenotypic phenomena, differences in the mean egg size representing differences in adaptive size ranges for the ova. Reznick (1981, 1982) found that in the ovoviviparous poeciliids *Gambusia affinis* and *Poecilia reticulata* the genome of the mother determined offspring size (weight); and because the genome of the offspring did not influence its own size, the effects of the paternal genome are delayed one generation. Such delayed inheritance ("grandfather effects") should be the rule in oviparous and ovoviviparous fishes (Reznick, 1981). We predict that subsequent analysis of the mechanisms underlying the variations in egg size we have observed will reveal a genetic basis with associated grandfather effects as well as proximate phenotypic influences, resulting in different adaptive (genetically determined) size ranges within which egg size may vary temporally or spatially in response to environmental factors.

While the structure of egg-size variation in fishes is just now beginning to be elucidated in some detail, the operational factors and their roles in phenotypic and genotypic responses are poorly understood. Before the evolution of egg sizes in fishes can be understood, the structure of the variation and environmental correlates must be determined. Marsh (1984) came to a similar conclusion. While correlation does not necessarily indicate causation, our approach provides a basis for new investigations into the phenotypic and genotypic significance of egg-size variation in fishes.[1]

[1]Eugene Beckham, Herbert Boschung, Neil Douglas, Douglas Nester, David Nieland, and Patrick O'Neil provided locality data for some possible collection sites. David L. Bechler, Ben Morris, Douglas Nester and Marlene Nester, Felix G. Rabito, Jr., Lynn Sadler, and Allen Sanders aided in the collecting efforts for localities or areas we were unable to sample on our "mad dashes" to the East and West. Allen Sanders also helped with the sorting of the collections. Ira Giles and Mickey Plunkett, U.S. Geological Survey, and Robert Seyfarth, Mississippi Bureau of Pollution Control, provided unpublished water-quality and streamflow data or were helpful in locating them. Gerald E. Gunning reviewed the initial manuscript.

28. Alternative Mating Behaviors of Male Atlantic Salmon (*Salmo salar*), with Special Reference to Mature Male Parr

W. Linn Montgomery, George E. Goslow, Jr., Kathryn B. Staley, and James R. Mills

Abstract

Atlantic salmon (*Salmo salar*) exhibit several modes of male reproductive behavior, depending on the relative age and size of the male and on the presence or absence of larger male competitors. Multisea-winter males defend females against smaller male competitors. One-sea-winter males (termed grilse) similarly defend females when MSW are absent but sneak spawnings when the larger, older males are present. River-dwelling premigratory juveniles (parr) frequently mature sexually and sneak spawnings. Parr perform different behaviors depending on the presence or absence of sea-run males. When sea-run males are present, parr approach the spawning pair primarily in response to the male's quiver. When adult males are absent, parr attend the female more closely, approach her as she probes the nest site, and spawn with her. After spawning, parr frequently eat eggs they have presumably just helped fertilize and may thereby regain some of the nutrients or energy expended during sexual maturation and spawning. Similar systems in Pacific salmon may represent a case of iteroparity in species normally considered to be semelparous.

External fertilization in an aqueous medium provides an opportunity for direct sperm competition and, through this, for the evolution of alternative mating tactics among male fishes (Gross, 1984). In recent studies of such alternative tactics among fishes, emphasis has been placed on reef fishes, often in conjunction with studies on the adaptive significance of sequential hermaphroditism (Reinboth, 1973; Warner and Downs, 1977; Robertson and Warner, 1978; Warner and Hoffman, 1980; Shapiro, 1984), and on nest-building freshwater fishes such as the centrarchids (Gross, 1979, 1982, 1984; Dominey, 1980; Gross and Charnov, 1980) and salmonids (Gross, 1984, 1985). Typically, the attempts of strongly dominant males to sequester females or breeding sites are subverted by various sneak behaviors of younger, smaller, or otherwise subordinate males. These subordinates perform behaviors characteristic of the dominant individuals (in terms of position, orientation, and motor patterns) during the actual spawning event.

Precocious sexual maturation among parr (premigratory, juvenile *Salmo salar*) has increased in recent years (Montgomery and Naiman, 1981; Montgomery et al., unpub. data). Here we examine the significance of this potential alternative mating tactic. We summarize observations on mating behavior in Atlantic salmon and pay special attention to post-spawning phenomena that may help recover nutrients and energy expended during precocious maturation and spawning by parr.

Methods

We conducted studies of Atlantic salmon reproductive behavior at a small hatchery facility operated by the Canadian Department of Fisheries and Oceans on Noel Paul's Brook, a tributary of the Exploits River in central Newfoundland (fig. 28.1). Preliminary studies of spawning behavior took place 27–31 October 1981. More extensive studies of general reproductive behavior and of movements and distribution of parr spanned a six-week period from 2 October to 8 November 1984.

Associated with the hatchery facility at Noel Paul's Brook (NPB) is an observation chamber (approximately 2.5 m × 2 m) that allows one to manipulate the makeup of spawning groups under study and to film and observe their behavior from below the water line. During 1984 we also constructed a series of pens that allowed observation from above. All pens were 1 m wide × 2.5 m long × 0.3–0.5 m deep. Observations of behavior were dictated into a tape recorder for later transcription. In 1981 we filmed reproductive behaviors at 24 frames per second (fps) with a Bolex Super 8 camera. In

1984, 1,300 feet of 16 mm film were exposed at 24–70 fps with a Bolex H16 camera. Five spawning sequences, including selected pre- and postspawning behaviors, as well as various parr-adult interactions were filmed and subsequently analyzed frame by frame on an L&W digitizer.

Water from a raceway holding adults at the NPB facility flowed into a channel in which we studied changes in the distribution of parr during the spawning season (fig. 28.1). In 1984 we distinguished five areas in the channel according to hydrologic and substrate characteristics (zones 1 to 5, moving downstream) and seined these areas at least twice a week 3 October–November 4. Captured parr were removed and either sacrificed or held for later experiments; this allowed us to assess subsequent recolonization rates.

Preliminary feeding experiments were performed in 1984 to assess the potential impact of egg eating by parr. Eighteen parr were held individually in screen compartments that were placed in the inlet pond (fig. 28.1). Eggs obtained from spawnings in the observation pens were fed ad libitum to the parr; fresh eggs were introduced daily to replace those eaten. At the end of three days the eggs in each compartment were counted, and the number of eggs eaten by each parr was determined by subtraction. In a separate experiment we fed eight starved parr both recently fertilized eggs and a popular commercial brand of brilliant red-orange salmon eggs marketed as bait. Eggs were introduced individually so that the behavior of the parr toward them could be recorded. The parr were sacrificed after two days, and the number of eggs in each gut was counted.

Summary of Salmon Life History

Stages in Atlantic (*Salmo salar*) and Pacific (*Oncorhynchus* spp.) salmon life cycles have been given distinctive names that may lead to confusion in interpreting similarities and differences in their respective life histories. Our categories differ from recent attempts to apply developmentally meaningful terms to early life-history stages of fishes (Balon, 1975) but are in general agreement with the salmonid literature.

Females bury their eggs in the gravel of a nesting site, or redd. After hatching, the young alevins remain beneath the gravel, nourished by an attached yolk sac. Upon depletion of their yolk, fry emerge from the gravel to begin their first year of free-swimming life, during which they will grow to approximately 5 cm fork length (FL). After passing their first winter, they begin one to several years of life as river-dwelling parr (~ 7–16 cm FL). Many male parr will mature precociously and may spawn with returning adults. Those parr that emigrate to the sea are termed smolts. Some individuals return to their natal rivers to spawn after only a single year at sea. Atlantic salmon following this schedule are termed grilse, while their Pacific salmon analogs are called jacks. Male jacks are commonly referred to as "precocious males" in the Pacific salmon literature, but we believe that the term "precocious" should be reserved for the more striking case where male parr mature and take part in spawning. All adults we studied were grilse. Other individuals remain at sea for more than one year, and we refer to them as

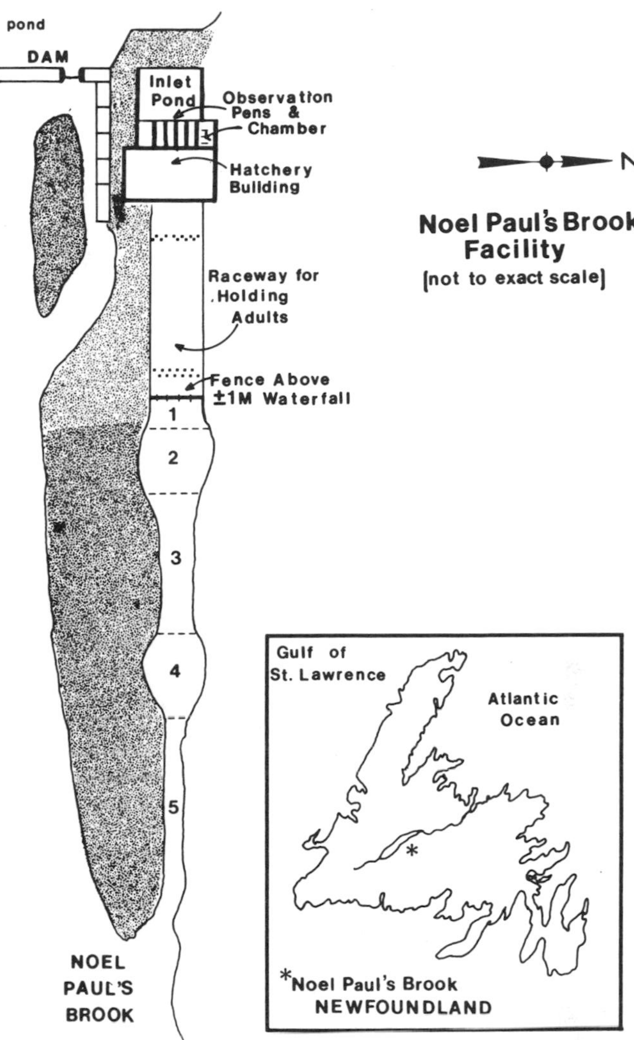

Fig. 28.1. Diagrammatic representation of the field station on Noel Paul's Brook, a tributary of the Exploits River in central Newfoundland (inset). The pond above the dam serves as the source of water for both Noel Paul's Brook and the spawning facility. Pens were constructed in the enclosed inlet pond; the observation chamber was built into the side of that pond. Water from the inlet pond flows beneath the hatchery building, down the raceway where adults were held, over a small barrier, and into a gravel-and-cobble channel that eventually empties into the brook. The channel was subdivided into five zones that could be distinguished on the basis of substrate and current. Dimensions of the zones were as follows: zone 1: 9 m × 3.5 m; zone 2: 19 m × 3.5 m; zone 3: 64 m × 3.2 m; zone 4: 23.2 m × 3.8 m and 7 m × 7 m (two sections); zone 5: 50 m × 3 m.

multisea-winter (MSW) salmon. Unlike Pacific species, which are considered semelparous spawners, Atlantic salmon may spawn as adults in more than one season. Although the phenomenon and its implications have received little attention, precocious sexual maturation by some Pacific salmon parr suggests that semelparity in these species is not absolute.

Summary of Atlantic Salmon Reproductive Behavior

Following their oceanic migrations, adult males and females converge on spawning sites in their natal rivers. The female digs a redd in the gravel by rolling to one side or the other, positioning the posterior half of her body into a sinusoidal waveform, and sharply undulating the tail. The resulting downward-directed jets of water cause a lateral displacement of sand and gravel beneath the fish. After each digging sequence she backs down into the redd to assess its condition with vertical probings of an erect anal fin. Bouts of digging are interspersed with periods of general inactivity accompanied by deep, rapid respirations (68–76/min); occasionally a female may chase foreign males or parr from the area of the redd. During this preparatory period the dominant male in attendance divides his time between periods of inactivity, chases directed at foreign males (adult or parr), and courtship of the female.

Courtship and other interactions between the adult male and female appear to be usually initiated by the male. The most common interaction involves contact with an inactive female, usually in the form of a nudge to her body or a glide-over or glide-under with continual contact where relative right-left positions in the stream are reversed. A more intense courtship pattern occurs when the male positions himself lateral to or slightly upstream of the female and qivers rapidly (approximately 90–110 Hz) for 2 to 5 seconds. A third interaction is particularly common during later stages of redd development, when the male approaches the female while she is in a stationary, probing position deep within the redd. At this time the anal fin of the female is in contact with the bottom of the redd. If the female ceases probing, the male withdraws; if she remains in the stationary position within the redd, the male takes up a parallel position beside her and spawning often ensues.

During spawning the main body axes of the pair are tilted upward anteriorly, and the caudal fins are raised to bring the vent into proximity with the substrate. Both individuals gape widely and begin to quiver (± 110 Hz) shortly before and during ejaculation of gametes. Release of gametes takes only a few seconds, after which both fish exit the redd. The male returns to his previous position and behavior of attendance, and the female moves slightly upstream to begin the digging that will cover the eggs and simultaneously prepare the next spawning site.

This pattern can be altered somewhat by subordinate, satellite males that perform various sneak spawning tactics to gain access to females and their gametes. Sneak behaviors may be exhibited by male grilse if they face competition with a large MSW male or by precociously mature parr. In both cases the subordinate males remain inconspicuous until spawning begins. They then enter the redd and release sperm.

Results and Discussion

Male Mating Behavior in Atlantic Salmon

Three general categories of reproductively active males exist, the categories based on age and size: multisea-winter salmon (MSW; ~ 70 cm FL, ~ 3.5–4 kg); grilse (one sea-winter: ~ 50 cm FL, ~ 1.5 kg); and precociously mature parr (~ 10–15 cm FL, ~ 15–30 g). This list does not, however, accurately represent the diversity of reproductive behaviors among male salmon, for at least two of these categories (grilse and parr) exhibit more than one type of spawning behavior.

MSW Salmon. At this point we know only that MSW males exhibit the dominant, defensive behavior described above (Jones, 1959; Ouellet, 1977). We cannot exclude the possibility that a smaller MSW male may also behave as an inconspicuous subordinate and spawn as a sneak when competing with a much larger MSW male; the behavior of grilse and parr, in fact, suggests that such a potential may exist.

Grilse. Male grilse spawn at a length and weight approximately 70% and 40%, respectively, of that exhibited by two-sea-winter fish and are often the prevailing spawners in many parts of the Atlantic salmon's range (Schiefer, 1971; Gibson, 1977). At NPB, we worked exclusively with grilse that exhibited dominant behavior in our enclosures. One male would dominate additional males and could switch between dominant and subordinate behavior (subordinate males tended to remain inactive and apart from dominants) when we changed the competitive environment by introducing or removing males or by changing the size or aggressiveness of male competitors. We never observed sneak spawning behavior by a subordinate grilse, but Ouellet (1977) makes it clear that grilse may perform such behavior. In a group of wild salmon spawning on Anticosti Island in the Gulf of Saint Lawrence, grilse were constantly harried by the dominant MSW male, yet they remained in the vicinity of the redd. During a spawning by the female and dominant male, the grilse entered the redd and assumed characteristic spawning positions lateral to the spawning pair. Parr present before the spawning could not be seen in the cloud of milt produced during the spawning, but both grilse and parr left the area of the redd following the spawning. Gross (1984) described similar sneak behavior by one-sea-winter Pacific salmon males (jacks) but did not report any involvement by parr.

Grilse can, therefore, perform both dominant and sneak spawning behaviors, depending on the nature of their male competitors. At present we cannot determine whether individual males (1) exhibit only one behavior, although both behaviors may be represented in the same or different populations, or (2) switch between behaviors depending on local conditions.

Precociously Mature Parr. Precociously mature male parr also exhibit two distinct modes of behavior that are de-

Table 28.1. Average Density of Parr (Adjusted to per 100 m²) in Channel Below Raceway Holding Adult Salmon at Noel Paul's Brook[a]

Zone	Area (m^2)	Week 1	2	3	4	5	6	Total Parr per Zone
1[c]	32	3.2	3.2	15.9	20.7	123.9	14.3	115
2	67	1.5	1.0	0	0	11.3	3.8	24
3	205	1.3	0.5	2.0	2.2	8.8	1.0	64
4	137	4.4	1.2	1.5	1.5	4.8	0.4	39
5[d]	150	0.7	0.2	0	1.0	3.7	0.4	18
Total parr per week		23	14	22	28	153	20	
Days sampled per week		2	3	2	2	2	2	
Recolonization rate[e]		2.7	1.8	3.7	3.5	51.0	4.0	

[a]Contingency table analysis indicates that weeks and zones are dependent (X^2 = 56.2, *df* = 20, $P < 0.001$).
[b]Collection dates for weeks 1–6, respectively, were: 3, 6 October; 9, 12, 14 October; 17, 20 October; 24, 28 October; 30, 31 October; 2, 4 November. Daily stripping of eggs and milt from adults began on 29 October.
[c]Zone 1 was within 1 m of a dam blocking upstream movement into the raceway.
[d]Zone 5 emptied into Noel Paul's Brook.
[e]Recolonization rate = captures/days since previous sampling, in parr/day moving into channel.

termined by the presence or absence of an adult male. Before spawning, parr tend to rest quietly on the substrate near the redd and may settle into and remain in the bottom of the redd as the female digs and probes (Jones and King, 1949; Jones, 1959; Montgomery et al., unpub. data). At the onset of spawning and in response to quivering behavior of an adult male, parr dart beneath the spawning pair and, at least sometimes, gape, twirl about in an exaggerated swimming action, and emit sperm. The second behavioral mode exhibited by parr occurs when adult males are absent. Then parr are more attentive to the female than when the male is present, and the parr enter the redd to spawn in response to probing by the female. Otherwise, parr spawning behavior in this context parallels that when a male is present.

Parr Reproductive Behavior: Noel Paul's Brook Studies

Behavior in the River. Weekly summaries of parr densities in the channel below the raceway that held adults reveal two basic patterns (table 28.1). First, as the spawning season approached, parr aggregated in the upstream zone immediately below the raceway holding adults (zone 1; fig. 28.1). Second, movements into the channel below the raceway increased dramatically in week 5 (recolonization rate of 51 fish moving into the channel per day versus 1.8–3.5 fish/day in weeks 1–4, before 29 October).

These patterns reflect a tendency for parr to move upstream, apparently in response to the presence of adults. Adults were initially brought to the NPB raceway in July. Nonetheless, a strong surge in entry and movement upstream in the channel did not occur until late October (week 5, 30–31 October), which coincided with the period when hatchery personnel began stripping eggs and milt from adults at the upstream end of the raceway (extensive daily stripping began 29 October).

Ripe male parr may respond more frequently to spawning or prespawning adults than do female parr. Most parr captured in the channel during our initial sampling period (week 1) were not running ripe, and many may have been females. Only 14 of 93 parr (15.1%) captured during that week were ripe, and a subsample of 16 individuals included only 4 males (table 28.2). In contrast, 141 (71.6%) of 197 parr captured in weeks 3–6 were ripe males, and only 32% of a subsample of 50 individuals were females.

King et al. (1939), Buck and Youngson (1982), and Dalley et al. (1983) describe similar upstream movements of mature male parr during autumn, while immature males and females moved downstream during the same period. Up-

Table 28.2. Summary of Weekly Collections of Parr from Channel Below Raceway, Noel Paul's Brook*

Year, week	No. Parr Captured	Percent Ripe Males	Size Range (mm): Not Ripe	Size Range (mm): Ripe Males	Sex Ratio: % Male (*N*)	Sex Ratio: Method
1981†	47	83.0	62–107	71–152	83.0(47)	% ripe males
1984						
1	93	15.1	77–117	39–134	25.0(16)	Subsample
3	15	86.7	82–120	84–87	93.3(15)	Entire sample
4	35	31.4	74–207	68–198	57.1(35)	Entire sample
5	147	79.6	75–153	61–240	79.6(147)	% ripe males

*Weeks as in table 29.1.
†1981 samples taken during the week equivalent to week 5 of 1984.

Table 28.3. Distribution of Parr Within Enclosures Related to Presence or Absence of Adult Salmon*

Combination	Zone 1 $\bar{x}$	Zone 1 SD	Zone 2 $\bar{x}$	Zone 2 SD	Zone 3 $\bar{x}$	Zone 3 SD	N
Parr only	51.8	14.8	24.6	7.7	23.6	7.1	498
Parr + males	68.0	14.1	19.0	8.4	13.0	8.5	440
Parr + females	72.9	4.9	14.3	5.7	12.8	10.6	426
Parr + females + males	58.5	13.5	32.4	5.1	9.0	9.7	343

(Columns other than Combination and N: Percent of Parr Observed in Given Zones.)

*Zone 1 was the downstream third of an enclosure, zone 3 the upstream third. Three experiments were conducted for each combination of parr, males, and females. For analysis, data from all three experiments in each case were combined. Entries are the mean ($\bar{x}$; SD = standard deviation) percent of observations occurring in the three zones; N is the total number of parr observed in the three experiments. Adults influence the distribution of parr (table $X^2 = 45.099$, $df = 2$, $P < 0.001$**); parr with males and parr with females are indistinguishable ($X^2 = 0.9$, $df = 2$, $P > 0.5$ NS); parr with both sexes and parr alone are distinguishable ($X^2 = 28.1$, $df = 2$, $P < 0.001$**).

stream movements correlate with immigration of adults into spawning streams and may be initiated by chemicals such as ovarian fluids (Newcombe and Hartman, 1973; Emanuel and Dodson, 1979). Contrasting patterns exhibited by mature and immature fish appear to relate to spawning and escape from severe winter conditions, respectively (Thorpe, 1981).

Prespawning Behavior. Observations in our pens confirm reports that parr tend to remain downstream of adults (table 28.3), although they showed a similar but weaker tendency to remain at the downstream end (zone 1) of the pens even when adults were absent. We cannot determine whether this latter tendency was due in some manner to our pens or to effects of adult salmon held slightly upstream but out of sight of our pens (concurrent experiments by another group of investigators). Parr positions and orientation differed somewhat when only one sex of adult was present and when both males and females were present. Parr were more evenly distributed in zones 1 and 2 when adults of both sexes were present and were more concentrated in zone 1 when only one sex was present. In the presence of both sexes parr often faced the adults rather than upstream as in other experiments.

Spawning Behavior. As indicated above, parr will spawn with an adult female whether or not an adult male is present. Previous reports (e.g., Jones and King, 1952) suggested that an adult male had to be present for courtship and spawning to occur. Parr exhibit different behavior when spawning with both sexes and when spawning with female alone.

In situations where an adult male is present, parr generally take up positions on or near the substrate and move only (1) to shift position, occasionally coming to rest in the redd, (2) to escape aggressive adults or parr, (3) to evade digging actions of the female, or (4) to dart at a drifting particle in the water column. Parr tend to associate more closely with the substrate when an adult male is present than when an adult male is absent.

Parr respond differently to behaviors involving preparation of the redd or spawning (table 28.4). When parr are in the presence of both male and female adults, they ignore glide (0% approached) and occasionally approach when the female digs (6.8%) or probes (9.1%). Parr may discern between digs during preparation of the redd (6.8%) and digs following spawning that function to cover eggs (0% response). The critical cue in this context appears to be the male's quiver. Quiver is both an intense courtship behavior of adult males and a consistent part of the spawning behavior before actual gametic release. Parr approached the adults on 210 (54%) of 389 observed displays of courtship quiver.

Parr respond differently when adult males are absent (table 28.4), and individual parr switch between these alternatives as males are introduced into or removed from experimental enclosures. When adult males are absent, parr pay moderate attention to prespawn (15.3%) and postspawn digs (10.5%). The most significant cue appears to be the female's probe (44.8% response). As the female backed into the redd following a dig, parr would converge on and frequently make contact with the area around her vent and anal fin. Jones and King (1949) mention a single observation of similar behavior. This behavior appears to parallel the approach of the adult male to a probing female, but we observed the other characteristic male courtship behavior, quiver, only once. On this occasion a parr approached the left dorsum of the female posterior to her dorsal fin and quivered; the female did not appear to respond. Jones and King (1949) also reported a single instance of parr quiver directed at the side of the female between anal and pelvic fins.

Table 28.4. Frequency of Approaches by Parr to Adults in Response to Common Adult Reproductive Behaviors

Adult Behavior	Percent Approach Responses†		Total Number of Observed Behaviors	
	Male Present	Male Absent	Male Present	Male Absent
Male-female glide	0	—	49	—
Female dig (prespawn)	6.8	15.3	307	72
Female probe	9.1	44.8	199	154
Male quiver	54.0	—	389	—
Male-female spawn	100.0	—	8	—
Female dig (postspawn)	0	10.5	10	86

*Adult behaviors are ranked approximately in the order they would appear during a courtship and spawning sequence.

†All instances when parr moved away from a digging female were excluded.

When spawning occurs, parr mill below the vents of the adult(s). We have not clearly distinguished sperm release by parr when they are with an adult male, but sperm clouds produced in the absence of an adult male make it clear that parr emit sperm. Others have recorded spent testes in male parr following the spawning season (Jones and King, 1952; Robertson, 1957; Mitans, 1973). Parr produced viable young in experiments involving mature male parr and castrated adult males (Jones and King, 1949) and when used as sires in hatchery crosses (Glebe et al., 1979). Nonetheless, there are few data that indicate the amount of sperm contributed by parr or their reproductive success. During late August-September, testes of maturing male parr from the Matamek River, Quebec, commonly constitute 15–20% of total body weight, in contrast to the 4–5% normally cited for migratory adults. Packed cell volumes for parr sperm may also be greater than that for adults (B. Glebe, pers. comm.). Both phenomena would be predicted for broadcast spawning fishes experiencing severe sperm competition (Warner and Robertsons, 1978).

Postspawning Behavior. Following a spawning event, both adult males and parr generally leave the redd and resume their previous positions, although parr often stay behind in the redd after adult males have departed. The female remains to dig and to cover the eggs. Parr exhibit one distinctive behavior at this time: they often eat eggs of the clutch they have presumably helped fertilize. Although cannibalism is well known (Rohwer, 1978; Polis, 1981), it appears rare to encounter vertebrate male mating systems where parental cannibalism of apparently viable progeny follows the act of fertilization so closely (cf. Rabito and Heins, 1985).

The adaptive significance of such egg eating remains unclear. Parents may regain some reproductive effort by eating progeny that are in some way handicapped and unlikely to survive (Polis, 1981). Previous observations indicated that parr would frequently ignore eggs resting on the substrate and that most eggs were eaten when they were thrown into the water column by digging actions of the female (Jones and King, 1949; Montgomery, unpub. data). Eggs in the water column would normally be swept downstream to eventual destruction. Gross (1979) describes similar behavior for cuckolding sunfishes. Further, the fraction of eggs fertilized by a single parr may be low so that an eaten egg would probably represent offspring of a competitor rather than one's own. Finally, Saunders and Sreedharan (1978) demonstrated that tissue lipid levels are lower in mature male parr than in nonmature males and females, and several sources give evidence for unexplained reductions in overwinter survival of mature parr (Dalley et al., 1983; Montgomery et al., unpub. data). Acquisition of lipids from eggs could reduce such mortality if overwinter survival is linked to energy or essential lipid stores.

Eggs could contribute significantly to nutrition of parr. During *ad libitum* feeding experiments over a three-day period, 18 ripe male parr ate 16.2 eggs on average (SD = 13.8, range = 0–41). Eight ripe male parr collected from the spawning channel in 1981 contained an average of 16 eggs (SD = 10.1, range = 3–28). Glebe et al. (1979) recorded averages of 1,066–1,576 Joules/egg for salmon populations from New Brunswick.

Consumption of eggs by parr is a concern for some salmon managers who see them as having a serious impact on spawning output of adults (J. Pratt, pers. comm.), but their calculations usually consider an instantaneous count of eggs in a parr gut as a daily ration. Our preliminary investigations suggest that estimates of daily rations based on instantaneous counts of eggs in the gut are overestimates. We fed eggs individually to eight starved parr. Of the eggs introduced (N = 83), 45 were eaten immediately. Dissections of these parr two days later yielded 60 eggs, most of them in the stomach and anterior intestine. In most cases eggs were ruptured, and egg membranes remained in the stomach or anterior intestine. Bait eggs appeared to rupture less readily than fresh eggs. Thus eggs may have an extended gut-residence time.

Summary of Parr Reproductive Behavior. Within-river movements by parr in apparent response to adults have been documented (Thorpe, 1981), but the cues to these movements are generally unknown. Our data indicate that strong movements may be stimulated by gametes or associated chemicals in the water.

Once in proximity to adults, parr tend to remain downstream until they receive specific cues that release approach behavior. When adult males are present, parr respond primarily to the courtship and spawning quiver. When adult males are absent, parr approach when the female probes. This later mode of behavior is similar to that of the adult male; the courtship quiver is rarely performed by parr. In any event, probe and quiver are the final behaviors to be expressed before release of gametes, depending on whether adult males are present or absent.

Parr position during spawning is markedly different from that of the adult male in terms of simple proximity to the source of eggs. During ejaculation the male vent is generally several centimeters above the substrate and to the side of the female. During the same period parr are usually much closer to the female's vent. Also sperm from the adult male travels several centimeters in a tight stream before breaking up into a cloud; this stream is directed ventrally rather than laterally toward the eggs. This factor may introduce a delay in the fertilizing capability of the adult male that would allow parr an advantage. Thus parr may fertilize a significant proportion of eggs.

In terms of general life-history theory, trade-offs take place between (1) reproductive (fertilization) success and (2) various types of energy or nutrient allocation to growth or reproduction (courtship, defense, testis growth, etc; Gadgil and Bossert, 1970; Schaffer, 1974; Pianka and Parker, 1975; Stearns, 1976; Horn, 1978; Bell, 1980; Reznick, 1983). Postspawning events that may help recover prespawning costs have largely been ignored, but ingestion of eggs by parr may represent such a phenomenon. Eating eggs that are floating in the water column probably has little effect on reproductive success of adult or male parr, since such eggs tend to be swept downstream to destruction or ingestion elsewhere. Eggs may, however, contribute to the postspawning survival of parr by recharging nutrient or energy stores depleted as testes develop or spawning ensues.

Parallels in Other Salmonids

The incidence of male spawning at younger ages or smaller sizes than dominant males has been recognized for some time in Pacific salmon, including *Oncorhynchus gorbuscha*, *Oncorhynchus keta*, *Oncorhynchus nerka*, and *Oncorhynchus tshawytscha* (Rutter, 1909; Robertson, 1957; Gebhards, 1960; Hanson and Smith, 1967; Everest and Chapman, 1972; Ivankov et al., 1975; Utoh, 1976; Goetz et al., 1979; Schroder, 1981; Chebanov, 1982), steelhead (Everest, 1973), and various trout (Smith, 1941; Greeley, 1932). Most of these studies report sneak behavior by subordinate males that spawn in the presence of dominant adults in systems parallel to that involving MSW Atlantic salmon and grilse.

Precocious male parr have been reported in *O. tshawytscha*, *Oncorhynchus kisutch*, and *Oncorhynchus masu* (Rutter, 1909; Robertson, 1957; Gebhards, 1960; Everest and Chapman, 1972; Utoh, 1976); a similar situation may obtain with small (15–26 cm), nonanadromous *O. nerka*, termed kokanee (Hanson and Smith, 1967). Like Atlantic salmon, Pacific salmon parr have been observed in the presence of spawning adults, often attempting to enter redds (Gebhards, 1960; Everest, pers. comm.). Other parallels between these two groups include the incidence of egg eating (reported in *O. tshawytscha*; Gebhards, 1960), viability of eggs fertilized by male parr (Robertson, 1957; Ivankov et al., 1975), and possible iteroparity (Gebhards, 1960). Such striking similarities suggest that a more complex array of alternate male mating tactics exists in Pacific salmon species than has been previously appreciated.[1]

[1] Initial work on the biology of mature male parr in Quebec was supported by the Woods Hole Oceanographic Institution Matamek Research Program and by a WHOI Postdoctoral Scholar fellowship to Montgomery. Funding for research at Noel Paul's Brook in Newfoundland was provided by Northern Arizona University in 1981 and by a National Geographic Society grant (#2850–84) to Montgomery in 1984. We sincerely thank the Canadian Department of Fisheries and Oceans for permission to use their facilities of NPB and are particularly grateful to C. Bourgeois, M. O'Connell, J. Davis, J. Pratt, D. Scott, G. Ralph, and the entire crew at NPB for logistic support and friendship.

29. Relationships Between Genetic Parameters and Life-History Characteristics of Stream Fish

Earl G. Zimmerman

Abstract

Correlations between five major genetic and eight biological features for 14 species of stream fish were analyzed to determine relationships between these two groups of parameters. Similarity matrices generated from the two data sets were not significantly correlated; however, discriminant analysis revealed that F_{ST}, an indicator of population heterogeneity, and percent of polymorphic loci, an indicator of population variation, were significant predictors for biological features such as vertical distribution, social structure, and trophic position. Population heterogeneity was higher but polymorphium was lower for benthic species, indicating greater population subdivision and lower genetic variation within populations of these forms. The demonstrated relationships between genetics and natural history and the resulting population structure and demography appear to be biologically meaningful with respect to patterns of genic adaptation in the diverse assemblage of stream fish studied.

Estimates of genetic variability assessed by electrophoresis indicate that a large amount of within- and between-population variation exists in a variety of species, including fish. Over the past 20 years various hypotheses have been proposed to explain this variation, including the opposing views of neutralists (Kimura, 1968, 1969; Kimura and Ohta, 1971; King and Jukes, 1969) and selectionists (Hedrick et al., 1976; Johnson, 1971, 1974; Nevo, 1978; Powell, 1971; Selander and Kaufman, 1973). While both views can be supported by experimental and theoretical approaches, recent investigators have begun to examine genetic variation in light of other factors that could account for observed patterns. For instance, Nevo et al. (1983) examined relationships between two measures of genetic variation, heterozygosity and polymorphism, and ecological, demographic, and life-history characteristics for 1,111 species of vertebrates, invertebrates, and plants. They found nonrandom trends between genetic variation and biological parameters among widely varying taxa. Genetic diversity was positively correlated with a larger geographic and climatic range and broader habitat requirements.

One important feature of fish populations that has emerged from these studies is that there are varying degrees of population subdivision over relatively small geographic areas. Population subdivision has been demonstrated in striped bass, *Morone saxatilis* (Morgan et al., 1973); bluegills, *Lepomis machrochirus* (Avise and Smith, 1974); darters, *Etheostoma radiosum* (Echelle et al., 1975); red shiners, *Notropis lutrensis* (Wooten and Zimmerman, 1985); salmonids (Utter et al., 1973); and mosquitofish, *Gambusia affinis* (Smith et al., 1983; Kennedy et al., 1985; McClenaghan et al., 1985). Some of these studies present possible environmental-genetic correlations with genetic variation; however, other factors such as demographic factors and stochastic processes may shape the genome of many species. Hence environmental patchiness and social behavior may contribute to population subdivision (Hartl, 1980). Social and behavioral relationships to genetic variation, as well as stochastic processes, have been investigated in mosquitofish (Brown, 1982; Kennedy et al., 1985; Smith et al., 1983); however, few fish species have been studied as extensively.

Classical explanations, especially the tendency to rely on a single phenomenon, for the existence of certain patterns to genetic variation in fish populations do not fully account for much of the variation demonstrated thus far. The purpose of this chapter is to examine genetic structure of populations in a variety of small fish species and to consider it in relation to a number of life-history or biological characteristics. Five genetic structure parameters, H, P, F_{ST}, F_{IS}, and F_{IT} were selected since they represent measures of individual variation, species variation, population subdivision (heterogeneity), reduction in heterozygosity owing to inbreeding, and reduction in heterozygosity owing to nonrandom mating and to subdivision itself, respectively (Hartl, 1980). Eight biological characteristics were selected: (1) vertical distribution in the water column, (2) habitat stream order, (3) preferred substrate, (4) preferred stream gradient, (5) water quality, (6) social structure, (7) trophic position, and (8) size of geographic range. The null hypothesis tested was that no overall or individual relationships existed between these genetic and biological parameters.

Materials and Methods

Data on genetic variation obtained by electrophoresis of soluble proteins for 14 small stream-fish species (table 29.1) were used in the analysis. Methods of electrophoresis for species in this analysis follow Zimmerman and Wooten (1981). While studies of genetic variation in small stream fish are numerous, certain requirements for calculations of the genetic parameters were necessary. Only species for which heterozygosity values and data for at least 15 gene loci per population were available could be used. Gynogenetic forms were excluded. Data available from the literature were limited in certain cases. For instance, heterozygosity values for each variable locus are rarely presented but are necessary for calculation of F_{IS} and F_{IT}. Therefore, mean heterozygosity (H) was used. Calculation of these parameters using H provided slightly different values; however, all deviations were proportional and in the same direction. F_{ST}, F_{IS}, and F_{IT} were calculated according to Hartl (1980) as: $F_{ST} = H_T - H_S/H_T$, $F_{IS} = H_S - H_I/H_S$, and $F_{IT} = H_T - H_I/H_T$, where H_I represents the average observed heterozygosity (H), H_S represents the heterozygosity of an equivalent random-mating subpopulation ($\overline{2pq}$), and H_T represents the heterozygosity in an equivalent random-mating total population ($2\bar{p}\bar{q}$). Values of F_{ST}, F_{IT}, P, and H were arc sine–transformed for all statistical analyses. In addition, all values were weighted by the number of variable loci.

Biological parameters for each species were obtained from the literature. Often these were limited to casual observations and could not be quantified consistently. The result was that each species was assigned a nominal value for each parameter. For instance, a value of 1 was assigned to benthic species, 2 for a mid-column species, and a 3 for top swimming species. In some instances assignment of a 1 or 2 for alternate designations might include an assignment of a 3 for species that occur over both categories. The latter was true for species that occur over multiple stream orders, substrates, stream gradients, or water qualities or were omnivorous feeders.

Several statistical procedures were used for data analysis; unless otherwise indicated, the SAS statistical package (Barr et al., 1976) was used. Many of the applications assume absence of correlated characters. Character correlations were established with the Spearman rank correlation procedure. Similarity matrices based on genetic or biological parameters for the 14 species were generated from NT-SYS (Rohlf et al., 1974). In turn, these matrices were used to construct dendrograms of genetic and biological similarity by the unweighted pair-group method (UPGMA) of NT-SYS; and the congruence between genetic and biological matrices was examined with the use of Mantel analysis (Mantel, 1967; Sokal, 1979). Principal components analysis of each data set was performed using NT-SYS. Stepwise discriminant analysis (Klecka, 1980) was used to determine those genetic parameters that best predicted the biology of the fish species. Level of accuracy for prediction of the genetic parameters was determined by discriminant analysis. Significance of results from all analyses was tested at the 0.05 probability level.

Results

Data accumulated on 14 species of small stream fish included a wide taxonomic range of six families and eleven genera (table 29.1). This permitted an analysis of fish occurring over a broad range of habitat types from high gradient, clear streams to low gradient, high-silt-load streams and rivers. The assemblage includes one top swimmer (*Gambusia* sp.), eight benthic forms (*Etheostoma* spp., *Hypentelium* sp., *Thoburnia* sp., *Campostoma* spp., *Pimephales* sp., and *Cot-*

Table 29.1. Populations Sampled, Number of Loci Examined, and Source of Genetic Data for 14 Species of Stream Fish

Species	Number of Populations	Number of Loci	Source
Campostoma anomalum	7	17	Zimmerman et al. (1980)
C. oligolepis	5	17	Zimmerman et al. (1980)
Hypentelium nigricans	3	40	Buth (1980)
Etheostoma microperca	5	23	Buth et al. (1980)
E. proeliare	4	23	Buth et al. (1980)
Thoburnia rhothoeca	2	34	Buth (1979b)
Cottus confusus	16	33	Zimmerman and Wooten (1985)
Astyanax mexicanus	6	17	Avise and Selander (1972)
Notropis lutrensis	8	20	Wooten and Zimmerman (1985)
N. venustus	4	20	Calhoun (1981)
Nocomis micropogon	2	43	Goodfellow et al. (1984)
Pimephales vigilax	5	20	Zimmerman (unpub. data)
Rhinichthys cataractae	2	43	Goodfellow et al. (1984)
Gambusia affinis	13	14	Smith et al. (1983, pers. comm.)

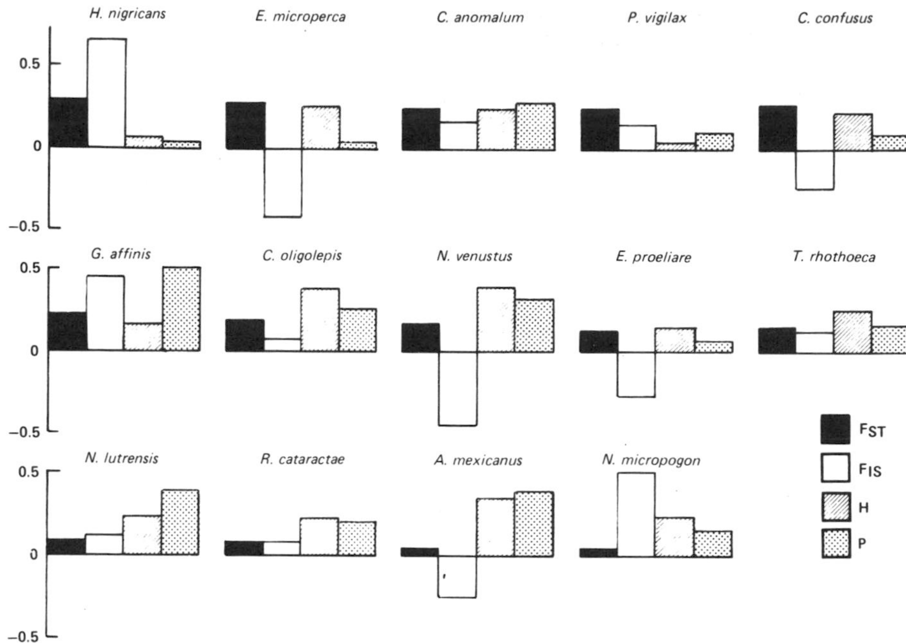

Fig. 29.1. Variation in four genetic parameters for 14 species of small stream fish.

tus sp.), and four mid-column species (*Nocomis* sp., *Notropis* spp., *Astyanax* sp). General patterns in the data are readily evident. Most of the benthic forms occur in riffle areas of smaller headwater streams and sometimes have rather limited distributions. Exceptions to this are *Etheostoma proeliare, Campostoma anomalum, Pimephales vigilax,* and *Hypentelium nigricans*. The benthic forms tend to be more solitary and have smaller population sizes. The mid-column species are generally those that occur in larger, clear to silty streams and congregate in schools.

Initial analysis for correlated characters revealed that biological parameters such as stream order, substrate, and stream gradient were highly correlated with other parameters. Removal of these three left vertical distribution, social structure, trophic level, geographic distribution, and water quality as five biological features to compare to genetic features. Similarly, along the genetic parameters, F_{IT} was significantly correlated to the remaining four and was removed from further analysis.

Values of F_{ST} ranged from a low of 0.010 to a high of 0.289 (fig. 29.1). Lowest values were found in species such as *Nocomis micropogon* and *Astyanax mexicanus*, indicating little population subdivision in these species. Highest values of F_{ST}, and hence the greatest amount of population subdivision, were found for *H. nigricans, Etheostoma microperca, C. anomalum, P. vigilax,* and *Cottus confusus*. High positive values of inbreeding within subpopulatons (F_{IS}) and within the total (F_{IT}) were observed for *P. vigilax, H. nigricans,* and *G. affinis,* with lowest inbreeding levels in *Rhinichthys cataractae, N. lutrensis* and *Campostoma oligolepis* (fig. 29.1). Negative values of F_{IS} and F_{IT} were found in several species, including *E. microperca, E. proeliare, C. confusus, A. mexicanus,* and *Notropis venustus*. Genetic variation, measured by proportion of loci heterozygous in the average individual (*H*) and percent of polymorphic loci (*P*), was highest in *N. venustus, C. oligolepis,* and *A. mexicanus*. *Hypentelium nigricans* and *P. vigilax* exhibited lowest levels of genetic variation (fig. 29.1).

The resulting data sets were subjected to separate cluster analyses. The phenogram constructed from the biological parameter matrix presents three major clusters (fig. 29.2). One cluster includes *A. mexicanus, N. lutrensis, N. venustus, N. micropogon, P. vigilax,* and *R. cataractae*. *Campostoma anomalum, C. oligolepis, H. nigricans, E. microperca, E. proeliare, C. confusus,* and *Thoburnia rhothoeca* comprise a second cluster, with *G. affinis* occupying a sole position in a third cluster. Principal components analysis provided an indication of the importance of variation in the biological features in placing the species in a character space and provides some indication of their relative importance in species placement in the phenogram as well. Highest character loadings in factor 1 were for vertical distribution and social structure. The order of contributions in factor 1 was vertical distribution > social structure > water quality > geographic distribution > trophic position. Trophic position accounted for most of the variation in factor 2, and geographic distribution was the major contributor in factor 3.

The phenogram generated from the genetic parameters was not similar to that constructed from biological characters (fig. 29.3). Two major clusters, one including *A. mexicanus, N. venustus,* and *C. oligolepis* and another including *C. anomalum, N. lutrensis, R. cataractae, T. rhothoeca,* and *N. micropogon,* were evident. The rest of the species were placed in a rather loose assemblage. Principal components analysis indicated that highest character loadings in factor 1 were, in order of decreasing importance, heterozygosity > F_{IS} > polymorphism > F_{ST}. Variation in the second factor was accounted for by F_{ST} > polymorphism > F_{IS} > heterozygosity, while F_{ST} accounted for most of the variation in factor 3. As expected, the correlation between the biological and genetic parameter matrices in the Mantel analysis was not significant (t = 0.192).

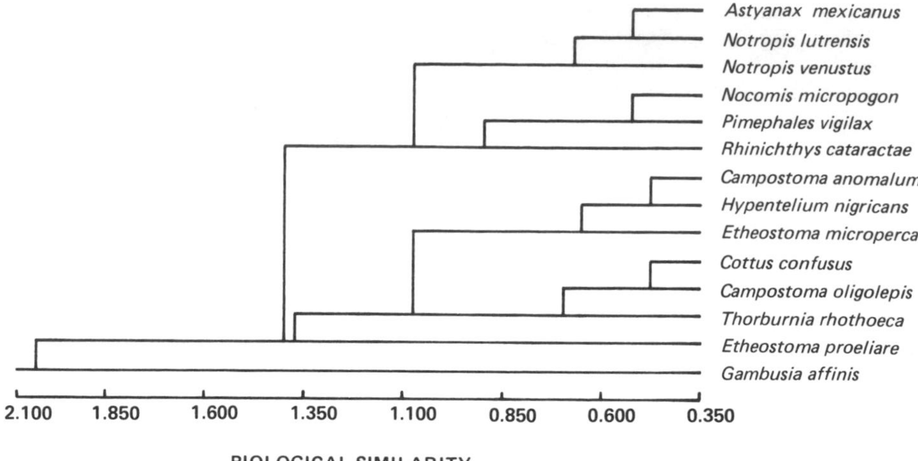

Fig. 29.2. Phenogram of biological relationship of 14 species of small stream fish.

While the combination of all genetic parameters was not correlated to the biological characteristics, it is meaningful to ask whether a subset of genetic variables might produce a discrimination model or predictor of biological similarity. With the use of the original three clusters of species established from the multivariate analysis of biological data the best model (combination of characters) for placement of species was determined by stepwise discriminant analysis (Klecka, 1980) of uncorrelated genetic parameters. Results indicated that, while F_{IS} and heterozygosity were poor predictors, polymorphism ($F = 7.71, P = 0.008$) and F_{ST} ($F = 4.80$, $P = 0.031$) were significant predictors in the model with correlations coefficients of 58% and 47%, respectively.

Finally, with the use of polymorphism and F_{ST} as classification variables, a discriminant model was generated to classify each species into the biological clusters determined from the multivariate analysis. In effect, this procedure tested the accuracy of polymorphism and F_{ST} for placing species into their respective biological clusters. An initial test for homogeneity of within-group covariance matrices resulted in a nonsignificant chi-square value ($\chi^2 = 0.040, P = 0.094$), and a pooled covariance matrix was used in the discriminant function. The analysis indicated that the posterior probability of placing each species in its respective biological cluster was accurate 83% and 86% of the time for clusters 1 and 2, respectively. In each case one species from each cluster was placed in an alternate cluster in the posterior probability model. Placement of the species in their respective clusters with the use of polymorphism and F_{ST} had a predictability of about 85%.

Discussion

Relationships between biological characters and genetic parameters were demonstrated for 14 species of stream fishes. Herein I consider these relationships in the context of the ecology and population biology of the species examined.

While the two matrices and phenograms derived from the separate data sets are not congruent, patterns within the sets are evident. For instance, the phenogram constructed from the biological data exhibits a major cluster comprised of obligate benthic fish that inhabit clear, high-gradient streams (fig. 29.2). Species such as *E. microperca, C. oligolepis, C. confusus,* and *T. rhothoeca* are restricted to riffles or gravelly substrates. Therefore, their preferred habitat may often be patchy, resulting in linearly disjunct populations. These species are solitary and rarely occur in large numbers in a single

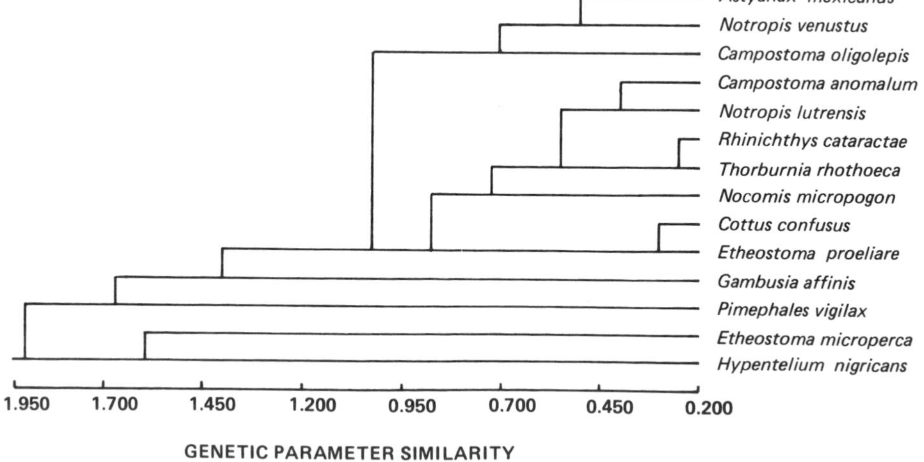

Fig. 29.3. Phenogram of genetic parameter relationships for 14 species of small stream fish.

riffle. Because of small effective population sizes, subpopulations of these species should be subject to stochastic events such as genetic drift, founder effect, and bottlenecks. F_{ST} values among these taxa ranged from 0.129 to 0.289 with a mean of 0.219, and these are concomitant to greater genetic heterogeneity indicative of a high degree of population subdivision in these species.

A second major cluster in the biological phenogram included fish that occur in larger congregations in a wider variety of stream types (fig. 29.2). Species such as *A. mexicanus, N. micropogon,* and the two species of *Notropis* often school in the mid-column of lower-gradient streams. This cluster also included *R. cataractae* and *P. vigilax,* which live primarily on the bottom, where they feed on a variety of plant and animal material. The latter two species are not as restricted in their local distributions as are other benthic species, often occurring throughout continuous habitats. Therefore, the species in this cluster tend to be more broadly distributed in their preferred habitat, are subject to greater gene flow, and should be more homogeneous genetically. *Pimephales vigilax* had a higher F_{ST} than other species with which it clustered. Nevertheless, F_{ST} values among these fish ranged from 0.010 to 0.249 with a mean of 0.100.

The remaining species, *G. affinis*, was the sole member of the third biological cluster. This top-swimming form occurs in a variety of habitats, primarily low-gradient streams or standing, often isolated, pools and ponds or reservoirs. F_{ST} for this species was high, 0.203, indicative of a high degree of population subdivision. McClenaghan et al. (1985) reported a similar F_{ST} (0.196) for populations over the Savannah River drainage. They suggested that selection accounted for little of the population heterogeneity and that stochastic processes play a more important role in structuring the genome of *G. affinis*. This was also suggested by Kennedy et al. (1985), who found a high degree of population subdivision in mosquitofish from isolated pools over short distances.

The phenogram constructed from the five genetic parameters displayed heterogeneous clusters of species with differing biologies (fig. 29.3). This resulted from the lack of concordance of certain of the genetic parameters, especially F_{IS} and heterozygosity. For instance, species such as *C. oligolepis* and *R. cataractae* had the lowest F_{IS} values and thus lowest levels of inbreeding but were grouped in different biological clusters. Highest levels of inbreeding were for *H. nigricans* and *P. vigilax*, also members of different biological clusters. The latter species also had the lowest levels of heterozygosity, while *C. oligolepis* and *N. venustus* had the highest and were clustered separately as well. No significant correlation was found between matrices of the two data sets in the Mantel analysis.

The high degree of variability in F_{IS} and F_{IT} values merits some interpretation. High positive F_{IS} values suggested departure from Hardy-Weinberg expectations caused by a deficiency of heterozygotes within populations owing to inbreeding. High positive values were found for *P. vigilax, H. nigricans, N. micropogon,* and *G. affinis* (fig. 29.1). Avise and Smith (1974) reported high F_{IS} values across drainages for bluegill populations coupled with low F_{ST} values. They suggested that elevated F_{IS} values were statistical artifacts in their study. However, the above species also had the highest F_{ST} values in this study. High positive F_{IT} values indicated a greater number of homozygous individuals relative to that expected when data were pooled for all populations. F_{IT} provides an estimate of differentiation owing to inbreeding and population subdivision, and the highest F_{IT} values were found for the same species that had high F_{IS} values.

High negative F_{IS} or F_{IT} values indicate an excess of heterozygotes within subpopulations and within the total, respectively. Such values were characteristic of both species of *Etheostoma, C. confusus, A. mexicanus,* and *N. venustus* (fig. 29.1). Explanations for heterozygote excesses in these species might include selection favoring heterozygotes or fusion of subpopulations with alternately fixed or common alleles. None of the studies used for this analysis presented evidence that either mechanism occurred, and this phenomenon warrants further investigation in these species.

The two genetic variables that were the best predictors of biological clustering in the stepwise discriminant analysis were F_{ST} and polymorphism. Correlations between these genetic variables and biological features were tested with a Spearman rank correlations procedure. F_{ST} was significantly correlated ($r^2 = 0.67, P = 0.009$) with trophic position of the species, while polymorphism was significantly correlated with vertical distribution ($r^2 = 0.86, P = 0.000$) and social structure ($r^2 = 0.77, P = 0.001$).

High degrees of interpopulation heterogeneity should be expected for species such as *Etheostoma* spp., *C. confusus, H. nigricaus,* and *T. rhothoeca* that typically occur in a patchy environment, whereas heterogeneity should be lower for species that are widespread over continuous environments that are not as conducive to the formation of isolated demes. While values of F_{ST} averaged higher for species occurring in patchy habitats, polymorphism in these taxa averaged about half (0.135) that for fish existing in continuous habitat (0.263). This is similar to results of Nevo et al. (1983), who found that heterozygosity was lower in less mobile species whose distribution was patchy rather than continuous. The reasons for such a pattern are not readily apparent; nevertheless, certain hypotheses can be suggested. First, lower levels of polymorphism might be expected in fish species that are specialized to a narrow niche, such as isolated riffles. In contrast, a more variable genome would be expected for species of fish acting as generalists or occurring over a broader range of patches in a stream or river. This is concordant with Levins's (1968) hypothesis that genetic variation should be high in species that occur in heterogeneous environments. Second, isolation of populations of small effective size, as must occur in the benthic forms examined, offers increased opportunity for stochastic events and inbreeding to shape their genomes. These mechanisms often reduce genetic variation and would be less likely to impact the genomes of fish that occur over continuous habitats where gene flow can occur more readily. Inbreeding (F_{IS}) in the benthic forms was high only for *H. nigricans*, while this variable was also high for species such as *P. vigilax, N. micropogon,* and *G. affinis*, which occur as bottom-, mid-, and top-swimming species, respectively. Thus concordance of high levels of inbreeding and low polymorphism was not typical for these species. Nevertheless, opportunities for directional selection in a narrow habitat and genetic drift, founder effect, and/or bottlenecking to contribute to genomic structuring should be common in subdivided populations of benthic fish, effectively reducing polymorphism.

The arguments offered above are not without problems. Certain aspects of the data analysis are undoubtedly open to criticism, and justly so. For instance, more discrete quantification of a larger set of biological parameters would have been preferred. However, the unavailability of comparable data for a variety of species in any such study necessitates resorting to use of fewer characters defined in only broad detail. Nevertheless, correlations of genetic parameters with the generalized biological parameters of these fish were high. Notwithstanding the limitations of the data, the fact that genetic parameters such as F_{ST} and polymorphism had about 85% probability of placing species in their respective biological clusters in the discriminant model is significant. Even more significant is the fact that the relationship of these parameters to the limits of a fish species' habitat tolerance or preference presents a biologically meaningful scenario of the combined roles of gene flow, balancing selection, stochastic events, and population structure in shaping their genome. Any of these phenomena may act in concert or individually over time to alter the adaptive peak of a population. This is, of course, the shifting balance theory of Wright (1977, 1978).

This investigation demonstrates the need for more thorough analyses of the genetic structures and life histories of stream-fish populations. Analyses should include a synthesis of different data sets into an evolutionary framework that does not rely on single factors to explain natural phenomena.[1]

[1] I wish to thank T.L. King, R. Ward, and M.C. Wooten for their help in the statistical analyses, their insight into various conclusions presented, and their constructive comments of early drafts of this chapter. This work was supported by a Faculty Research Grant from North Texas State University.

30. Genotypic and Phenotypic Aspects of Niche Diversification in Fishes

Robert C. Vrijenhoek, Gudrun Marteinsdottir, and Russell Schenck

Abstract

Aspects of niche diversification are compared in two groups of fishes that inhabit areas of low fish-species diversity. Reduced interspecific competition should facilitate diversifying mechanisms that reduce the stress of intraspecific competition, but genetic recombination opposes the production of discrete sympatric species. Polymorphic niche subdivision in *Poeciliopsis* is maintained by cloning, a rapid and efficient mechanism for eliminating antagonistic recombination. Diverse assemblages of all-female clones constitute a major portion of the fish fauna in desert streams of northwestern Mexico. In contrast, ecological diversification among Arctic charr (*Salvelinus alpinus*) in Icelandic lakes apparently results from developmental plasticity. Recombination does not oppose a purely phenotypic means for diversification, but we cannot completely exclude genetic involvement in this instance, despite the lack of electrophoretic differentiation among discrete charr forms. Evolutionary costs and benefits of genotypic and phenotypic means of niche diversification are discussed.

The biotic and physical conditions that a species encounters may change substantially over time and space, forcing shifts, compressions, or expansions in its geographical distribution and use of resources. What factors permit a species to endure such changes in its intra- and inter-specific milieu? With a few notable exceptions (see Van Valen, 1965; Levins, 1968; MacArthur, 1972; Roughgarden, 1972; Loeschke, 1984) ecologists have paid little attention to the roles that both genetic and nongenetic variability may play in competitive interactions within and between species. It is foolish to pretend that species are fixed entities that do not respond to new competitive regimes. Yet it is equally simpleminded to consider species as genetically unconstrained entities with all the time and variability necessary to evolve optimal solutions to new challenges (Lewontin, 1979). To what extent is genotypic variation involved in niche shifts and niche diversification? How much of a role does phenotypic plasticity play? In this chapter we examine both genotypic and phenotypic factors affecting niche diversification in two very different fishes. For stream-dwelling populations of *Poeciliopsis* (Poecliidae) in northwestern Mexico diversification is clearly genotypic, through the production of distinct asexual clones. For lake-dwelling populations of Artic charr, *Salvelinus alpinus* (Salmonidae), in Iceland, diversification is phenotypic, apparently resulting from developmental plasticity. However, a unifying feature ties together the niche structure of these fishes: both live in areas of low fish-species diversity. We believe that, because of weak interspecific competition in these environments, diversifying mechanisms that decrease the stress of intense intraspecific competition will be strongly favored.

Several theoretical models and many empirical data suggest that this is a tenable argument. For a particular resource dimension (e.g., food or space) one can describe niche width as the variance in resources used by a particular species. Roughgarden (1972) provided a phenotypic model for the evolution of niche width. Applying the logic of analysis of variance, he partitioned niche width into two components: (1) the "within-phenotype component" (WPC), which is the breadth of resources taken by any particular phenotype, and (2) the "between-phenotype component" (BPC), which is the difference in resource use by different phenotypes. Thus total niche width of a species (WPC + BPC) can be expanded by increasing one or both of its components. At the extremes, for two species with equally broad niches, one species might be composed of a polymorphic array of specialists (high BPC, low WPC) and the other composed of monomorphic generalists (low BPC, high WPC).

What happens when a sexually reproducing species invades an underexploited heterogeneous environment? Initially colonists experience an ecological vacuum because of their low density and a competitive vacuum because of the lack of potentially competitive species (Pianka, 1974b). Colonization of species-depauperate environments is often accompanied by ecological release (MacArthur and Wilson, 1967). Variant individuals often exploit less strongly contested or even marginal resources, as compared with related populations in species-packed environments. At first, such niche expansions may result entirely from behavioral plasticity (WPC), but, given sufficient time and an adequate base of genetic variation, the BPC of niche width may also expand by natural selection and thus result in more efficient exploitation of continuously distributed resources (Roughgarden, 1972). In a patchy environment, however, disruptive selection is less effective in maintaining discrete phenotypes because genetic recombination ensures that multilocus genotypes are reshuffled in each generation (Felsenstein, 1981).

Cloning, as observed in *Poeciliopsis*, is an efficient solution to the problem of "antagonistic recombination" (Felsenstein, 1981) because it effectively isolates whole genomes in one step. Given a sufficient source of clonal variation, ecological release is likely to proceed more rapidly in asexual populations than in sexual populations, a factor that may contribute to the colonization abilities of asexual organisms (Roughgarden, 1972). According to the "frozen niche variation" model, recurrent origins of new clones from a genetically variable sexual ancestor provide the base of variation upon which interclonal selection acts to produce a structured assemblage of clones with reduced resource overlap (Vrijenhoek, 1979, 1984a, b). Similar models have been explored by Bell (1982) and tested in simulations by Case and Taper (1985). Examples of clonal niche diversification in *Poeciliopsis* and several other asexual animals were recently reviewed by Vrijenhoek (1984a) and Lynch (1984). Because asexuality is rare in animals, this avenue for niche diversification may be closed to most species (Williams, 1975).

An alternative means for expanding the BPC is through developmental plasticity. Developmental plasticity has several advantages over genotypic forms of niche diversification in sexual populations. Plasticity avoids the problem of antagonistic recombination. Furthermore, in fluctuating or unpredictable environments, plasticity may be less costly because each form is produced in proportion to the environmental stimuli that induce it. While the capacity to be phenotypically plastic undoubtedly has an underlying genetic basis, divergent forms coexisting in a population may be genotypically identical. For example, all individuals may contain a set of "switch" genes that are triggered by environmental stimuli during early development (Wagner and Mitchell, 1964). We know very little about genetic processes that permit environmentally controlled phenotypic variation or "polyphenisms" (Sheppard, 1975), but see Collins and Cheek (1983) and Shapiro (1984) for recent reviews. Thus we advance our argument by citing examples rather than mechanisms or theory. Among vertebrates the larval salamander, *Ambystoma tigrinum*, exhibits a clear example of trophic polyphenism. Broad-gaped "cannibal" morphs sometimes appear in populations largely composed of "typical" larvae (Collins et al., 1980). The "cannibal" morph is indiced by crowding, and it feeds on the "typical" form (Collins and Cheek, 1983). A similar polyphenism may occur in the Mexican goodeid fish *Ilyodon furcidens* (Turner et al., 1983). Populations in the Río Armeria contain an *A* morph having a narrow mouth and a *B* morph having a wide mouth. Breeding studies have not revealed whether genetic factors or developmental mechanisms are responsible for these dichotomous trophic states. The Cuatro Ciénegas cichlid fish, *Cichlasoma minckleyi*, may also be a good candidate for polyphenism. This species exhibits two dentitional morphs, one having generalized filliform teeth on the pharyngeal bones and the other having snail-crushing molariform teeth. Profound functional shifts in the feeding apparatus derive from relatively minor changes in morphology (Liem and Kaufman, 1984). Experimental studies have not revealed genetic factors controlling these distinct trophic polymorphisms (Kornfield, pers. comm.), and developmental studies of other polymorphic cichlids suggest that plasticity may be involved. In both *Astatorheochromis alluaudi* and *Cichlasoma citrinellum* feeding on hard as opposed to soft diets can induce similar dentitional differences (Greenwood, 1965; Axel Meyer, pers. comm.). These examples provide useful models for our study of Icelandic charr, and we wonder how many more models are hidden in species names or are referred to as "species flocks" because of a tendency to associate morphological differentiation with reproductive isolation.

Sonoran *Poeciliopsis*

Ecologically diverse forms of small viviparous fishes in the genus *Poeciliopsis* (Poeciliidae) inhabit unpredictable desert streams in northwestern Mexico. Our ecological studies focus on the Río del Fuerte near the Sonora-Sinaloe border, where only five species of topminnows occur (table 30.1). *Poecilia butleri, Poeciliopsis latidens* and *Poeciliopsis prolifica* occur in large, permanent streams (Miller, 1960), but little is known of their ecology. An even more depauperate fish fauna inhabits arroyos and springs in the upper reaches of the Arroyo de Jaguari. *Poeciliopsis monacha* and *Poeciliopsis lucida* are the only sexually reproducing topminnows occuring there, and hybridization between them has produced diverse assemblages of clonally reproducing all-female biotypes (Schultz, 1969). The triploid all-female biotypes are gynogenetic. Sperm from males of a related sexual species is required to activate cleavage of triploid eggs, but inheritance of the triploid genotype is strictly clonal (Schultz, 1967; Cimino, 1972a; Vrijenhoek, 1972; Moore, 1977). The diploid all-female biotypes are hybridogenetic, that is, having a modified form of meiosis that transmits only a haploid *monacha* genome between generations and reestablishes diploidy through fertilization by sperm from *P. lucida* males (Schultz, 1961, 1966, 1969; Cimino, 1972b; Vrijenhoek, 1972). Because the haploid *monacha* (M) genome is cloned and the *lucida* (L) genome is sexually derived, at Kallman's suggestion we refer to distinct M genotypes of the ML hybrids as "hemiclones" (Vrijenhoek et al., 1978). Dynamics of the sperm-dependent relationship between sexual and clonal forms of *Poeciliopsis* have been explored in laboratory experiments, computer simulations, and analytical models (Moore, 1984).

Table 30.1. Ecological Characteristics of the Poeciliid Fishes Inhabiting the Rio del Fuerte

Species	Primary Diet	Adult Female Size Range, SL* (mm)	Typical Habitat
Poeciliopsis monacha	Omnivorous	25–35	Springs and arroyos
P. lucida	Deposit feeder	25–40	Open, sunny streams
P. latidens	Unknown	25–35	Riverine currents
P. prolifica	Unknown	25–30	Peripheral pools
Poecilia butleri	Filamentous algae	25–50	Open, sunny streams

**Poeciliopsis* are sexually dimorphic with adult males generally 19 to 25 mm SL.

Spatial segregation contributes to resource partitioning among sexual and clonal forms of *Poeciliopsis* inhabiting the Arroyo de Jaguari and its feeder streams (Vrijenhoek, 1978; Schenck and Vrijenhoek, 1986). Two reproductive complexes, each composed of a sexual host and two sperm-dependent clones, inhabit this stream (table 30.2). The *lucida* complex occurs only in the highly productive downstream portion of this river. The *monacha* complex completely dominates less productive arroyos and headwater springs that feed this river. Within the *monacha* complex members segregate according to stream order and productivity. Clone MML/II is most frequent in sunny and productive downstream areas but is rare in headwater springs and rocky arroyos. Females of *P. monacha* and clone MML/I show the opposite trend. On a local basis within individual pools, adults of both clones MML/I and MML/II are consistently more frequent in the current, and adult *P. monacha* females are more frequent in still-water areas. Striking spatial differences among adults occur over distances of only a few meters, and they are consistent despite seasonal changes in fish density and frequencies. A separate analysis during the reproductive season revealed that juveniles of *P. monacha* and MML/II behaved similarly to their adults (table 30.3), but clone MML/I juveniles sharply reverse the adult pattern. These demographic aspects of niche displacement require further investigation.

Food habits and aggressive behavior of these forms are currently being examined (Schenck, unpub. data). Both clones MML/I and MML/II increased the proportion of insects in their diet when they were feeding in currents, but *P. monacha* females did not. High levels of aggression occurred among these forms, but we have not yet determined whether aggression is specifically or randomly directed. Thus interference competition appears to structure patterns of spatial segregation and diets in these fishes. Seasonal shifts in dietary overlap were apparent within this complex. When aquatic insects were abundant, significant dietary differences among forms of *Poeciliopsis* were often apparent. However, in seasons when aquatic insect larvae were rare, all fish were deposit feeders, eating the rapidly replenished microfloral assemblage that covers the walls and bottoms of pools.

Substantial differences also occur among members of the *lucida* complex. Females of *P. lucida* and hemiclone ML/VII segregate on a scale related to local habitat patchiness, but hemiclone ML/VIII females were more equitably distributed throughout the stream (Schenck and Vrijenhoek, 1986). An ongoing study of predatory behavior found that *P. lucida* was the least efficient predator, hemiclone ML/VII was intermediate, and hemiclone ML/VIII was the most efficient (K. Spindler, unpub. data). Natural food habits of these forms corroborate the laboratory findings (Schenck, unpub. data). *Poeciliopsis lucida* and ML/VII were primarily deposit feeders. Hemiclone ML/VIII, the most efficient predator in laboratory experiments, was also the most insectivorous of these forms in nature (Schenck, unpub. data) and the most aggressive of eight Río Fuerte clones tested in independent laboratory studies (strain T70-3Cw; Keegan-Rogers and Schultz, 1984).

Additional studies of these and other clones are under way in our laboratory and in the laboratory of R. J. Schultz. To date, all carefully designed ecological, behavioral, and physiological studies of *Poeciliopsis* clones have revealed differences that might contribute to spatial and temporal partitioning of resources and to differential survival and reproduction in the heterogeneous environments of these desert streams (reviewed in Schultz, 1982; Vrijenhoek, 1984a).

Icelandic Charr

The extraordinary variability in morphological and life-history characteristics of Arctic charr, *Salvelinus alpinus* (Salmonidae) has led to considerable controversy over its status as a single species. Divergent, landlocked populations

Table 30.2. Members of the *Poeciliopsis Monacha* and *P. Lucida* Complexes of the Arroyo de Jaguari

Sexual Host	All-female biotype	Ploidy	Reproduction	Clones
Poeciliopsis monacha	*P. 2 monacha-lucida*	3*n*	Gynogenesis	MML/I, MML/II
P. lucida	*P. monacha-lucida*	2*n*	Hybridogenesis	ML/VII, ML/VIII

Table 30.3. Habitat Selection Among Forms of the *Poeciliopsis Monacha* Complex in the Arroyo de los Plátanos

Age and Habitat	Percent of Frequency				N	χ^2
	Poecliopsis Monacha Females	Clone MML/I	Clone MML/II	*P. Monacha* Males		
Adults						
Current	55.3	28.7	6.9	9.1	1,000	108.4†
Pool	74.3	14.4	3.1	8.2	1,407	(DF = 3)
Total (N)	1,598	490	112	207	2,407	
Juveniles						
Current	39.6‡	38.4	22.0	—	152	10.2§
Pool	43.3	53.3	3.3	—	60	(DF = 2)
Total (N)	80	90	35	—	212	

*The hypothesis of no association between the form of fish and habitat was examined with a contingency test.
†$P \leq 0.001$.
‡Males and females were undifferentiated; thus, all *P. monacha* were placed in this category.
§$P \leq 0.01$.

occur throughout islands and continental regions of the North Atlantic and along the coastline of the Arctic Ocean (Vladykov, 1963; Behnke, 1980; Johnson, 1980). Discrete forms differing in habitat selection, growth rate, age and size at maturity, time of spawning, coloration, and body proportions often coexist in single lakes (Fridriksson, 1939; Frost, 1965; Hindar and Jonsson, 1982; Klemetsen and Grotnes, 1980; Lamby, 1941; Nordeng, 1983; Skreslet, 1973; review in Johnson, 1980). The multiple sympatric forms in some lakes may represent separately invading stocks or species that evolved in allopatry during pre- and inter-glacial periods (Henricson and Nyman, 1976; Nyman, 1972; Klementsen and Grotnes, 1980) or perhaps during or since the last glacial period (Behnke, 1972, 1980). Alternatively, they may be ecologically plastic forms that derive from a single genetically uniform population (Jonsson and Hindar, 1982; Nordeng, 1983; Savvaitova, 1980).

Arctic charr are the predominant fish inhabiting the large, oligotrophic, species-depauperate lakes of Iceland. In one such lake, Thingvallavatn, the only other fishes are brown trout (*Salmo trutta*) and three-spine sticklebacks (*Gasterosteus aculeatus*). At least five Icelandic lakes contain two or more discrete forms of charr. Thingvallavatn is exceptional because six forms have been described (Saemundsson, 1904, 1917; Fridricksson, 1939). More recent studies of morphology, growth, and reproduction in charr from Thingvallavatn revealed four discrete forms: a benthos-feeding dwarf charr (8–15 cm at maturity), a planktivorous pelagic charr (18–20 cm), a piscivorous large charr (25–50 cm), and a mollusk-eating large charr (25–50 cm; Skulason, 1983). Both the dwarf and the large mollusk-eating charr are characterized by blunt snouts and subterminal mouths, while the pelagic and the large piscivorous charr have pointed snouts and terminal mouths (Skulason, 1983; Marteinsdottir and Vrijenhoek, unpub. data).

Charr from Thingvallavatn were analyzed electrophoretically with the use of protein products of 32 presumptive gene loci (Marteinsdottir, 1984). Because our initial sample was

Fig. 30.1. The sympatric adult forms of Arctic charr in Thingvallavatn. Top to bottom: large mollusk eater, large piscivore, pelagic, and dwarf form.

Table 30.4. Allelic Frequencies at Polymorphic Loci in Sympatric Forms of Icelandic Arctic Charr from Thingvallavatn*

Locus (Allele)	Large, 1980	Large, 1981	Pelagic, 1980	Pelagic, 1981	Dwarf, 1981	χ^2
Mdh-3, 4 (*F*)	0.674	0.654	0.600	0.653	0.500	2.2 NS†
(± 1 SE)	(0.069)	(0.066)	(0.069)	(0.067)	(0.112)	(Df = 4)
Est-2 (*F*)	0.833	0.729	0.714	0.792	0.800	2.5 NS
(± 1 SE)	(0.076)	(0.064)	(0.069)	(0.058)	(0.089)	(Df = 4)
Sample size (*N*)	26	25	26	26	10	
Heterozygosity, %:	2.7	2.7	2.6	2.6	3.1	
Polymorphic loci, %:	6.2	6.2	6.2	6.2	6.2	

*Estimates of average heterozygosity and percentage of polymorphic loci (95% criterion) are given. Chi-square test of homogeneity among groups is based on a contingency analysis of allelic numbers.

†Not significant.

small, we separated mature adults on the basis of body size. The two large forms, piscivorous and mollusk-eating, were pooled and compared with samples of pelagic and dwarf charr (fig. 30.1). Only two gene loci (Mdh-3, 4 and Est-2) were polymorphic (frequency of variant allele greater than 0.05). Within each of the three size classes the phenotypic distribution of polymorphic allozymes fit Hardy-Weinberg equilibrium (HWE) expectations. As such, there is no indication that the composite "large" group consisted of more than a single panmictic unit. Furthermore, allele frequencies at the two polymorphic loci were not significantly different between any of the three sympatric forms within years or between forms in different years (table 30.4). No significant deviation from HWE expectations were observed when all individual genotypes were pooled across the three life-history forms (table 30.5). This result indicates a lack of population genetic subdivision and suggests that the three forms constitute a single panmictic unit. Ongoing comparisons with adequate samples of the large piscivorous and large mollusk-eating forms have produced the same result, and we are currently examining charr from other Icelandic lakes (Marteinsdottir and Vrijenhoek, unpub. data).

Although striking differences in ecological, morphological, and life-history characteristics exist among charr forms within a lake, they appear to share a common gene pool. Similar results have been repoted for Scandinavian charr where also two loci (Mdh-4,5 and Est-2) of 37 were polymorphic (Andersson et al., 1983). Andersson's results did not support the existence of more than one discrete stock in Lake Gardiken, where two had been previously described (Gydemo, 1979). Breeding studies provided additional evidence that discrete sympatric forms of charr may not differ genetically. Nordeng (1983) found that all discrete forms, previously recognized as an anadromous versus small and large residents, can develop from a single parent of any of these types. Ecological studies have described niche shifts depending on the presence or absence of potentially competitive species. Nilsson (1977) demonstrated the ability of charr to switch feeding habits when co-occurring with brown trout. Two sympatric charr forms in Norway showed dietary separation when food was scarce, but they fed on similar food items in the same habitat when food production was high (Hindar and Jonsson, 1982).

Despite the lack of electrophoretic differentiation among charr forms, we cannot completely rule out genetic involvement. For example, Thingvallavatn is considered to be only 9,000 years old (Saemundsson, 1965), and the time since the initial invasion by charr may not have been sufficient for an accumulation of electrophoretically detectable genetic variation. Genetic differentiation may have occurred in restricted subsets of genes affecting growth and morphology. Carson (1975) suggested that species might have "open" and "closed" genetic systems. An open system of neutral or "quasineutral" genes (perhaps allozymes) might be permissive to gene flow, but a closed system (perhaps genes affecting growth and development) might be protected from extensive recombination through strong epistatic selection. Any degree of habitat-specific or phenotype-specific mating preferences of charr forms would help protect the closed system from antagonistic recombination and might eventually lead to speciation (Rosenzweig, 1978; Felsenstein, 1981; Rice, 1984).

Table 30.5. Observed and Expected (in Parentheses) Genotypic Frequencies at Mdh-4,5 and Est-2 Loci for Pooled Samples, Including All Charr Forms in 1980 and 1981 Samples

Loci	*F/F*	*F/S*	*S/S*	*N*	χ^2 (*DF* = 1)
Mdh-4,5					
Pooled 1981 samples	24 (23.9)	29 (29.2)	9 (8.9)	62	0.003 NA*
Pooled 1980 samples	19 (19.4)	23 (22.2)	6 (6.4)	48	0.056 NA
Est-2					
Pooled 1981 samples	33 (34.1)	23 (20.7)	2 (3.1)	58	0.705 NA
Pooled 1980 samples	27 (27.2)	16 (15.6)	2 (2.2)	45	0.037 NA

*Not significant.

Summary and Conclusions

The mechanisms of niche diversification used by Icelandic charr and Sonoran *Poeciliopsis* differ completely, yet we believe that primary attention should focus on a common feature of their respective environments. Both fish inhabit geographical areas that have low fish-species diversity. Reduced interspecific interactions in these competitive vacuums facilitate disrupting mechanisms that in turn reduce the stress of relatively intense intraspecific competition. Polymorphic niche subdivision in populations of *Poeciliopsis* is maintained by cloning. Diverse multiclonal assemblages of these unisexual-hybrid forms often constitute a major portion of the fish fauna in the heterogeneous springs and streams of Sonora, Mexico (Vrijenhoek, 1979, 1984a, b). Ongoing studies of predatory behavior, spatial patchiness, and food habits reveal significant differences in resource use among coexisting clones and their sexual ancestors (Vrijenhoek, 1978; Schenck and Vrijenhoek, 1986). However, cloning in these fish has not led to externally visible polymorphismsas extreme as those found in the charr. We can distinguish among clones only through electrophoresis or tissue-grafting experiments, and the ecological differences among clones are subtle compared to the morphological and life-history differences among charr forms.

The extraordinary degree of life-history and morphological differentiation among sympatric charr forms led many investigators to consider them legitimate species, and local fishermen have common names for them. The sympatric forms segregate trophically during the periods of most intense feeding, but unfortunately information on spatial separation during spawning are insufficient to permit evaluation of randon mating. Although we cannot exclude the hypothesis that the phenotypic variation detected among these forms has a genetic basis, lines of evidence reviewed herein suggest that such a hypothesis may be unnecessary.

Our ideas concerning charr may also pertain to other fish "species flocks." Assemblages of closely related endemic forms of fishes occur in a number of the world's larger lakes (see Echelle and Kornfield, 1984), and they have often been cited as examples of explosive speciation (Mayr, 1963) and punctuational evolutionary events (Greenwood, 1984). "Competitive speciation" (Rosenzweig, 1978) has been suggested as a mechanism for these adaptive radiations that presumably followed invasion of newly formed lakes by a few generalized riverine species (Smith and Todd, 1984; Barbour and Chernoff 1984). Are all the closely related morphotypes in these flocks reproductively isolated species, or are many of them just polyphenic forms belonging to a smaller number of developmentally plastic species? As in our study of charr, electrophoretic studies often fail to reveal "diagnostic" allelic differences among putative species in these flocks; but this failure is not due to an absence of potentially discriminating variation (Kornfield and Carpenter, 1984; Humphries, 1984; Sage et al., 1984). Fish populations inhabiting lakes and rivers can undergo substantial genetic differentiation without distinct geographical or reproductive barriers (Avise and Felley, 1979; Imhof et al., 1980; White and Turner, 1984). The fact that many of the discrete morphological and ecological forms in the putative "species flocks" have not diverged genetically should lead one to question their species status. We agree with Turner and Grosse (1980) that the number of "species" in these flocks may be grossly overestimated as a result of uncritical inferences from morphological studies. These fascinating assemblages of differentiated forms must be reinvestigated and the hypothesis of developmental plasticity treated more seriously.

Various mechanisms exist for niche expansion in response to intraspecific competitive interactions and disruptive selection in species-depauperate environments. Whichever course an invading species takes is dependent on many factors. Mechanisms for cloning may not be present in many species; but for taxa in which asexuality is possible, cloning can potentially contribute to rapid niche expansion (Roughgarden, 1972; Bell, 1982). Asexuality is generally more common in recently colonized habitats, disturbed habitats, and other environments that are characterized by low biotic diversity (Vandel, 1928; Suomolainen, 1950; Ghiselin, 1974; Glesenser and Tillman, 1978). Similarly, mechanisms for developmental plasticity may not be present in many animals, but the role of broadly plastic, "general purpose genotypes" is well documented for many colonizing plant species (Baker, 1965). Fishes are not as rigid in their reproductive and developmental processes as many other vertebrates, particularly birds and mammals. Asexuality occurs broadly in many fish taxa (see Schultz, 1977; Moore, 1984), and developmental plasticity may be more widespread than is presently realized.[1]

[1]The manuscript benefited from discussions with Jim Collins, Karel Liem, Irv Kornfield, and Axel Meyer. We thank F. Allendorf for helping interpret the electrophoretic patterns in charr. We are indebted to the National Science Foundation, which has provided uninterrupted support for the *Poeciliopsis* studies over the past eleven years, and to the Departmento de Pesca, which provided collecting permits (13 and 4962) for the Mexican studies. Special thanks go to Gudbjorn Einarsson for providing samples and valuable information concerning local charr populations.

31. Genetic Variation, Divergence, and Relationships in the Subgenus *Xenisma* of the Genus *Fundulus*

James S. Rogers and Robert C. Cashner

Abstract

Electrophoretic analysis of 24 loci was performed on nearly 300 specimens of *Fundulus (Xenisma) catenatus, Fundulus stellifer, Fundulus rathbuni,* and *Fundulus julisia*. Four additional species representing two other nominal subgenera were included in the study as outgroups. All species analyzed were electrophoretically distinctive, and there were several intraspecific differences in populations of *F. catenatus* and *F. stellifer*. *Fundulus stellifer* populations from the Tallapoosa River were separable from Coosa and Alabama river populations by complete allelic differences at 6 loci.

A phylogenetic analysis of the data revealed relationships among *F. catenatus* populations different from those suggested by morphology and further revealed that *F. julisia* is the sister group of the other three species, *F. rathbuni* is the sister group of *F. catenatus–F. stellifer,* and the Tallapoosa *F. stellifer* is the sister group of *F. catenatus*.

Populations of *Xenisma* have significantly lower heterozygosities than populations of the outgroup taxa, probably owing to the reduced opportunity for gene flow between populations in the upland streams inhabited by *Xenisma* relative to the lowland streams and estuaries inhabited by the out-groups.

The subgenus *Xenisma* of the genus *Fundulus* consists of five closely related species distributed primarily in streams draining the Central Highlands and the Piedmont Province of the eastern United States (fig. 31.1). Williams and Etnier (1982) diagnosed *Xenisma* and considered it to represent a monophyletic group comprised of the presumably extinct whiteline topminnow, *Fundulus albolineatus*; the northern studfish, *Fundulus catenatus;* the southern studfish, *Fundulus stellifer;* the speckled killifish, *Fundulus rathbuni;* and the Barrens topminnow, *Fundulus julisia*.

Fundulus julisia and *F. catenatus* are the only two species of *Xenisma* currently found syntopically, though Thomerson (1969) accepted a record of *F. stellifer* and *F. catenatus* from West Fork Chickamauga Creek (Tennessee River drainage in northern Georgia), and distribution maps indicate syntopy for *F. catenatus* and the extinct *F. albolineatus* (Shute, 1980).

In recognizing *Xenisma* as a monophyletic group, Williams and Etnier (1982) essentially followed earlier arrangements by Miller (1955) and Brown (1957). Williams and Etnier rejected expansion of *Xenisma* to include such species as *Fundulus diaphanus, Fundulus waccamensis,* and *Fundulus seminolis* (the subgenus *Fontinus*, after Brown [1957]), the brackish-water forms *Fundulus majalis* and *Fundulus similis,* and *Fundulus parvipinnis, Fundulus lima,* and *Fundulus persimilis* from California and Mexico (after Farris [1968] and Chen [1971]). Wiley (1985) in a phylogenetic analysis recognized *Xenisma* (sensu Williams and Etnier, 1982) as one of four monophyletic groups resolvable in *Fundulus*.

Thomerson (1969) recognized eight populations of *F. catenatus* on morphological criteria (Virginia, Green River, Cumberland River, Tennessee River, Indiana, Ozark, Ouachita, and Homochitto River; fig. 31.1). He considered *F. stellifer* to be the allopatric replacement of *F. catenatus* in the southeastern United States and recognized six populations with contiguous ranges (upper Coosa River, middle Coosa River, Alabama River, Cahaba River, Tallapoosa River, and Chattahoochee River; fig. 31.1).

Our purposes in this study were (1) to examine the electrophoretic variation in *F. catenatus* and *F. stellifer* to determine whether the morphologically distinctive populations of these two species were also distinctive electrophoretically, (2) to determine phylogenetic relationships within *Xenisma* using members of other nominal subgenera of *Fundulus* as out-groups, and (3) to compare the average heterozygosity in the essentially allopatric stream dwelling species of *Xenisma* with that of the wider-ranging coastal forms such as *F. majalis, F. similis, Fundulus heteroclitus* and *Fundulus grandis*.

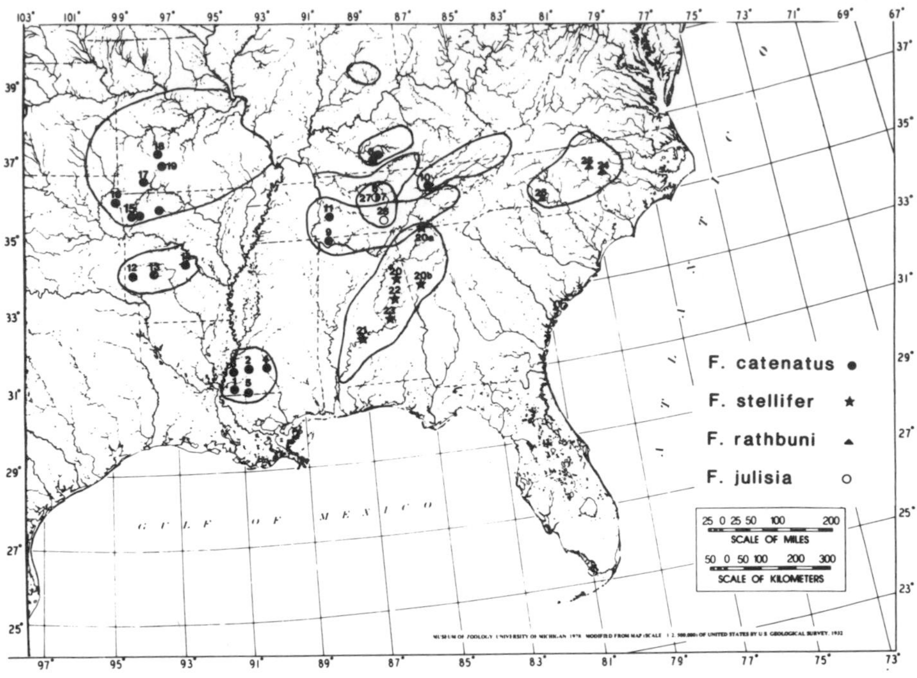

Fig. 31.1. Distributions and collection localities for the four extant species of *Xenisma*. The locality numbers correspond to those of appendix, tables 31A.1–A.7.

Materials and Methods

Collections

Nineteen samples of *F. catenatus* were collected from six of the eight populations recognized by Thomerson (1969). Populations of *F. stellifer* from the middle Coosa, Tallapoosa, Alabama, upper Coosa and Chatahoochee rivers were sampled. *Fundulus julisia* was collected from both drainages in its range, and *F. rathbuni* was taken from the Neuse, Cape Fear and Pee Dee drainages in North Carolina (collection sites for all extant *Xenisma* are shown in fig. 31.1 and identified by number in appendix, tables 31A.1–A.7). Localities for species used as out-groups are as follows: *F. majalis,* Pamlico Sound, North Carolina; *F. similis*, Grand Isle, Plaquemines Parish, Louisiana; *F. grandis,* Lake Pontchartrain, Orleans Parish, Louisiana; *F. heteroclitus,* Chesapeake Bay, North Hampton County, Virginia.

All specimens in the analysis were collected between 1980 and 1984. Specimens were immediately frozen on dry ice or in liquid nitrogen and kept frozen until they were dissected. Voucher specimens and carcasses are maintained in the vertebrate collection or the frozen tissue collection of the Department of Biological Sciences, University of New Orleans (UNO). Complete collection data for vouchers are available from the authors.

Samples of skeletal muscle, liver, and eye dissected from each specimen were individually wrapped in aluminum foil and stored at $-60°$ C until they were needed for electrophoresis.

Electrophoresis

Electrophoretic variation in 24 isozyme loci from skeletal muscle, liver, and eye (table 31.1) was assayed by starch gel electrophoresis according to the methods described in Stein et al. (1985), using only the tris-critrate buffer system. Enzyme names and numbers follow Harris and Hopkinson (1978). Enzyme and locus abbreviations (table 31.1) are modified from those suggested by Buth (1983) to produce locus designations that consist of no more than four characters but retain most of the desired information. This terminology facilitates the use of locus and allele symbols directly on figures rather than substituting numbers or single letters for them, which forces the reader to refer repeatedly to a list of equivalences. In our system the enzyme name is represented by a two- or three-letter abbreviation with the first letter capitalized, the locus is designated by an unhyphenated suffix consisting of one capitalized letter, and the intracellular localization (mitochondrial or supernatant), where recognized, is indicated by an unhyphenated prefix consisting of a single lower case letter (*m* or *s*, respectively). Alleles are designated by lower-case letters assigned in the order in which the alleles were discovered and appended to the locus designations as superscripts.

Three enzyme loci in this study cannot be readily assigned homologies to comparable loci of other vertebrates. The one peptidase (PepA) of our study is a tripeptidase (substrate, leu-gly-gly) and a dimer. The peptidase referred to as *A* in some other vertebrates is a dipeptidase (Harris and Hopkinson, 1978; D. Buth, pers. comm.). However, the major tripeptidase (called *B*, at least in human beings) is a monomer

Table 31.1. Enzyme Systems and Loci Examined

Enzyme	Locus Abbreviation	EC Number	Tissue
Glucose phosphate isomerase		5.3.1.9	
	GpiA		Muscle
	GpiB		Muscle
Phosphoglucomutasc		2.7.5.1	
	PgmA		Muscle
Lactate dehydrogenase		1.1.1.27	
	LdhA		Muscle
	LdhB		Eye
	LdhC		Eye
Malate dehydrogenase		1.1.1.37	
	sMdA		Muscle
	sMdB		Muscle
	mMdA		Muscle
Glycerol-3-phosphate dehydrogenase	GpdA	1.1.1.8	Muscle
Isocitrate dehydrogenase		1.1.1.42	
	mIdA		Muscle
	sIdA		Liver
Malic enzyme		1.1.1.40	
	MeA		Muscle
	MeB		Muscle
Aspartate aminotransaminase		2.6.1.1	
	sAtA		Liver
	sAtB		Muscle
	mAtA		Liver
Peptidase (leu-gly-gly)		3.4.11	
	PepA		Muscle
Creatine kinase		2.7.3.2	
	CkA		Muscle
Alcohol dehydrogenase		1.1.1.1	
	AdhA		Liver
Adenylate kinase		2.7.4.3	
	AkA		Muscle
6-phosphogluconate dehydrogenase	PgdA	1.1.1.44	Muscle
Mannose phosphate isomerase		5.3.1.8	
	MpiA		Liver
Sorbitol dehydrogenase		1.1.1.14	
	SdhA		Liver

(Harris and Hopkinson, 1978). Therefore, we have arbitrarily called our peptidase PepA.

Buth (1984) reports that cyprinid fishes have two malic enzyme loci, a mitochondrial form predominating in muscle tissue and a supernatant form found principally in liver. However, both malic enzyme loci that we discovered in *Xenisma* predominate in muscle. Therefore, we have arbitrarily labeled them MeA and MeB with no intracellular designation.

Data Analysis

Several groups of samples that were electrophoretically identical or nearly so were aggregated: (1) three samples of *F. catenatus,* all designated as locality 15, from the White River, Arkansas; (2) three samples of *F. catenatus* (localities 17–19) from the White River and Missouri River, Missouri; and (3) three samples of *F. rathbuni* (localities 24–26) from the Neuse, Pee Dee, and Cape Fear rivers, North Carolina. This resulted in 28 population samples, 24 for *Xenisma* and 4 from the outgroups. Two additional samples (localities 20a and 20b) were added later in the study and were not included in the data analysis. However, they are nearly identical in allozyme composition to *F. stellifer* from the Coosa River (locality 20; see app. tables 31A.1–A.7) and can be considered part of that sample.

The electrophoretic variation within and between the 28 samples was analyzed with the aid of three computer programs: a modified version of BIOSYS-1 (Swofford and Selander, 1981), MINT (F. J. Rohlf, State University of New York, Stony Brook), and a modified version of PHYLAL (Rogers, 1984). All computations were performed on the DEC-10 computer of the UNO Computer Research Center.

Results

Allozyme Variability

Of the 24 loci assayed, only 1 LdhB, showed no variation within or between population samples. The variation of the other 23 loci, expressed as allele frequencies, is tabulated in appendix tables 31A.1—A.7.

Relationships of Taxa

Several phylogenetic trees were derived from the allele frequencies by the method of Rogers (1984), with the use of a modified form of Cavalli-Sforza and Edwards (1967) chord distance rather than the Rogers (1972) distance. The modified chord distance for multiple loci is the arithmetic mean of the single-locus distances. Tree topologies were derived by several means, including the distance Wagner procedure (Farris, 1972; Swofford and Selander, 1981), the TRETOP subroutine of PHYLAL (Rogers, 1984), and manual manipulation of the latter two topologies. In each case the ancestral allele frequencies were optimized by the hyperboloid approximation procedure (Rogers, 1984). Figure 31.2 depicts the phylogenetic tree that was derived from the distance Wagner topology. It has a total length (TL) of 3.03. A slightly longer tree (TL = 3.04) was produced by modifying the tree of fig. 31.2 to make Tallapoosa *F. stellifer* the sister group of Coosa *F. stellifer* rather than of *F. catenatus*. A considerably longer tree (TL = 3.22) was produced by the TRETOP subroutine of PHYLAL (Rogers, 1984). Other hand-modified trees were also found to be longer than the tree in fig. 31.2.

Figure 31.3 is a tree produced by consolidating population samples of *Xenisma* into the indicated groups, consolidating out-group samples into two groups (*majalis-similis* and *grandis-heteroclitus*), and performing a character Wagner analysis (Farris, 1970) of the presence or absence of alleles in "significant" frequencies in the 11 resulting groups. An allele was assumed to be present in significant frequency in an ingroup if it had a frequency $\geqslant 0.20$ and in an outgroup if it had a frequency of $\geqslant 0.10$. The lower threshold frequency for outgroups was imposed to produce a more conservative estimate of derived character states in the ingroup.

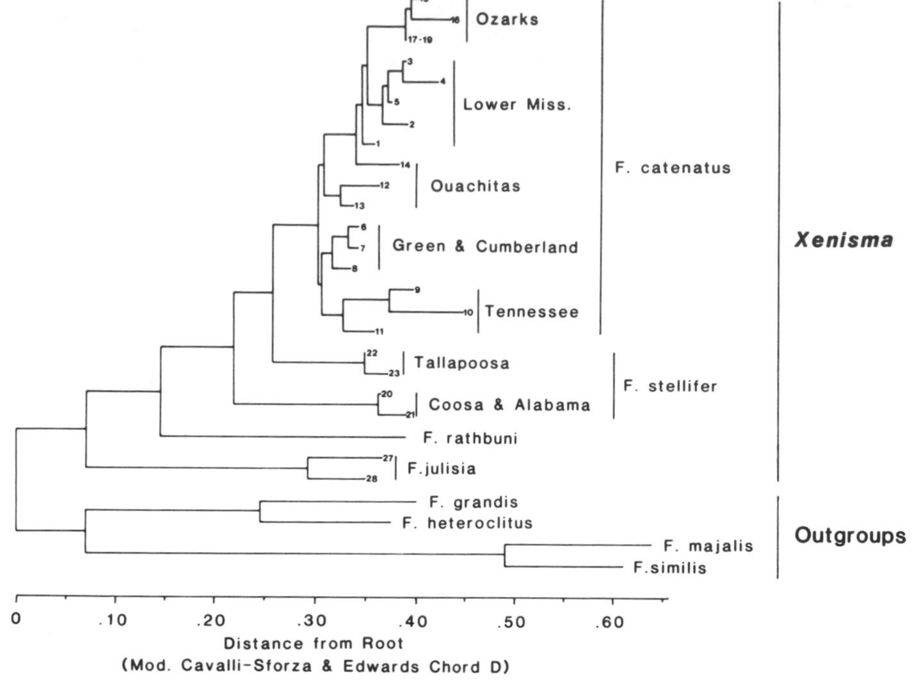

Fig. 31.2. Phylogenetic tree for populations of the four extant species of *Xenisma* and out-groups derived from allele frequencies at 24 allozyme loci by the distance Wagner procedure (Farris, 1972; Swofford and Selander, 1981) with the use of a modified form of Cavalli-Sforza and Edwards's (1967) chord distance with branch-length optimization by the hyperboloid approximation procedure (Rogers, 1984). Numbers for certain populations of *Xenisma* correspond to those of appendix, tables 31A.1–A.7, and fig. 31.1.

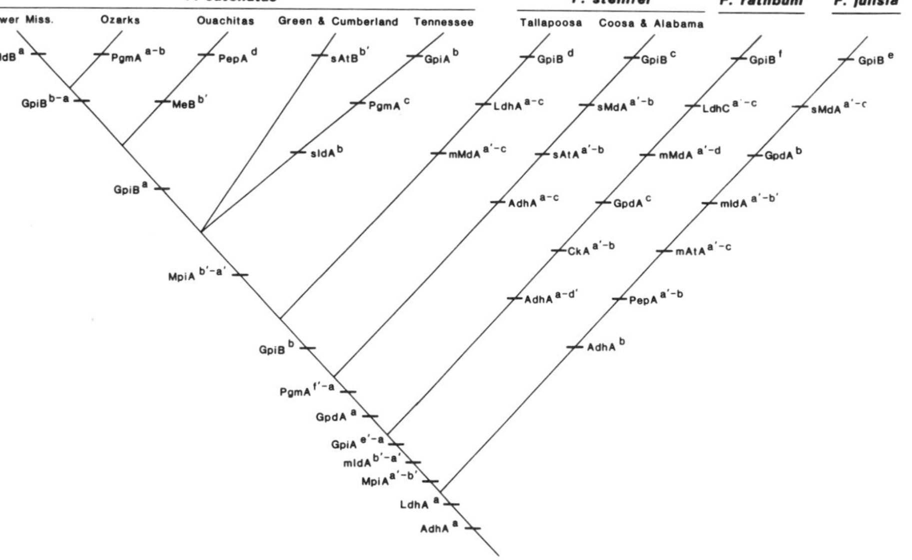

Fig. 31.3. Phylogenetic tree for the grouped populations and taxa of *Xenisma* derived from allozyme data by the character Wagner procedure (Farris, 1970). Allele and locus terminology is as explained in the text and in table 31.1 and appendix, tables 31A.1–A.7. An allele indicated by an apostrophe, e.g., a', is found in an out-group at a frequency ≥ 0.10. Two alleles separated by a hyphen, e.g., a'–b, indicate that the allele on the left is replaced by the allele on the right at that point on the tree. An allele indicated alone appears at that point on the cladogram without replacing another. See text for other details.

Table 31.2. Average Nei's (1972) Genetic Distance Within and Between Taxa of *Xenisma*

Taxon	Number of Populations	Average Distance				
Fundulus catenatus	19	0.074 (0.000–0.223)				
F. stellifer						
Tallapoosa	2	0.200 (0.136–0.290)	0.004			
Coosa & Alabama	2	0.276 (0.230–0.395)	0.289 (0.283–0.294)	0.004		
F. rathbuni	1	0.431 (0.400–0.527)	0.404 (0.403–0.406)	0.468 (0.464–0.472)	—	
F. julisia	2	0.448 (0.391–0.539)	0.609 (0.557–0.664)	0.560 (0.554–0.575)	0.667 (0.675–0.674)	0.057

Mickovich and Mitter (1981) have argued that the coding of single alleles as independent characters with two states (presence or absence) may sometimes be unrealistic, since "it does not prohibit a hypothetical intermediate (electromorphotype) without alleles at a locus." We think that this is not a valid criticism. The apparent absence of alleles from a locus for an ancestor simply implies the absence of any of the alleles that were included in the analysis. Ancestral taxa certainly may have possessed alleles that are no longer present in their descendants. Similarly, they may have possessed combinaions of extant alleles that are not observed in their descendants. To assert that we may never invoke these unobserved characters is to misuse "Occam's Probative," which simply cautions us that "plurality is not to be posited without necessity" (Boehner, 1964). Coding of alleles as independent characters produces ancestors with "no" alleles in exactly those situations (i.e., unique alleles in two or more sister taxa) in which the assumption that ancestors must have one and only one of the states observed in their descendants would leave us unable to identify an ancestral state for that locus. In any case, the presence-absence coding of our data revealed essentially the same cladistic relationships as the analysis of allele frequencies (compare fig. 31.3 to 31.2), which did assume that only observed alleles may be present in ancestors. Table 31.2 contains average Nei's genetic distances (Nei, 1972) for comparison with all other allozyme studies.

Heterozygosity

Mean heterozygosities (unbiased estimate; Nei, 1978) for all ingroup and out-group taxa are presented in table 31.3. The degree of heterozygosity of the outgroups is about three times that of the ingroups.

Table 31.3. Mean Heterozygosity (Unbiased Estimate; Nei, 1978) in *Xenisma* and Out-Groups

Taxon	Mean Heterozygosity*		
Xenisma	0.028		
Fundulus catenatus		0.029	
Lower Mississippi			0.026
Ozarks			0.009
Ouachitas			0.038
Green and Cumberland			0.029
Tennessee			0.057
F. stellifer		0.019	
Tallapoosa			0.024
Coosa and Alabama			0.015
F. rathbuni		0.007	
F. julisia		0.050	
Out-groups	0.114		
F. majalis		0.102	
F. similis		0.115	
F. grandis		0.070	
F. heteroclitus		0.170	

*Each mean is the unweighted average of the heterozygosities of the individual population samples included in the group.

Discussion

Relationships of Taxa

One unexpected result of this study was the discovery of the rather large genetic dissimilarity of Tallapoosa River *F. stellifer* to *F. stellifer* from the Alabama River drainage (including upper and middle Coosa rivers) and the Chattahoochee River. The average genetic distance (table 31.2) between the Tallapoosa and other *F. stellifer* populations lies well within the range of average genetic distances between species within 10 other genera of bony fishes (Avise and Aquadro, 1982). More important than the particular distance value, however, is the complete absence of shared alleles at six loci, GpiB, LdhA, sMdA, mMdA, sAtA, and AdhA (appendix tables 31A.1–A.3, A.5, A.7) indicating the absence of gene flow between these populations at present and probably for many generations past.

The phylogenetic trees (figs. 31.2, 31.3) partly corroborate Wiley's (1986) conclusion that *F. stellifer* is the sister group of *F. catenatus*, since *F. catenatus* and *F. stellifer* share two uniquely derived alleles, PgmA^{a} and GpdA^{a} (fig. 31.3; appendix, tables 31A.2, A.4). However, the trees indicate that *F. stellifer* may be paraphyletic, the Tallapoosa River population being the true sister group of *F. catenatus* and the other *F. stellifer* populations being the sister group of the *F. catenatus*–Tallapoosa clade. It is easy to understand how *F. catenatus* and *F. stellifer* could have differentiated allopatrically since stream capture has probably occurred several times between various parts of the present Tennessee and Coosa rivers (Fenneman, 1938; Thornbury, 1965). It is much more difficult to explain why the Tallapoosa *F. stellifer* should be more closely related than other *F. stellifer* to *F. catenatus* since the Tallapoosa River is now geographically completely separated from the nearest *F. catenatus* populations by the Coosa River. We could produce a tortuous ad hoc hypothesis that would "explain" the situation; however, we only point out that the phylogenetic trees may simply be wrong. As noted above, modifying the phylogenetic tree of fig. 31.2 to make the two distinct populations of *F. stellifer* sister groups of one another produces an only slightly longer tree. Also, the one allele (GpiB[b]) that unites Tallapoosa *F. stellifer* with *F. catenatus* on the tree of fig. 31.3 is present in an out-group (*F. similis*), although in low frequency, and thus may have been plesiomorphous for all of *Xenisma*.

Wiley (1986) was unable to resolve the relationship of *F. rathbuni* and *F. julisia* to the *catenatus-stellifer* clade. Our analysis shows that *F. rathbuni* is the sister group of *catenatus-stellifer* and that *F. julisia* is the sister taxon of all the rest of *Xenisma*. The relationship of *F. rathbuni* to the *catenatus-stellifer* clade is supported by the sharing of one uniquely derived allele (GpiA[a]), the sharing of the fixed state for one allele (mIdA[a]), and the sharing between *F. rathbuni* and *F. stellifer* of the fixed state for an allele (MpiA[b]) that ancestrally was polymorphic with another allele (MpiA[a]) (fig. 31.3; app. tables 31A.1, A.4, A.7). It is likely that *F. rathbuni* originated from the invasion of ancestral *Xenisma* from the west through stream capture, since the drainage divided between Atlantic and Gulf drainages in this region has probably migrated westward owing to steeper slope and faster erosion on the Atlantic side (Thornbury, 1965).

The monophyly of *F. catenatus* is supported primarily by all of its populations sharing the fixed state for an allele (MpiA[a]) that is present in two outgroups (*F. grandis* and *F. heteroclitus*) and present in polymorphic condition in *F. julisia* (fig. 31.3, appendix table 31A.7). Within *F. catenatus*, the populations generally fall into the groups recognized by Thomerson (1969) on the basis of morphology. However, the Ouachitas and the lower Mississippi (= Homochitto of Thomerson) are "slightly" paraphyletic; and the Green and Cumberland groups are very closely related (fig. 31.2). The close relationship of the Green and Cumberland populations may be due to their currently being tributaries of the Ohio River and possibly to capture of some Green River tributaries by the Cumberland (Fenneman, 1938).

The cladistic relationships of populations of *F. catenatus* (fig. 31.3) indicate that the disjunction between the Green-Cumberland and Tennessee populations is roughly the same age as that between these "Tennessee Highlands" (Wiley and Mayden, 1985) populations and the Interior Highlands populations (Ouachitas and Ozarks). The Interior Highlands populations were once continuous with each other and with the lower Mississippi population (Mayden, 1985; Wiley and Mayden, 1985). The relationships also show that the separation of the Ouachitas from the Ozarks by the Arkansas River before the Sangamon interglacial (Mayden, 1985; Wiley and Mayden, 1985) occurred before the disjunction of the lower Mississippi population. Alternatively, the lower Mississippi population may have been established by larval drift.

The cladistic relationships within *Xenisma* generally conform to Wiley and Mayden's (1985) "pre-Pleistocene hypothesis" of vicariance speciation of Central Highlands fishes and their non-Highlands relatives. Specifically, the cladogram and present distributions of *Xenisma* taxa suggest the following hypothesis of allopatric speciation events: (1) the separation of *F. julisia* from other *Xenisma* occurred by a pre-Pleistocene disjunction of the ancestral *Xenisma*, (2) the "western" *Xenisma* subsequently established sympatry with *F. julisia* by eastward dispersal, (3) *F. rathbuni* originated by introduction of "western" *Xenisma* into Atlantic Slope drainages by stream capture, (4) Coosa-Alabama-Chatahoochee and Tallapoosa *F. stellifer* originated by one or two invasions of these stream systems by "western" *Xenisma* from the Tennessee River, and (5) disjunction of *F. catenatus* populations occurred as the result of changes in topography and drainage systems brought about by Pleistocene glaciation.

Heterozygosity

Many hypotheses have been proposed to explain variation in heterozygosity between populations and taxa, including population size, time since founding of population (or since the last population bottleneck), and differences in "niche breadth" (Soule, 1976). Perhaps heterozygosities are lower in *Xenisma* than in the out-groups (table 31.3) partly because species of *Xenisma* have relatively restricted ranges (or a range that consists of several disjunct populations as in *F. catenatus*) and live primarily in upland streams above the fall line with limited opportunity for gene flow between stream systems. Thus the species of *Xenisma* have smaller effective population sizes than those of the out-group species with

Table 31.4. Mean Heterozygosity in Species of *Notropis* (Avise, 1977), Classified by Extent of Geographical Distribution and Whether or Not Distribution Is Primarily on Coastal Plain

		II	
		Not Primarily on Coastal Plain	Primarily on Coastal Plain
I	Restricted range	0.050 (N = 14 spp.)	0.039 (N = 7 spp.)
	Wide Range	0.057 (N = 16 spp.)	0.090 (N = 9 spp.)

Source	df	ANOVA F	Probability
Cells	3	3.24	0.031
I–II	1	4.29	0.044
II–I	1	1.38	0.246
I × II	1	3.91	0.055

their relatively broad continuous ranges in Coastal Plain streams, estuaries, and inshore marine waters. A reanalysis of Avise's (1977b) data for *Notropis* lends some additional support to this hypothesis. In table 31.4 we classify 46 species of *Notropis* according to two criteria, geographical extent of range and whether or not the range is primarily on the Coastal Plain. This was done by inspecting the range maps of these species provided by Lee et al. (1980). Even with such rough approximations, the wide-ranging *Notropis* have significantly higher heterozygosities than do those with restricted ranges, and wide-ranging species that primarily inhabit the Coastal Plain have higher heterozygosities than those of species that live primarily in upland areas. Some *Xenisma,* such as *F. rathbuni*, may also have low heterozygosity owing to the founder effect or to genetic drift during a period of small population size after a founder event, when speciation was the result of introduction of an ancestral population into a new stream system by stream capture.[1] The low heterozygosities and the significant genetic differentiation between mostly allopatric taxa within *Xenisma* are probably the product of the same factor, limited opportunity for gene flow between stream systems in upland areas.[1]

[1]We thank Hank Bart, Brooks Burr, Keith Goodfellow, Jim Grady, Gene Helfman, David S. Lee, Rick Mayden, Larry Page, Ray Paschall, Sharon Reiley, Michael M. Stevenson, Royal Suttkus, Dave Swofford, Werner Weiland, and Ed Wiley for field assistance. Special thanks are extended to Dave Swofford, Dave Etnier, and Randy and Peggy Shute for kindly sharing critical material of rare species or populations. We benefited from discussions with Jim Williams, John Ramsey, and Carter Gilbert and thank them for so freely sharing their knowledge of southeastern fishes. Jamie Thomerson and Ed Wiley provided support and encouragement and helped improve this study in a number of ways. We thank William Matthews and Julian Humphries for their assistance in the initial stages of the project. We acknowledge the assistance of Royal Suttkus, TU; Robert R. Miller and Doug Nelson, UMMZ; Herbert Boschung, UAIC; John Ramsey, AU; and Donald Scott, UGA, in allowing us to examine specimens under their care. Financial support for this study was provided by the American Philosophical Society in a grant to RCC and by Sigma Xi. For defraying some of the expenses of travel and laboratory supplies, we express our sincere thanks to Michael Poirrier and to Richard Olsen, Graduate Dean, University of New Orleans. Janet Forbes deserves our gratitude for typing countless drafts of tables and the final manuscript.

Table 31A.1. Allele Frequencies of Two Loci in *Xenisma* and Out-Groups

Species and Populations	GpiA							GpiB											
	N	*a*	*b*	*c*	*d*	*e*	*f*	*N*	*a*	*b*	*c*	*d*	*e*	*f*	*g*	*h*	*i*	*j*	*k*
Fundulus catenatus																			
1. Buffalo B., Miss.	9	1.000						9	1.000										
2. Homochitto R., Miss.	5	1.000						5	1.000										
3. Cole's Cr., Miss.	12	1.000						12	1.000										
4. Pearl R., Miss.	4	1.000						4	1.000										
5. Amite R., Miss.	6	1.000						6	1.000										
6. Green R., Ky.	12	1.000						12		1.000									
7. Cumberland R., Tenn.	5	1.000						5		1.000									
8. Cumberland R., Tenn.	5	1.000						5		1.000									
9. Tennessee R., Ala.	13	0.769	0.231					13		0.692	0.308								
10. Clinch R., Tenn.	5		1.000					5		1.000									
11. Buffalo R., Tenn.	9	1.000						9		1.000									
12. Cossatot R., Ark.	11	1.000						11		1.000									
13. Caddo R., Ark.	13	1.000						13	0.192	0.808									
14. Saline R., Ark.	10	1.000						10	0.950	0.050									
15. White R., Ark.	19	0.974		0.026				19	1.000										
16. Illinois R., Okla.	10	0.700		0.300				10	1.000										
17–19. White and Missouri R., Mo.	25	1.000						25	1.000										
F. stellifer																			
20. Coosa R., Ala.	13	1.000						13			1.000								
20a. Conasauga R., Tenn.	10	1.000						10			1.000								
20b. Chattahoochee R., Ga.	10	1.000						10			1.000								
21. Alabama R., Ala.	6	1.000						6			1.000								
22. Tallapoosa R., Ala.	4	1.000						4		0.875		0.125							
23. Tallapoosa R., Ala.	6	1.000						6		0.667		0.333							
F. rathbuni																			
24–26. Neuse, Pee Dee, and Cape Fear R., N.C.	23	1.000						23						1.000					
F. julisia																			
27. Cumberland R., Tenn.	6					1.000		6			0.250		0.750						
28. Elk R., Tenn.	9					1.000		9					1.000						
29. *F. majalis*	4						1.000	4									1.000		
30. *F. similis*	4						1.000	4		0.125					0.250	0.625			
31. *F. grandis*	4				0.750	0.250		4											1.000
32. *F. heteroclitus*	4					1.000		4									0.500	0.125	0.375

Table 31A.2. Allele Frequencies of Three Loci in *Xenisma* and Out-Groups

Species and Populations	PgmA											LdhA						LdhC			
	N	*a*	*b*	*c*	*d*	*e*	*f*	*g*	*h*	*i*	*j*	*N*	*a*	*b*	*c*	*d*	*e*	*N*	*a*	*b*	*c*
Fundulus catenatus																					
1. Buffalo B., Miss.	9	1.000										9	1.000					8	1.000		
2. Homochitto R., Miss.	5	0.900	0.100									5	1.000					5	1.000		
3. Cole's Cr., Miss.	12	1.000										9	1.000					4	1.000		
4. Pearl R., Miss.	4	0.875	0.125									4	1.000					4	1.000		
5. Amite R., Miss.	6	1.000										3	1.000					4	1.000		
6. Green R., Ky.	12	0.875	0.125									9	1.000					2	1.000		
7. Cumberland R., Tenn.	5	1.000										5	1.000					5	1.000		
8. Cumberland R., Tenn.	5	1.000										5	1.000					5	1.000		
9. Tennessee R., Ala.	13	0.231		0.769								13	1.000					5	1.000		
10. Clinch R., Tenn.	5			0.900		0.100						5	1.000					5	1.000		
11. Buffalo R., Tenn.	9	0.556		0.444								9	1.000					9	1.000		
12. Cossatot R., Ark.	11	1.000										11	1.000					6	1.000		
13. Caddo R., Ark.	13	1.000										11	0.955	0.045				5	1.000		
14. Saline R., Ark.	10	1.000										10	1.000					5	1.000		
15. White R., Ark.	19		1.000									18	1.000					13	1.000		
16. Illinois R., Okla.	25		1.000									10	1.000					10	1.000		
17–19. White and Missouri R., Mo.	25		1.000									25	1.000					25	1.000		
F. stellifer																					
20. Coosa R., Ala.	13	1.000										10	1.000					7	1.000		
20a. Conasauga R., Tenn.	10	1.000										10	1.000					10	1.000		
20b. Chattahoochee R., Ga.	10	1.000										10	1.000					10	1.000		
21. Alabama R., Ala.	6	0.833					0.167					6	1.000					6	1.000		
22. Tallapoosa R., Ala.	4	1.000										4			1.000			4	1.000		
23. Tallapoosa R., Ala.	6	1.000										6			1.000			6	1.000		
F. rathbuni																					
24–26. Neuse, Pee Dee, and Cape Fear R., N.C.	23						1.000					23	1.000					23		1.000	
F. julisia																					
27. Cumberland R., Tenn.	6				0.083		0.917					6	1.000					5	1.000		
28. Elk R., Tenn.	9						0.778	0.222				9	1.000					9	1.000		
29. *F. majalis*	3					1.000						4				1.000		5			1.000
30. *F. similis*	4					0.750			0.125	0.125		4				1.000		3			1.000
31. *F. grandis*	4						0.875				0.125	4					1.000	4	1.000		
32. *F. heteroclitus*	4				0.125		0.875					4					1.000	3	1.000		

Table 31A.3. Allele Frequencies of Three Loci in *Xenisma* and Out-Groups

Species and Populations	sMdA						sMdB					mMdA						
	N	*a*	*b*	*c*	*d*	*e*	*N*	*a*	*b*	*c*	*d*	*N*	*a*	*b*	*c*	*d*	*e*	*f*
Fundulus catenatus																		
1. Buffalo B., Miss.	9	1.000					9		1.000			9	1.000					
2. Homochitto R., Miss.	5	1.000					5	0.300	0.700			5	1.000					
3. Cole's Cr., Miss.	12	1.000					12	0.875	0.125			12	1.000					
4. Pearl R., Miss.	4	1.000					4	1.000				4	1.000					
5. Amite R., Miss.	6	1.000					6	0.417	0.583			6	1.000					
6. Green R., Ky.	12	1.000					12		1.000			12	1.000					
7. Cumberland R., Tenn.	5	1.000					5		0.900	0.100		5	1.000					
8. Cumberland R., Tenn.	5	1.000					5		1.000			5	1.000					
9. Tennessee R., Ala.	13	1.000					13		1.000			13	1.000					
10. Clinch R., Tenn.	5	1.000					5		1.000			5	1.000					
11. Buffalo R., Tenn.	9	0.778		0.056	0.167		9		1.000			9	1.000					
12. Cossatot R., Ark.	11	1.000					11		1.000			11	0.773	0.227				
13. Caddo R., Ark.	13	1.000					13		1.000			13	1.000					
14. Saline R., Ark.	10	1.000					10		1.000			10	1.000					
15. White R., Ark.	19	1.000					19		1.000			19	1.000					
16. Illinois R., Okla.	10	1.000					10		1.000			10	1.000					
17–19. White and Missouri R., Mo.	25	1.000					25		1.000			25	1.000					
F. stellifer																		
20. Coosa R., Ala.	13		1.000				13		1.000			13	1.000					
20a. Conasauga R., Tenn.	10		1.000				10		1.000			10	1.000					
20b. Chattahoochee R., Ga.	10		1.000				10		1.000			10	1.000					
21. Alabama R., Ala.	6		1.000				6		1.000			6	1.000					
22. Tallapoosa R., Ala.	4	1.000					4		1.000			4			1.000			
23. Tallapoosa R., Ala.	6	1.000					6		1.000			6			1.000			
F. rathbuni																		
24–26. Neuse, Pee Dee, and Cape Fear R., N.C.	23	1.000					23		1.000			23				1.000		
F. julisia																		
27. Cumberland R., Tenn.	6			1.000			6		1.000			6	1.000					
28. Elk R., Tenn.	9			1.000			9		1.000			9	1.000					
29. *F. majalis*	4	1.000					4		1.000			4					1.000	
30. *F. similis*	4	1.000					4		1.000			4						1.000
31. *F. grandis*	4	1.000					4		0.125			4	1.000					
32. *F. heteroclitus*	4	0.875				0.125	4		1.000			4	1.000					

Table 31A.4. Allele Frequencies of Three Loci in *Xenisma* and Out-Groups

Species and Populations	GpdA								mIdA				sIdA					
	N	*a*	*b*	*c*	*d*	*e*	*f*	*g*	*N*	*a*	*b*	*c*	*N*	*a*	*b*	*c*	*d*	*e*
Fundulus catenatus																		
1. Buffalo B., Miss.	9	1.000							9	1.000			9	1.000				
2. Homochitto R., Miss.	5	1.000							5	1.000			5	1.000				
3. Cole's Cr., Miss.	9	1.000							9	1.000			4	1.000				
4. Pearl R., Miss.	3	1.000							3	1.000			4	1.000				
5. Amite R., Miss.	3	1.000							3	1.000			3	1.000				
6. Green R., Ky.	9	1.000							9	1.000			3	1.000				
7. Cumberland R., Tenn.	5	1.000							5	1.000			5	1.000				
8. Cumberland R., Tenn.	5	1.000							5	1.000			5	1.000				
9. Tennessee R., Ala.	5	1.000							13	1.000			6	0.333	0.667			
10. Clinch R., Tenn.	5	1.000							5	1.000			5	0.600	0.400			
11. Buffalo R., Tenn.	9	1.000							9	1.000			7	1.000				
12. Cossatot R., Ark.	11	1.000							11	1.000			3	1.000				
13. Caddo R., Ark.	9	1.000							12	1.000			3	1.000				
14. Saline R., Ark.	5	1.000							10	1.000			5	1.000				
15. White R., Ark.	16	1.000							18	1.000			4	1.000				
16. Illinois R., Okla.	10	1.000							10	1.000			7	1.000				
17–19. White and Missouri R., Mo.	25	1.000							25	1.000			25	1.000				
F. stellifer																		
20. Coosa R., Ala.	10	1.000							10	1.000			8	1.000				
20a. Conasauga R., Tenn.	10	1.000							10	1.000			10	1.000				
20b. Chattahoochee R., Ga.	10	1.000							10	1.000			10	1.000				
21. Alabama R., Ala.	6	1.000							6	1.000			4	1.000				
22. Tallapoosa R., Ala.	4	1.000							4	1.000			4	1.000				
23. Tallapoosa R., Ala.	6	1.000							6	1.000			6	1.000				
R. rathbuni																		
24–26. Neuse, Pee Dee, and Cape Fear R., N.C.	23			1.000					23	1.000			15	0.933	0.067			
F. julisia																		
27. Cumberland R., Tenn.	5		1.000						6		1.000		5	1.000				
28. Elk R., Tenn.	9		1.000						9		1.000		9	1.000				
29. *F. majalis*	4				1.000				3	0.333		0.667	4		0.125	0.875		
30. *F. similis*	4				0.875			0.125	4	0.375	0.500	0.125	3			1.000		
31. *F. grandis*	4						1.000		4	1.000			3				1.000	
32. *F. heteroclitus*	4					1.000			4	1.000			3	0.500			0.333	0.167

Table 31A.5. Allele Frequencies of Four Loci in *Xenisma* and Out-Groups

Species and Populations	MeA					MeB				sAtA					sAtB				
	N	*a*	*b*	*c*	*d*	*N*	*a*	*b*	*c*	*N*	*a*	*b*	*c*	*d*	*N*	*a*	*b*	*c*	*d*
Fundulus catenatus																			
1. Buffalo B., Miss.	8	1.000				8	1.000			8	1.000				8	1.000			
2. Homochitto R., Miss.	5	1.000				5	1.000			5	1.000				5	1.000			
3. Cole's Cr., Miss.	9	1.000				9	1.000			4	1.000				12	1.000			
4. Pearl R., Miss.	3	1.000				3	1.000			4	1.000				3	0.667	0.333		
5. Amite R., Miss.	3	1.000				3	1.000			3	1.000				6	1.000			
6. Green R., Ky.	9	1.000				9	1.000			5	1.000				12	0.417	0.583		
7. Cumberland R., Tenn.	5	1.000				5	1.000			5	1.000				5	0.400	0.600		
8. Cumberland R., Tenn.	5	1.000				5	1.000			5	1.000				5	0.900	0.100		
9. Tennessee R., Ala.	12	1.000				12	1.000			3	1.000				12	1.000			
10. Clinch R., Tenn.	5	1.000				5	1.000			5	1.000				5	1.000			
11. Buffalo R., Tenn.	9	1.000				9	1.000			9	1.000				9	0.944		0.056	
12. Cossatot R., Ark.	11	0.818	0.182			11	0.545	0.455		1	1.000				6	1.000			
13. Caddo R., Ark.	9	0.944	0.056			9	0.889	0.111		5	1.000				6	1.000			
14. Saline R., Ark.	10	1.000				10	1.000			5	1.000				10	1.000			
15. White R., Ark.	16	1.000				16	1.000			5	1.000				17	1.000			
16. Illinois R., Okla.	10	0.350			0.650	10	1.000			9	1.000				10	1.000			
17–19. White and Missouri R., Mo.	25	1.000				25	1.000			25	1.000				25	1.000			
F. stellifer																			
20. Coosa R., Ala.	10	1.000				10	1.000			5		1.000			13	1.000			
20a. Conasauga R., Tenn.	10	1.000				10	1.000			10		1.000			10	1.000			
20b. Chattahoochee R., Ga.	10	1.000				10	1.000			10		1.000			10	1.000			
21. Alabama R., Ala.	6	1.000				6	1.000			4		1.000			6	1.000			
22. Tallapoosa R., Ala.	4	1.000				4	1.000			4	1.000				4	1.000			
23. Tallapoosa R., Ala.	6	1.000				6	1.000			6	1.000				6	1.000			
F. rathbuni																			
24–26. Neuse, Pee Dee, and Cape Fear R., N.C.	23	0.978			0.022	23	1.000			23	1.000				23	1.000			
F. julisia																			
27. Cumberland R., Tenn.	6	0.833		0.167		6	1.000			5	1.000				6	1.000			
28. Elk R., Tenn.	9	1.000				9	1.000			9	1.000				9	1.000			
29. *F. majalis*	3	1.000				3		1.000		5	0.200			0.800	3	0.833			0.167
30. *F. similis*	4	1.000				4		1.000		3				1.000	4	1.000			
31. *F. grandis*	4	1.000				4	1.000			3			1.000		4		1.000		
32. *F. heteroclitus*	4	0.875			0.125	4	0.125		0.875	3			1.000		4	0.125	0.875		

Table 31A.6. Allele Frequencies of Four Loci in *Xenisma* and Out-Groups

Species and Populations	mAtA						PepA								CkA			AkA		
	N	*a*	*b*	*c*	*d*	*e*	*N*	*a*	*b*	*c*	*d*	*e*	*f*	*g*	*N*	*a*	*b*	*N*	*a*	*b*
Fundulus catenatus																				
1. Buffalo B., Miss.	8	0.813			0.188		9	1.000							8	1.000		9	1.000	
2. Homochitto R., Miss.	5	0.600			0.400		5	1.000							5	1.000		5	1.000	
3. Cole's Cr., Miss.	4	1.000					3	1.000							9	1.000		9	1.000	
4. Pearl R., Miss.	4	1.000					1	1.000							2	1.000		2	1.000	
5. Amite R., Miss.	3	1.000					4	1.000							3	1.000		3	1.000	
6. Green R., Ky.	5	1.000					5	1.000							9	1.000		9	1.000	
7. Cumberland R., Tenn.	5	1.000					3	1.000							5	1.000		5	1.000	
8. Cumberland R., Tenn.	5	1.000					5	1.000							5	1.000		5	0.900	0.100
9. Tennessee R., Ala.	3	1.000					2	1.000							3	1.000		3	1.000	
10. Clinch R., Tenn.	5	1.000					4	1.000							5	1.000		5	1.000	
11. Buffalo R., Tenn.	9	1.000					9	1.000							9	1.000		9	1.000	
12. Cossatot R., Ark.	1	1.000					3	1.000							6	1.000		6	1.000	
13. Caddo R., Ark.	5	1.000					5	1.000							5	1.000		5	1.000	
14. Saline R., Ark.	5	1.000					5	0.100		0.200	0.700				5	1.000		5	1.000	
15. White R., Ark.	5	1.000					7	0.929	0.071						16	1.000		16	1.000	
16. Illinois R., Okla.	9	1.000					10	1.000							10	1.000		10	1.000	
17–19. White and Missouri R., Mo.	25	1.000					25	1.000							25	1.000		25	1.000	
F. stellifer																				
20. Coosa R., Ala.	5	1.000					5	1.000							11	1.000		11	1.000	
20a. Conasauga R., Tenn.	10	1.000					10	0.850		0.150					10	1.000		10	1.000	
20b. Chattahoochee R., Ga.	10	1.000					10	0.950		0.050					10	1.000		10	1.000	
21. Alabama R., Ala.	4	1.000					6	0.750				0.250			6	1.000		6	1.000	
22. Tallapoosa R., Ala.	4	1.000					4	1.000							4	1.000		4	1.000	
23. Tallapoosa R., Ala.	6	0.750		0.250			6	1.000							6	1.000		6	1.000	
F. rathbuni																				
24–26. Neuse, Pee Dee, and Cape Fear R., N.C.	21	1.000					23	1.000							23		1.000	23	1.000	
F. julisia																				
27. Cumberland R., Tenn.	5		0.700	0.300			5		1.000						6	1.000		6	1.000	
28. Elk R., Tenn.	9		1.000				9		1.000						9	1.000		9	1.000	
29. *F. majalis*	5	0.900				0.100	3	0.667		0.333					3	1.000		3	1.000	
30. *F. similis*	3	1.000					4	0.750		0.250					4	1.000		4	1.000	
31. *F. grandis*	3	1.000					4	0.250				0.375	0.375		4	1.000		4	1.000	
32. *F. heteroclitus*	3	1.000					1					0.500		0.500	4	1.000		4	1.000	

Table 31A.7. Allele Frequencies of Four Loci in *Xenisma* and Out-Groups

Species and Populations	AdhA						PgdA				MpiA					SdhA			
	N	*a*	*b*	*c*	*d*	*e*	*N*	*a*	*b*	*c*	*N*	*a*	*b*	*c*	*d*	*N*	*a*	*b*	*c*
Fundulus catenatus																			
1. Buffalo B., Miss.	9	1.000					9	1.000			9	1.000				9	1.000		
2. Homochitto R., Miss.	5	1.000					5	1.000			5	1.000				5	1.000		
3. Cole's Cr., Miss.	4	1.000					3	1.000			4	1.000				4	1.000		
4. Pearl R., Miss.	4	1.000					4	1.000			4	1.000				4	1.000		
5. Amite R., Miss.	2	1.000					3	1.000			2	1.000				2	1.000		
6. Green R., Ky.	5	1.000					4	1.000			3	1.000				3	1.000		
7. Cumberland R., Tenn.	3	1.000					3	1.000			3	1.000				3	1.000		
8. Cumberland R., Tenn.	5	0.900			0.100		5	1.000			5	1.000				5	1.000		
9. Tennessee R., Ala.	3	1.000					3	1.000			3	1.000				3	1.000		
10. Clinch R., Tenn.	2	1.000					4	1.000			2	1.000				2	0.250	0.750	
11. Buffalo R., Tenn.	9	0.889	0.111				9	1.000			9	1.000				9	1.000		
12. Cossatot R., Ark.	1	1.000					5	1.000			1	1.000				1	1.000		
13. Caddo R., Ark.	5	1.000					2	1.000			5	1.000				5	1.000		
14. Saline R., Ark.	5	1.000					5	0.900	0.100		5	1.000				5	1.000		
15. White R., Ark.	5	1.000					9	1.000			2	1.000				2	1.000		
16. Illinois R., Okla.	9	1.000					10	1.000			9	1.000				9	1.000		
17–19. White and Missouri R., Mo.	25	1.000					25	1.000			25	1.000				25	1.000		
F. stellifer																			
20. Coosa R., Ala.	5			1.000			2	1.000			5		1.000			5	1.000		
20a. Conasauga R., Tenn.	10			1.000			10	1.000			10		1.000			10	1.000		
20b. Chattahoochee R., Ga.	10			1.000			10	1.000			10		1.000			10	1.000		
21. Alabama R., Ala.	3			1.000			6	1.000			3		1.000			4	1.000		
22. Tallapoosa R., Ala.	4	1.000					4	1.000			4		1.000			4	1.000		
23. Tallapoosa R., Ala.	6	1.000					6	1.000			6		1.000			6	1.000		
F. rathbuni																			
24–26. Neuse, Pee Dee, and Cape Fear R., N.C.	21				1.000		23	1.000			20		1.000			22	1.000		
F. julisia																			
27. Cumberland R., Tenn.	6		1.000				6	1.000			5	0.900	0.100			5	1.000		
28. Elk R., Tenn.	9	1.000					9	1.000			9	0.667	0.278	0.056		9	1.000		
29. *F. majalis*	4	0.125			0.875		3			1.000	5		1.000			4			1.000
30. *F. similis*	3					1.000	4			1.000	3		0.833		0.167	2			1.000
31. *F. grandis*	3					1.000	4	1.000			4	1.000				4	1.000		
32. *F. heteroclitus*	2					1.000	4	0.750		0.250	3	1.000				3	1.000		

32. Summary of the Symposium

Clark Hubbs

The most general conclusion from this symposium is that stream fishes respond to diverse stimuli. This is not surprising, because streams vary widely. Each stream has specific constraints on its inhabitants. For some streams, physical factors are more restrictive than biotic factors, and for others the converse is true. The unique nature of individual streams is best illustrated by contrasting flood events. Catastrophic floods in Arizona (Minckley and Meffe, chap. 12) are vastly different from benign flood events in Minnesota (Coon, chap. 10), Missouri (Finger and Stewart, chap. 11), or Mississippi (Ross et al., chap. 6) (= physical control). In the latter group flooding may benefit fish diversity, whereas only a limited number of species can withstand torrential Arizona floods. Yet it is these floods that often "benefit" native Arizona fishes by decimating or eliminating introduced fishes (= biotic control). It is tempting to categorize floods into benign and catastrophic; however, all levels of intermediacy occur.

Many of the chapters address stream-fish community structure. Most studies focus on small clear streams with relatively few fish species to facilitate observations and to reduce the number of interactions involved. Although reducing the environmental complexities is often a prequisite for obtaining meaningful data, each investigator must remember the message in Li et al. (chap. 24) that actions elsewhere in the stream (the Columbia River basin) may impact trophic interactions in a small headwater tributary stream thousands of kilometers away. The whole system must be considered when we are evaluating a part. For example, what is the impact of acid rain on trophic dynamics of stream fishes in Maine?

Selection of study sites can benefit from prior studies. Fish-community ecologists are familiar with Brier Creek, Oklahoma; Black Creek, Mississippi; and Jordan Creek, Illinois. Although there are enormous benefit from sequential studies of the same stream, the possibility remains that those streams are atypical in one or more parameters. Perhaps Buncombe Creek, Oklahoma; Red Creek, Mississippi; or Salt Creek, Illinois, would provide quite different results—I doubt they would, but emphasis on one stream is often at the expense of studies on diverse streams.

In many ways stream-fish ecology has lagged behind similar studies on other taxa. It is more difficult to observe fishes than most terrestrial vertebrates, especially when the water is turbid. Innovative use of snorkling and scuba devices has helped enormously in the understanding of fish activities. In general, fishes differ from most reptiles, birds, and mammals (and to some degree amphibians) by having much smaller offspring (and many more). It is difficult to assess the relative abundance of larval darters (8 mm ±) or cyprinids (7 mm ±) in streams (they are hard to find in quiet water and much less easily observed when nonlaminar flow of streams distorts vision or directional pull of nets). In contrast, fishes may be relatively more abundant and diverse in limited areas of a stream. Rapid recruitment facilitates experimental manipulations that can confirm observations. Fishes are an extremely diverse group of organisms amenable to laboratory experiments.

The diversity of stream fishes is part of our national heritage. Unfortunately, the future is not promising, especially for large river fishes. Will those faunas survive? Stream-fish declines have long been reported, and here we have additional examples. Reservoirs tend to favor lacustrine over riverine fishes. Intense agricultural practices increase stream siltation, yet reservoirs act as settling basins and clear silt-laden streams and may decimate native fishes adapted to the turbid waters of the Colorado River (Minckley and Meffe, chap. 12) and the Missouri River (Pflieger and Grace, chap. 21). Industrial and mining wastes dumped into streams degrade habitats. Stream channelization results in a substantial decrease in fish diversity (Schlosser, chap. 3). Water diversions dry stream beds (Cross and Moss, chap. 20). Successfully introduced fishes must occupy one or more niches, especially when the river regimes have been altered (Minckley and Meffe, chap. 12). Clear-cutting has been shown to have an impact on coldwater fish forms; now we know there is a warmwater-fishes effect as well (Rutherford et al., chap. 22). Commercial (or sports) fish captures would be expected to alter fish abundances; now we know that commercial fish captures may deplete natural fertilization many kilometers away (Li et al., chap. 24). Major fish kills are obvious and easy to document. Subtle changes are probably more pervasive and very difficult to document. If we replace *Notropis whipplei* with *Notropis lutrensis,* many workers might not notice the change, but that change should be a danger signal that environmental degradation is under way. The well-documented and highly controversial threats of extinction—*Percina tanasi* and *Cyprinodon diabolis*—or the actual extinctions—tecopa pupfish and *Gambusia amistadensis*—are often fishes with relatively restriced ranges, but problems with *Notropis orca, Ptychochilus grandis, Cyprinodon pecosensis, Scaphirhynchus albus,* or even *Polyodon spathula* suggest that wide-ranging stream fishes may obtain similar notoriety and even Supreme Court hearings. These difficulties even extend to receiving water: Has streamflow decline influenced the abundance of *Chasmistes*? Yes. Of *Cynoscion macdonaldi*? Yes.

Sheldon (chap. 25) has shown that many fishes are rare in each tributary stream and that when interstream migrations are inhibited, serious problems may result. I am even more distressed, for Michael Soule's (1983) calculations on inbreeding depression suggest that even moderately rare fishes may be in trouble if interstream gene flow is reduced. Will small stream fishes survive? Those factors exacerbate the already diminished Tombigbee fauna eloquently reported by Boschung (chap. 23).

Li et al. (chap. 24) have persuasively argued that the whole system must be considered in evaluating any part of the system and that historical events also need to be considered (e.g., does cutting 400-year-old trees impact allochthonous food availability?). In contrast, studies of existing simple systems permit analyses of interaction webs far less complex than those for a whole river stream. Both approaches are appropriate.

Rapid advances in the study of body form will help us unravel the function of shape (and movement) in fish swimming and behavior. Stream fishes have body-form constraints (Douglas, chap. 18), and similar morphologies occur in quite distinct taxa (Strauss, chap. 17). The importance of fish size in stream-fish-community structure is a common theme among authors with diverse approaches (Douglas, chap. 18, and Strauss, chap. 17, on influence of fish size on community structure; Li et al., chap 24 and Moyle and Herbold, chap. 4, on special size-related community structure of western fishes; the separation of fishes into "adult" species and "juvenile" species by Gorman, chap. 5; the obvious size relations of the various predation studies [Werner, 1986]). Before this symposium I would have discounted size as a major factor in fish-community structure, because fishes tend to have continuous growth. A posteriori considerations provide a logical basis for size as a major factor in community structure. Habitat size, prey capture, predation avoidance, etc., are in accord with the major role of size shown in this symposium. Fish size has an approximate association with habitat size. Small streams (or stream systems) have only small fishes. Large fishes occur in large streams (or lakes and oceans). Other vertebrate taxa may have giant forms on islands; fishes do not.

What happens to the fish when currents or bursts of speed impact bouyancy has been addressed by Gee (chap. 19). Fish must adjust swim-bladder size rapidly to ensure that they remain at the same level of the water column. This factor applies not only to fishes moving between pools and riffles but also to stationary fishes when streamflow varies. These data also pose questions about why fishes became physoclistous and reduced their capacity to change swim-bladder size quickly. Applications of the Reynolds number to streamfish movements opens a variety of research opportunities. The mandatory low Reynolds numbers of larval fishes (Blaxter, 1986; Webb and Weihs, 1986), which drastically reduce their ability to swim against stream currents, may have an association with parental upstream migration distances. Larval fishes with relatively high Reynolds numbers may have less parental upstream migration than those with quite low Reynolds numbers. Use of eddies and other escapes from stream laminar flow will allow behavior to play a major role for larval fishes or even adult fishes adjusting their bouyancy for different current speeds. Analyses of larval drift in streams must consider the potential of swimming against currents and fish behavior in calculations of stream recruitment.

Two somewhat different themes, extrinsic (physical) and intrinsic (biotic) control, were the foci of several papers. Some, such as Gorman (chap. 5), detail interactions in one stream reach and show how fishes partition habitats at one place (in this instance with replications). Many others show that species interactions differ with localities within a stream (Felley and Felley, chap. 7; Schlosser, chap. 3) or differ between nearby streams (Fisher and Pearson, chap. 9) or between seasons (Finger and Stewart, chap. 11; Hlohowskyj and Wissing, chap. 13; Angermeier, chap. 7); these variations often involve differences in community structure (Fisher and Pearson, chap. 9; Matthews et al., chap. 16). A simplistic summary is that stream-fish abundance is dependent on physical (the stream) and biological (the community) factors. These factors are dependent upon time of day (Fraser et al., chap. 15) and season (Finger and Stewart, chap. 11) and among years (Ross et al., chap 6). Much of what has been summarized has been known for many years; thus we have a quantification of the knowledge of a good field-fish naturalist. This is not a negative comment but rather an illustration of how our science has advanced. We now have documentation of why I went to a specific stream site to obtain a desired fish. I knew where to go; now I have insight into why the fish I selected was (and is) there.

I provide a few words of caution. If the data do not show a difference, it does not prove that the elements are the same; rather, it shows that the results do not demonstrate a difference. We may be measuring the wrong parameter. It may seem that stream temperature is the critical factor, but that factor is inversely associated with dissolved oxygen and the actual limiting factor may be oxygen (Matthews, chap. 14). I have caught *Etheostoma* and *Gambusia* in the same seine haul; careful examination showed that one is at the top and the other at the bottom of the water column and that my seine artificially combined fishes from all levels of the water column. If *Percina* "prefers" large rocks and *Etheostoma* "prefers" small rocks, then a current index will show darter habitat segregation when rock size is associated with current, but not when rock size is independent of current in that stream at that time. In the former example a spurious association may result, in the latter an artificial co-occurrence could be reported. In summary, if the results are concordant with common sense or the "experience" of prior workers, fine. If the results deviate from what might be expected, proceed with caution. Either set of observations could have been incorrect, or an unknown condition may have altered circumstances sufficiently to provide contradictory results.

The faunal contrasts may be local or regional. Moyle and Herbold (chap. 4) have shown that fish assemblages in western North American are quite distinct from those in eastern North American (though headwater trout streams are quite similar). In many ways western North American stream fishes are like those of Europe. The results stimulate a few questions. Would East Asian stream fishes resemble those of eastern North American more than those of Europe? I think Europe is the closer parallel. Would analysis of assemblages on either side of the Appalachians show differences? I think yes. Would eastern North American fishes have more or less parental care in the south (i.e., equivalent south latitude of the Yaqui)? I think more.

The understanding of the community ecology of stream fishes has advanced substantially in the last few years, and the discussions in the symposium show that progress is accelerating. It is amply evident that stream fishes do a variety of things: *Campostoma* controls vegetation, but only some *Micropterus* control *Campostoma* (Matthews et al., chap. 16). *Semotilus* adults influence behavior of *Semotilus* young (who wants to be eaten?) (Fraser et al., chap. 15). Are stream fishes regulated by stochastic or deterministic factors? The proper answer is yes. Depending on circumstances, stochastic or deterministic factors are the most important. The interesting questions now revolve about when and where do the controls differ. My intuitive feeling is that Arizona biologists would obtain more stochastic results and Mississippi biologists more deterministic results. Those catastrophic Arizona floods (Minckley and Meffe, chap. 12) are quite distinct from the more benign floods reported by Ross et al. (chap. 6) and Coon (chap. 10). The systems also differ in that eastern streams drain into larger streams that can dampen the impact of local rains, and western streams often empty into ephemeral playa lakes. What would be the result of a flash flood (= rise of 10 m elevation in one hour) in a stream (e.g., the Guadalupe River) with downstream low-gradient permanent flow? Drastic drop in abundance, especially in the benthic invertebrates and slow (= 5 years) recovery—also a hybrid swarm, (Hubbs, 1985). The results of floods vary with area and predictability of the catastrophic event.

How does the historical biogeography of the fauna relate to its present composition? Mayden (chap. 26) has made an initial effort to provide a chronological development of the fauna of the mountain streams that have been the foci of many community ecology papers in this symposium. The slightly different electrophoretic (Rogers and Cashner, chap. 31) and morphologic (Williams and Etnier, 1982) taxonomic arrangements for *Fundulus* challenge biogeographic interpretations. If *F. julisia* rather than *F. rathbuni* is the sister group to other *F. catenatus* relatives, the trans-Appalachian separation could follow the separation of *F. julisia* rather than precede that event. If *F. catenatus* from the lower Mississippi is closer to the Ozark population than to the Ouachita population, then a lowlands connection must have played a major role in the distribution of these primarily highland fishes.

Other fruitful areas of investigation are also apparent. Do genetic (= isozyme variation) responses show environmental or evolutionary responses? Often (Zimmerman, chap. 29). Do genetic studies parallel morphological variations in stream fishes? Often (Rogers and Cashner, chap. 31). Do genetic data provide evolutionary insight not available from morphologic studies? Often (the *Poeciliopsis* results of Vrijenhoek et al., chap 30 show less morphological variation than electrophoretic). At times genetic variation does not equal morphological variation (the *Salvelinus* results of Vrijenhoek et al., chap. 30, recall the classic studies by Turner [1974] on *Cyprinodon* and the revolutionary insight of Kornfield et al. [1982] into *Cichlosoma* diversity). These and other tools yet to be exploited (genetic probes, etc.) or yet to be developed will provide even more insight into stream-fish biology.

Stream fishes will long remain a challenge. I pose the following food for thought. How do gymnotids partition the resources in the depths of the Amazon and Orinoco? Or even do they partition the resources? Why do fishes (the best examples live in streams) change their morphometrics (Tåning, 1952) depending on environmental conditions during early ontogeny? Why do some streams have more biomass concentrations in one reach than in another (Angermeier, chap. 7)? Diversity is commonly associated with stream order and stream size. What about "200 Springs Creek," which begins in a series of big springs and then branches into many smaller channels? How does that stream order impact diversity? We must also consider what happens at the end (= the estuary).

Are stream fishes reproductively mundane? Clearly, the answer from this symposium is no. *Menidia* does not sacrifice its somatic resources for reproduction; rather, they grow more slowly (Hubbs, 1982), but *Oncorhynchus* certainly does sacrifice somatic tissues for reproduction (Li et al., chap. 24). If males are so inclined, salmon can be reproductively precocious (Montgomery et al., chap. 28). All stream-fish enthusiasts would claim *Poecilia formosa* and the various hybridogenic *Poeciliopsis* spp. as stream fishes. Stream fish do everything; even gynogenesis has been reported recently for fish in northeastern streams by Dawley and Schultz (1984). Stream fish vary their reproductive investment geographically (Heins and Baker, chap. 27) or seasonally as recently reported by Marsh (1984). In summary, stream fishes provide intellectually stimulating raw material for scientific contributions, occupy fun habitats, and are a pleasure to study (= bright colors). I have enjoyed working with various stream fishes, and the enthusiasm and thoughts expressed by the contributors to this book signify the best in science.

Literature Cited

Abrams, P. 1980. Some comments on measuring niche overlap. Ecology 61:44–49.

Adams, G. I., C. Butts, L. W. Stephenson, and W. Cook. 1926. Geology of Alabama. Geol. Surv. Ala. Spec. Rep. 14. University, Ala.

Adamson, S. W., and T. E. Wissing. 1977. Food habits and feeding periodicity of the rainbow, fantail, and banded darters in Four Mile Creek. Ohio J. Sci. 77:164–69.

Alexander, R. M. 1961. Visco-elastic properties of the tunica externa of the swimbladder in Cyprinidae. J. Exp. Biol. 38:747–57.

———. 1966. Physical aspects of swimbladder function. Biol. Rev. 41:141–76.

———. 1972. The energetics of vertical migration of fishes. Symp. Soc. Exp. Biol. 26:273–94.

———. 1977. Swimming, p 222–48. *In*: Mechanics and energetics of animal locomotion. R. M. Alexander and G. Goldspink (eds.). Academic Press, New York.

Allan, J. D. 1982. The effects of reduction in trout density on the invertebrate community of a mountain stream. Ecology 63:1444–55.

Allee, B. J. 1974. Spatial requirements and behavioral interactions of juvenile coho salmon (*Oncorhynchus kisutch*) and steelhead trout (*Salmo gairdneri*). Unpub. PhD Diss., Univ. Washington, Seattle.

Allen, K. R. 1969. Distinctive aspects of the ecology of stream fishes: A review. J. Fish. Res. Board Canada 26:1429–38.

Allen, R. L., K. T. Beiningen, F. Cleaver, D. C. Lavier, D. W. Ortman, L. A. Phinney, K. Thompson, F. Vincent, and R. J. Wahle. 1976. Investigative reports of Columbia River fisheries projects. Pacific Northwest Regional Commission, Portland, Oreg.

Allendorf, F. W., and S. R. Phelps. 1980. Loss of genetic variation in a hatchery stock of cutthroat trout. Trans. Amer. Fish. Soc. 109:537–43.

Anderson, G. R. V., A. H. Ehrlich, P. R. Ehrlich, J. D. Roughgarden, B. C. Russell, and F. H. Talbot. 1981. The community structure of coral reef fishes. Amer. Nat. 117:476–95.

Andersson, L., N. Ryman, and G. Stahl. 1983. Protein loci in the arctic charr, *Salvelinus alpinus*: Electrophoretic expression and genetic variability patterns. J. Fish. Biol. 23:75–94.

Andrewartha, H. G., and L. C. Birch. 1954. Distribution and abundance of animals. Univ. Chicago Press, Chicago.

Andrusak, H., and T. G. Northcote. 1971. Segregation between adult cutthroat trout (*Salmo clarki*) and Dolly Varden (*Salvelinus malma*) in small coastal British Columbia lakes. J. Fish. Res. Board Canada 28:1259–68.

Angermeier, P.L. 1982. Resource seasonality and fish diets in an Illinois stream. Env. Biol. Fish. 7:251–64.

———. 1983. The importance of cover and other habitat features to the distribution and abundance of Illinois stream fishes. Unpub. PhD Diss., Univ. Illinois, Champaign.

———. 1985. Spatio-temporal patterns of foraging success for fishes in an Illinois stream. Amer. Midl. Nat. 114:342–59.

———, and J. R. Karr. 1984. Relationships between woody debris and fish habitat in a small warmwater stream. Trans. Amer. Fish. Soc. 113:716–26.

Anonymous. 1976. Missouri River bank stabilization and navigation project. Draft environmental statement continuing construction and operation and maintenance. US Army Corps of Engineers, Omaha, Nebr.

Arnold, G. P. 1969. The reactions of the plaice (*Pleuronectes platessa* L.) to water currents. J. Exp. Biol. 51:681–97.

———, and D. Weihs. 1978. The hydrodynamics of rheotaxis in the plaice (*Pleuronectes platessa* L.). *Ibid.* 75:147–69.

Atchley, W. R. 1982. Some genetic aspects of morphological variation, pp. 346–63. *In*: Numerical taxonomy. J. Felsenstein (ed.). NATO A.S.I. Series G, Ecological Sciences, No. 1. Springer-Verlag, New York.

———, J. J. Rutledge, and D. E. Cowley. 1981. Genetic components of size and shape. II. Multivariate covariance patterns in the rat and mouse skull. Evolution 35:1037–55.

Avise, J. C. 1977a. Is evolution gradual or rectangular? Evidence from living fishes. Proc. Natl. Acad. Sci. 74:5083–87.

———1977b. Genic heterozygosity and rate of speciation. Paleobiology 3:422–32.

———, and C. F. Aquadro. 1982. A comparative summary of genetic distances in the vertebrates: Patterns and correlations. Evol. Biol. 15:151–85.

———, and J. Felley. 1979. Population structure of freshwater fishes. I. Genetic variation of the bluegill (*Lepomis macrochirus*) populations in manmade reservoirs. Evolution 33:15–26.

———, and R. K. Selander. 1972. Evolutionary genetics of cave-dwelling fishes of the genus *Astyanax*. *Ibid* 26:1–19.

———, and M. H. Smith. 1974. Biochemical genetics of sunfish. I. Geographic variation and subspecific intergradation in the bluegill, *Lepomis machrochirus*. *Ibid.* 28:12–56.

Bagenal, T. B. 1969. Relationship between egg size and fry survival in brown trout, *Salmo trutta*. L. J. Fish Biol. 1:349–53.

———. 1978. Aspects of fish fecundity, pp. 75–101. *In:* The biological basis of freshwater fish production. S. D. Gerking (ed.). John Wiley & Sons, New York.

Bailey, R. M. 1955. Differential mortality from high temperature in a mixed population of fishes in southern Michigan. Ecology 36:526–28.

Baker, H. G. 1965. Characteristics and modes of origin of weeds, pp. 147–72. *In:* Genetics of colonizing species. H. G. Baker and G. L. Stebbins (eds.). Academic Press, New York.

Baker, J. A., and S. T. Ross. 1981. Spatial and temporal resource utilization by southeastern cyprinids. Copeia 1981:178–89.

Balon, E. K. 1975. Reproductive guilds in fishes: A proposal and definition. J. Fish. Res. Board Canada 32:821–64.

Baltz, D. M., and P. B. Moyle. 1982. Life history characteristics of tule perch (*Hysterocarpus traski*) populations in contrasting environments. Env. Biol. Fish. 7:229–42.

———, and ——— 1984. Segregation by species and size classes of rainbow trout, *Salmo gairdneri*, and Sacramento sucker, *Catostomus occidentalis*, in three California streams. *Ibid.* 10:101-10.

———, ———, and N. J. Knight. 1982. Competitive interactions between benthic stream fishes, riffle sculpin, *Cottus gulosus*, and speckled dace, *Rhinichthys osculus*. Canad. J. Fish. Aquatic Sci. 39:1502–11.

Barber, W. E., and W. L. Minckley. 1966. Fishes of Aravaipa Creek, Graham and Pinal counties, Arizona. Southwest. Nat. 11:315–24.

Barbour, C. D., and B. Chernoff. 1984. Comparative morphology of the Pescados Blancos (Genus *Chirostoma*) from Lake Chapalla, Mexico, pp. 111–28. *In:* Evolution of fish species flocks. A. A. Echelle and I. Kornfield (eds.). Univ. Maine Press, Orono.

Barlow, G. W. 1958a. High salinity mortality of desert pupfish, *Cyprinodon macularius*. Copeia 1958:231–32.

———. 1958b. Daily movements of desert pupfish, *Cyprinodon macularius* in shore pools of the Salton Sea, California. Ecology 39:580–87.

———. 1961. Social behavior of the desert pupfish, *Cyprinodon macularius*, in the field and in the laboratory. Amer. Midl. Nat. 65:339–59.

Barnes, J. R., and G. W. Minshall (eds.). 1983. Stream ecology—application and testing of general ecological theory. Plenum Press, New York.

Barr, A. J., J. H. Goodnight, J. P. Sall, and J. T. Hetwig. 1976. A user's guide to SAS. SAS Institute, Raleigh, N.C.

Barrett, P. J. 1983. Systematics of fishes of the genus *Tilapia* (Perciformes: Cichlidae) in the lower Colorado River basin. Unpub. MS Arizona State Univ., Tempe.

Becker, C. D., and M. P. Fugihara. 1978. The bacterial pathogen, *Flexibacter columnaris*, and its epizootiology among Columbia River fish: A review and synthesis. Amer. Fish. Soc. Monogr. No. 2.

Becker, G. C. 1983. Fishes of Wisconsin. Univ. Wisconsin Press, Madison.

Bedinger, M. S. 1978. Relation between forest species and flooding, pp. 427–35. *In:* Wetland functions and values: The state of our understanding. P. E. Greeson, J. R. Clark, and J. E. Clark (eds.). Amer. Water Res. Assoc., Minneapolis, Minn.

Beets, J. P. 1979. Population dynamics of the stoneroller minnow, *Campostoma anomalum anomalum* (Rafinesque) in streams of a five-county area in upper East Tennessee. Unpub. MS Thesis, Univ. Tennessee, Knoxville.

Behnke, R. H. 1972. The systematics of salmonid fishes of recently glaciated lakes. J. Fish. Res. Board Canada 29:639–71.

———. 1980. A systematic review of the genus *Salvelinus*, pp. 441–81. *In:* Charrs, Salmonid fishes of the genus *Salvelinus*. E. K. Balon (ed.). Dr. W. Junk Publishers, The Hague, Netherlands.

Beitinger, T. L., and L. C. Fitzpatrick. 1979. Physiological and ecological correlates of preferred temperature: preferenda versus optima. Amer. Zool. 19:319–29.

Bell, G. 1980. The costs of reproduction and their consequences. Amer. Nat. 116:45–76.

———. 1982. The masterpiece of nature: The evolution and genetics of sexuality. Univ. California Press, Berkeley.

Bennett, D. H., P. M. Bratovich, W. Knox, D. Palmer, and H. Hansel. 1983. Status of the warmwater fishery and the potential of improving warmwater fish habitat in the lower Snake Reservoirs. US Army Corps Eng., Final Rep. Contract No. DACW68-79-C0057.

Benson, N. G. 1968. Review of fishery studies on Missouri River main stem reservoirs. US Fish and Wildl. Serv. Res. Rep. 71.

Berezay, G., and J. H. Gee. 1978. Buoyancy response to changes in water velocity and its function in creek chub (*Semotilus atromaculatus*). J. Fish. Res. Board Canada 35:295–99.

Berner, L. M. 1951. Limnology of the lower Missouri River. Ecology 32:1—12.

Berra, T. M., and G. E. Gunning. 1970. Repopulation of experimentally decimated sections of streams by longear sunfish, *Lepomis megalotis megalotis* (Rafinesque). Trans. Amer. Fish. Soc. 99:776–81.

Bilton, H. T. 1971. A hypothesis of alternation of age of return in successive generations of Skeena River sockeye salmon (*Oncorhynchus nerka*). J. Fish. Res. Board Canada 28:513–16.

Birch, L. C. 1960. The genetic factor in population ecology. Amer. Nat. 94:5–24.

Bisson, P., and C. Bond. 1971. Origin and distribution of the fishes of Harney Basin, Oregon. Copeia 1971:268–81.

Black, E. C. 1953. Upper lethal temperatures of some British Columbia freshwater fishes. J. Fish. Res. Board Canada 10:196–210.

Black, G. F. 1980. Status of the desert pupfish, *Cyprinodon macularius* (Baird and Girard) in California. Calif. Dept. Fish Game, Inland Fish., Endang. Species Prog. Spec. Pub. 80–81, Sacramento.

Black, J.D. 1949. Changing fish populations as an index of pollution and soil erosion. Trans. Ill. State Acad. Sci. 542:145–84.

Blaxter, J. H. S. 1966. Utilization of yolk by herring larvae. J. Mar. Biol. Assoc. U.K. 46:219–34.

———. 1969. Development: Eggs and larvae, pp. 177–252. *In:* Fish physiology, Vol. 3. W. S. Hoar and D. J. Randall (eds.). Academic Press, New York.

———. 1986. The development of sense organs and behavior in teleost larvae with special reference to feeding and predator avoidance. Trans. Amer. Fish. Soc. 115:98–114.

———, and G. Hempel. 1963. The influence of egg size on herring larvae (*Clupea harengus* L.). J. Cons. Perm. Int. Explor. Mer. 28:211-40.

Boag, P. T., and P. R. Grant. 1981. Intense natural selection in a population of Darwin's finches (Geospizinae) in the Galápagos. Science 214:82–85.

Boecklen, W. J., and C. NeSmith. 1985. Hutchinsonian ratios and lognormal distributions. Evolution 39:695-98.

Boehner, P., ed. 1964. Introduction, pp. ix–li. *In:* Philosophical writings: *A* selection: William of Ockham. Bobbs-Merrill Co., Indianapolis.

Bookstein, F. L., B. Chernoff, R. L. Elder, J. M. Humphries, G. R. Smith, and R. E. Strauss. 1985. Morphometrics in evolutionary biology: the geometry of size and shape change with examples from fishes. Spec. Pub. 15, Acad. Natl. Sci. Philadelphia, Pa.

Boschung, H. T. 1973. A report on the fishes of the upper Tombigbee River, Yellow and Indian creek systems of Alabama and Mississippi. First Supplemental Report, Continuing Environmental Studies, Vol. 7, Appendix C. Army Corps of Engineers, Mobile District, Mobile, Ala.

———. 1984. A study of the fishes of the Upper Tombigbee River drainage system south of the Columbus Lock and Dam, Tennessee-Tombigbee Waterway. Army Corps of Engineers, Mobile District, Mobile, Ala.

———, and T. S. Jandebeur. 1974. A report on the fauna of the Cypress Creek watershed, with emphasis on the fishes. US Dept. of Agriculture, Soil Conservation Service, Auburn, Ala.

———, and P. O'Neil. 1981. The effects of forest clearcutting on fishes and macroinvertebrates in an Alabama stream, pp. 200–17. *In:* The Warmwater Streams Symposium. C. F. Bryan, G. E. Hall, and G. B. Pardue (eds.). Southern Division, American Fisheries Society, Lawrence, Kans.

Bottom, D. L., P. J. Howell, and J. D. Rodgers. 1985. The effects of stream alterations on salmon and trout habitat in Oregon. Oreg. Dept. Fish Wildl., Internal Rep.

Bottrell, C. E., R. H. Ingersol, and R. W. Jones. 1964. Notes on the embryology, early development, and behavior of *Hybopsis aestivalis tetranemus* (Gilbert). Trans. Amer. Microscop. Soc. 83:391–99.

Bottroff, L., J. A. St. Amant, and W. Parker. 1969. Addition of *Pylodictis olivaris* to the California fauna. Calif. Fish Game 55:90.

Bovee, K. D. 1978. Probability-of-use criteria for the family Salmonidae. US Fish Wildl. Serv., Biol. Serv. Prog. FWS/OBS-78/07, Washington, D.C.

———. 1981. A users guide to the instream flow incremental methodology. M. US Fish Wildl. Serv., Biol. Serv. Prog. FWS/OBS-80/52, Washington, D.C.

———, and T. Cochnauer. 1977. Development and evaluation of weighted critia, probability-of-use curves for instream flow assessments: Fisheries. US Fish Wildlife Serv. Biol. Serv. Prog. FWS/OBS-77/63, Washington, D.C.

———, and R. T. Milhous. 1978. Hydraulic similation in instream flow studies: Theory and technique. US Fish Wildl. Serv. Biol. Serv. Prog. FWS/OBS-78/33. Washington, D.C.

Brandt, S. B. 1980. Spatial segregation of adult and young-of-the-year alewives across a thermocline in Lake Michigan. Trans. Amer. Fish. Soc. 109:469–78.

———, J. J. Magnuson, and L. B. Crowder. 1980. Thermal habitat partitioning by fishes in Lake Michigan. Canad. J. Fish. Aquatic Sci. 37:1557–64.

Brattstrom, B. H. 1968. Thermal acclimation in anuran amphibians as a function of latitude and altitude. Comp. Biochem. Physiol. 24:93–111.

Breder, C. M., Jr. 1960. Design for a fry trap. Zoologica 45:155–59.

Brett, J. R. 1952. Temperature tolerance in young Pacific salmon, genus *Oncorynchus*. J. Fish. Res. Board Canada 9:265–323.

———. 1956. Some principles in the thermal requirements of fishes. Quart. Rev. Biol. 31:75–87.

———. 1971. Energetic responses of salmon to temperature. A study of some thermal relations in the physiology and freshwater ecology of sockeye salmon (*Oncorhynchus nerka*). Amer. Zool. 11:99–113.

Breukelman, J. 1940. The fishes of northwestern Kansas. Trans. Kans. Acad. Sci. 43:357–75.

Brockelman, W. Y. 1975. Competition, the fitness of offspring, and optimal clutch size. Amer. Nat. 109:677-99.

Brooks, D. R. 1985. Historical ecology: A new approach to studying the evolution of ecological associations. Ann. Mo. Bot. Gard. 72:660-80.

Brown, D. E., N. B. Carmony, and R. M. Turner. 1981. Drainage map of Arizona showing perennial streams and some important wetlands. Ariz. Game Fish Dept., Phoenix.

Brown, J. H. 1984. On the relationship between abundance and distribution of species. Amer. Nat. 124:255-79.

———, D. W. Davidson, J. C. Munger, and R. S. Inouye. 1986. Experimental community ecology: The desert granivore system, pp. 41–61. *In:* Commnity ecology. J. Diamond and T. J. Case (eds.). Harper & Row, New York.

———, and C. R. Feldmeth. 1971. Evolution in constant and fluctuating environments: Thermal tolerances of desert pupfish (*Cyprinodon*). Evolution 25:390–98.

———, and A. Kodric-Brown. 1977. Turnover rates in insular biogeography: Effect of immigration on extinction. Ecology 58:445–49.

Brown, J. L. 1957. A key to species and subspecies of the cyprinodont genus *Fundulus* in the United States and Canada east of the Continental Divide. J. Wash. Acad. Sci. 47:69–77.

Brown, K. L. 1982. Demographic and genetic characteristics of dispersal in the mosquitofish, *Gambusia affinis* (Family Poeciliidae). Unpub. PhD Diss., Univ. Georgia, Athens.

Brown, M. E. 1946. The growth of brown trout (*Salmo trutta* Linn.). I. Factors influencing the growth of trout fry. J. Exp. Biol. 22:118-29.

———. 1957. Experimental studies on growth, pp. 361–400. *In:* The physiology of fishes, Vol. 1. M. E. Brown (ed.). Academic Press, New York.

Bruns, D. A., and W. L. Minckley. 1980. Distribution and abundance of benthic invertebrates in a Sonoran desert stream. J. Arid Environ. 3:117–31.

Bryan, C. F., D. J. DeMont, D. S. Sabins, and J. P. Newman, Jr. 1976. Annual report: a limnological study of the Atchafalaya Basin. Louisiana Coop. Fish. Res. Unit, Louisiana State Univ., Baton Rouge.

———, D. S. Sabins, F. M. Truesdale, and C. R. Demas. 1974. Annual report: A limnological survey of the Atchafalaya Basin. Louisiana Coop. Fish. Res. Unit, Louisiana State Univ., Baton Rouge.

———, F. M. Truesdale, and D. S. Sabins. 1975. Annual report: A limnological study of the Atchafalaya Basin. Louisiana Coop. Fish. Res. Unit, Louisiana State Univ., Baton Rouge.

Bryant, E. H. 1977. Morphometric adaptation of the housefly *Musca domestica* L., in the United States. Evolution 31:581–96.

Buchanan, D. V., R. M. Hooton, and J. R. Moring. 1981. Northern squawfish (*Ptchocheilus oregonensis*) predation on juvenile salmonids in sections of the Willamette River basin, Oregon. Canad. J. Fish. Aquatic Sci. 38:360–64.

———, J. E. Sanders, J. L. Zinn, and J. L. Fryer. 1983. Relative susceptibility of four strains of summer steelhead to infection by *Ceratomyxa shasta*. Trans. Amer. Fish. Soc. 112:541–43.

Buchanan, T. M. 1973. Key to the fishes of Arkansas. Ark. Game and Fish Comm., Little Rock.

Buck, R. J. G., and A. F. Youngson. 1982. The downstream migration of precociously mature Atlantic salmon, *Salmo salar* L., parr in autumn: Its relation to the spawning migration of mature adult fish. J. Fish Biol. 20:279–88.

Bull, C. J., and W. C. Mackay. 1976. Nitrogen and phosphorus removal from lakes by fish harvest. J. Fish. Res. Board Canada 33:1374–76.

Bull, W. B. 1979. Threshold of critical power in streams. Bull. Geol. Soc. Amer. 86:1489–98.

———. 1981. Soils, geology, and hydrology of deserts, pp. 42–58. *In:* Water in Desert Ecosystems, D. E. Evans and J. L. Thames (eds.). Dowden, Hutchinson, and Ross, Stroudsburg, Pa.

Bulmer, M. G. 1975. The statistical analysis of density dependence. Biometrics 31:901–11.

Burke, T. D., and J. W. Robinson. 1979. River structure modifications to provide habitat diversity, pp. 556–61. *In:* The mitigation symposium: A national workshop on mitigating losses of fish and wildlife habitats. G. A. Swanson (ed.). Gen. Tech. Rep. RM-65, Rocky Mtn. Forest and Range Exp. Stn., Fort Collins, Colo.

Burkham, D. E. 1970. Precipitation, streamflow, and major floods at selected sites in the Gila River drainage basin above Coolidge Dam, Arizona. USGS Prof. Pap. 655-B:1–33.

———. 1972. Channel changes of the Gila River in Safford Valley, Arizona, 1846–1970. USGS Prof. Pap. 655-G:1–24.

———. 1976a. Flow from small watersheds adjacent to the study reach of the Gila River phreatophyte project, Arizona. USGS Prof. Pap. *Ibid.* 655-I:1–27.

———. 1976b. Hydraulic effects of changes in bottomland vegetation on three major floods, Gila River in southeastern Arizona. USGS Prof. Pap. 655-J:1–25.

———. 1976c. Effects of changes in an alluvial channel on the timing, magnitude, and transformation of flood waves, southeastern Arizona. USGS Prof. Pap. 655-K:1–14.

Burns, C. V. 1975. Temperatures of Kansas streams. Kans. Water Res. Board Tech. Rep. 12:1–220.

Burr, B. M. 1980a. *Campostoma anomalum* (Rafinesque). Stoneroller, pp. 143–44. *In:* Atlas of North American freshwater fishes. D. S. Lee et al. (eds.). N.C. State Mus. Nat. Hist., Raleigh.

———. 1980b. A distributional checklist of the fishes of Kentucky. Brimleyana 3:53–84.

———, and R. C. Cashner. 1983. *Campostoma pauciradii*, a new cyprinid fish from southeastern United States, with a review of related forms. Copeia 1983:101–16.

———, and W. W. Dimmick. 1983. Redescription of the bigeye shiner *Notropis boops* (Pisces: Cyprinidae). Proc. Biol. Soc. Wash. 96:50–58.

———, and L. M. Page. 1986. Zoogeography of fishes of the lower Ohio–upper Mississippi basin, pp. 287–324. *In:* Zoogeography of North American freshwater fishes. C. H. Hocutt and E. O. Wiley (eds.). Wiley Interscience, New York.

Burton, G. W., and E. P. Odum. 1945. The distribution of stream fish in the vicinity of Mountain Lake, Virginia. Ecology 26:182–94.

Bustard, D. R. 1975. Preferences of juvenile coho salmon (*Oncorhynchus kisutch*) and steelhead trout (*Salmo gairdneri*). *Ibid.* 32:681–87.

———, and D. W. Narver. 1975. Aspects of winter ecology of juvenile coho salmon (*Oncorhynchus kisutch*) and steelhead trout (*Salmo gairdneri*). *Ibid.* 32:667–80.

Buth, D. G. 1979a. Biochemical systematics of the cyprinid genus *Notropis*. I. The subgenus *Luxilus*. Biochem. Syst. Ecol. 7:69–79.

———. 1979b. Genetic relationships among the torrent suckers, genus *Thorburnia*. *Ibid.* 7:311–16.

———. 1980. Evolutionary genetics and systematic relationships in the catostomid genus *Hypentelium*. Copeia 1980:280–90.

———. 1983. Duplicate isozyme loci in fishes: origins, distribution, phyletic consequences, and locus nomenclature, pp. 381–400. *In:* Isozymes: Current topics in biological and medical research. M. C. Rattazzi, J. G. Scandlios and G. S. White (eds.) Alan R. Liss, New York.

———, B. M. Brooks, and J. R. Schenck. 1980. Electrophoretic evidence for relationships and differentiation among members of the percid subgenus *Microperca*. Biochem. Syst. Ecol. 8:297–304.

Caldwell, R. D. 1969. A study of the fishes of the Upper Tombigbee River and Yellow Creek drainage systems of Alabama and Mississippi. Unpub. PhD Diss., Univ. Alabama, University.

Calhoun, S. W. 1981. The role of genic, behavioral, and biochemical mechanisms in the adaption of minnows of the genus *Notropis* (Cyprinidae) to temperature. Unpub. MS Thesis, North Texas State Univ., Denton.

———, T. L. Beitinger, and E. G. Zimmerman. 1981. Similarity in selected temperatures of two allopatric populations of blacktail shiner, *Notropis venustus* (Cyprinidae). Southwest. Nat. 26:441–42.

———, E. G. Zimmerman, and T. L. Beitinger. 1982. Stream regulation alters acute temperature preferenda of red shiners, *Notropis lutrensis*. Canad. J. Fish. Aquatic Sci. 39:360–63.

Capinera, J. L. 1979. Qualitative variation in plants and insects: effect of propagule size on ecological plasticity. Amer. Nat. 114:350–61.

Caraco, T., S. Martindale, and H. R. Pulliam. 1980. Avian flocking in the presence of a predator. Nature 285:400–401.

Carlander, K. D. 1977. Handbook of freshwater fishery biology, Vol. 2. Iowa State Univ. Press, Ames.

Carlson, D. M., W. L. Pflieger, L. Trial, and P. S. Haverland. 1985. Distribution, biology, and hybridization of *Scaphirhynchus albus* and *S. platorynchus* in the Missouri and Mississippi rivers. *In:* the sturgeon symposium. S. Doroshov (ed.). Env. Biol. Fish. 14:51–59.

Carnes, B. A., and N. A. Slade. 1982. Some comments on niche analysis in canonical space. Ecology 63:888–93.

Carothers, S. W. 1977. Importance, preservation, and management of riparian habitat: An overview, pp. 2–4. *In:* Importance, preservation, and management of riparian habitat: A symposium. R. R. Johnson and D. A. Jones (tech. coords.). US For. Serv. Gen. Tech. Rep. RM-43, Rocky Mtn. For. Range Exp. Sta., Ft. Collins, Colo.

———, R. R. Johnson, and S. Aitchison. 1974. Population structure and social organization of southwestern riparian birds. Amer. Zool. 14:97–108.

Carson, H. 1975. The genetics of speciation at the diploid level. Amer. Nat. 109:73–92.

Carver, D. C. 1975. Life history of the spotted bass, *Micropterus punctulatus* (Rafinesque) in Six-mile Creek, Louisiana. La. Dept. Wildl. Fish., Fish. Div. Bull. 13.

Case, M. L., and T. J. Taper. 1985. On the coexistence and evolution of asexual and sexual competition. Evolution. 40:366–87.

Case, T. J., J. Faaborg, and R. Sidell. 1983. The role of body size in the assembly of West Indian bird communities. *Ibid.* 37:1062–74.

Cashner, R. C., and R. D. Suttkus. 1977. *Ambloplites constellatus*, a new species of rock bass from Ozark Uplands of Arkansas and Missouri with a review of western rock bass populations. Amer. Midl. Nat. 98:147–61.

Caswell, H. 1976. Community structure: A neutral model analysis. Ecol. Monogr. 46:327–54.

Caughley, G., and J. H. Lawton. 1981. Plant-herbivore systems; pp. 132–66. *In:* Theoretical ecology: Principles and applications, 2d ed. R. M. May (ed). Saunders, Philadelphia.

Cavalli-Sforza, L. L., and A. W. F. Edwards. 1967. Phylogenetic analysis and estimation procedures. Evolution 21:550-78.

Cederholm, C. J., and N. P. Peterson. 1985. The retention of coho salmon (*Oncorhynchus kisutch*) carcasses by organic debris in small streams. Canad. J. Fish. Aquatic Sci. 42:1222–25.

Cerri, R. D. 1983. The effect of light intensity on predator and prey behaviour in cyprinid fish: factors that influence prey risk. Anim. Behav. 31:736–42.

———, and D. F. Fraser. 1983. Predation and risk in foraging minnows: Balancing conflicting demands. Amer. Nat. 121:552–61.

Chaney, E. 1978. A question of balance: Water/energy-salmon and steelhead production in the upper Columbia River basin. Northwest Res. Inform. Center, Eagle, Idaho.

Chapman, D. W. 1965. Food and space as regulators of salmonid populations in streams. Amer. Nat. 100:345–57.

Chebanov, N. A. 1982. Spawning behavior of the humpbacked salmon *Oncorhynchus gorbuscha* with different ratios of sexes at the spawning ground. Ekologiya 1:57–66.

Cheetham, A. H., and J. E. Hazel. 1969. Binary (presence-absence) similarity coefficients. J. Paleontol. 43:1130–36.

Chen, T. R. 1971. A comparative chromosome study of the genus *Fundulus* (Teleostei, Cyprinodontidae). Chromosoma 32:436–53.

Chermock, R. L. 1955. First record of the shovelnose sturgeon, *Scaphirhynchus platorynchus*, from the Tombigbee River, Alabama. Copeia 1955:154.

Cherry, D. S., K. L. Dickson, and J. Cairns, Jr. 1975. Temperature selected and avoided by fish at various acclimation temperatures. J. Fish. Res. Board Canada 32:485–91.

———, ———, ———, and J. R. Stauffer. 1977. Preferred, avoided, and lethal temperatures of fish during rising temperature conditions. *Ibid.* 34:239–46.

Chiasson, A. G., and J. H. Gee. 1983. Swim bladder gas composition and control of buoyancy by fathead minnows (*Pimephales promelas*) during exposure to hypoxia. Canad. J. Zool. 61:2213–18.

Chorley, R. J. 1962. Geomorphology and general systems theory. USGS Prof. Pap. 500-B:1–10.

de Ciechomski, J. D. 1966. Development of the larvae and variations in the size of the eggs of the Argentine anchovy, *Engraulis anchoita* Hubbs and Marini. J. Cons. Perm. Int. Explor. Mer. 30:281–90.

Cimino, M. C. 1972a. Meiosis in triploid all-female fish (*Poeciliopsis* Poeciliidae). Science 175:1484–86.

———. 1972b. Egg production, polyploidization, and evolution in a diploid all-female fish of the genus *Poeciliopsis*. Evolution 26:294–306.

Cincotta, D. A., and J. R. Stauffer, Jr. 1984. Temperature preference and avoidance studies of six North American freshwater fish species. Hydrobiologia 109:173–77.

Clarkson, D. B. 1979. Estimating the standard errors of rotated factor loadings by jackknifing. Psychometrika 44:297–314.

Clay, W. M. 1975. The fishes of Kentucky. Kentucky Dept. Fish Wildl. Recources, Frankfort.

Clemmer, G. H. 1971. The systematics and biology of the *Hybopsis amblops* complex. Unpub. PhD Diss., Tulane Univ., New Orleans, La.

Coburn, M. M. 1982. Anatomy and relationships of *Notropsis atherinoides*. Unpub. PhD Diss., Ohio State Univ., Columbus.

Cochran, W. G. 1953. Sampling techniques. John Wiley & Sons, New York.

Cody, M. L., and J. M. Diamond (eds.). 1975. Ecology and evolution of communities. Belknap Press, Cambridge, Mass.

———, and H. A. Mooney. 1978. Convergence versus nonconvergence in Mediterranean-climate ecosystems. Ann. Rev. Ecol. Syst. 9:265–321.

Cohan, D. R., B. W. Anderson, and R. D. Ohmart. 1978. Avian population responses to salt cedar along the lower Colorado River, pp. 371–382. *In* Strategies for protection and management of floodplain wetlands and other riparian ecosystems. R. R. Johnson and J. F. McCormick (tech. coords.). US For. Serv. Gen. Tech. Rep. WO-12, US Foreign Service, Washington, D.C.

Cole, J. J. 1982. Interactions between bacteria and algae in aquatic ecosystems. Ann. Rev. Ecol. Syst. 13:291–314.

Cole, L. C. 1954. The population consequences of life history phenomena. Quart. Rev. Biol. 29:103–37.

Coleman, G. A. 1929. A biological survey of the Salton Sea. Calif. Fish Game 15:218–27.

Collette, B. B. 1962. The swamp darters of the subgenus *Hololepis* (Pisces, Percidae). Tulane Stud. Zool. 9:115–211.

Collins, J. P., and J. E. Cheek. 1983. Effect of food and density on development of typical and cannibalistic salamader larvae in *Ambystoma tigrinum nebulosum*. Amer. Zool. 23:77–84.

———, J. B. Mitton, and B. A. Pierce. 1980. *Ambystoma tigrinum:* A multi-species conglomerate? Copeia 1980:666–75.

Collins, J. P., C. Young, J. Howell, and W. L. Minckley. 1981. Impact of flooding in a Sonoran desert stream including elimination of an endangered fish population (*Poeciliopsis o. occidentalis,* Poeciliidae). Southwest. Nat. 26:415–23.

Colwell, R. K., and D. W. Winkler. 1984. A null model for null models in biogeography, pp. 344–59. *In:* Ecological communities: Conceptual issues and the evidence. D. R. Strong, D. Simberloff, L. G. Abele and A. B. Thistle (eds.). Princeton University Press, Princeton, N.J.

Connell, J. H. 1975. Some mechanisms producing structure in natural communities, pp. 460–90. *In:* Ecology and evolution of communities. M. Cody, and J. M. Diamond (eds.). Harvard Univ. Press, Cambridge, Mass.

———. 1978. Diversity in tropical rain forests and coral reefs. Science 199:1302–10.

———. 1980. Diversity and the coevolution of competitors, or the ghost of competition past. Oikos 35:131-38.

———, 1983. On the prevalence and relative importance of interspecific competition: Evidence from field experiments. Amer. Nat. 122:661-96.

———, and W. P. Sousa. 1983. On the evidence needed to judge ecological stability or persistence. *Ibid.* 121:789–823.

Connor, E. F., and E. D. McCoy. 1979. The statistics and biology of the species-area relationship. *Ibid.* 113:791–833.

———, and D. Simberloff. 1979. The assembly of species communities: Chance or competition? Ecology 60:1132–40.

Constantz, G. D. 1979. Life history patterns of a livebearing fish in contrasting environments. Oecologia 40:189–201.

———. 1981. Life history patterns of desert fishes, pp. 237–90. *In:* R. J. Naiman and D. L. Soltz. Fishes in North American Deserts. John Wiley & Sons, New York.

Cook, F. A. 1959. Freshwater fishes in Mississippi. Miss. Game Fish. Comm., Jackson.

Cooley, M. E., B. N. Aldridge, and R. C. Euler. 1977. Effects of the catastrophic flood of December 1966, North Rim area, eastern Grand Canyon, Arizona. USGS Prof. Pap. 980:1–43.

Coon, J. C., R. R. Ringe, and T. C. Bjornn. 1977. Abundance, growth, distribution and movements of white sturgeon in the mid-Snake River. Office Water Res. Technol. Tech. Rep., Project B-026-IDA.

Coon, T. G. 1982. Coexistence in a guild of benthic stream fishes: The effects of disturbance. Unpub. PhD Diss., Univ. California—Davis.

Courtney, W. C., Jr., J. E. Deacon, D. W. Sada, R. C. Allen, and

G. L. Vinyard. 1985. Comparative status of fishes along the course of the pluvial White River, Nevada. Southwest. Nat. 30:503-524.

———, D. A. Hensley, J. N. Taylor, and J. A. McCann. 1984. Distribution of exotic fishes in the continental United States, pp. 41–77. *In:* Distribution, Biology, and Management of Exotic Fishes. W. R. Courtenay, Jr., and J. R. Stauffer, Jr. (eds.). Johns Hopkins Univ. Press, Baltimore.

Coutant, C. C. 1973. Effects of thermal shock on vulnerability of juvenille salmonids to predation. J. Fish Res. Board Canada 30:965–73.

Cowles, R. B. 1934. Notes on the ecology and breeding habits of the desert minnow, *Cyprinodon macularius* Baird and Girard. Copeia 1934:40–42.

Cragin, F. W. 1885. Preliminary list of Kansas Fishes. Bull. Washburn Lab. Nat. Hist. 1:105–11.

Craig, J. A., and R. L. Hacker. 1940. The history and development of the fisheries of the Columbia River. Bull. Bur. Fish. 49:133–216.

Crawshaw, L. I. 1975. Attainment of the final thermal preferendum in brown bullheads acclimated to different temperatures. Comp. Biochem. Physiol. 52A:171–73.

———. 1979. Responses to rapid temperature change in vertebrate ectotherms. Amer. Zool. 19:225–37.

Crear, D., and I. Haydock. 1971. Laboratory rearing of the desert pupfish, *Cyprinodon macularius*. Fishery Bull. 69:151–56.

Crisp, D. T., R. H. K. Mann, and P. R. Cubby. 1984. Effects of impoundment on fish populations in afferent streams at Cow Green Reservoir. J. Appl. Ecol. 21:739–56.

Cross, F. B. 1967. Handbook of fishes of Kansas. Univ. Kansas Mus. Nat. Hist., Misc. Pub. 45.

———, and L. M. Cavin. 1971. Effects of pollution, especially from feedlots, on fishes in the upper Neosho River basin. Contrib. No. 79 Kansas Water Resources Res. Inst.

———, and S. G. Haslouer. 1984. *Pimephales vigilax* (Pisces, Cyprinidae) established in the Missouri River basin. *Ibid.* 87:105–107.

———, and D. G. Huggins. 1975. Skipjack herring, *Alosa chrysochloris,* in the Missouri River basin. Copeia 1975:382–85.

———, F. J. DeNoyelles, S. C. Leon, et al. 1982. Report on the impacts of commercial dredging on the fishery of the lower Kansas River. Rep. to US Corps Engrs., Kansas City District, Kansas City, Mo.

———, O. T. Gorman, and S. G. Haslouer. 1983. The Red River shiner, *Notropis bairdi*, in Kansas with notes on depletion of its Arkansas River cognate, *Notropis girardi*. Trans. Kans. Acad. Sci. 86:93–98.

———, R. L. Mayden, and J. D. Stewart. 1986. Fishes in the western Mississippi Basin (Missouri, Arkansas, and Red rivers), pp. 363–412. *In:* Zoogeography of North American freshwater fishes. C. H. Hocutt and E. O. Wiley (eds.). John Wiley & Sons, New York.

———, R. E. Moss, and J. T. Collins. 1985. Assessment of dewatering impacts on stream fisheries in the Arkansas and Cimarron rivers. Kansas Fish and Game Comm., Nongame Wildlife Contract 46:1–161.

Cross, J. N. 1975. Ecological distribution of the fishes of the Virgin River (Utah, Arizona, Nevada). Unpub. MS Thesis, Univ. Nevada, Las Vegas.

Cross, R. D., R. W. Wales, and C. T. Traylor. 1974. Atlas of Mississippi. Univ. Press of Mississippi, Jackson.

Crosswhite, F. S., and C. D. Crosswhite. 1982. The Sonoran Desert, pp. 163–320. *In.* Reference Handbook on the Deserts of North America. G. L. Bender (ed.). Greenwood Press, Westport, Conn.

Crow, J. H., and K. B. MacDonald. 1978. Wetland values: Secondary production, pp. 146–61. *In:* Wetland functions and values: The state of our understanding. P. E. Greeson, J. R. Clark, and J. E. Clark (eds.). Am. Water Res. Assoc., Minneapolis, Minn.

Crump, M. L. 1981. Variation in propagule size as a function of environmental uncertainty for tree frogs. Amer. Nat. 117:724–37.

———. 1984. Intraclutch egg size variability in *Hyla crucifer* (Anura: Hylidae). Copeia 1984:302–308.

de la Cruz, A. A. 1978. Production and transport of detritus in wetlands, pp. 162-74. *In:* Wetland functions and values: The state of our understanding. P. E. Greeson, J. R. Clark, and J. E. Clark (eds.). Am. Water Res. Assoc., Minneapolis, Minn.

Cuker, B. E. 1983. Competition and coexistence among the grazing snail *Lymnaea, chironomidae,* and microcrustacea in an arctic epilithic lacustrine community. Ecology 64:10–15.

Cummins, K. W. 1962. An evaluation of some techniques for the collection and analysis of benthic samples with special emphasis on lotic waters. Amer. Midl. Nat. 67:477–504.

———. 1978. Ecology and distribution of aquatic insects, pp. 29–31. *In:* An introduction to the aquatic insects of North America. R. W. Merritt and K. W. Cummins (eds.). Kendall/Hunt, Dubuque, Iowa.

Cupp, P. V., Jr., and E. D. Brodie. 1972. Intraspecific variation in the critical thermal maximum of the plethodontid salamander, *Eurycea quadridigitatus*. Amer. Zool. 12:689.

Currie, D. J., and J. Kalff. 1984. Can bacteria outcompete phytoplankton for phosphorus? A chemostat test. Microbial Ecol. 10:205–16.

Curry, K. D., and A. Spacie. 1984. Differential use of stream habitat by spawning catostomids. Amer. Midl. Nat. 111:267-79.

Curry, R. R. 1972. Rivers—geomorphic and chemical overview, pp. 9–31. *In:* River Ecology and Man. R. T. Oglesby, C. A. Carlson, and J. A. McCann (eds.). Academic Press, Inc., New York.

Cvancara, V. A., S. F. Stieber, and B. A. Cvancara. 1977. Summer temperature tolerance of selected species of Mississippi River acclimated young of the year fishes. Comp. Biochem. Physiol. 56A:81–85.

Czaya, E. 1981. Rivers of the world. Van Nostrand Reinhold Co., New York.

Daiber, F. C. 1982. Animals of the tidal marsh. Van Nostrand Reinhold Co., New York.

Dalley, E. L., C. W. Andrews and J. M. Green. 1983. Precocious male Atlantic salmon parr (*Salmo salar*) in insular Newfoundland. Canad. J. Fish. Aquatic Sci. 40:647–52.

Damann, K. E. 1951. Missouri River Basin plankton study, 1950. Federal Security Agency, Public Health Serv., Env. Health Center, Cincinnati, Ohio.

Davis, B. J., and R. J. Miller. 1967. Brain patterns in minnows of the genus *Hybopsis* in relation to feeding habits and habitat. Copeia 1967:1–39.

Davis, J. C. 1975. Minimal dissolved oxygen requirements of aquatic life with empahsis on Canadian species: A review. J. Fish. Res. Board Canada 32:2295–2332.

Dawley, R. M., and R. J. Schultz, 1984. Unisexuality and polyploidy in hybrids of *Phoxinus eos* and *Phoxinus neogaeus* (Cyprinidae). Abstracts 64th Annual Meeting ASIH: 101.

Dawson, W. R. 1967. Interspecific variation of physiological responses of lizards to temperature, pp. 230–57. *In:* Lizard ecology: A symposium. W. W. Milstead (ed.) Univ. Missouri Press. Columbia.

Deacon, J. E. 1968. Endangered non-game fishes of the West: Causes, prospects, and importance. Proc. Ann. Conf. West.

Assoc. State Game Fish Comm. 48:534–49.

———. 1979. Endangered and threatened fishes of the west. Great Basin Nat. Mem. 3:41–64.

———, and W. G. Bradley. 1972. Ecological distribution of fishes of Moapa River in Clark County, Nevada. Trans. Amer. Fish. Soc. 101:408–19.

———, and W. L. Minckley. 1974. Desert fishes, pp. 385–488. *In:* Desert Biology, Vol. 2. G. W. Brown, Jr. (ed.). Academic Press, New York.

———, and B. L. Wilson. 1967. Daily activity cycles of *Crenichthys baileyi,* a fish endemic to Nevada. Southwest. Nat. 12:31–44.

———, G. Kobetich, J. D. Williams, S. Contreras-Balderas, *et al.* 1979. Fishes of North America: Endangered, threatened, or of special concern. Fisheries (Bethesda, Md.) 4:29–44.

Dendy, J. S. 1945. Predicting depth distribution in three TVA storage type reservoirs. Trans. Amer. Fish. Soc. 75:65–71.

Denoncourt, R. F., and E. L. Cooper. 1975. A review of the literature and checklist of fishes of the Susquehanna River drainage above Conowingo Dam. Proc. Pa. Acad. Sci. 49:121–25.

Diamond, J. M. 1978. Niche shifts and the rediscovery of interspecific competition. Amer. Sci. 66:322–31.

———. 1986. Laboratory experiments, field experiments, and natural experiments, pp. 3–22. *In:* Community Ecology. J. Diamond and T. J. Case (eds.). Harper & Row, New York.

———, and T. Case. 1986. Ecological Communities. Harper & Row, New York.

Dikeman, N. J., and M. E. Earley. 1982. Statistical abstract of Oklahoma. Center for Economic and Management Research, Univ. Oklahoma, Norman.

Dill, L. B., and A. H. G. Fraser. 1984. Risk of predation and the feeding behaviour of juvenile coho salmon (*Oncorhynchus kisutch*). Behav. Ecol. Sociobiol. 16:65–71.

Dixon, W. J. (ed.). 1983. BMDP Statistical Software. Univ. California Press, Berkeley.

Doan, K. H. 1938. Observations on dogfish (*Amia calva*) and their young. Copeia 1938:204.

Dolan, R., A. Howard, and A. Gallenson. 1974. Man's impact on the Colorado River in Grand Canyon. Amer. Sci. 62:392–401.

Dominey, W. J. 1980. Female mimicry in male bluegill sunfish—a genetic polymorphism? Nature 284:546–48.

Donnelly, K. 1978. Simulations to determine the variance and edge-effect of total nearest neighbor distance, pp. 91–95. *In:* Simulation methods in archaeology. I. Hodder (ed.). Cambridge Univ. Press, London.

Douglas, M. E. 1978. Systematics, ecology, and evolution of sunfish and minnows: A multivariate morphometric analysis of speciose and depauperate phylads. Unpub. PhD Diss., Univ. Georgia, Athens.

———, and J. C. Avise. 1982. Morphological divergence in fishes: Tests of gradual *vs.* rectangular modes of evolutionary change. Evolution 36:224–32.

Douglas, N. H. 1974. Freshwater fishes of Louisiana. La. Wildl. and Fish. Comm., Claitor's Publ. Div., Baton Rouge.

Dowling, H. G. 1956. Geographic relations of the ozarkian amphibians and reptiles. Southwest. Nat. 1:174–89.

Downhower, J. F. 1980. Mate preference in female mottled sculpins. Anim. Behav. 28:728–34.

———, L. Brown, R. Pederson, and G. Staples. 1983. Sexual selection and sexual dimorphism in mottled sculpins. Evolution 37:96–103.

Durbin, A. G., S. W. Nixon, and C. A. Oviatt. 1979. Effects of the spawning migration of the alewife, *Alosa pseudoharengus*, on freshwater ecosystems. Ecology 60:8–17.

Dussault, G. V., and D. L. Kramer. 1981. Food and feeding ecology of the guppy, *Poecilia reticulata* (Pisces: Poeciliidae). Canad. J. Zool. 59:684–701.

Echelle, A. A., and I. Kornfield (eds.). 1984. Evolution of Fish Species Flocks. Univ. Maine Press, Orono.

———, and G. D. Schnell. 1976. Factor analysis of species associations among fishes in the Kiamichi River, Oklahoma. Trans. Amer. Fish. Soc. 105:17–31.

———, A. F. Echelle and L. G. Hill. 1972a. Interspecific interactions and limiting factors of abundance and distribution in the Red River pupfish, *Cyprinodon rubrofluviatilis*. Amer. Midl. Nat. 88:109–30.

———, ———, and B. A. Taber, 1976. Biochemical evidence for congeneric competition as a factor restricting gene flow between populations of a darter (Percidae: *Etheostoma*). Syst. Zool. 25:228–35.

———, ———, M. H. Smith, and L. G. Hill. 1975. Analysis of genic continuity in a headwater fish, *Etheostoma radiosum* (Percidae). Copeia 1975:197–204.

———, D. Mosier, and L. G. Hill. 1972b. Aspects of the feeding ecology of *Fundulus zebrinus kansae*. Proc. Okla. Acad. Sci. 52:6–9.

Edlund, A.-M., and C. Magnhagen. 1981. Food segregation and consumption suppression in two coexisting fishes, *Pomatoschistus minutus* and *P. microps:* an experimental demonstration of competition. Oikos 36:23–27.

Elser, A. A., M. W. Gorges and L. M. Morris. 1980. Distribution of fishes in southeastern Montana. Montana Department of Fisheries, Wildlife, and Parks, and US Dept. of the Interior, Bureau of Land Management.

Emanuel, M. E., and J. J. Dodson. 1979. Modification of the rheotropic behaviour of male rainbow trout (*Salmo gairdneri*) by ovarian fluid. J. Fish. Res. Board Canada 36:63–68.

Engen, S. 1979. Abundance models: Sampling and estimation, pp. 313–32. *In:* Statistical distributions in ecological work. J. K. Ord, G. P. Patil and C. Taillie (eds.). International Cooperative Publishing House, Fairland, Md.

Erman, D. C. 1973. Upstream changes in fish populations following impoundment of Sagehen Creek, California. Trans. Amer. Fish. Soc. 103:626–29.

Etnier, D. A. 1971. Food of three species of sunfish (*Lepomis:* Centrarchidae) and their hybrids in three Minnesota lakes. *Ibid.* 100:124–28.

———, W. C. Starnes, and B. H. Bauer. 1979. Whatever happened to the silvery minnow (*Hybognathus nuchalis*) in the Tennessee River? Proc. Southeast. Fishes Council 2(3):1–3.

Evans, J. W., and R. L. Noble, 1979. The longitudinal distribution of fishes in an east Texas stream. Amer. Midl. Nat. 101:333-43.

Everest, F. H. 1973. Ecology and management of summer steelhead in the Rogue River. Fish. Res. Rep. 7, Oregon State Game Commission, Corvallis.

———, and D. W. Chapman. 1972. Habitat selection and spatial interaction by juvenile chinook salmon and steelhead trout in two Idaho streams. J. Fish. Res. Board Canada 29:91–100.

———, and J. R. Sedell. 1983. Natural propagation and habitat improvement. Vol. I. Oregon Supplement. A: Evaluation of fisheries enhancement projects on Fish Creek and Wash Creek. Bonneville Power Admin., Final Rep., Contract No. DE-A179-83BP11968.

Fajen, O. F. 1962. The influence of stream stability on homing behavior of two smallmouth bass populations. Trans. Amer. Fish. Soc. 91:346–49.

Falconer, D. S. 1981. Introduction to Quantitative Genetics, 2d ed. Longman House, New York.

Farringer, R. T., III; A. A. Echelle; and S. F. Lehtinen. 1979. Reproductive cycle of the red shiner, *Notropis lutrensis*, in central Texas and south central Oklahoma. Trans. Amer. Fish Soc., 108: 271–76.

Farris, J. S. 1968. The evolutionary relationship between the species of two killifish genera *Fundulus* and *Profundulus* (Teleostei, Cyprinodontidae). Unpub. PhD Diss., Univ. Michigan, Ann Arbor.

———. 1970. Methods for computing Wagner trees. Syst. Zool. 19:88–92.

———. 1972. Estimating phylogenetic trees from distance matrices. Amer. Nat. 106:645–68.

———. 1981. Distance data in phylogenetic analysis, pp. 3–23. *In:* Advances in cladistics: Proceedings of the first meeting of the Willi Hennig Society. V. A. Funk and D. R. Brooks (eds.). New York Botanical Garden, New York.

Fausch, K. D. 1984. Profitable stream positions for salmonids: Relating specific growth rate to net energy gain. Canad. J. Zool. 62:441–51.

———, and R. J. White. 1981. Competition between brook trout (*Salvelinus fontinalis*) and brown trout (*Salmo trutta*) for position in a Michigan stream. Canad. J. Fish. Aquatic Sci. 38:1220–27.

Feinsinger, P., E. E. Spears, and R. W. Poole. 1981. A simple measure of niche breadth. Ecology 62:27–32.

Feldmeth, C. R., E. A. Stone, and J. H. Brown. 1974. An increased scope for thermal tolerance upon acclimating pupfish (*Cyprinodon*) to cycling temperatures. J. Comp. Physiol. 89:39–44.

Feller, W. 1968. An Introduction to Probability Theory and Its Applications. Vol. 1. John Wiley & Sons, New York.

Felley, J. D. 1984. Multivariate identification of morphological-environmental relationships within the Cyprinidae (Pisces) Copeia 1984:442–55.

———, and L. G. Hill. 1983. Multivariate assessment of environmental preferences of cyprinid fishes of the Illinois River, Oklahoma. Amer. Midl. Nat. 109:209–21.

Felsenstein, J. 1981. Skepticism toward Santa Rosalia, or why there are so few kinds of animals. Evolution 35:124–38.

Feminella, J. W., and W. J. Matthews. 1984. Intraspecific differences in thermal tolerance of *Etheostoma spectabile* (Agassiz) in constant versus fluctuating environments. J. Fish Biol. 25:455–61.

Fenneman, N. M. 1938. Physiography of eastern United States. McGraw-Hill Book Co., New York.

Ferguson, R. G. 1958. The preferred temperature of fish and their midsummer distribution in temperate lakes and streams. J. Fish. Res. Board Canada 15:607–24.

Findley, J. S. 1973. Phenetic packing as a measure of faunal diversity. Amer. Nat. 107:580–84.

———. 1976. The structure of bat communities. *Ibid.* 110:129–39.

———, and H. Black. 1983. Morphological and dietary structuring of a Zambian insectivorous bat community. Ecology 64:625–30.

Finger, T. R. 1982a. Interactive segregation among three species of sculpins (*Cottus*). Copeia 1982:680–94.

———. 1982b. Fish community-habitat relations in a central New York stream. J. Freshw. Ecol. 1:345–52.

Finnell, J. C., R. M. Jenkins, and G. E. Hall. 1956. The fishery resources of the Little River system, McCurtain County, Oklahoma. Okla. Fish. Res. Lab. Rep. No. 55.

Fisher, H. J. 1962. Some fishes of the lower Missouri River. Amer. Midl. Nat. 68:424–29.

Fisher, R. A. 1930. The genetical theory of natural selection. Clarendon Press, Oxford.

Fisher, S. G., and W. L. Minckley, 1978. Chemical characteristics of a desert stream in flash flood. J. Arid Environ. 1:25–33.

———, L. J. Gray, N. B. Grimm, and D. E. Busch. 1982. Temporal succession in a desert stream ecosystem following flash flooding. Ecol. Monogr. 52:93–110.

Fisk, L. O. 1972. Status of certain depleted inland fishes. Calif. Dept. Fish Game, Admin. Rep. 72-1, Sacramento.

Flanagan, C. A. 1981. Fourier morphometrics of reef fishes of the Gulf of California. Unpub. PhD Diss., Univ. Arizona, Tucson.

Fogel, M. M. 1981. Precipitation in the desert, pp. 219–34. *In:* D. E. Evans and J. L. Thames (eds.). Water in desert ecosystems. Dowden, Hutchinson and Ross, Stroudsburg, Pa.

Fontaine, T. D., III, and S. M. Bartell. 1983. Dynamics of lotic ecosystems. Ann Arbor Science, Ann Arbor, Mich.

Forbes, R. H. 1902. The river-irrigating waters of Arizona—their character and effects. Univ. Ariz. Agric. Exp. Sta. Bull. 44:143–214.

Forbes, S. A. 1880a. The food of fishes. Bull. Illinois State Lab. Nat. Hist. 1:19–70.

———. 1880b. The food of the darters. Amer. Nat. 14:697–703.

———. 1883. The food of the smaller fresh-water fishes. Bull. Illinois State Lab. Nat. Hist. 6:65–94.

———. 1887. The lake as a microcosm. Bull. Peoria Sci. Assoc. 1887:77–87.

———, and R. E. Richardson. 1908. The fishes of Illinois. Illinois State Laboratory of Natural History, Urbana, Il.

Ford, J. C. 1982. Water quality of the lower Missouri River, Gavins Point Dam to mouth. Missouri Dept. of Natural Resources, Jefferson City, Mo.

Fowler, L. G. 1972. Growth and mortality of fingerling chinook salmon as affected by egg size. Prog. Fish-Cult. 34:66–69.

Frankel, O. H., and M. E. Soule. 1981. Conservation and evolution. Cambridge Univ. Press, Cambridge.

Fraser, D. F. 1983. An experimental investigation of refuging behaviour in a minnow. Canad. J. Zool. 61:666–72.

———, and E. E. Emmons. 1984. Behavioral response of blacknose dace (*Rhinichthys atratulus*) to varying densities of predatory creek chub (*Semotilus atromaculatus*). Can. J. Fish. Aquatic Sci. 41:364–70.

———, and F. A. Huntingford. 1986. Feeding and avoiding predation hazard: The behavioral response of the prey. Ethology 73:56–68.

———, and T. N. Mottolese. 1984. Discrimination and avoidance reactions towards predatory and nonpredatory fish by blacknose dace, *Rhinichthys atratulus* (Pisces: Cyprinidae). Z. Tierpsychol. 66:89–100.

———, and T. E. Sise. 1980. Observations of stream minnows in a patchy environment: A test of a theory of habitat distribution, Ecology 61:790–97.

———, and R. D. Cerri. 1982. Experimental evaluation of predator-prey relationships in a patchy environment: Consequences for habitat-use patterns in minnows. *Ibid.* 63:307–13.

Fredrickson, L. H. 1978. Lowland hardwood wetlands: Current status and habitat values for wildlife, pp. 296–306. *In:* Wetland functions and values: The state of our understanding. P. E. Greeson, J. R. Clark, and J. E. Clark (eds.). Am. Water Resources Assoc., Minneapolis, Minn.

———. 1979. Floral and faunal changes in lowland hardwood forests in Missouri resulting from channelization, drainage and impoundment. US Fish and Wildl. Serv. FWS/OBS-78/91.

Fridriksson, A. 1939. On the Murta in Thingvellir Lake in relation to the charr and trout in that lake. Natturufraedingurinn 9:1–36. In Icelandic.

Frost, W. E. 1965. Breeding habits of Windermere charr, *Salvelinus williugbi* (Gunther) and their bearing on speciation in these fish. Proc. R. Soc. Edinb. B. 163:232–84.

Fry, F. E. J. 1947. Effects of the environment on animal activity.

Univ. Toronto Stud. Biol. Ser. 55, Publ. Ontario Fish. Res. Lab. 68:1–62.

Fryer, G., and T. D. Iles. 1972. The cichlid fishes of the Great Lakes of Africa. T. F. H. Publications, Neptune City, N.J.

Funk, J. L. 1955. Movement of stream fishes in Missouri. Trans. Amer. Fish. Soc. 85:39–57.

———, and J. W. Robinson. 1974. Changes in the channel of the lower Missouri River and effects on fish and wildlife. Mo. Dept. Conserv. Aquatic Ser. No. 11, Jefferson City, Mo.

Gadgil, M., and W. Bossert. 1970. Life historical consequences of natural selection. Amer. Nat. 104:1–24.

Gale, W. F., and W. G. Deutsch. 1985. Fecundity and spawning frequency of captive tessellated darters—fractional spawners. Trans. Amer. Fish. Soc. 114:220–29.

Gall, G. A. E. 1974. Influence of size of eggs and age of female on hatchability and growth in rainbow trout. Calif. Fish. and Game 60:26-35.

Gallagher, R. P. 1979. Local distribution of ichthyoplankton in the lower Mississippi River. MS Thesis, Louisiana State Univ., Baton Rouge.

Garrett, G. P. 1982. Variation in the reproductive traits of the Pecos pupfish, *Cyprinodon pecosensis*. Amer. Midl. Nat. 108:355–63.

Gatz, A. J. 1979a. Community organization in fishes as indicated by morphological features. Ecology 60:711–18.

———. 1979b. Ecological morphology of freshwater stream fishes. Tulane Stud. Zool. Bot. 21:91–124.

———. 1981. Morphologically inferred niche differentiation in stream fishes. Amer. Midl. Nat. 106:10–21.

Gebhards, S. V. 1960. Biological notes on precocious male chinook salmon parr in the Salmon River drainage, Idaho. Prog. Fish Cult. 22:121–25.

Gee, J. H. 1968. Adjustment of buoyancy by longnose dace (*Rhinichthys cataractae*) in relation to velocity of water. J. Fish. Res. Board Canada 25:1485–96.

———. 1970. Adjustment of buoyancy in blacknose dace, *Rhinichthys atratulus*. *Ibid*. 27:1855–59.

———. 1972. Adaptive variation in swimbladder length and volume in dace, genus *Rhinichthys*. *Ibid*. 29:119–27.

———. 1974. Behavioral and developmental plasticity of buoyancy in the longnose, *Rhinichthys cataractae*, and blacknose, *R. atratulus* (Cyprinidae) dace. *Ibid*. 31:35–41.

———. 1977. Effects of size of fish, water temperature and water velocity on buoyancy alteration by fathead minnows, *Pimephales promelas*. Comp. Biochem. Physiol. 56A:503–508.

———. 1983. Ecologic implications of buoyancy control in fish, pp. 140–76. *In:* Fish biomechanics. P. W. Webb and D. Weihs (eds.). Praeger Publishers, New York.

———, and P. A. Gee. 1976. Alteration of buoyancy by some Central American stream fishes, and a comparison with North American species. Canad. J. Zool. 54:386–91.

———, and T. G. Northcote. 1963. Comparative ecology of two sympatric species of dace (Rhinichthys) in the Fraser River system, British Columbia. J. Fish. Res. Bd. Canada 20:105–18.

———, K. Machniak, and S. M. Chalanchuk. 1974. Adjustment of buoyancy and excess internal pressure of swimbladder gases in some North American freshwater fishes. J. Fish. Res. Board Canada 31:1139–41.

———, R. F. Tallman, and H. J. Smart. 1978. Reactions of some great plains fishes to progressive hypoxia. Canad. J. Zool. 56:1962–66.

Geo-Marine, Inc. 1981. A three-month impingement study conducted at the Iatan Plant on the Missouri River. Unpub. rep. prep. for Kansas City Power and Light Co.

Geraghty, J. J., D. W. Miller, F. V. D. Leeden, and F. L. Troise. 1973. Water atlas of the United States. Water Information Center, Port Washington, N.Y.

Gerking, S. D. 1950. Stability of a stream fish population. J. Wildl. Manage. 14:193–202.

———. 1959. The restricted movement of fish populations. Biol. Rev. 34:221–42.

Ghent, A. W. 1983. Tau as an index of similarity in community comparisons: An approach permitting the hypothesis of unequal species abundance. Canad. J. Zool. 61:687–90.

Ghiselin, M. T. 1974. The economy of nature and the evolution of sex. Univ. California Press, Berkeley.

Gibbons, J. R. H., and J. H. Gee. 1972. Ecological segregation between longnose and blacknose dace (Genus *Rhinichthys*) in the Mink River, Manitoba. J. Fish Res. Board Can. 29:1245–52.

Gibbs, R. H. 1957. Cyprinid fishes of the subgenus *Cyprinella* of *Notropis*. III. Variation and subspecies of *Notropis venustus* (Girard). Tulane Stud. Zool. 5:175–203.

Gibson, R. J. 1977. Matamek Annual Report for 1976. Woods Hole Oceanographic Institution, Tech. Rep., WHOI-77-28. Woods Hole, Mass.

Gilbert, C. H. 1885. Second series of notes on the fishes of Kansas. Bull. Washburn Lab. Nat. Hist. 1:97–99.

———. 1886. Third series of notes on Kansas fishes. *Ibid*. 1:207–211.

Gilbert, C. R. 1980. Zoogeographic factors in relation to biological monitoring of fish, pp. 309–55. *In:* Biological monitoring of fish. C. H. Hocutt and J. R. Stauffer, Jr. (eds.). D. C. Heath, Lexington, Mass.

Gilliam, J. F. 1982. Habitat use and competitive bottlenecks in size-structured fish populations. Unpub. PhD Diss., Michigan State Univ., East Lansing.

Girard, C. 1857. Researches upon the cyprinoid fishes inhabiting the fresh waters of the United States, west of the Mississippi Valley. Proc. Acad. Nat. Sci. Phila. 8:165–213.

Glebe, B. D., T. D. Appy, and R. L. Saunders. 1979. Variation in Atlantic salmon *(Salmo salar)* reproductive traits and their implications in breeding programs. Intern. Counc. Explor. Sea, C. M. 1979/M:23.

Glesener, R. R., and D. Tilman. 1978. Sexuality and the components of environmental uncertainty: clues from geographic parthenogenesis in terrestrial animals. Amer. Nat. 112:659–73.

Glova, G. J. 1978. Pattern and mechanism of resource partitioning between stream populations of juvenile coho salmon (*Oncorhynchus kisutch*) and coastal cutthroat trout (*Salmo clarki*). Unpub. PhD Diss., Univ. British Columbia, Vancouver.

Goel, N. S., and N. Richter-Dyn. 1974. Stochastic Models in Biology. Academic Press, New York.

Goetz, F. W., E. M. Donaldson, G. A. Hunter, and G. M. Dye. 1979. Effects of estradiol-17 and 17-methyltestosterone on gonadal differentiation in the coho salmon, *Oncorhynchus kisutch*. Aquaculture 17:267–78.

Goodfellow, W. L., Jr.; C. H. Hocutt; R. P. Morgan II; and J. R. Stauffer, Jr. 1984. Biochemical assessment of the taxonomic status of "*Rhinichthys bowersi*" (Pisces: Cyprinidae). Copeia 1984:652–59.

Gorman, O. T. 1976. Diversity and stability in the fish communities of some Indiana and Panama streams. MS Thesis, Purdue University, West Lafayette, Ind.

———. 1983. The determinants of habitat segregation among Ozark minnows. Unpub. PhD Diss., Univ. Kansas, Lawrence.

———, and J. R. Karr. 1978. Habitat structure and stream fish communities. Ecology 59:507–15.

Gorsuch, R. L. 1974. Factor analysis. W. B. Saunders Co., Philadelphia.

Gould, S. J. 1967. Evolutionary patterns in pelycosaurian reptiles: A factor analytical study. Evolution 21:385–401.

Goulding, M. 1980. The fishes and the forest, explorations in Amazonian natural history. Univ. California Press, Berkeley.

Grabowski, S. J., S. D. Hiebert, and D. M. Lieberman. 1984. Potential for introduction of three species of nonnative fishes into central Arizona via the Central Project: A literature review and analysis. US Bur. Reclam. Res.-Eng. Cent. Rep. REC-ERC-84-7.

Grant, J. W. A., and P. W. Colgan. 1983. Reproductive success and mate choice in the johnny darter, *Etheostoma nigrum* (Pisces: Percidae). Canad. J. Zool. 61:437–46.

Grant, P. R. 1971. Variation of tarsus length of birds on islands and mainland regions. Evolution 25:599–614.

———. 1986. Interspecific competition in fluctuating environments, pp. 173–91. *In:* Community Ecology. J. Diamond and T. J. Case (eds.). Harper & Row, New York.

Gray, G. A., G. M. Sonnevil, H. C. Hansel, C. W. Huntington, and D. E. Palmer. 1984. Feeding activity, rate of consumption, daily ration and prey selection of major predators in the John Day Pool. Bonneville Power Admin. 1982 Ann. Rep., Contract.

Gray, J. 1928. The growth of fish. II. The growth-rate of the embryo of *Salmo fario*. J. Exp. Biol. 6:110–24.

Gray, L. J. 1980. Recolonization pathways and community development of desert stream macroinvertebrates. Unpub. PhD Diss., Arizona State Univ., Tempe.

———. 1981. Species composition and life histories of aquatic insects in a lowland Sonoran Desert stream. Amer. Midl. Nat. 106:229–42.

———, and S. G. Fisher. 1981. Postflood recolonization pathways of macroinvertebrates in a lowland Sonoran Desert stream. *Ibid.* 106:249–57.

Gray, R. H., and D. D. Dauble. 1977. Checklist and relative abundance of fish species from the Hanford Reach of the Columbia River. Northwest Sci. 51:208–15.

Greeley, J. R. 1927. Fishes of the Genesee Region with annotated list, pp. 47–66. *In:* E. Moore, ed. A biological survey of the Genesee River system. New York Dept. of Conserv., Albany.

———. 1932. The spawning habits of brook trout and rainbow trout and the problems of egg predators. Trans. Amer. Fish. Soc. 62:239–48.

Green, R. H. 1971. A multivariate statistical approach to the Hutchinsonian niche: bivalve molluscs of central Canada. Ecology 52:543–56.

———. 1974. Multivariate niche analysis with temporally varying environmental factors. *Ibid.* 55:73–83.

———. 1979. Sampling design and statistical methods for environmental biologists. John Wiley & Sons, New York.

Greenberg, L. A. 1983. An experimental analysis of habitat utilization in stream fishes. Abstract, 63rd Annual Meeting, American Society of Ichthyologists and Herpetologists, Tallahassee, Florida.

Greenwood, P. H. 1965. Environmental effects on the pharyngeal mill of a cichlid fish, *Astatorheochromis alluaudi* and their taxonomic implications. Proc. Linn. Soc. Lond. 176:1–10.

———. 1984. African cichlids and evolutionary theory, pp. 141–54. *In:* Evolution of fish species flocks. A. A. Echelle and I. Kornfield (eds.). Univ. Maine Press, Orono.

Gregg, K. L. (ed.). 1952. The road to Santa Fe.[Journal and diaries of George Champlin Sibley and others pertaining to the surveying and marking of a road from the Missouri frontier to the settlements of New Mexico, 1825–27]. Univ. New Mexico Press, Albuquerque.

Gregory, S. V. 1983. Plant-herbivore interactions in stream systems, pp. 157–89. *In:* J. R. Barnes and G. W. Minshall (eds.). Stream ecology—application and testing of general ecological theory. Plenum, New York.

Grinnell, J. 1917. Field tests and theories concerning distributional control. Amer. Nat. 51:115-28.

Gross, M. R. 1979. Cuckoldry in sunfishes (Lepomis: Centrarchidae). Canad. J. Zool. 57:1507–1509.

———. 1982. Sneakers, satellites, and parentals: Polymorphic mating strategies in North American sunfishes. Z. Tierpsychol. 60:1–26.

———. 1984. Sunfish, salmon, and the evolution of alternative reproductive strategies and tactics in fishes, pp. 55–75. *In:* G. W. Potts and R. J. Wooton (eds.). Fish reproduction: Strategies and tactics. Academic Press, New York.

———. 1985. Disruptive selection for alternative life histories in salmon. Nature 313:47-48.

———, and E. L. Charnov. 1980. Alternative male life histories in bluegill sunfish. Proc. Natl. Acad. Sci. 77:6937–40.

Grossman, G. D. 1982. Dynamics and organization of a rocky intertidal fish assemblage: The persistence and resilience of taxocene structure. Amer. Nat. 119:611–37.

———, M. C. Freeman, P. B. Moyle, and J. O. Whitaker, Jr. 1985. Stochasticity and assemblage organization in an Indiana stream fish assemblage. *Ibid.* 126:275–85.

———, P. B. Moyle, and J. O. Whitaker, Jr. 1982. Stochasticity in structural and functional characteristics of an Indiana stream fish assemblage: A test of community theory. *Ibid.* 120: 423–54.

Grubb, T. C., Jr., and L. Greenwald. 1982. Sparrows and a brushpile: Foraging responses to different combinations of predation risk and energy cost. Anim. Behav. 30:637–40.

Guillory, V. 1979. Utilization of an inundated floodplain by Mississippi River fishes. Florida Sci. 42:222–28.

Gunning, G. E., and T. M. Berra. 1969. Fish repopulation of experimentally decimated segments in the headwaters of two streams. Trans. Amer. Fish. Soc. 98:305–308.

Gunsolus, R. T. 1978. The status of Oregon coho and recommendations for managing the production, harvest, and escapement of wild and hatchery-reared stocks. Oreg. Dept. Fish Wildl. Internal Rep.

Gutentag, E. D., F. J. Heines, N. C. Krothe, R. Luckey, and J. D. Weeks. 1984. Geohydrology of the High Plains aquifer in parts of Colorado, Kansas, Nebraska, New Mexico, Oklahoma, South Dakota, Texas, and Wyoming. Regional Aquifer System Analysis, USGS Prof. Paper 1400-B.

Gydemo, R. 1979. Population genetics studies on Arctic charr in the county of Vasterbotten. Part 2. Report for the Local Board of Agriculture of the County of Vasterbotten, Sweden. Mimeogr. in Swedish.

Haase, E. F. 1974. Survey of floodplain vegetation along the lower Gila River in southwestern Arizona. J. Ariz. Acad. Sci. 7:75–81.

Hagen, D. W. 1964. Evidence of adaptation to environmental temperatures in three species of *Gambusia* (Poeciliidae). Southwest. Nat. 9:6–19.

Hairston, N. G. 1980. Evolution under interspecific competition: Field experiments on terrestrial salamanders. Evolution 34:409–20.

———, F. E. Smith, and L. B. Slobodkin. 1960. Community structure, population control, and competition. Amer. Nat. 94:421–25.

Hall, C. A. S. 1972. Migration and metabolism in a temperate stream ecosystem. Ecology 53:585–604.

Hall, D. J., and E. E. Werner. 1977. Seasonal distribution and abundance of fishes in the littoral zone of a Michigan Lake. Trans. Amer. Fish. Soc. 106:545–55.

Hall, H. D. 1979. The spatial and temporal distribution of icthyoplankton of the upper Achafalaya Basin. Unpub. MS Thesis, Louisiana State Univ., Baton Rouge.

Hall, J. D., and C. O. Baker. 1982. Rehabilitating and enhancing stream habitat: 1. Review and evaluation: Influence of forest and rangeland management on anadromous fish habitat in western North America. USDA Forest Serv. Gen. Tech. Rep. PNW-138.

Hall, L. W., Jr.; C. H. Hocutt, and J. R. Stauffer, Jr. 1978. Implication of geographic location on temperature preference of white perch, *Morone americana*. J. Fish. Res. Board Canada 35:1464–68.

Halyk, L. C., and E. K. Balon. 1983. Structure and ecological production of the fish taxocene of a small floodplain system. Canad. J. Zool. 61:2446–64.

Hanski, I. 1982a. Dynamics of regional distribution: the core and satellite species hypothesis. Oikos 38:210–21.

———. 1982b. On patterns of temporal and spatial variation in animal populations. Ann. Zool. Fennici 19:21–37.

———. 1985. Single-species spatial dynamics may contribute to long-term rarity and commonness. Ecology 66:335–43.

Hanson, A. J., and H. D. Smith. 1967. Mate selection in a population of sockeye salmon (*Oncorhynchus nerka*) of mixed age groups. J. Fish. Res. Board Canada 24:1955–77.

Hanson, D. L., and T. F. Waters. 1974. Recovery of standing crop and production rates of a brook trout population in a flood damaged stream. Trans. Am. Fish. Soc. 103:431–39.

Harper, J. L. 1981. The meaning of rarity, pp. 189–203. *In:* The biological aspects of rare plant conservation. H. Synge (ed.). John Wiley & Sons, New York.

———, P. H. Lovell, and K. G. Moore. 1970. The shapes and sizes of seeds. Ann. Rev. Ecol. Syst. 1:327–56.

Harper, R. J., K. M. McMaster, and L. G. Beckman. 1980. Assessment of fish stocks in Lake F. D. Roosevelt. Ann. Rep. US Bur. Reclam. Contract No. WPRS-0-07-10-X0216.

Harrel, R. C., B. J. Davis, and T. C. Dorris. 1967. Stream order and species diversity of fishes in an intermittent Oklahoma stream. Amer. Midl. Nat. 78:428–36.

Harrell, H. L. 1978. Response of the Devil's River fish community to flooding. Copeia 1978:60–68.

Harris, H., and D. A. Hopkinson. 1978. Handbook of enzyme electrophoresis in human genetics. North-Holland Pub. Co., Amsterdam.

Harris, L. D. 1984. The fragmented forest. Univ. Chicago Press, Chicago.

Hart, D. D. 1985. Causes and consequences of territoriality in a grazing stream insect. Ecology 66:404–14.

Hart, J. S. 1952. Geographic variations of some physiological and morphological characters in certain freshwater fish. Univ. Toronto Biological Series No. 60.

Hartl, D. L. 1980. Principles of population genetics. Sinauer Associates, Sunderland, Mass.

Hartley, P. H. T. 1948. Food and feeding relationship in a community of fresh-water fishes. J. Anim. Ecol. 17:1–14.

Harvey, P. H., R. K. Colwell, J. W. Silvertown, and R. M. May. 1983. Null models in ecology. Ann. Rev. Ecol. Syst. 14:189–211.

Hathaway, E. S. 1927. The relationship of temperature to the quantity of food consumed by fishes. Ecology 8:428–34.

Hawkins, C. P., M. L. Murphy, and N. H. Anderson. 1982. Effects of canopy, substrate composition and gradient on the structure of macroinvertebrate communities in the Cascade Range streams of Oregon. *Ecology* 63:1840–56.

———, M. L. Murphy, N. H. Anderson, and M. A. Wilzbach. 1983. Density of fish and salamanders in relation to riparian canopy and physical habitat in streams of the northwestern United States. Canad. J. Fish. Aquatic Sci. 40:1173–85.

Hay, O. P. 1887. A contribution to the knowledge of the fishes of Kansas. Proc. US Natl. Mus. 10:242–53.

Hedrick, P. W., M. Ginevan, and E. P. Ewing. 1976. Genetic polymorphism in heterogeneous environments. Ann. Rev. Ecol. Syst. 7:1–32.

Hefley, H. M. 1937. Ecological studies on the Canadian River floodplain in Cleveland County, Oklahoma. Ecol. Monogr. 7:345–402.

Heindl, L. A., and R. A. McCullough. 1961. Geology and the availability of water in the lower Bonita Creek area, Graham County, Arizona. USGS Wat.-Suppl. Pap. 1589:1–56.

Heins, D. C. 1979. A comparative life history of a closely related group of minnows (*Notropis*, Cyprinidae) inhabiting streams of the Gulf coastal plain. Unpub. PhD Diss., Tulane Univ., New Orleans, La.

———. 1985. Life history traits of the Florida sand darter, *Ammocrypta bifascia*, and comparisons with the naked sand darter, *Ammocrypta beani*. Amer. Midl. Nat. 113:209-16.

———, and G. H. Clemmer. 1975. Ecology, foods and feeding of the longnose shiner, *Notropis longirostris* (Hay), in Mississippi. *Ibid.* 94:284–95.

———, and D. R. Dorsett. 1986. Reproductive traits of the blacktail shiner, *Notropis venustus* (Girard), in southeastern Mississippi. Southwest. Nat. 31:185–89.

———, and F. G. Rabito, Jr. 1986. Spawning performance in North American minnows: Direct evidence of the occurrence of multiple clutches in the genus *Notropis*. J. Fish Biol. 28:343–57.

Helfman, G. S. 1978. Patterns of community structure in fishes: Summary and overview. Env. Biol. Fish. 3:129–48.

———. 1981. The advantage to fishes of hovering in shade. Copeia 1981:392–400.

Helwig, J. T., and K. A. Council. 1979. SAS user's guide. SAS Institute, Raleigh, N.C.

Hempel, G., and J. H. S. Blaxter. 1967. Egg weight in Atlantic herring (*Clupea harengus* L.). J. Cons. Perm. Int. Explor. Mer. 31:170–95.

Hendrickson, D. A., and W. L. Minckley. 1985. Cienegas—vanishing climax communities of the American Southwest. Desert Plants 6:131–75 + cover photos.

———, W. L. Minckley, R. R. Miller, D. J. Siebert, and P. H. Minckley. 1980. Fishes of the Rio Yaqui Basin, Mexico and the United States. J. Arizona-Nevada Acad. Sci. 15:65–106.

Hendrickson, J. A., Jr. 1981. Community-wide character displacement reexamined. Evolution 35:794–809.

Hennig, W. 1966. Phylogenetic systematics. Univ. Illinois Press, Urbana.

Henricson, J., and L. Nyman. 1976. The ecological and genetical segregation of two species of dwarfed charr (*Salvelinus alpinus* L.) species complex. Inst. Freshw. Res. Drottningholm. Rep. 55:15–37.

Herbold, B. 1984. Structure of an Indiana stream fish association: Choosing an appropriate model. Amer. Nat. 24:561–72.

Hertz, P. E., R. B. Huey, and E. Nevo. 1983. Homage to Santa Anita: Thermal sensitivity of sprint speed in agamid lizards. Evolution 37:1075–84.

Hespenheide, H. A. 1973. Ecological inference from morphological data. Ann. Rev. Ecol. Syst. 4:213–29.

———. 1975. Prey characteristics and predator niche width, pp. 158–80. *In:* The ecology and evolution of communities. M. L. Cody and J. L. Diamond (eds.). Harvard Univ. Press, Cambridge, Mass.

Hesse, L. W., Q. P. Bliss, and G. J. Zuerlein. 1982. Some aspects of the ecology of adult fishes in the channelized Missouri River with special reference to the effects of two nuclear generating plants, pp. 225–78. *In:* The middle Missouri River. L. W. Hesse (ed.). Missouri River Study Group, Norfolk, Nebr.

———, G. L. Hergenrader, H. S. Lewis, S. D. Reetz, and A. B. Schlesinger (eds.). 1982. The middle Missouri River. Missouri River Study Group, Norfolk, Nebr.

Hicks, D. B., and J. W. DeWitt. 1970. A system for maintaining constant dissolved oxygen concentrations in flowing-water experiments. Prog. Fish Cult. 32:55–57.

Hill, J., and G. D. Grossman. 1987. Home range estimates for three North American stream fishes. Copeia 1987:376–80.

Hill, L. G. 1968. Oxygen preference in the spring cavefish, *Chologaster agassizi*. Trans. Amer. Fish. Soc. 97:448-54.

———. 1969. Reactions of the American eel to dissolved oxygen tensions. Texas J. Sci. 20:305–15.

———. 1970. Resistance of the plains killifish, *Fundulus kansae* (Cyprinodontidae) to heat death at various salinities. Proc. Okla. Acad. Sci. 50:75–78.

———. 1971. Preference behavior of the Red River pupfish to acclimation salinities. Southwest. Nat. 16:55–63.

———, and W. J. Matthews. 1980. Temperature selection by the darters *Etheostoma spectabile* and *Etheostoma radiosum* (Pisces: Percidae). Amer. Midl. Nat. 104:412–15.

———, A. A. Echelle, and G. D. Schnell. 1973. Effects of dissolved oxygen concentrations on locomotory reactions of the spotted gar, *Leipsosteus oculatus* (Pisces: Lepisosteidae). Copeia 1973:119-24.

———, W. J. Matthews, and G. D. Schnell. 1978. Locomotor reactions of two cyprinidontid fishes to differences in dissolved oxygen concentrations. Southwest. Nat. 23:397-400.

———, G. D. Schnell, and J. Pigg. 1975. Thermal acclimation and temperature selection in sunfishes (Centrarchidae). *Ibid.* 20:177–84.

Hindar, K., and B. Jonsson. 1982. Habitat and food segregation of dwarf and normal Arctic charr (*Salvelinus alpinus*) from Vangsvatnet Lake, western Norway. Canad. J. Fish. Aquatic Sci. 39:1030–45.

Hirshfield, M. F. 1980. An experimental analysis of reproductive effort and cost in the Japanese medaka, *Oryzias latipes*. Ecology 61:282–92.

———, and C. R. Feldmeth. 1980. Genetic differences in physiological tolerances of Amargosa pupfish (*Cyprinodon nevadensis*) populations. Science 207:999–1001.

Hixon, M. A. 1980. Competitive interactions between California reef fishes of the genus *Embiotoca*. Ecology 61:918–31.

Hlohowskyj, I., and A. M. White. 1983. Food resource partitioning and selectivity by the greenside, rainbow, and fantail darters (Pisces: Percidae). Ohio J. Sci. 83:201-208.

———, and T. E. Wissing. 1985. Seasonal changes in the critical thermal maxima (CTMax) of fantail (*Etheostoma flabellare*), greenside (*Etheostoma blennioides*), and rainbow (*Etheostoma caeruleum*) darters. Canad. J. Zool. 63:1629–33.

———, and ———. Seasonal changes in low oxygen tolerance of fantail, *Etheostoma flabellare*, rainbow, *Etheostoma caeruleum*, and greenside, *Etheostoma blennioides*, darters. Env. Biol. Fishes. In press.

Hjort, R. C., and C. B. Schreck. 1982. Phenotypic differences among stocks of hatchery and wild coho salmon, *Oncorhynchus kisutch*, in Oregon, Washington, and California. Fish. Bull. 80:105–19.

———, P. L. Hulett, L. D. LaBolle, and H. W. Li. 1984. Fish and invertebrates of revetments and other habitats in the Willamette River, Oregon. US Army Eng. Waterways Exp. Stat., EWQOS Tech. Rep. E-84-9.

———, B. C. Mundy, P. L. Hulett, H. W. Li, C. B. Schreck, R. A. Tubb, H. W. Horton, L. D. LaBolle, A. G. Maule, and C. E. Stainbrook. 1981. Habitat requirements for resident fishes in the reservoirs of the lower Columbia River. US Army Corps Eng., Final Rep. Contract No. DACW57-79-C-0067.

Hocott, C. H., and E. O. Wiley (eds.). 1986. Zoogeography of North American freshwater fishes. Wiley Interscience, New York.

Hoffmaster, J. L. 1985. Geographic distribution of *Ceratomyxa shasta* in the Columbia River Basin and susceptibility of salmonid stocks. Unpub. MS Thesis, Oregon State Univ., Corvallis.

Hokanson, K. E. F. 1977. Temperature requirements of some percids and adaptations to the seasonal temperature cycle. J. Fish. Res. Board Canada. 34:1524–50.

Holmes, W. G. 1984. Predation risk and foraging of the hoary marmot in Alaska. Behav. Ecol. Sociobiol. 15:293–301.

Holt, R. D. 1977. Predation, apparent competition, and the structure of prey communities. Theoret. Pop. Biol. 12:197–229.

Hom, C. L. 1982. The effect of grazing by the snail, *Goniobasis clavaeformis* Lea on aufwuchs in artificial streams. Unpub. MS Thesis, Univ. Tennessee, Knoxville.

Honess, C. W. 1923. Geology of the southern Ouachita Mountains of Oklahoma. Part II. Geography and Economic Geology. Oklahoma. Geol. Surv. Bull. 32:1–76.

Hoppe, D. M. 1978. Thermal tolerance in tadpoles of the chorus frog *Pseudacris triseriata*. Herpetologica 34:318–21.

Horn, H. S. 1978. Optimal tactics of reproduction and life-history, pp. 411–29. *In:* Behavioral ecology: An evolutionary approach. J. R. Krebs and N. B. Davies (eds.). Blackwell, London.

Horn, M. H., S. N. Murray, and T. W. Edwards. 1982. Dietary selectivity in the field and food preferences in the laboratory for two herbivorous fishes (*Cebidichthys violaceus* and *Xiphister mucosus*) from a temperate intertidal zone. Mar. Biol. 67:237-46.

———, and M. A. Neighbors. 1984. Protein and nitrogen assimilation as a factor in predicting the seasonal microalgal diet of the monkeyface prickleback. Trans. Amer. Fish. Soc. 113:388–96.

Horton, J. S. 1977. The development and perpetuation of the permanent tamarisk type in the phreatophyte zone of the southwest, pp. 124-27. *In:* R. R. Johnson and D. A. Jones (tech. coords.). Importance, preservation, and management of riparian habitat: A symposium. US For. Serv. Gen. Tech. Rep. RM-43, Rocky Mtn. For. Range Exp. Sta., Fort Collins, Colo.

Horton, R. E. 1945. Erosional development of streams and their drainage basins: Hydrophysical approach to quantitative morphology. Bull. Geol. Soc. Amer. 56:275–370.

Horwitz, R. J. 1978. Temporal variability patterns and the distributional patterns of stream fishes. Ecol. Monogr. 48:307–21.

Hoyt, W. A., and W. B. Langbein. 1955. Floods. Princeton Univ. Press, Princeton, N.J.

Hubbs, C. 1964. Effects of thermal fluctuations on the relative survival of greenthroat darter young from stenothermal and eurythermal waters. Ecology 45:376–79.

———. 1967. Geographic variations in survival of hybrids between etheostomatine fishes. Bull. Texas Mem. Mus. 13:1–72.

———. 1982. Life history dynamics of *Menidia beryllina* from Lake Texoma. Amer. Midl. Nat. 107:1–12.

———. 1983. Handbook of darters (review). Copeia 1983:581.

———. 1985. Darter reproductive seasons. *Ibid.* 1985:56–68.

———. 1985. Use of darter hybrids in home aquaria. American Currents. Nov. 1985:7–10.

———, and N. E. Armstrong. 1962. Developmental temperature tolerance of Texas and Arkansas-Missouri *Etheostoma spectabile* (Percidae, Osteichthyes), *Ibid.* 43:742–44.

———, and E. A. Delco, Jr. 1960. Geographic variations in egg complement of *Etheostoma lepidum*. Texas J. Sci. 12:3–7.

———, and W. F. Hettler. 1959. Fluctuation in some central Texas fish populations. Southwest. Nat. 3:13–16.

———, and M. V. Johnson. 1961. Differences in egg complement of *Hadropterus scierus* from Austin and San Marcos. *Ibid.* 6:9–12.

———, and K. Strawn. 1957. The effects of light and temperature on the greenthroat darter, *Etheostoma lepidum*. Ecology 38:596–602.

———, M. M. Stevenson, and A. E. Peden. 1968. Fecundity and egg size in two central Texas darter populations. Southwest. Nat. 13:301–24.

Hubbs, C. L. 1922. Variations in the number of vertebrae and other meristic characters of fishes correlated with the temperature of water during development. Amer. Nat. 56:360–72.

———. 1926. The structural consequences of modifications of the developmental rate in fishes, considered in reference to certain problems of evolution. *Ibid.* 60:57–81.

———. 1934. Racial and individual variation in animals, especially fishes. *Ibid.* 68:115–28.

———. 1940. Speciation of fishes. *Ibid.* 74:198–211.

———. 1941. The relation of hydrological conditions to speciation in fishes, pp. 182–95. *In:* A symposium on hydrobiology. Univ. Wisconsin Press, Madison.

———. 1951. The American cyprinid fish *Notropis germanus* Hay interpreted as an intergeneric hybrid. Amer. Midl. Nat. 45:446–54.

———. 1964. History of Ichthyology in the United States after 1850. Copeia 1964:42–60.

———, and W. F. Hettler. 1964. Observations of the toleration of high temperatures and low dissolved oxygen in natural waters by *Crenichthys baileyi*. Southwest. Nat. 9:245–48.

———, and R. R. Miller. 1948. Two new, relict genera of cyprinid fishes from Nevada. Occ. Pap. Mus. Zool. Univ. Mich. 507:1–30.

———, and A. I. Ortenburger. 1929. Further notes on the fishes of Oklahoma with descriptions of new species of Cyprinidae. Pub. Univ. Okla. Biol. Surv. 1:17–43.

———, R. C. Baird, and J. W. Gerald. 1967. Effects of dissolved oxygen concentration and light intensity on activity cycles of fishes inhabiting warm springs. Amer. Midl. Nat. 77:104–15.

Huct, M. 1959. Profiles and biology of western European streams as related to fish management. Trans. Amer. Fish. Soc. 88:115–63.

Hucts, M. J. 1947. Experimental studies on adaptive evolution in *Gasterosteus aculeatus* L. Evolution 1:89–102.

Hull, C. H., and N. H. Nie. 1981. SPSS update 7-9. McGraw-Hill Book Co., New York.

Humphries, J. M. 1984. Genetics of speciation in pupfishes from Laguna Chichancanab, Mexico, pp. 129–40. *In:* Evolution of fish species flocks. A. A. Echelle and I. Kornfield (eds.). Univ. Maine Press, Orono.

———, F. L. Bookstein, B. Chernoff, G. R. Smith, R. L. Elder, and S. G. Poss. 1981. Multivariate discrimination by shape in relation to size. Syst. Zool. 30:291–308.

Hutchinson, G. E. 1957. Concluding remarks. Cold Spring Harbor Symp. Quant. Biol. 22:415–27.

———. 1959. Homage to Santa Rosalia, or "Why are there so many kinds of animals?" Amer. Nat. 93:145–59.

———. 1961. The paradox of the plankton. *Ibid.* 95:137–46.

———. 1968. When are species necessary? pp. 177–86. *In:* Population biology and evolution. R. C. Lewontin (ed.). Syracuse Univ. Press, Syracuse, N.Y.

———. 1978. An introduction to population ecology. Yale Univ. Press, New Haven, Conn.

Hutchinson, V. H. 1961. Critical thermal maxima in salamanders. Physiol. Zool. 34:92–125.

———. 1976. Factors influencing thermal tolerances of individual organisms, pp. 10–26. *In:* Thermal Ecology II. G. W. Esch and R. W. McFarlane (eds.). ERDA Symp. Ser. 40.

———, and J. Maness. 1979. The role of behavior in temperature acclimation and tolerance in ectotherms. Amer. Zool. 19:367–84.

Hynes, H. B. N. 1970. The Ecology of Running Waters. Univ. Toronto Press, Toronto.

———. 1975. The stream and its valley. Vech. Int. Ver. Limnol. 19:1–15.

Imhof, M. R., R. Leary, and H. E. Brooke. 1980. Population or stock structure of lake whitefish, *Corregonus clupeaformis*, in northern Lake Michigan as assayed by isozyme electrophoresis. Canad. J. Fish. Aquatic Sci. 37:783–93.

Ingersoll, C. G., and D. L. Claussen. 1984. Temperature selection and critical thermal maxima of the fantail darter, *Etheostoma flabellare*, and johnny darter, *Etheostoma nigrum*, related to habitat and season. Env. Biol. Fish. 10:131-38.

———, I. Hlohowskyj, and N. D. Mundahl. 1984. Movements and densities of the darters *Etheostoma flabellare*, *E. spectabile* and *E. nigrum* during spring spawning. J. Freshwater Ecol. 2:345–51.

Inhat, J.M., and R. V. Bulkley. 1984. Influence of acclimation temperature and season on acute temperature preference of adult mountain whitefish, *Prosopium williamsoni*. Env. Biol. Fish. 11:29–40.

Ivankov, V. N., V. A. Mitrofanor, and V. P. Bushuyer. 1975. An instance of the pink salmon (*Oncorhynchus gorbuscha*) reaching maturity at an age of less than one year. J. Ichthyol. 15:497–99.

Ives, R. L. 1936. Desert floods in the Sonoyta Valley. Amer. J. Sci. 32:349–60.

Jackson, J. K. 1984. Aquatic insect emergence from a desert stream. Unpub. MS Thesis, Arizona State Univ., Tempe.

Jahns, R. H. 1949. Desert Floods. J. Eng. Sci. 12:10–14.

Jaksic, F. M. 1981. Recognition of morphological adaptations in animals: The hypothetico-deductive method. BioScience 31:667-70.

James, F. C., R. F. Johnston, H. O. Wamer, G. J. Niemi, and W. J. Boecklen. 1984. The Grinnellian niche of the wood thrush. Amer. Nat. 124:17–30.

Jandebeur, T. S. 1975. Fish species diversity, occurrence and abundance in the North River drainage system of Alabama. Unpub. PhD Diss., Univ. Alabama, University.

Javaid, M. Y., and J. M. Anderson. 1967a. Influence of starvation on selected temperature of some salmonids. J. Fish. Res. Board Canada 24:1515–19.

———, and ———. 1967b. Thermal acclimation and temperature selection in Atlantic Salmon, *Salmo Salar*, and rainbow trout, *Salmo Sairdneri*. *Ibid.* 24:1507–14.

Jenkins, R. E., E. A. Lachner, and F. J. Schwartz. 1972. Fishes of the central Appalachian drainages: Their distribution and dispersal, pp. 43–117. *In:* The distributional history of the biota of the southern Appalachians. P. C. Holt (ed.). Virginia Poly. Inst., Blackburg, Res. Monogr. 4.

John, K. R. 1963. The effect of torrential rains on the reproductive cycle of *Rhinichthyes osculus* in the Chiricahua Mountains, Arizona. Copeia 1963:286–91.

———. 1964. Survival of fish in intermittent streams of the Chiricahua Mountains, Arizona. Ecology 45:112–19.

Johnson, G. B. 1971. Metabolic implications of polymorphism as an adaptive strategy. Nature 232:347–48.

———. 1974. Enzyme polymorphism and metabolism. Science 184:28–37.

Johnson, J. H., and E. Z. Johnson. 1982. Diel foraging in relation to available prey in an Adirondack mountain fish community. Hydrobiologia 96:97–104.

Johnson, L. 1980. The Arctic charr, *Salvelinus alpinus*, pp. 15–98. *In:* Charrs, salmonid fishes of the genus *Salvelinus*. E. K.

Balon (ed.). Dr. W. Junk Publishers, The Hague, Netherlands.

Johnson, R. I. 1978. Systematics and zoogeography of *Plagiola* (= *Dysnomia* = *Epioblasma*), an almost extinct genus of freshwater mussels (Bivalvia: Unionidae) from middle North America. Bull. Mus. Comp. Zool. 148:239–320.

Jolicoeur, P. 1975. Linear regressions in fishery research: Some comments. J. Fish. Res. Board Canada 32:1491–94.

———, and J. E. Mosimann. 1963. Size and shape variation in the painted turtle. A principal component analysis. Growth 24:339–54.

Jones, A. N. 1975. A preliminary study of fish segregation in salmon spawning streams. J. Fish Biol. 7:95–104.

Jones, J. W. 1959. The salmon. Collins, London.

———, and G. M. King. 1949. Experimental observations on the spawning behaviour of the Atlantic salmon (*Salmo salar* Linn.). Proc. Zool. Soc. Lond. 119:33–48.

———, and ———. 1952. The spawning of the male salmon parr (*Salmo salar* Linn. juv.). *Ibid.* 122:615–19.

Jones, K., and W. D. P. Stewart. 1969. Nitrogen turnover in marine and brackish habitats. IV. Uptake of the extracellular products of the nitrogen-fixing alga Calothrix scopulorum. J. Mar. Biol. Assoc. U.K. 49:701–16.

Jonsson, B., and K. Hindar. 1982. Reproductive strategy of dwarfed and normal arctic charr (*Salvelinus alpinus*) from Vangsvatnet Lake, Western Norway. Canad. J. Fish. Aquatic Sci. 39:1404–13.

Jordan, D. S. 1891. Report of explorations in Colorado and Utah during the summer of 1889, with an account of the fishes found in each of the river basins examined. Bull. US Fish Comm. 9:1–40.

———, and B. W. Evermann. 1896–1900. The fishes of North and Middle America. Pts. 1–4. Bull. US Nat. Mus., No. 47.

———, and S. E. Meek. 1885. List of fishes collected in Iowa and Missouri in August, 1884, with descriptions of three new species. Proc. US Nat. Mus. 8:1–17.

Jordan, P. R. 1968. Summary and analysis of sediment records in relation to St. Louis harbor sedimentation problem. Open File Rep. USGS, Water Resources Div.

———. 1979. Statistical summary of streamflow data for Kansas streams in the Kansas River Basin. Kansas Water Resources Board, Topeka. Tech. Rep. 14B:1–334.

———. 1982. Rainfall-runoff relations and expected streamflow in western Kansas. Kansas Water Office, Topeka. Bull. 25:1–42.

Juday, C., W. H. Rich, G. I. Kemmerer, and A. Mann. 1932. Limnological studies of Karluk Lake, Alaska 1926–1930. Bur. Fisheries, Bull. No. 12.

Jumars, P. A. 1980. Rank correlation and concordance tests in community analyses: an inappropriate null hypothesis. Ecology 61:1553–54.

Kallemeyn, L. W., and J. F. Novotny. 1977. Fish and fish food organisms in various habitats of the Missouri River in South Dakota, Nebraska, and Iowa. Fish and Wildl. Serv., US Dept. Interior, Biol. Serv. Prog. FWS/OBS-77/25, Yankton, S.Dak.

Kaplan, R. H. 1980. The implications of ovum size variability for offspring fitness and clutch size within several populations of salamanders (*Ambystoma*). Evolution 34:51–64.

———, and W. S. Cooper, 1984. The evolution of developmental plasticity in reproductive characteristics: An application of the "adaptive coin-flipping" principle. Amer. Nat. 123:393–410.

Karr, J. R., and K. E. Freemark. 1983. Habitat selection and environmental gradients: dynamics in the "stable" tropics. Ecology 64:1481–94.

———, and ———. 1985. Disturbance and vertebrates: an integrative perspective, pp. 153–68. *In:* Natural disturbance: the patch dynamics perspective. S. T. A. Pickett and P. S. White (eds.). Academic Press, New York.

———, and F. C. James. 1975. Ecomorphological configurations and convergent evolution in species and communities, pp. 258–91. *In:* Ecology and evolution of communities. M. L. Cody and J. M. Diamond (eds.) Belknap Press, Cambridge, Mass.

Keast, A. 1966. Trophic interrelationships in the fish fauna of a small stream. Great Lakes Res. Div., Univ. Michigan., Publ. No. 15:51–79.

———. 1978a. Feeding interrelations between age-groups of pumpkinseed (*Lepomis gibbosus*) and comparisons with bluegill (*L. macrochirus*). J. Fish. Res. Board Canada 35:12–27.

———. 1978b. Trophic and spatial interrelationships in the fish species of an Ontario temperate lake. Env. Biol. Fish. 3:7–31.

———, and D. Webb. 1966. Mouth and body form relative to feeding ecology in the fish fauna of a small lake, Lake Opinicon, Ontario. J. Fish. Res. Board Canada 23:1845–74.

Keegan-Rogers, V., and R. J. Schultz. 1984. Differences in courtship aggression among six clones of unisexual fish. Anim. Behav. 32:1040-44.

Kelly, P. J., Jr. 1975. Stream channelization and fish diversity in Luxapalila River in Alabama and Mississippi. Unpub. PhD Diss. Mississippi State Univ., Mississippi State.

Kendall, A. W., Jr.; E. H. Ahlstrom; and H. G. Moser. 1984. Early life history stages of fishes and their characters, pp. 11–22. *In:* Ontogeny and systematics of fishes. Am. Soc. Ichth. Herp. Spec. Pub. 1.

Kennedy, P. K., M. L. Kennedy, E. G. Zimmerman, R. K. Chesser, and M. H. Smith. 1985. Biochemical genetics of mosquitofish. V. Perturbation effects on genetic organization of populations. Copeia 1985:118–25.

Kesseli, J. E., and C. B. Beaty. 1959. Desert flood conditions in the White Mountains of California and Nevada. Tech. Rep. EP-198, US Army Qtrmstr. Res. Eng. Cent., Nantick, Mass.

Kimura, M. 1968. Evolutionary rate at the molecular level. Nature 217:624–62.

———. 1969. The rate of molecular evolution considered from the standpoint of population genetics. Proc. Natl. Acad. Sci. 63:1181–88.

———, and T. Ohta. 1971. Theoretical aspects of population genetics. Princeton Univ. Press, Princeton, N.J.

Kincaid, H. L. 1976. Effects of inbreeding on rainbow trout populations. Trans. Amer. Fish. Soc. 105:273–80.

King, C. E. 1964. Relative abundance of species and MacArthur's model. Ecology 45:716–27.

King, G. M., J. W. Jones, and H. J. Orton. 1939. Behaviour of mature male salmon parr (*Salmo salar*). Nature 143:162.

King, J. L., and T. H. Jukes. 1969. Non-Darwinian evolution. Science 164:788–98.

King, T. L., E. G. Zimmerman, and T. L. Beitinger. 1985. Concordant variation in thermal tolerance and allozymes of the red shiner, *Notropis lutrensis*, inhabiting tailwater sections of the Brazos River, Texas. Env. Biol. Fish. 13:49–57.

Kinne, O. 1960. Growth, food intake and food conversion in a euryplastic fish exposed to different temperatures and salinities. Physiol. Zool. 33:288–317.

———, and E. M. Kinne. 1962a. Rates of development in embryos of a cyprinodont fish exposed to different temperature-salinity-oxygen combinations. Canad. J. Zool. 40:231–53.

———, and ———. 1962b. Effects of salinity and oxygen on developmental rates in a cyprinodont fish. Nature [London] 193:1097–98.

Klecka, W. R. 1975. Discriminant analysis, pp. 434–67. *In:* Statistical package for the social sciences. H. H. Nie et al. (eds.). McGraw-Hill, New York.

———. 1980. Discriminant analysis. Sage Univ. Pap. Ser. Quant. App. Soc. Sci., Ser. No. 07-019. Sage Publications, London.

Klemetsen, A., and P. Grotnes. 1980. Coexistence and immigration of two sympatric arctic charr, pp. 757–63. *In:* E. K. Balon (ed.). Charrs, salmonid fishes of the genus *Salvelinus*. Dr. W. Junk Publishers, The Hague, Netherlands.

Kodric-Brown, A. 1977. Reproductive success and the evolution of breeding territories in pupfish (*Cyprinodon*). Evolution 31:750–66.

———. 1981. Variable breeding systems in pupfishes (Genus *Cyprinodon*): Adaptation to changing environments, pp. 205–35. *In:* Fishes in North American deserts. R. J. Naimen and D. L. Soltz (eds.). John Wiley & Sons, New York.

Kornfield, I., and K. E. Carpenter. 1984. Cyprinids of Lake Lanao, Philippines: Taxonomic validity, evolutionary rates and speciation scenarios, pp. 69–84. *In:* Evolution of fish species flocks. A. A. Echelle and I. Kornfield (eds.). Univ. Maine Press, Orono.

———, D. C. Smith, P. S. Gagnon, and J. N. Taylor, 1982. The cichlid fish of Cuatro Cienegas, Mexico: Direct evidence of conspecificity among distinct morphs. Evolution 36:658–64.

Korte, P. A., and L. H. Fredrickson. 1977. Loss of Missouri's lowland hardwood ecosystem. Trans. N. Am. Wildl. Nat. Res. Conf. 42:31–41.

Kotler, B. P. 1984. Risk of predation and the structure of desert rodent communities. Ecology 65:689–701.

Kour, E. L., and V. H. Hutchison. 1970. Critical thermal tolerances and heating and cooling rates of lizards from diverse habitats. Copeia 1970:219–29

Kowalski, K. T., J. P. Schubauer, C. L. Scott, and J. R. Spotila. 1978. Interspecific and seasonal differences in the temperature tolerance of stream fish. J. Thermal Biol. 3:105–108.

Kraatz, W. C. 1923. A study of the food of the minnow, *Campostoma anomalum*. Ohio J. Sci. 23:265–83.

Krakowiecki, J. M. 1972. A microbial, chemical, physical and historical study of the pollutants of the Missouri River, 6 June 1972–11 August 1972. Project Rep., NSF Grant GY-9627, Benedictine College, Atchison, Kans.

Kramer, D. L., D. Manley, and R. Bourgeois. 1983. The effect of respiratory mode and oxygen concentration on the risk of predation in fishes. Canad. J. Zool. 61:653–65.

Krumholz, L. A. 1948. Reproduction of the western mosquitofish, *Gambusia affinis* (Baird and Girard), and its use in mosquito control. Ecol. Monogr. 18:1–43.

Kuehne, R. A. 1962. A classification of streams, illustrated by fish distribution in an eastern Kentucky creek. Ecology 43:608–14.

———, and R. W. Barbour. 1983. The American darters. Univ. Press Kentucky, Lexington, Ky.

———, and R. M. Bailey. 1961. Stream capture and the distribution of the percid fish *Etheostoma sagitta,* with geologic and taxonomic considerations. Copeia 1961:1–8.

Kushlan, J. A. 1976. Environmental stability and fish community diversity. *Ibid*. 57:821–25.

Lachner, E. A., and R. E. Jenkins. 1971a. Systematics, distribution, and evolution of the chub genus *Nocomis* Girard (Pisces, Cyprinidae) of eastern United States, with descriptions of new species. Smithson. Contrib. Zool. 85:1–97.

———, and ———. 1971b. Systematics, distribution, and evolution of the *Nocomis biguttatus* species group (Family Cyprinidae: Pisces) with a description of a new species from the Ozark Upland. *Ibid*. 91:1–28.

Lack, D. 1947. The significance of clutch size. Parts I–II. Ibis 89:302–52.

———. 1948. The significance of litter-size. J. Anim. Ecol. 17:45–50.

———. 1954. The evolution of reproductive rates, pp. 143–56. *In:* Evolution as a process. J. S. Huxley, A. C. Hardy, and E. B. Ford (eds.). Allen and Unwin, London.

Lafleur, R. A. 1956. A biological and chemical survey of the Calcasieu River. Unpub. MS Thesis, Louisiana State Univ., Baton Rouge.

Lambou, V. W. 1959. Fish populations of backwater lakes in Louisiana. Trans. Amer. Fish. Soc. 88:7–15.

Lamby, K. 1941. Zur Fischereibiologie des Myvatn, Nord-Island. Z. Fisch. 39:749–805.

Larimore, R. W. 1961. Fish population and electro fishing success in a warmwater stream. Jour. Wildl. Manag. 25:1-12.

———, and P. W. Smith. 1963. The fishes of Champaign County, Illinois as affected by 60 years of stream change. Ill. Nat. Hist. Surv. Bull. 28:299–382.

———, W. F. Childers, and C. Heckrotte. 1959. Destruction and re-establishment of stream fish and invertebrates affected by drought. Trans. Amer. Fish. Soc. 88:261–85.

———, Q. H. Pickering, and L. Durham. 1952. An inventory of the fishes of Jordan Creek, Vermilion County, Illinois. Ill. Nat. His. Surv. Biol. Note No. 29. Urbana, Ill.

Larson, J. S., M. S. Bedinger, C. F. Bryan, S. Brown, R. T. Huffman, E. L. Miller, D. G. Rhodes, and B. A. Touchet. 1981. Transition from wetlands to uplands in southeastern bottomland hardwood forests, pp. 225–73. *In:* Wetlands of bottomland hardwood forests. J. R. Clark and J. Benforado (eds.). Elsevier Scientific Publishing Co., New York.

Larson, R. J. 1980. Competition, habitat selection, and the bathymetric segregation of two rockfish (*Sebastes*) species. Ecol. Monogr. 50:221–39.

Laughlin, D. R., and E. E. Werner. 1980. Resource partitioning in two coexisting sunfish: Pumpkinseed (*Lepomis gibbosus*) and northern longear sunfish (*Lepomis megalotis peltates*). Canad. J. Fish. Aquatic Sci. 37:1411–20.

Lawlor, L. R. 1980. Structure and stability in natural and randomly constructed competitive communities. Amer. Nat. 116:394–408.

Lawton, J. H., D. R. Strong. 1981. Community patterns and competition in folivorous insects. *Ibid*. 118:317–38.

LeCren, E. D. 1969. Estimates of fish populations and production in small streams in England, pp. 269–80. *In:* Symposium on salmon and trout in streams. T. G. Northcote (ed.). Univ. British Columbia, Vancouver.

Lee, D. S., et al. (eds.). 1980. Atlas of North American freshwater fishes. N.C. State Mus. Nat. Hist., Raleigh.

Lelek, A. 1981. Population dynamics of fishes in the changing streams, pp. 193–209. *In:* R. Cuinat, ed. Dynamique de populations et qualité de l'eau.

Lennon, R. E., and P. S. Parker. 1955. Electric shocker development on southeastern trout waters. Trans. Amer. Fish. Soc. 85:234–40.

———, and ———. 1960. The stoneroller, *Campostoma anomalum* (Rafinesque), in the Great Smoky Mountains National Park. *Ibid*. 89:263–70.

Leopold, L. B. 1962. Rivers. Amer. Sci. 50:511–37.

———. 1969. The rapids and pools—Grand Canyon, pp. 131–45. *In:* The Colorado River and John Wesley Powell. USGS Prof. Pap. 669-D.

———, and T. Maddock. 1955. The hydraulic geometry of stream channels and some physiographic implications. Amer. Sci. 252:1–57.

———, M. G. Wolman, and J. P. Miller. 1964. Fluvial processes in geomorphology. W. H. Freeman and Co., San Francisco.

Levene, H. 1960. Robust tests for equality of variance, pp. 278–92. *In:* Contributions to probability and statistics. I. Olkin, S. G. Ghurye, W. Hoeffding, W. D. Madow, and H. B. Mann (eds.). Stanford Univ. Press, Stanford, Calif.

Levin, S. A. 1974. Dispersion and population interaction. Amer. Nat. 108:207–28.

Levins, R. 1966. The strategy of model building in population biology. Amer. Sci. 54:421–31.

———. 1968. Evolution in changing environments: Some theoretical explorations. Monographs in Population Biology No. 2.

Princeton Univ. Press, Princeton, N.J.

———. 1969. Thermal acclimation and heat resistance in *Drosophila* species. Amer. Nat. 103:483–99.

———, and D. C. Culver. 1971. Regional coexistence of species and competition between rare species. Proc. Nat. Acad. Sci. USA 68:1246–48.

Lewis, D. D. 1963. Desert floods—a report of southern Arizona floods of September, 1962. Ariz. Land Dept., Wat. Res. Rep. 13:1–30.

Lewis, W. M., and D. R. Helms. 1964. Vulnerability of forage organisms to largemouth bass. Trans. Amer. Fish. Soc. 93:315–18.

Lewontin, R. C. 1966. On the measurement of relative variability. Syst. Zool. 15:141–42.

———. 1979. Fitness, survival, and optimality, pp. 3–21. *In:* Analysis of ecological systems. D. H. Horn, R. Mitchell, and G. R. Stairs (eds.). Ohio State Univ. Press, Columbus.

Li, H. W., and P. B. Moyle. 1976. Feeding ecology of the Pit sculpin, *Cottus pitensis*. Proc. S. Calif. Acad. Sci. 75:111–18.

———, and ———. 1981. Ecological analysis of species introductions into aquatic systems. Trans. Amer. Fish. Soc. 110:772–82.

———, C. B. Schreck, and R. A. Tubb. 1984. Comparison of habitats near spur dikes, continuous revetments, and natural banks for larval, juvenile, and adult fishes of the Willamette River. Water Resources Res. Inst., WRRI-95.

Licht, P., W. R. Dawson, and V. H. Shoemaker. 1966a. Heat resistance of some Australian lizards. Copeia 1966:162–69.

———, V. H. Shoemaker and A. R. Main. 1966b. Observations on the thermal relations of western Australian lizards. *Ibid.* 1966:97–110.

Liem, K. F., and L. S. Kaufman. 1984. Intraspecific macroevolution: Functional biology of the polymorphic cichlid species *Cichlasoma minckleyi*, pp. 203–216. *In:* Evolution of fish species flocks. A. A. Echelle and I. Kornfield (eds.). Univ. Maine Press, Orono.

Likens, G. E. 1983. A priority for ecological research. Bull. Ecol. Soc. Amer. 64:234–43.

Lister, D. B., and H. S. Genoe. 1970. Stream habitat utilization by cohabiting underyearlings of chinook (*Oncorhynchus tshawytscha*) and coho (*O. kisutch*) salmon in the Big Qualicum River, British Columbia. J. Fish. Res. Board Canada 27:1215–24.

Livingstone, D. A., M. Rowland, and P. E. Bailey. 1982. On the size of African riverine fish faunas. Amer. Zool. 22:361–69.

Lobel, P. S. 1980. Herbivory by damselfishes and their role in coral reef community ecology. Bull. Mar. Sci. 30:273–89.

Lobon-Cervia, J., and T. Penczak. 1984. Fish production in the Jarama River, Central Spain. Hol. Ecol. 7:128–37.

Loeschke, V. 1984. The interplay between genetic composition, species number, and population sizes under exploitative composition, pp. 235–46. *In:* Population biology and evolution. K. Wohrman and V. Loeschcke (eds.). Springer-Verlag, Heidelberg.

Loiselle, P. V., and G. W. Barlow. 1978. Do fishes lek like birds? *In:* Contrasts in behavior, pp. 31–75. E. S. Resse and F. J. Lightner (eds.). John Wiley & Sons, New York.

Lotrich, V. A. 1973. Growth, production, and community composition of fishes inhabiting a first-, second-, and third-order stream of eastern Kentucky. Ecol. Monogr. 43:377–97.

Lowe, C. H., D. S. Hinds, and E. A. Halpern. 1967. Experimental catastrophic selection and tolerances to low oxygen concentration in native Arizona freshwater fishes. Ecology 48:1013–17.

Lowe-McConnell, R. H. 1975. Fish communities in tropical freshwaters. Longman, New York.

Lubchencho, J. 1978. Plant species diversity in a marine intertidal community: Importance of herbivore food preference and algal competitive abilities. Amer. Nat. 112:23–39.

———. 1982. Effects of grazers and algal competitors on fucoid colonization in tide pools. J. Phycol. 18:544–50.

———. 1983. *Littorina* and *Fucus*: Effects of herbivores, substratum heterogeneity, and plant escapes during succession. Ecology 64:1116–23.

Lutterbie, G. W. 1976. The darters of Wisconsin. Unpub. MA Thesis, Univ. Wisconsin, Stevens Point.

Lynch, M. 1984. Destabilizing hybridization, general-purpose genotypes and geographical parthenogenesis. Quart. Rev. Biol. 59:257–90.

McAllister, D. E., S. P. Platania, F. W. Schueler, M. E. Baldwin, and D.S. Lee. 1985. Ichthyofaunal patterns on a geographic grid, pp. 17–51. *In:* Zoogeography of North American freshwater fishes. C. H. Hocutt and E. O. Wiley (eds.). John Wiley & Co., New York.

MacArthur, R. H. 1957. On the relative abundance of bird species. Proc. Natl. Acad. Sci. 43:293–95

———. 1972. Geographical ecology: Patterns in the distribution of species. Harper & Row, New York.

———, and R. Levins. 1967. The limiting similarity, convergence, and divergence of coexisting species. Amer. Nat. 101:377–85.

———, and E. O. Wilson. 1963. An equilibrium theory of insular zoogeography. Evolution 17:373–87.

———, and ———. 1967. The theory of island biogeography. Princeton Univ. Press, Princeton, N.J.

McAuliffe, J. R. 1984. Resource depression by a stream herbivore: Effects on distributions and abundances of other grazers. Oikos 42:327–33.

McCarthy, M. S. 1986. Age determination in razorback sucker, *Xyrauchen texanus* from Lake Mohave, Arizona-Nevada. Unpub. MS Thesis., Arizona State Univ., Tempe.

McCauley, R. W. 1958. Thermal relations of geographic races of Salvelinus. Canad. J. Zool. 36:655–62.

McClenaghan, L. R., Jr.; M. H. Smith; and M. W. Smith. 1985. Biochemical genetics of mosquitofish. IV. Changes of allele frequencies through time and space. Evolution 39:451–60.

MacDonald, P. O., W. E. Frayer, and J. K. Clauser. 1979. Documentation, chronology, and future projections of bottomland hardwood habitat loss in the lower Mississippi alluvial plain, Vol. I. Basic report. US Fish and Wildlife Service, Washington, D.C.

McFadden, J. T., E. L. Cooper, and J. K. Anderson. 1965. Some effects of environment on egg production in brown trout (*Salmo trutta*). Limnol. Oceanogr. 10:88–95.

McFarlane, R. W., B. C. Moore, and S. E. Williams. 1976. Thermal tolerance of stream cyprinid minnows, pp. 141–44. *In:* Thermal Ecology II. G. W. Esch and R. W. McFarlane (eds.). ERDA Symp. Ser. 40.

Machniak, K., and J. H. Gee. 1975. Adjustment of buoyancy by tadpole madtom, *Noturus gyrinus*, and black bullhead, *Ictalurus melas*, in response to a change in water velocity. J. Fish. Res. Board Canada. 32:303–307.

McIntire, C. D., and J. A. Colby. 1978. A hierarchial model of lotic ecosystems. Ecol. Monog. 31:51–104.

McLaughlin, T. G. 1943. Geology and ground-water resources of Hamilton and Geary counties, Kansas. Kans. Geol. Survey, Bull. 49:1–220.

MacLean, J., and J. J. Magnuson. 1977. Species interactions in percid communities. J. Fish. Res. Board Canada 34:1941–51.

MacMahon, J. A., D. J. Schimpf, D. C. Andersen, K. G. Smith, and R. L. Bayn, Jr. 1981. An organism-centered approach to some community and ecosystem concepts. J. Theor. Biol. 88:287–307.

MacNally, R. C. 1983. On assessing the significance of interspecific competition to guild structure. Ecology 64:1646–52.

McNaughton, S. J. 1979. Grazing as an optimization process: Grass-ungulate relationships in the Serengeti. Amer. Nat.

113:691–703.

———. 1984. Grazing lawns: Animals in herds, plant form, and coevolution. *Ibid.* 124:863–86.

———, M. B. Coughenour and L. L. Wallace. 1979. Interactive processes in grassland ecosystems, pp. 167–193. *In:* J. R. Estes, R. J. Tyrl, and J. N. Brunken (eds.). Grasses and grasslands: Systematics and ecology. Univ. Oklahoma Press, Norman, OK.

McPhail, J. D. 1967. Distribution of freshwater fishes in Western Washington. Northwest Sci. 41:1–11.

———, and C. C. Lindsey. 1970. Freshwater fishes of northwestern Canada and Alaska. Bull. Fish. Res. Board Canada. 173.

Magnuson, J. J., L. B. Crowder, and P. A. Medvick. 1979. Temperature as an ecological resource. Amer. Zool. 19:331–43.

Mahon, R. 1984. Divergent structure in fish taxocenes of north temperate streams. Canad. J. Fish. Aquatic Sci. 41:330–50.

———, and E. K. Balon. 1985. Fish production in warmwater streams in Poland and Ontario. *Ibid.* 42:1211–15.

———, and M. Ferguson. 1981. Invasion of a new reservoir by fishes: Species composition, growth and condition. Canad. Field Nat. 95:272–75.

Maitland, P. S. 1965. The feeding relationships of salmon, trout, minnows, stone loach and three-spined sticklebacks in the River Eudrick, Scotland. J. Anim. Ecol. 34:109–33.

Mann, R. H. K. 1971. The populations, growth, and production of fish in four small streams in southern England. J. Anim. Ecol. 40:155–90.

———, and C. A. Mills. 1979. Demographic aspects of fish fecundity, pp. 161–77. *In:* Fish phenology: Anabolic adaptiveness in teleosts. P. J. Miller (ed.). Symp. Zool. Soc. Lond. 44, Academic Press, London.

———, C. A. Mills, and D. T. Crisp. 1984. Geographical variation in the life-history tactics of some species of freshwater fish, pp. 171–86. *In:* Fish Reproduction. R. Wooton (ed.). Academic Press, New York.

Mantel, N. 1967. The detection of disease clustering and a generalized regression approach. Cancer Res. 27:209–20.

Marsh, E. 1980. The effects of temperature and photoperiod on the termination of spawning in the orangethroat darter (*Etheostoma spectabile*) in central Texas. Texas J. Sci. 32:129–42.

———. 1984. Egg size variation in central Texas populations of *Etheostoma spectabile* (Pisces: Percidae). Copeia 1984:291–301.

———. 1986. Effects of egg size on offspring fitness and maternal fecundity in the orangethroat darter, *Etheostoma spectabile* (Pisces: Percidae). *Ibid.* 1986:18–30.

———, and W. L. Minckley. 1982. Fishes of the Phoenix metropolitan area in central Arizona. N. Amer. J. Fish. Mgmt. 24:395–402.

———, and ———. 1985. Aquatic resources of the Yuma Division, lower Colorado River, Arizona-California. Final Rep. Contract 2-07-30-X0214, US Bur. Reclam., Lower Colo. R. Reg., Boulder City, Nev. Ariz. State Univ., Tempe.

Marteinsdottir, G. 1984. Electrophoretic and morphological variation in Icelandic arctic charr (*Salvelinus alpinus* L.) Unpub. MS Thesis, Rutgers Univ., New Brunswick, N.J.

Martin, F. D. 1984. Diets of four sympatric species of *Etheostoma* (Pisces: Percidae) from southern Indiana: Interspecific and intraspecific multiple comparisons. Env. Biol. Fish. 11:113–20.

Matheson, R. E., Jr., and G. R. Brooks, Jr. 1983. Habitat segregation between *Cottus bairdi* and *Cottus girardi:* An example of complex inter- and intraspecific resource partitioning. Amer. Midl. Nat. 110:165–76.

Mathur, D. P., R. M. Schutsky, E. J. Purdy Jr., and C. A. Silver. 1981. Similarities in acute temperature preferences of freshwater fishes. Trans. Amer. Fish. Soc. 110:1–13.

Mathur, E., and C. A. Silver. 1980. Statistical problems in studies of temperature preference of fishes. Canad. J. Fish. Aquatic Sci. 37:733–37.

Matthews, W. J. 1977. Influence of physio-chemical factors on habitat selection by red shiners, *Notropis lutrensis* (Pisces: Cyprinidae). Unpub. PhD Univ. Oklahoma, Norman.

———. 1982. Small fish community structure in Ozark streams: Structured assembly patterns or random abundance of species? Amer. Midl. Nat. 107:42–54.

———. 1985. Critical current speeds and microhabitats of the benthic fishes *Percina roanoka* and *Etheostoma flabellare*. Env. Biol. Fish. 12:303–308.

———. 1986a. Fish community structure in a temperate stream: Stability, persistence, and a catastrophic flood. Copeia 1986:388–97.

———. 1986b. Geographic variation in thermal tolerance of a widespread minnow (*Notropis lutrensis*) of the North American midwest. J. Fish Biol. 28:407–17.

———, and G. L. Harp. 1974. Preimpoundment ichthyofaunal survey of the Piney Creek watershed, Izard County, Arkansas. Ark. Acad. Sci. Proc. 28:39–43.

———, and L. G. Hill. 1977. Tolerance of the red shiner, *Notropis lutrensis* (Cyprinidae), to environmental parameters. Southwest. Nat. 22:89–99.

———, and ———. 1979a. Influence of physico-chemical factors on habitat selection by red shiners, *Notropis lutrensis* (Pisces: Cyprinidae). Copeia 1979:70–81.

———, and ———. 1979b. Age specific differences in the distribution of red shiners (*Notropis lutrensis*) over physicochemical ranges. Amer. Midl. Nat. 101:366–72.

———, and ———. 1980. Habitat partitioning in the fish community of a southwestern river. Southwest Nat. 25:51–66.

———, and J. Maness. 1979. Critical thermal maxima, oxygen tolerances and success of cyprinid fishes in a southwestern river. *Ibid.* 24:374–377.

———, and H. W. Robison. 1982. Addition of *Etheostoma collettei* (Percidae) to the fish fauna of Oklahoma and of the Red River drainage of Arkansas. Southwest. Nat. 27:215–46.

———, and J. T. Styron, Jr. 1981. Tolerance of headwater vs. mainstream fishes for abrupt physicochemical changes. Amer. Midl. Nat. 105:149–58.

———, J. R. Bek, and E. Surat. 1982a. Comparative ecology of the darters *Etheostoma podostemone, E. flabellare*, and *Percina roanoka* in the upper Roanoke River drainage, Virginia. Copeia 1982:805–14.

———, W. D. Shepard, and L. G. Hill. 1978. Aspects of the ecology of the duskystripe shiner, *Notropis pilsbryi* (cypriniformes, Cyprinidae), in an Ozark stream. Amer. Midl. Nat. 100:247–52.

———, M. E. Power, and A. J. Stewart. 1986. Depth distribution of *Campostoma* grazing scars in an Ozark stream. Env. Biol. Fish. 17:291–97.

———, E. Surat, and L. G. Hill. 1982b. Heat death of the orangethroat darter, *Etheostoma spectabile* (Percidae), in a natural environment. Southwest. Nat. 27:216–17.

Maule, A. G., and H. F. Horton. 1984. Feeding ecology of walleye, *Stizostedion vitreum vitreum* in the mid-Columbia River, with emphasis on the interactions between walleye and juvenile anadromous fishes. Fish. Bull. 82:411–18.

———, and H. F. Horton. In press. Probable causes of the rapid growth and high fecundity of walleye in the mid-Columbia River. *Ibid.*

Maurakis, E. G., and W. S. Woolcott. 1984. Seasonal occurrence patterns of fishes in a thermally enriched stream. Va. J. Sci. 35:5–21.

May, R. M. 1973. Stability and Complexity in Model Ecosystems. Princeton Univ. Press, Princeton, N.J.

———. 1974. On the theory of niche overlap. Theoret. Pop. Biol. 5:297–332.

———. 1975. Patterns of species abundance and diversity, pp. 81–120. *In:* Ecology and evolution of communities. M. J. Cody and J. M. Diamond (eds.). Harvard Univ. Press, Cambridge, Mass.

Mayden, R. L. 1983. Madtoms, America's miniature catfishes. Trop. Fish Hobbyist 31:67–73.

———. 1985a. Biogeography of Ouachita Highland fishes. Southwest. Nat. 30:195–211.

———. 1985b. Phylogenetic studies of North American minnows, with emphasis on the subgenus *Cyprinella,* genus *Notropis* (Teleostei:Cypriniformes). Unpub. PhD Diss., Univ. Kansas, Lawrence.

———. 1987. Pleistocene glaciation and historical biogeography of North American central highland fishes, pp. 141–51. *In:* Quaternary environments of Kansas. Kansas Geol. Surv. Guidebook No. 5.

———, and S. J. Walsh. 1984. Life history of the least madtom, *Noturus hildebrandi* (Siluriformes:Ictaluridae), with comparisons to related species. Amer. Midl. Nat. 112:349–68.

Mayr, E. 1963. Animal species and evolution. Belknap Press, Harvard Univ., Cambridge, Mass.

Meek, S. E. 1892. A report upon the fishes of Iowa, based upon observations and collections made during 1889, 1890, and 1891. Bull. US Fish. Comm. 10:217–48.

Meffe, G. K. 1983. Ecology of species replacement in the Sonoran topminnow (*Poeciliopsis occidentalis*) and the mosquitofish (*Gambusia affinis*) in Arizona. Unpub. PhD Diss., Arizona State Univ., Tempe.

———. 1984. Effects of abiotic disturbance on coexistence of predatory-prey fish species. Ecology 65:1525–34.

———. 1985. Predation and species replacement in American Southwestern fishes: A case study. Southwest. Nat. 30:173–87.

———, and W. L. Minckley. In press. Persistence and stability of repeatedly disturbed assemblages in a Sonoran Desert stream. Am. Midl. Nat.

———, D. A. Hendrickson, and J. N. Rinne. 1982. Description of a new topminnow population in Arizona, with observations on topminnow/mosquitofish co-occurrence. Southwest. Nat. 27:226–28.

———, ———, W. L. Minckley, and J. N. Rinne. 1983. Factors resulting in decline of the endangered Sonoran topminnow *Poeciliopsis occidentalis* (Atheriniformes: Poeciliidae) in the United States. Biol. Conserv. 25:135–59.

Melton, M. A. 1965. The geomorphic and paleoclimatic significance of alluvial deposits in southern Arizona. J. Geol. 73:1–38.

Mendelson, J. 1975. Feeding relationships among species of *Notropis* (Pisces: Cyprinidae) in a Wisconsin stream. Ecol. Monogr. 45:199–230.

Menge, B. A., and J. P. Sutherland. 1976. Species diversity gradients: Synthesis of the roles of predation, competition and temporal heterogeneity. Amer. Nat. 110:351–69.

Metcalf, A. L. 1959. Fishes of Chatauqua, Cowley and Elk counties, Kansas. Univ. Kans. Pub. Mus. Nat. Hist. 11:345–400.

———. 1966. Fishes of the Kansas River system in relation to the zoogeography of the Great Plains. Univ. Kansas Pub. Mus. Nat. Hist. 17:23–189.

Meyer, J., and G. S. Helfman. 1983. Fish schools: An asset to corals. Science 220:1047–49.

———, and E. T. Schultz. 1985. Migrating haemulid fishes as a source of nutrients and organic matter on coral reefs. Limnol. Oceanogr. 30:146–56.

Michevich, M. F., and C. Mitter. 1981. Treating polymorphic characters in systematics. A phylogenetic treatment of electrophoretic data, pp. 45–58. *In:* Advances in cladistics: Proceedings of the first meeting of the Willi Hennig Society. V. A. Funk and D. R. Brooks (eds.). New York Botanical Garden, New York.

Miles, D. B., and R. E. Ricklefs. 1984. The correlation between ecology and morphology in deciduous forest passerine birds. Ecology 65:1629–40.

Milinski, M. 1985. The patch choice model: No alternative to balancing. Amer. Nat. 125:317–20.

———, and R. Heller. 1978. Influence of a predator on the optimal foraging behaviour of sticklebacks (*Gasterosteus aculeatus* L.). Nature 275: 642–44.

Miller, A. C. 1982. Effects of differential fish grazing on the community structure of an intertidal reef flat at Enewetak Atoll, Marshall Islands. Pac. Sci. 36:467–82.

Miller, G. L. 1983. Trophic resource allocation between *Percina sciera* and *P. ouachitae* in the Tombigbee River, Mississippi. Amer. Midl. Nat. 110:299–313.

Miller, K., and G. C. Packard. 1974. Critical thermal maximum: Ecotypic variation between montane and piedmont chorus frogs (*pseudacris triseriata,* Hylidae). Experientia 30:355–56.

———, and ———. 1977. An altitudinal cline in critical thermal maxima of chorus frogs (*Pseudacris triseriata*). Amer. Nat. 11:267–77.

Miller, P. 1979. Adaptiveness and implications of small size in teleosts. Symposium Zool. Soc. London 44:263–306.

Miller, R. J. 1984. The occurrence of *Notropis hubbsi* in Oklahoma. Okla. Acad. Sci. 64:45.

———, and H. W. Robison. 1973. The fishes of Oklahoma. Oklahoma State Univ. Press, Stillwater.

Miller, R. R. 1946. The need for ichthyological surveys of the major rivers of western North America. Science 104:517–19.

———. 1955. An annotated list of the American cyprinodontid fishes of the genus *Fundulus* with the description of *Fundulus persimilis* from Yucatan. Occ. Pap. Mus. Zool. Univ. Mich. 658:1–25.

———. 1959. Origin and affinities of the freshwater fish fauna of western North America, pp. 187–222. *In:* Zoogeography. C. L. Hubbs (ed.). Amer. Assoc. Adv. Sci. Publ. 51, Washington, D. C.

———. 1960. Four new species of viviparous fishes, genus *Poeciliopsis* from northwestern Mexico. Occ. Pap. Mus. Zool. Univ. Mich. 433:1–9

———. 1961. Man and the changing fish fauna of the American Southwest. Pap. Mich. Acad. Sci., Arts, Lett. 46:365–404.

———. 1964. Extinct, rare and endangered American freshwater fishes. Proc. 16 Internat. Congr. Zool. 8:4–16.

———. 1968. Rare and Endangered World Freshwater Fishes. Internat. Un. Conserv. Nature Nat. Res., Surv. Serv. Comm., Morges, Switzerland.

———. 1969a. Red Data Book. Vol. 4. Pisces, freshwater fishes. *Ibid.*

———. 1969b. Conservation of fishes of the Death Valley system in California and Nevada. Trans. Calif.-Nev. Sec. Wildl. Soc. 1969:107–22.

———. 1972. Threatened freshwater fishes of the United States. Trans. Amer. Fish. Soc. 101:239–52.

———, and C. H. Lowe. 1964. Part 2. Annotated check-list of the fishes of Arizona, pp. 133–151. *In:* The Vertebrates of Arizona. C. H. Lowe (ed.). Univ. Arizona Press, Tucson (reprinted, 1967, as Part 2. Fishes of Arizona, *op. cit.*).

———, and E. P. Pister. 1971. Management of the Owens pupfish, *Cyprinodon radiosus* in Mono County, California. Trans. Amer. Fish. Soc. 100:502–509.

Miller, W. H., L. R. Kaeding, and H. M. Tyus. 1983a. Windy Gap fishes study. First Ann. Rept. Coop. Agreement 1-16-0006-82-959(R), N. Colo. Water Conserv. Dist., Municip. Subdist., Grand Junction, Colo. Final Rep. Mem. Understand. 9-07-40-L-1016, US Bur. Reclam., Upper Colo. R. Reg., Salt

Lake City, Utah. US Fish Wildl. Serv., Salt Lake City, Utah.
———, H. M. Tyus, and C. A. Carlson, eds. 1982. Fishes of the upper Colorado River system: Present and future. Amer. Fish Soc., Bethesda, Md.
———, ———, and C. W. McAda. 1983b. Movement, migration and habitat preference of radiotelemetered Colorado squawfish: Green, White and Yampa rivers, Colorado and Utah. Final Rep. Mem. Understand. 9-07-40-L-1016, US Bur. Reclam., Upper Colo. R. Reg., Salt Lake City, Utah. US Fish Wildl. Serv., Salt Lake City, Utah.
———, J. J. Valentine, D. L. Archer, H. M. Tyus, R. A. Valdez, and L. R. Kaeding. 1982. Colorado River fishery project, part I. Summary report. *Ibid.*
Mills, W. P., III. 1976. Ichthyofauna of Whiskey Chitto Creek, southwest Louisiana. MS Thesis, Univ. Southwestern Louisiana, Lafayette.
Minckley, W. L. 1963. The ecology of a spring stream, Doe Run, Meade County, Kentucky. Wildl. Mongr. 11.
———. 1973. Fishes of Arizona. Ariz. Game Fish Dept., Phoenix.
———. 1979a. Aquatic habitats and fishes of the lower Colorado River, southwestern United States. Final Rep. Contr. 14-06-300-2529, US Bur. Reclam., Lower Colo. R. Reg., Boulder City, Nev. Arizona State Univ., Tempe.
———. 1979b. Hydrology and climate, pp. 17–38. *In:* Resource Inventory for the Gila River complex, eastern Arizona. W. L. Minckley and M. R. Sommerfeld (eds.). Final Rept. Contr. YA-512-CT6-216, US Bur. Land Mgmt., Safford, Ariz., District. Arizona State Univ., Tempe.
———. 1981. Ecological studies of Aravaipa Creek, central Arizona, relative to past, present and future uses. Final Rep. Contr. YA-512-CT6-98, US Bureau Land Mgmt., Safford, Ariz., District. *Ibid.*
———. 1982. Food relations of introduced fishes of the lower Colorado River, Arizona-California. Calif. Fish Game 68:78–89.
———. 1983. Status of the razorback sucker, *Xyrauchen texanus* Abbott, in the lower Colorado River basin. Southwest. Nat. 28:165–87.
———. 1985. Native fishes and natural aquatic habitats of US Fish Wildlife Service Region II, west of the Continental Divide. US Fish Wildl. Serv., Albuquerque, N. Mex.
———, and D. E. Brown. 1982. Wetlands, pp. 222–77, 333–41 + Lit. Cited. *In:* Biotic communities of the American Southwest, United States and Mexico. D. E. Brown (ed.). Desert Plants 4.
———, and T. O. Clark. 1982. Vegetation of the Gila River Resource area, eastern Arizona. *Ibid.* 3:124–40.
———, and ———. 1984. Formation and destruction of a Gila River mesquite bosque. *Ibid.* 6:23–30.
———, and R. W. Clarkson. 1979. Fishes, pp. 510–31. *In:* Resource Inventory for the Gila River complex, eastern Arizona. W. L. Minckley and M. R. Sommerfeld (eds.). Final Rept. Contr. YA-512-CT6-216, US Bur. Land Mgmt., Safford, Ariz., District. Arizona State Univ., Tempe.
———, and F. B. Cross. 1959. Distribution, habitat, and abundance of the Topeka shiner, *Notropis topeka* (Gilbert) in Kansas. Amer. Midl. Nat. 61:210–17.
———, and J. E. Deacon. 1968. Southwestern fishes and the enigma of "endangered species." Science 159:1424–32.
———, and J. N. Rinne. In press. Large organic debris in hot desert streams: An historical review. Desert Plants 9.
———, D. A. Hendrickson, and C. E. Bond. 1986. Geography of western North American freshwater fishes: Description and relationships to intracontinental tectonism, pp. 519–613 + Lit. Cited. *In:* Zoogeography of North American Freshwater Fishes. C. H. Hocutt and E. O. Wiley (eds.). John Wiley & Sons, New York.
———, J. N. Rinne, and J. E. Johnson. 1977. Status of the Gila topminnow and its co-occurrence with mosquitofish. USDA, For. Serv. Res. Pap. RM-198:1-8.
Minshall, G. W., K. W. Cummins, R. C. Peterson, and C. E. Cushing. 1985. Developments in stream ecosystem theory: Canad. J. Fish. Aquatic Sci. 42:1045–55.
———, and J. N. Minshall. 1977. Microdistribution of benthic invertebrates in a Rocky Mountain (USA) stream. Hydrobiol. 55:231–49.
Mitans, A. R. 1973. Dwarf males and the sex structure of a Baltic salmon (*Salmo salar* L.) population. J. Ichthyol. 2:192–97.
Mitsch, P. P. 1978. Interactions between a riparian swamp and a river in southern Illinois, pp. 63–72. *In:* Strategies for protection and management of floodplain wetlands and other riparian ecosystems. R. R. Johnson and J. F. McCormick (eds.). US Fish and Wildl. Serv. Gen. Tech. Rep. W0-12.
Mittelbach, G. G. 1981. Foraging efficiency and body size: A study of optimal diet and habitat use by bluegills. Ecology 62:1370–86.
Montgomery, W. L. 1980. The impact of non-selective grazing by the giant blue damselfish, *Microspathodon dorsalis,* on algal communities in the Gulf of California, Mexico. Bull. Mar. Sci. 30:290–303.
———, and R. J. Naiman. 1981. Implications of changes in Atlantic salmon populations from the Matamek River, Quebec. Intern. Counc. Explor. Sea, Anadr. Catadr. Fish Comm. 1981/M:19.
———, T. Gerrodette, and L. D. Marshall. 1980. Effects of grazing by the yellowtail surgeonfish, *Prionurus punctatus,* on algal communities in the Gulf of California, Mexico. Bull. Mar. Sci. 30:901–908.
———, S. D. McCormick, R. J. Naiman, R. F. Whoriskey, and G. F. Black. 1983. Spring migratory synchrony of salmonid, catostomid, and cyprinid fishes in Riviere a la Truite, Quebec. Canad. J. Zool. 61:2495–2502.
Moore, G. A. 1944. Notes on the early life history of *Notropis girardi.* Copeia 1944:209–14.
———. 1950. The cutaneous sense organs of barbeled minnows adapted to life in the muddy waters of the Great Plains region. Trans Amer. Microscop. Soc. 69:69–95.
Moore, J. A. 1949. Geographic variation of adaptive characters in *Rana pipiens* Schreber. Evolution 3:1–24.
Moore, W. S. 1977. A histocompatibility analysis of inheritance in the unisexual fish *Poeciliopsis 2 monacha-lucida.* Copeia 1977:213–23.
———. 1984. Evolutionary ecology of unisexual fishes, pp. 329–98. *In:* Evolutionary genetics of fishes. B. J. Turner (ed.). Plenum Press, New York.
Morgan, R. P., II; T. S. Y. Koo, and G. E. Krantz. 1973. Electrophoretic determination of populations of the striped bass, *Morone saxatilis,* in the upper Chesapeake Bay. Trans. Amer. Fish. Soc. 102:21–32.
Moring, J. R., K. J. Anderson, and R. L. Youker. 1981. High incidence of scale regeneration by potadromous coastal cutthroat trout: Analytical implications. *Ibid.* 110:621–26.
Morris, R. F. 1959. Single-factor analysis in population dynamics. Ecology 40:580–88.
Moshenko, R. W., and J. H. Gee. 1973. Diet, time and place of spawning, and environments occupied by creek chub (*Semotilus atromaculatus*) in the Mink River, Manitoba. J. Fish. Res. Board Canada 30:357–62.
Mosimann, J. E., and F. C. James. 1979. New statistical methods for allometry with application to Florida red-winged blackbirds. Evolution 33:444–59.
———, and J. D. Malley. 1979. Size and shape variables, pp. 175–89. *In:* Multivariate methods in ecological work. L. Orloci, C. R. Rao, and W. M. Stiteler (eds.). Intl. Co-op. Publ. House, Fairland, Md.

Mosteller, F., and J. W. Tukey. 1968. Data analysis, including statistics, pp. 80–203. *In:* G. Lindzey and E. Aronson (eds.). The handbook of social psychology. 2d ed. Addison-Wesley Publishing Co., Reading, Mass.

Moyle, J. B., and W. D. Clothier. 1959. Effects of management and winter oxygen levels on the fish population of a prairie lake. Trans. Amer. Fish. Soc. 88:178–85.

Moyle, P. B. 1976a. Fish introductions in California: History and impact on native fishes. Biol. Conserv. 9:101–18.

———. 1976b. Inland Fishes of California. Univ. California Press, Berkeley.

———. 1985. Fish introductions in North America: Patterns and ecological impact, pp. *In:* H. Mooney (ed.). Biological invasions of North America. Springer-Verlag, New York.

———, and D. M. Baltz. 1985. Microhabitat use by an assemblage of California stream fishes: Developing criteria for instream flow determinations. Trans. Am. Fish. Soc. 114:695–704.

———, and J. J. Cech, Jr. 1982. Fishes: An introduction to icthyology. Prentice-Hall, Englewood Cliffs, N.J.

———, and H. W. Li. 1979. Community ecology and predator-prey relationships in warmwater streams, pp. 171–81. *In:* Predator-prey systems in fisheries management. R. H. Stroud and H. E. Clepper (eds.). Sport Fishing Institute, Washington, D.C.

———, and R. Nichols. 1973. Ecology of some native and introduced fishes of the Sierra Nevada foothills in central California. Copeia 1973:478–90.

———, and ———. 1974. Decline of the native fish fauna of the Sierra Nevada foothills, central California. Amer. Midl. Nat. 92:72–83.

———, and F. R. Senanayake. 1984. Resource partitioning among the fishes of rainforest streams in Sri Lanka. J. Zool. Lond. 202:195–223.

———, and B. Vondracek. 1985. Presistence and structure of the fish assemblage in a small California stream. Ecology 66:1–13.

———, D. M. Baltz, and B. A. Barton. In press. The Frankenstein Effect: Impact of introduced fishes on native fishes in North America, pp. *In:* The Role of Fish Culture in Fisheries, R. H. Stroud (ed.). Spec. Pub. Am. Fish. Soc. Washington, D.C.

———, H. W. Li, and B. A. Barton. 1985. The Frankenstein effect: Impact of introduced species on native fishes in North America. In press.

———, J. J. Smith, R. D. Daniels, and D. M. Baltz. 1982. Distribution and ecology of stream fishes of the Sacramento–San Joaquin drainage system. California: A Review. Calif. Publ. Zool. 115:225–56.

———, H. W. Li, and B. A. Barton. 1986. The Frankenstein effect: Impact of introduced fishes on native fishes in North America, pp. 415–26. *In*: The role of fish culture in fisheries. Manuscript. R. H. Stroud (ed.). Am. Fish Soc. Bethesda, Md.

———, J. J. Smith, R. D. Daniels, and D. M. Baltz. 1982. Distribution and ecology of stream fishes of the Sacramento–San Joaquin drainage system. California: A Review. Calif. Publ. Zool. 115:225–56.

Mulaik, S. A. 1972. The foundations of factor analysis. McGraw-Hill, New York.

Mulholland, P. J., J. D. Newbold, J. W. Elwood and C. L. Hom. 1983. The effect of grazing intensity on phosphorus spiralling in autotrophic streams. Oecologia 58:358–66.

Mullan, J. W., and R. L. Applegate. 1970. Food habits of five centrarchids during filling of Beaver Reservoir. Bureau Sports Fish. Wildl., Tech. Pap. 50:1–16.

Mundy, P. R. 1973. The occurrence, abundance and distribution of populations of larval fishes in Wheeler Reservoir, Alabama. Unpub. MS Thesis, Univ. Alabama, University.

———, and H. T. Boschung. 1981. An analysis of the distribution of lotic fishes with application to fisheries management, pp. 266–75. *In:* The warmwater streams symposium. L. A. Krumholz (ed.).Southern Div. Amer. Fish. Soc. Allen Press, Lawrence, Kans.

Murphy, G. I. 1968. Pattern in life history and the environment. Amer. Nat. 102:390–404.

Murphy, M. L., and J. D. Hall. 1981. Varied effects of clear-cut logging on predators and their habitat in small streams of the Cascade Mountains, Oregon. Canad. J. Fish. Aquatic Sci. 38:137–45.

———, C. P. Hawkins, and N. H. Anderson. 1981. Effects of canopy modification and accumulated sediment on stream communities. Trans. Amer. Fish. Soc. 110:469–78.

Murray, G. E. 1961. Geology of the Atlantic and Gulf Coastal Provinces of North America. Harper & Brothers, New York.

Muus, B. J. 1967. Freshwater fish of Britain and Europe. Collins, London.

Myers, G. S. 1964. A brief sketch of the history of ichthyology in America to the year 1850. Copeia 1964:33–41.

Naiman, R. J. 1983. The annual pattern and spatial distribution of aquatic oxygen metabolism in boreal forest watersheds. Ecol. Monogr. 53:73–94.

———, and D. L. Soltz (eds.). Fishes in North American Deserts. John Wiley & Sons, New York.

Neave, N. M., C. L. Dilworth, J. G. Eales, and R. L. Saunders. 1966. Adjustment of buoyancy in Atlantic salmon parr in relation to changing water velocity. 23:1617–20.

Neel, J. K. 1951. Interrelations of certain physical and chemical features in a headwater limestone stream. Ecology 32:368–91.

———, H. P. Nicholson, and A. Hirsch. 1963. Mainstem reservoir effects on water quality in the central Missouri River 1952-1957. US Dept. Health, Educ., and Welf. Pub., Kansas City, Mo.

Nei, M. 1972. Genetic distance between populations. Amer. Nat. 106:283–92.

———. 1978. Estimation of average heterozygosity and genetic distance from a small number of individuals. Genetics 89:583–90.

Nelson, G., and N. I. Platnick. 1978. The perils of plesiomorphy: widespread taxa, dispersal, and phenetic biogeography. Syst. Zool. 27:474–77.

Nevo, E. 1978. Genetic variation in natural populations. Theor. Pop. Biol. 13:121–77.

———, A. Beiles, and R. Ben-Shlomo. 1983. The evolutionary significance of genetic diversity: Ecological, demographic and life history correlates, pp. 13–213. *In:* Evolutionary dynamics of genetic diversity. G. S. Mani (ed.). Springer-Verlag, Berlin.

Newbold, J. D., J. W. Elwood, R. V. O'Neill, and A. L. Sheldon. 1983. Phosphorus dynamics in a woodland stream ecosystem: A study of nutrient spiralling. Ecology 64:1249–65.

Newcombe, C., and G. Hartman. 1973. Some chemical signals in the spawning behavior of rainbow trout *(Salmo gairdneri)*. J. Fish. Res. Board Canada 30:995–97.

Nie, N. H., C. H. Hull, J. G. Jenkins, K. Steinbrenner, and D. H. Bent. 1975. Statistical package for the social sciences. McGraw-Hill, New York.

Nigro, A. A., T. T. Terrell, and L. G. Beckman. 1981. Assessment of the limnology and fisheries in Lake F. D. Roosevelt. Annual Report US Bur. Reclam. Annu. Rep. Contract No. WPRS-0-07-10-X0216.

Nikolskii, G. V. 1969. Theory of fish population dynamics. Oliver and Boyd, Edinburgh, Scotland.

Nilsson, N. A. 1977. Interaction between trout and charr in Scandinavia. Trans. Amer. Fish. Soc. 92:276–85.

Nisbet, R. M., and W. S. C. Gurney. 1982. Modelling Fluctuating Populations. Wiley, New York.

NOAA [National Oceanic and Atmospheric Administration]. 1975–82. Climatological data, Oklahoma. Vols. 76–91. US Government Printing Office, Washington, D.C.

———, Environmental Data and Information Service. 1981. Climatological data, Missouri. Vol. 85 (2–8). US Government Printing Office, Washington, D.C.

———. 1982. Climatological data, Missouri. Vol. 86 (2–8). US Government Printing Office, Washington, D.C.

Nordeng, H. 1983. Solution to the "charr problem" based on Arctic charr *(Salvelinus alpinus)* in Norway. Canad. J. Fish. Aquatic Sci. 40:1372–87.

Northcote, T. G. 1954. Observations on the comparative ecology of two species of fish, *Cottus asper* and *Cottus rhotheus,* in British Columbia. Copeia 1954:25–28.

Northwest Power Planning Council. 1981. Recommendations for fish and Wildlife. Portland, Oreg.

Noy-Meir, I. 1975. Stability of grazing systems: An application of predator-prey graphs. J. Ecol. 63:459–81.

Nyman, L. 1972. A new approach to the taxonomy of the *Salvelinus alpinus* species complex. Inst. Freshw. Res. Drottningholm Rep. 52:103–31.

Nyquist, D. 1963. The ecology of *Eremichthys acros*, an endemic thermal species of cyprinid fish from northwestern Nevada. Unpub. MS Thesis, Univ. Nevada, Reno.

Oklahoma State Department of Agriculture. 1982. Oklahoma forest resources issue, an assessment of concerns and opportunities facing forestry in the 80's. Okla. State Dept. Agric., Forestry Division.

Oklahoma State Department Health. 1977. Surface water quality assessment for Oklahoma—water year 1977. Report 305B.

Olmstead, F. H. 1919. Gila River flood control—a report of flood control of the Gila River in Graham County, Arizona. US 65th Cong., 3rd sess., Sen. Doc. 436:1–94.

Olund, L. J., and F. B. Cross. 1961. Geographic variation in the North American cyprinid fish, *Hybopsis gracilis*. Mus. Nat. Hist., Univ. Kansas. Publ. 13:323–48.

O'Neil, P. E., M. F. Mettee, and J. S. Williams. 1981. A study of the fishes in related streams that drain lands of federal minerals ownership, Tuscaloosa, Fayette and Walker counties, Alabama. Geo. Survey Ala., Bull. 119:1–92.

Orth, D. J., and O. E. Maughan. 1982. Evaluation of the incremental methodology for recommending instream flows for fishes. Trans. Amer. Fish. Soc. 111:413–45.

———, R. N. Jones, and O. E. Maughan. 1983. Considerations in the development of curves for habitat suitability criteria. *In:* Symposium: Acquisition and utilization of aquatic habitat inventory information. W. Div., Amer. Fish. Soc., Fort Collins, Colo.

Otto, R. G. 1973. Temperature tolerance of the mosquitofish, *Gambusia affinis* (Baird and Girard). J. Fish Biol. 5:575–85.

Ouellet, G. 1977. Fraie en groupe de quatre saumons Atlantiques sur l'Île d'Anticosti. Naturaliste Canadien 104:507–10.

Owen, J. B., D. S. Elsen, and G. W. Russell. 1981. Distribution of fishes in North and South Dakota basins affected by the Garrison Diversion Unit. Fish. Res. Unit, Dept. Biol., Univ. North Dakota, Grand Forks.

Paerl, H. W. 1978. Microbial organic carbon recovery in aquatic ecosystems. Limnol. Oceanogr. 23:927–35.

Page, L. M. 1974. The subgenera of *Percina* (Percidae: Etheostomatini). Copeia 1974:66–86.

———. 1976. The modified midventral scales of *Percina* (Osteichthyes: Percidae). J. Morph. 148:255–64.

———. 1981. The genera and subgenera of darters (Percidae: Etheostomatini). Occ. Pap. Mus. Nat. Hist. Univ. Kan. 90:1–69.

———. 1983. Handbook of darters. T. F. H. Publishers, Neptune City, N.J.

———, and D. W. Schemske. 1978. The effect of interspecific competition on the distribution and size of darters of the subgenus *Catonotus* (Percidae: *Etheostoma*). Copeia 1978:406–12.

———, and G. S. Whitt. 1973. Lactate dehydrogenase isozymes, malate dehydrogenase isozymes and tetrazolium oxidase mobilities of darters (Etheostomatini). Comp. Biochem. Physiol. 44B:611–23.

Paine, M. D., J. J. Dodson, and G. Power. 1982. Habitat and food resource partitioning among four species of darters (Percidae: *Etheostoma*) in a southern Ontario stream. Canad. J. Zool. 60:1635–41.

Paine, R. T. 1966. Food web complexity and species diversity. Amer. Nat. 100:65–75.

Paloumpis, A. A. 1956. Stream havens save fish. Iowa Conserv. 15:60.

———. 1958. Responses of some minnows to flood and drought conditions in an intermittent stream. Iowa State Coll. J. Sci. 32:547–61.

Pardue, G. B., M. T. Huish, and H. R. Parry, Jr. 1975. Ecological studies of two swamp watersheds in northeastern North Carolina: A prechannelization study. Water Resources Research Inst., Univ. North Carolina, Raleigh.

Peach, N. W., and R. W. Pool. 1965a. Human and material resources of McCurtain County: A profile for growth and development. Technology Use Studies Center Pub., Southeastern State College, Durant, Okla.

———, and ———. 1965b. Human and material resources of Pushmataha County: A profile for growth and development. Technology Use Studies Center Pub., Southeastern State College, Durant, Okla.

———, ———, and J. D. Tarver. 1965. County building block for regional analysis. Oklahoma Research Foundation, Oklahoma State Univ., Stillwater, Okla.

Peckarsky, B. L. 1983. Biotic interactions or abiotic limitations? A model of lotic community structure, pp. 303–23. *In:* Dynamics of lotic ecosystems. T. D. Fontaine III and S. M. Bartell (eds.). Ann Arbor Science, Ann Arbor, Mich.

Peterson, N. M. 1978. Biological characteristics of wild and hatchery steelhead trout, *Salmo gairdneri,* in two Oregon rivers. Unpub. MS Thesis, Oregon State Univ., Corvallis.

Pflieger, W. L. 1971. A distributional study of Missouri fishes. Mus. Nat. Hist., Univ. Kans. Pub. 20:225–570.

———. 1975. The Fishes of Missouri. Missouri Dept. of Conservation, Jefferson City, Mo.

———. 1978. Distribution and status of the grass carp *(Ctenopharyngodon idella)* in Missouri streams. Trans. Amer. Fish. Soc 107:113–18.

Pianka, E. R. 1973. The structure of lizard communities. Ann. Rev. Ecol. Syst. 4:53–74.

———. 1974a. Niche overlap and diffuse competition. Proc. Nat. Acad. Sci. 77:2141–45.

———. 1974b. Evolutionary Ecology. Harper & Row, New York.

———, and W. S. Parker. 1975. Age-specific reproductive tactics. Amer. Nat. 109:453–64.

Pielou, E. C. 1975. Ecological diversity. John Wiley & Sons, New York.

Pierson, M., and C. A. Schultz. 1984. A report on the fishes of Bull Mountain Creek, with comments on the status of rare species. Proc. Southeast. Fishes Council 4(3):1–3.

Pister, E. P. 1974. Desert fishes and their habitats. Trans. Amer. Fish. Soc. 103:531–40.

———. 1976. A rationale for the management of nongame fish and

wildlife. Fisheries 1:11–14.
———. 1979. Endangered species: Costs and benefits. Environ. Ethics 1:341–52.
———. 1981. The conservation of desert fishes, pp. 411–45. *In:* R. J. Naiman and D. L. Soltz. Fishes in North American Deserts. John Wiley & Sons, New York.
Platnick, N. I., and G. Nelson. 1978. A method of analysis for historical biogeography. Syst. Zool. 27:1–16.
Platt, J. R. 1964. Strong inference. Science 146:347–53.
Polis, G. A. 1981. The evolution and dynamics of intraspecific predation. Ann. Rev. Ecol. Syst. 12:225–51.
———. 1984. Age structure component of niche width and intraspecific resource partitioning: Can age groups function as ecological species? Amer. Nat. 123:541–64.
Poss, S. G., and R. R. Milller. 1983. Taxonomic status of the plains killifish, *Fundulus zebrinus*. Copeia 1983:55–67.
Powell, J. R. 1971. Genetic polymorphisms in varied environments. Science 174:1035–36.
Power, M. E. 1981. The grazing ecology of armored catfish (Loricariidae) in a Panamanian stream. Unpub. PhD Diss., Univ. Washington, Seattle.
———. 1983. Grazing responses of tropical freshwater fishes to different scales of variation in their food. Envir. Biol. Fishes 9:103–15.
———. 1984a. Depth distributions of armored catfish: predator-induced resource avoidance? Ecology 65:523–28.
———. 1984b. Habitat quality and the distribution of algae-grazing catfish in a Panamanian stream. J. Anim. Ecol. 53:357–74.
———, and W. J. Matthews. 1983. Algae-grazing minnows *(Campostoma anomalum)*, piscivorous bass *(Micropterus* spp.), and the distribution of attached algae in a small prairie-margin stream. Oecologia 60:328–32.
———, and A. J. Stewart. In press. Flood reset of an algal assemblage in prairie-margin stream: Resistance and recovery of dominant taxa. Amer. Midl. Nat.
———, W. J. Matthews, and A. J. Stewart. 1985. Grazing minnows, piscivorous bass and stream algae: Dynamics of a strong interaction. Ecology 66:1448–56.
Preston, F. W. 1962a. The canonical distribution of commonness and rarity: Part I. *Ibid.* 43:185–215.
———. 1962b. The canonical distribution of commonness and rarity: Part II. *Ibid.* 43:410–32.
———. 1980. Noncanonical distributions of commonness and rarity. *Ibid.* 61:88–97.
Price, M. V. 1986. Structure of desert rodent communities: a critical review of questions and approaches. Amer. Zool. (in press).
Price, P. W., C. N. Slobodchikoff, and W. S. Gaud. 1984. A new ecology: Novel approaches to interactive systems. John Wiley & Sons, New York.
Probst, W. E., C. F. Rabeni, W. G. Covington, and R. E. Marteney. 1984. Resource use by stream-dwelling rock bass and smallmouth bass. Trans. Amer. Fish. Soc. 113:283–84.
Propst, D. L., K. R. Bestgen, and C. W. Painter. 1985a. Ichthyofaunal survey of the Gila–San Francisco basin, New Mexico, a status report, 1982–1983. Final Rep. Contrs. 519-71-102, 519-71-05, and 516-72-24(102), N.Mex. Dept. Game Fish Endang. Species Prog., Santa Fe.
———, P. C. Marsh, and W. L. Minckley. 1985b. Arizona survey for spikedace *(Meda fulgida)* and loach minnow *(Tiaroga cobitis)*: Fort Apache and San Carlos Apache Indian reservations and Eagle Creek, May 1985. US Fish Wildl. Serv., Albuquerque, N.Mex.
Quinn, J. H. 1958. Plateau surfaces of the Ozarks. Proc. Ark. Acad. Sci. 11:36–43.
Rabinowitz, D. 1981. Seven forms of rarity, pp. 205–17. *In:* The biological aspects of rare plant conservation. H. Synge (ed.). John Wiley & Sons, New York.
Rabito, F. G., Jr., and D. C. Heins. 1985. Spawning behaviour and sexual dimorphism in the North American cyprinid fish *Notropis leedsi,* the bannerfin shiner. J. Nat. Hist. 19:1155–63.
Rahel, F. J., J. D. Lyons, and P. A. Cochran. 1984. Stochastic or deterministic regulation of assemblage structure? It may depend on how the assemblage is defined. Amer. Nat. 124:583-89.
Rampe, J. J., R. D. Jackson, and M. R. Sommerfeld. 1985. Physiochemistry of the upper Gila River watershed: II. Influence of precipitation runoff and flood events on the San Francisco River. J. Ariz.-Nev. Acad. Sci. 19 (1984):115–20.
Raney, E. C., and E. A. Lachner. 1946. Age, growth, and habits of the hog sucker, *Hypentelium nigricans* (LeSueur), in New York. Amer. Midl. Nat. 36:76–86.
———, and E. A. Lachner. 1947. *Hypentelium roanokense,* a new catostomid fish from the Roanoke River in Virginia. Amer. Mus. Nat. Hist., No. 1333:1–15.
Ratliff, D. E. 1983. *Ceratomyxa shasta:* Longevity, distribution, timing, and abundance of the infective stage in central Oregon. Canad. J. Fish. Aquatic Sci. 40:1622–32.
Raymond, H. L. 1979. Effects of dams and impoundments on migrations of chinook salmon and steelhead from the Snake River, 1966 to 1975. Trans. Amer. Fish. Soc. 108:505–29.
Reagan, R. E., and C. M. Conley. 1977. Effect of egg diameter on growth of channel catfish. Prog. Fish-Cult. 39:133–34.
Reed, R. J. 1968. Mark and recapture studies of eight species of darters in three streams of northwestern Pennsylvania. Copeia 1968:172–75.
Reetz, S. D. 1982. Phytoplankton studies in the Missouri River at Fort Calhoun station and Cooper nuclear station, pp. 71–84. *In:* The Middle Missouri River. L. W. Hesse (ed.). Missouri River Study Group, Norfolk, Nebr.
Reeves, G. 1985. Interaction and behavior of the redside shiner *(Richardsonius balteatus)* and the steelhead trout *(Salmo gairdneri)* in Western Oregon: The influence of water temperature. Unpub. PhD Diss., Oregon State Univ., Corvallis.
Reeves, J. D. 1953. The fishes of the Little River system in Oklahoma Unpub. PhD Diss., Oklahoma State Univ., Stillwater.
Reimers, P. E., and C. E. Bond. 1967. Distribution of fishes in tributaries of the lower Columbia River. Copeia 1967:541–50.
Reinboth, R. 1973. Dualistic reproductive behavior in the portogynous wrasse *Thalassoma bifasciatum* and some observations on its day-night changeover. Helgol. wiss. Meeresunters. 24:174–91.
Reisenbichler, R. R., and J. D. McIntyre. 1977. Genetic differences in growth and survival of juvenile hatchery and wild steelhead trout, *Salmo gairdneri*. J. Fish. Res. Board Canada 34:123–28.
Reynolds, J. B. 1983. Electrofishing, pp. 147–63. *In:* Fisheries Techniques. L. A. Nielsen and D. L. Johnson (eds.). Amer. Fish. Soc., Bethesda, Md.
Reynolds, W. W. 1977. Temperature as a proximate factor in orienting behavior. J. Fish. Res. Board Canada 34:734–39.
———, and M. E. Casterlin. 1976. Thermal preferenda and behavioral thermoregulation in three centrarchid fishes, pp. 185–90. *In:* Thermal ecology II. G. W. Esch and R. W. McFarlane (eds.). ERDA Symp. Series 40.
———, and ———. 1979. Behavioral thermoregulation and the "final preferendum" paradigm. Amer. Zool. 19:211–24.
Reznick, D. 1981. "Grandfather effects": The genetics of interpopulation differences in offspring size in the mosquito fish. Evolution 35:941–53.
———. 1982a. The impact of predation of life history evolution in

Trinidadian guppies: Genetic basis of observed life history patterns. Evolution 36:1236–50.

———. 1982b. Genetic determination of offspring size in the guppy *(Poecilia reticulata)*. Amer. Nat. 120:181–88.

———. 1983. The structure of guppy life histories: The trade-off between growth and reproduction. Ecology 64:862–73.

———, and J. A. Endler. 1982. The impact of predation on life history evolution in Trinidadian guppies. Evolution 36:160–70.

Rice, W. R. 1984. Disruptive selection on habitat preference and the evolution of reproductive isolation: A simulation study. *Ibid.* 38:1251–60.

Richards, R. P., W. W. Reynolds, and R. W. McCauley (eds.). 1977. Temperature preference studies in environmental impact assessments: An overview with procedural recommendations. J. Fish. Res. Board Canada 34:729–61.

Richey, J. E., M. A. Perkins and C. R. Goldman. 1975. Effects of kokanee salmon *(Oncorhynchus nerka)* decomposition on the ecology of a subalpine stream. *Ibid.* 32:817–20.

Richmond, M. C., and E. G. Zimmerman. 1978. Effect of temperature on activity of allozymic forms of supernatant malate dyhydrogenase in the red shiner, *Notropis lutrensis*. Comp. Biochem. Physiol., Series B61:415–19.

Ricker, W. E. 1973. Linear regressions in fishery research. J. Fish. Res. Board Canada 30:409–34.

———. 1975. A note concerning Professor Jolicoeur's research. J. Fish. Res. Board Canada 32:1494–98.

Ricklefs, R. E. 1979. Ecology, 2d ed. Chiron Press, New York.

———, and G. W. Cox. 1977. Morphological similarity and ecological overlap among passerine birds on St. Kitts, British West Indies. Oikos 29:60–66.

———, and K. O'Rourke. 1975. Aspect diversity in moths: A temperate-tropical comparison. Evolution 29:313–24.

———, and J. Travis. 1980. A morphological approach to the study of avian community structure. Auk 97:321–38.

———, D. Cochran, and E. R. Pianka. 1981. A morphological analysis of the structure of communities of lizards in desert habitats. Ecology 62:1474–83.

Rinne, J. N. 1975. Hydrology of the Salt River and its reservoirs, central Arizona. J. Ariz. Acad. Sci. 10:75–86.

———, and W. L. Minckley. 1985. Patterns of variation and distribution in Apache trout *(Salmo apache)* relative to co-occurrence with introduced salmonids. Copeia 1985:285–92.

Robertson, D. R., and R. R. Warner. 1978. Sexual patterns in the labroid fishes of the Western Caribbean, II: The parrotfishes (Scaridae). Smithson. Contrib. Zool. 255:1–26.

Robertson, O. H. 1957. Survival of precociously mature king salmon male parr *(Oncorhynchus tshawytscha* juv.) after spawning. Calif. Fish and Game 43:119–29.

Robins, C. R., R. M. Bailey, C. E. Bond, J. R. Brooker, E. A. Lachner, R. N. Lea, and W. B. Scott. 1980. A list of common and scientific names of fishes from the United States and Canada, 4th ed. Amer. Fish. Soc. Spec. Publ. No. 12:1–174.

Robinson, G. D., W. A. Dunson, J. E. Wright, and G. E. Mamolito. 1976. Differences in low pH tolerance among strains of brook trout *(Salvelinus fontinalis)*. J. Fish Biol. 8:5–17.

Robinson, T. W. 1965. Introduction, spread, and areal extent of salt-cedar *(Tamarix)* in the western states. USGS Prof. Pap. 491-A:1–20.

Robison, H. W. 1985. *Notropis snelsoni,* a new cyprinid from the Ouachita Mountains of Arkansas and Oklahoma. Copeia 1985:126–34.

———, and G. L. Harp. 1971. A pre-impoundment limnological study of the Strawberry River in northeastern Arkansas. Ark. Acad. Sci. Proc. 25:70–79.

———, and ———. 1985. Distribution, habitat and food of the Ouachita madtom, *Noturus lachneri,* a Ouachita River drainage endemic. Copeia 1985:216–20.

Rodnick, K. J. 1983. Seasonal distribution and habitat selection by the redside shiner, *Richardsonius balteatus,* in a small Oregon stream. Unpub. MS Thesis, Oregon State University, Corvallis.

Rogers, J. S. 1972. Measures of genetic similarity and genetic distance. Stud. Genet. 7. Univ. Texas Publ. 7213:145–53.

———. 1984. Deriving phylogenetic trees from allele frequencies. Syst. Zool. 33:52–63.

Rohlf, R. J., J. Kishpaugh and K. Kirk. 1974. NT-SYS: Numerical taxonomy system of multivariate statistical programs. State Univ. New York, Stony Brook.

Rohovec, J. S., and J. L. Fryer. 1979. Fish health management in aquaculture, pp. 15–36. *In:* Aquaculture: A modern fish tail. P. C. Klingeman (ed.). Oregon Water Resource Research Institute, Seminar Series, SEMIN WR 026–79.

Rohwer, S. 1978. Parent cannibalism of offspring and egg raiding as a courtship strategy. Amer. Nat. 112:429–40.

Root, R. B. 1967. The niche exploitation pattern of the blue-gray gnatcatcher. Ecol. Monogr. 37:317–50.

Rose, D. R., and A. A. Echelle. 1981. Factor analysis of associations of fishes in Little River, central Texas, with an interdrainage comparison. Amer. Midl. Nat. 106:379–91.

Rosen, D. E., and R. M. Bailey. 1963. The poeciliid fishes (Cyprinodontiformes), their structure, zoogeography, and systematics. Bull. Amer. Mus. Nat. Hist. 126:1–126.

Rosenzweig, M. L. 1978. Competitive speciation. Biol. J. Linn. Soc. 10:275–89.

Ross, H. H., and W. E. Ricker. 1971. The classification, evolution, and dispersal of the winter stonefly genus *Allocapnia*. Ill. Biol. Monogr. 45:1–166.

Ross, M. R. 1983. The frequency of nest construction and satellite male behavior in the fallfish minnow. Env. Biol. Fish. 9:65–70.

Ross, S. T. 1986. Resource partitioning in fish assemblages: a review of field studies. Copeia: 1986. 352–88.

———, and J. A. Baker. 1983. The response of fishes to periodic spring floods in a southeastern stream. Amer. Midl. Nat. 109.1–14.

———, and F. G. Howell. 1977. Aquatic survey of Black Creek. Project report submitted to the South Mississippi Electric Power Association, Hattiesburg.

———, and F. G. Howell. 1982. Aquatic survey of Black Creek: Fishes, 1975–1981. Project report submitted to South Mississippi Electric Power Association, Hattiesburg.

———, W. J. Matthews, and A. A. Echelle. 1985. Persistence of stream fish assemblages: Effects of environmental change. Amer. Nat. 126:24–40.

Roughgarden, J. 1972. Evolution of niche width. *Ibid.* 106:683–718.

———. 1974. Species packing and the competition function with illustrations from coral reef fish. Theoret. Pop. Biol. 5:163–86.

———. 1979. Theory of population genetics and evolutionary ecology: An Introduction. Macmillan, New York.

———. 1983. Competition and theory in community ecology. Amer. Nat. 122:583–601.

Ruhr, C. E. 1956. Effects of stream impoundment in Tennessee on the fish populations of tributary streams. Trans. Amer. Fish. Soc. 86:144-57.

Rutherford, D. A., A. A. Echelle, and O. E. Maughan. 1985. An addition to the fish fauna of Oklahoma: *Erimyzon sucetta* (Catostomidae). Southwest. Nat. 30:305–306.

Rutter, C. 1909. Natural history of the Quinnat salmon, a report on investigations in the Sacramento River, 1896–1901. Bull. US

Fish Comm. 22:65–141.
Ryman, N., and G. Stahl. 1980. Genetic changes in hatchery stocks of brown trout *(Salmo trutta)*. Canad. J. Fish. Aquatic Sci. 37:82–87.
Saemundsson, B. 1904. Fiskirannsoknir, 1902. Andvari 1904:80–102.
———. 1917. Fiskirannsoknir, 1915–1916. *Ibid.* 1917:125–28.
Saemundsson, K. 1965. Ur sogu Thingvallavatns. Natturufraedingurinn 35:103.
Sage, R. D., P. V. Loiselle, P. Basasibwaki, and A. C. Wilson. 1984. Molecular versus morphological change among cichlid fishes of Lake Victoria, pp. 185–202. *In:* Evolution of fish species flocks. A. A. Echelle and I. Kornfield (eds.). Univ. Maine Press, Orono.
Sale, P. 1974. Overlap in resource use, and interspecific competition. Oecologia 17:245–56.
———. 1977. Maintenance of high diversity in coral reef fish communities. Amer. Nat. 111:337–59.
———. 1979. Habitat partitioning and competition in fish communities, pp. 323–31. *In:* Predator-prey systems in fisheries management. H. Clepper (ed.). Sport Fishing Institute, Washington, DC.
Salt, G. W. 1983. Roles: Their limits and responsibilities in ecological and evolutionary research. Amer. Nat. 122:697–705.
——— (ed.). 1984. Ecology and evolutionary biology: A round table on research. Univ. Chicago Press, Chicago.
Sammarco, P. W. 1983. Effects of fish grazing and damselfish territoriality on coral reef algae. I. Algal community structure. Mar. Ecol. Prog. Series 13:1–14.
Sanders, J. E., J. L. Fryer, and R. W. Gould. 1970. Occurrence of the myxosporidian parasite *Ceratomyxca shasta* in salmonid fish from the Columbia River Basin and Oregon coastal streams, pp. 133–41. *In:* A symposium on diseases of fishes and shellfishes. S. F. Snieszko (ed.). Amer. Fish. Soc. Spec. Publ. 5.
S.A.S. Institute. 1982. SAS user's guide: Basics, statistics. SAS Institute, Cary, N.C.
Saunders, R. L. 1965. Adjustment of buoyancy in young Atlantic salmon and brook trout by changes in swimbladder volumes. J. Fish. Res. Board Canada 22:335–52.
———. 1981. Atlantic salmon *(Salmo salar)* stocks and management implications in the Canadian Atlantic provinces and New England, USA. Canad. J. Fish. Aquatic Sci. 38:1612–25.
———, and A. Sreedharan. 1978. The incidence and genetic implications of sexual maturity in male Atlantic salmon parr. Intern. Counc. Explor. Sea, C.M. 1978/M:23.
Savvaitova, K. A. 1980. Taxonomy and biogeography of charrs in the Palearctic, pp. 281–94. *In:* E. K. Balon (ed.). Charrs, salmonid fishes of the genus *Salvelinus*. Dr. W. Junk Publishers. The Hague, Netherlands.
Schaffer, W. M. 1974. Selection for optimal life histories: The effects of age structure. Ecology 55:291–303.
———. 1979. The theory of life-history evolution and its application to Atlantic salmon. Symp. Zool. Soc. Lond. 44:307–26.
———, and P. F. Elson. 1975. The adaptive significance of variations in life history among local populations of Atlantic Salmon in North America. Ecology 56:577–90.
———, and M. D. Gadgil. 1975. Selection for optimal life histories in plants, pp. 142–57. *In:* Ecology and evolution of communities. M. L. Cody and M. M. Diamond (eds.). Belknap Press, Cambridge, Mass.
Schenck, R. A., and R.C. Vrijenhoek. 1986. Spatial and temporal factors affecting coexistence among sexual and clonal forms of *Poeciliopsis*. Evolution 40:1060–70.
Schiefer, K. 1971. Ecology of Atlantic salmon, with special reference to occurrence and abundance of grilse on north shore Gulf of St. Lawrence rivers. Unpub. PhD Diss., Univ. Waterloo, Ontario.
Schlosser, I. J. 1982a. Fish community structure and function along two habitat gradients in a headwater stream. Ecol. Monogr. 52:395–414.
———. 1982b. Trophic structure, reproductive success, and growth rate of fishes in a natural and modified headwater stream. Canad. J. Fish. Aquatic Sci. 39:968–78.
———. 1985. Flow regime, juvenile abundance, and the assemblage structure of stream fishes. Ecology 66:1484–90.
———, and L. A. Toth. 1984. Niche relationships and population ecology of rainbow *(Etheostoma caeruleum)* and fantail *(E. flabellare)* darters in a temporally variable environment. Oikos 42:229–38.
Schmulbach, J. C., G. Gould, and C. L. Groen. 1975. Relative abundance and distribution of fishes in the Missouri River, Gavins Point Dam to Rulo, Nebraska. Proc. S.Dak. Acad. Sci. 54:194–222.
Schoener, A., and T. W. Schoener. 1981. Biological correlates of the species-area relation. I. Amer. Nat. 188:335–60.
Schoener, T. W. 1965. The evolution of bill size differences among sympatric congeneric species of birds. Evolution 19:189–213.
———. 1970. Nonsynchronous spatial overlap of lizards in patchy habitats.Ecology 51:408–18.
———. 1974. Resource partitioning in ecological communities. Science 185:27–39.
———. 1975. Presence and absence of habitat shift in some widespread lizard species. Ecol. Monogr. 45:233–58.
———. 1976. The species-area relation within archipelagos: Models and evidence from island land birds. Proc. 16th Int. Ornith. Congr., Canberra, pp. 629–42.
———. 1982. The controversy over interspecific competition. Amer. Sci. 70:586–95.
———. 1983a. Field experiments on interspecific competition. Amer. Nat. 122:240–85.
———. 1983b. Rate of species turnover decreases from lower to higher organisms: A review of the data. Oikos 41:372–77.
———. 1984a. Size differences among sympatric, bird-eating hawks: A worldwide survey, pp. 254–81. *In:* Ecological communities: Conceptual issues and the evidence. D. R. Strong, D. Simberloff, and L. Abele (eds.). Princeton Univ. Press, Princeton, N.J.
———. 1984b. Counters to the claims of Walter et al. on the evolutionary significance of competition. Oikos 43:248–51.
———. 1985. Some comments on Connell's and my reviews of field experiments on interspecific competition. Amer. Nat. 125:730–40.
———. 1986d. Patterns in terrestrial vertebrate versus arthropod communities: Do systematic differences in regularity exist? pp. 556–86. *In:* Community ecology. J. Diamond and T. J. Case (eds.). Harper & Row, New York.
———. 1986c. Overview: Kinds of ecological communities—ecology becomes pluralistic, pp. 467–79. *In:* Community Ecology. J. Diamond and T. J. Case (eds.). Harper & Row, New York.
———. 1986a. Resource partitioning, chap. 6. *In:* Community ecology—pattern and process. J. Kikkawa and D. Anderson (eds.). Blackwell Scientific Publishers, Oxford.
———. 1986b. Mechanistic approaches to community ecology: A new reductionism? Amer. Zool. (in press).
———, and A. Schoener. 1983. Distribution of vertebrates on some very small islands: I. Occurrence sequences of individual species. J. Anim. Ecol. 52:209–35.
Schoenherr, A. A. 1977. Density dependent and density independent regulation of reproduction in the Gila topminnow, *Poeciliopsis o. occidentalis* (Baird and Girard). Ecology

58:438–44.

———. 1979. Niche separation within a population of freshwater fishes in an irrigation drain near the Salton Sea, California. Bull. S. Calif. Acad. Sci. 78:46–55.

———. 1981. The role of competition in the replacement of native species by introduced fishes, pp. 173–203. *In:* R. J. Naiman and D. L. Soltz (eds.). Fishes in North American deserts. John Wiley & Sons, New York.

Schonewald-Cox, C. M., S. M. Chambers, B. MacBryde, and L. Thomas (eds.). 1983. Genetics and conservation. Benjamin/Cummings Publishing Co., Menlo Park, Calif.

Schreiber, D. C., and W. L. Minckley. 1981. Feeding interrelationships of native fishes in a Sonoran desert stream. Great Basin Nat. 41:409–26.

Schroder, S. L. 1981. The role of sexual selection in determining overall mating patterns and mate choice in chum salmon. Unpub. PhD Diss., Univ. Washington, Seattle.

Schultz, R. J. 1961. Reproductive mechanisms of unisexual and bisexual strains of the viviparous fish *Poeciliopsis*. Evolution 15:302–25.

———. 1966. Hybridization experiments with an all-female fish of the genus *Poeciliopsis*. Biol. Bull. 130:415–29.

———. 1967. Gynogenesis and triploidy in the viviparous fish *Poeciliopsis*. Science 157:1564–67.

———. 1969. Hybridization, unisexuality, and polyploidy in the teleost *Poeciliopsis* (Poeciliidae) and other vertebrates. Amer. Nat. 103:605–19.

———. 1977. Evolution and ecology of unisexual fishes. Evol. Biol. 10:277–331.

———. 1982. Competition and adaption among diploid and polyploid clones of unisexual fishes, pp. 103–19. *In:* Evolution and genetics of life histories. H. Dingle and J. P. Hegmann. (eds). Springer-Verlag, New York.

Schultz, D. C., and T. G. Northcote. 1972. An experimental study of feeding behavior and interaction of coastal cutthroat trout (*Salmo clarki clarki*) and Dolly Varden (*Salvelinus malma*). J. Fish. Res. Board Canada 29:555–65.

Scott, D. P. 1962. Effect of food quality on fecundity of rainbow trout, *Salmo gairdneri*. *Ibid*. 19:715–31.

Scott, W. B., and E. J. Crossman. 1973. Freshwater Fishes of Canada. Fish. Res. Board Canada Bull. 184:1–966.

Sedell, J. R., and K. J. Luchessa. 1982. Using the historical records as an aid to salmonid habitat enhancement, pp. 210–23. *In:* Proc. Acquisition and utilization of aquatic habitat inventory information. Oct. 28–30, 1981, Portland, Ore. West. Div. Am. Fish. Soc., Bethesda, Md.

Seegrist, D. W., and R. Gard. 1972. Effects of floods on trout in Sagehen Creek, California. Trans. Am. Fish. Soc. 101:478–82.

Seghers, B. H. 1974. Geographic variation in the responses of guppies (*Poecilia reticulata*) to aerial predators. Oecologia 14:93–98.

Selander, R. K., and D. W. Kaufman. 1973. Genic variability and strategies of adaptation in animals. Proc. Natl. Acad. Sci. 70:1875–77.

Shaffer, W. M., and M. D. Gadgil. 1975. Selection for optimal life histories in plants, pp. 142–57. *In*: Ecology and evolution of communities. M. L. Cody and J. M. Diamond (eds.). Belknap Press, Cambridge, Mass.

Shafland, P. L., and W. M. Lewis. 1984. Terminology associated with introduced organisms. Fisheries 9:17–18.

Shannon, C. E. 1948. A mathematical theory of communication. Bell Syst. Tech. J. 27:379–423.

Shapiro, A. M., 1984. The genetics of seasonal polyphenism and the evolution of "general purpose genotypes" in butterflies, pp. 16–30. *In:* Population biology and evolution. K. Wohrmann and V. Loeschcke (eds.). Springer-Verlag, Berlin.

Shapiro, D. Y. 1984. Sex reversal and sociodemographic processes in coral reef fishes, pp. 103–18. *In:* Fish reproduction: Strategies and tactics. G. W. Potts and R. J. Wootton (eds.). Academic Press, London.

Sheldon, A. L. 1966. Longitudinal succession and diversity of the fishes of Owego Creek, New York. Unpub. PhD Diss., Cornell Univ., Ithaca, N.Y.

———. 1968. Species diversity and longitudinal succession in stream fishes. Ecology 49:193–98.

Shelford, V. E. 1911. Ecological succession: Stream fishes and the method of physiographic analysis. Biol. Bull. 21:9–35.

Shepard, T. E., and B. M. Burr. 1984. Systematics, status, and life history aspects of the ashy darter, *Etheostoma cinereum* (Pisces: Percidae). Proc. Biol. Soc. Wash. 97:693–715.

Sheppard, P. M. 1975. Natural Selection and Heredity, 4th ed. Hutchinson, London.

Shiozawa, D. K. 1983. Density independence versus density dependence in streams, pp. 55–77. *In:* Stream ecology: Application and testing of general ecological theory. J. R. Barnes and G. W. Minshall (eds.). Plenum, New York.

Shmida, A., and M. V. Wilson. 1985. Biological determinants of species diversity. J. Biogeogr. 12:1–20.

Shute, J. R. 1980. *Fundulus albolineatus* Gilbert, p. 507. *In:* D. S. Lee et al. (eds). Atlas of North American freshwater fishes. North Carolina State Museum of Natural History, Raleigh.

Sibley, George Champlin. 1952. *See* Gregg, K. L. (ed.).

Siebert, D. J. 1980. Movements of fishes in Aravaipa Creek, Arizona. Unpub. MS Thesis, Arizona State Univ., Tempe.

Siegel, S. 1956. Nonparametric statistics for the behavioral sciences. McGraw-Hill, New York.

Sigler, W. F. 1958. The ecology and use of carp in Utah. Utah St. Univ. Agric. Exp. Sta., Bull. 405:1–63.

Sih, A. 1980. Optimal behavior: Can foragers balance two conflicting demands? Science 210:1041–43.

———. 1982. Foraging strategies and the avoidance of predation by an aquatic insect, *Notonecta hoffmanni*. Ecology 63:786–96.

———, P. Crowley, M. McPeek, J. Petranka, and K. Strohmeier. 1985. Predation, competition, and prey communities: A review of field experiments. Ann. Rev. Ecol. Syst. 16:269–311.

Silverberg, R. 1975. The stochastic man. Harper & Row, New York.

Silvey, W., J. N. Rinne, and R. Sorenson. 1984. Index to the natural drainage systems of Arizona—a computer compatible digital identification of perennial lotic waters. USDA, For. Serv. Wildl. Unit Tech. Rep., Fort Collins, Colo.

Simberloff, D. S. 1970. Taxonomic diversity of island biotas. Evolution 24:23–47.

———. 1982. The status of competition theory in ecology. Ann. Zool. Fenn. 19:241–53.

———. 1983. Competition theory, hypothesis testing, and other community ecological buzzwords. Amer. Nat. 122:626–35.

———, and W. Boecklen. 1981. Santa Rosalia reconsidered: Size ratios and competition. Evolution 35:1206–28.

Simons, D. B. 1979. Effects of stream regulation on channel morphology, pp. 95–111. *In:* J. V. Ward and J. A. Stanford (eds.). The ecology of regulated streams. Plenum Press, New York.

———, R. Li, et al. 1984. Analysis of channel degradation and bank erosion in the lower Kansas River. Rep. to US Army Engineer District, Kansas City, Mo., MRD Sediment Series no. 35, Sept. 1984.

Sinclair, D. F. 1985. On tests of spatial randomness using mean nearest neighbor distance. Ecology 66:1084–85.

Skreslet, S. 1973. The ecosystem of the arctic lake Nordlaguna. Jan

Mayen Island. Part 3. Ecology of arctic char. *Salvelinus alpinus*. Astarte 6:43–45.

Skulason, S. 1983. Utlit, Voxtur og aexlunarliffraedi mismunandi gerda bleikjunnar, *Salvelinus alpinus* (L.) i Thingvallavatni. Report Thingvallavatns Research Group, and BS-Honor thesis, Univ. of Iceland, Reykjavik.

Slade, N. A. 1976. Statistical detection of density-dependence in a series of sequential censuses. Bull. Ecol. Soc. Am. 57:35.

———. 1977. Statistical detection of density dependence from a series of sequential censuses. Ecology 58:1094–1102.

Slatkin, M. W. 1974. Competition and regional coexistence. Ecology 55:128–34.

Slizeski, J. J., J. L. Anderson, and W. G. Dorough. 1982. Hydrologic setting, system operation, present and future stresses, pp. 15–38. *In:* The middle Missouri River. L. W. Hesse (ed.). Missouri River Study Group, Norfolk, Nebr.

Slobodchikoff, C. N., and J. E. Parrott. 1977. Seasonal diversity in aquatic insect communities in an all-year stream system. Hydrobiol. 52:143–51.

Slobodkin, L. B., and H. L. Sanders. 1969. Benthic marine diversity and the stability-time hypothesis. Brookhaven Symp. Biol. 27:82–95.

Small, J. W., Jr. 1975. Energy dynamics of benthic fishes in a small Kentucky stream. Ecology 56:827–40.

Smart, H. J., and J. H. Gee. 1979. Coexistence and resource partitioning in two species of darters (Percidae), *Etheostoma nigrum* and *Percina maculata*. Canad. J. Zool. 57:2061–71.

Smartt, R. A. 1978. A comparison of ecological and morphological overlap in a *Peromyscus* community. Ecology 59:216–20.

Smith, C. C. 1975. The coevolution of plants and seed predators, pp. 53–77. *In:* Coevolution of animals and plants. L. E. Gilbert and P. H. Raven (eds.). University of Texas Press, Austin.

———, and S. D. Fretwell. 1974. The optimal balance between size and number of offspring. Amer. Nat. 108:499–506.

Smith, C. L., and C. R. Powell. 1971. The summer fish communities of Brier Creek, Marshall County, Oklahoma. Amer. Mus. Novitates No. 2458:1–30.

Smith, G. R. 1978. Biogeography of intermontane fishes, pp. 17–42. *In:* K. T. Harper and J. L. Reveal (eds.). Intermountain biogeography: A symposium. Great Basin Nat. Mem. 2.

———. 1981a. Effects of habitat size on species richness and adult body sizes of desert fishes, pp. 125–71. *In:* R. J. Naiman and D. L. Soltz (eds.). Fishes in North American deserts. John Wiley & Sons, New York.

———. 1981b. Late Cenozoic freshwater fishes of North America. Ann. Rev. Ecol. Syst. 12:163–93.

———, and T. N. Todd. 1984. Evolution of species flocks of fishes in north temperate lakes, pp. 45–68. *In:* Evolution of fish species flocks. A. A. Echelle and I. Kornfield (eds.). Univ. Maine Press, Orono.

Smith, J. J. 1982. Fishes of the Pajaro River System. Univ. Calif. Pub. Zool. 115:83–170.

Smith, M. L. 1981. Late Cenozoic fishes in the warm deserts of North America: A reinterpretation of desert adaptations, pp. 11–38. *In:* R. J. Naimen and D. L. Soltz (eds). Fishes in North American deserts. John Wiley & Sons, New York.

Smith, M. W., M. H. Smith, and R. K. Chesser. 1983. Biochemical genetics of mosquitofish. I. Environmental correlates, and temporal and spatial heterogeneity of allele frequencies within a river drainage. Copeia 1983:182–93.

Smith, O. R. 1941. The spawning habits of cutthroat and eastern brook trouts. J. Wildl. Mgmt. 5:461–71.

Smith, P. W. 1971. Illinois streams: A classification based on their fishes and an analysis of factors responsible for disappearance of native species. Ill. Nat. Hist. Surv. Biol. Note 76.

———. 1979. The fishes of Illinois. Univ. Illinois Press, Urbana.

Sneath, P. H. A., and R. R. Sokal. 1973. Numerical taxonomy: The principles and practices of numerical classification. W. H. Freeman and Co., San Francisco.

Snyder, G. K., and W. W. Weathers. 1975. Temperature adaptations in amphibians. Amer. Nat. 109:93–101.

Sokal, R. R. 1979. Testing statistical significance of geographic variation patterns. Syst. Zool. 28:227–32.

———, and C. A. Braumann. 1980. Significance tests for coefficients of variation and variability profiles. Syst. Zool. 29:50–66.

———, and F. J. Rohlf. 1981. Biometry. W. H. Freeman, San Francisco.

———, and D. E. Wartenberg. 1983. A test of spatial autocorrelation analysis using an isolation-by-distance model. Genetics 105:219–37.

Solemdal, P. 1967. The effect of salinity on buoyancy, size and development in flounder eggs. Sarsia 29:431–42.

Soltz, D. L. 1979. Our disappearing desert fishes. Nat. Conserv. News 29:8–12.

Soulé, M. 1976. Allozyme variation: Its determinants in space and time, pp. 60–77. *In:* Molecular evolution. F. J. Ayala (ed.). Sinauer Associates, Sunderland, Mass.

———. 1983. What do we really know about extinction? pp. 111–24. *In:* Genetics and conservation. C. M. Schonewold-Cox, S. M. Chambers, B. MacBryde, and W. L. Thomas (eds). Cummins, Menlo Park, Calif.

———, and B. A. Wilcox. 1980. Conservation biology. Sinauer Associates, Sunderland, Mass.

Sousa, W. P. 1979. Experimental investigations of disturbance and ecological succession in a rocky intertidal algal community. Ecol. Monogr. 49:227–54.

———. 1984a. Intertidal mosaics: Patch size, propagule availability, and spatially variable patterns of succession. Ecology 65:1918–35.

———. 1984b. The role of disturbance in natural communities. Ann. Rev. Ecol. Syst. 15:353–91.

Spellerberg, I. F. 1973. Critical minimum temperatures of reptiles, pp. 239–47. *In:* Effects of temperature on ectothermic organisms. W. Wieser (ed.). Springer-Verlag, Berlin.

Spranger, M. S. 1984. The Columbia Gorge, a unique American treasure. Washington State Univ. Cooperative Extension and Washington Sea Grant Program.

Stainbrook, C. E. 1982. Selected life history aspects of American shad (*Alosa sapidissima*) and predation on young-of-the-year shad in Lake Umatilla of the Columbia River. Unpub. MS Thesis, Oregon State Univ, Corvallis.

Stalnaker, C. B. 1979. The use of habitat structure preferenda for establishing flow regimes necessary for maintenance of fish habitat, pp. 321–37. *In:* J. V. Ward and J. A. Stanford (eds.). The ecology of regulated streams. Plenum Press, New York.

———, and J. L. Arnette (eds.). 1976. Methodologies for the determination of stream resource flow requirements: An assessment. US Fish Wildl. Serv., Washington, D.C.

Stamps, J. A. 1983. The relationship between ontogenetic habitat shifts, competition and predator avoidance in a juvenile lizard (*Anolis aeneus*). Behav. Ecol. Sociobiol. 12:19–33.

Starnes, W. C., and D. A. Etnier. 1986. Drainage evolution and fish biogeography of the Tennessee and Cumberland rivers drainage realm, pp. 325–61. *In:* Zoogeography of North American freshwater fishes. C. H. Hocutt and E. O. Wiley (eds.). Wiley Interscience, New York.

Starrett, W. C. 1950a. Distribution of the fishes of Boone County, Iowa, with special reference to the minnows and darters. Amer. Midl. Nat. 43:112–27.

———. 1950b. Food relationships of the minnows of the Des Moines River, Iowa. Ecology 31:216–33.

———. 1951. Some factors affecting the abundance of minnows in the Des Moines River, Iowa. *Ibid.* 32:13–27.

Stauffer, J. R., B. M. Burr, C. H. Hocutt, and R. E. Jenkins. 1982. Checklist of the fishes of the central and northern Appalachian Mountains. Proc. Biol. Soc. Wash. 95:27–47.

———, D. S. Cherry, K. L. Dickson, and J. Cairns, Jr. 1975. Laboratory and field temperature preference and avoidance data of fish related to the establishment of standards, pp. 119–39. *In:* Fisheries and energy production. Vol. 2. S. B. Saila (ed.). Lexington Books, Lexington, Mass.

———, K. L. Dickson, J. Cairns, Jr., and D. S. Cherry. 1976. The potential and realized influences of temperature on the distribution of fishes in the New River, Glen Lyn, Virginia. Midl. Monogr. 40:1–40.

———, D. R. Lispi, and C. H. Hocutt. 1984. The preferred temperatures of three *Semotilus* species. Arch. Hydrobiol. 101:595–600.

Stearns, S. C. 1976. Life-history tactics: A review of the ideas. Quart. Rev. Biol. 51:3–47.

———. 1977. The evolution of life history traits: A critique of the theory and a review of the data. Ann. Rev. Ecol. Syst. 8:145–71.

———. 1980. A new view of life history evolution. Oikos 35:266–81.

———. 1983. The genetic basis of differences in life-history traits among six populations of mosquitofish (*Gambusia affinis*) that shared ancestors in 1905. Evolution 37:618–27.

———. 1984. Heritability estimates for age and length at maturity in two populations of mosquitofish that shared ancestors in 1905. *Ibid.* 38:368–75.

Stein, D. W., J. S. Rogers, and R. C. Cashner. 1985. Biochemical systematics of the *Notropis roseipinnis* complex (Cyprinidae: Subgenus *Lythrurus*). Copeia 1985:154–63.

Stein, R. A. 1979. Behavioral response of prey to fish predators, pp. 343–53. *In:* R. H. Stroud and H. Clepper (eds.). Predator-prey systems in fisheries management. Sport Fishing Institute, Washington, D.C.

———, and J. H. Magnuson. 1976. Behavioral response of crayfish to a fish predator. Ecology 57:751–61.

———, P. E. Reimers, and J. D. Hall. 1972. Social interaction between juvenile coho (*Oncorhynchus kisutch*) and fall chinook (*O. tshawytscha*) in Sixes River, Oregon. J. Fish. Res. Board Canada 29:1737–48.

Stephenson, L. W., and W. H. Monroe. 1940. The Upper Cretaceous deposits Miss. Geol. Surv. Bull. 40:1–296.

Stevens, L., B. T. Brown, J. M. Simpson, and R. R. Johnson. 1977. The importance of riparian habitat to migrating birds, pp. 156–64. *In:* R. R. Johnson and D. A. Jones (tech. coords.). Importance, preservation, and management of riparian habitat: A symposium. US For. Serv. Gen. Tech. Rep. RM-43, Rocky Mtn. For. Range Exp. Sta., Fort Collins, Colo.

Stewart, D. B., and J. H. Gee. 1981. Mechanisms of buoyancy adjustment and effects of water velocity and temperature on ability to maintain buoyancy in fathead minnows, Pimephales promelas, Rafinesque. Comp. Biochem. Physiol. 68A:337–47.

Stewart, E. M. 1983. Distribution and abundance of fishes in natural and modified bottomland hardwood wetlands. Unpub. MS Thesis, Univ. Missouri, Columbia.

Strahler, A. N. 1945. Quantitative geomorphology of erosional landscapes. Compt. Rend. 19th Intern. Geol. Congr., Sec. 13:341–54.

———. 1957. Quantitative analysis of watershed geomorphology. Trans. Amer. Geophys. Un. 38:913–20.

Strauss, R. E., and F. L. Bookstein. 1982. The truss: Body form reconstructions in morphometrics. Syst. Zool. 31:113–35.

Strong, D. R. 1980. Null hypotheses in ecology. Synthèse 43:271–85.

———. 1983. Natural variability and the manifold mechanisms of ecological communities. Amer. Nat. 122:636–60.

———, D. Simberloff, L. G. Abele, and A. B. Thistle (eds.). 1984. Ecological communities, conceptual issues and the evidence. Princeton Univ. Press, Princeton, N.J.

———, L. A. Szyska, and D. S. Simberloff. 1979. Tests of community-wide character displacement against null hypotheses. Evolution 33:897–913.

Sugihara, G. 1980. Minimal community structure: An explanation of species abundance patterns. Amer. Nat. 116:770–87.

Summerfelt, R. C. 1967. Fishes of the Smoky Hill River, Kansas. Trans. Kans. Acad. Sci. 70:102–39.

Suomolainen, E. 1950. Parthenogenesis in animals. Adv. Genet. 3:193–253.

Surat, E., W. J. Matthews, and J. R. Bek. 1982. Comparative ecology of *Notropis albeolus, N. ardens,* and *N. cerasinus* (Cyprinidae) in the upper Roanoke River drainage, Virginia. Amer. Midl. Nat. 107:13–24.

Suttkus, R. D. 1980. *Notropis candidus,* a new cyprinid fish from the Mobile Basin, and a review of the nomenclatural history of *Notropis shumardi* (Girard). Bull. Ala. Mus. Nat. Hist. 5:1–15.

———. 1985. Identification of the percid, *Ioa vigil* Hay. Copeia 1985:225–27.

Suzumoto, B. K., C. B. Schreck, and J. D. McIntyre. 1977. Relative resistances of three transferrin genotypes of coho salmon (*Oncorhynchus kisutch*) and their hematological responses to bacterial kidney disease. J. Fish. Res. Board Canada 34:1–8.

Svardson, G. 1949. Natural selection and egg number in fish. Ann. Rep. Inst. Freshwater Res., Drottningholm 29:115–22.

Swaidner, J. E., and T. Berra. 1979. Ecological analysis of fish distribution in Green Creek, a spring-fed stream in northern Ohio. Ohio J. Sci. 79:84–92.

Swanson, F. J., S. V. Gregory, J. R. Sedell, and A. G. Campbell. 1982. Land-water interactions: The riparian zone, pp. 267–91. *In:* Analysis of coniferous forest ecosystems in the Western United States. R. L. Edmonds (ed.). US/IBP Synthesis Series 14. Hutchinson Ross Publishing Co., Stroudsburg, Pa.

Swarts, F. A., W. A. Dunson, and J. E. Wright. 1978. Genetic and environmental factors involved in increased resistance of brook trout to sulfuric acid solutions and mine acid polluted waters. Trans. Amer. Fish. Soc. 107:651–77.

Sweet, J. G., and O. Kinne. 1964. The effects of various temperature-salinity combinations on the body form of newly hatched *Cyprinodon macularius* (Teleostei). Helgolander Wissenschaftliche Meeresuntersuchungen 11:49–69.

Swift, C. C. 1970. A review of the eastern North American cyprinid fishes of the *Notropis texanus* species group (subgenus *Alburnops*), with a definition of the subgenus *Hydrophlox*, and materials for a revision of the subgenus *Alburnops*. Unpub. PhD Diss., Florida State Univ., Tallahassee.

Swofford, D. L., and R. B. Selander. 1981. BIOSYS-1: a FORTRAN program for the comprehensive analysis of electrophoretic data in population genetics and systematics. J. Hered. 72:281–83.

Taning, A. V. 1952. Experimental study of meristic characters in fishes. Biol. Rev. 27:169–93.

Tallman, R. G., and J. H. Gee. 1982. Intraspecific resource partitioning in a headwaters stream fish, the pearl dace *Semotilus margarita* (Cyprinidae). Env. Biol. Fish. 7:243–49.

Taylor, J. N., W. R. Courtenay, Jr., and J. A. McCann. 1984. Known impacts of exotic fish introductions in the continental United States, pp. 322–73. *In:* W. R. Courtenay, Jr., and J. R. Stauffer, Jr. (eds.). Distribution, biology, and management of exotic fishes. Johns Hopkins Univ. Press, Baltimore, Md.

Taylor, L. R., and I. P. Woiwod. 1980. Temporal stability as a density-dependent species characteristic. J. Anim. Ecol. 49:209–24.

Thomas, D. L. 1970. An ecological study of four darters of the genus *Percina* (Percidae) in the Kaskaskia River, Illinois. Ill. Nat. Hist. Surv. Bull. 70:1–18.

Thomerson, J. E. 1969. Variation and relationships of the studfish *Fundulus catenatus* and *F. stellifer* (Cyprinodontidae Pisces). Tulane Stud. Zool. Bot. 16:1–21.

Thompson, B. A., and R. C. Cashner. 1980. *Percina ouachitae* (Jordan and Gilbert), yellow darter, p. 732. *In:* Atlas of North American freshwater fishes. D. S. Lee et al. (eds.). North Carolina State Museum of Natural Hist., Raleigh.

Thompson, D. H., and F. D. Hunt. 1930. The fishes of Champaign County—a study of the distribution and abundance of fishes in small streams. Ill. Nat. Hist. Surv. Bull. 19:5–101.

Thomson, B. W., and H. H. Schumann. 1968. Water resources of the Sycamore Creek watershed, Maricopa County, Arizona. USGS Water Supply Pap. 1861:1–53.

Thomson, J. D. 1980. Implications of different sorts of evidence for competition. Amer. Nat. 116:719–26.

Thornbury, W. D. 1965. Regional geomorphology of the United States. John Wiley & Sons, New York.

Thorpe, J. E. 1981. Migration in salmonids, with special reference to juvenile movements in freshwater, pp. 86–97. *In:* Salmon and trout migratory behavior symposium. E. L. Brannon and E. O. Salo (eds.). Univ. Washington, Seattle.

Timmons, T. J., W. E. Garrett, W. D. Davies, and W. L. Skeleton. 1982. Fisheries studies on Gainesville and Aliceville lakes on the Upper Tombigbee River system, Alabama-Mississippi. Third Supplemental Environmental Report, Tennessee-Tombigbee Waterway, Vol. 10, App. K. Army Corps of Engineers, Mobile, Ala.

Toft, C. A., and P. J. Shea. 1983. Detecting community-wide patterns: Estimating power strengthens statistical inference. Amer. Nat. 122:618–25.

Tomelleri, J. R. 1984. Dynamics of the woody vegetation along the Arkansas River in western Kansas, 1870–1983. Unpub. MS Thesis, Fort Hays State Univ., Hays, Kans.

Toth, L. A., D. R. Dudley, J. R. Karr, and O. T. Gorman. 1982. Natural and man-induced variability in a silverjaw minnow (*Ericymba buccata*) population. Amer. Midl. Nat. 107:284–93.

Tramer, E. J. 1978. Catastrophic mortality of stream fishes trapped in shrinking pools. *Ibid.* 97:469–78.

Trautman, M. B. 1939. The effects of man-made modifications on the fish fauna in Lost and Gordon Creeks, Ohio, between 1887–1938. Ohio J. Sci. 39:275–88.

———. 1942. Fish distribution and abundance correlated with stream gradients as a consideration in stocking programs. Trans. N. Amer. Wildl. Conf. 7:211–33.

———. 1957. The fishes of Ohio. Ohio State Univ. Press, Columbus.

———. 1981. The fishes of Ohio, rev. ed. Ohio State Univ. Press, Columbus.

———, and D. K. Gartman. 1974. Re-evaluation of the effects of man-made modifications on Gordon Creek between 1887 and 1973 and especially as regards its fish fauna. Ohio J. Sci. 74:162–73.

Trendall, J. T. 1982. Covariation of life history traits in the mosquitofish, *Gambusia affinis*. Amer. Nat. 119:774–83.

Tschaplinski, P. J., and G. F. Hartman. 1983. Winter distribution of juvenile coho salmon (*Oncorhynchus kisutch*) before and after logging Carnation Creek, British Columbia, and some implications for overwinter survival. Canad. J. Fish. Aquatic Sci. 40:452–61.

Turelli, M. 1981. Niche overlap and invasion of competitors in random environments. I. Models without demographic stochasticity. Theoret. Pop. Biol., 20:1–56.

———. 1986. Stochastic community theory: A partially guided tour. *In:* Lecture Notes in Mathematical Ecology. T. G. Hallam and S. A. Levin (eds.). Springer-Verlag, Berlin.

Turner, B. J. 1974. Genetic divergence of Death Valley pupfish species: Biochemical versus morphological evidence. Evolution 28:281–94.

———, and D. J. Grosse. 1980. Trophic differentiation in *Ilyodon*, a genus of stream-dwelling goodeid fishes: Speciation versus ecological polymorphism. *Ibid.* 34:259–70.

———, T. A. Grudzien, K. P. Adkisson, and M. M. White. 1983. Evolutionary genetics of trophic differentiation in goodeid fishes of the genus *Ilyodon*. Env. Biol. Fish. 9:159–72.

Tyus, H. M. 1985. Homing behavior noted for Colorado squawfish. Copeia 1985:213–15.

———, C. W. McAda, and B. D. Burdick. 1982. Green River fishery investigations: 1979–1981, pp. 1–100. *In:* Colorado River fishery project, pt. II. Field investigations. Final Rep. Mem. Understand. 9-07-40-L-1016, US Bur. Reclam., Upper Colo. R. Reg., Salt Lake City, Utah. US Fish Wildl. Serv., Vernal, Utah.

Ultsch, G. R., H. Boschung, and M. J. Ross. 1978. Metabolism, critical oxygen tension, and habitat selection in darters (*Etheostoma*). Ecology 59:99–107.

Upper Colorado River Biological Subcommittee. 1984. Rare and endangered Colorado River fishes sensitive areas. Rep. Upper Colo. R. Coord. Counc. US Fish Wildl. Serv., Salt Lake City, Utah.

US Department of the Interior. 1984. Endangered and threatened wildlife and plants: Proposed endangered status and critical habitat for the desert pupfish (*Cyprinodon macularius*). Fed. Regist. 49:20739–44.

US Fish and Wildlife Service. 1984. Recovery plan for Gila and Yaqui topminnow (*Poeciliopsis occidentalis* Baird and Girard). US Fish and Wildlife Service, Albuquerque, N.Mex.

———. 1985. Recovery plan for woundfin. *Plagopterus arqentissimus* Cope (Revised). *Ibid.* US Fish and Wildlife Service, Albuquerque, N.Mex.

US Geological Survey. 1978. Water resources data for Arkansas, water year 1977. USGS Water Data Rep. AR-77-1. Washington, D.C.

———. 1979. Water resources data for Tennessee. USGS Water Data Rep. TN-78-1. Washington, D.C.

———. Water-supply records for Arizona and New Mexico. Published periodically. US Geological Survey, Phoenix, Ariz., and Santa Fe, N.Mex.

US Weather Bureau. 1948–55. Climatological Data Oklahoma. Vols. 59–64. U.S. Government Printing Office, Washington, D.C.

Utoh, H. 1976. Study of the mechanism of differentiation between the stream resident form and the seaward migratory form in Masu salmon, *Oncorhynchus masou* Brevoort. I. Growth and maturity of precocious masu salmon parr. Bull. Fac. Fish. Hokkaido Univ. 26:321–26.

Utter, F. M., H. O. Hodgins, F.. W. Allendorf, A. G. Johnson, and J. L. Mighell. 1973. Biochemical variants in Pacific Salmon and rainbow trout: Their inheritance and application in population studies, pp. 329–39. *In:* Genetics and mutagenesis of fish. J. H. Schroder (ed.). Springer-Verlag, Berlin.

Valdez, R., P. Mangan, M. McInerny, and R. P. Smith. 1982b. Tributary report: Fishery investigations of the Gunnison and Dolores rivers, pp. 321–62.

———, ———, R. P. Smith, and B. Nilson. 1982a. Upper Colorado River investigation (Rifle, Colorado, to Lake Powell, Utah), pp. 101–280. *In:* Colorado River fishery project, part

II. Field investigations. Final Rep. Mem. Understand. 9-07-40-L-1016, US Bur. Reclam., Upper Colo. R. Reg., Salt Lake City, Utah. US Fish and Wildlife Service, Grand Junction, Colo.

Vandel, A. 1928. La parthénogénèse géographique. Contribution à l'étude biologique et cytologique de la parthénogènése naturelle. Bull. Biol. France Belg. 62:164–81.

Vandermeer, J. H. 1969. The community matrix and the number of species in a community. Amer. Nat. 104:73–83.

———. 1972. On the covariance of the community matrix. Ecology 53:187–89.

van der Valk, A. G., C. B. Davis, J. L. Baker, and C. E. Beer. 1978. Natural fresh water wetlands as nitrogen and phosphorus traps for land runoff, pp. 457–67. *In:* Wetland functions and values: The state of our understanding. P. E. Greeson, J. R. Clark, and J. E. Clark (eds.). American Water Resources Association, Minneapolis, Minn.

Vannote, R. L., G. W. Minshall, K. W. Cummins, J. R. Sedell, and C. E. Cushing. 1980. The river continuum concept. Canad. J. Fish. Aquatic Sci. 37:130–37.

Van Valen, L. 1965. Morphological variation and the width of the ecological niche. Amer. Nat. 99:377–89.

———. 1978. The statistics of variation. Evol. Theor. 4:33–43.

Vladykov, V. D. 1963. A review of Salmonid genera and their broad geographical distribution. Trans. Royal Soc. Canada Ser. 4,1, Sec. 3:459–504.

Vogel, S. 1981. Life in moving fluids: The physical biology of flow. Princeton Univ. Press, Princeton, N.J.

Vrijenhoek, R. C. 1972. Genetic relationships of unisexual hybrid fishes to their progenitors using lactate dehydrogenase isozymes as gene markers (*Poeciliopsis,* Poeciliidae). Amer. Nat. 106:754–66.

———. 1978. Coexistence of clones in a heterogeneous environment. Science 199:549–52.

———. 1979. Factors affecting clonal diversity and coexistence. Amer. Zool. 19:787–97.

———. 1984a. Ecological differentiation among clones: The frozen niche variation model, pp. 217–31. *In:* Population biology and evolution. K. Wohrman and V. Loschcke (eds.). Springer-Verlag, Heidelberg.

———. 1984b. The evolution of clonal diversity in *Poeciliopsis,* pp. 399–430. *In:* Evolutionary genetics of fishes. B. J. Turner (ed.). Plenum Press, New York.

———, R. A. Angus, and R. J. Schultz. 1977. Variation and heterozygosity in sexually vs. clonally reproducing populations of *poeciliopsis*. Evolution 31:767–81.

———, ———, and ———. 1978. Variation and clonal structure in a unisexual fish. Amer. Nat. 112:41–55.

Wagner, B. A. 1984. Status and habitat utilization of the peppered shiner *Notropis perpallidus* (Pisces: Cyprinidae). Unpub. MS Thesis, Oklahoma State Univ., Stillwater.

Wagner, R. P., and H. K. Mitchell. 1964. Genetics and Metabolism. John Wiley & Sons, New York.

Walberg, C. H., G. L. Kaiser, and P. L. Hudson. 1971. Lewis and Clark Lake tailwater biota and some relations of the tailwater and reservoir fish populations, pp. 449–67. *In:* Reservoir fisheries and limnology. G. D. Hall (ed.). Amer. Fish. Soc. Spec. Pub. No. 8:1–734.

Wallace, J. C., and D. Aasjord. 1984. An investigation of the consequences of egg size for the culture of Arctic charr, *Salvelinus alpinus* (L.). J. Fish Biol. 24:427–35.

Walsh, S. J., and B. M. Burr. 1985. Biology of the stonecat, *Noturus flavus* (Siluriformes: Ictaluridae), in central Illinois and Missouri streams, and comparisons with Great Lakes populations and congeners. Ohio Acad. Sci. 85:85–96.

Walter, C. M. 1971. Everyone can't live upstream: A contemporary history of the water quality problems on the Missouri River (Sioux City, Iowa to Hermann, Missouri). US Environmental Protection Agency, Region VII, Kansas City, Mo.

Walter, G. H., P. E. Hulley, and A. J. F. K. Craig. 1984. Speciation, adaptation and interspecific competition. Oikos 43:246–48.

Ward, G. M., and K. W. Cummins. 1979. Effects of food quality on growth rate and life history of *Paratendipes albimanus* (Meigen) (Diptera: Chironomidae). Ecology 60:57–64.

Warner, R. R., and T. F. Downs. 1977. Comparative life histories: Growth vs. reproduction in normal males and sex-changing hermaphrodites in the striped parrotfish, *Scarus croicensis*. Proc. Third Internat. Sym. Coral Reefs, 1 (Biol.):275–82.

———, and S. G. Hoffman. 1980. Local population size as a determinant of mating system and sexual composition in two tropical reef fishes (*Thalassoma* spp.). Evolution 34:508–18.

———, and D. R. Robertson. 1978. Sexual patterns in the labroid fishes of the Western Caribbean. I: The wrasses (Labridae). Smithson. Contrib. Zool. 254:1–27.

Warren, C. E., and W. J. Liss. 1983. Systems classification and modeling of streams. US Environ. Prot. Agency Rep. CR807187 and USFSF RM-80-144-CA.

Waters, T. F. 1983. Replacement of brook trout by brown trout over 15 years in a Minnesota stream: Production and abundance. Trans. Amer. Fish. Soc. 112:137–46.

Watkinson, A. R. 1985. On the abundance of plants along an environmental gradient. J. Ecol. 73:569–78.

Webb, P. W., and D. Weihs. 1986. Locomotor functional morphology of early life history stages. Trans. Amer. Fish. Soc. 115:115–27.

Wedel, W. R. 1970. Some environmental and historical factors of the Great Bend aspect, pp. 131–42. *In:* Pleistocene and Recent environments of the central Great Plains. W. Dort and J. K. Jones, Jr. (eds.). Univ. Press of Kansas, Lawrence.

Weinstein, M. P., K. L. Heck, Jr., P. E. Giebel, and J. E. Gates. 1982. The role of herbivory in pinfish (*Lagodon rhomboides*): A preliminary investigation. Bull. Mar. Sci. 32:791–95.

Welcomme, R. L. 1979. Fisheries ecology of floodplain rivers. Longman, New York.

———. 1984. International transfers of inland fish species, pp. 22–40. *In:* W. R. Courtenay, Jr., and J. R. Stauffer, Jr. (eds.). Distribution, biology and management of exotic fishes. Johns Hopkins Univ. Press, Baltimore, Md.

Welton, J. S., C. A. Mills, and Z. L. Rendle. 1983. Food and habitat partitioning in two small benthic fishes, *Noemocheilus barbatulus* and *Cottus gobio* L. Arch. Hydrobiol. 94:434–54.

Wendler, H. O., and G. Deschamps. 1955. Logging dams on coastal Washington streams. Fish. Res., Wash. Dep. Fish:1–13.

Werner, E. E. 1980. Niche theory in fisheries ecology. Trans. Amer. Fish Soc. 109:257–60.

———. 1984. The mechanisms of species interactions and community organization in fish, pp. 360–82. *In:* Ecological communities: Conceptual issues and the evidence. D. R. Strong, Jr., D. Simberloff, L. G. Abele and A. B. Thistle (eds.). Princeton Univ. Press, Princeton, N. J.

———. 1986. Species interactions in freshwater fish communities, pp. 344–67. *In:* Community Ecology. J. Diamond and T. J. Case (eds.). Harper & Row, New York.

———, and J. F. Gilliam. 1984. The ontogenetic niche and species interactions in size-structured populations. Ann. Rev. Ecol. Syst. 15:393–425.

———, and D. J. Hall. 1976a. Niche shifts in sunfishes: experimental evidence and significance. Science 191:404–406.

———, and ———. 1976b. Species packing and niche complementarity in three sunfishes. Amer. Nat. 111:553–78.

———, and ———. 1977. Competition and habitat shift in two sunfishes (Centrarchidae). Ecology 58:869–76.

———, and ———. 1979. Foraging efficiency and habitat shifts in competing sunfishes. *Ibid.* 60:256–64.

———, J. F. Gilliam, D. J. Hall, and G. G. Mittelbach. 1983. An experimental test of the effects of predation risk on habitat use in fish. *Ibid.* 64:1540–48.

———, D. J. Hall, D. R. Laughlin, D. J. Wagner, L. A. Wilsmann, and F. C. Funk. 1977. Habitat partitioning in a freshwater fish community. J. Fish. Res. Board Canada 34:360–70.

———, G. G. Mittelbach, D. J. Hall, and J. F. Gilliam. 1983. Experimental tests of optimal habitat use in fish: The role of relative habitat profitability. Ecology 64:1525–39.

Wharton, C. H., W. M. Kitchens, E. C. Pendelton, and T. W. Sipe. 1982. The ecology of bottomland hardwood swamps of the southeast: A community profile. US Fish Wildl. Serv. FWS/OBS-81/37.

Wheeler, A. 1969. The fishes of the British Isles and northwest Europe. Michigan State Univ. Press, East Lansing.

———. 1977. The origins and distribution of the freshwater fish of the British Isles. J. Biogeogr. 4:1–24.

———. 1978. Key to the fishes of northern Europe. F. Warne, London.

Whitaker, J. O., Jr. 1977. Seasonal changes in food habits of some cyprinid fishes from the White River at Petersburg, Indiana. Amer. Midl. Nat. 97:411–18.

White, M. M., and B. J. Turner. 1984. Microgeographic differentiation in a stream population of *Goodea atripinnis* (Goodeidae) from the Mexican Plateau. Env. Biol. Fish. 20:123–27.

Whiteside, B. G., and R. M. McNatt. 1972. Fish species diversity in relation to stream order and physicochemical conditions in the Plum Creek drainage basin. Amer. Midl. Nat. 88:90–101.

Whitley, J. R., and R. S. Campbell. 1974. Some aspects of water quality and biology of the Missouri River. Trans. Mo. Acad. Sci. 7–8:60–72.

Whittaker, R. H. 1972. Evolution and measurement of species diversity. Taxon 21:213–51.

Wiens, J. A. 1977. On competition and variable environments. Amer. Sci. 65:590–97.

———. 1980. Patterns of morphology and ecology in grassland and shrubsteppe bird populations. Ecol. Monogr. 50:287–308.

———. 1984. On understanding a non-equilibrium world: Myth and reality in community patterns and processes, pp. 439–57. *In:* Ecological communities: Conceptual issues and the evidence. D. R. Strong, Jr., D. Simberloff, L. G. Abele, and A. B. Thistle (eds.). Princeton Univ. Press, Princeton, N.J.

———, and J. R. Rotenberry. 1980a. Bird community structure in cold shrub deserts: Competition or chaos? *In* Acta XVII Congr. Internat. Ornithol., pp. 1063–70. Berlin.

———, and ———. 1980b. Patterns of morphology and ecology in grassland and shrubsteppe bird populations. Ecol. Monogr. 50:287–308.

Wilbur, H. M. 1977. Propagule size, number, and dispersion pattern in *Ambystoma* and *Asclepias*. Amer. Nat. 111:43–68.

Wilcox, B. A., and D. D. Murphy. 1985. Conservation strategy: The effects of fragmentation on extinction. *Ibid.* 125:879–87.

Wiley, E. O. 1981. Phylogenetics. The theory and practice of phylogenetic systematics. Wiley Interscience, New York.

———. 1986. A study of the evolutionary relationships of *Fundulus* topminnows (Teleostei: Fundulidae). Amer. Zool. 26:121–30.

———, and R. L. Mayden. 1985. Species and speciation in phylogenetic systematics, with examples from the North American fish fauna. Ann. Missouri Botanical Gardens 72:596–635.

Williams, C. B. 1964. Patterns in the balance of nature. Academic Press, New York.

Williams, G. C. 1959. Ovary weights of darters: A test of the alleged association of parental care with reduced fecundity in fishes. Copeia 1959:18–24.

———. 1966. Adaptation and natural selection. Princeton Univ. Press, Princeton, N.J.

———. 1975. Sex and Evolution. Princeton Univ. Press, Princeton, N.J.

Williams, J. D. 1975. Systematics of the percid fishes of the subgenus *Ammocrypta*, with descriptions of two new species. Bull. Ala. Mus. Nat. Hist. 1:1–56.

———. 1981. Threatened desert fishes and the endangered species act, pp. 447–75. *In:* R. J. Naiman and D. L. Soltz (eds.). Fishes in North America deserts. John Wiley & Sons, New York.

———, and D. A. Etnier. 1977. *Percina* (*Imostoma*) *antesella,* a new percid fish from the Coosa River system in Tennessee and Georgia. Proc. Biol. Soc. Wash. 90:6–18.

———, and ———. 1978. *Etheostoma aquali,* a new percid fish (subgenus *Nothonotus*) from the Duck and Buffalo rivers, Tennessee. *Ibid.* 91:463–71.

———, and ———. 1982. Description of new species, *Fundulus julisia,* with a redescription of *Fundulus albolineatus* and a diagnosis of the subgenus *Xenisma* (Teleosti: Cyprindontidae). Occ. Pap. Mus. Nat. Hist. U. Kans. 102:1–20.

Williams, J. E., D. B. Bowman, J. E. Brooks, A. A. Echelle, R. J. Edwards, D. A. Hendrickson, and J. J. Landye. 1985. Endangered aquatic ecosystems on North American deserts, with a list of vanishing fishes of the region. J. Ariz.-Nev. Acad. Sci. 20:1–62.

Willson, M. F. 1969. Avian niche size and morphological variation. Amer. Nat. 103:531–42.

Wilson, D. S. 1975. The adequacy of body size as a niche difference. *Ibid.* 109:769–84.

Winegar, H. H. 1977. Camp Creek channel fencing—plant, wildlife, soil, and water response. Rangeman's J. 4:10–12.

Winger, P. V. 1981. Phyiscal and chemical characteristics of warmwater streams: a review, pp. 32–44. *In:* The warmwater streams symposium. L. A. Krumholtz (ed.). Southern Division, American Fisheries Society. Allen Press, Lawrence, Kans.

Winkler, P. 1979. Thermal preference of *Gambusia affinis affinis* as determined under field and laboratory conditions. Copeia 1979:60–64.

Winn, H. E. 1958. Comparative reproductive behavior and ecology of fourteen species of darters (Pisces-Percidae). Ecol. Monogr. 28:155–91.

Winter, G. W., C. B. Schreck, and J. D. McIntyre. 1980. Resistance of different stocks and transferrin genotypes of coho salmon, *Oncorhynchus kisutch,* and steelhead trout, *Salmo gairdneri* to bacterial kidney disease and vibriosis. Fish. Bull. 77:795–802.

Wooley, R. R. 1946. Cloudburst floods in Utah, 1850–1938. USGS Water Supply Pap. 994:1–128.

Wooten, M. C., and E. G. Zimmerman. In press. Adaptation in a generalist species. I. Genetic variation in the red shiner, *Notropis lutrensis*.

Wright, H. E., Jr. 1970. Vegetational history of the central plains, pp. 157–72. *In:* Pleistocene and Recent environments of the central Great Plains. W. Dort and J. K. Jones, Jr. (eds.). Univ. Press of Kansas, Lawrence.

Wright, S. 1954. The interpretation of multivariate systems, pp. 11–33. *In:* Statistics and mathematics in biology. O. Kempthorne, T. A. Bancroft, J. W. Gowen, and J. L. Lush (eds.). Iowa State Univ. Press, Ames.

———. 1968. Evolution and the genetics of populations, Vol. 1. Univ. Chicago Press, Chicago.

———. 1977. Evolution and the genetics of populations. Vol. 3. Experimental results and evolutionary deductions. Univ. Chicago Press, Chicago.

———. 1978. Evolution and the genetics of populations. Vol. 4. Variability within and among natural populations. Univ. Chicago Press, Chicago.

Wydoski, R. S., and R. R. Whitney. 1979. Inland fishes of Washington. Univ. Washington Press, Seattle.

Wylie, G. D. 1985. Limnology of lowland hardwood wetlands in southeast Missouri. Unpub. PhD Diss., Univ. Missouri, Columbia.

Wynes, D. L., and T. E. Wissing. 1982. Resource sharing among darters in an Ohio stream. Amer. Midl. Nat. 107:294–304.

Yant, P. R., J. R. Karr, and P. L. Angermeier. 1984. Stochasticity in stream fish communities: An alternative interpretation. Amer. Nat. 124:573–82.

Zammuto, R. M., and J. S. Millar. 1985. Environmental predictability, variability and *Spermophilus columbianus* life history over an elevational gradient. Ecology 66:1784–94.

Zar, J. H. 1974. Biostatistical analysis. Prentice-Hall, Englewood Cliffs, N.J.

Zaret, T. M. and A. S. Rand. 1971. Competition in tropical stream fishes: Support for the competitive exclusion principle. Ecology 52:336-42.

Zimmerman, E. G., and M. C. Wooten. 1981. Allozymic variation and natural hybridization in sculpins, *Cottus confusus* and *Cottus cognatus*. Biochem. Syst. Ecol. 9:341–46.

———, and M. C. Richmond. 1981. Increased heterzygosity at the MDH-B locus in fish inhabiting a rapidly fluctuating thermal environment. Trans. Amer. Fish. Soc. 110:410–16.

———, R. L. Merritt, and M. C. Wooten. 1980. Genetic variation and ecology of stoneroller minnows. Biochem. Syst. Ecol. 8:447–53.

Zinn, J. L., K. A. Johnson, J. E. Sanders, and J. L. Fyer. 1977. Susceptibility of salmonid species and hatchery strains of chinook salmon (*Oncorhynchus tshawytscha*) to infections by *Ceratomyxa shasta*. J. Fish. Res. Board Canada 34:933–36.

The Contributors

Paul L. Angermeier
Department of Ecology, Ethology, and Evolution, University of Illinois, Champaign, Ill.

John A. Baker
Environmental Laboratory, US Army Corps of Engineers, Waterways Experiment Station, Vicksburg, Miss.

Carl E. Bond
Department of Fisheries and Wildlife, Oregon State University, Corvallis, Oreg.

Herbert Boschung
Department of Biology, University of Alabama, University, Ala.

Robert C. Cashner
Department of Biological Sciences, University of New Orleans, New Orleans, La.

Kathleen E. Clark
Department of Biological Sciences, University of Southern Mississippi, Hattiesburg, Miss.

Thomas G. Coon
School of Forestry, Fisheries, and Wildlife, University of Missouri—Columbia, Columbia, Mo.

Frank B. Cross
Museum of Natural History, University of Kansas, Lawrence, Kans.

Debra A. DiMattia
Department of Biology, Siena College, Loudonville, N.Y.

Michael Edward Douglas
Department of Zoology and Museum, Arizona State University, Tempe, Ariz.

James Duncan
Department of Biology, Siena College, Loudonville, N.Y.

Anthony A. Echelle
Department of Zoology and Oklahoma Cooperative Fisheries Research Unit, Oklahoma State University, Stillwater, Okla.

James D. Felley
Department of Biological and Environmental Sciences, McNeese State University, Lake Charles, La.

Susan M. Felley
Department of Biological and Environmental Sciences, McNeese State University, Lake Charles, La.

Terry R. Finger
School of Forestry, Fisheries and Wildlife, University of Missouri—Columbia, Mo.

William L. Fisher
Water Resources Laboratory, University of Louisville, Louisville, Ky.

Douglas F. Fraser
Department of Biology, Siena College, Loudonville, N.Y.

John H. Gee
Zoology Department, University of Manitoba, Winnipeg, Manitoba, Canada.

Owen T. Gorman
Department of Biological Sciences, Northern Illinois University, DeKalb, Ill.

George E. Goslow, Jr.
Department of Biological Sciences, Northern Arizona University, Flagstaff, Ariz.

Timothy B. Grace
Missouri Department of Conservation, 1110 College Avenue, Columbia, Mo.

David C. Heins
Department of Biology, Tulane University, New Orleans, La.

Bruce Herbold
Department of Wildlife and Fisheries Biology, University of California, Davis, Calif.

Ihor Hlohowskyj
Department of Zoology, Miami University, Oxford, Ohio.

Clark Hubbs
Department of Zoology, University of Texas at Austin, Austin, Tex.

Hiram W. Li
Department of Fisheries and Wildlife, Oregon State University, Corvallis, Oreg.

Gudrun Marteinsdottir
Department of Biological Sciences and Bureau of Biological Research, Rutgers University, New Brunswick, N.J.

William J. Matthews
Biological Station and Department of Zoology, University of Oklahoma, Kingston, Okla.

Eugene Maughan
Department of Zoology and Oklahoma Cooperative Fisheries Research Unit, Oklahoma State University, Stillwater, Okla.

Richard L. Mayden
Department of Biology, University of Alabama, Tuscaloosa, Ala.

Gary Meffe
Savannah River Ecological Laboratory, Aiken, S.C.
James R. Mills
Department of Biological Sciences, Northern Arizona University, Flagstaff, Ariz.
W. L. Minckley
Department of Zoology, Arizona State University, Tempe, Ariz.
W. Linn Montgomery
Department of Biological Sciences, Northern Arizona University, Flagstaff, Ariz.
Randall E. Moss
Oklahoma Cooperative Fisheries Research Unit, Oklahoma State University, Stillwater, Okla.
Peter B. Moyle
Department of Wildlife and Fisheries Biology, University of California, Davis, Calif.
William D. Pearson
Water Resources Laboratory, University of Louisville, Louisville, Ky.
William J. Pflieger
Missouri Department of Conservation, 1110 College Avenue, Columbia, Mo.
Mary E. Power
University of California, Entomology and Parasitology, Berkeley, Calif.
Eric Rexstad
Department of Fisheries and Wildlife, Oregon State University, Corvallis, Oreg.
James S. Rogers
Department of Biological Sciences, University of New Orleans, New Orleans, La.
Stephen T. Ross
Department of Biological Sciences, University of Southern Mississippi, Hattiesburg, Miss.
D. Allen Rutherford
Department of Zoology and Oklahoma Cooperative Fisheries Research Unit, Oklahoma State University, Stillwater, Okla.
Isaac J. Schlosser
Department of Biology, University of North Dakota, Grand Forks, N.Dak.
Russell A. Schenck
Department of Biological Sciences and Bureau of Biological Research, Rutgers University, New Brunswick, N.J.
Thomas W. Schoener
Department of Zoology, University of California, Davis, Calif.
Carl B. Schreck
Department of Fisheries and Wildlife, Oregon State University, Corvallis, Oreg.
Andrew Sheldon
Department of Zoology, University of Montana, Missoula, Mt.
Kathryn B. Staley
Department of Biological Sciences, Northern Arizona University, Flagstaff, Ariz.
Arthur J. Stewart
Environmental Sciences Division, Oak Ridge National Laboratory, Oak Ridge, Tenn.
Elaine M. Stewart
School of Forestry, Fisheries and Wildlife, University of Missouri—Columbia, Columbia, Mo.
Richard E. Strauss
Division of Fishes, Museum of Zoology, University of Michigan, Ann Arbor, Mich.
Robert C. Vrijenhoek
Department of Biological Sciences and Bureau of Biological Research, Rutgers University, New Brunswick, N.J.
Thomas E. Wissing
Department of Zoology, Miami University, Oxford, Ohio.
Earl G. Zimmerman
Department of Biological Sciences, North Texas State University, Denton, Tex.

Indexes

Index of Scientific Names

Subject Index